WAR DOG

WAR DOG

FIGHTING OTHER PEOPLE'S WARS

The Modern Mercenary in Combat

By
AL J. VENTER

Foreword by
FREDERICK FORSYTH

Philadelphia & Newbury

Published in the United States of America in 2008 by
CASEMATE
1016 Warrior Road, Drexel Hill, PA 19026

and in the United Kingdom by
CASEMATE
17 Cheap Street, Newbury, Berkshire, RG14 5DD

ISBN 978-1-932033-90-8

Cataloging-in-Publication data is available from the Library of
Congress and from the British Library.

Printed and bound in the United States of America

For a complete list of Casemate titles, please contact

United States of America
Casemate Publishers
Telephone (610) 853-9131, Fax (610) 853-9146
E-mail casemate@casematepublishing.com
Website www.casematepublishing.com

United Kingdom
Casemate-UK
Telephone (01635) 231091, Fax (01635) 41619
E-mail casemate-uk@casematepublishing.co.uk
Website www.casematepublishing.co.uk

CONTENTS

Foreword *by Frederick Forsyth* — vii

Acknowledgments — xiii

Prologue — 1

PART I: A THIN LINE
1 Helicopter Gunships in Sierra Leone's War — 25
2 Neal Ellis: Jungle Warrior — 49
3 Strike on Makeni and British Involvement — 69
4 Combat Flights Into the Interior — 93
5 Radio Intercepts and the Inevitable SAMs — 115
6 The United Nations Debacle in West Africa — 131
7 Strange Bedfellows in Mercenary Wars — 155

PART II: MAELSTROM IN THE JUNGLE
8 More Mercs—More Wars — 191
9 Mercenaries in Bosnia, Lebanon and Elsewhere — 207
10 Early Mercenary Activity in the Congo — 241
11 Soldiers of Fortune During Mobutu's Rule — 257
12 Nellis and His War Dogs in the Congo — 279
13 Zimbabwe's Mercenaries in Congo's War — 295
14 Biafra's War and More Foreign Intervention — 321

PART III: THE RISE OF THE PROFESSIONALS
15 Executive Outcomes in Angola — 349
16 How Executive Outcomes Ran Its Wars — 387
17 The Mercenary Air War in Angola — 405
18 Taking Angola's Diamond Fields from the Rebels — 425
19 An American Warrior Dies in Africa — 445
20 Executive Outcomes Moves North — 461
21 Gunship Combat in West Africa — 487
22 Sierra Leone's Diamond War — 513
23 War Dogs Hit a Rebel Base in the Jungle — 539
24 A Future for Private Military Companies — 553

Epilogue — 579
IPOA Code of Conduct — 595
Notes — 599

MAPS

Sierra Leone 114

Africa 190

The Democratic Republic of the Congo (Zaire) 240

Central and Southern Africa 256

Angola's Cafunfo Diamond Fields 479

Freetown and Environs 538

FOREWORD

By Frederick Forsyth

These are interesting times in which we live. We've all recently seen the consequences of the botched attempt by a fairly large group of South African mercenaries headed by former British SAS officer Simon Mann to invade Equatorial Guinea.

But may I, with due modesty, point to my novel of 1974 *The Dogs of War*? That was a blow-by-blow manual for the invasion of that very same island of Fernando Po, as it was called before it gained its independence from Spain in 1968.

After exploring all the options when writing that novel, I became convinced that a mercenary invasion by air would not succeed. I was right, because it didn't work for "Mad" Mike Hoare and his group when they tried to take the Seychelles in 1981, and it certainly didn't work almost a quarter century later for the boys from Pretoria in Equatorial Guinea.

In both cases, I believe the plotters ignored the basics by trying to come in by plane. I was always convinced that the attackers would need the freedom and invisibility of the ocean to launch such an operation.

Invasion from the water is an obvious option because until you arrive, nobody knows you're there. Also, you do all your training and kitting-up onboard. The ocean is ideal for target practice, getting your weapons battle-ready, perhaps removing manufacturer's grease and that sort of thing. In other words, you prepare. And when you come in over the horizon and your target island is ahead of you, your men are landed and they storm the capital.

Not long after *The Dogs of War* was published, Bob Denard invaded Grand Comores by trawler out of Le Havre and he did exactly that. In the back pocket of every one of the forty mercenaries involved in that action was a paperback copy of *Les Chiens de Guerre*, the French edition of my book. The same with Hoare's ill-fated party. Both teams, I was told afterwards, used my novel as a manual. They'd pull the book out and keep referring to the text, asking each other, what do we do now? What comes next?

Why Simon Mann made such an evident cock-up leaves me baffled. Anyway, what he managed to demonstrate is how not to conduct a putsch on a tropical island.

There is no question that a good deal of what appeared in my original novel came from time that I spent in Biafra reporting on that dreadful conflict, first for the BBC and then, after I had resigned, independently. There was a steady flow of mercenary hopefuls entering the enclave, though only a handful stayed the distance.

The first group arrived at the behest of French President Charles de Gaulle, who, you will recall, had no real interest in Nigeria, it being a former British territory. Having virtually nothing to lose, he made a speech that was not so much helpful as favorable toward the breakaway Republic of Biafra. That was followed by an offer of French mercenaries.

General Odumegwu Ojukwu, the British-trained Biafran leader told me at the time that he simply had to accept because it would have been a considerable rebuff to the French to tell them and their mercenaries to get lost. It was also unfortunate that Paris charged him a hefty quarter of a million pounds, money he so desperately needed for his war effort.

So Roger Faulckes, a very distinguished Indo-China veteran who'd also been in the Foreign Legion and had every gallantry medal in the book, arrived in Biafra a short while later. The group was comprised of about thirty-five, perhaps forty men.

It didn't take anybody long to realize that these veterans actually knew very little, either about Biafra or the kind of problems they were likely to encounter in that breakaway state. In fact, it seemed as if they thought they were going on a picnic. To their horror, on their very first trip south, they ran straight into an ambush east of Port Harcourt.

Ojukwu told me later, as we sat talking late into the night with coffee and brandy, that immediately after extricating themselves from that mess, they did an abrupt u-turn and headed straight back to the airport. One of their representatives came into his office afterwards, sat down and told him that he wished to withdraw all his men. The Biafran leader had no option but to say yes. Nor did he get any of his money back.

Return to Europe the French soldiers did. Ojukwu said afterwards that it was probably the shortest military assignment in the history of warfare. A couple of the men decided to stay, one of them an ex-

Legionnaire by the name of Rolf Steiner. The other was a burly Belgian national, Marc Goossens. Both men went on to play useful roles in this terrible internecine conflict, though Steiner eventually overstepped the bounds and was abruptly hustled out of the country. He refused to go, but ended up in restraints when they put him onboard an aircraft headed for Libreville.

Meanwhile, a few more unlikely war dogs dribbled in, all of them volunteers. One was Alec Gay, a Scott. There was also Taffy Williams, a South African, though ethnically Welsh. An Italian who had been fighting in the Congo until a short while before, George Norbiatto, also showed up but he was later killed while on a solo op when he went down the Imo River, south of Port Harcourt. Finally there was Armand Ianarelli, a Corsican from Paris who later secured a more comfortable assignment as bodyguard to Madame Claude in Paris; she was then the world's most famous procuress of top-class call girls.

Another German, Christian Oppenheim, joined the group later. Unlike the others, his job was to fly a twin-engine B-26 light bomber that crashed on its second raid over Lagos. The Biafrans had no bombs of their own so they improvised and used hollowed-out fire extinguishers with a couple of fins welded onto them to guide them downward. Packed with industrial explosives, these devices were fitted with impact fuses with the hope that they'd land nose downwards and explode.

The mercenary group that ended up in Biafra was an unusual bunch. We'd all get together evenings and after a few drinks Taffy Williams would tell us that we were all crazy to be there and that he was the only certifiably sane person in the group. What he omitted to tell us was that he'd got the certificate to prove it after being released from a lunatic asylum sometime in his obscure past.

Getting *Dogs of War* published in the early 1970s wasn't something that just happened.

After Harold Harris of Hutchinson accepted *Day of the Jackal*, he came to me with what I thought was a stunning proposal and said that he was prepared to offer me a three-book contract. I'd get five hundred pounds down and six thousand pounds each for books Two and Three. Also, the money was up front, so that I'd have something to live on while I researched and wrote. I didn't yet know what a "three-book project" was, but it sounded good. Harold explained that it was *Jackal* plus two more and he suggested that I come up with some ideas for the other two.

I saw him a short while later and said that I had what I thought were two very good plots. The first had its roots in the world of Simon Weisenthal, who was Europe's real-life Nazi hunter. The book that resulted there eventually became *The Odessa File,* which was also filmed under that title. Essentially it dealt with hunting down a Nazi butcher from the Hitler period who had disappeared. It was all very topical because similar events had taken place in the snatching of Adolf Eichmann from Argentina in 1960.

The third book was more problematic because it involved a bunch of white mercenaries in West Africa who invaded a country and took it over. But that sort of thing hadn't happened. Not yet anyway, even though Bob Denard and a group of mercenaries had already tried and failed to take the West African country of Togo. He'd also attempted to invade the Congo from Angola with forty-four of his men on bicycles and that little episode became a traditional mess.

Both events provided me with the concept of a rather unusual military take-over involving a group of armed mercenaries who seized a state by force. I realized that I'd have to have a tycoon behind it, hence my invention of the character Sir James Manson. There also had to be a reason why and, of course, vast profits to motivate all these people into doing something like that in the first place. So in *Dogs of War* I created a mountain of platinum in the interior of the target country. Platinum is more valuable than gold; it was years before the genuine discovery of oil under the sea around Equatorial Guinea.

At that point I had to look about for the most basic, most indefensible West African republic I could think of. I remembered the establishment of the Biafran International Red Cross air bridge between breakaway Biafra and Equatorial Guinea and I thought, why not set the whole thing on that offshore island republic?

I went further. You take that island country by force and suddenly you're into another league. You have your own republic. You've now got a government that can issue visas, passports, its own currency, as well as a seat at the United Nations. It's a massive power tool if you happen to be a businessman. So why not fund a group of mercenaries to do your bidding? They're totally deniable if something goes wrong. Then you take them in and topple your tyrant, just like the South Africans intended doing in Equatorial Guinea in 2004 where they were hoping to oust a particularly brutal, incompetent and savage dictator by the name of Teodoro Obiang Nguema. Back in 1973, the man in charge was his equally foul uncle, Francisco

Macias Nguema, whom Teodoro toppled and shot.

I had to look at getting weapons for these people and considered the most logical way of doing it. I thought that it had to be Antwerp or Hamburg, then the two European centers of black market arms trafficking. Or even the Soviet Omnipol group, at the time the biggest communist outlet for weaponry. But I was also aware that they would only supply to customers of whom Moscow approved and that mercenaries probably wouldn't fit the mold. So I focused on the Europeans, people who would deal with anybody as long as they had money, as I knew they had already done with Biafra.

In my investigations I came up with the names of several real-life arms dealers including a certain Otto Schluter of Hamburg. He was a nasty individual, so I changed the character's name to Schleicher, which means to slither, like a snake, which, I must confess, was appropriate. He was the ultimate slitherer and in the book he provided my group of mercenaries with all the weapons they needed for the job.

At this point I had one of my old mercenary friends from Biafra as my advisor. It was he, in fact, who first suggested that the group go in by sea because they would almost certainly have been stopped if they had tried to fly in from Europe. They would also have found it extremely difficult to ship their weapons out by air. He mentioned that for about a hundred and fifty thousand quid it would be possible to buy a real little rust bucket out of Genoa.

He then suggested that you get some washed up sea captain who had possibly been beached and who'd have liked to get back to sea. Once you've hired your mercenaries, like Denard did by word of mouth in some of the bars that these people frequent, away you go. Out on the open sea, you use inflatable boats to take on your twenty or so mercenaries, the sort of craft that you're going to need for the invasion anyway.

Obviously you'd have to do a bit of homework or you'd end up like Denard. The first time he invaded the Comores in 1978, he actually found that they'd landed on the wrong island when he and his men initially went ashore. When they grabbed someone and asked him the way to Moroni the capital, the poor fellow pointed across the horizon and said "That way!" Denard couldn't leave the man there so they took him along.

Before dawn the next day they were off the target city, which needed a couple of hours to secure.

So I went back to Harold and gave him a few details about the third book and he exclaimed, "Wow, is this possible?" I answered yes. According to my advisors, it was absolutely feasible, I told him. His immediate reaction was that it was one of the most ingenious things he'd heard . . . a bunch of mercenaries actually taking over a country?

The funny thing about recent events in Equatorial Guinea is that had the South Africans actually managed to get ashore at Malabo, they would probably have captured both Nguema and the country in an hour because at the time that tin pot dictator's defense structure was centered around an emasculated praetorian guard that was responsible for the security of the nation. Nguema was so paranoid about being murdered by his own people that while his bodyguards were issued with weapons, they weren't given a single round of ammunition. He kept all that locked in a cellar below his throne room, where he also safeguarded his foreign reserves.

Had the South Africans under the mercenary leader Nic du Toit pulled it off, it would have been a double coup: they'd have had the country and the money. And let us not forget that immense lake of oil upon which Equatorial Guinea is perched, the reason why Mark Thatcher—the son of a former British PM, and his friend Simon Mann—were first tempted into that eventually calamitous project.

All of this concerns the plausible fiction I've been fortunate to provide for publishers and movies. At the base of my research has lain the capability of these "mercenaries," a rare breed of men who don't shun warfare but are attracted to it, whether for wealth or merely for the thrill of combat.

In this work, Al Venter has delved into the real-life exploits of the *War Dogs*—whether South African or Rhodesian, French, British, Russian or American—to illuminate how the privateers have continued to conduct battle in the wake of the Colonial Age. The true stories in this work are more impressive than fiction, and in terms of Africa, this book should be on the must-read list for the U.S. State Department and British Foreign Office.

FREDERICK FORSYTH
Hertfordshire,
September 2005

ACKNOWLEDGMENTS

I have walked a circuitous route in putting this book together. It is the exploits of many men, the occasional woman and more than enough wars, insurgencies, revolts and coups for a dozen generations of bloodlettings. My span of activity as a military correspondent covers almost forty years of it.

While most of what is here is contemporary, I've had to look back a little. We need to remember that the modern mercenary, war dog, private military contractor, freebooter et al., really only emerged when people like "Mad" Mike Hoare and my old friend Bob Denard started to do their thing in the early 1960s. These days there are many thousands of people willing to put their lives on the line for a monthly paycheck (at last count, some thirty thousand of them in Iraq alone) and some of the old timers are no longer around. Quite a lot of them are dead, killed in the line of duty.

Among the latter is the American mercenary Bob MacKenzie, who I got to know quite well when he was still around. We were together in the war in El Salvador for a spell, and before that I'd met him in Rhodesia. Bob was killed while in command of the first mercenary unit to go into action in Sierra Leone. As a freelance military contractor hired by a British private military company (PMC), Bob had offered his services to the Freetown government. His job, stated in his contract, was to put down a military uprising in the interior of this tiny West African state that, in normal circumstances, any enthusiast could probably cycle across in two or three days.

It was not to be, because things went against him from the start. Having been wounded in a contact, Bob was taken alive by the rebels. Word has it that after he'd died following a particularly barbaric torture session, they tore out his heart and ate it. Sybil, his lovely wife, survived their posting to the lonely army outpost at Mile 91, which as the name implies, lies ninety-one miles beyond Freetown. She gave willingly of their experiences during that brief West African sojourn as well as some of her photos.

Many of the soldiers of fortune I have encountered over the years were veterans of a succession of conflicts. These are people like helicopter gunship pilot Neall Ellis, or more popularly, "Nellis," without whose friendship this book wouldn't have happened. Neall and I have walked a long road together, the last time in northern Oregon watching salmon twirl in the Columbia River before he went on to more adventures in Baghdad and I returned to Africa. There is also the indomitable Ron Reid-Daly who not only achieved an MBE fighting communist terrorists with the SAS in Malaya, but went on to become the founding commander of the Selous Scouts.

There was also Lafras Luitingh, himself a rugged warhorse who made a few million dollars from organizing a group of mercenary fighters under the banner of Executive Outcomes (EO). That group went on to battle it out in a succession of campaigns in Angola and Sierra Leone.

Mauritz le Roux, one of his fellow combatants in the historic Soyo operation (which set the seal for EO's military participation in Angola) did even better as a corporate warrior since he today runs a huge PMC concern in Baghdad. To Mauritz (who features within these pages in the debacle that took him and Nellis to the Congo) I owe much for correcting earlier misconceptions about what really happened at Soyo. His involvement highlights one of the problems associated with war reporting. If you weren't there yourself, people tell it the way they want you to record it, which is not always the truth. Then, when those lies appear in print, it's your credibility that takes a knock.

Others to whom I am indebted include a former British officer with the Scots Guards, Colonel Tim Spicer, whose writings have provided valuable insights to what went on with Sandline when he still ran that show. His latest gambit as head of London's Aegis Defence Services managed to achieve a huge Pentagon contract to act as the "coordination and management hub" for the fifty plus private security companies in Iraq.

Let's not forget the likes of former SADF Reconnaissance Regiment (and Executive Outcomes) veteran Colonel Bert Sachse, together with my old friend Arthur Walker, the only man, in twenty-one years of conflict, to *twice* be awarded the Honoris Crux in gold.

Then there are people like Jim Maguire, Charlie "Tatties" Tate and Carl Dietz, as well as the incorrigible Peter McAleese, with whom I took a lot of fire at Cuamato in southern Angola. In his classic book on freelance fighting, *No Mean Soldier*, Peter went on to record his adventures as a contract soldier in places as diverse as Rhodesia, Angola and in the drug wars of Colombia. That book was published several years ago by Orion Publishing in the UK and for aficionados of the genre it's well worth a read.

Lt-Colonel Rob Symonds, British Military Liaison Officer at the High Commission in Freetown during the period that I flew combat with Nellis, deserves a slot of his own. Though hardly in the mercenary mold, he showed great empathy for the efforts of these people trying to stop the rot in West Africa. Rob had a difficult role there, balancing strictures imposed by his Whitehall bosses with the often immediate operational demands in a country where nothing happened by the book. At the end of the day, it was Rob who showed us how the professional does it.

Another fine source for what went on, this time in the Congo, is my old friend Dave Atkinson, formerly a gunship pilot for Mugabe at a time when that tyrant went to the aid of Kabila. "Double Dave" is now instructing aspirant pilots in Lesotho.

Some of these veterans, like Duncan Rykaart, former British SAS operator Fred Marafano, Roelf van Heerden, Nick van den Bergh, Hennie Blaauw, Harry Carlse, Juba Joubert, Carl Dietz, Andy Brown, Simon Witherspoon (who spent time in an African jail as a result of his involvement in a planned insurrection in Equatorial Guinea), the indomitable Du Preez brothers—Louis and Nico—as well as Cobus Claassens, originally served with Executive Outcomes. I was hosted by many of them when I spent time with that organization in Angola and Sierra Leone. Others will recognize in these pages the shenanigans that some of them initiated while fighting under foreign flags, and a few, like French secret service agent "Christophe," would rather that I did not mention their real names.

War dogs come from just about everywhere. George Yazid, who for a while (because, as he claims, "I had nothing better to do at the time") flew combat with Neall Ellis, holds joint Irish/Sierra Leonian nationality. Before going to the Sharp End beyond Freetown, George originally studied electronics in Canada. There was also Ethiopian flight engineer Sindaba Nemera Meri and the rest of his team from Addis Ababa who employed their quite remarkable skills to keep Sierra Leone's aging Hinds in the air long after both machines might otherwise have been relegated to the scrap heap.

And then there is my not-so-old comrade-in-arms Hassan Ahmed Hussein, who we would all refer to, though never disparagingly, as "our tame Shi'ite." While he was serving as our Mi-24 side-gunner I was able to watch him in action from up close many times. Hassan must be one of the most ruthless combatants that I've met and his aggression under fire is legend.

In the late 1990s, during one of the rebel incursions into Freetown, he and Neal Ellis, using the only helicopter in the country still able to fly, rescued hundreds of civilians trapped behind enemy lines and brought them to safety, taking quite a few knocks themselves in the process. Had this been a conventional war, they would probably have shared the kind of kudos that most nations bestow on those who "go beyond the call of duty." Don't take my word for it: rather, judge for yourself since many of their exploits are within these pages.

Several of my fellow scribes also deserve credit. Topping the list is Jim Penrith who, while still bureau chief with the Argus Africa News Service in Nairobi in the 1960s, took me in his charge. So did the indomitable Henry Reuter, though sadly he is no longer with us.

Nor is my old *rafiki* Mohammed Amin. He was killed when a bunch of radicals hijacked an Ethiopian airliner out of Addis Ababa in which he was traveling to Nairobi, and crashed it off one of the tourist beaches in the Comores Archipelago. Many is the night that I "camped out" in the sitting room of the tiny apartment that Mo and Dolly used as their office and home near the main bus station in the Kenyan capital—but that was long ago, before he moved off tangentially to become one of the wealthiest journalists I've known. With Amin's sometime help I would cover all of East Africa, from Zanzibar, the eastern Congo and Burundi to Idi Amin's Uganda and the Tanzanian Army invasion that finally ousted that dreadful monster.

It was also "Mo" who got me through the Sudan and, before that, Somalia and on to Yemen. And let's not forget another old pal, Michael Knipe, then a plucky Southern Africa correspondent for the London *Times*. We went overland through a badly ravished Mozambique where Lisbon was fighting a rearguard action to salvage what was left of its African colonies. Before that, I'd spent a month covering Lisbon's wars in Angola with Cloete Breytenbach, and that sojourn eventually became the subject of the very first book I wrote. In Portuguese Guinea afterward I was to cross paths with Jim Hoagland of *The Washington Post* and Peter-Hannes Lehman of Germany's *Der Spiegel*. Of course, Gerry Thomas still deserves all the accolades I can muster for his incisive reporting at the start.

In more recent times there has been *The Daily Telegraph*'s Chris

Munnion, and briefly in Sierra Leone, Anton la Guardia, as well as Chris McGreal of London's *Guardian*, whom I sense has a better handle on developments in West Africa than most. Like Mark Doyle of the BBC, McGreal likes to follow the action. Nor should I forget Bob Morrison: he made *Combat & Survival* what it is today.

I also ended up sharing some astonishing confidences about what was then going on in Charles Taylor's Liberia with Jim Rupert, formerly Africa correspondent of *The Washington Post*. Jim's revelations about the groups of South African and Israeli seditionists who supported this wicked psycho were appalling. I visited Liberia often over the years, the first time in 1965 when the elaborately named William Vacanarat Shadrack Tubman benignly ruled. That was an era when one could still travel alone through the remotest regions of Africa. Most times I slept, unarmed, on the side of the road and my biggest worry was not malaria, but rather, where I would get my next meal.

All that took place on my second overland trip through Africa, the first being across East Africa. I traveled from Johannesburg to London and the trip lasted almost six months. Some of it was spent in Liberia, then still a delightfully quaint place. My path took me from the Ivoirean capital Abidjan, through the recently mercenary-embattled Toulepleu (on the border with the Ivory Coast) to Monrovia on the Liberian coast. Along the way—serious logging of Africa's forests had not yet started—I spent time in the kind of primeval jungle country that these days you only read about. Part of the journey, I'd imagine, was similar to that undertaken decades before by Graham Greene, though in my case without the hardships, because he was on foot. Greene's overland efforts eventually found form in his classic work, *Journey Without Maps*.

While I took many of the photos in this book, others come from people like Cobus Claassens Arthur Walker, Werner Ludick, Danny O'Brien, Dave McGrady, Craige Grice, Mike Draper, Hennie Blaauw and a few others who passed on pictures over a few ales and who I may have neglected to formally thank.

Two colleagues who didn't make it were Reuter's correspondent Kurt Schork and AP cameraman Miguel Gilmoreno. Tragically, both men were killed in an ambush in Sierra Leone while the events recorded here were taking place. I've lost a lot of colleagues as a consequence of violent action over the years. Among them were people like the photographer Ken Oosterbroek, Nicholas Della Casa (I gave Nic his first job in news gathering) the redoubtable Danny Pearl, George

De'Ath (who covered Beirut with me: he on the Muslim side and me with the Christians), George Cole in the Congo, who was shot in the approaches to Stanleyville, Priha Ramrakha in Biafra, Michael Kelly in Iraq—the first American journalist to die in Gulf War 2—and a lot of others besides. The deaths of Schork and Gilmoreno seemed different. We were shaken because of what had happened out there in the jungle that day. Rather sharply, we were reminded that this kind of work is dangerous.

Kurt, a Rhodes Scholar at Oxford with former President Bill Clinton, had been in Iraq, Afghanistan, Bosnia, Chechnya and East Timor. For his part, Miguel Gil Moreno de Mora was a Barcelona-trained lawyer who threw away everything to follow the action. In the process, he won his share of awards as a cameraman for Associated Television News (APTN). This book pays tribute to both these brave souls and the rest of my mates who went on to take the long walk.

At Jane's Information Group in London there are editors and friends to thank for help accorded over the years. Having written for *International Defense Review* for more than thirty years, it was natural that a former editor, Clifford Beal, should have initiated my second phase with the company. When he moved on to *Jane's Defence Weekly*, he passed that mantle on to Peter Felstead, then putting out *Jane's Intelligence Review*. At one stage I was doing work for all three publications. That trend continued after Mark Daly took over as editor-in-chief at IDR.

Thanks must also go to Michael Grunberg, a planning and financial boffin of repute who spent a lot of time putting both Sandline International and Executive Outcomes on the map. Having read some of the proofs, he dispelled myths and misconceptions galore about what mercenaries do. Also in London, or rather on the western outskirts of that great city—along the upper reaches of the Thames in Richmond—is one of the computer whiz kids of our time. Hanno Gregory pulled my chestnuts out of the fire computer-wise often enough and a gracious thanks for his efforts, always at short notice.

The same with Bruce Gonneau of Durban who did his thing in helping to complete the photo sections. Bruce's help has been incalculable with some of my earlier books as well: a truly-inspired graphic artist.

Among my American friends, two literary stalwarts, Don McLean and Tom Reisinger, are among the most helpful people I know.

The same with Jim Morris, a much-wounded Special Forces vet—

and an accomplished author in his own right with a turn of phrase that often awes us lesser mortals (even if he does go on a bit about Montagnards and continues to believe that there's something to be said for living in Los Angeles). Morris has always been ready to speak to the world on the web when I needed something in a hurry. He then went on to edit my next book, *Cheating Death*, which deals with cops who got themselves shot and survived.

Essentially, that book is about the history of concealable body armor, something that another compadre, Richard Davis, invented more than three decades ago. To date, Richard's brainchild—emulated by some, brazenly and illegally copied by others—went on to save the lives of three thousand Americans, the majority of them men and women working in law enforcement.

In an altogether another league is Dana Drenkowski, the only merc pilot I know who Libya's Muammar Qadhaffi hired as a combatant. His story is included here as well. So is Dave McGrady's, together with a few of the things that French Foreign Legionnaire Phil Foley has done. And Robin (Hawkeye) Hawke—recently commissioned into a U.S. Special Forces unit—whose experiences as a hired gun in Sierra Leone's earlier days are certain to provide a few unusual insights. Hawkeye's story, macabre one moment and almost poetically lyrical the next, is worthy of much more attention than it has so far achieved: it is a truly epic tale. So is Tom Staley's, who added a vignette, as did Hank Kenealy who, while operating as a communications geek for the U.S. State Department, sometimes found himself in unusual places.

His story about a couple of stateside ham radio operators who, when all conventional radio communications with Freetown were cut, tapped into the ether in order to keep U.S. Embassy communications with Washington alive, must be a classic. I deal with that little episode in the Prologue.

Danny O'Brien often came up with the unusual. An enterprising former Special Forces operator turned corporate bigwig, Danny today runs one of the most successful private military companies on the globe, International Charter Incorporated of Oregon (more commonly called ICI, though not be confused with Britain's Imperial Chemical Industries). The first time I saw an ICI chopper it was a Russian-built Mi-8MTV with American flags painted on both sides of the fuselage, parked on the helipad at Freetown's military headquarters.

During the course of finishing this work I also touched base with another of America's finest, Gary Jackson, who today devotes a good deal of energy and effort at the helm of Blackwater USA. Doug Brooks, President of IPOA (International Peace Operations Association) is someone else who came up with the goods.

Floyd Holcolm, who recently found himself in an unusual Special Forces liaison role in Iraq, has been a singular—if sometimes critical—source of inspiration. Floyd speaks Mandarin, Arabic and Farsi, and is a member of that new breed of combat elite that the American military establishment has recently nurtured to cope with the ever-variable face of war. He and I propped up the bar at The Schooner in Oregon's Astoria often enough, regaling Mark (America's best barkeep), Peter Marsh, the lovely Cynthia, Jennifer Genge, Wayne Symonds, Matt (or as he prefers, Cap'n Matt) Stein, as well as the rest of the gang with some of our improbable "war stories." Also in Astoria, Steve Forester and Patrick Webb at *The Daily Astorian* have always been on hand with advice and information, as has Police Chief Rob Deupree.

The intrepid Suzie Sizemore of Seaside, Oregon, to whom this book is dedicated, pulled so many good things out of the hat during difficult times. A lovely, spiritual soul, she had a way of making things happen. Bless you my precious friend.

There are also my Chinook friends in Washington. That includes my walking-buddy, Joyce Otterson, who has always cast a critical eye over my work and I am deeply in debt to you my dear. A bow must go, too, to the man I still regard as the best wordsmith in the business, my old editor and friend, Jack Shepherd-Smith, who, when the world was still young and innocent, taught me most of what I know about syntax.

And Steven Smith, with whom I worked for many months in getting out my previous book on Iran's putative atom bomb program. At very short notice he came in and helped with the American version of this one. Others who served in getting aspects of *War Dog* together include Willem Steenkamp, David Williams and Larry O'Donoghue. I must also remember Clare, Larry's delightfully innovative daughter for keeping me in touch with the old country.

I have left Freddie Forsyth till almost last for good reason. Freddie and I shared some of our earliest impressions of conflict in Africa—if not together, then within an AK-rifle shot of one another. Both of us were reporting from Biafra toward the end of that nasty affair that left a million people dead, though Freddie had been there from the start. I suspect that neither of us came out of that experience emotionally intact; I certainly did not. Unlike me, this polymath and former Reuters and BBC correspondent put his experiences to good use. Having been one of the last whites to leave the rebel enclave in late 1969, he celebrated that Christmas and New Year's in London and then settled down in a friend's pad with his rickety old Olivetti portable and set to work. Thirty-five days later Freddie emerged with the first draft of *The Day of the Jackal.*

By the time that this work appears in the U.S., another Forsyth offering—this one titled *The Afghan*—should be almost done. While doing research for his latest work, he spent a bit of time with me and my friends at the estuary of the Columbia River in Washington. Being the raconteur that he is, what a delightful few days those were.

In a peculiar way, I also owe David Cornwell, aka John le Carré, a special vote of thanks. David wanted to talk about some of the goings-on to be found within these covers. His own book, due out in the summer of 2006 and titled *The Mission Song*, involves mercenaries as one of its themes, though it is set in London, a Danish island and, inevitably, the Congo Republic. So, together with his lovely wife Jane, we met for lunch in Hampstead and the rest of the afternoon was spent in a briefing session on the subject of today's private military companies.

Until then, I'd prevaricated a little with this edition, but that fortuitous get-together over maps, African reference works, parts of an unfinished manuscript, the nature and tactics involved in this kind of unconventional warfare, and, I thought, even an English-Swahili dictionary, instilled in me the resolve to sit down and finish this book, which has been years in gestation. A few months later it was done.

Linked to this side of things as well, was the husband and wife team Duane and Rebecca Sentgeorge. What lovely support I had from those delightful people, as well as Ryker and Katrina.

I've left David Farnsworth, my often intrepid, always helpful publisher till now because he and Sarah deserve the biggest toast of all. This book originally saw light under the auspices of David when I was still in South Africa. He kept at it by an extremely subtle process of coercion, persuasion and hard-assed business acumen, fueled by the occasional dram of a good quality vintage Fonseca. In so many ways, this book is a tribute to Philadelphia's Casemate Publishers, a small company that the two of them resurrected and restructured into one of the largest distributors of military books on the American continent.

And so to Caroline Delius, my lovely, wild "free spirit," as she likes to call herself, who became almost iconic during the final stages of the book. Thank you darling one. Here's to our next trudge through the heather atop our beautiful Isle of Bute.

AL J. VENTER
Rothesay, Western Isles
January 2006

PROLOGUE

"Ending the slaughter of innocent civilians in Sierra Leone is
the job some three hundred well-equipped and motivated
[PMC] soldiers managed to do a few years ago."

Ed Royce, Chairman, U.S. Senate Africa Subcommittee

Conflict attracts a peculiar brand of adventurer. Tom Staley, one of
Africa's old hands who spent time in some strange wars in West
Africa, told me the intriguing story of a flight crew that went on one
of many relief missions in Liberia. They were using a beat-up old
Russian Mi-8 helicopter that had probably seen service with the Soviet
Air Force in Afghanistan in the 1980s.

The three men, headed by my old buddy Danny O'Brien of
International Charters Incorporated of Oregon, took this machine—
together with a bunch of about twenty officials onboard—into
Zwedru, a remote village in Liberia's interior. Recalling the incident at
his home near Fort Lewis south of Seattle, Danny remembered it as
having been unscheduled: there was no curriculum, script or template
to get by.

"It was one of those typical 'hey you!' missions that always results
in trouble. But this was the Department of State calling the shots and
we did what they told us to do."

Waiting on the ground when the helicopter finally arrived at a very
remote jungle encampment were four hundred or more agitated, upset
and none-too-happy Liberian Political Council (LPC) guerrillas. Just
two hours before Danny got there, this untidy band of Krahn fighters
(all of whom had previously been closely associated with the recently-
very-dead, former Liberian leader Sergeant Samuel Doe) had come
under surprise attack by forces loyal to Charles Taylor's NPFL.
Obviously, there had been casualties and the survivors were in a fury.

"Actually, we found out afterward that they had received no word
of us coming. Our job was to take in a delegation that was supposed

1

to sort out some kind of political impasse. Consequently they had no idea why a helicopter would suddenly swoop in from nowhere. Our chopper could just as easily have been one of Taylor's. We were pretty lucky not to have been shot down when we first circled the football field where we eventually put the wheels down."

Having unloaded his passengers, all of whom went into town under rebel escort, Danny and his guys sat back and waited for them to do their business and return. Meanwhile, they were getting a lot of attention. Every move these aviators made was being observed by a group of irregulars, many who were perhaps eight or ten years old. Each one of them was armed with an assortment of infantry squad weapons that included AKs, RPGs and RPD machine guns. One of the crew recalled afterward that while it was still early in the day, it was pretty clear that this bunch had been mixing their brew. Either that or they'd been smoking something, because soon afterward the taunting started.

"They'd wave their Kalashnikovs about like crazies and we knew that we couldn't hang about indefinitely because things could get worse," Danny recalled. But he couldn't simply up sticks and haul out of there without his "cargo."

Then the leader of this crazy band—gimlet-eyed and brutish—stepped forward and used his weapon to indicate that the helicopter wasn't going anywhere. With that, the three men were pulled from their machine, beaten and robbed of everything, including their wedding rings. The hapless trio was finally stripped naked, with some of the women brawling over who would get their clothes. One of the biggest fights erupted over a pair of colored jockeys.

"Things deteriorated quickly when shots were fired between our legs . . . there was no particular aim, they'd just let rip. Each time they'd laugh like hell because they could see we were shitless."

More beatings followed. Then some of the ringleaders argued about whether the victims should be shot or possibly cut up with machetes, and since those doing the talking were dead serious, this was worrying. Others ransacked the helicopter, ripping out the radio and a good deal of equipment with it, all of which eventually cost a mint to replace. Not that the savages would have any use for the stuff in some dark African jungle, O'Brien contemplated.

Hearing shots, Danny and crew were eventually rescued by the leader of this guerrilla group. She had been on the ground when the helicopter arrived. A tough woman who preferred to be known by her *nom de guerre* "Attila" was, as O'Brien remembers, large in proportion, voice and energy as well as being Number Two within that particular rebel group

"Gun in hand, she marched fixed-eyed at the rioting mob, fired several shots in the air and told her bodyguards to grab the ringleaders. She promptly ordered them to be taken behind some buildings and executed," said O'Brien.

"Now," she screamed. "Kill them now!"

Not long afterward, Danny O'Brien and his crew—without a pair of underpants between them—were allowed to take both the delegation and their helicopter back to Monrovia.

Africa is full of such stories. Anton la Guardia, for a while Africa correspondent with London's *Daily Telegraph*, visited us in Freetown in 2000 and mentioned another group of fliers he'd seen that day. He'd watched them climb into a helicopter, also an Mi-8 and possibly the same one that had been involved in the Liberian fracas. The men onboard were clutching AK-47s, he said when he joined us for sundowners on the patio of Nellis' villa.

"They're mercenaries, aren't they?" he queried.

They weren't, we replied. The men were armed because at that stage of Sierra Leone's civil war it was a given that nobody flew into the interior without protection. For almost a decade, this former British colony was a place where a person's life sometimes wasn't worth the trainers on his feet. Or possibly the Swatch on his or her arm.

It's an ugly word, mercenary. Though hardly the rough and tough of the quotidian, it conjures up images of mindless brutality, the murder of innocents. To others, it's a call to arms.[1]

Since the abolition of war is a prime example of an ethical problem with which science is powerless to deal, conflict in all its forms has a following, though within the constraints of what is today "politically incorrect," you'd be lucky to find anyone willing to admit that he killed for cash.

Military historian Sir John Keegan is of the view that that people forget that one of the supreme British heroes, General Charles Gordon, served in the Middle East as a mercenary. Moreover, he did so with government approval, both under the Chinese Emperor as well as under orders of the Khedive of Egypt. So too with Colonel Pulaski, hero of the American artillery corps, who fought under a foreign flag and got paid for it, as did Lafayette.

The Persian Emperor Darius used regiments of Greek mercenaries against Alexander the Great, while German freebooters have fought for the highest bidder just about forever. You might recall that Britain's George III hired battalions of Germans to subdue his rebellious American colonists and they were apparently very good at it.

The most illustrious of the lot could very well have been the audacious Admiral Cochrane on whom the British novelist C.S. Forester based the life of his fictitiously famous Captain Horatio Hornblower. The real-life Lord Cochrane was a dominant figure in early 19th-century maritime history. His naval career, at turns, was both brilliant and controversial, and what a memorable calling it was!

Drummed out of the Royal Navy after what was termed "inappropriate" political and financial activities, he went on to Chile where he commanded that country's fleet against Spain. Later, in 1827, he led the Greek Navy against Turkish control before being accepted back into the Royal Navy. This time round, he returned to serve his regent as an admiral and that, too, is the stuff of legend.[2]

On to the modern period, I suppose that Gurkhas could feasibly be classified as mercenaries. So are all the British officers and men who served in the Sultan of Oman's armed forces, and some are still doing so. The same with my good friend Colonel Brian Robinson, a former commanding officer of the Rhodesian SAS. These days Brian is answerable about border security to the Abu Dhabi royal family in a part of the world where there was almost none prior to 9/11. What's more, Brian likes what he does, especially since the United Arab Emirates sits on one of the busiest crossroads to the east of Suez.

There have been military badhats, of course, as there always are when conflict looms and people don't deliver. But then that's the story of most wars.

Not so with the small group of South African mercenaries attached to the almost whimsically named Executive Outcomes (EO) who went into Sierra Leone in 1995 and brought that country back from the brink of catastrophe. Speak to them today and they'll tell you, almost to a man, that they're proud of what they did. They'll recall the lives they saved and the unthinkable rapes and amputations that they were instrumental in preventing. They'll mention too, that the first time around, they mercilessly battered into submission the rebel RUF leader—the late Foday Sankoh—a mass murderer whose place in the Valhalla of megalomaniacal tyrants is secure.

But in the end, it didn't help. The South Africans had hardly gone home before Sankoh—by now forgiven his revolutionary fervor, welcomed back into the fold and even handed a ministerial post in the Freetown government—launched the bloodiest campaign of all in his bid to achieve power.

Ultimately it was the British who rolled up rebel successes, and while London would never publicly admit it, the Royal Marines and the Paras as well elements from the SAS and the SBS did so by spilling an awful lot of rebel blood.

To others in the business of "hired guns," cause is irrelevant. For most of these professionals, it's a question of money. Like it or not, the concept of being paid to fight is almost as old as civilization itself.

Let us also not forget that being a mercenary is the world's second oldest profession, which could be why it attracts all types: the sad, the bad, the dangerous and the mad. The majority of today's freelance fighters are none of these: they are professionals and, in the main, they are not particularly unhappy with what they do. In fact, speak to a few of them and likely as not you'll find that apart from long periods away from home, most prefer the job to anything else on offer. It is worth noting that, in 2005, the U.S. Army offered bonuses of $150,000 to experienced men who signed on again, which says something about the attractions of freelance contract work: it is attracting a lot of professional soldiers.

Many independent contractors—including quite a few who appear within these pages—today serve in support roles in places like Afghanistan, Angola, the Sudan, Nigeria, Algeria, Colombia and Iraq. Their jobs are usually associated with protecting from harm non-governmental organizations (NGOs), embassies, hospitals, oil drilling rigs, police stations, contract companies and the like. As we are also now aware, they are not shy to retaliate when they're being shot at.

In an ambush in Iraq's Falluja in April 2005, a dozen contractors attached to a South African private military company drove off about sixty attackers without one of their members being hurt. It was a violent exchange of gunfire that went on for several minutes and the Iraqis who'd initiated the ambush took some serious casualties including several of their number killed.

Advertisements for private military operators appear all over. You just have to know where to look. "Job Number 96" was posted by DynCorp International on January 4, 2005. It read as follows:

Job Title: WPPS (Worldwide Personnel Protection Service)
Openings: Continuous openings
Contact: Bill Greenhalgh via e-mail
bgreenhalgh04@yahoo.com
Salary: $177,000 one year contract

Qualifications:
US Citizen
Applicant must have a minimum of 1 year verifiable experience in personal protective security employment in one of the following organizations:
• US Secret Service
• Department of State Diplomatic Security
• US Military (MP, CID)
• Civilian law enforcement (local/state SWAT assignments)
• Executive Protection
• For qualification to serve in certain assignments in Central Asia, Special Operations Force experience is required (Delta, SEAL, Green Berets, Rangers, Force Recon, AST, Para-Jumpers)
• Military experience is preferred
• Ability to communicate confidently and be understood in English
• Valid US driver's license
• Unblemished background with ability to obtain government security clearance
• Excellent medical and dental health
• Be able to possess a valid passport from home country
• Must be able to pass DOS/Diplomatic Security weapons qualifications
• Must be able to successfully complete a high-risk training/evaluation course
• Must submit to psychological evaluation and pre-employment drug screening

Three weeks later, a company rather nostalgically calling itself OSS and listing an address at 2521 Raeford Road, Fayetteville, North Carolina, advertised for an Antiterrorism Training Instructor. The location given was: Antiterrorism Training Detachment (ATD), D-2-1st SWTD (A), Fort Bragg, NC.

Prerequisites listed were: Antiterrorism Instructor Qualification Course (AIQC) Graduate as well as Individual Terrorism Awareness Course (INTAC) Graduate with:
- Instructor Training Course (ITC) Graduate
- Secret clearance
- Special Forces qualified
- Possess or able to obtain a US passport
- Pass an over-forty physical

While there was no mention of remuneration, salary scales were roughly in line with what DynCorp was offering.

Clearly this is big money if you know where to get it, especially if you've been struggling along at $5,000 or $6,000 a month for most of your professional career in the military.

The truth is that when anybody starts scratching about, likely as not he'll find that there are lots of mercenaries who are doing their thing. For instance, foreigners have been involved in a string of civil wars that seem to have dragged on forever in the Congo and they're still at it. For more than forty years, this huge, largely ungovernable state has been torn apart by a succession of internecine struggles that have reduced just about everybody to penury. There are also those of the view that mercenaries have actually helped to prolong the carnage, which could just be true because a host of influences have played discordant roles in what was once a Belgian king's personal fief.

Others are similarly involved in Asia, the East Indies, South and Central America, some of the more unsettled parts of Eastern Europe, the Middle East, Africa and elsewhere.

Mercenaries have also been used to quell violence in the oil-rich Nigerian delta. With religious differences escalating in that country, bets are on that Africa's most populous nation is going to host more of these contractors.

Danny O'Brien's ICI actually handled a support and training contract on behalf of the U.S. State Department in Nigeria recently. While flying about eastern Nigeria, he saw a region the size of Wales being laid to waste. As he recalled, he covered hundreds of miles on both sides of the great Benue River which empties into the Niger, "and all I saw was one village after the other that had been torched by the Nigerian Army . . . hundreds of miles of terrain seemed to have been abandoned by its original inhabitants."

That was only the start of it, Danny O'Brien feared. As he likes to point out, things can only deteriorate when zealots start to kill their fellow countrymen because they are of the wrong religious persuasion. This is something about which Danny knows a lot, because his helicopters also work Darfur.

I've written a good deal about this subject in recent years, and though Abuja might argue otherwise, Danny O'Brien's reasoning is spot-on.[3] As he says, Nigeria is fertile ground for more such violence, especially when the one side is Christian and the other Muslim. Moreover, things begin to happen when those who perceive themselves to be oppressed decide that they need outside help to counter such injustices. It is only a question of time, he muses.

Not all discord is so easily delineated. It is sometimes difficult to categorize the individual roles of people involved in this kind of activity. For instance, South Africa's Islamic fundamentalist *Qibla*—the military wing of that country's fundamentalist PAGAD (the word is an acronym for People against Gangsterism and Drugs)—recruited hundreds of young Muslims to "fight the hated infidel in Palestine." With the passion of the possessed, their spokespeople in South Africa maintained that these recruits would help "liberate sacred ground from the Zionist enemy," which underscores another issue: in the realm of polemics, one man's freedom fighter is often somebody else's terrorist. Also, one can hardly label that kind of fanatic a "soldier of opportunity," even if he is paid for his efforts.

Ideologues apart, war dogs come from many countries, among them Germany, the United States, France, Australia, Italy, Croatia, Britain, Serbia, South Africa, Zimbabwe, the Ukraine and Namibia. In fact, just about every nation on earth is represented. While covering the Rhodesian war in the 1970s, I even met a young man serving in the Rhodesian Light Infantry (RLI) from the Seychelles Islands, a soporific Indian Ocean haven of peace. He claimed that he was having a grand time fighting for Ian Smith, and he did well enough to be decorated for valor.

Rhodesia presented the international community with some of the best examples of government-coordinated mercenary activity. In Chris Cocks' book *Fireforce*—it covers four years of his very personal wartime experiences as a combatant in the RLI and to my mind, the work is still among the best to emerge from that conflict—he makes the case for the Rhodesian Army having been second only to the French Foreign Legion in assimilating foreigners into operational fighting ranks. As a national force, the RLI had a bigger proportion of expatriates than any other army in modern times, with the exception of the Legion. As Cocks described:

> There was a wide diversity of characters in 3 Commando. By tradition, most foreign volunteers served in the ranks and at one stage I was the only born Rhodesian in 11 Troop. And Americans, of course, many of them Vietnam veterans resplendent with arrays of medals. But we were not overly impressed by such dazzling displays and told them they looked like Christmas trees. Understandably, they ignored our taunts and wore their decorations with pride.
>
> There were Canadians and Australians and New Zealanders, some of whom had fought in Vietnam. And we had Frenchmen, Belgians and Germans too, many of them ex-Legionnaires. Earlier there had been a lot of South Africans, but their numbers began to dwindle as their own bush war intensified in South West Africa and Angola. The majority of overseas recruits came from Great Britain and Ireland, from a variety of regiments like the Paras, Royal Marines, Special Air Service and the Brigade of Guards. The British adapted well to Rhodesian conditions and many served with distinction and were decorated for valor.
>
> All foreign volunteers, in most cases, were professional soldiers. It is true that a few liked to think of themselves as mercenaries (or mercs) but they weren't really . . . if they had been, they would have been soldiers "without fortune," if only because they got the same pay and served under the same conditions of service as Rhodesian-born regular soldiers. Like everyone else, they paid income tax to the Rhodesian exchequer. Added to that, they were allowed to remit only a small percentage of their salaries to their own countries.
>
> The volunteers came for many and varied reasons. For some it was the action and adventure. For others it was glory. Many arrived in the belief that they were fighting to stop the spread of international communism. And there were a few who were there just for the love of killing . . .

One of the more notable figures in this period was British Major André Dennison who, before Rhodesia, had served with some distinction with 22 Special Air Service Regiment in Borneo. His exploits in penetrating dense jungle on patrol in South Asia with the legendary Sergeant Eddie Lillico earned him high praise from General Walter Walker. Dennison was then detached as part of a contingent of eighty British officers and senior NCOs, seconded to the 3rd Battalion of the Malaysian Rangers. Stints in Europe, Cyprus, the Malawi Rifles, Northern Ireland and elsewhere followed.

Major Dennison joined the 2nd Battalion of the Rhodesian African Rifles in October 1975, commanding A Company until he was killed in action almost four years later.

An interesting aside here is that while serving in Rhodesia, Dennison met the American war photographer Sarah Barrell, an intrepid go-getter who had spent a good while in Vietnam. As one wag wrote, "Her obituary would describe her as a beautiful blonde . . . who collected wars and war heroes." John le Carré is believed to have cast her as the American photo-journalist "Lizzie Worthington" in *The Honorable Schoolboy*, though when I asked him about this, he simply smiled.

Having arrived in southern Africa after the wars in Cambodia and Lebanon, Barrell moved on to Rhodesia, met Dennison and the two fell deeply in love. Her friends believed that, at last, he'd given meaning to her life. Then Dennison was killed, an incident compounded by the fact that he was accidentally shot by one of his own men during a contact.

Two days after his funeral, the beautiful Sarah returned to her apartment in Salisbury, sat down on her bed and shot herself with the same .38 that her lover had given her for protection. She was thirty-three years old.

Richard Wood documents Dennison's adventures in Rhodesia in another fine book to emerge from that war titled *The War Diaries of André Dennison* (Ashanti Publishing, 1989).

As Chris Cocks suggested in his own writings, the cause of the commercial combatant, generally, is transparent and is usually defined by the monthly paycheck. Sometimes it is coupled to the promise of being able to mine mineral concessions in the interior, which was the case in Angola, Uganda, both Congos and Sierra Leone, as well as a few other places where diamonds and precious metals are the common denominator.

When the violence in Kosovo was at its worst, experienced veterans from many countries fought on one side or the other, most times for a pittance. Some got involved as much for kicks as for the experience or cash. All were labeled mercenaries.

That analogy would also have held for Iraqi fighter pilots at the controls of Sudanese Air Force jet bombers. Those Arab airmen were well rewarded for their services, on top of which they avoided hardships imposed by UN sanctions on their own country. There are numerous reports of them dropping explosives (and in several cases, chemical nerve agents) on to the heads of groups of emaciated Nilotic recalcitrants.

The way I've been reading events in the Sudan more recently, it would seem that the majority of these tribespeople would almost certainly prefer to be Christian and dead than suffer the vagaries of the kind of militant Islam propagated by a Khartoum regime that regards anything that is not Moslem with abhorrence. It is also a government that punishes those of its citizens that are not Islamic, which is one of the reasons why the U.S. State Department recently declared the killings in the Sudan to be genocidal. Halfway through the first decade of the new millennium, these random killings continue.

So too, with those who volunteered to fight in Chechnya and Macedonia. And with Pakistan's *Hizbul Mujahadeen*, an organization that has been at war with the Indian Army in mountainous Kashmir for many years and employs religious "Party of God" recruits who emanate from places like Afghanistan, the Sudan, Yemen, Chechnya, Saudi Arabia and the Philippines.

A hefty crowd of Islamic militants put the seal on that embroilment when, two weeks after the destruction of the Twin Towers in New York, they detonated a car bomb at the entrance to the state legislature in Jammu-Kashmir. Twenty-five people were killed in that explosion and a hundred wounded. A couple of months later, this same group of hotheads almost triggered a nuclear war by trying to assassinate a couple of dozen Indian parliamentarians in New Delhi. It was a close call and the region remains tentative. Looking at subsequent developments, it seems likely to stay that way.

Still more military freelancers fly helicopters and other aircraft and they do so for a huge array of foreign forces. They have been active in places like Ethiopia, the Philippines, Sri Lanka, Afghanistan, Liberia, Angola, Libya, Iraq, Eritrea, Columbia, Sierra Leone and many other places besides. Quite a few are my friends and, together, we've occasionally taken what American vets like to call "incoming."

There was a time when the majority of mercenaries were white, or at least of European or American or Antipodean extraction. Today there are many times more black soldiers of fortune being paid to fight in Africa than there are bloody-minded contractual killers from the West. A number of them, in places like Liberia, the Ivory Coast and the Congo especially, don't have the same kind of entrenched religious convictions that you are likely to encounter in the Middle East. Quite a few are only interested in carnage: they like to kill people. Anarchists, some would call them.

Still, there are those soldiers of fortune that have done much to glorify the cause of fighting for foreign flags. A tiny handful tower above the rest.

Rolf Steiner, a German and former French Foreign Legionnaire who I met in Biafra where he called himself "The Last Adventurer," was one of them. Rolf espoused several causes, usually of the underdog. In his day he fought in Algeria, the Congo, Biafra and, finally, for the primitive tribespeople in southern Sudan.

Things didn't work out as planned and this German adventurer was captured by government troops. They put on a very public trial in Khartoum and sentenced him to a jail term that should have meant his death. They released him after a few years because he had only one lung, claiming to having lost the other at Dien Bien Phu, which, Freddie Forsyth said, wasn't true. Whatever the reason, Steiner was a very sick man when the Sudanese let him go; they feared repercussions had he died on them. That was the way it was among professional soldiers thirty years ago, when it was principle, not ideology that mattered.

It's instructive that had he not been white, Rolf Steiner would probably have been shot, as was another of his associates, the psychotic "Colonel" Callan.

In moments of crass stupidity, Callan—a Cypriot Greek whose real name was Costas Georgiou (we called him "Crazy Callan" in Angola)—caused the death in an ambush in northern Angola of several people I'd got to know along the way, including George Bacon, then working undercover for the CIA.

Peter McAleese, as tough a Scot as they come—or as somebody described him, "a typical Glaswegian mixture of Catholic Scottish and Irish"—was fighting for this same rebel unit as Callan in northern Angola. His only regret was that he didn't ice the man when he could have. Having served in Britain's Parachute Regiment, and later in the

SAS (before he saw combat as a war dog on four continents) it would have been a cinch, he confided. Trouble was, he didn't immediately recognize Callan's incipient lunacy.

In Angola in the mid-1970s, McAleese, like the rest, saw a good deal of action. His book details events that led up to that monumentally flawed effort to counter Fidel Castro's advances into the Angolan interior. The merc force was routed and the Cubans stayed in Angola for fifteen more years.

McAleese talks at length about the dreaded Callan and why things happened the way they did. As he elaborates, a mainly British force of "irregulars"—many of whom had no military experience whatever—was hired in London by a bunch of opportunists and almost overnight was flown to the Congo. On the same night that they arrived in Kinshasa, the group was hurriedly led to a cluster of buses and driven straight across the border into Angola. Their job, they weren't instructed until it was too late, was to halt the momentum of a powerful Cuban–led mechanized force heading their way.

Without any armor for support or even a single piece of artillery— they had only a handful of obsolete bazookas to hand—this exhausted and fearful little band of recruits awaited the arrival of one of the biggest mobile columns seen in Africa since the end of World War II. They and their rebel hosts got a thrashing from which the Angolan opposition never recovered.

The results make for grim reading, but the outcome was predictable. After a week, nearly half the force of almost a hundred and fifty mercenaries was dead, wounded or missing. As one of those who survived recounted afterward, "It had to happen . . . most of them didn't know sugar from shit."

Having failed to acquit themselves against government forces, their schizoid leaders—headed by Callan—set about murdering fourteen of their own. Of those who were later captured by the Angolans, four—including the American Danny Gearheart and Callan—were executed by Angolan firing squads.

Clearly, here was a story made for dishing dirt, and the media gloried in it. They splashed the episode, especially the part about mercenaries killing each other. Murray Davies of London's *Daily Mirror* was taken by the Luanda government to northern Angola where it had all taken place and he headed his story: "I Saw the Horror of Massacre Valley."

The way McAleese tells it, the event is a textbook version of how not to fight a freelance war. Together with those who managed to get back across the border into the Congo a couple of days after the final MPLA thrust, he reckons he's lucky to be alive. Among this group was Robin Wright, a perky little American colleague from *The Los Angeles Times* then based in southern Africa. She told her story afterward to Chris Munnion of *The Daily Telegraph* and admitted having emerged from that hellhole by a whisker. Then, having had enough of Africa, Robin went on to write books about Iran. We saw quite a bit of Robin on network television during events that took place in Afghanistan following September 11, and thereafter in Iraq.

Throughout his book, MacAleese's mién epitomizes the concept of the modern no–nonsense professional fighting man. He also questions the rationale as to why soldiers of fortune are held in such derision, especially among those who know little about the military. This tough, outspoken Scot encapsulates the mentality of so many of these professional fighters when he said: "I've never soldiered for profit. During all my service in three regular armies, my pay was unimpressive by modern standards. I went from one fighting zone to another, but today I receive no pension. Nor do I have funds from any other source. I've done it for the adventure, because I've always been a professional soldier and because I love a fight. I've never been happier than in action."

As a mercenary, McAleese saw a good deal of action in Rhodesia's war. Afterwards, he fought for a while with elite South African Defence Force units and then for a handful of other nations. His closest brush with death, he admits, occurred when he tried to assassinate the Colombian drug lord Pablo Escobar.

The mercenary ideal—already vilified by excesses committed by South African soldiers of fortune fighting for 5 Commando in Katanga (Callan's Angolan debacle came later)—never retrieved either its glamour or the mystique in which some of these people had basked before.

The achievements of the early years, when small groups of foreign soldiers put loosely armed bands of disorganized Simba rebels in the Congo to flight and brought stability to a huge chunk of Central Africa, were subsumed by scandal. In part, this is why some Western governments continue to be vigorously opposed to private military companies getting involved in African—or any other—wars. As one British minister phrased it succinctly, "The opportunity for abuse predominates."

When it happens, he said, it was impossible to ignore either the violence or the brutal excesses. Very often it was white on black, "which, in the post-colonial era is both reprehensible and indefensible." Looking at some of the events surrounding the Angolan tragedy, you can hardly argue otherwise.

Yet, for all this, there is a handful of war dogs who have served with distinction. And even if we don't like what they did, we must acknowledge their skills, tenacity and accomplishments as professional soldiers.

The most notable individual in this category must surely be Bob Denard, a warrior king out of Homer who made a career of involving himself in a variety of trouble spots all over Africa and beyond. His tally included Togo (an unsuccessful attempt at toppling the Lome government), Chad, Biafra and Angola as well as Mobutu Sese Seko's Congo. Then, in March 1975, with a small band of about forty "volunteers," he sailed all the way from France, rounded the southern tip of Africa and in a short, sharp exchange of fire, took possession of an entire Indian Ocean archipelago. Though the Comores is little more than a cluster of islands, these were difficult Cold War times. Yet he managed to hold on to power for almost a decade. In another age, Kipling might have described him as "the man who would be king."

The miracle is that the *Antinea*, a dilapidated old rust bucket in which this intrepid group of Frenchmen managed their remarkable ten thousand-mile voyage around the Cape, actually made it to this island group to the north of Madagascar. The rest of what happened in a country that experienced twenty or more coups in its first quarter-century of independence is history: there were three more attempted putsches while I was working on this book, two of them involving more groups of French mercenaries.

Denard's arrival in his original 1970s endeavor was well timed. The Comorean leader, a crazy demagogue by the name of Ali Soilih, was schizoid and to many it was "written" that he should die. One of his last public edicts was that the nation should pray to him and not to Allah. Always the opportunist, the French mercenary leader grabbed the moment and promptly declared himself boss of the republic. Since he had some local support, the foreign-backed coup went unchallenged.

Denard took matters further when, sensitive to public opinion— and obviously, to score points with those who mattered in this staunchly Muslim state—he converted to Islam. Within a short while he married a couple of local beauties and raised a family. Finally, years

later—after the French Navy had driven him out and before returning
to France to stand trial—he and his entourage took refuge in South
Africa, wives, children and all. His story has the makings of a marvelous epic and I'm surprised that Hollywood hasn't grabbed it.

While still in power, I visited Denard at his lovely villa on the
north of Grande Comore, the main island. The idea was that I should
make a television documentary about the place, but this being impossible without his blessing, I sought the help of another of his old compadres, former submarine flotilla commander Rear Admiral Theo
Honiball. Theo and Bob were old pals, the two having got to know
each other in France while the admiral—then a captain—took delivery
of the first of a squadron of Daphne Class submarines for the South
African Navy.

As so often happens in the impalpable world of spooks and favors,
Theo obliged and handed me a letter of introduction, which I presented to Denard's office on the morning of my arrival in Moroni, the
Comorian capital. Though the hawk-eyed Frenchman was skeptical at
first, I was warmly welcomed once formalities had been cleared.

In Denard, I discovered a man who had a blokishness about him
that implied trust. We became friends and he even approached me
later in Johannesburg to publish his memoirs covering all his exploits.
Though he offered me English-language publication rights, I couldn't
help him because I was about to leave for Washington.

One of the first questions I'm usually asked when I mention
Denard is: was this archetypal mercenary really the fire-eater that so
many of his enemies (and some of his friends) said he was?

I'd like to think that the answer rests, in part, with another of the
old veterans of an age of which, I fear, we might have seen the last.
That man is Ron Reid-Daly—Uncle Ron to his friends, of Selous
Scouts fame.

It is perhaps significant that the roots of both men—within their
respective military establishments—go deep. Denard first fought with
the French and Reid-Daly served well enough while attached to the
British Army in Malaya to be awarded a gong by the Queen. And let's
face it, there aren't too many militant recalcitrants who are able to
sport an MBE. In other respects the two stalwarts are a lot alike,
though Reid-Daly—with his bred-in-the-bones élan—would offer you
a feisty bunch of fives if you were to call him a merc.

Both men, totemic images in their own right, had outstanding military careers. Both share an encyclopedic knowledge of the kind of his-

torical events that affect us all. Even more important, both men are gentlemen in the classical mold. Whenever my wife would enter the room, they'd get up and stay on their feet until she was seated, something you don't see too often these days. Also, they've kept themselves astonishingly fit well into old age, which is why the irrepressible Ron is still sometimes seen in the company of women thirty years his junior.

More important, both Denard and Reid-Daly, while active militarily, clearly understood the dynamics of conflict. There were times when they could ask their men to do just about anything and, when push came to shove, they often did. Indeed, these two old veterans tended to stand out in the crowd, and even those who totally opposed their ideals would defer to them.

Colonel Ronald Francis Reid-Daly went on to command the armed forces of South Africa's now-defunct Transkei government where they made him a general. His second-in-command in Umtata was an American Vietnam vet by the name of Bob MacKenzie, the same man I mentioned earlier who was wounded, tortured and eaten in Sierra Leone.

Interestingly, MacKenzie's bizarre ending was not an isolated incident. By all accounts, eating human flesh in some African conflicts is a lot more widespread than most imagine. In its official full-page obituary notice of Foday Sankoh, the revolutionary who led the rebels in Sierra Leone, Britain's *Economist* recorded that one of Sankoh's campaigns was called "Operation Pay Yourself" and involved the rebels actually "eating the flesh and drinking the blood of freshly killed victims."[4]

As Colonel Bert Sachse, Executive Outcomes commander in Sierra Leone, was to discover during his own tour of duty, there were many instances of prisoners having been eaten by their captors. His comment when I interviewed him was that "This activity wasn't exactly limited only to the rebels: our own Sierra Leone troops sometimes ate members of the opposing forces . . . it was really the only red meat they got." Give them some slack, Sachse suggested, "because they were very discreet the way they went about doing it."

That all happened a decade ago. The war in Sierra Leone went on to claim thousands more victims, almost all of them innocents (see Chapter 19).

African conflicts are sometimes enmeshed in imponderables that even governments do not anticipate until it is too late.

Henry Kenealy, erstwhile communications officer at the U.S. Embassy in Freetown, has a stock of stories of his own emanating from time spent serving the State Department. He recalls something that took place during the 1997 putsch when members of the Sierra Leone Army grabbed power. It was a messy affair and thousands died: anybody caught in the open or on the streets became targets.

As Hank tells it, nobody could get to the embassy because of the fighting: "It was a Sunday morning and we were all at home. Worse, nobody had expected anything even remotely as violent as this. The same with communications: the power was down and there were none. Since all domestic phone lines in Sierra Leone were programmed by SierraTEL and because of cable thefts and fraud, any kind of foreign call—including those from the embassy—were out. We couldn't even tell our bosses in Washington what was happening, though they'd obviously heard the news on the BBC." Consequently, the US Embassy and its entire staff was, as they say, "in quarantine."

Using his private Yeasu FT-747GX HF radio—Kenealy's ham call sign is 9L1HK—he ran phone patches through two radio hams in the United States to the State Department's switch board. Eventually he was able to retrieve an Inmarsat phone and, at the end of it, the HF set was used to coordinate the evacuation of embassy staff to the USS *Kearsarge*, an American warship lying off the West African coast. The two amateurs got a commendation from the Secretary of State for their efforts that involved an ongoing and extremely tense drama played out with almost no sleep over several days.

A lot else in Africa has changed as well. Where once there were European governments divvying up the conquered playing fields, some of the more recent players have included individuals like the cerebrally challenged Charles Taylor, who—when still running things in Liberia—made Idi Amin look civilized. Nor were this tyrant's excesses restricted to his own country: none of the horrific sequences played out in Sierra Leone in the decade that followed—together with a quarter-million deaths, most of them innocents—would have happened without Taylor's personal say-so.

A late UN report pointed to this despot as having hired Serb, Libyan, Ukrainian and South African mercenaries—together with regular soldiers from half a dozen African states. All were there to do his bidding and they were paid very well for their efforts. Their sole objective, the document states, was to foster revolt across the border.

CNN television, in one of the remarkable docu-dramas of our times titled "Cry Freetown," excluded nothing when the network showed us what these savages were capable of. For sport, *The Economist* records, some of the young rebels, many of them still pre-teen kids in sneakers, "would place bets as to the sex of an unborn baby. And then they would slit open the mother's stomach to find out."

Conditions weren't helped by some of the European mercenaries hired to counter this carnage. A number of Serbs and Croats that we encountered in the Congo in the late 1990s were, if anything, little more than thugs with distorted visions of "sorting out" Africa. Like Callan's mob in Angola twenty-five years before, their military background was rudimentary and not a few were racists. There were times when they openly insulted their black officers, irrespective of the fact that they were the ones who passed on the pay packets filled with dollars each month.

While the names change, most of the basics of unconventional warfare remain more or less what they have always been. People are hired to fight for obscure causes (and some not so obscure, like the ongoing genocide in Darfur, and Biafra before that), and usually it is accomplished with vigor. So, too, in Colombia where South American drug barons muster squads of mercenaries to achieve paramilitary objectives that invariably result in people dying. Most of these often have nothing to do with the either the "cause" or the government. The almost-defunct IRA has been especially active in this regard.

Squads of Catholic Irish dissidents are known to have trained Colombian rebel forces in counterinsurgency procedures. It matters little that there are moments when they are arrayed against the very same Catholic Americans who, for decades, helped fund the original IRA crusade back home.

Indeed, according to a seventy-page report titled "Global Trends 2015," and released by the U.S. Central Intelligence Agency, international affairs in the foreseeable future are likely to be increasingly determined by large and powerful organizations rather than governments, especially in the Third World. Langley reckons that these could involve alliances between the world's most influential crime syndicates such as the Mafia and Chinese triads.

Worse, the use of mercenaries is implicit in the muscle needed to implement these policies. The Agency adds that their income will come from narcotics, alien dispersal, toxic materials and hazardous waste smuggling, illicit arms, military technologies and so on.

The mercenary of today is consequently a very different person from many of the characters who liked to masquerade under the usually derogatory epithet of previous times.

While Executive Outcomes was active in Sierra Leone and Angola, the men on the ground could expect to earn at least $1,000 a month, while the average field commander took home very much more. Since then, those amounts have quintupled, and in some cases, as in Afghanistan and Iraq, have increased tenfold.

It was (and still is) very different in the air. Helicopter gunship pilots like Charlie Tate, Juba Joubert, Arthur Walker or Neall Ellis could, in theory, notch up as much as $100,000 a year. As with their land-bound counterparts, it was all tax free, though in point of fact, contracts rarely lasted long enough to score that well. Also, living conditions, food, water and other facilities that the majority of Western forces take for granted were (and still are) almost always substandard.

Executive Outcomes liked to hire what it regarded as "the best of the bunch," the majority of them tough counterinsurgency specialists with about a decade or more of solid, unconventional bush combat experience. Feeding and keeping a medium-sized force in the field also presents its own set of problems.

While rations in Angola were sometimes passable, EO units in Sierra Leone had to learn to eat like the locals. Much of the time—especially once you got into the interior, beyond Freetown—there was simply little else available but cassava root, plantain and, on a feast day, cane rat.

"You get used to it," said the never-churlish Cobus Claassens, who spent a year with EO fighting the rebels in Sierra Leone. These days there are some West African dishes that he cannot do without, which helps, because he's still in Freetown.

Establishing an effective communications system for a newly arrived fighting force is another issue faced by mercenary groups, wherever they might be deployed. Also, things aren't made any easier when those involved cannot speak the lingo. In places like the Congo (French) and Angola (Portuguese), being able to communicate can be crucial if you are to survive, never mind the need to maintain radio comms with an outlying military post where the commander might have proved himself to be rabidly anti-white. It gets worse when he also controls the only supply of aviation fuel for a couple of hundred miles. Every one of the men involved in these remote, isolated conflicts has his stock of war stories.

Most of the airmen active in Angola and Sierra Leone in recent years had to take inordinate risks, if only to survive. As one of them phrased it, they'd spent years at the combat coalface and chance was a constant factor. But then so was merely living in Africa, so what the hell, as one exclaimed when he was about to embark on his third tour of duty with EO.

Also, these were hardly the ordinary sort of folk that you get to mix with at your local Wal-Mart. The average merc is a breed apart. His life of choice is most times infused with a relentless and sometimes reckless desire for a scrap. And then, once it's over, many of these professionals simply don't fit in with society back home. Others become loners. Inherently, the majority are suspicious creatures, but then that's perhaps symptomatic of most of the military, especially where it involves the press.

In essence, the mercenary types that I've encountered in a score of wars over the past four decades have not been all that different from any regular U.S. Army, British Parachute Regiment or United Nations soldier from countries all over. Sitting in with a planning group at the U.S. Army Operational HQ in Somalia in the early 1990s was not very different from being with a crowd of Her Majesty's Royal Marines at an Order Group at Lungi Airport ten years later.

So, too, on operations in El Salvador. We'd gather around a large colorful map on the wall of the control room at military headquarters in the eastern city of San Miguel when that insurgency was at its worst, and discuss the day's events. This was another thing organized by the indomitable Bob MacKenzie. Similarly, while flying combat in a rickety old Mi-24 helicopter gunship with Neall Ellis in Sierra Leone in the summer of 2000, we shared an operations center and a map room with British Army elements (including Special Forces) at Cockerill Army Barracks in Freetown. Apart from the setting and the faces of the guards outside all being black, there weren't many aspects of this headquarters' infrastructure that would have been out of place back in the UK.

Interestingly, Whitehall did ask a few questions about what it termed "the mercenary connection." But it is also true that as the war progressed, the bowler-hatted ones were never really kept abreast of what was taking place on the ground in this West African state. It stayed that way until it was over.

It's to be expected, perhaps, that mercenaries—as with most regular troops, officers and men alike—tend to share something of a common empathy that sets them apart from the rest of the public. After all, that is what first prompted them to enlist and don a uniform.

To some it is the appeal of tradition. To others, it's the lore of yesterday's battles. To a rare few it's the discipline. Mercs, like those attached to regular armies, have similar foibles.

So, too, with their aspirations. Back home, both sets of individuals have families, wives, girlfriends—and in one or two notable cases, even among "hired guns"—boyfriends.

Many of them are parents. Their fears for the future are similar to those that preoccupy the rest of us. And while government forces are—and always have been—subject to the rule of law, mercenaries have increasingly been made answerable for what they do "out there."

One of the last documents signed by the outgoing Clinton administration was a Human Rights bill involving war crimes. Ultimately that legislation—which has serious international ramifications—will bring some of the transgressors who ignored these tenets to justice.

The "brutality of war," as Slobodon Milosovic discovered to his astonishment at The Hague not very long ago, no longer sanitizes inhumanity, no matter who you are.

PART I

Ongoing wars in Afghanistan and Iraq continue to dominate the headlines. Concurrently, notable changes in the manner in which military events are unfolding elsewhere have taken place. Today, when some wayward African dictator becomes restless or a South American warlord fosters insurrection, the world's major powers are more inclined to look the other way. They are too focused on tamping down the worldwide Islamic terror threat. The possibility that the Pentagon will dispatch forces to assist some troubled Third World government is much less likely today than it was in our pre-9-11 world. Just getting the USS *Iwo Jima* to assist with a regime change in Liberia in August 2003 was difficult. For the difficult times we live in, it was also unusual. Thus, where security has become an issue in maintaining stability in some far- flung state, another solution must be sought. And since it was the Dogs of War that cleared the bramble patch in the old days, once again, it seems, it will be their job to instill a measure of order in such places when things begin to fall apart.

1

HELICOPTER GUNSHIPS IN SIERRA LEONE'S WAR

"For the mercenary is a simplistic fellow. Not for him the strutting parades of West Point, the medals on the steps of the White House or perhaps a place at Arlington. He simply says: 'Pay me my wage and I'll kill the bastards for you.' And if he dies, they will bury him quickly and quietly in the red soil of Africa and we will never know. . . ."

Frederick Forsyth, "Send in the Mercenaries,"
Wall Street Journal, May 15, 2000

Anybody on the wrong side of sixty who believes that he can contribute something by going to war in a helicopter gunship in one of the most remote corners of the globe has got to be a little crazy. Or he's into what aficionados like to term "wacky backy." In my case, neither condition applies.

For five hectic weeks in the summer of 2000 I did exactly that, flying combat in West Africa with a bunch of mercenaries against rebels trying to take over the country of Sierra Leone. Although I was shot at as often as the others, my role was not as a combatant. Officially I was an observer, reporting for various publications in the stable of Britain's Jane's Information Group, including *Jane's International Defence Review* as well as *Jane's Defence Weekly*. In doing this, I was strapped into the gunner's seat just ahead of the pilot on a rickety old Russian-built Mi-24 that leaked when it rained.

The commander of that bird was Neall Ellis (whom we affectionately called Nellis). We had flown together twenty years earlier during the bloody Angolan War. In those days he flew a French-built Alouette helicopter, the same type of gunship that had played such a significant role at Cuamato, a small town inside Angola that witnessed the hard hand of war from both the ground and the sky. In those days the gunships were flown by people like Arthur Walker and Heinz Katzke. These aviators made a name for themselves in a conflict that escalated

25

several notches beyond a simple counterinsurgency. Their goal was to oppose the aggressive activities conducted by communist forces led by Fidel Castro's Cuban Army and Air Force. The operations in that remote southern African theater took the form of irregular battles that one rarely read about in news reports of the day.

The fighting in Sierra Leone was different—and much more so after the turn of the millennium. Every day of the week, Sundays included, we'd fly one or more strike missions a day, taking the gunship sometimes deep into the jungle interior of a country roughly the size of Ireland. Other times we'd strike at targets not far from the capital Freetown itself.

The war was especially brutal on the ground where most of the victims were innocents. Aloft, we were the masters and it stayed that way as long as a batch of white-painted United Nations helicopters that had arrived a short while before I got to Freetown had not yet been armed. A fully equipped squadron of the more potent Indian Air Force Mi-24 variants that eventually became part of the UN detachment was still being assembled at Hastings, one of Sierra Leone's smaller domestic airports, not far from the capital.

To paraphrase Shakespeare, our problems arrived in battalions. While the rebels attached to Foday Sankoh's Revolutionary United Front (RUF) did not have an air force of their own, they made do with what they could cadge from those who supported their cause. As we were to constantly observe from radio intercepts, there were a number of foreigners who backed Sankoh's revolt and were not averse to using their more sophisticated hardware when it suited their purposes. An occasional Mi-8 flown by South African and Russian mercenaries would slip into Sierra Leonian airspace from Liberia, usually headed for rebel outposts in the northern part of the country.

The ostensible object of these flights was to haul men and material, but the real reason behind their presence was diamonds. Tens of millions of dollars in raw stones were being illegally mined under rebel supervision in the northern Kono region. The rebel-backed helicopter gunships zipped in and out of the country, fast and low, to snatch large diamond parcels. The existence of Sierra Leone's precious stones was the primary reason Liberian President Charles Taylor provided the RUF with military support. A cunning and ruthless operator, Taylor— who had come to power after a lengthy civil war—had but one purpose in mind: helping the rebels to take Freetown. By doing so, all of Sierra Leone's diamond fields would eventually have been under his control.

By any yardstick, flying combat in Sierra Leone was an experience. The rebels had the run of almost everything beyond Freetown. Also, it was accepted by everyone onboard that if we were shot down or forced to land behind enemy lines, we would probably not survive. With our weapons—including a pair of belt-fed GPSG machine guns—we would certainly have been able to keep going for a while, assuming, of course, that we would survive the initial impact. But we were under no illusion that beyond the confines of Freetown and its environs we would be in our adversary's back yard. They would have had the additional advantage of numbers: the four of us, no matter how well-armed would hardly have been a match for a squad of guerrillas, no matter how badly trained or doped. Personally, had I been faced with the options of a fight or making a run for it, I would probably have taken the gap towards the Guinea frontier. Its most distant point—considering that Sierra Leone is only fractionally bigger than New Jersey—the trudge through the jungle could never have been more than a hundred miles: perhaps three or four days on foot. One tends to think about such things when flying over endless stretches of tropical forest when you have the prospect of what might be a pretty bloody confrontation ahead.

Certainly, each one of us was also aware that Ellis had a price on his head: at the time I flew with him it was a bounty of a million US dollars, though there was a little muted discussion in Freetown's watering holes as to whether that meant dead or alive. Several reports subsequently claimed that the reward was actually double that. Travelling about with this war dog each day, to and from work and back home from the pubs and sometimes Hassan's place, quite often very late at night was probably a bit of a risk, but the truth is, nobody ever gave us more than a passing glance.

During the course of dozens of operational flights we saw a good share of action, with Nellis and the boys doing the necessary each time we encountered rebels. Through it all, we were lucky. Our worst afflictions during this period were mild bouts of malaria.

In retrospect, the Sierra Leone experience was neither as odious nor as repulsive as I might have expected, even though, on a day-to-day, sortie-by-sortie basis, we were able to account for sizable numbers of the enemy. It is also true that none of us felt anything for those who came into our sights, if only because Nellis was eliminating the same bloody cretins who were systematically mutilating children. In this regard, it was telling that when we'd return to Freetown after a flight and the people asked us whether we'd been successful, they would embrace us no matter how we answered. Each one of them was aware of the dreadful stories that emerged each day from the jungle that encroached to the edges of this huge suppurating conurbation.

It was that kind of war. And for two years, Nellis' lone helicopter gunship was about all the majority of the population had on which to precariously pin their hopes.

By the time that I became involved, the ground war had been going on for several years. Casualties had been heavy on both sides, sometimes with a Nigerian Army-backed "peacekeeping mission" (ECOMOG) providing support, sometimes not. We had little doubt about the nature of the enemy. As one UN observer succinctly explained in an off-the-record briefing, "The majority of the rebels are mindless cretins who make a fetish of cutting off the limbs of children." He went on to declare the rebels "simple-minded bastards," some of whom, he explained, believed that such actions were appropriate when they needed to amuse themselves during a slow day in the jungle.

Flying with Nellis could be a taxing experience, with some sorties that left us drained after only a couple of hours in the air. We had our moments, obviously, especially when we hovered over enemy positions or occupied towns after being told by British military intelligence (under whose auspices Nellis operated) that the rebels had deployed SAMs. Conventional anti-aircraft weapons, I was soon to discover, was the norm, but since recent events in Chechnya had demonstrated that this hardware was a match for anything more conventional forces could field, such occasions would marvelously exercise the imagination.

Occasionally we would return to base with a hole or two in our fuselage, though at least once the damage was self-inflicted. During an attack on one of the more active rebel towns to the east of Freetown, Hassan, our starboard side-gunner, swung his machine gun in too wide an arc and stitched a set of holes into the starboard drop tank. Fortunately it was empty. Had it not been—with us using tracers—the upshot of that little episode over enemy territory might have been different. Nor was it a lone occurrence. The pair of Mi-24 helicopters operated by Nellis and his pals for the Sierra Leone Air Wing was probably more often patched than any comparable choppers then operational in Asia, Africa or Latin America.

While the Air Wing's day-to-day regimen was dictated largely by events in the field—much of it coupled to intercepts of enemy radio messages, which came into the special ops room around the clock—there was always something new happening at Cockerill Barracks. The headquarters of the Sierra Leone military was a large, futuristic-looking structure at the far end of a festering lagoon that fringed one of Freetown's outlying suburbs. From there, the country's only operational pilot flew from a single, heavily defended helipad on the grounds of this expansive military establishment that dated from World War II.

Most of the sorties launched during my own sojourn in Sierra Leone were routine, quick in-and-out strikes on specific targets. Still, things could get hectic. There were days when the crew went up three times in quick succession, occasionally timing the last mission to return just as the sun dipped below the horizon beyond Cape Sierra Leone on which much of this city lies.

On one of my early flights, we'd been ordered to scramble on short notice. Since I was the newcomer, Nellis relegated me to the back of the chopper with the side-gunners. I'd barely had time to shower and change, but I went aloft anyway in a T-shirt, jeans, and a pair of flip-flops. It was a bad decision. I spent much of that flight dodging chunks of sizzling hot metal as brass shell casings clattered onto my exposed feet from two very active general purpose machine guns (or in official British Army terminology, GPMGs). I should have known better because I'd been in a similar situation in Angola a few years before while covering that conflict with Executive Outcomes, a mercenary firm based out of Pretoria, South Africa. At the time we were in an Angolan Air Force Mi-17.

The bloodiest chapter of Sierra Leone's brief post-independent history is now on record, but the war could easily have gone the other way. Because the government had been unprepared for any kind of conflict, hostilities from the outset tended to favor the rebels. It remained that way until a lightning deployment codenamed "Operation Palliser," involving Britain's Quick Reaction Force (QRF) pushed a powerful body of rebels into West Africa. Tony Blair's government was serious about countering a military insurrection in what until the 1960s had been one of the jewels in the British Imperial crown.

The British strike force was initially composed of eight hundred men of the 1st Parachute Battalion Parachute Regiment, which was later replaced by a Royal Marine detachment. Additional support came from a variety of Royal Air Force and Royal Naval elements, including the aircraft carrier HMS *Illustrious* as well as the helicopter carrier HMS *Ocean*. C-130 Hercules transport planes from RAF Lyneham, and RAF Tristars from 216 Squadron operating out of Brize Norton, were tasked to shift most of the combatants and lighter hardware, with much of it arriving by sea a month later.

With only a few hours' advance notice, four RAF HC Mk2 Chinooks were flown in pairs more than 3,000 miles to Dakar, on the Atlantic coast of Africa. The epic deployment had set out from RAF Odiham, home of the British Chinook force. The crews of each of these giant helicopters were ordered to fly twenty-three hours within a thirty-six hour window of opportunity. In order to make this possible, the Chinooks were equipped with two 800-gallon Robinson internal extended-range tanks. Each aircraft had replacement crewmen from all three squadrons, each of whom assisted in some important way on what is now recognized as the longest self-deployment in the history of the RAF helicopter force.

From the beginning, just about everybody involved militarily in Sierra Leone knew they were up against an extremely aggressive insurgent group accustomed to meeting little if any resistance from government forces. However, when the war flared up again in late 1998 (there had been several earlier conflicts, one of which involved Executive Outcomes and South African mercenaries) the RUF quickly demonstrated that it was better trained and equipped than it had been in the past. Because of earlier results, Sankoh's rebel army was motivated to achieve its single objective: the control by force of the entire country. The rebels' combat ability was evident: they succeeded virtually every time they set out to capture a position held by Sierra Leone security forces. Within a month of initiating hostilities in 1998, Sankoh's revolutionaries could go just about anywhere they wanted except the capital of Freetown.

Foday Sankoh's twisted path to power as the head of the Revolutionary United Front meandered through several countries and spanned decades. The radicalized 1970s student leader served for a time as a corporal in the army and later as a television cameraman. His anti-establishment criminal behavior, however, landed him in jail. When he was freed, Sankoh fled with fellow Sierra Leonean exiles to Libya in the 1980s, where President Muammar Gadhaffi was busy spreading revolutionary instability by stirring up West African dissidents like Sankoh. Seething with anger against those with more wealth and anxious to lead his own rebellion, Sankoh crafted an alliance with Liberia's Charles Taylor, who was planning his own internal coup. Taylor's horrific eight-year uprising seized the presidency in neighboring Monrovia in 1998.

With the support of Charles Taylor, Liberia's rogue president, Foday Sankoh had used the two years following a ceasefire—which the mercenary group Executive Outcomes had brought into effect—to totally revamp his revolutionary forces. During this impasse, President Gadhaffi provided generous material and financial support, and he obviously had reasons of his own for doing so. Other countries linked to the rebels were Burkina Faso (formerly Upper Volta) and, to a lesser extent, the Sudan. It was then too that al-Qaeda emerged as a factor in the war, using diamonds mined by Sierra Leone's large Lebanese community to finance Osama bin Laden's aspirations. This could very well have a bearing on why Britain took such drastic steps to defeat the rebels, though you won't get anybody in London to acknowledge it.

We now know that the RUF employed Russian, Ukrainian, South African and other African mercenaries. Deployed operationally, many of these people were responsible for combat command and control as well as logistics and communications. For their part, the South Africans concentrated their efforts on imparting many of the principles they had used to good effect in their own wars in Namibia and Angola, which was one of the reasons why the rebels initially gained as much ground as they did.

The "hired guns" were not working their trade for free. Virtually every mercenary wielding a rifle or piloting a craft was also into diamonds, which was what the fighting was about. President Taylor's cut was about one-half of the gemstones carried, flown or shipped across the border. His take was so large it explains why, within the comparatively short time of three or four years, Liberia emerged in London, Johannesburg, Antwerp, and Tel Aviv as a diamond exporting country of some significance.

And the war dragged on. On two occasions the rebels fought their way to within spitting distance of the gates of Freetown. Both times RUF forces were beaten back by a single helicopter gunship flown by Nellis, the government's lone South African mercenary pilot. Far from their own supply lines running out of Liberia—but protected by enough heavy weapons to start another war—the rebels did not have the proper weaponry to counter Nellis' airborne firepower. Our gun-ship had a 57mm rocket pod under each of its winglets together with a four-barreled 12.7mm Gatling Gun System mounted in the nose. The latter could fire nearly four thousand rounds a minute. It was impressive to behold such a weapon from a distance, as we sometimes did when we'd touch down in a town and Nellis would have us stay on the ground while he "cleaned up" outside. His favorite tactic was to fire the quad in half-second bursts. That alone was enough to tear-up everything in its path and a good reason why the Gatling was always the most feared weapon dominating Sierra Leone's skies.

Beyond the perimeters of the grotesque Hell that some of us got to know as Freetown—a dirty, dusty, overcrowded conurbation with two million-plus refugees, all of them perched precariously atop rows of hills overlooking the sea—Foday Sankoh for a long while was little more than a rebel-in-waiting. In this regard he was identical to a dozen or so other militants who threatened governments up and down an unstable and debilitated Africa. There was, however, one striking difference between this aspiring oligarch and the rest. Sankoh craved legality. As some of his lieutenants were to report after the war, he dreamt of acceptance by the world at large. With it, he knew, came a seat at the United Nations and many of its ancillary bodies. Further, he would have had his own people ensconced in the Sierra Leone embassies in London, Washington and elsewhere. Foday Sankoh held throughout that the only way he could achieve his goal was to "own" his own capital, and that was Freetown. Fortunately, the squalid city on the northeast tip of a small peninsula jutting into the Atlantic Ocean remained just beyond his reach—and much of that was Nellis' doing.

Still, it was a near-run thing. Had Sankoh got what he wanted, it's more likely than not that he and his cohorts might today be dealing cards with representatives not only of the British Crown, but with the rest of the world. Sankoh's representative would have had a vote on par with that of the United States in the United Nations General Assembly. It was Nellis and his Hind in the end that preserved the status quo.

Operating as a scribe out of Cockerill Barracks in Freetown presented me with few problems. It soon became clear that my presence at the heli-base was an unusual departure for the Sierra Leone command, if only because I was the first journalist to become part of a combat team. But then, as Nellis himself pointed out to his commanders, I was his friend. Moreover, he stressed, the war was going badly for the government and Freetown needed to counter an effective public relations campaign launched by the rebels—again with Gadhaffi's cash. Nellis had twice saved the struggling nation from being overrun by those same rebels, so when the South African pilot elaborated on such things, hardly anybody complained, at least overtly.

The Jane's cachet, too, helped my cause. Once my articles began to appear abroad, British advisors operating out of Cockerill—including a sprinkling of SAS operators (specially-trained British commandos) and military intelligence boffins—tacitly accepted my presence. The result was that thereafter nobody, apart from some flying officers off the carriers lying at anchor with eight or nine other Royal Navy ships in Freetown Bay, gave me or my graying beard a second glance as we went about our work.

Ours was a tight, almost intimate little clique. The group included former SAS sergeant Fred Marafano. Decorated for his role in freeing hostages trapped in the Iranian Embassy in London some years before, Marafano had seen and done it all on four continents. There was also Hassan the side gunner, who had inadvertently poked a few holes in our own bird. Hassan, a native of Lebanon, was a proud Muslim and what made him even more unusual was that he firmly believed that Hezbollah, the terrorist group operating with Iranian financial support back home, would ultimately save the world. Given the circumstances under which we operated, we couldn't disabuse him of his notion. He was, after all, covering our backs. He was also one of the most competent gunners I'd met in any war.

Another member of the team was a mysterious young thirty-something Frenchman known only as "Christophe." He would come and go from Paris as it pleased him, there one month, gone the next. We eventually concluded that if nothing else, he was a likely candidate to have been working for France's *Direction Generale de la Securite Exterieure*, though to be fair, that was little more than speculation. When the numbers tally, however, you reach your own conclusions.

No one in Freetown examined "Christophe's" credentials too closely. Nor, for that matter, did they run a check on mine, though Whitehall would have definitely have taken the trouble to check us all out at some stage or another. Our team included several Sierra Leonian side-gunners, all of them tough, committed fighting men who had seen both sides of the ongoing conflict.

Though subject to the kind of military discipline that one would expect in any fighting force, there were a lot of surprises. For instance, I was nonplused the first time I was taken into Cockerill Barracks by Nellis' driver: we didn't even rate a second glance from the guards. I wasn't armed and I wasn't wearing a uniform. I was actually wearing shorts. In fact, I didn't even own a flying suit. Yet none of the black troops who were manning the gates so much as blinked when we drove through without stopping—even though they had never seen me before. It was peculiar to be so casually accepted as one of the gang in one of the most sensitive military establishments on Africa's West Coast.

As I discovered, the only "authority" needed was a white skin, which in a black African country gripped by conflict was hardly another first. European mercenaries involved in African struggles tend to generate respect among the locals, especially when they were all that stood between a populace sleeping in their own beds at night and the kind of lunacy that RUF rebels were capable of generating.

My biggest personal concern that first day was how to strap my six-foot-two-inch frame into the gunner's seat of the M-24, or in NATO-speak, the Hind. It was clearly built for smaller, more compact folk. The routine was fixed: slip the left foot into the appropriate groove on the fuselage and then a hard twist to the right, toward another indentation just inside the cockpit. That done, I would end up with one leg on either side of the joystick. For somebody who doesn't even like to travel on the London Underground when it's crowded, it took fortitude.

The view from up front was daunting. Until then I'd been relegated to the back with the side-gunners, where I had less of an observer's perspective of the war than from where I was now perched. The small fan blowing into my face didn't help dissipate the fog of humidity that enveloped us as we waited for Nellis to "wind her up."

Naturally my curiosity got the best of me, especially since this was my first time up front. The array of dials and switches on all sides was rather intimidating, especially since they were all labeled in Cyrillic script. In my immediate line of sight was a gyroscopic device, digital-age complicated. More dials cluttered several rows of panels to my right and left. The black-painted optics of the helicopter's computerized gun sights hovered at two o'clock. Though I flew often, I never understood any of it

Most obtrusive was the joystick. As Nellis had shown me earlier, this device was decorated with toggles in several colors, like the handles on some of those machines in any amusement arcade. The one that activated the Gatling, he specified, was bright red. "You touch it and it's going to fire. So you don't because that's my job." That was fine with me, I replied. The quiet-spoken pilot could be emphatic when it suited him. Earlier, he'd explained which buttons fired the helicopter's rockets and that, too, was taboo for this passenger.

Moments later we were under orders. If I had doubts about what I was doing, it was too late. I'd be letting everyone down if I pulled out now. In any event, Nellis had stipulated that if I didn't like it I should tell him beforehand so he could put somebody else in my place. Whoever flew under the front bubble had several in-flight roles, every one of them critical.

From the moment Nellis' threw the first switch it took only minutes to become airborne. The ground crew checked out everything and then stood clear. While Western helicopters have set procedures to prepare for take-off—with things invariably arranged in an ergonomically friendly order—it is very much otherwise with Russian choppers. The first two circuit breakers Nellis activated were on either side of and behind his seat. The next, in sequence, was on his left, followed by another in the center, then to the right again, and so on.

He never complained about the Russian whirlybird, but I knew that this was one of the reasons why he was keen to get his hands on a surplus Aerospatiale Puma to do some of the transport work into the interior of this heavily forested country. Also, he told me, you could see the ground a lot better from the French chopper than the Russian, which was especially helpful when flying into some of the more difficult LZs, where we'd approach through disproportionately tiny spaces flanked by some of the tallest trees in Africa.

On the Mi-24, meanwhile, I had to attend to my own set of chores. My first job after lift-off was to push down hard on a small circuit breaker at my left elbow to arm our weapons' systems. I would only do that after we entered Injun country, roughly six or eight minutes out of base.

Most pre-flight briefings in the Operations Center at Cockerill—unless there was a specific task that involved other aircraft or possibly liaison with ground forces—were brief. Never one for formality, Nellis had developed a sharp eye and a gambler's instinct for risk, all of it rather resourcefully disguised by an urbane, insouciant style. He would sit at his desk and poke fingers at us.

As the pilot, he would first discuss fuel with his Russian-trained Ethiopian ground crew. One by one they'd go through some of the technical issues encountered after each flight, such as a problem they'd encountered the day before that involved a smoking exhaust. That seemed to indicate oil in a part of the engine where it shouldn't have been.

Nellis turned to me. "You got water?" he asked while his eyes scanned a map on his desk. He did not see me nodding in reply.

"Something to eat?"

"We going out that long?" I asked.

"No, but you'll need food in case we go down."

"All I have is a can of bully beef."

He didn't answer.

The regular gang traveled light. Most times they didn't take much of anything other than a single bottle of water, which was enough for a couple hours of flying. Somehow they just knew that they were going to get back, but then so does every aircrew in just about every war.

I was fractionally more skeptical. From day one, I never went up without a handful of water purifying tablets and my precious Shell Petroleum road map of Sierra Leone which, word had it, the rebels also used for navigation. If it came to that, at least I'd know how to get to Guinea.

"Side arms?" Nellis quizzed the others with a studied air of disregard. Each member of the crew had an AK-47 as standard issue. For "luck," one of the gunners cradled a compact little Czech 9mm submachine gun. When dismantled, it could be hidden inside a car's glove compartment.

The evening before, Hassan had given me the rundown of what to expect should there be problems. Whatever happened, he thought, we'd have enough firepower to fight our way out of almost any mess. The problem was that the GPMGs we carried onboard, stacked under the seats of the main compartment behind the cockpit when not in use, were comparatively heavy as these things go. Their ammunition cases were in obtuse, sharp-edged wooden cases, which would have made for awkward lugging in difficult terrain if we had to extricate ourselves from a dangerous situation on the ground in a hurry.

"If anything happens, you've got to help fight," the Lebanese gunner told me with a wry smile. There were no ifs or buts about it, he suggested almost as an afterthought. One time he joked that since I was a journalist, I needn't worry: "Just show them your Press Card," he chuckled before turning to other matters. Hassan had never been one for the media, which he had grown to distrust from his experiences in Lebanon, but going down in the jungle, even he admitted, was a very serious matter. Which was why he took time out to explain what would be required of me if something happened. He had seen firsthand what the rebels did to people they considered their enemy. Anybody who emerged from a downed helicopter, as he chirped, "would be fair game."

Not yet thirty, Hassan Ahmed Hussein had a sometimes sanguine view of the world, especially since he came from a society dominated as much by the chador as by the mullahs. Looking like a Corsican bandit, Hassan could charm a bird out of a tree. He was also a good man to have at your side in a tight spot. What became evident once I began mixing socially within this community was that Hassan's reputation preceded him wherever we went. The last time the rebels had raided the town, Hassan had almost single-handedly evacuated hundreds of expatriate families from under the noses of the enemy. It was no accident that he was held in such high regard by everybody with whom he came into contact in Freetown.

Hassan had arrived in Sierra Leone by accident, having left Monrovia a short while before the Sierra Leone conflict got serious. Involved in undercover work for the Nigerians in the uprising that eventually brought Charles Taylor to power, a crooked Nigerian commander who owed Hassan money shopped him to Taylor's people and he had to leave Liberia in a hurry. Tipped off that the president's honchos were coming after him, Hassan slipped out of a window at the back of his villa just as they broke down the front door. Like Nellis and the rest of the boys, Hassan knew little else but war.

Once the Hind had lifted-off and headed out over the bay, there was none of the inertia of protracted custom. Nellis flew over several hardscrabble hotspots held by Sankoh's people and peppered those we'd been told were hot, first with rockets and then with bursts from the Gatling. That went fine until the 12.7mm jammed. It was my job to "unjam" it, but nothing I had been told to do worked. Nellis reverted to projectiles again, and when they were gone, we headed back to base.

The gods smiled that musty tropical morning in West Africa and all went as planned. The crew got its share of kills.

Going to battle in the nose of a Hind, with my feet almost nudging the Gatling breech, must rank right up there as one of the ultimate combat experiences. It was certainly very different from flying in the rear with the side-gunners where our vision was largely restricted to the Hip's half dozen portholes on each side of the fuselage. In contrast, my view of the war during those few dozen sorties when I was seated up front was superb, if only because I had the proverbial gunner's-eye view of the war, like the pilot observing just about everything ahead of us and almost as much below.

To qualify to sit just ahead of Nellis in the nose, I was briefed that my first job was to spot enemy fire and movement. Everything else was secondary, Nellis said, accentuating the need for vigilance. Flying in single-ship operations meant that we had to be extra alert because, as he stated blandly, "We're completely on our own."

The helicopter's Gatling gun got us out of most of the hotspots we ran into, poking as it did out of the fuselage immediately ahead of my seat. Dating from the Soviet era, this was the deadliest weapon in the Sierra Leonian armory. I'd been warned that it made a lot of noise, and for me this was somewhat worrying. Already half-deaf from a life-time of covering conflicts, I feared what its blast would do to my ears. The two side-gunners at the rear with their GPMGs, in contrast, were relatively distant from the quad up front, and from where they stood behind the pilot, the Gatling roared rather than barked.

Being virtually on top of the weapon, however, was something else. I'd considered stuffing my ears to deaden the blast, but once in the air I had other important tasks to perform. The instructions arrived in a string of commands on the intercom. Nellis' last words to all of us before lift-off were almost always the same: "Just be sharp and we'll be OK." He wasn't one for throwing platitudes about.

That afternoon we went out again. A four-second run down Cockerill's concrete runway and we were in the air, banking sharply to the right over the huge putrid mangrove swamp that separated the barracks from Lumley Beach. Once we'd topped the bridge at Cockle Bay—the one that links Aberdeen to Freetown—we were over open water and one of the largest natural harbors in the world. This was the same bay that had sheltered Allied convoys during two world wars and, more recently, a Royal Navy task force headed for the Falklands in the early 1980s.

The city's low hills began to emerge out of the haze to our right, clut-tered with more tin shacks than you are likely to find in many cities in

Africa, Lagos and Johannesburg combined. A lazy smoky haze covered parts of the city. Our destination was Lungi, Sierra Leone's only international airport. Along the way we skimmed a sea as flat as Antibes in August, broken intermittently by a couple of deep-sea trawlers at anchor, as well as dug-outs fishing for grouper and 'cuda. There was also a flotilla of larger "Pam Pam" motorized boats that ply this coast all the way up to Dakar and beyond.

The gunship was a familiar sight over these waters and as we passed, the natives raised their oars in salute and yelled lustily in Krio. Because of the roar of our rotors we would never hear the natives as we zipped past, but others told us their cries were always the same: "Nellis, you de man!"

How they loved him. There were quite a few others in that part of the globe who called this former South African Air Force pilot "Peacemaker."

After refueling at Lungi we headed for the interior, going in low and passing within hailing distance of one of the partially sunk car ferries the rebels had destroyed the last time they had come to town. For the rest, a primeval world whizzed by beneath us. It was simultaneously beautiful and captivating. An immediate impression, flying low, about thirty feet above the topmost layer of greenery to avoid enemy missiles, was that very little of it had had changed since time began. Now and again a cluster of forest giants would force us higher and a couple of times Nellis would almost clip the tops of palms. There were moments when we were so close to the triple-canopied forest that I might have stuck out my hand and touched it.

From our vantage point, as we headed into enemy country and the interior, there was little discernible movement in the bush below and, rather astonishingly, few signs of any kind of life. There were no people, no huts, and no animals that we could spot from the air. For much of the time we were aloft, we seemed to be caught in an ambiance that was both fascinating and mysterious. It was also forbidding—shaped, as some of the old codgers would say, by the Hand of God.

The coastal plain that we straddled was mostly flat, punctuated here and there by a thousand streams that would begin and end in the kind of putrefying swampland that I'd previously only seen in films about Vietnam or Cambodia. I imagined what it would be like to be forced down in that totally alien environment. I was certain that even if we survived the impact, never mind the crocs, it would have been difficult to reach dry ground.

Gradually the countryside sloped upward. Below were serried rows of ordered wilderness that stretched away as far as vision would allow. Ahead lay the Wara Wara Mountains, which escalated into Guinea. In contrast to the coast, the carpet of jungle in the north was almost unbroken, dotted here and there by granite outcrops that seemed to punctuate the furry carpet of green, very much like the gomos the Rhodesian Army had used for observation sites during their insurgent war. The rest of the country, laced with rivers, was simply beautiful. What a pity man had desecrated it with war.

Apart from flying and navigating across some of the most rugged tropical terrain anywhere (all very orthodox and military with grid map references and zero times), Nellis liked to handle the larger weapons himself. Usually he used manual sights because so few of our attacks were pre-planned.

Once we entered the "operational area" my role was threefold. First, as noted earlier, I had to throw the switch that armed our weapons systems. Second, I would activate our anti-missile jamming equipment, in a flash if needs be. Third, in the event of a stoppage, the Gatling had to be re-cocked. There were three booster cartridges coupled to three settings installed by its original Soviet manufacturers. And when the time came to push buttons, Nellis could be pretty direct over the mike about what needed to be done. And fast.

While the sortie earlier in the day had produced nothing of substance, our afternoon mission was based on a call for backup from a Sierra Leone Army unit deployed near Port Loko. A small, strategically situated town on the "horseshoe" road that links the capital with Lungi Airport, Port Loko had consistently come under fire from the rebels in recent months. Early word from the base to which we were headed indicated that a squad of government troops had been ambushed and its commander had reported the attack. That was why we were scrambled.

Though the history books had not yet recorded any of it, the region we were then traversing had seen more than its share of drama. Weeks before, four of my colleagues had been ambushed at a road junction a couple of hours' drive north of Freetown. Two of them, Kurt Schork, an American with Reuters, and AP cameraman Miguel Gilmoreno, a Spanish national, were killed in the attack. The incident accentuated the army's tenuous hold on the region as the balance of power continued to seesaw. Once the newspapers got wind of the story, Sierra Leone's media did its best to shape public opinion. If government forces scored a hit, all of Freetown would rejoice. Were it a rebel success that might result in their close approach to the capital, the townspeople would stop buying non-essentials and instead go for that extra bag of rice to hide under the bed. Whenever bad news hit, a gloom of war so palpable you could almost sense despair settled on this mountainside African city.

As we headed toward our target more reports filtered in. This was no enemy feint. By all accounts we were heading towards a large force of rebels backed by vehicles that had Dshka heavy machine guns mounted on their cabs. Most were 12.7mm caliber, like our own, but single-barreled and unmistakable with their long muzzle-breaks up front. The radio reported some 23mm AAA.

Since headquarters had patched into the action by radio, I listened while an army captain with the nom de guerre "Scorpion" kept us briefed. His voice, high-pitched at times as he gave his version of events, verged on hysteria. We'd been given some idea of what was happening earlier, while still on the ground. Colonel Tom Carew, the Sierra Leone Army Chief of Defense Staff (CDS), had visited Nellis' office shortly before we left and told him that one of the units patrolling towards the town of Mange had come under fire. The rebels were following up in large numbers, Nellis learned.

From the maps that covered the walls of Nellis' ops center, it was clear that the target was a good deal closer to Guinea than Freetown. By vehicle, with roadblocks in place—even if the army had the fire-power to back it up, which it didn't—it would have taken some solid fighting and perhaps a full day to cover the distance. The Hind took twenty minutes.

We were still on the approaches to Port Loko, which was little more than a collection of mud huts with thatched roofs along the main road leading into the interior, when Nellis fired his first salvo. I could-n't immediately see what he was aiming at, but eight 57mm projec-tiles—four from each pod—roared in toward a clump of palms. A moment later we banked sharply to the right and then left again as Nellis took evasive action. He followed up with one or two brief bursts from the Gatling.

Interestingly, the "chin gun" didn't sound at all like an automatic weapon. Rather, when fired, it uttered a low-pitched roar almost like an unmuffled heavy-duty truck going down a hill. You could feel the effects of the blast from its four barrels each time Nellis pulled the trig-ger, almost as if he had eased back on the throttle. The racket wasn't as harsh as I'd been expecting, and I reckoned I could live with it.

As we continued circling the jungle below the reason for the scrap became clear. Government forces were indeed being attacked, but the situation wasn't as bad as Scorpion had made out. From what we had been able to follow through our headsets, Scorpion's men were being spearheaded by an unconventional and well-motivated group of tribal fighters known colloquially as Kamajors, which literally translated means "hunters." Before the war, these tough, seasoned warriors roamed the forests of West Africa, keeping themselves and their families alive with what they were able to bag in the bush. They were originally armed with shotguns, a few single-action rifles of World War I vintage, and now and again a two hundred-year-old blunderbuss. These days, however, they matched the firepower of the enemy and cradled Kalashnikovs.

While we were heading in their direction, Nellis learned that the Kamajors had been attacked from a rebel emplacement on the road northwest of the place. It was perhaps a dozen clicks (about seven miles) or so from Rogberi Junction where Schock and Gilmoreno had been killed. Indeed, Nellis later told me, it wasn't impossible that the same bunch of killers were responsible.

Moments after we arrived over the area Hassan spotted a white truck. It had probably been taken from the UN a few weeks before, only this one was heading down the road toward the Kamajors—fast! Mounted on its cab was a heavy Dshka machine-gun, the classic Russian anti-aircraft weapon. As Hassan later recalled, even from where we were hovering, he couldn't miss the gun's distinctive ribbing that ran down almost the full length of the barrel.

Nellis gained height, banked and leveled off, all the while keeping the vehicle in sight. He followed that maneuver with another salvo. Moments later he swung low over the target to find that the vehicle had swerved into a palm as it skidded off the road. It was now little more than a charred statistic. A few yards away lay a bloodied body, spread-eagled on the road. There were more rebel dead nearby in an open patch surrounded by tall clumps of elephant grass.

I thought I spotted green tracer fire coming up at us from a heavily foliated area, but Nellis wasn't sure. Clearly the enemy was still active, but by then the pilot's attention was focused elsewhere. He was looking at another target and we braced hard as he threw the machine into a tight two-G turn, almost clipping the tops of a stand of mahogany trees. Hassan and his Sierra Leonian counterpart, Lieutenant

Schenks, had to hold on tight in the back because, unlike in Western attack helicopters, they weren't strapped in. When the crew wasn't doing what was required of them when flying from one point of the compass to another, they'd use beer crates for seats.

In his debrief Nellis explained the action: "I had a good idea where all this was happening. Headquarters had indicated that it was somewhere along the road to Mange." Mange was not a big place, but it had long been an important staging area for the rebels in the north. The notorious Rogberi Junction was perhaps twelve miles away in the opposite direction. The truck, he explained, stood out sharply against the red gravel road, throwing up dust as it raced down. "You couldn't miss it."

Apart from two or three people sitting in the vehicle's cab with the driver, another rebel with an AK was balanced perilously on the hood, right up front. There were half a dozen or more of them clustered around the anti-aircraft gun in the back.

"That promised trouble," said Nellis. "I had to get us in and out again quickly. Fortunately I saw them before they spotted us."

The gunship fired first. Nellis could see that the driver—suddenly aware of our approach—reacted smartly by slamming on his brakes. Unexpectedly, it had the effect of hurling the man on the hood headlong into the road ahead. Then, in what must have been a blind moment of panic, the driver put his foot down hard and drove over the prostrate figure. Nellis recalled seeing the truck lurch twice as two sets of wheels went over his body. By now both our side-gunners were firing independently.

The enemy—"gooks," as the guys referred to them—kept emerging from the bush below, desperate on escape. I could hear Hassan curse each time he needed to change ammo belts, which was often. Spent 7.62mm brass casings started to pile up at his feet. Contrary to some reports, the British automatic weapons used by Hassan and Schenks were good, even though their barrels smoked like cigars after prolonged bursts of fire. Though they were in play just about every day of the war while I was about, we never had a jam.

For more than an hour we were in the air exchanging fire. Nellis would often carve a wide arc with the Hind, gaining a bit of height to better observe the terrain before taking us in again, low and fast. Depending on priorities, he would turn, level out and send in a line of rockets or perhaps use the heavy machine gun. The boys at the back would follow up with their GPMGs each time we banked and the routine would be repeated two, three or more times depending on circumstances. A lot hinged on whether there was enemy hardware or vehicles about, and Nellis would hammer away until he was satisfied that whatever he was targeting was destroyed.

As with most things in Sierra Leone's war, flak jackets onboard were optional. Only side-gunner Schenks wore body armor, but then he was regarded as something of a pessimist within our ranks. I should have worn something, but in the clinging heat and hundred percent West African humidity, that sort of protection was more than just constrictive. Because the Hind was air-conditioned, however, it wasn't nearly as stifling as I'd imagined it would be once we were airborne.[1]

With both sides exchanging blows, enemy fire slackened markedly once we'd arrived, the crew soon settled into something of a routine. Either Nellis would spot for targets, or Hassan or Schenks would report something suspicious below. From their positions at the back they had a more lateral view of the battle, while the two of us under our bubbles could only cover our forward envelope. Our flying helmets made it impossible to look behind.

Following a tradition that has become standard in many Third World wars, this South African pilot rarely moved about the operational area at anything but treetop height. Traveling just above the foliage at about a hundred-and-sixty knots (184 mph) was routine, though he would often raise the nose of the machine slightly once the scrap was on. This tactic could be hairy. A British Special Forces observer based at Cockerill's operations center went up several times in the Hind and he surmised that going into action with Nellis was a bit like flying into Germany with the Dambusters during World War II. The same officer returned to base after one particularly hectic foray over Makeni to inform us that the altimeter had almost constantly registered zero.

Officially, taking British military personnel out in the Hind was forbidden: Whitehall strictly prohibited any of its soldiers flying with mercenaries. Nevertheless, conditions in combat are changeable and there was nothing that offered better reconnaissance opportunities than Nellis' craft. So the British used Nellis when they could. In any event, operating as we were on the edge of the beyond, who in London would ever know?

Fighting over an under-populated and heavily foliated region has its advantages. In places the bush was so thick that it created huge natural arcs over smaller, open patches of ground. In that sort of country it was difficult to deploy heavy weapons. Of course, we knew that these were around, but usually the men manning the heavier weapons couldn't see what they were firing at until it was too late.

This was also true with anti-aircraft missiles or Manpads—especially the former Soviet Strela-2 (SA-7 "Grail"). Because of the lead-time needed to activate their intricate electronics systems, these anti-aircraft weapons were all but useless in the jungle. According to British intelligence, some of the surface-to-air missiles (SAMs) had been flown into Liberia from Libya and the Ukraine, though most had come by land from Ouagadougou, the capital of Burkina Faso, in numbers deliberately fudged.

Something similar had happened in the 1970s and 1980s in South Africa's border wars along the Angolan frontier. There, Soviet-backed insurgent armies had for decades tried to bring down a South African Air Force helicopter using ground-to-air missiles. There were many close calls and, while a few choppers and other aircraft were lost by conventional ground fire, the Angolans fired an arsenal of Russian SAMs over the years and not one was successful. Sierra Leone, in contrast, offered a different set of permutations, especially when Nellis covered open ground or struck at some of the towns in rebel hands.

Gradually, as the months passed and hostilities intensified, Nellis' Hind became the Freetown government's most potent weapon. It was the first time in modern warfare that a lone pilot at the controls of a helicopter had actually turned a war on its head—though Nellis will concede today that there were times when he thought he was done for.

In an earlier sortie around Newton, about a month before I arrived—the town lies just beyond a line of hills surrounding the capital—he and the crew were ambushed one early morning. Because Nellis was the one obstacle that stood in Sankoh's way in his bid to take Freetown, the rebels went to considerable lengths to try and shoot him down. On this particular morning they set up a Dshka, together with a double-barreled 14.5mm anti-aircraft gun, near a tall building in the middle of town. The idea was to effectively cover both arcs of the Mi-24s approach. They were aware, too, that Nellis followed the same flight path when "going to work" each day. He did so purposely. As he explained, his "predictable" flight path was designed to draw enemy fire in the hope they would use their heavier weapons.

"Then, I can see what I'm aiming at . . . and I can take them out."

And that's what eventually happened. For once, as Nellis remembers it, the rebels were prepared to fight. Normally they ran for cover whenever his helicopter appeared. According to Hassan, the first thing the crew saw was a string of tracers coming at them the moment Newton came into view. "You couldn't miss the telltale, red tracers of the 14.5s," he explained, adding that it made for an impressive display in the early morning sky. "The moment the firing started we knew that it was serious," he declared.

Nellis reacted by throwing the chopper into an arc. "What was really bad," continued Hassan, "was that the tracers just kept on coming; there seemed to be no end to them." He vividly recalled how they all believed, at least for a time, that some of the projectiles were going through their tail rotors (though this was not the case). Since a 14.5mm shell will penetrate the steel of any armored vehicle, it would certainly demolish a helicopter—especially if a rotor, the tail boom or the hydraulics take a hit.

It was over almost as soon as it had started. The Hind soon crossed a nearby row of hills and was out of range. "What happened next," explained Hassan, "was like something out of a film." Nellis turned the helicopter around again and standing off almost a mile from the small community, he launched two salvoes of rockets, first at one side of the building adjacent to the heavy stuff, and then at the other.

"After that we went in fast," Hassan explained, "firing the Gatling. Then we let them have it with a beautiful bunch of rockets."

And so it went for the rest of the time that we worked the area around Port Loko that afternoon. Nellis would bank hard as soon as something came into view. If he didn't use the Gatling, more rockets would follow. With thirty-two projectiles in each pod, the Hind was capable of firing eight salvos of eight each time he took her out, but on this occasion, he would rarely fire clutches of more than four at a time, most times in pairs to conserve firepower. Gradually, after an hour in the air, the pace slackened. Nellis would ease down low and for a while we'd nudge the jungle before he'd look for something else to hit. It was almost as if he was getting his second wind.

Weaving around enough to make me squeamish, Nellis waited until we could see a small force of government troops approaching along the road where we'd hit the truck. It was their job to secure the vehicle and the heavier stuff. After dealing with them by radio, Nellis headed north again, this time making for the riverside town of Mange; it was from there that the rebels had initially launched their raid.

This compact little settlement emerged from the jungle only a few minutes later. In the soft light of dusk, the setting wa the last rays of the sun reflecting off images below as growth and what had once been a palm plantation was the sort of place, I couldn't help thinking as we l have liked to visit before the war. More of a village t dominated by a disproportionately large, whitewas...... three-story mosque, Mange was quaint compared to the rest. It was a pity, I reflected at the time, that the rebels had a hold on it.

In his approach, Nellis fired a couple of rockets at a position on the outskirts and seconds later looped around to come in again. I didn't see any retaliatory fire, but Nellis assured me there was. His objective had been a small stand of buildings protected by sandbags at the southern end of a large bridge that had earlier been identified by Cockerill as having been used by the rebels as a vehicle checkpoint. Banking once more Nellis swooped in for a final pasting and in the process hit several more buildings.

Ten minutes later we were on the approaches to Lungi to refuel. We had just about used up the last of our ammunition. By the time we got back to the base at Cockerill the Hind had been out for just under two hours. Throughout the sortie I hadn't once been able to stretch my legs. And being very long, they did need intermittent stretching.

A report was later brought to the ops room indicating that the day's kills (confirmed body counts) totaled fourteen, though there were almost certainly more. Ground forces would also have accounted for their share. More of the dead would be found days later when, following their noses, troops would be led to half-devoured, decomposing corpses strewn about in the undergrowth. Their buddies would have crudely hidden them in the dense growth before pulling out, though in the tropics it is impossible to hide the stench.

While there might have been more fatalities, there was no way then of knowing for certain. In any event, not many of the wounded were likely to have survived the night. Without treatment, septicemia would set in from any significant wound to the torso and, in that climate, would kill a man in six hours, sometimes sooner. Add to that the everyday reality that the conflict in Sierra Leone—irrational and uncompromising as it was—was not one that favored prisoners of war. Very few captives survived for long. Some were eaten; "fresh chop" they call it in West Africa.

What was clear to anyone who stayed in Sierra Leone for any length of time was that this was an extraordinarily difficult country which to fight. On my previous visit with the mercenary group Executive Outcomes in 1995, Fred Marafano warned that West Africa's jungles were "the absolute worst imaginable." He spoke from hard experience, for he'd spent more than twenty years in the British Army and had seen combat in some of the world's harshest conditions.

While in uniform Marafano, a Fijian-born national, had been posted just about everywhere. He'd soldiered in the rain forests of South and Central America as well as Borneo, the Gulf, Northern Ireland, and the Middle East. West Africa, he said, was very different. He was adamant that the jungle that started on the outskirts of Freetown and went on in an unbroken line all the way to the frontiers of Guinea and Liberia, was the most inhospitable place on the planet. In contrast with the Amazon and Southeast Asia's rain forests, he declared, Sierra Leone's jungles "with their spikes that clawed" were totally unforgiving.

"The jungle here is impossible for us and equally daunting for them," he told me. The only way to really get about was on properly made roads or tracks through the thick bush, many of them created by generations of everyday usage. Stop using them, he explained, "and the jungle will reclaim a road in three months."

Approaching sixty, the man everybody in Sierra Leone knew simply as Fred had a coolness in his dark eyes that was belied by a fixed smile. Marafano had always been one for accepting the most difficult option, if only, as he put it, "because it's usually the quickest route to success." That, he stated, was even more pertinent when there was a war on the go.

Marfano had been fighting rebels in Sierra Leone the first time I met him six years before. And he was still at it this second time around. Meantime, he'd made a life for himself in Freetown with his young wife and a new baby. When his missus started worrying about her parents who lived up-country in a town that was periodically over-run by the RUF, Marfano singlehandedly led a combat team composed of about a hundred of his Kamajor followers halfway across the country to liberate the place.

"I kicked them out of the area to ease her mind," he nonchalantly explained.

2

NEAL ELLIS:
JUNGLE WARRIOR

"When hostilities in Sierra Leone took off again on May 6, 2000, Neall Ellis was among the first of the combatants to go into action. He was sometimes averaging three or four combat missions a day in the government Hind helicopter gunship. Twice, he was sent operational six times in a twenty-four hour period, the last sortie taking place after dark where he used night vision goggles to spot rebel concentrations. His logbook shows that over an eight-week time frame, he clocked up more than 130 combat missions. Pilots in the majority of the world's air forces—unless they are in a major war—rarely see that much action during the course of their careers."

Lt. Colonel Rob Symonds, former Military Liaison Officer,
British High Commission, Freetown.

At the heart of just about everything that happened in Sierra Leone's war in 2000 was the Air Wing operations room at Cockerill Barracks. More properly known as the corps operations center, it was a home away from home for Neall Ellis. An untidy place that had a certain disordered charm about it, the barracks was a combination office, social club, intelligence clearing house, telephone answering service, map room, and conference center. Situated well away from the main block at Army Headquarters, his expansive, sparsely furnished ground floor office was visited by as many senior British officers in camouflage as there were top Sierra Leonian army commanders. Because of the Nellis connection—the South African was clearly regarded as a mercenary in London's eyes—the Ministry of Defense would have quickly abrogated any unofficial arrangement if they caught wind of it. Obviously some of the brass back home knew what was going on, but it was a convenient arrangement while hostilities lasted.

Cockerill Barracks was entered through a pair of steel doors. Immediately inside was a room, in the middle of which sat the desk of

Sindaba Nemera Meri, head of the Air Wing's four-man Ethiopian technical squad. It was Meri's responsibility to keep the country's two helicopter gunships in the air. Stashed against one of the far walls was a pile of automatic weapons, mostly AK-47s. While we were away on sorties, the steel doors remained locked.

Cardboard boxes, some of them half open, lay clustered about. Each was jammed with propaganda leaflets about to be dropped on enemy positions. Propaganda sheets were usually dispersed only after the ammo had been fired, and then with reluctance. Nellis had made it clear many times that he didn't like the idea of dropping pieces of paper in areas where the rebels were active. It might be justifiable if it saved lives, he argued, but the exercise unnecessarily exposed his crew to ground fire. "The gooks know when I'm dropping that shit," he remonstrated with one of the British officers. "It tells them that I'm not going to be using my guns." Still, Nellis went along with it because he was ordered to do so. His gunship made several pamphlet drops urging the rebels to come in under an amnesty brokered by the United Nations. All they had to do was bring their guns with them, which could be handed in for cash at any United Nations post.

Neall Ellis was not the archetypal soldier of fortune. A little more rotund than earlier in his career, his hair was cropped so close it was difficult to determine whether it was thinning,. When he talked about his "office" he was referring not to the barracks but to the helicopter he flew every day. He was soft-spoken, articulate, and well read. Few of us ever saw him angry, though like everybody else on Freetown's roads he could be pretty cantankerous behind the wheel. As I was to discover when I flew with him in attacks on rebel headquarters at Makeni (a fairly large town in the north), Nellis' often used explicit language, especially when he missed a target. He was never critical of his crew, however, even though we made mistakes.

Papers, maps, a laptop, electric bills, cardboard plates with scraps from a past meal, and several catalogues offering the latest killing machines from the former Soviet Union littered Nellis' desk. Most of the catalogues had Rosvoorouzhenie's imprint, a company that was formerly Moscow's State Corporation for Export and Import of Armaments and Military Equipment. Others were from Rosoboron-export, a successor company.

Tucked away almost unobtrusively in a pile of its own was a letter from a British weapons supply company. Addressed to Nellis, it offered the Air Wing a reconditioned Mi-24 engine for $545,000 cash.

In another corner lay the remains of a pile of British Army ration packs. A small refrigerator held the day's supply of butter, pita bread, sausage spread, or whatever else Hassan had managed to scrounge from the Lebanese supermarket in Wilkinson Street. The room was air-conditioned, but there were so many power cuts that refrigeration was essential. For that reason, smoking was only permitted outside, alongside the pad where the unit's second gunship was parked.

As noted in the previous chapter, the Hind we flew was also equipped with a Gatling and under-wing rocket pods, though on the second helicopter the latter were 80mm, as opposed to the 57mm explosive missiles with which we were "gunned up." The second "spare" helicopter saw little action, primarily because the larger rocket projectiles were in short supply and nobody was certain when more would be ordered. It wasn't air-conditioned, either. Whenever Nellis took it out he would come back drenched in sweat; it would sometimes take him an hour or two to recover from the draining experience. I refused to go up in it if it meant sitting up front. It was bad enough being squeezed into a confined space, but I was not about to endure that suffering without cool circulating air.

I wasn't the only one to suffer these rigors. Even with the air conditioning working, flying under the front bubble could do strange things to people. Mark von Zorgenfrei, an Executive Outcomes Mi-17 mercenary pilot with a lot of spare weight, gave it a bash a few years ago. As he admitted to the lads, he did it "just for the experience." Von Zorgenfrei let his co-pilot bring his own Hip back to Freetown while he flew in the front seat of Charlie Tate's Hind. As Tattie remembers, von Zorgenfrei suffered badly. "By the time we got back to base we thought he was having a heart attack." He never flew in either of the Hinds again.

By Nellis' own admission, his domain at Army Headquarters in Cockerill Barracks "kind of ran itself." Two or three times a day he would liaise with his bosses upstairs and things would start to happen. For a long time Nellis was on his own, fending off the occasional crisis and making do with what was available. Not long after I left, however, Whitehall appointed a Royal Air Force squadron leader to "supervise" Nellis' Air Wing team. The project was handled under a guise they termed their "Sierra Leone military training program." It was a shrewd move designed to avoid having the Royal Air Force linked in Parliament—or anywhere else—to Sierra Leone's low-key but prominent mercenary force.

The new RAF arrival, Nellis told me, was what was known in military jargon as "an advisor." At the same time, he admitted that the RAF man was running the show. "These guys see that the money the government owes us keeps on coming, which is good. And so we eat again." The guise, however, did not last long. A report appeared in a British newspaper claiming that the British military force in Sierra Leone was supporting a mercenary force. The thrust of the piece was that not only were the Brits fighting rebels, they were providing the mercenary force with material and tactical succor. Essentially, it was suggested, Whitehall was doing a repeat of the Sandline debacle. (A mercenary firm, Sandline International operated in West Africa with Ministry of Defence complicity.) Once he learned of the story, Nellis was convinced that London would backtrack on its support of his efforts in Sierra Leone. But then, to the surprise of all, the unexpected happened.

Several days later, a London newspaper report by Caroline Davies declared that the Ministry of Defence had stated that a British officer was in fact advising Sierra Leone on how to build up "a proper structured air wing" and that the gunship in question "belonged to the government, and not to mercenaries." The story went on: "If the Sierra Leonians haven't got anybody who can fly these helicopters and if they want to get South African nationals who can, then that's up to them. The RAF does not advise them on their role on a day-to-day basis," wrote Davies.

It was the first time that the British government had actually acknowledged it was in any way involved with irregular military forces like a private military company (PMC)—and that in an age when hired guns were still anathema throughout the civilized world. Also, the involvement was taking place on a continent where mercenary organizations had proliferated since the first black states were handed the right to govern themselves half a century earlier, which made the issue that much more contentious. But the Ministry of Defence had said its piece, and the matter was allowed to drop.

The consequences of the revelation were difficult to predict. One commentator was heard to suggest that this was possibly the shape of things to come on a continent that was in the process of unraveling. Since the appearance of the first news report there has been a flurry of articles advocating the use of PMCs in some of the world's more isolated wars, where any kind of traditional intervention would not make sense to, or garner the support of, the intervener's electorate. The wars recently triggered in Iraq and Afghanistan have served to train, enlarge and advertise private mercenary groups, and they have proliferated. At last count, in the fall of 2005, it was estimated that there were something like twenty thousand private military contractors operating out of Baghdad, about a quarter to a third of them South African nationals.

Nellis' ops center was very different from the rest of what was going on in Freetown's military headquarters at Cockerill. For starters, the place itself was different. It had its own distinctive atmosphere. For part of the day the wails and squeaks coming from the communications equipment in the radio shack next door saturated everything. Technicians working there—even when they weren't trying—would create noises that, anywhere else in the country, would have invoked demons. It was worse when there was a power outage and they were forced to revert to using batteries, which came around like clockwork several times each day. The job of the communications technicians was to monitor enemy radio transmissions, and they did so around the clock. Because this was sensitive work, Nellis' ops center was also the most heavily guarded area in the military complex, with an armed sentry on permanent duty outside the entrance.

Since we had to deal with the threat, it was Nellis—and usually the crew--who saw these intercepts as they came in. So did just about everybody else who visited the place, which must have had some effect on diminishing the level of security. But that had been a problem in this war from the start because secrets were never kept for long in the streets of Freetown. The majority of incoming messages were not coded and those few that were only took a while longer to filter into the operations center upstairs.

During most of the time they were active in Sierra Leone, the rebels used a Slidex code in their more important messages. As Nellis told me, it was an unusual practice because the system was cumbersome. It was his view that the use of this particular code reflected a South African presence in the enemy's ranks. The old South African Defence Force, he explained, was one of the last of the more sophisticated military establishments still using Slidex. In fact, he was of the view that it might have been some of his former SADF buddies that had passed it on to the Liberians.

To Nellis, the idea that some of his former colleagues were now working for the enemy was abhorrent. He felt such service was nothing short of betrayal. Nellis took it personally. "To be honest, it hurts," he admitted. During his service in places like Ondangua and in the Ruacana area during Namibia's border war days, or at the Swartkops Air Force base near Pretoria and elsewhere, these same people had been his buddies. "We were really one big family, wives and children included." he explained.

At the same time, it was no secret that some of the former Executive Outcomes hands had "gone over" to fighting for or training rebel forces, among them people with whom Nellis had previously served in Sierra Leone. That was still the case in 2002 when former SADF Reconnaissance Regiment Colonel Hennie Blaauw was spotted in Liberia helping Charles Taylor's forces quell a rebellion in the north. The money was good and since opportunities for this kind of work were limited, Blaauw and others grabbed the chance when it came about.

Carl Alberts, another Nellis' colleague, was among the first of the Executive Outcomes pilots to convert to flying Hinds. Alberts and Arthur Walker did so at the same time, after Executive Outcomes had launched its rescue mission of the Freetown government in 1995. After that phase of Sierra Leone's hostilities had ended and the rebels were forced to negotiate a truce, Arthur went home and stayed there. Alberts, however, did not. His was one of the names mentioned in a United Nations report on mercenaries operating illegally out of Liberia. Published in New York in late 2000, the UN document detailed his flying activities on Mi-8s for Charles Taylor. Although Alberts consistently denied having worked in Liberia, Western intelligence agents who helped source the UN report observed his activities with interest while in West Africa. Among his duties, the report disclosed, was making regular cross-border weapons deliveries to rebel units engaged in hostilities with the legitimate Sierra Leone government.

According to those who had worked with him, Alberts—five years earlier, while still with EO—had fought what some believed was a "good war" against Sierra Leone's rebels. He and Walker shared command of what was then Sierra Leone's single Hind. But that was before the Russians managed to sabotage their efforts, which they did once they learned the South African mercenary group had surreptitiously snatched their combat contract with the Sierra Leone government. It was more than an act of pique: the Russians saw to it that that particular Hind never flew again while EO remained in-country.

Afterward, Alberts (a likable opportunist) tried to enter Britain dressed as a priest. Tipped off, British security was waiting for him at

Heathrow and he was detained and put on the next plane home. The last anyone heard of Alberts was that he ran a bed and breakfast in the Cape, followed by a spell of fighting in the Ivory Coast, for which he was arrested by "The Scorpions," South Africa's crack security unit. His efforts in the Ivory Coast cost him a hefty fine.

It was clear to everyone that Nellis viewed Carl Alberts' "going over" to fight for Taylor with a certain rancor, though he was rarely prepared to be too upset about it. During their South African Air Force days, he and Alberts had fought in some of the bloodiest battles of the border war. As Nellis explained it, he would not judge the actions of an old friend. He pointed out that some of their friends had been killed and it could just as easily have been them. Of such things are strong bonds created. Even though it was clear that they went back a long way, Nellis reserved unmitigated venom, if not for the man— because they remained friends throughout—then for his actions.

There were many reasons why senior Sierra Leone staff officers would sidle down to Nellis' ops center to talk to him. For a start, he was the best source of intelligence in the region. Tucked into his cockpit, Nellis missed very little of what was going on in the jungle below. His reports were invariably an accurate, reasoned and balanced assessment of the activities of enemy ground forces. Much of it was based on the kind of subliminal instinct that comes with experience. Years of flying in primal environments added a distinctive edge to his reports.

That he was invariably spot-on, just about everybody concurred. For instance, from the air he could judge a man's actions simply by watching him—how he walked, what he was carrying, whether he was being evasive, and if he was friend of foe. Unlike most of us, Nellis could "read" the bush. Often he would identify a target and go in with weapons blasting, but it was only at the last moment that I would see his objective. Most of the time it was a vehicle or a building that had been cunningly camouflaged under heavy foliage or palm fronds. Nellis' actions certainly galvanized the mind, especially when we came under fire. On one occasion he strafed a position, targeting something in primitive forest that most of the handbooks would classify as impenetrable. I had no idea what his target was because I could not see anything. Only on his third pass did the target—whatever it was— explode in a fireball. I'd missed it completely. With time, Hassan became equally adept at spotting targets.

I recall an occasion when we passed a fairly large boat heading down the Little Scarcies River, not far from the Guinea border. It wasn't unlike several other partially enclosed motor craft plying hundreds of miles of inland waterways that sometimes made Sierra Leone's coastal plain remarkably similar to the Mekong Delta. This one was a bit bigger than a Pam Pam—but not large enough to be ocean going—and stopped in mid-stream as soon as we came into view. On the second pass, Nellis said he was going in. The boat blew up when its cargo of fuel ignited.

"How did you know it was an enemy vessel?" I later asked him.

"Because the first time around the crew was ready to swim for it," he explained. "They don't normally do that, so what else to conclude but that there was something illegal in the boat's hold?" Nellis shrugged, adding, "They were also armed and jumpy. In Sierra Leone, that just about says it all." He went on to explain that the entire region through which the Little Scarcies flowed was in rebel hands. "Whatever those crewmen had onboard was almost certainly destined for the RUF."

Although a rebel radio intercept proved he was correct about the boat, Nellis was always the first to admit that sometimes he made mistakes. "But you must remember that this is a very real war. It's not an exercise. Here, it's them or us, and never forget that a helluva lot of people are getting killed," he emphatically told a visitor to Cockerill who had made an issue about innocents being targeted.

As this West African conflict escalated, so did the manner in which it was being dictated. Strictly a ground war at the outset, the deployment of Sierra Leone's precious helicopter assets quickly brought about a discernable transition in insurgent tactics. At first, bold, opportunistic, and sometimes foolhardy tactics had been the norm. Once Nellis had begun to make his mark, rebel leaders reacted more cautiously, especially in trying to counter his gunship strikes.

Though RUF rebels had taken a forceful line at the beginning of the war (largely because they lacked opposition), they soon discovered that trying to counter Nellis' Air Wing would invariably extract a disproportionate cost in men and hardware. Consequently, instead of shooting back when they spotted Nellis' bird, they'd take cover as quickly as possible, especially in some of the more populated regions like Makeni and Bo.

While Sierra Leone's operational parameters in this African war might have been different from other conflicts, Nellis' prime objective was probably no different from those of the majority of East European pilots who, even today, continue to fight a succession of obscure internecine wars on both sides of the Caucasus. Hind helicopters have been used offensively in almost all of them. Most of the combat helicopters viewers see on TV in reports from Chechnya or Macedonia are Mi-24s. So, too, more recently, in the Ivory Coast and the eastern Congo.

A good deal bulkier than comparable Western combat helicopters and, to layman, not looking at all aerodynamic, the Hind—according to some of the pilots who fly it—does exactly the job for which it was designed. Because the Mi-24 is cheap and readily available in arms markets throughout the Middle East and Eastern Europe, it remains the most widely used ground-support helicopter in the world.

Anton La Guardia,[1] a writer with a critical eye for detail, in the tradition of the late James Cameron, phrased it well in an article on the war in Sierra Leone in the London *Sunday Telegraph*. "The gunship," wrote La Guardia, "strikes the fear of God into the rebels." The writer added, quoting Nellis, "They [the rebels] run into the bush as soon as they see it. And in Africa the man who makes the loudest noise wins the battle and this helicopter with all its weapons and engines makes a lot of noise." The *Telegraph* article went on to mention that at the height of the Sandline scandal over London's links to mercenaries hired by the Sierra Leone government, British officials would have quickly avoided Nellis. "Today, he is the toast of Freetown. British army officers, United Nations soldiers and government troops cannot praise his operations too highly." The Mi-24, La Guardia declared, was at the same time a deadly offensive weapon, a carrier of Special Forces, a platform for intelligence gathering and an instrument of psychological warfare when it dropped British-designed leaflets into rebel camps.

Nellis scoffed at the suggestion that being a mercenary was reprehensible, though there were those in Freetown at the time, blacks and whites alike, who employed much stronger language whenever his name came up. One of Nellis' favorite comments was that "the diagnosis of the problem was one thing, prescription quite another." Whenever the role of contract pilots was raised in the context of the Sierra Leone war (which was often, and usually in a bar), Nellis stressed that he was "performing a service." It frustrated him that others did not see it his way. "We're the guys who are saving lives, killing the bad guys," he remonstrated, a cynical smile creasing his lips. Then he would add contemptuously, "You don't think that doesn't make me feel good? Think again!" It was at times like this when I could detect a hardness around his eyes. Nellis was never really one for small talk if he didn't have a drink in his hand. And when he did, he'd go on all night!

Neall Ellis first flew combat with Executive Outcomes in Sierra Leone after heading back home from the Balkans in 1995. He returned to Freetown again as a government pilot three years later. In between, this former South African Air Force colonel was involved in an unsuccessful rearguard action while trying to rescue the regime of the dying Mobutu Sese Seko of Zaire (today the Democratic Republic of the Congo). It was quite an event at the time. Once that dictator and his people left the country, things really began to slide. Nellis and the rest of the flying team—based at Gbadolite in northern Zaire—only just managed to escape with their lives. When they finally emerged safely, Nellis and his partners were clad only in their underpants. We were fortunate to get out, he acknowledges.

As Nellis tells it, he, a French pilot friend of his, and Juba Joubert—one of his colleagues from the Angolan war with whom he had flown combat missions for several years—eventually had to steal a pirogue (similar to a small skiff) and paddle across the Congo River. That in itself was a remarkable feat because the great waterway is fast flowing in many places and miles wide. Eventually the trio was rescued in primitive bush country west of Bangui in the Central African Republic. A group of French paramilitary troops they'd managed to contact earlier on the Frenchman's satellite phone rescued them. (See Chapter 11 for more details.)

I only heard Nellis really fired up once on the subject of combat: "Smack 'em! Smack 'em again and then hit the fuckers once more, just to be sure!" he instructed one of the Sierra Leonian pupil pilots. Shoulders hunched and eyes afire, he reiterated it again for good effect. "Be it Sierra Leone, Angola or Sri Lanka," he told the man, "that's the only way to do it!"

Nellis' "smack 'em!" tactic was no different even when the heavy stuff began coming his way. He would lay the Hind off at a distance and use his height to hurl a salvo or two at those trying to take him out—and he rarely missed. As he explained, eight of those projectiles at a time would dislocate everything in an area half the size of a football field.

On the subject of war, Nellis had a premise of his own. It went something like this: "In conflict, all else being equal, raw aggression wins. Most times anyway." He was adamant that it worked for him, and he had certainly seen the consequences of his theory in action often enough to know it worked. Whenever his gunship approached a rebel position, those on the ground would often hurl everything aside and make a run for it. They would discard their weapons, vehicles, and supply packs in a frantic dash for cover. And Africa being Africa, the word got around. Within months Nellis was the stuff of legend on both sides of the front.

It was expected that when you flew combat with Neall Ellis, you'd need to accept the fundamental ground rule that avionics would have an altogether different application from just about anywhere else. Obviously the first consideration was our safety. If we were forced down, there would be no back-up. "We'll be utterly on our own in the jungle, assuming we survive the landing," Nellis explained to me before my first flight. He continued by telling me that it would be little more than luck if he had time to report our situation to one of the control towers before diverting the Hind into a bit of open ground and the reason was obvious the first time you went on a sortie with him. Flying over a carpet of greenery where the jungle seemed to go on forever, there were simply not that many patches of open earth that might have been suitable for an abrupt helicopter landing. Putting her down in water, for instance, would probably have been the end for us two up front: there was no easy way of exiting from either of the cockpit bubbles, though it had been done.

In order to survive a crash, we all knew that a soft landing would have been essential. Setting down a twelve-ton heavyweight with a rotor that had been shot away or only part of its boom, however, would be even more difficult. Once on the ground, we might hope that one of the British choppers would react and come out looking, but even that would have needed authority from the top, especially if an extensive (and expensive) air search were to be launched. In the nether world of "contract" flying, Nellis and his crew were very much aware that they were flying with virtually no insurance of any kind.[2]

The retrieval of a downed crew also depended on who was on duty at the time. Nellis was not everybody's favorite person, partly because there was very little about him that made for the gossamer stuff of money and ambition.

In theory, the UN command was expected to help the government Air Wing if it was in trouble, just as Nellis had come to their rescue several times in the past. In practice, the Blue Helmets would have liked nothing more than to see the end of the only freelance helicopter gunship pilot in the country, if only because Nellis' bold actions had so graphically illustrated the almost wanton impotence of the huge UN force. If Nellis took a hit and went down in the jungle in the interior, he could provide a bearing as to his whereabouts to anyone listening on the same frequency. It was what the people on the receiving end would do with that information that was problematic. Perhaps a UN chopper team would be put on the alert; perhaps not. The UN command structure—from Turtle Bay down, all the way to West Africa—was about as enthusiastic for what this mercenary pilot was doing as was Nellis for their shambolic "peacekeeping' efforts."

I was always amazed at the way Nellis moved about in a land where there were no navigational or flying aids. There were two rudimentary air traffic control systems in operation in the Freetown area: one for civilian and Air Wing activity centered at Lungi, the other a mobile unit operated by the UN at the chopper pad at the Mammy Yoko Hotel. The mobile unit should have been deployed at Cockerill, where there was a high-rise concrete tower built specifically for that purpose. The UN members, however, decided that they preferred something closer to headquarters. Government gunships across the narrow, mosquito-ridden swamp separating us from their base probably had something to do with the decision. Whatever happened, if we did crash, we'd have to talk to at least one of those stations. And even then, radio contact would be erratic.

Flying in Sierra Leone posed several problems, not the least of which was trying to figure out where you were. While there are some fine natural landmarks, especially among the mountains in the north and to the east of the country, a good deal of the south and central region was flat and it all looked the same. Elsewhere the terrain was undulating. Though there was always something in sight on the horizon, flying thirty feet above the jungle wasn't conducive to good navigation unless it was something that you'd been doing for a long while.

In contrast to flying in Sierra Leone, Nellis explained, Angola offered featureless terrain for hours on end because much of the southern part of the country is largely semi-arid. "In that kind of environment, we quickly learnt to use our maps." In Sierra Leone Nellis flew without a co-pilot, meaning he was in absolute control of the machine. As his crew, we helped with spotting and the occasional ancillary task, such as tripping circuit breakers or activating the helicopter's IR jamming system, but the rest was up to him. He not only flew the helicopter, but also picked out the targets and manually activated the Hind's weapons systems. Then, without any apparent reference to a marker, he would move across some of the wildest bush country in the world to the next target and do it all over again.

Flying directly to and from an objective over this green pea soup of a terrain taxed Nellis' skills. Sitting in front I should have been able to assist him, but I couldn't even begin to help. He was constantly forced to calculate fuel, distance, speed, reserves, and all the rest. And since there were no convenient army bases or towns where we could top off if we needed to, he couldn't afford to make a mistake. As far as I know, he never did.

Nellis always flew with a map on his lap, usually 1:250,000 scale when routing to the target and, as he got closer to the area, a more concise 1:50,000. When something came into view he logged it onto his portable GPS so that, if necessary, he could get back to the place later. Only then would he turn his attention to establishing whether the target was worth a strike.

Nellis' findings would be brought back to base, where CDS staff and British Army intelligence came and went throughout the day and night. These included grid and map references as well as an interpretation of events, enemy strengths, weaknesses, and deployment. Most of what he reported came from memory, which in itself was rather remarkable. Nellis did have the occasional lapse, however, such as forgetting where he'd put his keys. It was then that he would joke about suffering from what he termed "Tropical Halfheimers." It was a regular crack; usually he could only remember about a half of what had taken place the previous night.

One of the advantages about gadding about in helicopters in West Africa was that you never knew what was going to happen next. Every one of us onboard was aware that operational mishaps were all too regular in Africa's ongoing wars. We also knew that there had been numerous incidents involving South African gunship crews in Angola and Sierra Leone being shot down or having to put down for one reason or another; in most cases the crews survived. Nellis put that down not to luck but to good training.

Two who didn't survive were flying an Angolan Air Force Pilatus PC-7 ground attack aircraft, armed, like the Hind, with underwing rocket pods. At the controls in the summer of 1994 was SAAF veteran (and Executive Outcomes pilot) Louwrens Bosch. Behind him sat the base medic, Danny "Skeeries" Scheurkogel, who went up "for the ride." Exactly what happened has, with time, become confused with innuendo and conflicting reports. All that's certain is that the plane was hit and shortly afterward made a crash-landing in the heart of Unita country adjacent to the diamond-mining town of Cafunfo, which a short time before had been captured by an EO-led mechanized force. (See Chapter 18.) According to intelligence sources, the aircraft might have been downed by the more advanced SAM-14 Strela missile, which didn't rely solely on infrared emissions. It was widely known that the Angolan rebels had bought some of these Manpads in Eastern Europe.

No one knows what happened to the survivors, and to this day the rebels that survived that war refuse to talk. All we know was that if Bosch and Scheurkogel survived the initial crash, they would have been tortured and executed. Later intelligence "leaks" indicated that the guerrillas took at least one of them captive. Neither man's family was ever told what had happened, even though Nelson Mandela's government made several inquiries into the matter.

Obviously, something similar was in store for us if we ended up in rebel hands, which was one of the reasons Hassan was so furious when somebody stole his Colt .45 pistol out of his desk. It was his "last resort," he told me. Not altogether tongue-in-cheek, he begged Allah for reparation, calling down a loud and lengthy curse on the thief's head.

Nellis did not fly anywhere without his issue AK-47 and personal 9mm pistol for back-up. He also carried his GPS, as well as a tiny portable VHF radio he could use to speak to rescue aircraft—that is, if somebody came looking. It was only marginally reassuring that some weeks before I arrived, four officers—Major Phil Ashby, Royal Navy Lt. Cmdr. Paul Rowland, and Major Andy Samsonoff (Brits all three), and a New Zealand army signals officer named David Lingard—trudged to safety across some of the most difficult country in West Africa. The group had escaped from a camp that had been surrounded by an RUF rebel group armed with heavy weapons. Much of the country the four traversed was nearly impenetrable jungle. They left Magburaka, just south of Makeni, in the middle of the night and it took them four days to cover barely fifty miles to the nearest UN position. Moving only after dark, they spent daylight hours hiding in thick undergrowth because there were large groups of rebels looking for them. Afterward, hearing them recount their ordeal—no food, drinking swamp water "in which floated putrescence things," being devoured by mosquitoes—it was astonishing to learn what the human body could endure.[3]

Flying in West Africa is hazardous in other ways as well. Birds—especially when moving about just above the jungle canopy—were a major hazard faced by every flying crew. In that tropical haven there are some hefty species, and I was concerned that a bird strike could damage our machine. One moment we'd be ambling along at a hundred and sixty knots and the next, Nellis would slam the stick to the left or right and we'd shoot off tangentially. I needn't have worried because the armor-plated glass embedded in the Perspex bubble at head level in my gunner's seat was designed to take a hit from a soft-bodied creature. But it was unnerving. We would head in low and fast toward a strike and suddenly find a large vulture or a fish eagle directly ahead. At that speed, Nellis had a fraction of a second to react, which he did each time with alacrity. It says something for his ability as a pilot that we avoided contact at least half-a-dozen times during my tenure in West Africa.

There had been several bird strikes in the past. During the previous Executive Outcomes deployment, Charlie Tate, another SAAF mercenary who for a time worked for the company spent many hours in Sierra Leone in his Mi-17. He told me of several hits he sustained. Once, coming back from a three-ship mission in the interior, his chopper ingested a bird into the starboard engine. It was pretty big, he recalled, probably a crane. Within seconds he had one engine barking and the other overheating. That meant putting down—fast. First, however, he had to find some open ground, or at least a clearing large enough to accommodate the helicopter's almost seventy feet of rotors.

With the other two Mi-17s circling and ready to provide close air support should he need it, Tate brought his craft down in the largest space he could find. His tail boom absorbed most of the impact and the Hip's rotors disintegrated outward, as one of the other pilots commented afterwards, "in a brilliant display of flying metal." Tate was lucky, because there are numerous recorded instances of rotors slicing through the cockpit in a crash. Thankfully, there were no serious injuries.

Once the rest of the men were on the ground the third chopper managed to land nearby. Meanwhile, a situation report was sent to Lungi and a rescue effort was launched. Being West Africa, this took a while. Because of a known rebel presence in the area, it was decided to leave behind some of the troops they had been ferrying to guard the damaged helicopter. Aircrews had all been warned—just as we had—that the RUF had two immediate priorities: the first, to kill mercenary pilots; the second, to destroy their aircraft.

Once the Belorussian technical crew responsible for Air Wing maintenance arrived at the site, they quickly hauled the wreck onto a low loader. By using chains with the kind of excessive force that seemed to be part of their approach, these former Soviets damaged the airframe even more. Once the machine was loaded they headed back to Lungi; for once, nobody was hanging around until dark. Because of the rough handling, it took much longer to get the chopper back into service than it should have, though part of the reason one of the pilots suggested, was probably overtime pay. In fact, according to Nellis, it was the usual African story: aircraft are purchased, but nothing is budgeted for maintenance. Consequently, this helicopter never flew again.

At the time of Charlie Tate's downing, Executive Outcomes was economizing and most of the flights were single-pilot missions. Freetown had cut EO's budget to the core and air crews were told that there wasn't enough money for the customary air crew team of three—two pilots and an engineer. Budgets were a significant issue in every EO contract, but some of these cuts appeared to be unjustified—especially because they put lives at risk. These kinds of cutbacks were even more astonishing because each one of the principal players in this extremely successful private mercenary company made millions.

The directors would never cut back as they did had the crews been American or British, but then the South Africans were constantly being short-changed. For instance, only six pilots were hired for the duration during the course of the Executive Outcomes' twenty-one-month deployment in Sierra Leone. This tiny group of specialists was required to man three Mi-17s, and at the same time allow for one of the crews to return home on leave. The changeovers were handled on a rotational basis.

What exactly was it that drove Nellis to participate in this war? (Or as somebody else queried, "What was it that turned his crank?") It was a question most often asked by those who thought they knew him. His enemies were also curious about his motivations.

Nellis' customary reply was something along the lines that flying over the jungle was better than working for a living. He was being more honest than many people realized, because this South African mercenary loved the job. He must have, because he certainly wasn't getting paid when I was there. When I arrived in Freetown, I learned the government hadn't given Nellis anything more than the basics for nineteen months. By that time he and his crew were owed about a million dollars, an amount that increased by another fifty percent by the end of 2005.

"It'll come in time," he would say with a shrug. And in the end some of it did, but the country's military leaders never fully wiped his slate. It was culpable that the Sierra Leone government did not pay him because he'd go out on combat operations almost daily in one of the most dangerous locations in the world. In fact, the people of Freetown needed Nellis much more than he needed them. And yet, financially abused as he was, he stayed. Nellis knew as well as anyone that there were scores of contract pilots ready to fill his boots if he pulled out. If he stopped flying he conceded, he would have had to leave the country, likely without any recompense.

Flying combat as a freelancer wasn't Nellis' only concern. There were civilians in Freetown who hated him. They called him "the resident psychopath," a man who made a living killing people. While Nellis is certainly no mental case, it was difficult to argue with their latter point. As the man himself said, "They are right on the button on that score."

I have known Nellis for the best part of a quarter-century, but was much more familiar with the man than the warrior. Because I knew the Ellis family as well as I did, I saw things a lot differently than most. My wife and I had watched Nellis' four children—Kevin, Samantha, Justin, and Tracy—emerge from their formative years. Neall had helped me with my last book and had contributed sections on helicopter operations in other parts of the great African continent, Angola included.[4] We kept in regular touch, usually through his wife Zelda, who still lives in Cape Town. Because I had moved abroad, however, we'd seen little of each other in recent years. Once he'd settled in Freetown, contact became more regular.

On our first operational sortie together in Sierra Leone, I discovered that this professional loner possessed a somewhat disjointed philosophy about conflict. To my dismay, a good deal of it involved taunting the enemy, something akin to shaking a cape before a bull. He was hoping for a reaction—any reaction—that would expose what he termed "the enemy's underbelly." He relished pushing the Hind into a vulnerable position in the hopes that the rebels would use some of their bigger guns against him, perhaps even their twin-barreled ZPU-14-2s. That ploy came about while rocketing Makeni, a large town in north-central Sierra Leone that was very much in the hands of the rebels.

One sensed, too, while flying with him—and afterward, over a few ales—that there was something perverse about the possibility that the other side might retaliate. He'd light up, sit back, and admit that it really didn't enter into the equation.

"Of course they shoot at us, Al," he declared, "but then they do not have my experience." After a slight pause he added, "Anyway, I know how to retaliate. Those mothers don't!"

Nellis was hardly a braggart; he simply wasn't that sort of person. British pilots who flew with him and spent time in his company would tell you that Nellis was among the most self-effacing individuals they'd met. As one of them commented, "He's a very atypical war hero."

Nellis' off-the-cuff statements about what he did for a living were rarely more than a succession of statements of fact. Most stemmed from the way he read his war, colored by a couple of hundred sorties across an utterly cruel land that will carry its scars for generations.

Someone else was heard to say that this was a man who had long ago learned to sublimate his fears to the extent that some of his colleagues considered him reckless. Coping with the unknown had to be part of it, but he was also—as everybody was aware—relentless in the face of fire. Some of the things he did frightened me, and in the end there were operations that I preferred to sit out. Questions lingered about the way Nellis operated, like when he went in repeatedly against a variety of targets at Makeni and elsewhere. He did so without regard for Manpads, which military intelligence had repeatedly warned us the rebels had acquired. Still, he'd sometimes hover interminably over rebel concentrations, some of whom must have had us in their sights.

While the manner in which he fought his war wasn't everybody's recipe for survival—and it definitely wasn't mine because I refused to venture over Makeni with him after that first time—his actions ultimately gave him what he sought. In some of the engagements we knew that, SAMs apart, the enemy had strong stuff, even if they didn't use it to their best advantage.

There was, for instance, a surfeit of DShKM and gas-operated NSV 12.7mm heavy support weapons in RUF hands. We knew this because dozens had been taken from the UN units that had capitulated without argument during the early weeks of their deployment. They also had a few wheeled, twin-barreled 14.5mm KPVs, a very effective anti-aircraft weapon. Nellis would hover over likely rebel concentrations in the hope that they would use them. And occasionally, they did, usually to their detriment.

The Hind was causing so much damage that, just before I left the country, the rebel command from its Liberian headquarters upped the price on the South African's head to a couple of million dollars. Australian broadcaster Mark Corcoran, who reported on the conflict for Sydney's ABC network, said that he saw a message addressed to the mercenary pilot that said something along the lines of, "If we ever catch you, we'll cut your heart out and eat it." Of course, that sort of threat appealed to Nellis. In fact, said Corcoran, Nellis found it flattering. Nellis chuckled when told that the price on head had been increased, answering that anybody who knew Africa was aware that the chance of collecting any real money ranked somewhere between zero and nil. Like us, he knew there was nothing legal or binding about the ransom, but, as someone pointed out, who could be sure?

One thing the rebels did have was a rather illustrious name for Nellis' gunship. One man taken captive near Lunsar said that the helicopter had been dubbed "*Wor Wor* Boy" in Mende, a local African language. Loosely translated, it meant "Ugly Boy." That, too, pleased the man.

Despite all this, or perhaps because of it, pilots from a host of nations were eager to fly with him. Requests usually arrived in the form of telephone calls from friends or "friends of friends" from overseas. Most were from people who wanted to join him "just for the experience." Quite a few were willing to fly for free. But these were short-term options, and Nellis was wary about taking on someone who probably lacked the total commitment he required—especially in the difficult circumstances under which he operated. As Nellis discovered to his cost, beneath the brittle crust of some fliers' camaraderie there was occasionally a thinly-disguised streak of paranoia, particularly with some of the Americans who wafted through.

Sierra Leone was so far off the beaten tourist track that Nellis also had to question the motives of someone who would willingly buy a plane ticket to a country enmeshed in a particularly brutal war, simply for the sake of seeing what it was like. It didn't make sense, he reckoned, especially when those involved were throwing dollars about as if they owned the place while the rest of the lads were counting their pennies.

Outwardly at least, Nellis seemed to enjoy the company of just about everyone. He was a gregarious soul after a couple of toots and loved to exchange war stories, sometimes all night long. But some of the Americans worried Nellis. "They're different than the Europeans," he would ruminate, "a bit like Scandinavians." When I asked him to elaborate, he changed the subject. He later confided that he never really knew where he stood with many of them. Most of them, he sensed, viewed the world loftily, with the kind of detached amusement that didn't warrant close attention. Still, admitted the pilot, "I often ask myself what their real agenda was."

I knew what he meant. All of us were aware that some of the Americans who meandered across Africa might have been involved with Washington's multi-tiered intelligence services—CIA, DIA, State Department, and so on. Nellis didn't have to be told to be wary; that came with the job. Naturally, there was also the occasional American flier who was willing to sully his reputation with no questions asked. But once Nellis started to explain how things worked, and that the locals would kill you for the watch on your wrist, most were appalled that he would work in such terrible conditions. To some, it was a state of mind that fringed on the primordial.

Many of these newcomers, especially the Americans, were shocked when they discovered that the Sierra Leone government had no support system for the Air Wing if things went wrong. "Support system?" Nellis would reply cynically. "Shit, we don't even have the flares we need for our missile dispensers!"

The truth was that there was not enough money to pay for that kind of equipment, and by the time I arrived in Sierra Leone, the crew had learned to live without such essentials. Consequently, few American pilots hung about Freetown for long.

Looking back, perhaps it wasn't surprising that some of the non-governmental organizations with their own helicopters in Freetown got former Soviet pilots to fly for them.

3

STRIKE ON MAKENI AND BRITISH INVOLVEMENT

For more than three weeks, through Christmas 1998 and New Year's 1999, Neall Ellis flew the lone Mi-17 helicopter that they had christened "Bokkie" with its two well-oiled GPMGs onboard. This rickety old flying machine was all that stood between a depleted Nigerian ECOMOG force and the collapse of the Sierra Leone government. Without a break except to refuel, Nellis and his crew systematically penetrated rebel lines in and around Freetown—and sometimes further afield. Though "Bokkie" was never used offensively, the helicopter took some heavy retaliatory fire, though never enough to permanently ground her.

War had tainted Freetown long before I arrived. The city wasn't exactly burning, but there were big bangs, automatic fire, flares, and tracers going off in the outlying areas and occasionally in the middle of town. What had begun with the rebels sporadically probing army defenses—usually during the dark hours—ended with the capital of Sierra Leone facing a protracted urban revolt that resulted in terrible death and destruction. I am writing with 1999 in mind, because the RUF campaign had started in the Kono diamond fields in December 1998. Significantly, it wasn't the first time that Foday Sankoh's RUF rebels had tried to take charge.

American warships, meanwhile, were stationed off Africa's West Coast to evacuate the country's expatriates. Most Freetown residents were being airlifted to Lungi so that US aircraft wouldn't have to venture into the interior. For their part, the British weren't all that interested in what was going on. Not yet, anyway. To them, Sierra Leone was just one more in a large number of hotspots around the world. It was believed that matters would eventually settle down and work themselves out, just as they had in the past. What was going on along the west coast wasn't all that unusual; this was, after all, Africa. So Whitehall remained aloof to the goings-on until Washington pointed out that if the Sierra Leone military junta was toppled, the entire coast—Ghana, the usually stable Ivory Coast, and Nigeria—could go the same way.[1] This was bad news and helped Whitehall focus on the problem. Although not the most stable country on the African continent, Nigeria was a major oil supplier with almost all of it going to the West. With that in mind, and with unhealthy things taking place in the Middle East, West Africa suddenly started to matter to Britain's bean-counting mandarins.

For better or worse, it was Nigerian troops who were holding what was left of government ground in Freetown. This was significant because many of the Nigerian soldiers were hardly any better than the rebels. Meanwhile, Sierra Leone was forced to muddle through, which was remarkable considering the mess in which the country now found itself. If anything, Sierra Leone was on the brink of becoming ungovernable. Even a cursory glance at the facts drives that home: the army's efforts were disjointed and ineffectual because its soldiers were ill-disciplined and the majority barely trained; there was almost no domestic order because the police hadn't been paid for six months; Parliament remained suspended; the civil service had effectively ceased to exist; and the country's president had hotfooted hastily into exile, taking the customary fortune in diamonds with him.

That was roughly the time that Neall Ellis came into prominence. Initially he had been flying the Mi-17 that everybody knew as "Bokkie" for Sandline, a Private Military Company with headquarters in London. Things had been going fine until somebody took a photo of the helicopter being worked on by Royal Navy technicians in Freetown harbor and passed it on to one of British tabloids. Parliament came down hard and demanded an immediate end to "this mercenary activity." Sandline was out of there in record time and in lieu of a financial settlement package, the South African pilot was offered the Mi-17 instead. He accepted gratefully, even though he knew that the Hip was already overdue for a service. But there was a war in the offing and shrewd operator that Nellis is, he and his new-found partner, Hassan Ahmed Hussein, eventually made a million dollars in hauling refugees to safety. Ostensibly, they were working for ECOMOG who, with the Sierra Leone government, paid them.

It is worth noting that hostilities had begun earlier in Monrovia, the Liberian capital, when the South African mercenary helicopter pilot "Juba" Joubert, his Ethiopian flight engineer Sindaba, and former SAS operator Fred Marafano originally got the ball rolling in

October 1997 in conjunction with Sandline. It was Hassan that had actually got them started there and why Taylor wanted them all dead. They all fled across the border to nearby Freetown with rogue Nigerians right behind them.

For much of the preceding year, Neal Ellis' multiple tasks had been supplemented by an unusual and enterprising company that maintained its headquarters in Oregon. International Charter Inc. (ICI) operated a pair of Russian-built Mi-8MTVs out of Cockerill Barracks on the fringe of Freetown. It was no accident that Brian Boquist, at that time ICI's CEO (before he was elected to Congress in Oregon) decided to base his helicopters at the same military headquarters that Nellis used. Situated on the eastern edge of the capital, this was one of the few relatively secure places left in the country.

The South African's relationship with the American was, of necessity, equitable—the two men never knew when they would need each other. They had already worked together once in October 1998, when Nellis was put on standby to help ICI crews evacuate US Embassy staff from Liberia. Nellis commented later that he liked to stay in touch with such friends. He would down a few beers with them when the occasion presented itself and "help where I can. It was sort of the accepted thing to do."

Nellis is also generous in his praise for ICI. "Without them we would never have survived, and that's the kind of reality we all faced."

ICI's two Mi-8s were distinctive. Both had large United States flags painted on their fuselages—one on each side. The American flags did not dissuade the rebels in the least, and the two choppers were routinely hit by ground fire. One of ICI's crewmen (the pilots were East European) was heard to say in Paddy's Bar one night that the flags did nothing to stop enemy fire. "We could immerse both fucking birds in a pink bath and decorate them with polka dots and the bastards would still shoot at us," was how he phrased it. The man's frustration was obvious, though the palm wine he gulped by the tumblerful also had something to do with it. Paddy Warren, owner and chief factotum at Paddy's, would happily get just about any libation you asked for. He'd been doing that work for so long that somebody in London eventually decided to reward him with an MBE for his good work.

Some people in Sierra Leone were worried about ICI's role in the country. While ICI's involvement thus far had been constructive and had contributed a semblance of stability in the regions in which it operated, the company's ties to Washington were close enough to cause a huff among some of the more politically correct. As usual, European NGOs living in Freetown were vocal about their concerns and labeled the ICI crews "a bunch of spies." Part of the reason for this friction was that many of these do-gooders despised anything to do with the United States. They also resented a US presence in West Africa. In their minds, an American connection presupposed some kind of intelligence link. Its purpose had to be nefarious, they would claim. The fact that the ICI crews went about their business armed only heightened their suspicion. These were the same people that journalist Anton la Guardia had spotted when he was in-country—ICI crews sporting AK-47s on the chopper pad at Cockerill. But none of this was unique for a US company working in an African war zone.

ICI was only one of several Stateside combines that sometimes operated in an Africa beset by revolt. Another was Military Professional Resources, Inc., or MPRI for short. MPRI is a massive Washington-based organization offering all manner of military training and other programs. Like ICI, its detractors always like to say that the company has specific links to the Pentagon.

There is also Florida's AirScan, another US entity that flits about on the fringe of the world's trouble spots. For a long time, AirScan monitored developments in that tiny oil-rich enclave that, while it is twice the size of Rhode Island, lies north of the Congo River and is very much an integral part of Angola. That someone would want to keep an eye on Cabinda made sense because most of that country's oil also ends up in America.

Interestingly, AirScan did some reconnaissance work in Sierra Leone during 2002, contracted for the job by the mainly British group International Military Advisory and Training Team, IMATT (SL) with a headquarters element in Freetown.

ICI's primary job as a private military company under contract to the U.S. State Department was to run supplies into Sierra Leone's interior, mostly to towns and garrisons under siege by rebel forces. Since most of their tasks were in support of military operations, ICI's helicopters often returned to base "having grown holes in the fuselage." That little comment came after a particularly hairy run to the town of Kabala in the northern part of the country. Kabala was the same place that Nellis took us from time to time, where the rebels were well equipped and didn't mind using their hardware against "intruders."

ICI's motto is proudly proclaimed on its website: "Anytime . . . Anywhere." The company's specialty is operating in regions where few others are willing to take the risk, including Haiti, Liberia, the Sudan and Sierra Leone, together with a few others that the company does not list. As ICI unequivocally declares, "Our staff has worked on every continent." The well-connected company's contracts have even included presidential security details. At least one European diplomat in Freetown referred to ICI as "Africa's own Air America." His comment was prompted by the fact that the firm used to draw its staff almost exclusively from US Army Delta, Navy Seals and Special Operations' elite forces, though it now includes former South African Special Forces veterans among its crews. Another unusual departure is that ICI, an American concern, prefers to use Russian helicopters instead of those manufactured in the States. That is unusual, especially for the proud patriots on its pay sheets.

As Danny O'Brien, a former Special Forces operator and current CEO, told me at his home near Fort Lewis in Washington, there is good reason to fly these foreign birds. The Mi-8MTV used by ICI is a souped-up version of the original Mi-8 and offers five hundred more horsepower than the earlier, military model. It is also a tough and reliable transport chopper—the perfect choice for what he called "sustained, heavy use in harsh environments." Never mind that it has the additional advantage of being comparatively simple to convert to a basic form of gunship. Rocket pods, obviously, are optional.

Like the Hind, the Hips were originally built by the Soviets for durability. They're also the workhorses for dozens of air forces around the globe. When I questioned Nellis about flying birds that had been designed and produced by his nemesis, the Evil Empire, he was candid: "No sweat. You puts your oil and gas, you service the bitch regularly and she'll go forever; just got to treat her right."

Many Americans who knew about such things agree. ICI reckons that the Hip's straightforward engineering and reduced reliance on sensitive, high-maintenance technology "makes it an extremely reliable aircraft under any condition," explained Danny O'Brien. This also means less unscheduled downtime, more flying time, and better safety because the helicopter was essentially designed to fly for extended periods before it needs an overhaul. After a thousand hours in the air, the engine is sent back to Ukraine to be rebuilt, which can be done six times before a new one is installed. The procedure is unabashedly Russian and applies to a lot of other equipment developed during the Soviet era. As O'Brien succinctly put it, "It's simpler, it's more practical and most important of all, it's a lot cheaper."

One of ICI's professionals who made a living in some of the world's more isolated places—his CV includes wounds in Colombia, Haiti and elsewhere—was Robin Hawke. Having banged heads with the UN representative in Port-au-Prince, he was relocated to Sierra Leone by ICI.

In Freetown the man called himself Hawkeye, which was appropriate since he handled automatic weapons with the proficiency of a professional. It's worth mentioning that since his time in Sierra Leone, First Lieutenant Hawk again entered the US Military and served as an officer with a Special Forces unit in Afghanistan with the 19th Special Forces Group (Airborne). Undoubtedly, his experiences in West Africa found some kind of application against a Taliban-backed insurgency.

Hawkeye's job with ICI during the short time he worked in West Africa was that of a project manager. Simply put, he ran ICI's show. He was also willing to provide good backup if and when things turned nasty because he had good military experience in intelligence, communications and as a medic.

I got to know Hawkeye fairly well after he returned to the States. Writing under the pseudonym A.G. Hawke, he kept a remarkable diary of his experiences. Some of the excerpts from a chapter headed "Bad Prez, Bad Gen's, Bad Troops, and Bad Asses" could have been scripted for an Indiana Jones follow-up:

"As for us, we packed our heaters religiously, to dinners and showers and even in our compound hooch . . . the mere thought of dying on the toilet for the lack of a heater . . . and to make battlefield recovery feasible, we packed 9mm's to leave no distinct American signature. We carried our AK-47s in tennis racket cases . . . on us, if we felt the heat, near us if not . . . and always a grenade in the crotch for breaking contact in a bad situation. We went to war with only vests (body armor) and a mule pack full of magazines of ammo, grenades, smokes, strobes, gps, maps, compass, radios, mini-first aid and food. But mostly we were all water and weapons . . . it was too hot for all the crap typical US soldiers carry because you can't fight in that heat for very long . . . your guaranteed lethargy will get you killed faster than anything . . . travel light, better to fight . . . that's the way."

Hawkeye was a lot kinder to Freetown than most. "Lot of good ass was everywhere to be had," he wrote:

The women here are fine and, unlike many other African cesspools, AIDs is nearly unheard of here because the war has been raging so long, no tourists have been spreading the dreaded disease . . . and when you get nearly dead daily, somehow you need that to know you're alive. . . .

In an article subsequently published in Colonel Robert K. Brown's *Soldier of Fortune* magazine, Hawkeye painted a vivid picture of the kind of unconventional helicopter operations that were ongoing at a time when rebels dominated most of the country. As was to be expected, his path crossed with Nellis' often enough, especially since the ICI's Mi-8s were helping to evacuate civilians. Hawkeye wrote:

"We woke to the sounds of artillery and mortars in the distance, the sound of sporadic gunfire in the streets and the out-of-control chatter of everyone crying on all the radio channels. So we were asked to assist in getting the people out with our two helos and we did. We worked the better part of a day and evacuated the citizens. Then I had to send one of my choppers out of the country to the nearest safe haven (Guinea) with all my crew and staff and kit so that we could support an operation once we returned. Who knew when that would be, if ever? I stayed with my three best pilots and a minimum amount of kit. We would leave the next day, and since it was Christmas Eve, I didn't know if we'd see morning.

"Like something out of a bad movie, I watched our secondary chopper fly off into the sunset. I then heard the sound of machine-gun fire on the radio. Nellis, our South African chopper brother was taking fire. He (and Hassan Ahmed Hussein) had continued to try to help the Nigerian peacekeeping force as we evacuated the civilians and said he'd been hit and was going down fast.

"I had to help. Our base began to get the coordinates and I told the guys to kit up and get back into the cockpit. We fired up the turbines . . . I didn't know what would happen, but there was an understanding that we would do anything to help our buddies as they would us . . . so off we went.

"We flew out to get our friend and fortunately, though he'd taken rounds, he could land safely. Said he could make his repairs in the bush. So he only needed us to get his cargo out which consisted of some wounded troops. We landed, loaded and took off . . . he said he'd be up and running in fifteen minutes.

"Then he told us the news: 'Hey, Hawkeye . . .the wounded that you guys have just picked up are actually rebels who've defected back to our side!' "

Worse, both Nellis and Hawkeye knew that Liberian warlord
Charles Taylor had just posted that million-dollar price on each of the
choppers. There was also a massive reward waiting for anyone who
would bring home one of the crew members flying the Hips: any crew
member.

Hawkeye wrote about the presence of a group of white mercenaries working with the rebels and a white-painted rebel helicopter that
operated briefly in support of the RUF in the Freetown corridor. The
copter was based in the Liberian capital of Monrovia, and regularly
crossed into Sierra Leone airspace to support rebel operations. The
American and others crunched numbers and dates and deduced that
the intruder was probably being run by some of the old South African
crews who had flown combat for Executive Outcomes in Angola and
Sierra Leone five years before. They were acquiring reputations for all
the wrong reasons, he decided.

Hawkeye, meanwhile, wasn't so sure about another group of
whites reported to be working with the rebels, some on the very outskirts of Freetown. At first the Americans were dubious that there
were actually mercenaries operating with Sankoh's people. But the
reports kept coming in. The crews had their doubts. Hawkeye and his
crowd had been involved in the region for a long time and as he
explained, his people knew just about everybody they came across in
the interior. If it was happening, he said, if white outsiders were actually fighting with the rebels, the news could cause quite a stir because
it meant escalation of the war. At the same time, they were all aware,
the only way that Europeans could be attached to the rebel army was
if they had been brought in from the outside.

As we all discovered soon afterward, that was exactly what was
going on. About a dozen mercenaries of East European stock were
serving with the RUF (later joined by some South Africans and Serbs).
Most of the imported help were paid their dues in raw diamonds. "We
found this out when they brought in the heads of a couple of them
after a few battles," remembered Hawkeye. "It took us a while to discover that they were actually Serb military types on Taylor's payroll,
originally flown in by Gadhaffi's people in the hopes of changing the
course of the war. Earlier we'd thought they might be Spetznaz—
Russian Special Forces."

The American freelancer went on to describe a rather atypical
operation as the rebels approached Freetown. He had flown out on a
routine mission to pull out the dead and wounded from a government

position that had taken a pounding. "We called ahead on the radio, ensured that all was OK: good weather, security along the perimeter OK and so on. By the time we arrived thirty minutes later, the gooks had routed the entire ECOMOG force and, just then, lay waiting for us in ambush. Somehow, they'd been told that we were on our way . . . or, more feasibly, they monitored our transmissions."

Hawkeye continued: "We saw the village from the air and it looked like only ghosts lived there. We could see from where we hovered that something was seriously wrong. As soon as we started to pull away, the chopper came under some pretty heavy machinegun fire . . . no joy for the bastards that day. . . ." Upset that they hadn't been warned, Hawkeye and his crew headed down the main road leading away from the embattled town in search of what the American called "a lost army." Coming over a rise they found it. There were almost a thousand men, "all ass and elbows" running down the highway to escape the advancing rebels.

That evening, after several more confrontations, the American and his crowd tried to get the last batch of civilians across the bay to Lungi Airport. The first relief helicopters from an American task force began arriving to airlift the civilians to US naval ships waiting offshore. From there, they were finally shipped to the Gambia and Dakar in Senegal.

"We came in but the Nigerian Army at the hotel wouldn't allow us to land without charging us—as well as each of the refugees that we had onboard—some big bucks," complained Hawkeye. "They demanded, virtually at gunpoint, a thousand dollars from each of us if we wanted to leave. True capitalists! We landed anyway and told the people to ignore those assholes and get onboard."

Matters almost got out of hand when one of the soldiers shoved Hawkeye, who promptly punched the man in the face. "He was bleeding when he reached for his weapon but I drew on him first. The citizens that we'd brought out, meanwhile, afraid of the violence, refused to join us. So we left them there, in deadly fear of their own protectors. Time was tight and we still had to refuel and make ready for our own exodus the following morning."

Hawkeye thought little of the Nigerian soldiers, but he absolutely despised the rebels, whom he called "barely human" miscreants. With real rancor in his voice he added, "We all know what they did . . ." He was referring, of course, to their practice of eating captives.

Hawkeye had his own ideas about using Russians to fly ICI helicopters. Always outspoken, especially when he was convinced he was right, it was his view that the Russians work hard. "Fucking hard," he called it, "just like we Americans used to do a generation ago. Also, they're very much down to earth. Most important, these guys really are ballsy." In fact, he rated them right up there with the best chopper pilots he had ever flown with in half a dozen theaters of war. There was no doubt about it, added Hawkeye, the Russians were as competent as the Americans.

Hawkeye's comments (which outraged some and triggered nodding heads among others) might at least be partially explained by his motto, which went something like "Live, like you'll die tomorrow, learn like you'll live forever, love like you've never been hurt and laugh like no one is watching."

According to Hawkeye, his worst experience in Sierra Leone wasn't having people shoot at him. It was something more mundane: slopping blood out of the helicopter after each airlift of wounded from front-line positions. Although they flew with the occasional medic, the company didn't have the proper equipment for the job. "We sometimes had inches of blood caked in the back. Soggy pools of it would gather in every hole on the aluminum floor. It couldn't be left there, not overnight, and definitely not in that heat with all those flies and filth about." The American mustered teams of local workers and paid them extra to scrape the slime and blood away. Work was difficult to get in Freetown then—as it still is today—and he wasn't short of takers. "We had to use gallons of bleach each day. Afterward I started putting down wooden boards so that we would have some traction as the mucous gelled. Then we'd hose that floor pad down so that it'd drain into the swamp and feed the prawns. But it didn't always work that way, not with the old stuff that coagulated into lumps."

A strike on Makeni, the rebels' regional headquarters in the interior of the country, was something of a watershed adventure for me while flying with the Air Wing. Nellis loved to hit the place whenever he could. I visited it only once, from the air.

"I don't mind risks," I explained to Nellis, "but Makeni is at the very heart of the war. If we're going to be shot down, I'd rather it be as far away from the largest concentration of rebel forces in the country as possible. Then, at least, we'd have a sporting chance." Nellis only smiled in response.

Our flight path took us first to Rogberi Junction which, despite its notoriety following the death of our two colleagues, was really little more than a handful of shacks along a pot-holed road leading into the forbidding interior. It was manned by UN troops and they waved at us as we passed. From there we went on to Lunsar, which had been captured by Sierra Leone soldiers the day before. To the consternation of us all, it was lost again in a rebel offensive a few nights later. Considering the nature of the war, this was to be expected. The problem was that victories and defeats were quickly promulgated in Freetown, often at astonishing speed. Sometimes we would be flying back from a battle and learn on the radio that Freetown was jubilant at the news of a particular strike that had only taken place an hour earlier. How the hell did they know this so soon?

We believed the rebel intelligence network was a lot better than most people thought, and we weren't wrong. As expatriates, we were better placed to see the wood for the trees, and it was manifest that in this department the government really wasn't in kilter. In terms of media relations, for instance, the RUF was streets ahead of anything that all the President's men together might have contemplated. Also, Sankoh's men had an outstanding communications network.

Five years later I was able to discuss some of this with Mark Doyle, the BBC correspondent in Africa who spent a good deal of time in that horrific conflict. Though his reports were hardly favorable to the rebels, they treated him well whenever he crossed the lines. He was even allowed access to some of their fighting units. "They pretty well understood the nature of propaganda . . . the fact that they made me welcome in spite of some of my hostile reports in the past about their militants hacking off legs and arms is certainly indicative of that. Shrewd operators, some of the RUF command," was Doyle's opinion.

When bad news spread, whether it was true or false, it was almost like a fog; one could sense the gloom settling on the populace like a heavy shroud. It was also disheartening. As the word spread, some people would become breathless, others frantic. Most would cast their eyes about to see what their neighbors were doing in the hope of finding direction. As we are all aware, fear invariably breeds dislocation, especially when there are two million anxious people in trouble in a community where answers were rarely possible. Children would be called home, food gathered, contact with relatives or friends on the far side of town established. And as conditions deteriorated still more, terror would become almost palpable, not only in the civilian community but also within government.

The newly-arrived British military aid detachment—drawing upon its own experiences elsewhere, including Northern Ireland—was the first to observe that if this was not checked, the situation could rapidly get out of hand. We all knew that rumors and half-baked news spread rapidly, almost like a virus, as it had under previous leaders like Momeh and the delinquent Valentine Strasser, who was usually so spaced out on cocaine that it is surprising he was able to hold on to power as long as he did. If the news was black enough, the civilians might believe that President Kabbah and his diamond-dealing cartel were losing their grip. The next step would be the panic buying of essentials, but little else. The economy of Freetown would quickly collapse. Hassan's cousin owned a shoe store in the capital. During the week of the Lunsar incident, explained Nellis' gunner, his cousin sold almost nothing. "The people are very worried," he explained, "and so am I."

Lunsar, our first destination that afternoon, was the site of a long-abandoned iron-ore mine dominated by two large hills to its immediate south. There was evidence of government troops about as we flew over the place, but nobody had yet claimed the heights looming over the settlement. Nellis didn't like that at all. It was obvious that whoever held the place needed to dominate the high ground. And dominating it would not be that difficult, as Nellis had warned his superiors at Cockerill several times. The rebels had only to lug a heavy machine gun up the nearest hill to be able to target all of Lunsar. If they did that, "they'd have their own version of a gunship," he explained simplistically, trying not to insult their intelligence. Some Sierra Leone staff officers had spent time at Sandhurst—not that it seemed to make much difference in their approach to basic military tactics.

And that's exactly what the rebels did the next time they took Lunsar. The move underscored one of many contradictions symptomatic of this struggle. Both sides often overlooked the most obvious military options. The difference, however, was that the rebels appeared to us to be markedly less negligent in this regard. The mercenaries in their ranks were earning their pay.

Once past Lunsar we were into the badlands again: Makeni was about ten or fifteen minutes flying time away and Nellis instructed me to trip the passive infrared jammer switch. This was Manpad country.

Within minutes we spotted two United Nations armored personnel carriers (APCs) that had been captured by the rebels a month previously. Both were abandoned, probably for lack of fuel. A half-hearted attempt had been made to camouflage them with branches and shrubs, but their white-painted frames stuck out through the undergrowth like banners. There were gaping holes in their turrets where the heavier guns had been ripped free and transferred to the back of a rebel truck or van, like Mogadishu's "Technicals," or so we surmised.

Six or eight villages dotted the road to Makeni, though most did not show any signs of life. Once we spotted a cluster of huts with smoke. It was a communal fire and suggestive of the way the rebels liked to operate; in peacetime, for example, each hut used its own hearth. Nellis opened up on it and moments later the side-gunners reported that armed men were running out of adjacent buildings.

"They're headed for that clump of forest on the left!" Hassan called out over the intercom, his voice like a rasp. "They're not government," he added, since none of them were wearing camouflage. Nellis swung the chopper about and rocketed that clump of bush for good measure while the rest of us watched the thickets below for return fire.

The day's priority was not this small group of huts but Makeni and its RUF regional headquarters. While most of the rebel brass had decamped into the interior, army intelligence sources indicated that there were still some "heavies" about. Nellis' mission was to hit a cluster of two-story buildings near the center of the town that the rebels had commandeered about a month before. Back at base, defectors had pinpointed the site as a radio room as well as the RUF commander's office.

By West African standards Makeni was quite a big place, about a mile or two across. It was laid out in the traditional British colonial "tween-war" style, with an ordered focus toward the marketplace in the center of town. Forty years of independence had done little to alter the place, and I thought it resembled Kumasi in Ghana, though smaller. Similar to Lunsar, Makeni was dominated by a tall communication mast and a series of low hills rimming the skyline. One of these sported a rebel flag; Nellis suggested Hassan use it for target practice as he flew past. He had mentioned earlier that the town was about twenty miles from Malal Hills, where the bones of my friend Bob MacKenzie lay scattered. Out of curiosity, we flew over this low range of hills on the way back. As with so most of the area, there was no evidence of any living being.

With his initial reconnaissance complete, Nellis got busy. He pushed the Hind upward to about eight hundred feet before shoving the nose down, hard. Moments later a rocket salvo crashed into Makeni's central business district. We should have completed the job with the Gatling, but it jammed. Nellis cursed. Undeterred, he climbed again, swung the Hind around, and went in a second time. By now my mouth was dry.

When emerging from our dives I felt that we were at our most vulnerable. Then and during the tight turns—when the world below appeared to stand still—we must have presented the rebels with a pretty good target. But nothing happened and this was surprising, because intelligence reports had specifically warned that the rebels had 23mm quads and enough RPGs to intimidate any attacker. Worse, we were flying well within the weapon's thousand-yard destruct envelope.

Suddenly, Hassan screamed: "Trucks!" followed by a bearing on our flank. By the time Nellis had swung his nose round again and gained some height, a vehicle pool emerged a couple hundred yards from our initial target. We shouldn't have missed it the first time round. There were half a dozen trucks, vans, and Land Rovers, including a BRDM-60 personnel carrier. Nearby, a ten-tonner was parked in the shadow of a large building: almost all of them painted white and indicating more captured UN stock. Nellis' previous strikes were slightly off center, but this time his aim was spot-on. Pieces of metal, wood and plastic showered down as several columns of smoke rose into the sky. Before I could assess the damage, the South African had pulled his bird up and away to the right; it was no place to hover. We struck again at more targets on the edge of town before heading for home and I was glad to have Makeni at our back.

Because of its headquarters status and target-rich opportunities, Makeni regularly beckoned Nellis, almost like a siren song. He liked the challenge, the certainty of finding targets and, by inference, the kills that resulted. But there would come a time, I suggested once we were on the ground again, when they would hit back, if only for the hell of it. When that happened, I decided early on in the assignment, I'd rather be sitting quietly at Cockerill working on my laptop.

I never flew over Makeni again. The aggressor in my soul had become dormant. Treetop height at a hundred and sixty knots—for hours at a stretch, if necessary—took some getting used to. Frankly, a vulnerable, slow-moving SAM target over Makeni wasn't something I wanted to experience again. Nellis played on my fears for a long while afterward. "Dry mouth time, again, Al. You coming?" I'd shake my head and he would chuckle quietly to himself.

As noted earlier, the flight to Makeni that afternoon was over land that was almost totally deserted. Going home by a different route, we spotted a few locals; some were washing clothes by a stream. Elsewhere there was a family working their patch of land and pointedly, they ignored us. That was instructive, considering that a helicopter in Africa is an event. In his debrief back at base, Nellis suggested the reason was a rebel presence in the vicinity. He had the coordinates and would go back, perhaps the next day. Innocent civilians always waved, he argued. "Those people were worried about us," he declared emphatically. "They could very well have been gooks who put their weapons aside on our approach. It's the oldest gambit in insurgency," he continued. "Ask anybody who has flown combat in some of these far flung outposts."

By the time we got back to Lungi to refuel, the floor at the back was half-an-inch deep in spent brass.

Because Nellis flew the only helicopter in Sierra Leone that never returned to base without at least one strike at an RUF position, there were a lot of people at Cockerill eager to sit in on his debriefs. It was to be expected that there were also those in Freetown who would try and forge ties with the man, particularly within the diplomatic community. It was a standard routine: Nellis would be drinking at Paddy's or Alex's, and the first secretary of this embassy or the cultural officer of that embassy would greet him like somebody from the old country. It had about as much to do with getting to know the man as what he might reveal. Nellis wasn't yesterday's child and he accepted this faux familiarity with good humor.

The same could be said about the High Commission, though there was a special place in Nellis' heart for the British. Although Nellis was a native of South Africa, his antecedents had come from East Anglia and he had a British passport. London's emissaries often exploited this situation, almost ruthlessly at times. As author John Le Carré said of British foreign policy in *The Constant Gardener*, "It's all ritual and no faith."

But since Nellis is a likable fellow and many of those involved in military liaison work in Freetown had seen conflict—even if from a distance—there were a few bonds forged. Among those with whom Nellis shared confidences during my swing through Freetown, was Lt. Col. Rob Symonds, British Military Liaison Officer at the High Commission.

An interesting fellow, Symond's weathered face revealed absolutely nothing. Those who spent time with the man found that he could be simultaneously evasive and elliptical. Or, if the mood took him, explicit and just moments later, infuriatingly vague. To him it was all part of the job. I remember one night when we were having dinner at Alex's in Aberdeen's Man of War Bay, one of the few restaurants that maintained acceptable Western health standards. Symonds said something about Nellis' expertise with the Gatling.

Listening to Nellis' experiences, the colonel quoted the conventional wisdom regarding close air support crews within NATO. "No helicopter wing should go operational," he said, "unless there are at least three aircrews dedicated to each pair of gunships." That meant three pairs of cockpit crews and another three pairs of side-gunners, never mind ground crews. In Freetown, Symonds observed, Ellis' total complement was himself as pilot and a couple of side-gunners armed with machine guns. There wasn't even a co-pilot.

The consensus among just about everybody in Freetown—ethnics and expatriates alike—was that this veteran of South Africa's border wars had achieved an astonishing level of success. What's more, he and the crew had done so without back-up and it had been going on a while.

But Nellis was paying a price. He hadn't had a real break for more than two years. Moreover, he, Hassan, and the rest of the gang had only had a couple days off since the most recent bout of hostilities opened months earlier. Sometimes Nellis would show up so dizzy or disorientated that his crewmates would drive him home instead. The next day the pilot would be back at work.

"You can go on for so long and ignore the obvious," I told him. "Something has to give." It didn't help that Nellis had not even seen a doctor in five years. I urged him to take a few precautions. One of my suggestions was to thin his blood, even marginally. His condition so worried me that once I'd joined the group, I practically forced him to take an aspirin a day. Nellis was overweight, enjoyed his liquor, and did not eat or sleep properly. He had adrenaline for blood, and his was a classic prescription for a heart attack. I was aware that even with a complete set of controls before me in the gunners' seat, I'd be helpless if anything happened while we were in the air. I know marginally more about nuclear fission than about flying.

I'd mentioned his condition to several British officers serving with the Royal Navy task force. There must be doctors to spare, I suggested. Though they were initially enthusiastic, nothing came of it. It also didn't take me long to discover that while most of them admired the man for what he was doing, it didn't occur to them to arrange for Nellis to have a proper check-up. It would have been a small but valuable tribute to the one man who was fighting the hardest, especially since Nellis was also broke at the time. It was an entirely different battle to scrape together enough each month to pay the Ethiopians who were keeping the choppers in the air, especially when the government that they were protecting wasn't prepared to do its bit: *C'est l'Afrique.*

No slouch while at his post in Freetown, Rob Symonds was a different caliber of officer altogether. He was a participant in the war and would help where he could, playing a significant—though understated—role the hostilities. In intelligence matters, the Colonel was as eager to catch as to throw and his job early on was to head north out of Freetown each morning toward the badlands. Interestingly, he traveled in full camouflage uniform (which surprised us all), sometimes going through Rogberi and behind rebel lines. Mostly he tried to find out what was going on in the jungle and beyond. He worked alone and unarmed, his only "defense" a High Commission Land Rover painted white all over with two large Union Jacks painted on the doors, one on each side.

Symonds must have known what he was doing, though we all thought him a little demented to be moving about the dark and distant interior unescorted. Only after our two journalist colleagues were killed did he accept some help, usually in the form of another Land Rover with a few of the Special Forces operators in it, mostly SAS. But even then they would have been pushed had there been an ambush in that overgrown terrain where the jungle was often so dense that it deflected light. Our greatest concern was that Symonds might be taken hostage. Each day he set out for a new destination "to get the feel of things." Since he and Nellis were neighbors in the Cape Sierra Hotel compound, we'd afterward sit about in Nellis' backyard and talk about the day's events, usually over drinks, snacks, and swarms of mosquitoes. Anton La Guardia would sometimes join us for a natter.

Fit and wiry, "Colonel Rob" was one of the few people I knew who jogged and actually enjoyed his smokes. He was also heading for retirement; Sierra Leone was to be his last foreign posting. This British officer's simplest and most innovative ploy to win points, however marginal, was to try to get some of the hearts and minds of the locals on his side. His unlikely weapon in this campaign involved a bagful of old tennis balls. When he entered a village, he'd toss a few balls about to get the children scurrying after them and the exercise would delight everybody there since most had never handled a real ball before. Totally out of touch with civilization, their "balls" consisted mostly of rags and stuffing tied with string.

"You want one?" he would ask in an accent polished by years of associating with the right people. Of course they did. In this, these jungle kids were no different from their distant cousins in Brixton or the Bronx; one tennis ball represented their most prized possession. Then Symonds would say, with a candor these kids must have found disarming, "I will give you a ball, and you, in return, must give me a gun . . . one ball for one gun." The routine was always the same, with the parents often enthusiastic as interested bystanders.

The ploy was absurd, but it worked. Symonds rarely returned to Freetown without a Kalashnikov or two in his rig. Looking back, what made it scary was that this was the same area where the West Side Boys took a squad of British troops hostage not long afterward.[2] Time and again this enigmatic and calculating British diplomat was called upon to outface the enemy, and he was invariably successful.

Rob Symonds worried all of us by the way he went about his business. Many of us kept an eye out for his safe return, sometimes a little anxiously. He would go about his work with a deceptive half smile that belied the depth of his resolve and, in retrospect, I think it would be difficult to find that level of dedication among most military types, no matter what uniform they wore. Invariably, his work took him deep into the kind of primitive bush country where nobody would have been any the wiser if they'd shot him in the back and left his body for the animals to devour. We were all aware that this selfsame brutal scenario played itself out every day, sometimes twenty or thirty times over and quite often within walking distance of Freetown. Had the worst happened to this British intelligence officer in Sierra Leone's muggy interior, the killers would probably have eaten him themselves, as they did with my American friend Bob MacKenzie after they tortured and killed him (Chapter 19).

Doing what Symonds did, serving in an ultra-sensitive security position in Sierra Leone, placed the man in a class of his own. He was certainly in the same category as the occasional SAS operator visiting us at Cockerill. These were tough, resourceful people, and the demands made on them were often severe. Mostly they operated behind enemy lines and had limited recourse to rescue or assistance if things turned bad. Even so, it was a lot more than what Nellis could possibly hope for if the worst happened.

The actions of so many of these British officers repeatedly underscored the resolve of those who were attached to the Sierra Leone Army to do what they could to help that impoverished war-torn country. By now, I imagine, the good colonel has been properly rewarded for his efforts, though with Britain's security services such things are rarely made public.

While Whitehall knew and accepted the Hind's value to the war effort, it soon became apparent during the British military deployment to West Africa that British officers were to have no direct association with Neall Ellis. The word was that any contact—personal or operational—was to be limited to essentials. In fact, as I was subsequently told by the South African pilot, a letter was sent out from Army Headquarters in Britain very specifically warning British personnel not to even talk "to the mercenary element" in Freetown. The RAF Air Advisor in Sierra Leone at the time actually had to request a special waiver because he was discussing just about everything to do with the war with Neall Ellis every day. It took a little while, but in the end he got it.

This policy highlighted an event that took place shortly after the Royal Navy squadron arrived. Out of nowhere, Nellis was invited for dinner onboard the helicopter carrier HMS *Ocean*. Obviously his reputation preceded him. The invitation came with an offer to spend the night onboard; the shindig would end late and it would be difficult to get ashore afterward. Nellis was delighted, of course, because these were his sort of people. Anyway, he was already a familiar figure to the flight crews of both *Ocean* and *Illustrious*: they often sank a few together at Paddy's and he'd briefed some of the carrier pilots at Cockerill several times, as it later transpired.

The invitation was retracted just a day before the event. The fact that no explanation was offered only compounded the insult; the entire affair was the antithesis of just about everything British. Obviously, someone was looking over his shoulder at his pension, which was a pity because it was a deliberate slight and totally uncalled for. I sensed that it cut deep.

It was also no secret that London kept strict tabs on what Nellis might or might not be doing to contaminate Britain's fine upstanding military ethos. Very early one morning, Rob Symonds—still at his villa at the hotel—got a call from his London headquarters. The question was direct: had he, the British military attaché in Sierra Leone, flown in Nellis' Hind?

Whether he had or not—he never went up while I was around, so I don't know definitively one way or the other—was irrelevant. The inquiry reflected an intransigent British government mindset about all things unconventional. As Michael Grunberg of Sandline told me afterward, the policy wasn't all that surprising. The British government declared more than once in Parliament that it would have no truck with mercenaries, and sadly he added, "That's been symptomatic of Labor's convoluted African politics ever since Suez." Interestingly, Nellis took Joe Melrose, America's ambassador to Sierra Leone, on a flip (though unofficially, I imagine). That it was unorthodox, there is no doubt: one of the President's men flying over enemy territory with a merc!

Brigadier David Richards, Force Commander in Sierra Leone, was one senior British officer on a foreign posting who, as a journalist tartly commented, "shot from the lip." Richards also spoke about the advantage of having the Air Wing's helicopter on call at all hours. The Brigadier remarked during an interview I did for *Jane's Defence Weekly* that Nellis' dedication was "quite remarkable." All the more so, he added, since the man wasn't even from Sierra Leone, although he was permanently living there. The statement was underscored by a rebel radio intercept that same week: "Were it not for the government gunship," it declared, "the entire RUF command would be sleeping in the capital within three days."

The Brigadier's comments were especially noteworthy, coming as they did from an officer everyone acknowledged wasn't afraid to say what he thought, and in an establishment rarely known for its candor. Sierra Leone was a sensitive operation that involved the potential race card, as well as a dozen other imbroglios. With time, it became so bad that word games—semantics, really—became the norm with any statement issued by the High Commission. So in this regard, Richards was refreshingly different. As the front man for a rescue operation that could have gone horrifyingly wrong, he wasn't afraid to react when a situation demanded firm action, a character trait that did not endear him to many of the stuffed shirts back home. This youthful senior officer—who, in his previous deployment, had commanded the British contingent in East Timor—must have learned early on that style confessed grace; so, too, when briefing a bunch of cynical hacks. Every question, no matter how astute or absurd, was answered in full and usually with a smile that belied the gravity of what he knew was taking place in the country.

Richards' maverick nature proved popular with the locals. Indeed, according to British journalist Chris McGreal, by the time he arrived in West Africa, Richards was well on the way to enjoying the same appeal in Freetown as former British High Commissioner Peter Penfold. When this British official was abruptly recalled to London (after being accused of complicity in allowing mercenaries to break the UN arms embargo) his departure sparked violent demonstrations in the capital.

Not unexpectedly, the "hired guns" issue became a topic on the brigadier's watch, especially as more journalists arrived in Freetown and Nellis' successes became a topic at just about every bar in town. What was of interest this time around was that neither Nellis nor any members of his team had ever been labeled "mercenaries," either by the Sierra Leone government or by its military hierarchy. To British military forces and, for that matter, the offices of the British High Commission in Freetown, Nellis was a "contract pilot" and nothing more. In any event, the war had encroached too close to the capital for there to be any need to downplay his role.

Richards was questioned about this and his retort was unequivocal. The Hind had originally been acquired for the people of Sierra Leone, explained the general. "International funds had paid for it, some of which, no doubt, came from Britain. Having achieved that much, the people of this country obviously needed someone to fly it." Besides, he added,[3] "Ellis is under contract to a recognized government." Indian Army Major General Vijay Jetley, the United Nations Force Commander in Sierra Leone, said much the same thing. His utterances, coming from someone most of us referred to as "the resident artful dodger," were propounded in more evasive terms, largely because he could never being himself to acknowledge the role that Nellis had played in rescuing some of his men from a rebel attack immediately after the Indian contingent had been pushed into this debacle. "Ellis has a valid contract with this government," Jetley jousted when I asked him about it in his office at the Mammy Yoko Hotel across the way from Alex's Bar.

With all this fuss going on, Nellis went about each day doing his thing, and as even his adversaries had to concede, he was damned good at his job. He'd go out on a sortie, kill a bunch of rebels, and return to base. Apart from the British contingent at Cockerill Barracks (and as a consequence, the High Commission) the South African pilot would apprise his Sierra Leonian chiefs of anything he'd managed to learn along the way. That included his immediate boss, Colonel Nelson Williams, as well Brigadier Tom Carew, the Chief of Defense Staff. They, in turn, informed their minister who put the president in the picture. If it were really important, the Brigadier would be the first to know.

Regardless of the explanations, official and otherwise, the mercenary issue festered. I quickly learned that Ellis' very presence would sometimes provoke unwarranted questions and, on occasion, emotion. People would inquire about what his official position was within the country's military hierarchy. In supercilious fashion, they'd ask about the meaning of Brigadier Richards' term "contract pilot." Untold times Nellis was asked whether he actually was a mercenary. It's little wonder why he liked to change out of his flying suit before going to the pub.

While many perceived the rebels as villains, not everyone in Freetown agreed. The result was that while there were those who regarded Nellis as a hero, others were convinced that his motives were suspect. "Why else would he do what he did if he wasn't getting paid vast sums in diamonds?" was the inference wafting about Freetown.

Worse, it was regarded as chic in some circles on the West Coast to take a passive line about the war, even though only months before Sankoh's rabble had all but broken down the gates to Freetown. Even that little episode notwithstanding, the consequences of rebel actions could hardly be missed since so many of these disfigured creatures were all over town: everywhere you looked were amputees. It was astonishing, then, that so many non-governmental personnel in Freetown were outspoken in their hostility toward this pilot. Some declared Nellis an "unperson." Though Orwellian and ridiculous considering the circumstances, it was still of some concern. How could people think like this given what Sierra Leone was experiencing? Moreover, some of these people lived barely a stone's throw from where we did in Aberdeen. Just about everybody was aware that quite a few of them sympathized quite openly with the rebels. We also knew they were probably acting as conduits to some of the more influential rebel fellow travelers in town.

The rationale of people who thought this way seemed to be grounded in the belief that as long as Nellis remained part of the Sierra

Leonian military equation, there could never be peace. This kind of cockeyed logic made Nellis the cause of war, rather than a consequence of the fighting. It seemed a bit like listening to a group of historians discussing the origins of World War II without referencing Hitler.

One of the results of this friction was that some of these do-gooders believed that if they ignored Nellis long enough, his persona would eventually evaporate or, more seriously, someone might assassinate him. Others wrote nasty letters to the newspapers, cranking themselves up into high dudgeon. Quite a few expressed the opinion that Nellis was evil incarnate, a bloody murderer who should be handed over to the RUF. Of course it was also obvious to clear-thinking individuals that it was Nellis' actions that made it possible for these same people to stay on in Sierra Leone and keep their jobs. He and his boys actually prevented more barbarism from taking place.

Listening to what some of the rebels' victims went through might have been a bit of a corrective for those so powerfully opposed to the conflict, but that wasn't the end of it. Unless you were Medicins Sans Frontieres (MSF), Caritas, or one of those rare ministrants prepared to help the unfortunate, few members of the expatriate community ever took the trouble to lift the covers and look up close at conditions for themselves. Some actually went to a lot of trouble to avoid having anything to do with the military struggle, including some of its pathetic and utterly helpless victims. This surprised me because the refugee camps were right there in Murraytown, squarely in your face.

In fact, the Amputee and War Wounded Camp in that suburb was open to visitors at all hours. I went there several times and though I'd seen many things in my travels around the world, my visits there unsettled me—sometimes for days afterward. It's tough trying to communicate with a four-year-old with no arms, or a fat old lady who had had both her legs chopped off above her knees with machetes, something that couldn't have happened in a hurry because this was a very large woman.

Few of the pacifists made any effort to acquaint themselves with the consequences of rebel actions. Had they done so, they would probably have met a Swiss national by the name of Randin who lived nearby. A qualified prosthetic mechanic, Randin spent most of his days working with amputees, building limbs for those who had been brutalized. It was a slow process, he admitted, but he was finally getting somewhere by the time I went through his place the last time.

"We're sorrowfully short of cash and that kind of limits our output," he confided to me in the tin shack where he and his clutch of half a dozen Sierra Leonian assistants put in their eight- or ten-hour stints. It's salutary that they did so for next to nothing, day after day, in that soporific heat. There was no air conditioning within the confines of that awful place, and no complaints from his tiny band of volunteers either.

4

COMBAT FLIGHTS INTO THE INTERIOR

"If we want to put the world to rights and we're not prepared to risk our own forces in doing so, then we should consider the employment of private security forces. . . . If the South African mercenaries had been allowed to stay in Sierra Leone from '96 onwards, a lot of children would still have their hands today."

William Shawcross, author of *Deliver Us From Evil*,
on ABC TV, August 29, 2000

Nellis' view of conflict, especially his utterly unconventional approach to the role of the modern mercenary, reflects some of the unexpected results that can flow from refusing to bow before the Zeitgeist. That became clear in the way that he took his war to the enemy.

Almost from the start of this needless war, the town of Makeni had been the fulcrum on which both government and rebel forces hinged their options. Whoever held Makeni controlled almost all of the country's central regions, which was why both sides fought so hard for it. Thus it wasn't surprising that on at least two previous occasions, RUF insurgents had targeted Makeni after crossing into Sierra Leone from Liberia. As Nellis always said, you could be sure that going anywhere near the place would give you something to talk about afterward.

A couple of years before I got to West Africa that time round, Nellis, his former SAS operative buddy Fred Marafano, and their Ethiopian engineer Sindaba, were involved in an earlier phase of the war. That came after the South African mercenary group Executive Outcomes had been sent on their way and Foday Sankoh and his cohorts embarked on a new round of fighting in a bid to topple the government. Halfway through those hostilities, Neall Ellis and his partner Marafano, together with Sindaba, were ordered to take "Bokkie"—the antiquated erstwhile Soviet Mi-17 transport helicopter—to Makeni.

Robin Hawke (Hawkeye) and his American company ICI were still in the country. Up to that time, ICI Hips tended to fulfill most of the supply needs of the Nigerian Army, which was also involved in trying to bring some order to Sierra Leone. To a lesser degree, ICI—working in conjunction with another American company, Pacific Architects and Engineering (PAE)—also occasionally delivered supplies to Sierra Leone Army (SLA) units in the field. But that didn't happen too often since the loyalties of remote garrisons were most times suspect. Indeed, there were times when government forces would switch sides and support whichever force looked the most likely to take the day. It was essentially a question of survival, but inevitably, diamonds would be integral to the paradigm.

The sortie to Makeni was intended to bolster Nigerian defenses, which was exactly how Brigadier Tom Carew's predecessor phrased it when he issued orders. He didn't need to tell Nellis that Makeni was about to fall because just about everybody in Freetown already knew that. Rumors apart, it was no longer a secret that the rebels had taken the Kono diamond region and were advancing steadily toward the capital. Makeni lay spread-eagled along a single road that was vulnerable to a well-armed aggressor.

The persistent (and according to many, verified) reports that white mercenaries were operating with the rebels only made matters that much worse. According to initial intelligence reports, the advancing RUF army was extremely well equipped. Its armory had supplies that were superior to anything fielded either by government forces or the Nigerians, and almost all of it had come from Libya. This included large numbers of heavy machine guns, some of them mounted on the backs of pick-up trucks.

The military force that was supposed to have matters in hand for the Sierra Leone government was the brainchild of the Economic Community of West African States (ECOWAS). The West African "peacekeeping force" organized by ECOWAS was an armed Monitoring Group called ECOMOG, which by this time was composed almost entirely of Nigerians. Although primarily a ground force, ECOMOG had the support of a squadron of Nigerian Air Force Alpha jets. These could be useful, but they flew only during daylight hours and if the weather was right. As it stood, it looked as though ECOMOG would not be able to stop the advance.

Well aware that he was on his own after dark, and instead of trying to head off the RUF rebels on the outskirts of town, the Nigerian commander of the ECOMOG Brigade pulled his men back to Teko Barracks in the middle of Makeni. Even though he could, conditions allowing, call for support from the jets, it was clear to anyone who knew what was taking place on the ground that his men were on the verge of being overrun. His last link by radio with Cockerill Barracks informed headquarters that if Freetown didn't come to his aid "within hours," he'd be without ammunition and his troops would have to pull out and take their chances in the bush. Without significant and timely assistance, he warned, Makeni would be lost.

The ECOMOG commander's messages were clipped, informative, and under the circumstances, quite dramatic to everyone within earshot—including Nellis. Another message came through shortly afterward asking for an immediate casualty evacuation. The defenders had ten or twelve wounded soldiers, some of them in critical condition, as well as a much larger number of dead. He wanted them out. The Chief of Defense Staff turned to Nellis. "That, my man, is your job."

"After a search-and-rescue briefing with ICI's Hawkeye, we took off just after midday," recalled Nellis. "We had about three tons of ammunition stacked in several piles amidships to deliver to the Nigerians. It was intimidating that there wasn't even time to strap anything down. We just loaded it onboard and headed out."

From the start, radio communication with Makeni was intermittent. It was difficult for Nellis to get a complete picture not only of the security position, but also exactly what part of town the enemy had occupied. The only information coming in was that Teko barracks, then being held by ECOMOG forces, was under heavy attack.

"The situation was more desperate then we knew," recalled Nellis. "The last we'd heard was that the rebels had launched from the north. Early reports indicated that they were advancing down the road from Binkolo." From that scrap of information, the chopper pilot concluded that his best approach would be from the west. They'd use the high ground to mask the noise of their approach, he determined. "And if the Nigerians were trapped in their barracks, hopefully the bulk of the rebels would be concentrated in the north and the east," he explained. "With that in mind, I decided to fly a path just to the south of the barracks, make a tight lefthand turn and come in straight onto the landing zone."

The thirty-five minute flight to Makeni was uneventful until about ten miles outside the town. As the Hip approached, several huge columns of smoke were spotted rising into the air to the north. As far as Nellis was concerned, that was a good sign. If this really was the work of the rebels, it meant they were looting and burning, which, he reasoned, would divert them from their main task of ousting the ECO-MOG contingent.

"I gave Fred [Marafano] the customary two-minute call, increased power to max and took the machine down as low as possible," Nellis recalled as he made ready to enter Makeni airspace. For every one of the men onboard, the prospect of the fight ahead kicked in and, as Nellis quaintly phrased it, "It wasn't long before our sphincters tightened. This was serious stuff."

As he prepared to make his approach, Nellis radioed the ECO-MOG brigade commander. There was no reply. "I felt that it was unlikely that the situation had deteriorated to the point where everybody had pulled out, even though we'd heard nothing for a while on the radio. Rather than abort, I accepted that I had to go in." Marafano agreed. "We landed without picking up too much shit and Fred rushed to the back to help Mohammed, our rear gunner, open the doors. The two of them started throwing out ammunition." It was then that an unusual set of events began to unravel.

Usually in Africa, when a helicopter lands at one of the bush bases, soldiers emerge from every point of the compass. Even before the rotors had wound down, throngs of troops would welcome the aircrews. It was always an occasion, if only because helicopters brought men on the ground goodies like food, ammunition, mail, and the rest. If things weren't too hot, some commanders even flew out their mistresses to spend a few days in remote parts of the bush. Touching down at Makeni that afternoon was very different. "What immediately worried me was that nobody came anywhere near us when we touched down," Nellis explained. "Instead, there were a few troops lying in defensive positions between us and what seemed to be a clump of bushes that made up the outer perimeter of the unit's protection. Every one of them was firing at some unseen enemy around the pad." The situation was confusing, even for a veteran like Nellis. "For us new arrivals it didn't make sense, because although shots were being fired there was no hint of any great battle that we'd been anticipating. Also, at first glance, the camp seemed deserted.

After some time a few soldiers finally walked up and began helping the crew unload the ammunition. "Moments later an explosion in the trees next to the helipad rocked us, almost as if 'Bokkie' had taken a hit," continued Nellis. "It hadn't, but it was about as close as it got. Troops that had been helping us bolted for cover." It immediately became clear to everyone onboard that the Mi-17 helicopter was now someone's target.

A frantic Nigerian officer ran up to the ship. "Leave!" he screamed. "Go now!"

There was a problem, however. Nellis could not leave even if he'd wanted to. Most of the ammunition was still onboard and lifting off with that weight would have been impossible. And even if they were able to get into the hover, with fighting going on all around, a slow-moving helicopter would have made an ideal target. Meantime the rate of fire increased significantly. Nellis watched as rounds began to creep closer and strike the ground immediately ahead of his craft. And then it dawned on him: the Nigerian troops had not run up to the helicopter because he had set the Hip down between the troops holding the base and a fairly large group of attacking rebels.

Nellis beckoned towards Sindaba, his Ethiopian engineer. "Get back and tell Fred and the gunners to make quick work of what's left! We've got to get out of here. Now! So move it!" The Ethiopian moved towards the unloading crew and the pace picked up. As more crates of hardware were lifted from the helicopter, a bunch of Nigerian troops rushed forward to assist and this pleased the pilot. By now some of the wounded were being brought forward and taking them onboard was also underway; most were on improvised stretchers. Then, for a short time, the firing slackened.

A long time afterwards, Nellis was able to reflect on this terrifying situation: "We brought in three tons of ammo and that was a lot. Obviously, I wanted it hauled away from us quickly as possible, but with things happening all over the place, time seemed to drag. Each moment I expected to be hit by an RPG because, let's face it, the chopper was a target that invited attention. It wasn't like a man or a few troops on the ground: you could easily see the cockpit from two hundred yards away. We sort of drew the enemy towards us."

It surprised nobody that the lull didn't last. Within a short time hostilities on both sides intensified, the Nigerians having found new hope from the ammunition that had been brought in. Then RPG rockets passed over the helicopter with their grenades exploding in a succession of blasts that rocked the craft. Nellis could hear the irregular clank of shrapnel as it hit the fuselage, but so far they'd been lucky because the cockpit had taken no direct hits.

A few moments later Sindaba rushed forward. "We've to get out of here!" he shouted at Nellis, as he gesticulated with both hands. The man was desperate "Now! Go now," he urged. Experience had long ago revealed that the Ethiopian's level of agitation was directly proportionate to how bad things were. Excited or not, Nellis had never known the engineer to lose his head. Raising his voice and agitation was his way of coping with disaster, however imminent.

"The crates gone?" Nellis yelled back

"Negative," replied Sindaba. They still had some to go, he indicated, using his thumb and forefinger for indication.

Marafano called from the rear of the copter: "Nellis, we gotta get the fuck out of here!" There was an edge to the Fijian's voice that was about as serious as it gets with this former SAS operator. Like Sindaba, Marafano wasn't easily distressed. A short while later Sindaba appeared alongside the cockpit and signaled that they were ready to move.

"Back doors closed?" inquired the pilot. There was no reply because the Ethiopian had already dashed back to the rear to speed things up. More shells roared over the helicopter and ended in claps of thunder in a grove of mango trees behind.

"Let's go! Go!" shouted Marafano as Sindaba appeared alongside the cockpit again. "Go . . . go . . . yes, go quickly!"

As Nellis later recalled, "That was good enough for me. I pulled power, thinking that the aircraft was empty or nearly so. Instead, the engines wound up and the rotor revs came down to ninety-one percent. Anything below ninety is critical: that's when our electronics and autopilot kick out. Still, things seemed to be working, so the loss of revs meant that we must have been unusually heavy. Also, we had minimum fuel, so without the ammo we'd managed to unload, I surmised that we must have some very large number of casualties onboard.

"As I nursed the Hip through transition, just brushing the tops of trees at the edge of the landing pad, the shooting intensified still further. It seemed that the entire town had turned their guns on us. A lot of tracers started coming past my nose and in a gamble, desperate but pretty well calculated, I turned out towards the west. I had to try to get to a more open part of town because the gooks were doing what they could to bring us down."

As Nellis slowly gained altitude and his speed increased, he was surprised that the firing didn't slacken. In fact, there was more hardware heading their way, with the sudden addition of something new to the rebel arsenal. They could hardly miss the distinctive thuds of a Dshka heavy machine gun. "The fuckers had brought out the big stuff and there were still a lot of RPGs being hurled about," remembered Nellis. While some of the rounds exploded just above the cockpit, most detonated towards the rear. "Fortunately they weren't leading when they were shooting at us. Either that or they'd forgotten their basics, if they'd ever learnt them."

The crew was not yet in the clear. Nellis could feel that the helicopter was not responding as it should have. "I was doing what I could, but it wouldn't accelerate," Nellis explained. "I knew that I needed to fly as low as possible, over rooftops and between some of the big trees to reduce incoming fire, but we just seemed to be dragging along. I'd look down into the streets and could see those fuckers running about everywhere, out of houses, from behind buildings, out of vehicles, all of them pointing things at us."

At that moment, as if in slow motion, Nellis was transfixed when a rebel took aim at the helicopter with his RPG-7. "It looked like it was facing straight at me." But then, in a flash, he recalled, the attacker had dropped to the ground, almost as if he'd been tripped. "That was Fred doing his thing from behind. The Fijian had been consistently firing his GPMG and he'd seen the man taking aim and slotted him."

While trying to dodge fire, increase speed and keep his helicopter air-worthy, Nellis noticed that something else was amiss. Though Fred's machine gun was stuttering furiously to starboard, there was nothing happening to port where Mohammed, a Nigerian who'd joined the helicopter crew as a side-gunner a short while before, should have been working his GPMG. Since he wasn't connected to the Hip's internal intercom system, Nellis couldn't ask him why he wasn't doing his thing. "I presumed that he was trying to clear a stoppage. It had to be that because I knew that Mohammed was onboard: I'd seen him working at the back just before take-off. I thought he'd probably had other things to worry about just then, which was why he wasn't shooting."

Though it seemed longer—as it always does when you become a target —the entire episode from take-off had probably consumed two minutes at most. The helicopter seemed to be in the clear as far as enemy fire was concerned, but the machine still wasn't responding properly. Try as he might, Nellis wasn't able to coax more than a hundred miles an hour out of it, whereas under normal circumstances, he should, by then, have been able to increase airspeed to something approaching a hundred and fifty.

"I checked the instruments and on the face of it, everything was in the green. So there was nothing wrong there," Nellis explained. "Still, our performance wasn't anywhere near normal." Thinking perhaps they had taken a hit somewhere in the fuselage, the pilot used the mike to ask Marafano whether he spotted any battle damage. The Fijian replied that he wasn't sure. Anyway, he added, there were just too many people on board to do a proper check. Could even be underneath, he suggested, under the lumpen mass of wounded, dead and dying that covered every available square inch of the chopper's floor.

Now that matters had settled down in the rear, Marafano was able to tell Nellis about what had gone on on the ground alongside Teko barracks. While the ammunition was being unloaded, the Nigerian commanders had come under a consistent spate of heavy fire. Since their priorities were first, to try to stay alive and then to maintain order in fast-thinning ranks, they were too busy to do anything about their own deserting troops, many of whom had already clambered aboard prior to lift-off. As Marafano explained, he and Sindaba could see a bunch of soldiers climbing in through side doors while they and the rest of the loading gang labored at the back. There was little they could do since their job just then was to clear away three tons of supplies and get the hell out of Makeni.

"Instead of off-loading cargo," reported Marafano, "those cretins were trying to sneak out of Makeni. Obviously, the Hip was their most immediate option. Seeing a chance of escape from what was clearly a hopeless situation, they grabbed it. As it subsequently turned out, the majority of the deserters were in uniforms of the Sierra Leone Army."

The intruders were a rough, unsavory bunch. Many had left the diamond fields a few days before, mostly in a disorganized retreat in the general direction of Freetown. Few understood discipline or would accept orders. It was only then that Nellis realized why take-off had been so difficult and why their speed remained consistently below what it should have been. The Hip was dangerously heavy—beyond the emergency limit. "Actually, we were lucky to get off the ground," he commented dryly.

By now, flying level and heading back to base, the Mohammed issue seriously troubled Nellis. Where the hell was the man? "Is he onboard?" he asked Marafano again. The Fijian checked once more among the crumpled, huddled troops. He even looked over a couple of men who had died since take-off but he wasn't there. He also mentioned that the rear clamshell doors had been open the whole time they had been airborne, which was unusual. Both revelations jolted Nellis. "I realized then that one of the reasons for the low airspeed was because of drag produced by the huge gap at the rear of the fuselage." More important, he recalled, it was the first time in his career that he'd actually lost a crewman.

Mohammed's disappearance also puzzled Fred. He swore that he'd seen the man climb onboard when they pulled out. "I weighed a few options, or at least those that were left to me," he explained afterward and decided that in all likelihood, one of two things had occurred: Either Mohammed had fallen out the back as went into the hover or he'd been killed by gunfire and the others had kicked his body out the back. Neither scenario was unique in this kind of war, he conceded, but what Nellis could not do, he was also aware, was turn back to Makeni and look for him.

The intercom remained in the off position almost all the way back. The remaining helicopter crew were resigned to accepting that there was no immediate way to tell whether the Nigerian gunner had survived. Since the radio at Makeni wasn't manned, Nellis couldn't ask the Nigerians about it. Nellis knew that if the enemy had him, he was probably dead. They hated Nigerians—ECOMOG soldiers, especially—because they stood in the way of ultimate victory. Whenever they captured one alive, they tortured him until he was dead. Then, quite often, they ate him.

Out in the clear, the South African pilot set about computing his fuel reserves and distance to base. Because he had originally taken off from Freetown with only enough in his tanks for the designated task, it was clear that with the extra load and lower speed they weren't going to make it home in one hop. Flying to Lungi direct therefore, was not an option because his reserves were already down to scratch. "I decided to divert to Port Loko. It had been in ECOMOG hands earlier in the day, and for once I prayed that nothing had changed. In this war you never knew."

Nellis radioed Hawkeye and told him about the problem. He was diverting to Port Loko, he said. "If that base couldn't help, I hoped that the American would be there for me." Hawkeye answered in the affirmative.

Except for having to continually monitor fuel levels, the rest of the

flight was uneventful, until "Natasha," in a screeching wail that star-
tled some of the wounded to the rear, warned that they had a problem. "Natasha" was the simulated voice of the helicopter's cockpit
audio warning device: it was linked to the machine's fuel warning system. As Nellis likes to recall, there is not a pilot flying one of these
East European rotor craft who does not dread her very loud and
urgent remonstrations. Checking the gauge against the fact that they
were still about five minutes out of Port Loko when "Natasha" began
her tirade, Nellis reckoned they would make it. But since "Natasha"
persisted, Fred removed his headset to escape the noise. That particular Russian lady never turned him on.

"We got there in the end, just barely," Nellis said. He landed with
both fuel low-level lights on steady. As the wheels settled on the
ground, he lowered the collective and just about everybody in the rear
smiled. One or two of the wounded even raised a hand or an arm.
They were almost home.

The Makeni sortie was not yet over. "Suddenly I saw a shape out
of the corner of my eye," remembered Nellis. "I didn't know what it
was at first because it didn't look like anything I'd encountered during
the course of a normal landing before. It was a large piece of metal
that I immediately recognized as belonging to one of our rear doors.
It whizzed past the cockpit in a flurry of rotor wash and attached to it
was the body of a soldier."

It took some figuring to get to the bottom of it. Just before take-
off from Makeni, while Mohammed was behind the helicopter trying
to close the clamshell doors, some of the Nigerian troops were pushing hard at the opening in an effort to get onboard. In their fervor,
some successful, some not, they were able to prevent him from closing
the rear doors. And because the doors can only be shut from outside,
Mohammed and several others were still clinging to the fuselage when
Nellis took off. The majority of these stragglers, including
Mohammed, let go before the Mi-17 gained much height, but one man
hung on. Just beyond the sight of the others inside, he clung desperately to one of the clamshell doors and stayed there for the duration
of the flight to Port Loko.

As Nellis later explained, the man had spent thirty minutes watching Africa zip past below, with only space between him and the
ground. While the turbines roared and the rear doors remained open,
nobody could hear him scream over the cacophony of the flight. "But
they must have seen him from the ground, which was probably why

so many of them were shooting at us." That he survived at all was remarkable. Badly shaken but alive, the man picked himself up once the door had come to rest in the dirt around the helipad and smiled, almost as if he'd won the lottery. In some ways, he had.

Once safely down in Port Loko, Nellis walked around the helicopter to check for damage. Although there were holes everywhere, the Hip remained structurally sound and able to continue. First, however, the crew had to get rid of the "illegals" on board, which was tough. Most were interested only in getting to the next stop, Freetown. In the end it took some serious persuasion that included fisticuffs and the help of other troops at the base to eject the recalcitrants. Sticking AK-47 barrels into the ears of some of the more reluctant escapees helped speed up the process.

"Fortunately," said Nellis, "PAE had an efficient radio net that covered the Port Loko area and I was able to get into indirect comms with Hawkeye back at base. His last chopper hadn't yet left for Guinea and he was able to fly out a couple of drums of fuel. Had all this happened a day later, with the ICI crews out of the country, who knows what would have happened."

And then there was still the matter of Mohammed. Early the following morning, as it transpired, Cockerill Barracks received a signal from Makeni confirming that the Nigerian gunner was alive. Indeed, according to the message, Mohammed was waiting to be fetched from Makeni barracks, where he'd spent most of the night fighting a rearguard action against a large rebel force.. "The signal also confirmed what we already knew: the situation on the ground was big-time bad," said Nellis.

The following afternoon the South African and his crew were ordered back to Teko Barracks. It was to be a repeat operation: ammo supplies in, casualties out. The prospect of another flight into what had become a rather hot and beleaguered Makeni made nobody's day, but as they say, orders are orders. "None of us were too happy about the trip," said Nellis, "but we'd left behind one of our own, so it was a question of showing face." There could be no argument because that was what Nellis and his crew were being paid for.

He later recalled that while the flight out was routine enough, all he could make out from listening to radio chatter during finals was that the situation there was about as grim as it gets. There were some seriously bad things going down in Makeni, was how Fred phrased it. It would be another tough assignment.

"We were aware that overnight the rebels had occupied the rest of Makeni, which was fine by us because from past experience we knew that the enemy would gravitate toward areas where they could loot. To those primitives, pillage and rape came before the next battle, not after it," explained Nellis. The South African was determined to use the opportunity to duck in and out as quickly as possible. "So I decided that because our intelligence was sketchy, I'd use the same approach path. But this time, instead of heading for the usual LZ, I'd put the old bird down on an adjacent football field in the middle of the army barracks. While it was only about half normal size, it did have the advantage of some protection from buildings that before the war had housed married personnel. Also, it lay in a slight depression and would shield us to some extent from direct fire."

The sudden reappearance of a helicopter over Makeni surprised the rebels, so that Nellis and crew attracted little incoming fire. Setting down, therefore, was no problem. Because of what had happened the day before, the guys decided to keep the rear cargo doors sealed. Instead, Nellis instructed Fred to use the sliding door on the side of the fuselage instead. Though it would take longer, at least they'd be able to control exactly who did or did not get onboard. Mohammed arrived as the first of the ammo boxes was being pulled out onto the grass surrounding the improvised pad, a smile plastered all the way across his face. The boys were happy to see him, but as the firing picked up, he fell in with the others in furiously stripping the helicopter of its cargo. Every few minutes they would stop and fend off troops anxious to climb onboard, now and again with their side arms or rifle butts.

While this went on at a hectic pace, a succession of mortar shells began to fall into the area from the far side of the improvised helipad. Nellis and crew could hear the distinctive hollow crumps as they were being fired and this caused worry. So did the proximity of the attack. Fortunately, the aim of those handling the mortars was poor and most of the shells went wide.

More serious was a bit of intelligence that had come into the Air Wing shortly before Nellis and his men left base. Overnight reports spoke of the rebels having positioned a 14.5mm twin-barreled heavy machine gun on the hills above the town. Their attackers used it to fire into the barracks, but only at night because nobody was sure whether there were Nigerian Air Force jets around. Even though they flew only in daylight hours, they were an intimidating presence. The rebels would scatter wildly each time the Alphas arrived over Makeni on a strafing mission.

Mohammed told them afterward that the ZSU above town was manned by white mercenaries and had "caused a shithouse of damage" during the night. In the end, it was that weapon more than anything that broke the spirit of the Nigerian and Sierra Leone troops still trying to hold on in Makeni. It also prevented them from trying to muster a counterattack. The Nigerian side-gunner believed that one more night of that drama and their defenses might crack, which was why he was eager not to be left behind a second time. It was Nellis' view that if the rebels had decided to fire the 14.5mm while he and the boys were still on the deck, they could have easily crippled or destroyed the helicopter. But it didn't happen.

"Eventually the guys were done and I prepared for lift-off. But as soon as we passed through transition, we were exposed to even more ground fire than before, including a shower of RPGs," Nellis reported in his debrief later that day. "They threw everything they could at us." Once again, dodging between trees and rooftops, the pilot managed to avoid serious damage, though the Hip took several hits, one of them serious enough to worry the pilot because it was in the lower boom area. "We didn't pick up any major holes, though."

Once back at Cockerill, the crew reported on the previous day's events. While still on the ground, and after Fred and the Ethiopian engineer Sindaba had told him to close the rear doors and prepare for take-off, they told the CDS, Mohammed had been shouldered aside by some of the troops. The helicopter, they implied, was their passport to safety. Nobody was going to stop them from getting out. Consequently, with all the bodies pressing inward from outside, Mohammed hadn't been able to close the clamshell doors. Moments later the Mi-17 lifted off and hovered low for a few moments before moving ahead. At that stage, he and some of the others were still clinging onto the back step. Their original intention had been to make their way into the main cabin, but there wasn't space enough to do so. At the last moment, with the helicopter gaining height, the Nigerian gunner decided that to remain where he was, horribly exposed and still outside the main fuselage was probably not the best move.

He let go when the chopper was perhaps eight or ten feet off the ground. Five other soldiers did not. The last he saw of them, they were desperately clutching the outside of the fuselage as the machine hurtled away. As the Hind accelerated, wind sheer stretched out their bodies almost parallel to the ground. "I still don't know what happened to them," he told me later. "I can imagine that the slipstream eventually became too much and they fell to their deaths."

For the twenty hours or so that Mohammed was forced to sit out the attack and wait for his pals to return and the gang to return, he spent most of his time trying to bolster the morale of the troops around him. Moving from one group of defenders to another, he ensured that they had ammunition and water, which was just as well since a lot of rebel effort went into a counterattack that was launched once darkness set in. ECOMOG defensive capabilities, however, continued to deteriorate as the night progressed, he recalled.

In the end, something of a rout developed when Sierra Leone soldiers who were supposed to provide support were either unable to do so or flatly refused to counter the enemy. The majority had received little training and there wasn't a man among them who wasn't gripped by fear. Worse, the Nigerian troops refused to fight alongside them because most were afraid of being shot in the back. The Sierra Leone soldiers had already killed some of Mohammed's colleagues by firing blindly from behind at some real or imagined enemy, and the way he read it, it mattered little who might be in the way. Their standard rookie procedure was to set their AKs on full auto and let rip, usually in the direction of the enemy, but quite often off target.

For Mohammed, seeing Nellis and the gang disappear over the town the day before was cathartic. Considering what was just then taking place around him, he had to concede that the prospect of his getting out of Makeni was remote. Talking about it afterward, he said that it was a good thing they came back when they did: all signs pointed to the defenses being breached and overrun that night. And he was right. Early the next day Cockerill received reports that the main ECOMOG force had withdrawn from Makeni. They had left in a shambles with the rebels in close pursuit. The wounded left behind were butchered, many of them publicly and in the presence of children, while the entire spectacle deteriorated into an unspeakably barbaric ritual.

Reports of the massacre filtered through to the capital and triggered an immediate exodus of refugees to Guinea. It seemed as if anyone who could get a place on a boat out of Sierra Leone packed a bag and left. There was even a pirogue or two headed across the bay for Conakry.

Later that same day, Nellis and crew were ordered to resupply a

Nigerian contingent assisting Lifeguard Security, a small commercial security group that was then trying to hold on to the hydroelectric dam at Bumbuna. Cobus Claassens, another former South African Defence Force Parabat officer, was helping run that show and called Nellis on the radio. Everything went well enough, but on the return leg, Nellis changed channels to hear news from what was left of the ECOMOG force. "I was hoping that perhaps we'd pick up a distress call from some of the escaping troops. Sure enough, within seconds a transmission came through calling for help. The voice was urgent and none too coherent. He said he was part of a group of five that the rebels were chasing on foot."

If they were to live, Nellis was their only hope. "You couldn't miss the sounds of one big-time firefight over the radio," he remembered. "They must have been very close. Whoever was talking to us seemed to be almost past hope. He even had difficulty in giving us his location." As Nellis flew above the bush, the terrified soldier shouted breathlessly into the mike, "We're under the big tree next to the road!"

"Which tree? From where we are, I told him, there were many big trees within my view."

After searching a bit in the area southwest of Makeni, Nellis spotted a handful of soldiers running like a bunch of crazies down the main road. "They were being closely followed by a group of gooks shooting at them. They'd run, stop, raise their AKs and then start running again." Once the pilot had established that this was the party—though by now there were three of them, not five—Fred opened fire on the pursuers and they scattered. Most of the pursuers ended up taking cover in heavy bush alongside the road. Nellis meanwhile, searched for somewhere to put down his helicopter: he had to get the men on board as soon as possible because other groups of rebels were following behind. Finding an LZ a couple of hundred yards down the road and after loading up the three survivors, he set a course for home.

"It turned out that we had rescued the battalion commander," said Nellis. "The sound of gunshots that I'd heard during the transmission was from the rebel group chasing him, and they were barely a hundred yards behind. Had they got him, the RUF would have had themselves a pretty valuable asset: the man was one big fry!"

The Nigerian colonel was lucky indeed. Two or three minutes more and the chase would have been over. The three escapees were fortunate that Nellis and the chopper just happened to be over the area during those final, critical minutes. For a long time afterward, whenever Nellis met the man in town or at Cockerill, the Nigerian officer would be overwhelmed at seeing him again. It was the same each time they met. Several times the Nigerian hugged and kissed the South African when he ran into him in town. "We enjoyed more than a few ales as a consequence of that little episode . . . lucky man," Nellis admitted.

Freetown is the one city in the world where a rumor gone sour can panic the nation. We saw that when a sizable RUF force neared the capital in early May 2000. A United Nations spokesman warned that rebels were on their way.

"They're already at Hastings, on the outskirts of the city," he said in a broadcast. At first blush it was the sort of thing that can happen in any war, but what made it different this time was that it wasn't true. In fact, the police were holding their annual ball in the Hastings town hall that night, and they would have been the first to know. There was no doubt that the rebels intended to pay Freetown a visit, but just then they were still at Rogberi, about fifty miles north of the capital. Nonetheless, the statement had exactly the kind of effect for which the insurgents hoped. The UN official involved, a British national who will remain nameless, did not know it at the time, but his misguided intentions drove fear into the souls of two million people.

Once you're in Freetown, just about the only way out is by boat. The city is perched on a peninsula and the road from the interior ends at any one of the numerous bays fringing the sea. Some have illustrious names like Destruction Bay, Whiteman's Bay (evoking an era when Europeans stayed in one part of town and Africans in another), as well as several others that reflect a time when parts of the city were as English as dusty aspidistras in the church vestibule. It took stern action by Brigadier David Richards and his newly arrived military aid group to calm a situation that was already out of hand.

More history was made later that day. Because of urgent representations made to President Kabbah by Lieutenant-Colonel Rob Symonds, Nellis was sent out on a night mission in a bid to confront the enemy. To achieve this, the British Liaison Officer had to force his way past the President's bodyguards to put his case personally to Sierra Leone's head of state. He told him, "Sir, if you don't order up the Hind, the rebels will be in the city by morning." Carefully and with singular intent, Symonds detailed the nature of the threat and the need for effective and immediate counteraction. With that, President Kabbah ordered the British officer to task Nellis to do what was necessary.

Executive Outcomes had conducted many night operations in and around Freetown five years earlier (that mercenary force had the equipment to do so), but it was to be the first time since Neall Ellis had arrived in the country that he was ordered out after dark on a sortie. After that, it happened quite often. It was not all that surprising, therefore, shortly after HMS *Ocean* arrived off Freetown, that a brand new set of night vision goggles—complete with requisite batteries and instruction manual—mysteriously landed on his desk at Cockerill.

Talking about it afterward at one of our backyard chin-wagging sessions, Symonds told me that he would probably never be able to do again what he did that night. "Normally it is impossible to get anywhere near the President; his security people block anyone trying to get close. But they saw something desperate in my eyes as I approached them," he said mischievously, almost as if he had dared anybody to try to stop him. "I don't think they would have been able to, short of shooting me. But I know, too, that if I hadn't, we wouldn't be sitting here now." He gestured in a characteristically offhand manner toward Nellis and said something about him being the man to thank. Because of the Colonel's quick-thinking action in briefing President Kabbah, Nellis in his trusty old Hind had managed to halt the forward movement of a thousand- strong insurgent force.

The security situation that first week of May 2000 was already so bad that President Kabbah—like his delinquent predecessor Momeh—wasn't taking any chances. He, too, had a chartered helicopter—together with its expatriate pilot component—which sat on permanent standby on the lawn of his lodge. Nobody remembers seeing any bags of diamonds nearby, but even if they had they wouldn't be telling. It was not the sort of thing you talked about in Sierra Leone, not publicly at any rate. Do so, even today, and you're likely to have an accident.

Thanks largely to Nellis' preemptive action, it took the RUF three more days to get to Newton, the small town about thirty miles south of Rogberi where Nellis was later ambushed. By then the British Army had consolidated security around Freetown and, less than two years later, the RUF leadership was hauled up before international courts on charges of treason and much worse.

Terror in the streets of Freetown as the rebels approached was not always caused by the prospect of an unexpected enemy presence. More often, it came as the result—in the middle of the city—of an intra-factional firefight between the army and Kamajor irregulars, or even dissidents within the Sierra Leone Army (though at times there were battles involving all three).

Another real danger lay with the city's taxis. Half of Freetown's taxi drivers can't drive while the other half don't have a license to do so. Equally wicked were some of the soldiers at the wheels of United Nations vehicles— especially Jordanians, Bangladeshis, and Indians— where aggression on the city's narrow, rutted streets was dictated more by incompetence than blue-beret arrogance. We were all aware that bad driving caused a fire in the belly of some, but that was only a part of it.

Travel about Freetown while war raged in the surrounding hills, a city where most of its residents, to paraphrase the old homily, regard life as nasty, brutish and cruel, and you could not get away from an overriding tension that appears to dominate the atmosphere. A rippling groundswell of uncertainty followed wherever we went in streets where small buildings bespoke of decent frugality. Avoiding questions from locals was near impossible. Inevitably, the first question most locals asked was, "What you think of the situation?" The next was almost always, "Do you think the war will ever end?" Scratch a little deeper and it soon became clear that much of what had taken place was predictable. Just about everything that happened in this civil war was exactly what Foday Sankoh had hoped for when he originally planned his revolt while in exile in Libya with his co-conspirator Charles Taylor of Liberia. Back then, both were revolutionaries with a taste for clout and higher office.

Sankoh's first objective throughout, some of his disaffected lieutenants will tell you today, was to terrify the population on a scale that nobody could have imagined, never mind understood. Things like this happened elsewhere—Angola, the Congo, and Cambodia—but not in the delightfully quaint and historic Sierra Leone.

In order to put Sankoh's revolutionary fervor into perspective, one must accept that a series of carefully considered options had been thoroughly examined beforehand and then put into motion. His operations were done with a gusto that astonished everyone. Many of those who suffered at the hands of these barbarians remember one thing in particular: the crazy stares of the rebels. "They are like devils," said a man who had the betrayed look of the refugee.

The situation that prevailed at the time can best be illustrated by one of the more bizarre events of the final stages of the last rebel uprising. A Nigerian unit operating at the front arrested a man who was found with a bag of hands and feet cut from children. His haul also included a leg or two. When asked what it was all about, the sweaty vulgarian admitted that his commander had told him that if he could fill the bag with limbs, he would be promoted to captain. The Nigerian soldiers didn't waste much time with him and quickly did what they thought right. The sad thing is that there were dozens of similar stories and most are verifiable today. A lot of this came out in subsequent UN investigations, including allegations of cannibalism.

I spoke to some of the captured rebels in a holding cell at Cockerill Barracks. It was all very irregular, but a carton of cigarettes did the trick. A guard carrying an AK-47 stood nearby. One of the prisoners who appeared more erudite than the rest did most of the talking. He was relieved for the opportunity to emerge from the foul-reeking subterranean warren running beneath the length of the old gun emplacements. It was an evil, ominous place. Only later was it learned that deaths were rather commonplace there, not all of them caused by hostilities.

"Our ideas were simple and almost all were centered on Sankoh's intentions," declared the rebel in a fairly erudite rendition. And from what we now know, this rebel leader got most of this kind of inspiration from Liberia's equally murderous Charles Taylor. Sankoh's first priority, by his own admission, was to cause so much bloodshed as to bleed the country white. "When you go on long enough with such things, you can do just about anything you want with a helpless nation," he added. He was right, of course. But so were Hitler, Stalin, Idi Amin, Pol Pot, Robert Mugabe and a host of other bloody-minded tyrants.

Another rebel ploy quite widely used early on, was to use a razor blade to cut through the small muscle at the back of the neck. The result was crippling and caused the victim's head to plop forward onto his chest. There was no controlling it once the muscle was severed. Mercifully perhaps, the majority of those victims died, but there are still a few walking about Freetown. I have a picture of one of them with his neck seemingly stuck to his breastbone. I would have used it in this book as an illustration had it not been so gruesome. We found the poor fellow alongside the road near Koidu while I was operating with Executive Outcomes personnel.

In many places around the world this injury could have been repaired, though it's a complex, finicky surgical process. In Sierra Leone such skilled surgery is impossible and frankly, money is only part of it. The country has neither the assets nor the facilities to do anything to help these victims. There isn't even a proper Western-style hospital, never mind anything resembling a clinic way out in the bush beyond.

If you're sick and qualify as an expatriate with travel insurance, you might fly to Europe or South Africa for treatment. Alternatively, if you were lucky you could, at one stage, get checked into Choitram Hospital, the local UN facility run by what is left of the UN's Jordanian contingent. According to Nellis, this facility offers up-to-date clinical attention but you won't get in the door if you're not part of the UNAMSIL contingent or have money in your pocket. The Indian Army left soon after I did, which is sad because their doctors and specialists treated many tropical diseases and did a pretty good job of it, especially with malaria and other tropical bugs. For quite a time the British maintained an effective medical service, but that was restricted to their own military personnel and those working for the British government.

Targeting shortcomings like these—as well as huge gaps in rudimentary education, welfare, social services and much else—Sankoh systematically abused his fellow man with a vulgarity so ferocious that it surprised us all. As he was once reported to have said, "We will let the violence continue until the country begs us to stop." Worse, while the UN went on about so-called human rights inanities, he used that impasse to spill more blood and sharpen his tactics.

After three RUF invasions, the single biggest problem facing the country after a decade of war was the level of intimidation that pervaded every level of society. Evidence of it was everywhere: in the streets, in government offices and, as we observed for ourselves, daubed on peoples' faces. Once Sankoh had come into the reckoning, people started looking over their shoulders when they spoke to anyone outside the family circle. No one was sure who had ties to the RUF and who did not. For a while it was a bit like Afghanistan when the Taliban strode tall.

When that first bunch of insurgents crept stealthily across the Peninsula Mountains one night early in 1999, they linked up with people who had earlier professed horror at the brutal deeds committed by them. It turned out later—much to the dismay of the majority of

Freetown's residents—that some friends and neighbors had been card-carrying RUF cadres all along. Only after the Nigerians managed to take control did they uncover the fact that quite a few senior Sierra Leone officers had been consorting under the covers with the devil.

One of them, Colonel Nelson Williams, was Nellis' boss while I was with the unit. He and twenty others were sentenced to death when their dual roles were exposed. Following the Lome Accord of July 1999, all were pardoned and it came under what the legal pundits call a "blanket amnesty." The colonel, a bear of a man and as genial as a country squire, was the last person any of us might have suspected of consorting with these killers. But he did, and apparently held a top position in the rebel command. So, too, with some Nigerian senior commanders, but then Lagos has always been corrupt, prodigiously so since gaining independence from Britain almost half a century ago. I should know; I lived in Nigeria for almost a year.[1]

Another fifth columnist at Cockerill Barracks was the only Sierra Leonian pilot then able to fly a Hind, Major Arnold Bangura. Once he had declared himself for the RUF (he was recruited by one of Sankoh's deputies early on because of his purported flying skills), Bangura repeatedly attacked Nigerian positions with the Mi-24 and killed bagfuls of them. He, too, received a death sentence that was later commuted. Afterward he rejoined the Air Wing under Nellis, though he'd been demoted to lieutenant.

I wouldn't want to be in Bangura's position today. As anybody in West Africa will tell you, Nigerians are a bit like elephants: they have inordinately long memories. Some of my Nigerian pals in Lagos would sublimate their grievances only until they were able to do something about them. After all, revenge is a dish best served cold. The fact that Bangura was allowed to fly again during the RUF incursions that followed my visit in 2000 raised eyebrows. As one of the British liaison officers said, "Allow him into the cockpit and who knows where he's going to land the Hind. Monrovia?"

During my own stay in Freetown, Bangura was never allowed to touch the controls of either of the Hinds that operated out of Cockerill Barracks.

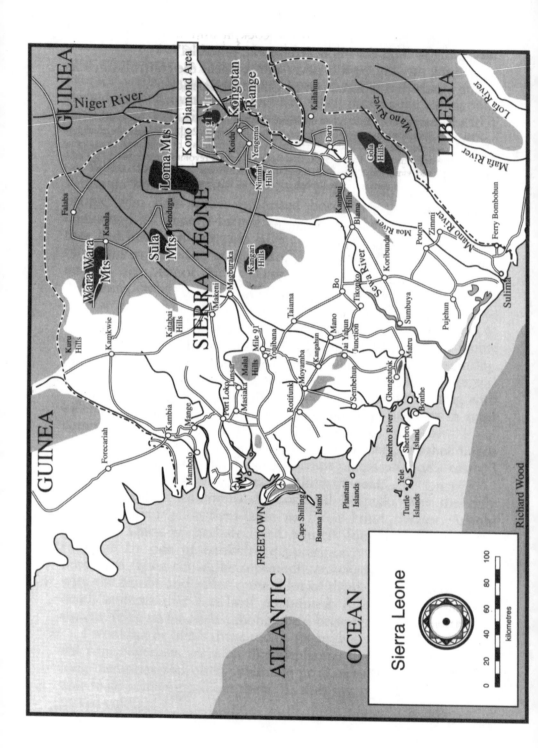

5

RADIO INTERCEPTS AND THE INEVITABLE SAMS

"Sometimes in Africa a heavy machine gun can
be as effective as ten tanks elsewhere . . ."

Lt. Colonel Tim Spicer, former chief executive of
Sandline and author of *Unorthodox Soldier*

Getting to Freetown to join Neall Ellis and his team wasn't easy. The journey underscored another Third World conundrum: working your way through Africa—except to recognized destinations like Kenya, Morocco or South Africa—is like an unaccompanied group tour through Hades. It can be almost as dangerous.

In the old days you could fly from London to Freetown by way of Senegal or Accra. Ghana Airways would take you all the way in relative comfort. But in the summer of 2000, Foday Sankoh's rebels targeted Sierra Leone's only international airport at Lungi and the international community got the message to steer clear.

Both Washington and London were cagey about the extent of the threat initially posed by the rebels. They, together with just about everybody else, advised their nationals to give the country a miss. Also, the word was out in the streets of Freetown that the rebels had surface-to-air missiles, or SAMs. That sort of knowledge dampened the desire of many to fly on an airliner in or out of Lungi. Nellis told me afterward that the RUF fired at least two of these supersonic devices in Sierra Leone airspace during the months preceding my arrival.

There was another problem. Until British forces arrived, the UN was supposed to be in control. Its job was to check everybody coming near Lungi or, at the very least, to set up some form of routine inspection system to vet people entering the airport and its environs. One would think such measures would have included looking in carry-on bags for weapons. But being the United Nations, nothing of the sort occurred. They not only nodded everybody through with cursory insouciance, but the blue helmeted "peacekeepers" also allowed hundreds of insurgents to inveigle their way through otherwise secure defenses. The majority who wished to do so simply came in, weapons and all. It took smart action on the part of the British Parachute Regiment to clear this rabble away.

In an ambush that the Paras got wind of before it happened, the rebels suffered some pretty hefty casualties. Nobody was hurt among the British troops who had been in the country only a few days, and Sankoh's rebels used the opportunity to slink away. A few came back, but they were just as smartly dispatched, no questions asked.

Travelling to Africa this time around wasn't all work. Flying from Portland, Oregon to Paris was a charm. It was the next two days that hurt, first to Bamako in Mali, and finally on to Conakry, which still wore its faded Marxist testimonials like decorations.

I went through there as a student in the 1960s, overland, from Abidjan to Dakar. It was a difficult call at the time, but it was cheaper than flying. In those days, Lenin was god in Sekou Toure's Guinea Republic and the main radio station in the capital was dubbed *Voix de la Revolution*. The political flavor of the day pretty well everywhere, you might recall, was Ché Guevara. More than three decades later things hadn't changed much. The Cold War was over, but Guinea-Conakry was still a one-party state. Presidential edicts emanating from government offices at the start of the new millennium would have done better justice to a youth rally in Havana. Otherwise, the political mood centered on foreign aid, profit, capitalism and free trade, though there was precious little evidence of any of it in the streets of the capital. As my Lebanese hotel manager told me, all of it sounded very good and that was about all that mattered to the fat cats who ruled the country out of the barrel of a gun. More important, making the right noises allowed Guinea to qualify for Western assistance.

Of course, there had been some changes in the interim, most of them nominal. Now that Washington and Moscow were talking, Russian (and American) handouts that made millionaires of despots were supposed to be a thing of the past. The only difference was that Conakry's poverty had become more obtrusive and as *Paris Match* phrased it, "gripping in its dinginess." Also, in an age of mass communication where Guinean housewives—if they have access to a television set at all—watch exactly the same soaps as you or I, the disparity of lifestyles displayed on the screen have made these people that much more desperate. They see the way we live and they resent it.

Profoundly. They know too, that few of them are ever likely to experience it for themselves, certainly not as long as they are trapped in an Africa shackled by poverty. This is one of the reasons why New York (and every other big city in America) is up to the craw with illegal African immigrants.

The images I picked up on the way in and out of Conakry from the airport this time around remain fixed in my mind. They included the stench, the noise, the babble, tons of garbage left in piles six feet deep on street corners, and more open-air markets than it seemed possible to crowd into the few open pieces of dirt passing for pavement. This Boston-sized city boasted acres of open suppurating drains, quite a few with children playing in them. Add to this abominable potpourri the most accomplished pickpockets outside Europe. Taken as a package, Conakry—just like Lagos, Johannesburg, Dar es Salaam, and every other black African city—offered some stunning Third World contrasts.

My arrival at Guinea International Airport was starkly different compared to the last time I visited the place more than thirty years before. Then, I traveled overland from Freetown to Conakry, crossing the border at a remote frontier post in the interior where Louis, a local expatriate Frenchman, offered me the best coffee south of the Sahara.

This time, the local United Nations representative, Komba (he of the unpronounceable last name), eased my passage through to the VIP lounge. He also took care of my passport and baggage, and generally smoothed my path into Conakry proper.

It wasn't that I was a member of UN: I'd simply phoned somebody at UN headquarters in New York before leaving for Africa and, because of the Jane's cachet, I qualified. My assignment, as I told them, was to cover Sierra Leone's developing mercenary war for *Jane's International Defence Review*. In truth, I could have been anybody throwing an identity about as I was never asked to show my credentials. But that too is Africa.

Leaving the next day was something else. I decided to take a commercial flight to Freetown. It was either that or a two-day wait for the scheduled UN Mi-26 helicopter flight. Consequently, I was on my own.

My hassles started as soon as I entered the gates of the airport terminal early the next morning. Before the guard would let me through he demanded *un petit cadeau*, literally, "a little something." He also wanted something for his buddy. And possibly, a little extra for his girlfriend. Then it was time for security checks, health, immigration, *sureté* and still more security, which at one stage involved a physical shakedown—as if anybody would contemplate hijacking Air Guinea's antiquated Antonovs. Eventually my hand luggage was put through a cranking old Soviet-era x-ray machine that must have figured in some 1970s-style Comintern largesse.

Along the way I had to pay a departure tax, together with an airport tax and another government "fee" and, naturally, take care of my porters. Ten of them made a grab for my bags as I stepped out of the taxi and I had to look sharp to keep track of them all. Some expected tips that were equivalent to ten dollars a throw. I had been warned that I could expect a con somewhere along the way and because of that, perhaps, it didn't happen.

Christophe—our French crewman with the Air Wing—had come through Conakry the week before and he wasn't so lucky. After being stopped by security, The Parisian was forced to empty his pockets. Meanwhile, his baggage and leather jacket were placed on the X-ray machine. It was only after he was in the air that he discovered a zipped pocket in the inside lining of his coat had been rifled and an envelope containing a thousand dollars—almost all of his money—was gone. Being a reticent type, he didn't say much about the incident at the time, though Nellis had to lend him a few bucks.

In Conakry, once through the hour-long security detail that quickly became officious, sixteen of us boarded a rickety old Czech Turbolet that had probably last experienced a proper service before it left its homeland a couple of decades before. After taking off, our Russian pilot stayed well offshore and he remained there until Lungi Airport was in sight. Then he put his left hand sharply down and, with a crunch, we plopped onto the runway. "Missiles," the pilot explained. "We don't be round for long with them."

Once clear of Sierra Leonian immigration, I made my way—military escort in tow—to the control tower, passing through a succession of dark corridors in Lungi's trashed terminal building. The floors were lined with dozens of stretchers covered with mosquito nets that belonged to soldiers from the occupying British force. Their stuff was everywhere, but it was well looked after because there were armed guards at every entrance, just as there were when the lads went for a dip off Freetown's Lumley Beach.

Lungi's control tower was under the command of an operations officer whose brogue was as broad as the Clyde. Since I could barely understand what he said, I could only speculate how the Russians managed, especially since there were a lot of them about. Moscow, it appeared, had been charged with bringing in a constant flow of supplies for the local United Nations contingent, which, at the time, was the largest in the world.

"Can you possibly contact 'Eagle Two?'" I asked the controller, citing Nellis' call sign. "You can tell him that I've arrived."

Neall and the gang had been expecting me, though they weren't sure when I'd get there. Flights out of Conakry were problematic at the time. Also, I'd purposely been vague with dates because of the Guinea connection. Even regular flights into Guinea were sometimes delayed because of strikes, as was the case with Air France when I tried to leave six or seven weeks later. Still, the Air Wing had arranged my visa through the Ministry of Defense the previous week, though what should have been free cost me $60.

Fifteen minutes later, Nellis and his Hind touched down alongside the tower. On his way back from a strike in the interior, Nellis sat there only long enough for Fred to bundle me, my bags and my cameras into the back. British troops in cammo gear came across to have a look at the gunship and were impressed by the stacks of spent shell casings piled around the feet of the side gunners. After an eight-minute flip across the bay, we were on the ground at Cockerill Barracks.

Once a British army outpost in one of London's far-flung African colonies, Cockerill had also been home in the mid-1990s to the mercenary organization Executive Outcomes. I had worked out of the place for the duration I'd been with EO in 1995 and, to my surprise, I quite liked it there. Indeed, with its barracks, bunkers, maritime defenses and historic gun emplacements, Cockerill reflected much of the colony's early history. The only difference was that in those days the fort had been in fine shape.

Now five years on, Cockerill presented a different picture. A grim and indefinable gloom hung over the place. It felt as though the headquarters had been condemned and was about to be torn down. The impressive old guns that once protected allied ships, lay rusted and encrusted with dirt alongside their original moss-covered emplacement. Their magazines now served as convenient garbage dumps and, going by the stench, as toilets.

Several abandoned and not so old armored fighting vehicles that would have seen round two in any reputable Western military force sat untended. Anywhere else and Cockerill would have been a lovely museum and people would have been enthused about this legacy. What hadn't changed were the dozens of brilliantly hued blue and yellow lizards doing their characteristic press-ups and scattering each time somebody approached.

Part of Cockerill's malaise could have been due to fighting that took place there in early 1998. Nigerian Air Force Alpha Jets bombed Cockerill then, in the hope of wiping out the invading rebel command. And since nobody had seen fit to repair the damage, many buildings were still heavily scarred. One structure had half its walls blown away.

On touchdown at headquarters, Nellis suggested that because of the delays and the heat, his driver Augustine would take me to his villa at the Cape Sierra Hotel. It was an opportunity to freshen up, he said. He added that we'd fly again later that afternoon. "Something's up," he confided with a sly grin.

I'd been coming to Freetown since the 1960s, the first time only weeks before Winston Churchill died. I even stayed at the raffish old City Hotel where Graham Greene is purported to have written lonely letters home as well as his classic *The Heart of the Matter*. While conflicts were tearing Europe and much of the Far East apart, Greene was putting out some of his best writing from there. Sadly, Greene is long gone. So is the hotel, which burned down in a rebel mortar attack. A mysterious Royal Navy submarine was also missing. It had been left to rot on the beach for so long, the sands of Freetown harbor eventually gobbled it up. While in Freetown to make an hour-long television documentary two decades earlier, part of the old sub could still be seen in Krio Bay, but the sea had long since claimed it.

Sierra Leone was a delightful country in the old days: friendly, rambunctious, unpredictable, and so typically West African. It was a time when "High Life" ruled and even Nigeria was regarded by those who went through it as a nice place. Like Ghana and Senegal, old Freetown was infused with an unpretentious bonhomie that quickly became infectious. People liked to go back there because they had left with memories that lingered. In West Africa everybody is aware that Sierra Leonians were once among the best-educated people along the coast, and in this regard I found Greene's association with Freetown interesting, if only because the historic link between Africa and the Caribbean fascinated him. One of his comments about the city struck me when he wrote about Freetown "having been left on a tropical beach to rot."

One quickly appreciated after only a short walk along the city's streets that there was another side to this West African coin. Freetown must be one of the unhealthiest places on earth with all manner of rampant tropical diseases. The place today is also squalid. And too hot, too muggy, and definitely much too humid. As one of my colleagues commented bitterly after a month in the place, it's one of those grim Equatorial stations where leather really does turn green after a week. And as in Douala in the Camerouns, you'll sometimes find mushrooms sprouting from the carpet of your hotel room.

Then there are the people, not very different today compared to when the rebels were banging at their gates. Also, not much had changed from my earlier visits, except that the crush of numbers had become overbearing. Even their leaders are of a similar ilk. Some were of the view that one generation of "pickaninnies" had simply replaced another and for all I knew, the youngsters who had been playing in the open drains along Boston Lightfoot Street, or where the sewers spilled into the bay when I visited Sierra Leone the first time round, now had their feet squarely under the table at State House.

Getting around Freetown was rarely a problem, even though there was never anything resembling a municipal bus service, then or now. Taxis have always been the preferred mode of transport, though you usually have to share a seat with half-a-dozen others. For as long as I can remember, Freetown also had its twelve-seater poda podas, a version of the mini-bus that might contain goats, baskets of poultry, or occasionally a scaly anteater brought through from up-country. Even today such fare draws good prices in the city market, even if slightly high. Like dugong and crocodile meat, these creatures are greatly prized.. In the old days, the acquisition of a haunch or a rump of goat or a cane or rat or three—sometimes the size of cats—was often the signal for a feast. The onset of war, however, resulted in fresh meat becoming scarce. Not so in the interior, where a basketful of crickets or locusts with palm wine is invariably considered good bush chop.

In the old days, because I couldn't afford better, I'd explore Freetown on foot. It was the only way to get a proper sight of the sprawling dilapidation that made a flummery of twentieth-century progress. Then, as now, this capital city is a tottering congeries of sagging structures, lost hopes and bleak prospects.

Things haven't changed much in the interim, though we know now that if Britain had been a little more circumspect about the problems that faced Sierra Leone at the start of the insurrection, the country would not have found itself in such a murderous muddle. It was

London's parliament that voted against supplying Sierra Leone with the weapons it desperately needed to defend itself against Foday Sankoh's guerrilla-backed revolution a couple of years earlier.

The issue wasn't fatuous or in any way ill-timed. Rather, it was a desperate plea for help—the same call, coincidentally, that came from Malaysia, Kenya, Saudi Arabia and others when they faced threats from outside. Even Zimbabwe, supporting an extreme and questionable war in the Congo for a long time, received the wherewithal to fight that Sierra Leone did not.

When the RUF rebels first began smashing the country's defenses apart, Sandline International, a British private military company (with which Nellis was associated) told Whitehall that it was willing to send armed men to Sierra Leone to fight the rebels. The South African mercenary concern, Executive Outcomes, with never more than two hundred men, had been there before and had done an outstanding job retaking Sierra Leone—together with its diamond fields around Kono—back from the rebels, and Sandline's directors argued they could do so as well.

By this time, some of Sandline's people had already arrived in West Africa but it was London that quickly stopped them from doing anything effective because the organization had been, as one British paper described it, "ideologically stigmatized." Sandline, horror of horrors, had done the unthinkable by recruiting mercenaries!

By the time I arrived this time, in the spring of 2000, the country's security problems had been magnified tenfold. There were half a dozen states—including Libya—who were providing Sankoh's RUF with money and arms. Consequently, a preponderance of Sierra Leone's defense establishment was tied down just trying to maintain a grip on the country. Had Sandline been allowed to do what it had hoped for in the first place, it could have halted Sierra Leone's slide toward anarchy within a month. It could also have saved an awful lot of lives

This radio intercept arrived while we were returning to base after a sortie in the northern part of the country:

Fm—c/s 076 (Fadugu)
To—c/s O83 (Makeni)
Info—c/s 077 (Bafodia) and c/s 085 (Koidu)
Subject—Sitrep

Sir, we have been engaged by the heligunship for the whole day, 16/6/00. It bombarded the entire township (Fadugu). The command vehicle was burnt down. It also bombarded when the Bn commander was about talk to the CNS at Bn HQ. The radio operator managed maneuver with the radio into the bush. Casualties nil. Firm regards.

Received Cockerill Barracks 2130 hrs 19/06/00

The message was prompted by Nellis' decision to take the Hind deep into the interior, almost as far north as the Guinea Republic frontier. It was an eventful two-and-a-half-hour flight under the front bubble and we were kept busy throughout. There were four strikes on rebel positions about which radio intercepts later said quite a lot.

It took us about an hour's flight to get to Fadugu, a small town northwest of the Kono diamond fields. Once there we went to work. Nellis' gunner, Hassan Ahmed Hussein, spotted a Land Rover that had a 12.7mm "heavy' mounted on its cab parked near some buildings. Since this was rebel territory, Nellis took the bait, sending in a batch of rockets and then used his Gatling. Three passes over the target and some of the surrounding buildings were reduced to junk. The rig blew up when its tank ignited on our last pass, which resulted in a column of black smoke spiraling upward between the palms.

It was this attack that had prompted the rebels to send the radio message that headquarters had intercepted. Nellis had done well; roadworthy four-by-fours were in short supply among rebel units in Sierra Leone, in part because of gunship attrition. Few replacements were making their way into the country from Liberia. We continued north again. I'd activated the IR jammer before this strike because Nellis had warned earlier that the place had seen a lot of action.

Flying low, it soon became clear that many of the small towns had been critically affected by the war. There were damaged structures everywhere, some of them gutted and roofless. It was a pitiable scenario because Sierra Leone had once been the showpiece of Britain's colonies in West Africa. Not as big or as bustling as Nigeria, or as potentially rich as the Gold Coast with its Ashanti goldfields, but the Crown had been kind to it, which was to be expected since relations with Britain went back four centuries.

Though Nellis rarely followed preordained in-flight routines—one of the reasons why he was still alive—we kept as close to the road as the jungle allowed. It was tarred and had been well maintained before the war. In several places we could see logs placed haphazardly across it, the classic rebel ambush tactic and as much a feature of insurgencies in Sierra Leone as in Angola, El Salvador, Malaya, Afghanistan, or, for that matter, Malaya two generations ago.

Five or six minutes out of Fadugu Nellis spotted what he had been looking for: a big pile of logs across a road and, to our surprise, a rebel ambush in place. There must have been about thirty enemy troops on the ground. "Brace yourselves!" he said over the intercom.

Nellis saw some of the enemy soldiers crouched low by the side of the road as he approached. Two heavy machine guns they had not bothered to camouflage had betrayed them. It was a mistake. As the pilot ruminated afterward, they'd probably been waiting for a convoy from the army base at Kabala to their immediate north. And while they might have been prepared for action, they were facing the wrong way. We came up behind them and were consequently unexpected.

As always, Nellis kept our profile low, very rarely venturing more than a hundred or so feet above the jungle. As a result, the rebels hadn't heard us coming as we peaked over one of the hills. He just took the Hind straight in, and because the foliage muffled our engine roar, it was too late for those waiting on the ground to do much more than flee. Those that could disappeared into the forest, with Nellis sending a salvo after them. More strikes followed, one of which torched some of the grass-roofed buildings in the process. We had no fear of killing innocents because the insurgents had devastated the area and the locals who had lived there before the war were long gone.

On the way back we passed over Kamakwie—the largest town that lay across our flight path. Hassan spotted a pair of trucks parked under a tree near the center of town. He passed on specifics over his mike: "Look to the right of the mosque . . . a large structure . . . four or five minarets . . . target two, three hundred yards to its south," he called. After a few moments I saw it too. The vehicles were partially hidden in brush topped by palm fronds and were difficult to make out until we were almost on top of them.

The tactic underscored one man's theory about insurgency: scouting for enemy in primitive terrain is something you get better at the longer you practice. Pulling up sharply, we were suddenly confronted by a blue, spanking new five-tonner parked just outside town. It stood in the middle of a clearing with neither camouflage nor protection. Out of rockets, Nellis stitched it with the Gatling, most of the shells going into the engine.

Being the rainy season, we cut across the paths of a succession of silvery black tropical rainstorms that rolled darkly across the land. This forced Nellis to avoid an occasional billowing bank of cumulonimbus on both sides, with the sky lit up intermittently by lightning strikes that were sometimes a little too close. Whenever storms caught us, the Hind leaked in spurts, even though we were supposed to be inside a sealed cockpit. Nellis would adjust the pressure and it would ease off, though my Nikon's light meter gave up soon afterward. So much for Soviet precision engineering, though perhaps the old girl was just beginning to show her age.

Although many of the gunship's gauges around me had a thin film of damp under the glass, Nellis ignored the problem. "Ultimately this must affect your operational parameters," I argued because not all the instruments worked. As it was, the Ethiopian ground crew had to pirate the other Hind for spares. They would move things around: a string-and-elastic-band solution since there was no cash for spares. Somehow, they managed because both choppers were never grounded at the same time. This mechanical miracle said a lot for Sindaba's crowd, as well as for the training the Soviets had given him and his guys back home in Addis Ababa.

The last action that afternoon (we were now running short of fuel) before we headed back to Cockerill was a strike against a defensive RUF position at the head of one of the diamond pans that suddenly appeared across our flight line. They must have heard us coming because everybody on the ground took cover, quickly, though not before we saw the last of them scampering away like rabbits. Hassan dealt with it, telling us afterward that one of the rebels had done an involuntary back flip somersault when he'd hit him with his PKM machine gun. The target went one way, he recounted, and his AK-47 the other. This was the sort of thing that pleased our Arab gunner.

Like all wars, this one was full of surprises. On the penultimate stage of the flight we unexpectedly ran into a gathering of RUF forces at Gbinti, a tiny spot on the map north of Port Loko. Clustered about a few huge ebony trees were half a dozen vehicles, some with AAA guns on the back. It was a big force sitting like proverbial ducks in a pond, and all we could do was gawk as we shot past. There wasn't enough fuel for us to go in and hot them, and anyway we were nearly out of ammunition.

Looking back, it would have been a bonus had we been able to engage them, because that same night a fairly large strike group—

probably the one we saw, because they had vehicles with 12.7s mounted on their cabs—struck at a government position about an hour's drive to the south. After picking up a half-dozen Sierra Leone Army field commanders at Port Loko we set back down in Cockerill. Nellis had less than five minutes flying time left in the tanks.

Once on the ground again Nellis and crew rushed off to check ammo supplies, leaving me alone in the operations room when three British officers arrived. All were Special Forces. They told me they were hoping Nellis would brief them on the mission. Since I was the next best thing, I stood in for him. Before of a 1:500,000-scale wall map—with a scattering of automatic weapons at my feet—I went through the afternoon's routine, including what we'd encountered at Gbinti and the trucks. The situation was a little absurd. There I was, not altogether an outsider but a scribbler to boot, briefing a crack combat group (that I later discovered were SAS) in the intricacies of what had taken place earlier in an ongoing counterinsurgency operation. We had a beer on it afterward.

There was another intercept waiting for us when we got back:

Fm—c/s 086 (Magburaka-Bunbuna Axis)
To—Bde. Comdr c/s 045 (Magburaka)
Subject—Information 25 June, 2000
    Sir, be informed that the men sent last as reinforcement Cmm have escaped. Furthermore there is no proper deployment toward Bumbuna and some towns under our area of control are vacant. Accept info and your action. Regards.
    Received at Cockerill Army Barracks 0916 hours

The message seemed of little consequence until Nellis pointed out that one of the targets rocketed several times the previous day had been at Magburaka. Earlier, the Hind had attacked a rebel column advancing on the town. From what we could see, they were driving civilians ahead of them like cattle—an improvised version of a human shield. As we approached, long and low, the civilians froze. The rebels, in contrast, ran into the bush. Fortunately our rockets diverged and exploded in the undergrowth on both sides of the road, killing some of the enemy. A rebel Sitrep arrived afterward and announced that there had been casualties.

"Their pagan gods abandoned them that day," Nellis chuckled.

After that, we got word that the gooks had packed up and gone back to their original bases.

Nellis' approach to combat never varied. Just before a mission his mién was as calm as if he was going to a movie. Carefully, methodically, he would go through his pre-flight checks, walking around the helicopter, pushing this and tugging at that. He also carefully examined all the spaces inside, which pilots are apt to do when somebody is willing to pay good money to destroy an adversary. Pipe bombs have killed a few fliers in Africa over the years. One was Bruce McKenzie, Kenya's last white cabinet minister. He was murdered by Idi Amin's goons with such a device while returning to Nairobi from Entebbe.

Once this routine was complete, Nellis gathered his ground crew to go over what had been done to the helicopter since his last flight: repairs, replacements and, most important, what they had not been able to fix.

I asked him once, almost as an afterthought, how he felt about waging nearly daily combat. Things were likely to happen in the end, I suggested.

His reaction was muted, and looking back, I don't believe he thought that much about it. He and the crew had been in so many enemy contacts and been fired at so often that they were a bit like Pavlov's hounds, though the work was never mindless. Having someone shoot at you focuses the mind, he laughed, though his eyes told me that he was serious.

One evening, weeks later, after a brief night out, Nellis tossed a paper across the table. "You want to know what's its like? There's part of the answer," he said. He had underlined an obituary notice in one of the British newspapers detailing events associated with the life of Air Vice-Marshal Sandy Johnstone. The write-up concerned a Spitfire raid on a chemical factory at Pachino, Sicily in World War II. "It was a strange overwhelming feeling of excitement that made your mouth run dry with the taste of it," explained Johnstone to someone long ago. The quote had come from Johnstone's autobiography.

And he was right: that was exactly what happened to me each time we saw action. Whenever I flew with Nellis into an attack and things became dodgy, my hands would tightly grip whatever they had in them at the time, usually my cameras. At the same time, my responses to his orders would quicken and my senses grew about as sharp as they've ever been.

Nellis told me once that he and the Hind were like one. It was at in flight, he explained, that he felt almost invincible. From his expression I could see that he meant it.

"I'll never die in a helicopter," he told me halfway through my stay. He really believed that he was far more likely to croak in a car accident. Africa's roads and drivers being what they are, it made sense.

Few people have had as much hot metal thrown at them as Neall Ellis. He had been involved in one conflict or another almost continuously since leaving university in his early twenties. After completing half the required hours for an officer's course in the Rhodesian Army, he joined the South African Air Force and flew jets, helicopter transports and gunships in the Namibian and Angolan border wars. At the end of that phase, he had achieved the rank of half-colonel and was then told by his white bosses in Pretoria—shortly after South Africa's first democratic post-apartheid elections—that there was no place for him in Nelson Mandela's new order.

The news was hurtful, coming as it did abruptly and without fanfare. So he left the SADF with his pension and, as he admits today, great hopes for what he would encounter on "civvy street." Following a spell in a commercial fishing venture that quickly turned sour, he lost everything. With his extensive experience and little else to lose, Neall Ellis became a mercenary, a profession which first took him to Bosnia. Now that he was into his fifties, fighting in Third World wars had become a way of life for him. "What the hell else am I qualified for?" he asked me once over dinner.

Nellis is extraordinarily good at what he does, which could be why he has survived for so long after being involved in a host of conflicts. He concedes, though, that he has had his share of breaks. Some years before, in a battle in Angola he found himself at the receiving end of three Russian SAM missiles fired at his helicopter in rapid succession from a hefty two-hundred-strong guerrilla strike group that the South Africans had waylaid. Within little more than a minute he'd dodged three oncoming SAM-7s, which, in itself, gives some idea of the man's super-keen eyesight and remarkable reflexes.

During that raid, the first time he spotted a Strela coming at him, he had only a moment to turn straight into its path, a successful tactic he and other South African Air Force pilots had discovered earlier. While such incidents aren't commonplace, even in Africa, they are significant because they do provide an insight into a developing trend in the world's smaller wars. Manpads—the ubiquitous SAM-7s, now superseded by more sophisticated SAM-14/16s—have been deployed in many of Africa's conflicts and, more recently, in Iraq as well as Afghanistan.[1] The only difference today is that whereas Strelas were never fitted with proximity fuses, the more modern versions of the missile are.

The contact involving the SAMs, as Nellis recalls, took place in a remote corner of southern Angola, not far from the Namibian border. A tiny spot on the map just north of the great Kunene River, the area is a barren, badly eroded region that the Portuguese originally called *Terras do Fim Mundo*. They were right, because this really is a "land at the end of the earth." At the controls of one of a pair of SAAF Alouettes, he and Angelo Maranta, his wingman, were giving close air support to a combat detail on the ground. Flimsy as these French helicopters might seem when compared to Russian combat choppers, they can still inflict an astonishing amount of damage. They always have.

The moment Nellis and Maranta reached the battlefield, the guerrillas retaliated. "The entire insurgent force was shooting at us at once. Our choppers were all that were in their sights!" Nellis recalled. "When they saw that they weren't having any effect—and by then the guys on the ground were hitting them—the majority of the insurgents tried to make a run for it. But they had nowhere to go. In that desolate terrain, even the few shrubs that dotted the countryside were sparse. There was no place to hide."

The two helicopter pilots methodically picked off targets at random. Nellis continued: "The first rounds from our choppers stopped the run and with that, the enemy ducked low for cover, such as it was. Then we almost caught it. I felt a powerful blast at the back as an RPG-7 exploded near the tail.

In clipped tones, Maranta screamed at Ellis over his radio, "SAM Nellis! Six o'clock! Swing left . . . hard!"

"I could see the distinctive thick, white-gray smoke trail of a Strela twirling up toward us and immediately put on more bank to find the firing position," explained Nellis. "As I turned through a hundred-and-eighty degrees, a second missile was on its way, this time heading straight for Maranta." It was Nellis' turn to shout: "SAM! Nine o'clock!"

"By then we had dropped so low that by the time I'd used my radio, the missile was already traveling at Mach 1.5. Maranta performed as much evasive action as time allowed and the missile passed harmlessly ahead of his machine.

"Things were gathering pace and by now we were coming under

heavy fire," continued the South African pilot. "Machine guns, RPG blasts and ground action—much of it accompanied by curtains of tracer fire, was deafening, even with our headsets on. Another Strela shot past our nose. Once we'd been able to spot from where that one had been launched, Coetzee, my gunner, killed the missile team. With our Pumas arriving with back-up squads—they were quite close to an LZ that I had identified earlier—I shifted my position to mark the spot with a smoke grenade. Then we both went into top-cover mode."

Altogether more than two hundred SWAPO fighters died that morning. It was the guerrilla organization's largest single loss to a small field force in any battle during two decades of consecutive border conflict. Many of the Angolan enemies subsequently captured by the South Africans were eventually "turned" to fight against their old comrades. It is possible that quite a few of these "turned gooks" ended up serving with Executive Outcomes elsewhere in Africa a decade later.

For their roles in "Op Super," both Nellis and his tech, Steve Coetzee were awarded South Africa's *Honoris Crux* (Cross of Honor), which, in general terms is perhaps only a couple of steps away from the highest British or American decorations for bravery under fire.

6

THE UNITED NATIONS DEBACLE
IN WEST AFRICA

"Just past the town of Mile 38, General 'One Man One Bullet'
and Major 'Prayer' are squatting under a palm tree, their rifles
leaning against their legs. The exhausted men from the Special
Forces of the Sierra Leone Army had just captured Masiaka, a
strategic town outside the Occra Hills."

Janine di Giovannie in *The Times*,
London, May 15, 2000

Things can go seriously wrong when a thirteen-thousand-strong UN
force in Sierra Leone is either unwilling or incapable of rescuing eleven
of its own who have been taken prisoner by a crazy bunch of malcontents who spend most of their waking hours stoned to the gills.

In the fall of 2000, after weeks of haggling with a rebel group that
called itself "The West Side Boys," London finally took matters in
hand. A strike force composed of a few hundred members of the
Parachute Regiment, backed by the SAS and Royal Marines' Special
Boat Service (SBS) were flown to West Africa in an attempt to pull the
UN's chestnuts out of the fire. In the short crackerjack operation that
followed that September, all the hostages were safely airlifted out of
the rebel jungle base where they were being held captive. It took these
professionals just twenty minutes to complete the job, though they lost
one of their own in the process.

Code-named Operation Barras, the attack on the West Side Boys'
(WSB) camp at the head of Rokel Creek was a masterstroke in planning and execution. Britain's *Sunday Times* said afterward that it was
"an extremely complex . . . textbook operation, worthy of study for
years to come." According to General Sir Charles Guthrie, Chief of
Britain's Defense Staff (himself a former SAS soldier), Operation
Barras "was one of the most complicated operations in which I have
ever been involved."

Deployed were three Chinook C-47s of the RAF's 7 Squadron

with machine guns mounted to port, starboard and on their retractable rear ramps, as well as two Lynx choppers from 657 Squadron to provide close air support. These helicopters were equipped with TOW missiles on their port pylons, and a gunner with a GPMG at the starboard door. Earlier, Gazelles had conducted reconnaissance and liaison missions.[1]

Nellis was also there with the government gunship. The Hind acquitted itself splendidly, accounting for its share of kills. In concert with the British choppers, the South African laid down covering fire for the attackers, some of whom had to wade chest-deep almost six hundred yards to reach their target, an excruciating experience in appalling temperatures and the kind of humidity that can enervate the soul.

The initial strike force of more than a hundred Paras was ferried into the target area in an unusually well coordinated, two-pronged dawn assault. One group was earmarked to destroy rebel positions on the south bank of a deeply foliated creek while the other pulled the remaining hostages out of Gberi Bana camp immediately to its north. Dozens of men of D Squadron, 22 SAS and SBS personnel had already infiltrated the area. Still more had gone in clandestinely several days before, a handful in scuba gear.

The primary British Special Forces role was to supply the attacking force with intelligence. Afterward, the group formed a succession of blocking groups to prevent the "Boys" from escaping. Working in pairs—as they had done often enough in Northern Ireland in the past—they spent most of the time in bulky, suffocating ghillie suits, which must have been hell in that furnace. Usually prostrate in a succession of shallow hollows half full of water, these professionals had long ago mastered the art of using the bush to clever advantage.

Early reports revealed how these soldiers subsisted on specially packed rations and urinated into cans during periods when they were immobile. Their real work began after dark. Using night vision goggles they went to work gleaning information for their superiors back in Britain. The intelligence they provided was so detailed that Northwood headquarters was able to construct a complete replica of the West Side Boys' camp that was used for planning the final onslaught.

The terrain—a mix of tropical forest, swamps, and restricted access through an extremely dense triple-canopied jungle—favored the rebels, dug in behind solid defenses. There were other problems like scorpions, snakes and the occasional crocodile. The men had to operate discreetly to avoid alarming troops of monkeys that would sometimes become inquisitive. Large flocks of birds, often including thousands of parrots that colonized the jungle, landed all around the intruders. If any of these creatures sounded the alarm, the rebels would certainly nose about.

Once the basics had been established, the rescue plan was presented to British Prime Minister Tony Blair. He was to give the green light four days before the launch. As Brigadier Andrew Stewart declared when discussing the operation afterward, "You cannot resolve a situation like this with a laser bomb from thirty thousand feet." Stewart and his planning staff monitored the minute-by-minute progress of the raid from the headquarters of Britain's Permanent Joint Headquarters northwest of London. Northwood was nearly three thousand miles from where it was all taking place.

The United States took more than a passing interest in the operation, especially since there were several squads of Green Berets in tropical Africa training national battalions in Special Force techniques—five in Nigeria and one each in Ghana and the Republic of Guinea. Since then, there have been more such developments. Writer Robert Kaplan provided a pretty good account of what Washington was up to on the "Dark Continent" in an unusually insightful article in *The Atlantic Monthly*.[2]

What triggered this activity at the head of a filthy, overgrown swamp that reeked of rot and human effluent was the capture a few weeks earlier of eleven British soldiers on patrol. Attached to the Royal Irish Regiment, the contingent commanded by Major Alan Marshall was in three Land Rovers on its way back to base at Benguema, north of Freetown. Marshall inexplicably ordered his men to turn off the main road onto a narrow dirt way leading to Magbeni. Unbeknown to the British, a large force of West Side Boys was waiting for them.

In the subsequent debriefing, Major Marshall explained that he had been told "only a few" rebels were in the village. When he and his men arrived, the rebel group pulled up a truck alongside the army vehicles, its twin-barreled 14.5mm heavy machine gun mounted on the cab. Marshall recalled afterward that facing his men were essentially a bunch of juveniles in uniform. Unwilling to kill "children armed with AKs," the British had no option but to surrender.

After stripping the newcomers of their weapons and uniforms,

"Brigadier" Foday Kallay, the self-appointed rebel leader, threatened to execute anybody who tried to escape. No amateur insurgent, Kallay was regarded by those who had dealings with him as a depraved little man in a permanent rage, partly because he seemed hooked on a combination of cocaine, ganga (pot), and an evil local brew resembling gin. On several occasions he would perform his own macabre little pantomime and go through an elaborate ritual as if he was about to execute one or more of his helpless captives. Major Marshall was beaten when he protested the inhumane treatment.

The British soldiers were very much aware that there was no guarantee that Kallay would not carry out his threats. When some of his own men had approached in a delegation and asked to be released so that they could turn themselves in to the UN, he summarily executed twenty-seven of them—"some of them right there, in front of us," reported one of the British soldiers afterward.

Not averse to a little bartering, he also arranged a meeting with a group of British officials in Freetown. Kallay and his bodyguards duly arrived—to the chagrin of the British—in one of the Land Rovers that his group had filched. After long discussions that went nowhere, the "Brigadier," as he insisted on being called, finally traded six of his hostages for a consignment of clothes, food and a satellite phone.

The meeting was Kallay's undoing. The phone went everywhere with him. He slept with it under his pillow, oblivious of the fact that the British had installed a miniature radio transmitter in the set that broadcast a DF beam. It was a brilliant piece of work since it only sent out a signal when it was switched off. When the time came, the attackers used it to zero in on Kallay's headquarters while he was asleep.

The size of the rescue effort was indicative of the resistance London anticipated they could expect from these reprobates. The six soldiers already released were extensively debriefed, with the result that London knew precisely what needed to be done.

Northwood was aware, for instance, that the hostages had been taken by open boat from Magbeni to a cluster of mud huts at a former palm oil plantation at Geri Bana on the north bank of the Rokel River. They were also aware of numbers and strong points. They knew how many guards there were, when and where they slept, and that there were about sixty well-equipped rebels on each of the two riverbanks armed with mortars, LMGs, and some heavy stuff. One of the three British Land Rovers—with its mounted 50mm caliber Browning—was dug in to provide flanking fire. Because just about everything centered about the leader's hut, his capture was a primary aim, second only to the rescue of the hostages.

In the words of the London *Times*, The assault "was brutal." A British press report said that "about twenty-five of the West Side Boys were killed." Someone else at Cockerill told me that the figure could be multiplied by five or six or more. While the hostages were airlifted out within twenty minutes, Para and Special Forces elements remained behind until nightfall. Asked what they had been doing, one of them answered nonchalantly, "Cleaning up." For his part in the action, Nellis admits to killing "a shithouse full of gooks" with his Hind in that follow-up.

British casualties were light. Only one soldier, a bombardier member of the SAS squad named Brad Tinnion, was killed when he took a hit in the back while exiting from one of the choppers. A dozen or so others were wounded, one seriously. Seven were hurt in a single mortar blast that might have caused serious casualties but for the soft soil in which it landed.

Yet for all its recent drama, Sierra Leone was not always at war. In the old days people referred to it as "Superlative Sierra Leone." When the country achieved its independence in 1961, its people were among the best educated and most prosperous in all of West Africa. The country had diamonds and gold in abundance, and Britain left it in excellent stead with a balanced budget and a population regarded around the world as among the friendliest to be found. From the sublime to the barbaric, how things have changed, but then that's the story of so much of Africa these days.

By the start of the new millennium (and the arrival of the latest bunch of RUF rebels from Liberia) almost nothing of the old order remained intact. In terms of atrocities, Sierra Leone's decade-old war at the time was the worlds worst. Its government was among the most corrupt, and its murderous excesses—tabulated daily by organizations such as Human Rights Watch and the International Committee of the Red Cross—rated among the most horrific on the planet. Aside from lopping off the hands and feet of children, the rebels were also charged with cannibalism. A mindless level of brutality prevailed that included the ritual execution of innocents.

As one enraged British hack fulminated, "What a mess: in a sense it's Pol Pot all over again, though without the ideology."

Into this bubbling cauldron stepped the United Nations. The organization was supposed to put a stop to it all. Instead, the world body compounded problems when they should have solved them.

For several years the UN was integral to the security equation in Sierra Leone, with billions of dollars spent in a West African operation that didn't ever look like it could be brought to a halt. Looking back, we are now able to accept that the UN did precious little and achieved even less because in the end it was the British who managed to turn the war around. Sadly, that appears to be something of a pattern elsewhere in the world.

Since the UN deployed its first international teams of peacekeepers in 1948 in the Middle East, more than a hundred countries have provided three-quarters of a million personnel for fifty-three operations around the globe. The dividends from these actions, well-intentioned though they might have been, are miniscule when compared to both the blood and the resources. East Timor, the transition to nationhood of Namibia, Mozambique, and a handful of others are among the few successful UN ventures, and in those cases only because the participants agreed to lay down their arms.

It is also true that very few outsiders who have seen UN forces operating in Third World countries have much to say for their efforts, except that just about everything the world body does is inordinately expensive. That also applies to UN activities today in the Middle East. One need only look closely at what they did in West Africa to understand why this is so.

UNAMSIL (United Nations Mission in Sierra Leone) was the world's largest single multinational "peacekeeping" operation of its time, involving nationals from more than twenty countries. Yet it quickly evolved in what was probably the most incompetent "peacekeeping" operation ever fielded. Some observers, when discussing the UN role with me while I was in country, charitably described UNAMSIL as "impotent." They would expound that it had an army that wouldn't fight (unless there were British elements involved), national units that refused to emerge from their camps, and a command structure—composed mainly of Indians and Nigerians—that would not (or perhaps, more correctly, could not) make the most fundamental decisions. This debacle had not only deteriorated to the point of farce by the time British Brigadier David Richards and his support group arrived, but the international group had itself begun to unravel. It was Richards' thankless job to bring cohesion to a situation that was all but lost.

While all this was going on, UN Secretary General Kofi Annan was trying to recruit more countries to send additional troop contingents to West Africa. He could find no takers. In the end, following the untimely and embarrassed departure of the Indian Force Commander (about which we shall hear more later) he appointed a Kenyan Army general to command UNAMSIL.

The UN in Freetown faced multiple problems from the very beginning, almost all of its own making. Apart from its multiple and diverse military components, there were God-knows how many civilian employees. Upon arrival, most of these people were handed keys to their own vehicles, the white-painted SUVs that crowded Freetown's forlorn and potholed streets. One result of this little extravagance was that more new Toyota Landcruisers were brought into Sierra Leone in the first six months of UNAMSIL's existence than had been commercially imported into the country in the previous quarter century. Almost all arrived by air, again flown in at UN expense.

Why spend millions of dollars on such a frivolous expense when nobody could or would go beyond the city limits without massive armored support? A fleet of smaller sedans (at a fraction of the outlay) would have been a better and cheaper option. But as they say, nothing is quite as much fun as spending someone else's money.

These excesses had their consequences. On Sundays, for instance, the beach along the Aberdeen seafront looked like a showcase for marketing white Japanese four-by-fours. Once the word got out about big-spending UN staffers—the majority with time to kill—prostitutes from just about every state in Africa gravitated to Sierra Leone. They arrived by boat from Ghana and Guinea, many took the chance and tried to entire the country overland through rebel lines, and a few even flew into Lungi, all of them attracted to the blue helmets and their civilian caretakers like bugs to a blanket.

The logistics that made these excesses possible created a yawning chasm in the finances of the UN, though in the words of some of the organization's officials, it didn't matter because American taxpayers paid for most it. Even to feed this monster required massive injections of cash, much of which found its way into Russian pockets. On any day of the week there would be a dozen or more giant Antonov-124s arriving at Lungi Airport loaded with supplies and equipment. These aircraft are immense, larger than your average 747 and twice as expensive to run.

Apart from vehicles, virtually all of the furniture and appliances needed for hundreds of UN offices came into Sierra Leone by air.

Added to that were scores of charters containing household goods, bedding, and whatever else was needed for the apartments of UN officials based there. In any other business, anywhere in the world, squandering resources on such a scale would have been regulated or possibly even made criminal. The truth is that the Sierra Leone operation was no different than any other UN effort, whether in West Africa, Sinai or Afghanistan.

Instead of importing all these needs, the UN could very easily have placed orders through any of the hundreds of small industries standing idle in Freetown because of the war. Local facilities could easily have been harnessed to manufacture many of the requirements. Having the locals produce items like cupboards, chairs, tables, desks and beds (wood was always available in abundance in Sierra Leone, even at the height of the war) would have served a double purpose: bundles of money could have been saved in freight costs alone, never mind that a sizable chunk of the population would have been employed. Implementing that measure would also have provided a useful cash injection into an economy crippled by years of fighting. Alas, logical decisions are rarely a UN priority.

The UN was forthcoming with all sorts of reasons why they did not use local industries. Nellis looked into the matter and was told that everything was acquired abroad because "local businesses did not have the resources or the infrastructure to utilize the indigenous people." Also it was claimed that only overseas organizations were capable of ordering and shipping the large quantities of logistical requirements. Sounds like a load of hogwash to this writer.

As Nellis commented, a cursory check on who got all these lovely contracts and exactly how they were allocated might reveal something interesting. Also, everything came into the county tax free, which certainly could not have helped the local economy. At the end of it, one needs to ask: was all this another UN scam at which that organization appears to be so unusually proficient?

The Sierra Leone UN operation was also cumbersome and top heavy. It was almost all chiefs and no Indians. To cop it all, the organization often appeared to be uncertain about its role in the conflict.

Everyone—from shoeshine boys in the center of town all the way up the employment chain—could hardly miss the fact that a fairly extensive ground war was being fought in the interior of the country. Indeed, there were some battles that were decided on the outskirts of town. But UNAMSIL was not prepared to admit that reality. Many of its officers would use euphemisms like "disturbances" or "emergency" to describe the war, even though on any given night you could lie in your bed and hear volleys of automatic rifle fire just beyond the city limits.

Consequently, I was not all that surprised when one of my journalist friends warned me soon after I got to Freetown that it simply wasn't kosher to inquire too closely about the purpose of a United Nations military presence in Sierra Leone. If I did, she said, I would be shunned. At the one and only press briefing I was allowed to attend, I had the temerity to ask that very question: "What is the actual role of the thousands of UN soldiers in the country at present?" I was summarily told that I was being provocative and never invited back.

Within UN ranks there was also a lot of uncertainty about the nature and the extent of the threat that existed from Sankoh's RUF forces. (It was instructive in a discouraging way that at press conferences these killers were never referred to as "rebels" or as "the enemy," but merely the RUF or sometimes as "the opposition.") Forthright questions about the actual role of the rebels or even crimes that might have been committed by their cadres were fudged, or in my case, fobbed off. As one British journalist suggested, we were given the sort of answers one would expect from a small town political meeting. "Most of the replies were evasive," he declared. Others were elusive, and not a few patently dishonest.

For example, in early September 2000, UNAMSIL's deputy force commander, Nigerian General Mohammed A. Garba[3] stated that Sankoh's rebels had "never once during the past year initiated any attack on a government position." Of course, that claim was not only preposterous, it was a lie. None of us could figure out what motivated him to go on record with such an inane declaration. It did nothing for the credibility of the second most powerful military man in Sierra Leone.

"You begin to wonder whose pay he's in and whether the promise of diamonds didn't have something to do with it," Nellis told me after hearing the UN General answer. "Hasn't he heard what's being going on at Lunsar? Or Makeni?" the South African queried cynically.

Everything dealing with the war and UNAMSIL's purported role in it came from the UN's luxurious headquarters at the Mammy Yoko Hotel, where only official personnel (and the occasional favored hack) were allowed to stay. These UN activities dealt mainly with ancillary administrative issues: unit strengths, vehicles, helicopter movements, base support, logistics, and visits by VIPs, of which there were a lot. Of course, there were also social functions and briefings galore, especially the former. When asked about UNAMSIL's contingency measures in the event of contact with armed groups of rebels, UN spokespeople would never be specific or in any way definitive. Invariably there was never a clear-cut reply to anything that might be considered contentious because there was obviously no fixed plan. Prevarication was the name of the game and axiomatically, there was also no strategy for victory.

As one Scandinavian naval officer attached to the world body discreetly explained one night after a boisterous session at Alex's, the senior UN command structure in Sierra Leone rarely bothered about the reality of what was going on in the interior. He was also candid enough to admit that he had found this surprising since it was the UN's very reason for being there in the first place.

"Why should they?" he commented sourly after ruminating on the issue. "No action would ever be taken against any UN commander who sat on his hands in the face of any kind of rebel provocation." This, he continued, "was one of the reasons why the RUF—before the British force arrived—was able to disarm and imprison hundreds of international peacekeepers. "UN policy in Sierra Leone is moribund," he declared. End of conversation.

It was London's task to counter this perception once British troops had arrived in the country. Conditions were the worst among some Third World units that were part of the UN mediating process. The Jordanians, especially, would move restlessly within—but never beyond—their designated areas in the tropical interior. It was their camp that the British Major Marshall had been visiting before being taken hostage with his squad.

We often had reports come in of Jordanian soldiers fraternizing with the West Side Boys. Sometimes they would let this rabble pass unchecked—together with their guns and sometimes heavier hardware—through any one of five checkpoints supposedly under the control of this Arab force. Rarely did their soldiers enforce criteria required of them in an area that had not only experienced years of bloodshed, but had also seen some of our colleagues killed. With time, the consensus grew that these Bedouins were actually quite terrified of the jungle, which, to many of them, was an almost mystical and overwhelming source of power. While they might have been brilliant soldiers in the desert sands of Arabia, all that green and gloom in West

Africa frightened the hell out of them. There were also reports of the Jordanians giving the WSBs food, medicine and blankets, and there were unconfirmed reports of them handing out ammunition as well.

Such matters became an issue with Chris McGreal of London's *Guardian* when he was assigned to cover West Africa. McGreal wrote an article that was critical of the Jordanians, and the BBC asked him about it.

"What they are doing," he answered, "is not United Nations policy. Rather, it's very much a relationship between the Jordanian peacekeepers and the West Side Boys, and quite probably one that's a convenience to use as a means of keeping the peace and making sure that they, too, are safe." McGreal added that the Jordanians might be vulnerable to an attack by the West Side Boys if they failed to get along with them. "It's a means of buying them off, so to speak."

He also stated that Sierra Leonian military officials had firsthand knowledge of the arrangement. Interestingly, no one ever contradicted him. "The UN cannot say that it's not informed about this situation," McGreal continued, pointing out that irregular WSB thugs "had hundreds of military and civilian hostages, quite a few of them abducted from villages where the militia remained active." Many women had been taken and raped, he wrote.

Then there was "Operation Thunderbolt," which made a mockery of any kind of UN military operation. A month before McGreal penned his piece, UN Command in Freetown declared that it had launched a "most effective" raid, code-named Operation Thunderbolt. According to the spokesman, it was an attack on the Occra Hills area in a bid "to stop the excesses and the abuses of the WSBs."

The raid was a farce, explained Nellis. "There was a lot of noise, radio chatter, helicopters flying around in circles, and UN movement on all the roads leading north. But the "Boys" had been tipped off and so made themselves scarce until the UN operation ended."

Privy to the upcoming operation, Jordanian officers had apparently told some of the rebels about the raid. The RUF fighters had asked that the Arabs warn their commanders of what was coming. That, too, was confirmed afterward by some of the rebels themselves when they returned to Freetown under amnesty and became part of the "peace process," such as it was.

Uncharacteristically, a UN official afterward admitted to McGreal: "I don't think collaboration is too strong a word to describe what is happening. . . . The Jordanians are feeding those guys and socializing with them without thinking that these rebels are the same ones killing people and raping girls." It was tough talk. According to others at Cockerill, it was true.

One night Nellis and I were stopped at a checkpoint on the way home from dinner with Hassan, an incident that might easily have gone badly adrift and which I deal with in a later chapter. An entire Jordanian battalion had passed us driving furiously into town, almost like they had been spooked. Without telling anybody, they'd simply abandoned their posts on the most strategic road in the country. Hunkered down in their Land Rovers with .50mm Brownings mounted on the rear, they charged past us as we waited to be searched. This was a worried bunch of Sunnis. Even the Nigerians knew better than to try and stop them. The issue was kept under wraps, but because nothing remains secret in Freetown, the media tackled it the next day and much subsequently emerged in the press. It was a scandal to the local press because such a bug-out affected their security as much as that of the Jordanians. Finally, as radio and newspaper scrutiny began to gather a momentum of its own, New York began to take notice.

It was then that the UN Secretary General ordered UNAMSIL to get off its collective butts and take some kind of initiative. Instructions arrived that from then on, the world body and its huge force were required to enforce peace rather than try to keep it.

Predictably, the battalion commanders from several countries objected. Heading that list were the Jordanians, while troops from Guinea, Kenya, and three or four other countries told the UN Supremo, General Jetley, that they had not come to Sierra Leone to fight. As usual, the Indian force commander did little more than shrug.

In Jetley's defense, Nellis reckoned that the UN Force Commander "was actually a warrior. He wanted to take the fight to the rebels. However, he was not given the authority by New York to enforce the peace." Anyway, he added, most of the UN commanders in Sierra Leone were simply not interested and that "the issue was burdened with politics!"

In fact, what should have happened was that the dissenting battalion leaders should have been sent home. Brigadier Richards was probably right when he told *Jane's Defence Weekly*[3] that the Indian Major General was "a prisoner to his own captives" who were (then) being held by the rebels somewhere in the interior of the country. But even when a group of UN troops being held hostage by Sankoh's brigands were eventually released—it took a British and Indian Air Force military strike involving Indian Air Force Hinds to achieve it—nothing changed. Jetley never spoke out about periodic Jordanian lapses, whereas in any other military force, charges of dereliction of duty would almost certainly have warranted court martial proceedings. Sadly, nothing like that took place in war-torn Sierra Leone. That's what happens when you mix a volatile military situation with politics and, in a different sense, we've seen the same sort of thing happening in parts of Iraq and Afghanistan these days.

Worse, everybody knew that the rebels read exactly the same newspapers that we did. It was consequently no secret which national detachments might succumb to intimidation. Thus, it wasn't that surprising that the West Side Boys successfully exploited Jordanian impotence and they did so with a dedicated, evil ruthlessness. They'd had the United Nations measure all the time.

William Shawcross encapsulated so much of this imbroglio brilliantly in his book *Deliver Us From Evil: Peacekeepers, Warlords, and a World of Endless Conflict*. Published about the time the UN first deployed in West Africa, it offers what might have been a case history for UNAMSIL. In his review of Shawcross' work for *Stars and Stripes*, noted American commentator David Isenberg, who knows more about PMCs than almost anybody I know, said, "After reading this book, nobody will ever again be able to contemplate a call to deploy United Nations peacekeepers without gagging." Nellis, having read the book himself, commented that unlike the international body, he was usually of a mind while heading the Air Wing to destroy rebels. In contrast, he observed, "The UN simply seems to move its assets about like chess pieces on a board, largely, one would imagine, for want of anything better to do."

The cost of this huge United Nations charade was stultifying. Jetley's budget for the first six months actually exceeded a quarter of a billion US dollars, or nearly $1.5 million a day. This was over and above the billion or so dollars it took to set the operation up in the first place. Worse, by the time the operation had staggered into its second year, UN Secretary General Kofi Annan had absolutely nothing to show for it. There wasn't even a glimmer of hope that any of it might lead to success. In fact, by the middle of the year 2000, things looked even more dismal than when I'd arrived. At least then we had been hitting rebel targets and doing so effectively several times a day. Once the UN arrived, in contrast, the operation became moribund.

To get a better perspective of United Nations machinations in this far-flung West African outpost one needs to examine the saga surrounding the West Side Boys in a little more detail, not only because there was much else happening on the periphery of this bush war, but until the British knocked the stuffing out of those bastards, this rebel bunch manipulated things with a a an astonishing measure of cunning and ruthlessness. For its part, the local UN command structure was incapable (or possibly unwilling) to accept what was happening. What emerges is a compendium of blunders, half-truths, lies and, as we have witnessed, lives lost.

The Occra Hills terror campaign that took place while Indian Army Major General Vijay Kumar Jetley ran the show in Sierra Leone eventually became big news.[5] What we know is that a catatonic bunch of rebels occupied a row of hills an hour or so out of Freetown. Though there were only a few hundred of them, these irregular thugs were committing the most awful crimes against humanity. Also, they were getting away with it.

On August 15, 2000—about a month after I'd left Sierra Leone, Neall Ellis sent me a copy of an e-mail he'd forwarded to IRIN, the African news agency. It detailed some of the atrocities then being perpetrated by these West Side Boys. Also referred to as Jungle Boys or "Junglers," they showed themselves to be a mindless bunch of killers. To gain admission to their ranks, you had to have murdered someone; anyone, your mother even, it didn't matter who. Then you had to kill again to be properly inducted.

Most of these psychos operated from hideouts in the Occra Hills, not far from the main road that links Freetown to Rogberi junction, though their gangs could occasionally be seen in the capital, which was one of the quirks of the war. Hawkeye mentions bars that he frequented where he knew that some of the fellow-patrons had fired on his helicopter that day. They'd even acknowledge his presence with a symbolic slashing of the throat, their lips miming: "next time!"

Nothing that "The Boys" did indicated equanimity. All that mattered was the number of lives taken and how many females—many of them young girls, some not even teenagers—they managed to keep as sex slaves.

Nellis' missive in trying to highlight what these brutes were doing was motivated by frustration. As he told me, everybody—and especially the UN—was aware of what was happening, "but there's nobody around who is prepared to do anything about it."

Like a crazed Mafia, the Junglers would extort money from those sections of the community who had least: these were mostly impoverished civilians caught in the crossfire.

Copies of his report went to Corrine Dufka, then a researcher for Human Rights Watch, who has since become a prominent international voice against injustice. In turn, I passed a copy of Nellis' brief on to Jim Rupert at *The Washington Post* who checked it out. Doug Farrer, the *Post*'s man in West Africa arrived in Freetown a week later to speak to Nellis.

Having investigated the matter for herself, Dufka told the French news outfit *Agence France Presse* that there had been an incident where a busload of civilians had been robbed by the "Junglers" in full view of a Jordanian Army detachment. It was their job to put a stop to such things, she pointed out. Also, they did nothing when two women were abducted within yards of their control post: the girls were snatched and forced to join the unit's harem in the jungle. A little undercover work afterward disclosed that there were hundreds of these "sex slaves" in Freetown, many of whom would eventually attest to this barbarism.

The gist of Nellis' original message was simple: he protested about the UN being either incapable or unwilling to stop these activities. The area in which the WSBs "worked," he explained, was within the Jordanian mandate. But apart from that Arab force symbolically manning roadblocks, its troops seemed to spend most of their time with their fingers up their noses or high on dope. According to the British Military Attaché, even getting them to build a toilet a healthy distance from their main encampment never happened. These were people, Rob Symonds concluded, who were terrified of the bush and everything that it represented.

This spate of incidents might have gone unnoticed in the kind of fluster that surrounds most Third World conflagrations, except that those same West Side Boys a week or so later kidnapped those eleven British soldiers and their two or three local aides. Also taken was a Sierra Leone Army liaison officer who had been traveling with them. From the start, the British press was harsh about cause and effect and it had good reason to be.

The apogee to what must be regarded as an ongoing catalogue of disasters came when Ms. Hirit Befecadu, Jetley's Ethiopian United Nations Spokesperson, appeared to take up her duties at the Mammy Yoko. Obnoxious in manner and bearing, she commented scathingly on Dufka's reports, saying that the story had been fabricated.

"It wasn't happening," she told journalists at a press briefing, which was absurd. Befecadu must have been the only person in Freetown who believed such rubbish. Either that or she was smoking something noxious. How could she miss observing the fact that Freetown just then overflowed with thousands of victims, many of whom were disfigured as a consequence of what these juvenile psychos had done to them?

To be charitable, being African herself, Ms. Befecadu might have been anesthetized by the violence in her own country. But that, in turn, begs the question: why would Kofi Annan—himself from Ghana—send to Freetown an intellectual cripple from one embattled black state to another to try to do a job that needed a measure of understanding, or, at the very least, solicitude? Judging by her performance—and it wasn't her only gaffe—while she remained "on seat" in West Africa, she reflected neither.

As one of the French journalists in our clique noted, she had operated in that hall of mirrors in New York City for so long that she didn't know fact from fiction. And he wasn't being tendentious. It might have helped if this refugee from the Manhattan cocktail circuit had taken her blinkers off. But then, as others have said, that's the UN style: once again the world body was the only one in step.

Cumulatively, all these events highlight another gap in the African military theater, in this case of intelligence.

More often than not, the bulk of the information that arrives in any kind of military campaign—be it in Basra or Darfur—is suspect, for no other reason than it often cannot be substantiated, at least not immediately. Out there, beyond the last serviceable track or bush trail, it's sometimes a lone pair of eyes peering through the undergrowth that will return with the most frightful tales. Or an informant could be broke: his story might have been "manufactured" to feed his family. This sort of thing takes place often enough in the developed world, never mind Africa. Just then it was happening in Sierra Leone. Whether something was done or not would usually dictate whether someone lived or died.

In this instance, Nellis' report was spiked. Had it not been, the capture of British soldiers might have been averted. This unfortunate action stemmed from the fact that Nellis' relations with Jetley's crowd was both acrimonious and tenuous. And for good reason.

On one hand, the South African pilot had been a major factor in helping the UN to establish a presence in West Africa in the days immediately after they arrived. On the other, now that his helicopter was no longer necessary to secure options, he might just as easily not have existed. This notwithstanding the fact that in the months that Jetley and his force had been in-country, Neall Ellis had saved the lives of numerous Indian Army soldiers involved in scrapes with rebel units in the interior. In one instance, he had used his Hind to drive more than a hundred RUF troops from the periphery of town to allow a relief convoy to reach the place where scores of UN soldiers had been under siege. Could it really have been lost on Jetley (or for that matter, the newly-arrived British contingent) that for a long while, this gunship pilot was the only effective pro-government combat element in the country?

Before the Indbat (Indian Battalion) was able to activate its own Hinds, it had a good deal of help from the Air Wing in Nellis' bid to provide UN ground forces with close air support, sometimes on a daily basis. Moreover, in doing so, the South African had used up a lot of government ammunition. That done—and the worst of the fighting dealt with—it was to be expected that the Air Wing would like a bit of the old quid pro quo. It needed to get back some of the hardware Nellis had expended in those operations. There were a couple of truckloads of SNEB 57mm rockets to start with—all of them pricey items and, to a country as impoverished as Sierra Leone, vital to its defense. All of it boiled down to self-preservation.

While some of the ammunition was eventually returned, the procedure was like root canal treatment. It would arrive in small consignments, sometimes a case of ammo at a time, and then only as a result of some heavy wrangling on the part of the British. The issue reeked of duplicity.

There was something indefinable about Jetley, a mild little man of indiscernible views. Asked to sum him up, someone might have answered that he filled a chair. Others called him pliable and indecisive. What he didn't do—as a member of the venerated Indian Army or not—was portray the very model of a modern major general.

Of course, the comment made by Sierra Leone's only contract helicopter pilot eventually filtered through to UN headquarters, and Nellis was hung out to dry. At the end of Jetley's period, while Nellis would mix socially with some of the UN flight crews—they couldn't help but all frequent the same bars out Aberdeen way—one sensed that they had been instructed to be wary of the South African. There were times when he might have been regarded, as the Americans would say, "attitudinally compromised."

Nellis had the ability after hours to be sociable with just about everybody. He was (and still is) that kind of guy. But if he sensed that he was being shafted, that was that. As far as he was concerned, that individual was dead. It didn't take long for Jetley to fall into that symbolic category. "Life's too short for crap," Nellis would say, usually under his breath. As Symonds commented after one of these brannigans, his bullshit threshold was at a permanent low.

Then, mid-September that year, came the event that shook the UN all the way back to Turtle Bay. In an unprecedented public announcement, Major General Jetley accused a group of senior Nigerian civil and military deputies serving under him in the Sierra Leone United Nations Command of "nepotism, corruption and collusion with the enemy." For once, Jetley was unequivocal. The Nigerians, he declared, were "far more interested in getting their hands on Sierra Leone's diamonds than they were in tackling the military problem at source." It took about a week after that little tirade for the Indian government to give notice that it was pulling its army out of the country. As a consequence you can be fairly certain that the international community won't be seeing Indian troops in any African peacekeeping operation for a generation or more to come.

As might have been expected, the squabble involved money. In Sierra Leone, the Nigerians would have preferred keeping the leadership in the peacekeeping role for themselves, as they had done earlier with ECOMOG. Also, there was a festering, ongoing issue of some of the soldiers from this West African state having been accused by some observers of not actually wanting the war to end. There were too many senior Nigerian officers who were making money from a variety of import/export businesses they had established in Freetown. It was also no secret that still more among them were into diamonds, almost all of it bought directly from rebel interests.

In his pronouncement on the subject, Jetley used some pretty strong language to censure his Nigerian deputies for putting personal gain before the mandate with which they had been entrusted by UN Headquarters in New York. To the credit of this officer, who was viewed by the majority of his detractors as a prevaricator, he was prepared to tie the Nigerian officer corps directly to Sierra Leone's illegal diamond trade.

Jetley: "The mission directive given to me and which I tried to follow implicitly, directly conflicted with the interests of not only the warring factions, but also the major players in the diamond racket like Liberia and Nigeria." As one diplomat in Freetown exclaimed when hearing the news: "Sounds like war talk to me."

In fact, what is astonishing is that the event came as something of a surprise because everybody in Freetown that mattered knew very well what the Nigerians were doing. The issue reeked of corruption. At the same time, while serving with ECOMOG forces in Liberia a couple of years before, the Nigerian Army had involved itself in similar illegal shenanigans. One Nigerian colonel ended up exporting about a million dollars of tropical hardwoods to Europe through an associate who went on to make him a director of his company.

And then, when it was all over, Jetley, by now back in New Delhi, was again questioned about these accusations by the BBC and once more he surprised everybody. He said he really couldn't remember saying what he did!

A postscript to that little exercise came afterward at the Cape Sierra Hotel. Jetley's role in the war came up for discussion among a bunch of journalists who were propping up the bar. Some of the comments weren't exactly flattering.

Said one choleric, rumpled old hack whose paper is famously to the left of center (and therefore usually in favor of everything that Kofi Annan does) that what was happening in Sierra Leone just then was really not that different from numerous other "peacekeeping" operations elsewhere. He'd seen a lot of them, he said. By reputation, I knew that he had. He reckoned that the deadlock that had enveloped Sierra Leone's war was no different to what was happening just about everywhere the world body was—or had been—active: South Lebanon, the Middle East, Angola, the Congo, Eritrea and elsewhere. And what did they have to show for it?

"Nothing! It's all been a monumental waste of money," he declared, looking at each one of us in turn.

Notably, he added, it was UN soldiers that stood helplessly by while seven thousand Muslims were massacred in the Bosnian town of Srebrenica only five years before. Our journalist friend was sure of his facts because he'd been there, too.

Compare all this with the previous mercenary operation in Sierra Leone when Executive Outcomes cleared most of the country of an RUF presence. The first of these war dogs were brought into the country from South Africa in early 1995. Twenty-one months later they had been successful enough to force Sankoh, by then driven out of the country, to sue for peace.

Throughout, EO never had more than two hundred men in the country at any one time. Usually it was something like seventy-five. In the end, this ragged, ultra-aggressive group of bearded toughies completed the task while taking minimal casualties themselves. Overall, there were perhaps a dozen of them killed or wounded. Also, the cost was a modest $35 million. Another report spoke of $62 million, which was never confirmed. Nor did any of the former EO directors ever get to talk about it. Either way it was a drop in a pisspot compared to what the UN had been splurging in a year.

Were Sandline given the green light to do the same three years later, the British firm was going to charge more than the original figure, perhaps $50 million, though again the figures are hazy. It would have been a more expansive operation anyway because the rebels were believed to have increased their fighting strength three or four-fold and Sandline would almost certainly have needed to use a larger force.

Specifics about the earlier EO operation only emerged much later. They are illuminating since it provides parameters within which this mercenary force operated. For a start, the EO squad that eventually set out from Freetown to take the Kono diamond fields in August 1995 was composed of a hundred-and-eighty-five men. Of these, about a dozen were white and the rest were black. Like the whites, these South African blacks were all veterans of decades of Angolan and Namibian conflict.

For close air support, the strike force had two Mi-17 gunship/troop carriers. One of them was "Bokkie," a veteran of half-a-dozen military campaigns, which was eventually taken over by Nellis in lieu of a settlement payment when the Sandline operation was aborted. Though used mainly in transport roles, the Hips could lay down a pretty heavy field of covering fire from its two, sometimes three, automatic weapons mounted to port, starboard and quite often in the rear.

EO's regulars were backed by two rattling old BMP-2 armored personnel carriers that offered muscle on the ground. It wasn't much, but enough to rout the rebels each time they were used. I was onboard one of them as an observer for *Jane's International Defense Review* when an EO team hit a rebel base in the Koidu area. Tactically, it was to become something of a touchstone for this kind of unconventional warfare: (see Chapter 23).

Not very long afterward, the rescue of more than two hundred members of a United Nations peacekeeping mission underscored the preeminence of the role of the combat helicopter in Third World wars. The operation took place in a remote and isolated corner of Sierra Leone in August, 2000.

Classic in style, this was British-planned and executed. It was also a brilliantly executed operation that involved a pair of RAF Chinooks as well as several Indian Air Force Mi-24 attack helicopters. UN flight crews had obviously been studying Nellis' tactics earlier in the war because they went in fast and low and hit everything on the ground that moved.

That it took place at all was remarkable. Until then, General Jetley had been reluctant to use his forces offensively. In particular, he had never deployed the Indian Air Force Hinds until a month or two before he went home because, he reckoned, all the aircraft in white UN livery would then come under attack. In theory he might have been right. But, as someone else asked, if that was the issue, then what the hell was he doing in Sierra Leone?

It took a concerted effort to get the man to do something about the deteriorating security position in the interior. The week before the August operation, *Jane's Defence Weekly* published an unflattering critique of his reluctance to curb rebel excesses.[6] As Brigadier Richards commented, he was in control of the biggest military force in a region twice the size of Europe and he was doing nothing with it.

What only became clear much later was that the British must have pulled a few strings, because when the first attack came it was a big one that totally routed the enemy. Its effect on the RUF morale was drastic enough to cause a spate of rebel desertions. A year later the war was over and almost all the rebel leaders who were in Sierra Leone at the time were in custody. Those who remained behind in Liberia went on to offer their services to President Charles Taylor in a bid to help quell an escalating domestic insurgency of his own.

By the middle of 2002, Liberia's woes had escalated and a succession of isolated jungle spats had become a civil war. Eventually that conflagration wavered and another started in the Ivory Coast.

Through it all, Lt-Col. Rob Symonds always liked to talk about the vital role of the helicopter in what he afterward termed "my little war." He made the point often enough that no single asset had been as pivotal in containing rebel assaults as the Air Wing's Mi-24 attack helicopter. The media of a dozen nations carried his comments.

The "child syndrome" that British forces encountered when they routed the West Side Boys was one of the more disturbing developments of what was taking place in Sierra Leone. It is a phenomenon that seems to be on the increase in Africa. Child rebels, it would appear, have always been more violent and unthinking in conflict than adults, evidence of which has been presented repeatedly in Sierra Leone, Liberia, Uganda and the Congo. In fact, the issue has presented itself wherever these supposed innocents are manipulated by warlords. In the Congo, for instance, it has been that way for generations. For all the other contradictions linked to Africa's so-called Imperial Era, even the more politically correct among us have to concede that it was never like that in Colonial times. But now, suddenly we're seeing a lot of it.

The media tends toward apoplexy whenever it sees dead kids following a firefight. Sadly, few bother to check the details. Case in point here is something experienced by ICI's Danny O'Brien during the first RUF invasion of Freetown in the late 1990s.

Having ferried members of Nigeria's ECOMOG Force into the airport area around Lungi, Sierra Leone's only international airport, he then helped them with ammo and weapons supplies. Following one such delivery, O'Brien was at Lungi when Sankoh's people launched a huge counterattack involving hundreds of rebels. As he told me, "They arrived in several trucks and a school bus. Without ceremony, the entire force was routed and quite a few of the attackers—some of whom were eight or nine—were killed." The rest were disarmed and herded together, by which time a bunch of journalists arrived.

"All that the press saw was the school bus. In fact, it was about all they looked at. What they found was a school bus with almost all of its windows shot out. The vehicle itself was riddled by bullets as were a number of children. Many were either dead, wounded or in custody. Our helicopter and its white crew was on the tarmac nearby and it soon became obvious that these scribes were going to reach their own conclusions about mercenaries.

"They didn't bother to ask us what had happened there. Naturally, the stories that appeared made a splash abroad," O'Brien recounted.

In both Freetown and Monrovia, the authorities concede that a lot more went on in the war in the interior than most of them could even begin to comprehend. One Swiss social worker admitted, "We will never know anything about some of the worst of the excesses, cannibalism, the murder of pregnant women and children."

For instance, the feared Small Boys Units of the RUF was notorious for carrying out grisly acts of violence, many of them unconscionable. Martin Coker, a neo-Marxist, British-educated spokesman for the RUF, told Steve Coll of *The Washington Post* in Buedu that he not only supported the use of children in war but he also abhorred the West's criticism of "child soldiers."

These were, as he quaintly phrased it, "elitist human rights activists," adding that those who protested about such things were out of touch.

"They fail to understand that in a people's army, families had to move together on the front lines—husband, wife and children, all fighting the people's war," he explained. It had nothing to do with terrorism, he is reported to have subsequently broadcast on "Radio Freedom: The Voice of the People's Army of Sierra Leone." This was an FM station in Buedu in the eastern corner of the country that Coker helped establish for the RUF Command. He offered no comment about the almost four thousand children that were subsequently declared missing by their parents.

John Sweeney, reporting from Freetown for the Johannesburg *Mail & Guardian*, was able to interview three twelve-year-olds who had been taken by the RUF. All were about nine or ten years old and were made to fight, having been specifically recruited for one of the organization's Small Boy Units. While all sides in involved in this carnage had SBUs, "people tell you that the RUF were the worst," Sweeney is on record as saying.

As a consequence of these developments, one of the problems that now face the international community is whether these underage Sierra Leonian terrorists were actually aware of what they have been accused of doing. Most of the perpetrators claim they were drunk or on drugs. There are no clear answers and the debate goes on, as it eventually will in the Ivory Coast, the Niger Delta, where another conflict looms because of oil, Darfur and elsewhere on a continent that knows no bounds to its misery. The population is also kept in line by death threats if they try to escape, or the threat of liquidation of their friends and possibly family—if their parents are still alive.

Significantly, this is a recurring problem in so many countries in Africa. In the early 1960s, as we are to see in subsequent chapters of this book, the Congo's "Simba" rebels who took European hostages in Stanleyville (today Kisangani) allowed the children among them to torture their victims. They raped nuns, often in public in the town square. Following the accession to power of President Mobutu, all prosecutions for these crimes were put on hold because it was maintained that "it was the adults who had unduly influenced these young people."

Some Belgian social workers objected and said at the time that that was simply not the case. They maintained that youngsters who were psychotic initiated many of the brutalities—including many hostage deaths.

The same holds for Uganda today. In early September 2000, a group of Lord's Resistance Army (LRA) rebels based in the southern Sudan killed nineteen people in attacks around the towns of Kitgum. LRA cadres near Gulu massacred others. Local villagers say that some of those involved were juveniles. Like adult LRA members, they were armed with AKs and RPG-7 rockets and took part in ritual killings of anybody who was suspected of being pro-government. No proof was needed: somebody just had to point a finger and that person was dead. It mattered not at all that according to the Geneva Convention such acts are of a terrorist nature and are categorized as war crimes.

The same kind of thing, but certainly not as widespread, took place in South Africa during the apartheid epoch. While children did not spearhead anti-government protests, they instigated a lot of the violence. Very few of these juveniles have ever been tried in the country's courts, even though some of the victims died after being "necklaced," a particularly brutal system of immolation, usually initiated by gangs of youths.[7]

7

STRANGE BEDFELLOWS IN MERCENARY WARS

Fm—Regional Cmdr North (Makeni)
To—Overall RUF S/L (Brigadier Issa Sesay)
Subject—Report dated today 20 June 2000

Sir, Our delegates were attacked today while on the way for
UCOWAS meeting in Lunsar. This attack was done by the
heli-gunship twelve (12) miles fm this location. Ten (10) KIA,
five (5) seriously wounded including radio operator Sheku
Compass with one hand cut off. Radio set battered beyond
repairs (c/s 072 Kovine). Immediate admin request. Medical
help for the brothers and immediate replacement of this operator. Accept info for ack.

Rebel message: Cockerill Barracks, June 20, 2000

About halfway through my stay in Sierra Leone, a signal was intercepted at Army headquarters following Nellis' ambush of a rebel convoy on the road between Lunsar and Makeni. The strike had killed
and wounded some of the key players in Foday Sankoh's rebel command. Ironically, the Nigerian commanding general in charge of UN
operations in this troubled West African state ended up losing his job
because of it.

The entire affair dripped duplicity, and it had a direct effect on the
course of the war. It surprised no one to learn afterward that once the
people involved in this double-cross were identified, Nellis used his
own initiative to bring the matter to a rapid conclusion. He ended it
in an opportunistic raid by relying more on gut instinct than military
intelligence.

The incident has all the features for an outstanding Hollywood
thriller: secret night meetings between the military leaders of opposing
forces, deals to subvert government authority, radio intercepts, phone
taps involving the British High Commission and its staff, and so forth.

The mercenary component added another dimension. Avarice, betrayal and deceit compounded the treachery. The trouble was that none of it was fiction pouring from a screenwriter's pen, and the survival of a nation hung in the balance. Some of the players—the Nigerians in particular—were interested only in how much loot, payable in diamonds, they could reap from the sorry episode. Their dubious commitment to Sierra Leone had always been about money, so there was nothing shocking about that.

After this sad little chapter, apart from getting a new boss, UN operations in this embattled West African state were restructured from the top down. Significantly, orders implementing these changes came directly from the office of the Secretary General, Kofi Annan. Ultimately, Whitehall was obliged to play a more forceful role, both in Freetown's internal politics and in the war itself, which was just as well because it was the large British military contingent in Sierra Leone that eventually forced the insurgency first to falter, and then fail altogether. But that took a while. In between, there was even more conspiracy, murder and pillaging.

Nellis' outline of the events that led up to this attack set the scene for what followed:

> A few days before June 19, we intercepted a radio message from the regional rebel headquarters in Makeni. This indicated that they'd been in contact with Nigerian General Garba, that irascible and totally unpredictable second-in-command of the UN here. Sankoh's people obviously weren't aware that we were monitoring his calls and we only did so because we'd had intelligence that he was dealing directly with the rebels. They were enemy, dammit!
>
> The message we'd got indicated that the rebels had been given Garba's satellite phone number and that a meeting was to be scheduled for the following week. The nub of it was that Garba had apparently suggested to the rebel command that New York wanted to deal, which, of course, was nonsense. But he went ahead anyway and said that it was his job to explore the possibility of all the parties involved in the war returning to the Lome Peace Accord.
>
> What he didn't tell the RUF was that the Freetown government had nothing to do with it. In fact, they didn't even know he was talking to the enemy, never mind the meeting

he'd arranged. Essentially, this was treason.

There were no specifics about any kind of time and place, but Garba suggested in one of the secret calls that the conference take place possibly in Makeni. It was to be between the rebel command, with representatives of several African countries present (again, under supposed UN auspices—for which you can read instead General Garba since it was to be his show). We got the impression fairly early on that the Nigerian general was determined to be present, if only for the rewards that he imagined this tidy bit of sedition would eventually bring.

By now, the government was aware of what Garba was up to but details were restricted to only a handful at the top and that included the President: this was one time they didn't want any leaks.

On Saturday, June 17, Army Intelligence determined a tentative date for Garba's little get-together. It was on for the following Monday, just two days ahead.

At that stage, everything pointed to it taking place at Lunsar although we couldn't be certain. It made good sense, though. The town was close enough for both sides to get to without too many problems and Garba could get there easily enough in one of the UN choppers. Also, Lunsar was relatively isolated and whatever took place there wouldn't draw attention, especially from the government or media. The probable time was set for about 1000 hours.

On the face of it then, it seemed that Garba had brokered an arrangement convenient to both himself and the rebels, Nellis told me with a grin that was as insouciant as it was wicked.

Nellis spoke to Colonel Tom Carew, his Chief of Defense Staff about the matter, confirming that the government was not a party to any meetings between the UN and the rebels. The reply inferred that the show was solely Garba's doing. Carew was emphatic when he and Nellis discussed the matter—as the CDS did occasionally with Nellis when he needed to get something off his chest that President Kabbah's government would never sanction anything like that, especially "if it were to take place in isolation of any ongoing efforts by Freetown to achieve a lasting political and military solution to the war."

Nellis could visualize how the meeting would go down. "We were aware that if it were to happen at all, the (bogus) UN delegation would most likely get there by UN helicopter," he explained. "Being second in charge of UNAMSIL, Garba could commandeer one at will without questions being asked and they'd take her in at a disused airfield near the RUF headquarters adjacent to Lunsar's old iron ore mine. My intention was to get airborne about fifteen or twenty minutes before they left and hope to hell that the rebels on the ground waiting for the delegates would believe that my rotors were those bringing the Nigerian and his entourage." Nellis continued: - "Obviously, I was also counting on them all to be gathered together in one area. I'd surprise them in the open, though I'd have to get in and out before the UN contingent arrived." The intention was that the UN helicopter would be greeted by a bunch of very freshly dead rebel bodies.

Nellis armed the Hind's Gatling and two pods of 57mm rockets, "courtesy of the United Nations." Ironically, these were the same munitions returned to Cockerill Barracks at General Jetley's behest only days earlier. By a curious twist, it was Garba who had signed the release.

Rather than use the other Mi-24 with its larger 80mm rocket pods (which make for a bigger killing radius) Nellis reckoned that the smaller projectiles would be the better option if he came in low and fast. That way, he'd be able to launch at the last moment and ensure sharper accuracy. It wasn't always possible to do that with 80mm projectiles, explained the South African. "They had a greater radius of impact and with them I'd have to stand off a bit. If we didn't fire from a reasonable distance with 80mm rockets, there was a chance that we'd take hits from our own shrapnel if we came in on a very low profile, which, under the circumstances, was essential."

On the day of the planned ambush, Nellis met for an early breakfast with his Deputy Minister of Defense, Chief Hinga Norman.[1] The pilot explained the situation in some detail. Nellis was well aware that almost nothing affecting the course of the war or those involved in it escaped Chief Norman's notice. The chief was also the same man who had been fingered as having been a secret RUF supporter during an earlier phase of hostilities, but had been pardoned after the Lome Accord had brought the war temporarily to a halt. Things had changed a lot since then, and Nellis sensed that the chief, in his new cabinet position, was now firmly on the right side.

Nellis outlined his plan of attack. He wanted his boss' opinion on the political implications if he were to take out an RUF convoy on its way to supposed "peace talks." If he were successful, he knew, there would be some very loud noises made afterward in the world media. And if his luck held, he would end up killing some top RUF men, including front-line commanders. Chief Hinga smiled at the news, sat back in his chair, and told Nellis not to worry himself with such things. That was his bailiwick, he added. "It's not us they're making peace with! You do what you have to do."

What Nellis actually wanted Chief Norman to do was officially sanction the strike. It was one thing to act on innuendo, and altogether something else to receive a direct order. A wily old battler and well into his sixties, the chief understood military procedures quite well, largely because he had served in the British Army when he was young. Before Nellis left the chief's office—and probably because the issue was so sensitive—the minister phoned UN Commander General Jetley. In the pilot's presence the defense minister asked him, almost in as many words, whether he was aware of any meetings with the rebels. The question put to Jetley was whether he was aware of any UN operation in the Lunsar area that day. The Chief explained that he wanted to task the Hind on a recce in that sector and was not able to guarantee the safety of anybody else that might be there.

"No," Jetley answered, his tone indicating annoyance. There was nothing happening, of that he was certain, he declared.

Chief Norman warned the Indian General that the Air Wing would be conducting an armed reconnaissance around Lunsar and that his government couldn't be held responsible for any attacks on unauthorized UN patrols operating in that area. Jetley accepted that position and didn't argue any of its finer details.

The conversation was enlightening, thought Nellis. If the Indian had been in any way a party to this conspiracy, he would almost surely have asked more questions or possibly he would have acted differently. There was nothing defensive about his responses. "Instead he seemed straight up and down. His immediate reactions—direct and to the point—told us pretty conclusively that he'd nothing to hide," explained Nellis. It was also significant that the deputy minister did not bother to call Jetley's Nigerian deputy, General Garba; everybody who mattered at Cockerill already knew of the Nigerian's involvement in the plot.

"Based on the Jetley response, Chief Norman gave me the clearance I sought," Nellis said. "I was to carry out an armed patrol of the road between Lunsar and Makeni. Being the wily politician, he never instructed me deliberately to seek and destroy any rebel convoy, but instead, stated that he had been given assurances by Jetley that nothing was expected so I should go ahead and do my job, which I did." Norman added one more thing. "He told me to use my discretion if any target presented itself," continued Nellis. "Those were his last words before I left his office."

The planning discussions at Cockerill had also helped clarify something that had been worrying everyone for some time: a deep-rooted animosity existed between Jetley and Garba. It was apparently a rift of long standing. The events that followed would eventually result in both men being relieved of their commands

Nellis' plan had a second phase. If nothing was happening at Lunsar by the time he got there, he would follow the Makeni road and see if there was anything or anybody moving along it. Cockerill was aware that if Garba got cold feet and decided to cancel, he would not be able to get a message through to the RUF command in time to stop the convoy.

As far as Nellis was concerned, it was a fine time for war. The visibility was perfect. It was one of those bright sunny West African days when a target can be seen for miles. Unfortunately, the clear weather cuts both ways: the rebels would be able to spot his chopper from a long distance.

The Air Wing actually planned for a late take-off, because time means nothing in Africa. "Pitching up for an appointment an hour late is normal," Nellis explained.

"Once over Lunsar, we saw nothing. There were no vehicles in the area, nor any groups of people either in town or in the surrounding area. It didn't make sense. What was immediately clear was that the RUF delegation was late. So, accepting the second option, down the road we flew. We clipped along less than fifty feet above the ground, staying low so that if anything was ahead, we'd surprise them. They'd be certain to have Triple-A mounted on their vehicles."

Nellis liked the odds. "The way I saw it, I was pretty certain that we'd have the advantage of surprise because the last thing the rebels would have been expecting was us hitting them from the air. After all, they did have Garba's word on it, and since he was the second most powerful military man in the country, the rebel command must have been confident that he would see to it that nothing was allowed to happen. In their minds, it was probably a given that he would ensure their safe passage. The meeting had been the UN's idea and that must have been a guarantee of sorts."

Shortly after passing over the village of Macut, about eight miles from the town of Makeni, the gunship breasted a low hill. At that moment Nellis spotted a four-vehicle convoy heading his way. In the lead was a Toyota Landcruiser escorted by a pair of motorcycles. A pick-up with a Dshka mounted on the back followed a couple of hundred yards behind the three lead vehicles with a five or six-man gun crew crowded around it.

Nellis' immediate instinct was to go right in. With the first bike in his sights, he delivered a burst with the Gatling. The target disintegrated and hurled what was left of the driver and bike in a crumpled heap into the bush. The second motorcycle wobbled perilously for a moment and then ran headlong into a ditch. Nellis locked the Landcruiser in his sights and shattered its windscreen. A split-second later its fuel tank exploded.

The driver of the rear pickup jumped on his brakes but Nellis was able to get in a short burst, most of which went wide. The entire attack had lasted only seconds.

Throwing the Hind hard to port, the pilot banked and came in again. Hassan shouted through the mike that the rebels were bombshelling from the last three vehicles which, Nellis anticipated, probably carried the main delegation. He recalled later, foliage and cover was the only option left to them. Another whoop from Hassan and the two side-gunners joined in. Both he and Lieutenant Schenks set about picking off targets with their GPMGs.

The next time Nellis brought the helicopter around, he used his rockets. A couple of rebels who had remained with the pickup were trying to swing the gun around, but they were struggling with what seemed to be a jam. A salvo of sixteen rockets went into the pickup, eight from each pod. "Thus were a few more gooks sacrificed for the cause," was how the South African later put it. Another low altitude turn and more rockets raked thickets where Hassan had spotted some of the rebels taking cover.

"After that strike there was no more resistance. We were able to concentrate on eliminating the other vehicles, and the individual members of the delegation who were still trying to escape. Because the bush wasn't as thick as elsewhere, Hassan spotted some of them trying to crawl along a gulley. He asked me to bank to starboard, and then set about doing the necessary," explained Nellis. "I knew that we would never be able to account for every single member of the party, but it was not for want of trying. Anyway, by then I'd had a stoppage on the Gatling and that ended the exercise. Also, we were out of rockets, so I decided to call it a day."

The flow of radio intercepts at Cockerill didn't stop for the rest of the day. They poured in from all over Sierra Leone—Makeni, Kono, everywhere. Some originated from Liberia, inquiring as to the where-abouts of a General Sesay. The rebel command was clearly rattled by the crippling strike. Intercepts the following day confirmed that Nellis had knocked out the convoy's communications on his first pass, re-moving the radio operator's hand in the process. As a result, no one at either Lunsar or Makeni had any idea of what had taken place, or even that there had been an attack. Only after dark—and then tenta-tively, for fear of a night strike—did another convoy set off from Makeni. Their orders were to find out what had happened to the RUF interim leader. With Foday Sankoh in jail by this time, Sesay had recently been appointed head of the rebel junta. Sesay was lucky: he had only been lightly hurt in the attack. Ten others were killed out-right, including several senior regional commanders. Early reports suggested that Brigadier General Maurice Kallon, the head of the northern axis of the RUF war effort, was dead, but this later proved false. Another battlefield commander, Dennis Mingo, alias "Super-man," was wounded in the attack. In fact, just about everybody in the convoy took some kind of hit, with several very badly wounded.

More damaging, especially to future United Nations/RUF rela-tions, was that Garba and his entourage never showed up at Lunsar. Had his group of "negotiators" at least made the attempt to do so, they might have had a case to argue. Neither did they indicate to any-one that they weren't going to make it. Garba and several others with him could have easily used their satellite phone to cancel, but they did not. The rebels, therefore, had good reason to believe they had been betrayed. And, of course, they had been. In their own words, "The Nigerian betrayed us." The consensus at Cockerill Barracks was that Garba was intimidated by Chief Hinga's questions to his boss. Nellis surmised that Jetley spoke to his Nigerian deputy about the call and the Fulani officer probably sensed a catastrophe about to erupt.

Once the strike was announced, Garba resorted to invective. He immediately launched a campaign of words against several British officers seconded to the Sierra Leone Army, accusing them of bugging his satellite phone and intercepting his messages. He followed that up with a bitter attack on Whitehall and Britain generally, claiming that Africa's cause had been betrayed. "They tried to undermine my command!" he told his deputy, spitting out the words in a characteristic display of unrestrained tribal fury.

Several choice comments were reserved for Colonel Mike Dent, the CDS's opposite number with the British military advisory contingent. Sitting across the table from him at the next staff meeting, Garba traded more insults. Undeterred, Dent apparently told the man to fuck himself.

Garba's troubles had only just begun. The rebels condemned him in their propaganda broadcasts for playing a double game. They had been led into a trap, they cried, and he would pay for the murders. At Cockerill the mood was upbeat, even though no one was fully aware of the details about how the rebel itinerary and dates had been leaked, or why the gunship was on the Makeni road when it was. Gradually aspects of the ambush filtered into town and the event was portrayed as "a great victory for President Kabbah."

Looking back, Nellis is not so certain his mission on the Makeni road was as successful as some made it out to be. The strike had indeed boosted the sagging morale of both the government and the army. The newspapers could not get enough of the story, though without the behind-the-scenes details. As more details emerged about the UN's—and, in particular, Garba's—duplicity, a visible rift appeared between the Nigerian and Indian factions in West Africa. Ultimately this divide led to New Delhi pulling its troops out of the UN force altogether, followed shortly afterward by Annan's declaration that the Jordanian contingent would leave as well. The moves depleted the UN "peacekeeping" strength in Sierra Leone by about a quarter, and obliged Britain to take on a more obtrusive security role. In spite of protests from the Tory opposition, by the end of that year the British government had a Royal Navy and Royal Marine strike force stationed semipermanently off the coast of West Africa. Also, the Nigerian Army in Sierra Leone was forced to temper its dealings with the RUF. Had these been allowed to continue, Kabbah's government would have been pushed further into isolation.

There were several results that troubled Nellis. First, both Jetley and Garba were aware that they had been duped; from then on, both refused to provide the Air Wing with any more help. Until the strike, the Hinds had been fueled at UN depots at both Lungi and Hastings Airports. Jetley saw to it that those facilities were put off-limits to the two Mi-24s. The same applied to ammunition, which led to some serious shortages a month or so later. Whitehall had to schedule several emergency arms deliveries by air and these too, were questioned in Westminster.

In the past, a grudging pact had existed between the Air Wing and the UN force, but relations hadn't been good since the first phase of the UN operation. There had been several fractious encounters in months past, and a deep suspicion between the two parties developed as a consequence. Jetley, who usually played the role of the panderer, treated Nellis and his crowd like adversaries. This was a very different situation compared to their previous relationship.

The consequence of Jetley's actions became more apparent a few weeks later, when Nellis' helicopter was ordered to attack a rebel target about two weeks after the ambush strike on the Makeni road. The South African accompanied Colonel Carew to Garba's office with requests for ammunition and spare parts. The moment the two men stepped inside the door the Nigerian became belligerent. "He refused us everything we'd asked for, saying that he wasn't prepared to give us any assistance whatever," recalled Nellis. He also accused the Air Wing of destroying his efforts in trying to secure a peace process.

"It didn't help that despite the CDS being present, he was being his usual insidious self and I wasn't in a position to say anything. Perhaps I should have congratulated him for being candid. At least we knew where we stood with each other," Nellis concluded.

It took the British military aid contingent and the Sierra Leone Army several months of fence-building before anything resembling a working relationship was put in place. Although the situation improved with time, the relationship never reverted to what it had been before the Makeni road strike.

The ongoing war and its daily rebel atrocities did not allow the impasse to go on indefinitely. Nellis' ambush might have scored some points, but the retaliating rebels intensified their barbarism in all the towns and villages under their control. Fortunately most of the civilian population had already fled.

Six weeks after the incident, the UN asked Nellis to take the Hind and attack a village in the eastern part of the country. Under Operation Kukri, the area had come under strong Indian Air Force Mi-24 fire during the rescue of a batch of UN soldiers being held hostage by RUF rebels. The Indian gunships razed the place. Nellis was told that there were still some rebel targets intact, including a radio center. "The idea was that I should hit the village the day after Op Kukri. Out of nowhere, Garba—all charm and snake oil—gives me a clearance to eliminate any infrastructures that were still intact and, as he said, I was to kill anyone found there. So, to me, it starts to smell bad."

Nellis was good at sniffing out rats, and to him this operation had all the hallmarks of a typical underhanded Nigerian move. By this time even the UN higher-ups in New York were aware that Garba was up to no good. His motive became clear soon enough. Garba's intent was to transfer blame for the destruction by UN gunships onto Nellis and the Air Wing. This, in turn, would allow the Nigerian general to tell the rebels that his people had never been involved in any attack. "I wasn't prepared to become Garba's scapegoat for any UN white-wash," Nellis said. "We had a fairly good measure of these people by then."

Stretching the limits of his own credibility, Nellis reported to the UN office at the Mammy Yoko Hotel later that same day that neither of his aircraft was serviceable, adding that it would be impossible to carry out any strikes for a day or two. The South African was convinced that had he gone ahead and made the attack as Garba suggested, pressure would have been placed on Kabbah's government to restrict all operational flights involving the Air Wing's Hinds. He and the rest of the crew might even have been expelled from Sierra Leone.

An incident that had taken place a short time earlier only served to compound Nellis' problems. Headquarters at Cockerill Barracks received information that the RUF was rebuilding several boats at Manowa Junction in order to transport captured ECOMOG and UN vehicles and equipment to Liberia. Nellis was given the job of knocking out all enemy assets associated with this venture, which he promptly did. After that attack, the rebels refused to continue negotiating with Jetley's staff for the release of Indian troops being held in Kailahun, a small town near the Guinea frontier that was also the focus of rebel communications.

This placed the UN Command in something of a quandary since the hostage situation in Kailahun had suddenly become desperate. A couple of hundred Indian and other nationals—all of them serving UN personnel—were being kept prisoner under dreadful conditions. They had minimal food and no medical supplies worthy of the name; many had come down with malaria. Although none of them had died, it was only a matter of time before the situation worsened. The Indian general was now in an untenable position, and for once he had no option but to do something. The operation that followed also involved elements of the RAF.

Nellis provided for me the background to some of these events, which clearly demonstrated the UN's predilection for prevarication and, not to put too fine a point on it, Jetley's chronic indecision. "With Operation Kukri, you need to remember that it was largely a case of Indian forces rescuing their Indian counterparts, with little involvement from the other units. The British made available their choppers together with Special Forces for reconnaissance and the rescue of MILOBS (military observers)," explained Nellis. "And then only because there was a British officer among the prisoners."

The operation was supposed to be a coordinated affair with the RAF and Indian Air Force choppers. Nellis continued: "They would go in together in what was planned as a surprise raid. However, there was a thick mist over the target early on the morning in question and Jetley insisted on a delay. He told the RAF that he wanted to allow for the viz to improve. The British refused and went in anyway." As Nellis tells it, "The Indian gunships followed hours later and by that time most of the RUF had fled the area. As it happened, the Chinooks did the job on their own. They performed like heroes, taking out all the hostages without loss."

Magnificent action photos of the operation snapped by British freelance photographer Patrick Allen showed these graceful giants hovering a few feet above the jungle while putting down suppressing fire and shooting off strings of anti-missile flares. It was an impressive display with the twin-rotor helos, each with two six-barrel Gatlings (one to port and the other to starboard), together with a GPMG on lowered ramps to the rear. Since all the guns onboard were 7.62mm NATO, the firepower was awesome.

In general, Nellis recalled afterward, "The perception was that Op Kukri didn't have too much of an effect because there was no followup. There was no attempt to dominate and hold ground taken in the attack. Consequently, the rebels reoccupied their original areas immediately afterward." But, as he remembers, "that it happened at all was remarkable. Until then, the UN General had been typically Indian in his behavior, the ultimate equivocator."

Yet not all Indian forces in Sierra Leone followed the example of their commanding general. Kashmir had long ago proved that the Indian Army could fight, and damn well too, if there was need.

Among Jetley's units in West Africa were two battalions that had been on active service in Kashmir. They had performed outstandingly against Pakistani-supported Hizbollah guerrillas in the mountainous enclave that included some of the most difficult fighting terrain in the world.

During my interview with General Jetley for *Jane's Defence Weekly*, he explained that bringing these men to Africa had been "something of a reward" for time spent in Kashmir. He was poker faced about it since, he said, the matter centered solely on economics. While serving on the Indian subcontinent, he explained, these men were paid only a fraction of what they got when they donned blue "peacekeeping" uniforms. With the UN, he declared, the basic salary was roughly $1,000 a month. "Money talks the same language wherever you are," said this effete little man who had a mental sail so rigged as to be swelled by the slightest puffery.

An interesting sidelight to Nellis' attack on the RUF convoy near Makeni involved a little socializing afterward with Lt-Col. Rob Symonds, the British Military Liaison Officer. Prior to the Makeni road attack (but only after he'd read the intercept that Garba's meeting was to take place) Nellis had casually questioned Symonds one evening as to whether he'd heard anything about a meeting between the rebels and the UN.

No, said the British officer, feigning indifference. Had Nellis heard anything? Negative. There were some rumors about, replied Nellis, but nothing concrete. Anyway, scuttlebutt on such issues was a feature of the Freetown scene.

Once Nellis ambushed the rebel column, he admitted to Symonds that same night that he'd actually known about Garba's actions all along. He hadn't wanted to mention it, he disclosed, because he feared that London might put the word out for him not to go ahead. Ironically, that was Symonds' position as well. The British Colonel was candid enough to admit to Nellis that he had also been aware of Garba's contacts with the RUF, but had stayed mum about it because he too feared that if he said anything, the people in charge might call the whole thing off. There must have been some pretty sophisticated monitoring devices installed at the High Commission in Freetown.

Flying combat in Africa can result in rich rewards. There are few restrictions, the money is usually good, nobody worries about dress codes, and the beaches are empty because tourists don't like being put at risk. Further, safety rules can be bent and there are almost none of the governances that might be encountered while flying over European or American airspace.

"The problem with crossing parts of West Africa in aircraft," explains Nellis, "is that there are people on the ground who sometimes like to shoot at you." He remembered one occasion when the rebels approached Freetown for the third or fourth time and Nellis had to use the Hind to haul in 1960s--vintage 105mm shell cases, charges, fuses, ammunition and food, as well as drums of diesel and petrol—all in the same load.

"This was the sort of stuff required by government units coming under rebel attack in the deep interior. We'd sometimes get there and the troops would be down to their last eight or ten cartridges per man," recalled the pilot. "Then, the moment we started making our approach, the fun would start. And sometimes we'd be subjected to a lot of ground fire." He reckons that a single tracer through his Hind could have set the lot off. Other times, as we saw before, gun-toting and often terrified soldiers would mob the crew as soon as they touched down. Blinded by fear, this was exactly the effect the rebels had been trying all along to cultivate. As the axiom goes, a fearful soldier doesn't always do what he's told.

This happened several times at Lunsar. Nellis would bring the chopper in and before they could even open the hatches, squads of soldiers would run up to the Hind and demand to be extradited. "Since the helicopter was their last option, it was pointless to talk about weight and space limitations, or that wounded were a priority," said Hassan.

"It didn't matter that we were armed—we had two or three AKs among us, together with the bigger stuff. Those making demands on us had a lot more firepower."

The last time something like this happened and it began getting out of hand, Hassan had a hard time trying to stop some of these crazies from running into the spinning tail rotor. It wasn't so much that he minded anybody's brains being splattered halfway across Africa. His concern was a more practical one: the Hind might not be able to get off the ground again after sending human bone and debris flying. Someone would then have to fly in a spare—if there was one—together with the technicians needed to replace it.

At Lunsar that evening, it was the third time that day that Nellis had taken the machine into action. It was also the day before the rebels would again overrun Lunsar. Nellis' chief concern was delivering the half-ton of ammunition he had on board. When his wheels touched ground, instead of helping off-load the ammo, the troops just stood about and watched while the crew did it themselves. "We simply had to," recalled Hassan. "Time was against us because it was already late. Also, if we didn't pull finger, we'd still be there."

Lieutenant Schenks was mad about the lack of assistance. "It didn't matter that we had brought them ammunition when they needed it most, not one of those bastards would help."

"It was a lot different when we started to wind the machine up again before lift-off," continued Hassan, who returned to Cockerill with scuffed knuckles. "Then they'd all come crowding around, some of them ugly. The only officer in the place was a Sierra Leone Army captain, and he had to warn his men off with a machine pistol. He had big balls, that guy. One man on his own in the middle of the jungle with a mutiny on his hands . . . you don't often see it that bad," the Shi'ite gunner recollected. It was a pretty close call. A few more seconds and the Hind might have been overrun with armed and angry troops. Even Hassan, veteran gunner that he was, was shaken by the time they got back to Cockerill.

After that incident Nellis refused to take calls to fly to Lunsar unless there was a responsible British officer on the ground, which was just as well because the rebels were massing in numbers on the outskirts of the place. Worse, they had already destroyed the Rolat road bridge between there and Rogberi, to their rear, which meant there was no avenue for a withdrawal from Lunsar. To Nellis, this indicated that there was at least someone involved with the rebels who knew something about planning, since it was way ahead of how the Sierra Leone Army—or for that matter, the rebels—had been used to operating in the past.

Judging solely from tactics used and the way the battle subsequently evolved, it was Nellis' view that someone else was pulling strings that day, and it wasn't rebels. "Some of the moves these people made were more than familiar—not RUF at all, which, like the SLA, does just about everything by the book, if they're sober, of course." The aviator was of the opinion that it was likely that South African mercenaries had trained his adversaries since several were known to be in the employ of the RUF. He probably even knew some of the men involved. We found out later this was indeed the case, and it annoyed us all.

Another time, a couple of years before, and shortly after the series of Makeni rescue incidents with the Nigerian ECOMOG force, Nellis and his crew had been tasked to go to Moyamba with "Bokkie," the Mi-17. The idea was to uplift as many of the Kamajors bush fighters as they could fit into the machine and take them to Freetown. With Makeni lost to the government, the rebels were again on the march toward the capital. The intention was to deploy these tough, aggressive veterans in the defense of the approaches to the city. But, as Nellis recounted, it did not work out as planned.

"We'd earlier lost one rear door and meantime, I'd had the other one removed as well. The result was that we were flying with the back of the aircraft wide open: not a good idea. We simply had no control over who might or might not have been trying to get onboard, especially when conditions were chaotic, which they often were. Also, we were sharply aware that Executive Outcomes had lost one of their helicopters through ill-disciplined soldiers running away from battle. That incident had almost got two crews killed. So when we finally did land at Moyamba, we had these Kamajors storming us, but for a different reason. Unlike the idiots at Lunsar, these guys actually wanted to fight and we'd been sent by their jungle gods to take them to war."

Nellis explained that it felt as though an entire company of Kamajors had squeezed in. Worse, not one of them would get off. When the crew was eventually able to do a head count, they found ninety-one of them onboard. Considered by one and all in Sierra Leone as mean bastards, their philosophy ran along the lines that whoever opposed their will was to be regarded as the enemy and killed.

'We were in something of a Catch-22 situation, and there was nothing we could do but sit it out," rationalized Nellis. "Since this mob refused to budge and there was no way I could take off, we'd reached a stalemate." He continued: "Basically, the LZ was a small football field surrounded by dozens of hundred-foot-high trees. Also, the outside air temperature was over a hundred, which didn't help either. And while 'Bokkie' wasn't underpowered, the Mi-17 definitely didn't have enough power to get out of a relatively confined area with that kind of load. It was well over twice the factory-recommended limit."

For a while the crew tried to entice some of the men to leave, but neither threats nor cajoling worked. Besides, it was dangerous to take too tough a line on these primitive tribesmen. "Our guys couldn't get

Hassan Ahmed Hussein, our Shi'ite gunner who brooked no opposition in any kind of action.
Author's collection

Neall Ellis, commonly known as "Nellis," at the controls of his Mi-24 "Hind."
Author's collection

"Bokkie," the trusty old Mi-17 "Hip" that EO and Nellis used to good effect in Sierra Leone.
Author's collection

Above and below left: The inscrutable terrain in which the Sierra Leone war was fought.

Author's collection

Right. Nellis and Hassan Ahmed Hussein at Cockerill Barracks discussing an upcoming mission. Note the Russian arms catalogs on the table next to the map.

Author's collection

Above and below. A rocket attack sequence taken by the author from the front bubble of Neall Ellis's Hind. Salvoes such as these could involve anything between 2 and 64 rockets being fired.

The target is a vehicle in the village with a 14.5mm machine gun mounted on the cab.

The first picture shows a cluster of eight rounds being fired. The second shows the vehicle hit and exploding in a ball of fire.

Author's collection

Opposite above: International Charter Incorporated of Oregon (ICI) operating former Soviet Mi-8 helicopters (flying the American flag!) over the jungle in Sierra Leone.

The pilots of both machines were Russians from Archangel.

Image courtesy of Nathan Jones.

Opposite below: The Sierra Leone Air Wing Mi-24 arriving back at Cockerill Barracks in Freetown.

Author's Collection

Above: Call-sign "Eagle Two," the Mi-24 that twice turned the war around in Sierra Leone.

Author's collection

Right: Fred Marafano in the bush with the Hind. When this shot was taken he was the front gunner on this machine.

Author's collection

Above: An Executive Outcomes column makes for the diamond fields in Sierra Leone. Note the Soviet-built AGS-17 grenade-launcher behind the driver and the BMP-2 APC following behind.

Photo: Cobus Claassens

Below: View from the sandbagged control tower at Lungi airport.

Author's collection

Above: "Christophe," the Sierra Leone Air Wing's irregular French side gunner (with Lt. Schenks pointing out a target) in action while firing at rebels in the Port Loko district.

Below: Preparing the helicopter gunship for an operation in the interior of Sierra Leone.

Russian mercenary pilot Nicolai Kagouk put the South Africans through their paces on the Mi-24 when they first arrived in Sierra Leone.
Author's collection

The rebels cleverly placed sheets of corrugated iron roofing across the tracks as an "early warning system." They would make an awful din when vehicles crossed them.
Author's collection

Executive Outcomes operational base at Koidu in the east. Note the Mi-17 on the heli-pad.
Author's collection

Above: American freebooter "Hawkeye" standing in front of one of ICI's Russian Built Mi-8 helicopters.
Image courtesy of Robin Hawke

Below: The rebel-held town of Wara Wara Hills in the north of the country takes a pasting from our Hind. Nellis wasn't concerned with collateral damage as most of the civilians had fled. Author's collection

In Appreciation of Outstanding Performance

ICI SECURITY LOGISTICS

N. Ellis

For your teamwork and outstanding contribution
to our efforts in Sierra Leone and the
evacuation of the U.S. Embassy, Monrovia, Liberia.

October 9th, 1998

Above left: A tribute from ICI to Nellis for his help in rescue efforts in Liberia.

Above: A British RAF Chinook on ops in Sierra Leone.

Left: British Lt. Colonel Rob Symonds (seated), discusses the day's events at Nellis's ready room in Cockerill Barracks. He was the military liaison officer at the British High Commission in Freetown.

Below: After Brigadier David Richards took control of security in Sierra Leone in 2000, order was quickly restored. Lungi airport, across the bay, soon resembled an army base.

Author's collection

Above: A tough bunch of mercs return after an action with Fred Marafano (second from right with Cobus Claassens on his right).

Below: Giant Antonov An-124s arrived at Lungi Airport each day with more equipment for an already bloated UN force.

Several Zimbabwe Air Force Helicopters (originally bought under the table from Israel) were shot down in Mugabe's Congo war which followed the ousting of the dictator Mobutu Sese Seko (below right).

Left: Former SAAF gunship pilot Dave Atkinson spent several spells fighting there with the ZAF.

Below left: One of Mugabe's generals involved in the bloody Congo debacle.

These Belgian paratroopers coordinated with Colonel Mike Hoare's legendary "Flying Geese" in the assault on the rebel stronghold of Stanleyville (today Kisingani) on the Congo River.

Above: Early operations in the Congo's Katanga province produced a mixed bag of combatants, including Mike Hoare's 5 Commando "flying column."

Left and left below: South African mercenaries bolstered this unconventional but extremely effective mobile force.

Below: Siegfied Müller was never seen without his Iron Cross, earned when he was a member of the SS.

Author's collection

Above: The dreaded "Colonel Callan" (back to camera) shortly before he was captured by a Cuban force and executed by firing squad.

Left: A Unita strike force uses what is left of the Angolan railroad to cover ground more quickly.

Below left: Portugese mercenaries in Angola after independence.

Below: Angolan Air Force MiG-21 shot down in eastern Angola by CIA-donated Stinger missiles.

Author's collection

Above: Mercenaries were also involved in Uganda's many conflicts, among them a large force of Libyans who, once the tyrant Idi Amin Dada had been ousted, were hunted wherever they were found and, like this one, butchered by locals.

Photo: Camerapix, Nairobi, courtesy of the late Mohammed Amin

Above right and below: These gruesome images speak for themselves.

Right: Some of the combatants were barely in their teens.

Author's collection

Above: Daniel Chipenda, head of "Chipa Esquadrao," takes the salute in Nova Lisboa (today Huambo). The author joined this unit to get his story.

Below: Dana Drenkowski—with 200 Vietnam missions in B-52's and F-4's behind him—was the only American pilot to be hired as a mercenary by Qaddafi. He is seen here with Jim Bolen bounty hunting in the Rhodesian war.

even one of them to stay. Also, they had been taking something powerful, which meant that they were about as spaced out as it can get," recalled the aviator. According to Nellis, the Kamajors weren't into dope or narcotics as we in the Western world understand drugs. Before each battle they would en masse go through a ritual of their own that involved drinking an extremely potent concoction that made them goofy. He thought it was probably something with a jungle methamphetamine base, though nobody was certain.

"These guys really were on cloud nine, and they were making a helluva din of it behind me. They could probably be heard singing and shouting a mile away," explained Nellis, who decided to try something else. "I realized then that the only way to get some of them back on the ground was to switch off and try to talk some sense to their leaders. We went through the motions, but that didn't work either."

By this time it was mid-afternoon, and the heat had been escalating, as it does in the tropics. Nellis knew it was like an oven in the rear, with all those people stuffed into a confined and airless compartment. They were jammed against each other like being stuffed into an overcrowded elevator. Perhaps nature would take care of the problem, he told Hassan.

"After an hour or so the racket began to ease. Some of the soldiers climbed out, all of them wet with sweat. Some went looking for water. Obviously there were quite a few who had dehydrated, which probably helped in the end," admitted the pilot. "Then it wasn't long before we managed to get a bit of order out of a situation that had been almost riotous. I promised their leader that we would take as many as we could in the first run and return immediately afterward to uplift the balance. That way we were able to select who was going to war and who wasn't, which was a complete reversal of our earlier experiences."

Hawkeye, the former American Special Forces veteran, had a stock of war stories of his own. Rampaging troops was nothing new to him. They had mobbed him several times. Working with International Charter Inc. of Oregon (ICI), the crew often took the Mi-8 to a distant military post on the edge of nowhere with the jungle a backdrop on all four sides. On touchdown, it was not unusual for the helicopter to be rushed by troops who, at gunpoint, would demand to be taken home. One time it was a bunch of government troops who boarded illegally the moment the helicopter landed. "That time, they simply refused to move," reported Hawkeye. "They pointed their muzzles at us and said that if we didn't get them out of there we'd die." It was a tough call, admitted the American. "Most times, though, we seemed to deal with it."

Hawkeye recalls landing near a contingent alongside the Rokel River, about thirty minutes north of Freetown (the same river that was later used as a base by the infamous West Side Boys). We knew that government forces had been taking a pasting from the rebels there and were falling back, almost all of them in disarray. Some of the younger men were discarding their uniforms and slipping back into the jungle. Others just fled as they were.

"We had come in to this position to take out some of their casualties," remembered the American freelancer. "Had that not been the reason, I wouldn't have considered getting near that hellhole. The trouble was, back at base they don't always go into any kind of detail about what we're likely to find there. So you get over the camp and look down and it all appears fine, but then you get on the ground and you find yourself in a disaster area! But a job's a fuckin' job," explained Hawkeye with a hollow laugh that echoed. Those who've been in a tight spot with him say that his guffaws get louder as the tension grows, a trait that tends to unsettle those who don't know him well. He continued: "Once we were firmly down, they really started to mob us. We just had to beat them back with our rifle butts, which was the only way we were able to stop them from swamping us. I broke a few bones that day."

Nor was that the end of it, since they still had to get out of there. As soon as the wounded had been uploaded Hawkeye turned toward the Russian pilot to signal to him get away pronto. Then the unthinkable happened. "One of those assholes grabbed Loneman, our rear-door gunner, and physically hauled him off the chopper." Only I wasn't to know it until later." Hawkeye explained that in the heat and kerfuffle of boarding, Loneman had somehow become separated from the rest and had taken up a position at the rear door. M-16 in hand, like the rest of the crew, he was trying to keep illegals away.

"I didn't actually see it happening. One moment the man was there and the next he's gone!" Hawkeye recalled. He explained that Loneman was one big, strong fellow and knew how to look after himself. Also, it wasn't the first time he'd had to use force to restrain a horde." "He was certainly a strange cat. On operations, he never had much to say and preferred to keep it like that, usually concentrating on the immediate task at hand. So we got on well and made a good team, which is what it's all about if you're going to survive in that crap."

Loneman had come to West Africa after volunteering for a tour of duty with ICI. Before that, he'd spent a while in the French Foreign Legion, one of the few Americans who could handle the pace there. Afterward he returned to the States and joined the 101st Air Assault Division. As experienced as Loneman was, Hawkeye knew the situation was critical. "At that moment, I had a big time problem on my hands: Loneman was missing and we were already into the hover. I turned to the pilot, but before I could catch his attention an M-16 flew through the back door and clattered against the bulkhead."

Confused, Hawkeye moved to the rear and peered over the edge to find Loneman hanging onto the chopper with one hand while desperately using the other to pry loose a couple of dozen fingers of other potential escapees who were gripping his legs. "There were three of them altogether, which gives you some idea of his strength," explained Hawkeye.

At about fifteen feet, the man at the bottom decided that this wasn't going to work and he let go. A few seconds later the number two guy slipped his grip and fell headlong to the ground. That left one more, "and he just wasn't going to let this opportunity go by in a hurry. By then we'd gained some height, perhaps forty or fifty feet. What I'd liked to have done was give our guy a hand, but then things were happening so fast."

"Obviously it couldn't last, so something had to happen, especially since the pilot still had no idea of the drama being played out behind him," continued Hawkeye. "The former Legionnaire shook the remaining man loose a second or two later, which was just as well because by then the Hip started topping trees at about ninety feet and there was a lot of incoming fire."

Like the athlete that he was, Loneman swung himself back onboard. "Only when we got back to base did he discover that his watch was gone and one of his ribs had been smashed," remembered his buddy. "That had happened when the soldiers pushed him over backwards. And that's when we knew damn well that the rebels really were coming for Freetown and that our people were losing the war.

"We never did tell our bosses what happened," admitted the American mercenary. "The guys in the States wouldn't have understood, and anyway, it was just too much of a close call. Medically I knew there was nothing to be done for Loneman's broken rib. I flew for him for a while until he'd healed enough to start operating again . . . doped him up enough to stand the pain, but still keep his wits."

The pilot later apologized to both of them. He knew it was a mess and reckoned that had circumstances been otherwise, it could have been avoided. What he didn't say was that if they had left Loneman behind, they would almost certainly have lost him.

Every helicopter team that has worked Sierra Leone has had similar experiences. During the course of Sierra Leone's four rebel invasions, there were probably enough close squeaks for somebody to publish a compendium of West African horror stories.

For instance, another time Hawkeye and crew reached a medevac site to find three truckloads of healthy soldiers, all of them desperate to get back to Freetown and beer. "This was a really terrified bunch of soldiers, we could see that even before we put our wheels down. But that wasn't our deal." Hawkeye remembered them "yelling like hellhounds, demanding a place on the chopper, but we ignored them while their buddies loaded the worst of the casualties onboard, some of whom would die on us before it was over. That done, almost the entire group piled onboard, some sixty or seventy of them."

There was no explaining or reasoning with this belligerent bunch. "What these assholes couldn't understand was that, in an ultra-extreme situation, a Russian Hip can take sixty men, which is about thirty over the limit. But then you're pushing your luck and you have additional factors like heat and humidity and getting into the hover. Still, they just kept coming. Soon they were three deep in the rear. We couldn't have lifted off had we tried."

There were other problems. First, the helicopter was low on fuel—really low. It was also getting dark. In the tropics, recalls Hawkeye, one minute there's light and the next there isn't. If the chopper was going to get out of there and make it back to base, the crew had only minutes to leave because there was no night vision equipment onboard. "I didn't even have to think about it before I threw off the man nearest me. Then I tackled the one next to him. I'd pushed off two more when a handful of them grabbed me by both arms and hurled me out the door!" Hawkeye was lucky in one regard: he still had his carbine. The problem was that everybody else was armed. Some soldiers were angry enough to turn their guns on him.

"I'd just picked myself up off the ground when the first man I'd ousted came at me, carbine in hand. He was bleeding from taking a hit when he'd exited, but I cuffed him with my butt and he went down again. Then his officer decided to rush me. With his muzzle at my chest, he said he was going to execute me." From that moment, recalled Hawkeye, everything moved at breakneck speed. Backing up toward the fuselage, he told the man that if he opened fire, he'd hit the chopper's fuel tanks and they'd all go up. For a moment that seemed to calm things.

The American decided to push his luck. "Look, Lieutenant. If we keep on arguing like this, nobody's going to get out because we can't fly in the fucking dark! You got me?" Hawkeye was shouting in his face. Those who could hear him over the roar of the rotors didn't argue. They couldn't.

Confident that he had their attention, he sketched a hasty plan. "Listen to me! We'll take thirty of your people out and that includes the wounded. Only thirty! No more! The worst of the casualties and you, Lieutenant. Then we'll come back for the others," he lied. Hawkeye knew he'd won when everybody stopped pushing. "It surprised us all that they acquiesced the way they did. A minute later we were airborne."

Fighting in remote regions also makes for strange bedfellows. Sometimes there would be a journalist or two asking for a ride to the front, and though Nellis liked to help—usually in the interests of creating what he termed "a more realistic image of what we're doing"— it wasn't always possible. Other times he had to use whatever help was available, particularly in the early days.

One of those who came along for the ride was George Yazid, a gangling, confident young man with long-boned walker's shanks. Though born in Sierra Leone, he had grown up with one foot in Ireland and the other in Africa. Jesuit educated in Ireland and trained in electronics in Canada, Yazid was a useful man to have around when some of the persnickety things that could go wrong with a helicopter did. He had a military background of sorts in, of all places, the Ghanaian Army, but what Nellis and the boys were doing was new to him. He told us all one jolly fine evening at Nellis' place that he thought he could learn something if he could attach himself to the Air Wing.

Yazid had mentioned to Nellis earlier that if he were ever stuck for help, he'd fly with him. Nellis liked hearing that because at that stage the South African really was short-handed. Juba, his co-pilot, had

gone to Europe, ostensibly to buy another helicopter. That meant
Nellis, single-handed, was flying the only Mi-17 that was still operational.

Yazid's offer came at an opportune time, not so much to assist
with the piloting, since Yazid cannot fly helicopters, but rather, to have
a Sierra Leone national onboard who could be trusted. He was also
required to negotiate with soldiers on the ground when things became
dicey. Since Yazid could speak the local lingo, he was well placed to
cool things at critical moments.

On their first sortie together, Nellis and Yazid flew to Daru at the
far end of the helicopter's fuel limitation envelope. The place was close
enough to the Liberian border to mean trouble: the only people there
were some Nigerian soldiers and a squad or two of Sierra Leone Army
troops who were so doped, he recalled, that they didn't know day
from night.

"We'd barely got down after coming in and we joined some of the
guys on the ground cooking their daily rice ration. That's when the
shooting started," began Nellis. Shots were coming in from everywhere and some of it was getting too close for comfort, he recalled.
Nellis suggested to his crew that they move out of there—fast. Yazid,
meanwhile, was seated in the co-pilot seat viewing the scene with a
kind of detachment better suited to a Sunday drive back home.
Surprised at his demeanor, Nellis leaned across and asked, "You aware
that we're being shot at?"

"Yeah. Reckon so," was Yazid's laconic retort. "But what's there
to do about it?" Point taken. His equanimity impressed the South
African, and with that, the Air Wing had an additional member of its
crew.

Just then, however, eager to get the out of there, Nellis upped the
revs. He was lifting off, indicating as much to the men outside by raising his hands in the usual way and it got their attention. With that, a
Sierra Leone Army sergeant major moved forward and brusquely
ordered a Nigerian soldier out of the engineer's seat. "Get up. I'm sitting there!" he barked before promptly sitting down between Yazid
and Nellis. He was a big fellow, Nellis recalled. Anyway, there was no
time to argue.

Nellis said, "Soon after take-off, we flew over some rebel lines
and, of course, they revved us. One round hit the helicopter and
passed through the floor, into the seat where the sergeant major was
perched. The bullet went right up his ass. He ended up on the floor

screaming like a stuffed pig, crying for God's protection, his mother, his wife and for anyone who cared to listen.

"Fred told him to shut up and carried on shooting. The corporal who'd been ousted from his seat up front by his senior was on the floor next to the wounded doubled up with laughter. Moral of the story—don't throw people out of their seats when there are people shooting at you."

"Fucker had it coming," exclaimed Yazid when he related the story. "Better him than me. But the bullet that hit him could just as easily have struck either Nellis or me, so it must have been close!"

George Yazid flew a lot with Nellis after that. He proved to be a useful acquisition, though the Air Wing never had any money to pay him. The two men saw good action and the newcomer used his new-found experiences to get a good job with another American organization that remains active in Sierra Leone today, Pacific Architects & Engineering (PAE) as their radio boffin.

Like the Oregon company, PAE's ties to Washington are indefinable and it didn't get you anywhere to ask about them. Interestingly, PAE got a contract to work in Afghanistan after the 2001 Coalition invasion, and recruited quite a number of former Executive Outcomes vets to work for them. Simon Witherspoon, a former member of the South African Reconnaissance Regiment of Angola fame, joined the company in Kabul. After that, Simon—one of the best operators in the business—got himself involved in the debacle of trying to unseat the Equatorial Guinea president and, with almost seventy others, found himself in a cell in Harare's hell-hole of a prison at Chikurubi.

One of the worst experiences Nellis and his people lived to tell about took place in January 1999. That was when the rebels were making a concerted push toward Freetown. They had already reached Waterloo, barely ten miles from Hastings, Freetown's other airport. If they achieved a breakthrough there, their chances of reaching the city proper were much improved. Clearly there would have been very little standing in their way because the regular army—such as it was—was already overextended.

It was touch and go for several days. The extent of the fighting can be gauged from the fact that the Guinea contingent attached to the multi-national ECOMOG force had deployed a squadron of Russian-built T-55 tanks and they were almost overrun. From the start it was a hard fight to keep the place, and both sides took heavy casualties.

Nellis was called upon to haul an ammunition re-supply to a battalion from the Guinea Republic and though fighting was heavy, there was no arguing. What it meant was taking the Hind into a dicey situation about which no one could tell him much of anything. Added to that, Nellis could speak no French and the Guineans couldn't, or possibly wouldn't, comprehend any English. Looking back, he agrees that it was a recipe for disaster.

"I asked for a sitrep[2] on their status and what the rebels were doing. Headquarters came back on the radio and said that all was 'Charlie Charlie'—in other words, cool and calm." At this point Nellis laughed nervously and continued: "My experience over previous weeks was that when anybody reported cool and calm it meant that their faces were cool from the wind while running away from battle. Calm came when whoever was doing the reporting got to an area where there was no fighting!"

Normally "Bokkie"—the Mi-17—had a Guinean liaison officer named Benson who flew onboard whenever the Air Wing re-supplied positions held by Conakry's soldiers. On that day though, when Nellis suggested that he should go with them, he suddenly found a dozen excuses for not flying, including having to see his dentist. "I smelt a rat," Nellis recalled.

"So we took off, anyway, the Hip loaded to the max with ammunition and a nagging suspicion that there was something not quite right. Still, we couldn't ignore that they'd said it was fine and who knows, perhaps it was."

Nellis knew that fairly often government or ECOMOG troops working in the interior were not always as forthright as they might have been while under attack. "They would be cagey about the real situation, which might give them a better chance of getting what they had asked for," explained the South African pilot. "Fred suggested that that was possibly to be expected."

Nellis was more circumspect. In his view they were exposed to real danger on just about every flight, and it wasn't necessary to compound issues by lying. In this case, though, it was a short hop across the hills and anyway, he had been into that particular LZ before without problems. He hoped they'd be in and out before anybody knew they'd arrived. The problem with Waterloo was that it lay between a succession of hills, so there was only one route in and out of the place, and that was directly over the town itself. If the rebels were in the area—as we expected them to be—there would be a tough reception.

An interesting sidelight to the sortie was that a short while before, the crew had to fork out their own money to buy new flying helmets, which was fine because they were state-of-the-art Gentex and had come from ICI in a barter deal. In contrast, if it had been government money, they would probably have gotten cheaper models. Nellis found that while the new helmets were the best things that had happened since the invention of the hamburger, they tended to deaden external noise, especially the crack of bullets passing close by.

"The sound of a near-miss is quite distinctive," he said, describing it as being a bit like a room full of typists madly banging away at their machines.

"This time, on short finals, I heard the sound of firing, but I wasn't too sure because Gentex helmets are super efficient. I asked Fred if the rebels were shooting at us. In reply to what was obviously a very stupid question—we could see the bastards running around all over the place with their AK's pointing at us—Fred's answer was, 'No Nellis, it's the radio crackling.'

"At least someone had a sense of humor. There was no going back, especially with three tons of ammo on board. So it was a question of ignoring incoming and concentrating on getting the old girl's wheels onto the ground."

As the South African tells it, the surface of the LZ had been churned into a fine powder by Guinean tanks, which wasn't helped by a helicopter coming into the hover. The rotors kicked up a brownout, which was both good and bad: Nellis couldn't see a thing, but neither could the enemy. Once down, nobody showed up to help the crew unload. Everybody around them was in the throes of a fierce exchange and, as with Makeni, none of the troops would leave their trenches to help.

"After a while a couple of soldiers did come up and they gave Fred and Mohammed a hand, but it was tense," continued Nellis. "Again, one of my fears was that we'd be hit by an RPG. So I kept the rotors going and anyway, dust was what we needed just then to obscure our goings-on from the people who were firing at us. In any other circumstance, we'd have made a damn good target."

Getting the load away took longer than the crew would have liked. As he recalled, "Everybody onboard was blinded by the fine dust that the rotors whipped up. We were worried too that somebody would walk into our tail rotor. If that happened we wouldn't have been able to fly out, not with damaged tail rotor blades." Once that task was finished, Nellis again had to pass once through a curtain of small arms fire to get clear. Fred, meanwhile, kept on doing his own thing, including dropping a rebel armed with an RPG pointed at the helicopter.

"We were flying through transition and moving relatively slowly," remembered Nellis. "He slotted the bastard just as he was about to pull the trigger." It must have been close, he admits.

There were several issues that continued to disturb those countries willing to provide the wherewithal to the Sierra Leone Army in its efforts to fight the rebels.

One of the immediate concerns of British officers seconded to the Sierra Leone Army was that nobody really knew how many of the enemy there were. Nor could Freetown's government answer questions about its own strength, except that by the time British units arrived it was budgeting for four thousand bags of rice a month to feed the force. One bag of rice feeds three soldiers for one month. It was widely accepted that the total was inflated by about a third, with senior officers pocketing the excess.

The same applied to ammunition. Nobody at Army headquarters took the trouble to plan for future needs. The British couldn't do it because it wasn't their war. Anyway, they were assigned to training, not operations. I would sit in the ops center and listen every other day to Nellis rail about the shortage of rockets and 12.7mm cartridges. As a result, much of our activity was dictated by what was left in the headquarters' magazines below the main building. It got so bad toward the end of my trip that in the latter phase, Air Wing's stocks had to be carefully monitored if the Hinds were to fly at all.

Three or four operational missions a day, at 64 rockets a sortie, gobbled up a lot of what was there. And it was almost a full-time job preparing new batches between flights. As Nellis started using up his supplies of 57mm projectiles, he was obliged to revert to the Air Wing's second Hind with its 80mm pods.

Six weeks after the start of the rebel offensive in 2000, things started to get serious. One letter would follow another to the CDS's office upstairs warning about shortages that were becoming imminent. Resupply, Nellis warned, wasn't something that could be done at short notice. Tenders had to be sought from arms dealers as well as governments abroad, and these needed to be weighed and tested. Only then could decisions be made on the basis of price, quality, availability, reliability of delivery and so on. When a source was eventually awarded a contract, there would be more haggling. The process was inevitably slowed because someone involved usually tried for a kickback or two. In addition, the stuff had to be freighted. The process could take months.

The result was that, twice following the May 2000 rebel incursions, the army didn't have enough ammunition to re-supply some of its garrisons in the interior. Several strategic strongpoints were lost because troops had to be pulled out when they were unable to counter rebel firepower. There were also times, largely at the urging of senior military staff attached to the British High Commission, that emergency stocks had to be rushed to Lungi by air from Britain.

It says something for those in London who recognized Sierra Leone's plight. They had no need to do so. Starving millions in Kenya were just as much a priority as the kinds of problems being experienced by this small but beleaguered West African state. At the end of it though, it was possibly the combined roles of Libya's Gadhaffi and Charles Taylor, the Liberian war lord, that forced London' hand—that and an incipient threat that indicated an al-Qaeda presence among some of those who were dealing in diamonds in Sierra Leone.

The bottom line was that the worst threat came from those abroad who were supplying the rebels with weapons and ammunition, and in this regard, the presidents of Libya and Liberia were well to the fore. By then the West was aware that if Gadhaffi and Taylor were allowed to get away with what they had stage-managed in Sierra Leone, there was no guessing where they would next try to ferment trouble. As it stood, parts of Guinea (which fringes on both Sierra Leone and Liberia) devolved into anarchy by early 2001. The Ivory Coast followed soon afterward.

Nellis' Air Wing faced many technical problems during the short while that I was there. As time passed, and with no money coming in, it gradually became more difficult to keep both Hinds airborne. As it was, there were some parts that Sindaba and his team cannibalized from another Hind in order to get Nellis' machine into the air. There were also problems with some of the Mi-24's weapons systems. They constantly acted up. There was barely a flight when the Gatling didn't jam, and even though I had been briefed how to get it going again from my seat under the gunner's bubble, this didn't always work. Because of this, the multi-barrelled 12.7mm needed much more attention than might have been accorded most heavy weapons. After each flight, every one of its parts had to be dismantled and washed down with aviation fuel and oiled. Before that could be done, its breeches had to be cleared and carefully checked.

The ground crew also needed to be certain that there wasn't something up the spout. But it didn't always happen the way the instruction book said it should. Once it was established that there was a round jammed in the breech, the entire barrel assembly had to be taken to the armory and mechanically cleared.

Twice while at Cockerill, the walls of the ops room were rattled by accidental discharges. The second time, a 12.7mm round went all the way through the concrete wall of the armory. Luckily there were no casualties in an area where there were usually soldiers loitering. We had no idea what its trajectory might have been, except that it must have missed the second Hind by a coat of paint. We searched an hour for holes in the fuselage and found none. Lucky!

While the 12.7mm Gatling installed in the Hind had a service life of about ten thousand rounds—when the service manual said it was supposed to be removed and destroyed—"Ours already had double that number of rounds through them. Consequently I didn't always shoot as straight as I would have liked," commented the South African.

Flying in the nose of the Mi-24 gunship can become addictive. Once Fred Marafano had gone to London on leave, I moved into the front bubble and remained there on the Air Wing's missions until the end of my stay. Nellis relented only when Tom Carew, the CDS, ordered a strike on Makeni and after I'd argued that whatever articles I was going to produce needed pictures.

The move to the chopper's nose was an entirely different experience from before, but at least I felt more secure there than at the back. Where the Mi-24 had an advantage was that its cockpit is enclosed in a titanium armor-plated capsule. Though a large caliber AP might pass right through it (and you), the armor did give some comfort of mind, even though we were aware that there was a sprinkling of large-caliber guns among the rebels. It was easy to spot them: quad-barreled ZPU 14.7 triple-A muzzles emit brilliant Christmas tree-shaped flames, sometimes ten or twelve feet long that you could see for miles. That's scary when somebody is aiming these things at you.

What we tended to look for were not only the distinctive signatures of tracers—green, in the case of former Eastern Bloc AK fire and red with 14.7 tracers—but also telltale muzzle-blasts on the ground. The pink, two-meter-long pencil-thin sheet of flame emitted by the 14.5, for instance, was unmistakable, even during daylight hours.

The first time Nellis mentioned these specifics was after somebody had hurled something heavy at us in Bendugu, one of the towns we strafed. He recognized it immediately.

"Twelve-seven," he shouted harshly. "To port, eleven o'clock."

I asked him afterward how he could be so certain that it was a Dshka. "What do you think, Venter? Those bastards have used them against me often enough!" He softened the retort by adding that with the experience he'd gained over the years, he could recognize them well enough.

About the time that I arrived in Freetown in the summer of 2000, there had been a spate of intelligence reports about the rebels deploying what the boffins called "operational" SAMs, or, in officialese, Manpads. Everybody was aware that there were Strelas (SAM-7s) in the region, the majority of which had been acquired illegally from the Ukraine. The word was that few had been completely assembled to include the most vital component of all: their trigger actions. Without them, obviously, these systems wouldn't work.

The missile customarily operates in a predetermined manner. Each SAM-7 is powered by its own battery that is linked to the trigger mechanism and is customarily kept separate from the missile. The weapon is only assembled when the operator intends to use it. Once the launcher has been switched on, you either use it or discard it. There is no going back. Later, more advanced Manpad versions have overcome this and other hurdles.

Essentially, it works like this: once an aircraft or a helicopter comes into view, the operator "locks on" to his target. He knows that this is achieved when the device emits a distinctive growling sound. Only then can he fire. The difficulty is that there are several stages to the process. The rigmarole involved can take a little while, and is one of the reasons why it's so difficult to use SAMs in areas with no clear field of vision. These missiles are almost useless in regions overgrown with trees or foliage, a category that includes almost all of Sierra Leone. This is why Nellis almost always flew low, practically scraping the treetops of the jungle.

Like everybody else in ops, I followed rebel radio intercepts with interest. This one came in after the Makeni raid:

Fm—c/s Pompay (Sparrow)
To—c/s Mike Mike (Daru)
Subject—Emphasy dated today 10/6/00
Ref my message this 1830 hrs to be relayed to c/s Satellite (Emperor). You are to ensure that they get the message today and to immediately dispatch the required items very fast. Otherwise let them be prepared to receive us at their point (Koidu Town). And let them also find experts for the trigger.

For easy reference, the radio room italicized the origins of the various call signs. Also, the intercept had been given a daytime reference number by air operations staff. This one had come in at 1948 hours on June 10, and we deduced that it referred to SAMs. That was the good news, a source at the High Commission explained. While the rebels had deployed ground-to-air missiles, their trigger mechanisms hadn't been part of the package. A crucial tactical element had been revealed by this intercept, and it pleased Nellis.

More worrying were other intelligence reports—coupled to what came in with more than a single defector—that mentioned missile triggers. Most claimed they were either already in the hands of "experts" or that they would be, in short order. It seemed that the main body of the launcher and its trigger, either by design or by accident, were never in the same place at the same time.

Issuing the weapon without being able to fire it didn't make sense. Some of the British officers felt that while some SAMs—particularly in and around the diamond fields—were possibly armed, Sankoh's rebels were holding most of them in reserve for the anticipated government push on Kono. If that happened, they said, they would definitely be used offensively. Also, the Kono region was fairly open country, and thus optimum for Strelas.

In any event, explained Nellis, the Kono region just then was nowhere near our area of operations. Koidu town, he intimated, was well prepared for an air strike and he wasn't prepared to try his luck, though he apparently did shortly after I left Freetown—three times, in fact, he told me afterward. Meanwhile, there were a lot of other things that demanded his attention.

Of prime importance to the head of the Air Wing, was whether the Hind faced the older Strela versions of the ground-to-air missile or the newer, more sophisticated SAM-14/16, or Gremlins. Later versions were fitted with more sophisticated homing devices that included proximity fuses. Unlike the SAM-7, they weren't solely dependent on infrared.

"I know I can cope with sevens," Nellis confidently told me when discussing the threat. But he wasn't at all confident about some of the later versions, or what was coming out of China. The British military advisory team at Cockerill shared his view. Thus, in mid-July, when RAF Chinooks burst onto Kailahun to rescue the more than two hundred United Nations peacekeepers who had been held for ten weeks by the RUF, they and their Indian Air Force Hind counterparts fired anti-missile flares like a 4th of July fireworks display.

Apart from daily search and destroy sorties against known enemy positions, Neall Ellis targeted regional rebel headquarters in half-a-dozen locations. Our strike on the regional capital in Makeni that day, however, was different. Normally, with me sitting in the gunner's seat in the nose, that should have been my job. But I remained the neutral observer for the duration.

Having returned to London afterward, one of the first questions I was asked by Clifford Beal, editor of *Jane' Defence Weekly*, was whether I had, as he phrased it, "crossed the line."

Obviously I hadn't, for the simple reason that military correspondents simply cannot do so. One has to remain aloof, and anyway it is not considered ethical. Should a correspondent identify with hostilities —one side or the other—he becomes a participant, though to be fair there are times when the distinction between right and wrong in a conflict becomes so smudged as to be irrelevant. Sierra Leone's bitter, brutal conflict wasn't one of them.[3]

So it went. Nellis or one of the gunners would spot something on the ground and we'd bank and go in, usually firing rockets the first time round. His accuracy was unerring. Interestingly, though both Mi-24s had less than 100 hours on the clock since their last overhauls, there was also an older, third Hind waiting for an overhaul at Lungi. But the government had no money for that craft. So it sat out the war gathering dust while Nellis' "Bokkie"—the veteran Mi-17—was used by he and Hassan to haul almost a thousand refugees out of Freetown across the bay to safety.

Something of a more personal nature bothered me for some of the time that I was flying up front: leg cramps, or to be more precise, muscle seizures that could practically make a grown man cry. For the duration of any flight we sat cooped up under the bubble, sometimes for two or more hours at a stretch. Strapped down in that confined space, we were never able to relax. In fact, it was such a close fit that it was hardly possible to move your butt, never mind stretch a leg.

Three days after arriving in Sierra Leone I ate something bad, which was hardly unusual in a society where health controls went out the window with the last elected government in the 1970s. It was serious enough to put me out of action for a day or two, and one of the immediate side effects was cramps. These powerful, constricting pains caused me to double up in agony. It didn't occur often, but when it did, everybody would know about it.

When I finally did fly again, it wasn't until I was strapped in and Nellis had started to wind her up that I remembered my dilemma. With horror, I realized that I wouldn't be able to move my legs if it happened. But I was spared that drama and things got better with time. Nellis had warned earlier that I'd have to live with it. "I can't have you unstrapping in the middle of a sortie," he warned. "I might have to take evasive action. Or the chopper could buck and you could fall on the stick," he said seriously. Traveling at treetop height meant that any maneuver had to be immediate. "There' no time for error," he added grimly.

Nellis and I were almost killed on one of my last nights in Freetown, ironically on the ground. It was a close call and the cause, as with most things in wartime, was communications—or rather the lack thereof. It's also a truism that the majority of people who are shot at military checkpoints are not intentionally killed.

We were stopped at a roadblock manned by Nigerian troops after having had a farewell dinner with Hassan and his friends in another part of town. It was a long trek home before the curfew came into effect, and it irked us that we had to wait in line for almost half an hour. Obviously, there was something up. The Nigerians manning the barriers were edgy and, as we had all discovered a long time before, Nigerians can be dangerously dysfunctional. This is especially true after dark when there's liquor and drugs about, which, in West Africa, was often.

These troops moved along our line of cars in varying states of agitation, some of them aggressively brandishing firearms and shouting orders in barely comprehensible English. What was also worrying was that they made a lot of people get out of their cars and some of them were subjected to body searches. It was probably weapons they were after, we concluded. Or maybe they had earlier caught someone with a pile of them, which would have explained their edginess.

That night, though, the majority of these troops—half-stoned and glassy-eyed—were more than their usual abrasive selves. In uniform, these West African soldiers can be as cocky as hell, and even more so when armed. I lived for almost a year at Apapa, a Lagos suburb, and was able to view the country and its people from up close, so this was nothing new. These days, however, I prefer to give Nigeria a miss.

In any event, it took a while before our turn came. Nellis, thinking the officer had recognized him and waved him on—he does the trip twice a day and has a nodding acquaintance with most of the security people in the city—put his car into gear and started to move ahead. Just then another Nigerian soldier hurled himself out of a grove of bushes lining the road. "Halt!" he called out hoarsely. "You stop!" he screamed, raising his FN.

"Didn't you hear your officer?" Nellis said quietly to the man. It's difficult to rattle that aviator, even in a tight situation. "He said we could go." I could see that even while this discussion continued, the momentum of our rig was carrying us forward.

Annoyed at having a white man disregard his orders, and perhaps a little confused by Nellis' defiance, the soldier jumped in front of us, his knees almost touching our bumper. With that, he put his weapon to his shoulder and leveled it at the driver's head. I was sitting in the back seat and I would probably have been directly in line had he fired. Nellis by now had fortunately put his foot on the brake, more in fear of running over the soldier than in any act of compliance. But we still hadn't come to a complete stop.

One hand out the window, the South African pilot remonstrated. "I've been told by your officer that I can go." He neither acquiesced nor was he disrespectful. It was a statement of fact.

A moment of indecision on the other man's part probably saved our lives. In his befuddled mind—we saw as we pulled away that he was unsteady on his feet—he'd perceived that we were trying to avoid the search. If he had pulled the trigger, he'd probably have gotten away with it. Seconds later, he stepped back and ran to a sandbagged position about twenty yards ahead. There he turned, his gun still pointing in our direction.

Nellis swung around in his seat to look at me but said nothing. There was no reason for any of it, but he wasn't going to do something stupid: not at that time of night and certainly not on the streets of Freetown.

It took a while for it all to be resolved. The police arrived, and since there wasn't one of them who didn't immediately recognize the only helicopter gunship pilot in the country, they didn't even glance at his military pass that allowed us to have weapons on board. We had Nellis' 9mm pistol, the minuscule Czech submachine gun that he normally took flying with him, and an AK-47 he routinely kept in his car. After speaking to the checkpoint commander, the police told us we could go.

It was then, after five weeks of flying with the Air Wing, that I finally felt that perhaps it was time to head home. Sierra Leone was starting to get to me.

PART II

"By definition, mercenaries have always been a dying breed."

British journalist Ian Bruce in *Comment*,
London, February 19, 2002

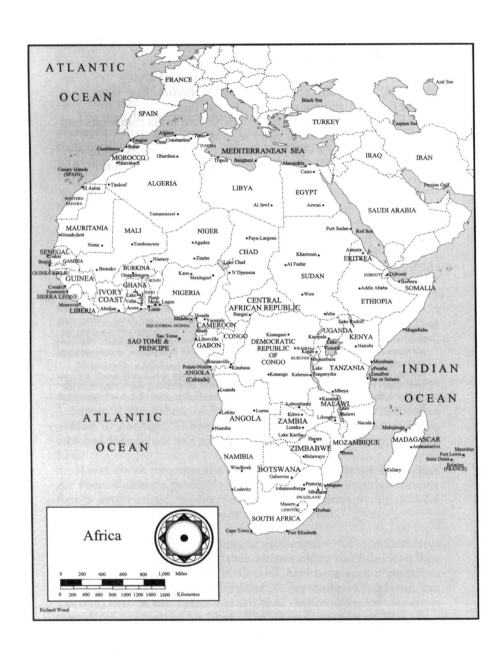

ATLANTIC

OCEAN

FRANCE

SPAIN

Aral Sea

Black Sea

TURKEY

Caspian Sea

Tangier
Algiers
Constantine
Tunis
Oran
Casablanca
Rabat
TUNISIA
MOROCCO
Marrakech
Ghardaia
MEDITERRANEAN SEA
Tripoli
Banghazi
Alexandria
Cairo

IRAQ

IRAN

Canary Islands
(SPAIN)
El Aaiun
Tindouf
ALGERIA
LIBYA
EGYPT
Persian Gulf

WESTERN
SAHARA

Al Jawf
Aswan

SAUDI ARABIA

MAURITANIA
Nouakchott
MALI
NIGER
Faya-Largeau
CHAD
Port Sudan
Red Sea

Nema
Tombouctou
Agadez
Khartoum
Asmera
ERITREA

SENEGAL
Dakar
GAMBIA
Niamey
Zinder
Lake Chad
N'Djamena
Al Fashir
SUDAN
DJIBOUTI
Djibouti

Banjul
Bamako
BURKINA
SOMALIA

GUINEA-BISSAU
Ouagadougou
BENIN
Kano
Maiduguri
Waw
Addis Ababa
Berbera

Conakry
Freetown
GUINEA
GHANA
Togo
NIGERIA
CENTRAL
Juba
ETHIOPIA
Mogadishu

SIERRA LEONE
IVORY
COAST
Lake
Volta
Port
Novo
Lagos
AFRICAN REPUBLIC
Lake Rudolf

Monrovia
Abidjan
Accra
Lome
Bangui

LIBERIA
Malabo
Douala
Yaounde
UGANDA

EQUATORIAL GUINEA
CAMEROON
Bath
Kisangani
Kampala
Lake
KENYA

SAO TOME &
PRINCIPE
Sao Tome
Libreville
CONGO
RWANDA
Kigali
Victoria
Nairobi

GABON
DEMOCRATIC
REPUBLIC
OF
CONGO
BURUNDI
Bujumbura
Mombasa

Pointe-Noire
Brazzaville
Kinshasa
Kananga
Kalemie
TANZANIA
Pemba
Zanzibar

ANGOLA
(Cabinda)
Lake
Tanganyika
Dar es Salaam
INDIAN

Luanda
Mbeya
OCEAN

Kasama

Lobito
Luena
Lubumbashi
MALAWI
Nacala
Mahajanga

ANGOLA
ZAMBIA
Kitwe
Lilongwe
Lake
Malawi

ATLANTIC
Namibe
Lusaka
MADAGASCAR

Lake Kariba
Harare
MOZAMBIQUE
Antananarivo
Mauritius

OCEAN
ZIMBABWE
Beira
Port Lewis
Saint Denis

NAMIBIA
Bulawayo
Reunion
(FRANCE)

Windhoek
BOTSWANA
Toliary

Gaborone

Luderitz
Johannesburg
Pretoria
Maputo
Mbabane
SWAZILAND

Maseru
LESOTHO
Durban

SOUTH AFRICA

Cape Town
Port Elizabeth

Africa

0   200   400   600   800   1,000   Miles

0   200 400 600 800 1000 1200 1400 1600   Kilometres

Richard Wood

8

MORE MERCS—MORE WARS

**"You must remember, this is Africa. They think nothing of
doing filthy, beastly things to each other."**

Lord Soames, British Governor in Salisbury, Rhodesia

Jim Penrith, one of the last of the Old Africa Hands, recalls how easy
it was to become a mercenary at a time when there were significant
parts of Africa in turmoil. Based in Nairobi, Penrith had worked for
several years for a South African newspaper group where so many of
us had cut our teeth and developed the knack of telling it like it was.
Penrith jotted down one of his own experiences circa 1969:

"I walked into the bar and saw this fellow downing *waragi* like
there was no tomorrow, grimacing when the potent banana-based fire-
water hit base. You needed a copper-lined gullet to drink that rough
Ugandan liquor and I shook my head when he invitingly waved the
bottle at me.

"I looked around the White Gardenia bar, my favorite watering
hole in the Kampala of the late 1960s, and seeing no one I knew, sat
down at his table. He had already made a serious dent in the *waragi*
but he appeared perfectly sober. I noticed that his heavily muscled
forearms and bush jacket collar had a fine coating of red murram dust.
He'd evidently driven a long way on border backroads.

"'So, *mon ami*, what are you doing in Uganda?' I knew from experience that the quickest way to terminate a conversation in jumpy
Uganda was to admit to being a visiting journalist.

"'Just looking around. Opportunities,' I said.

"He asked whether I'd ever been across the border into the Kivu
province of the eastern Congo. No, but I'd been in Katanga when the
Congo blew up in June 1960 after the Belgians abandoned their
colony overnight, taking even the electric plugs and light bulbs with
them. I mentioned several other places I'd visited in Central Africa
over the years, and let drop the names of some of the better-known

mercenary officers I'd bumped into. I didn't actually lie and say I'd been a mercenary, but nor did I mention that I'd been there as the Nairobi bureau chief of the Argus Africa News Service [AANS]. 'All that was in the days before things quietened down,' I said.

"He leant across the rickety table and gripped my arm. 'The Kivu, *mon ami*, is about to take fire, and I am looking for men to join the force of Jean Schramme.'

"The *waragi* now seemed to have loosened his tongue and I listened attentively as he outlined the plan that would see 'Black Jack' Schramme and his mercenaries drive Mobutu's *Armée Nationale Congolaise* out of the province and take over the major administrative center of Bukavu, on Lake Kivu. He said he was authorized to recruit throughout East Africa and offer generous pay in US dollars, deposited in a bank anywhere in Europe. I said I was interested and he asked me to meet him again in the bar in a week's time. The Kivu rebellion was scheduled to start two weeks after that.

"Back in my office in Nairobi I fired off a cable to London for transmission to Alan Syer, head of the AANS in Johannesburg. I told him of the planned uprising and said I intended to drive from Nairobi to Shangugu in Rwanda to wait there for the mercenary offensive to begin. I reckoned that I would be the only journalist on the spot when Schramme and the men known as *les Affreux*, 'The Frightful Ones,' stormed Bukavu.

"The reply astounded me. It said that our London office had checked with their sources and could find no hint or whisper that anything was likely to happen in peaceful Kivu. In effect, the AANS discounted the report of its own representative in Black Africa. They had listened to the mandarins thousands of miles away in London.

"A few days before Schramme's planned uprising I set out for Shangugu. Within forty-eight hours I was sitting on the verandah of a hotel perched on a rise looking out across Lake Kivu and down on the narrow bridge linking the sleepy little Rwandan village with the road into Bukavu. All seemed peaceful so I walked across the bridge into the Congo. A mile further on, the road turned around a bluff and I could see the sprawl of Bukavu. The next minute I was staring into the barrels of half a dozen Kalashnikovs held by Congolese soldiers who were screaming at me in a language I didn't understand, but whose meaning was quite clear. I turned around and slowly strolled back down the way I'd come. It was the longest walk I've ever taken.

"Back at the hotel I joined a knot of locals drinking beer under covered awnings waiting for the war to start. It was like sitting at a drive-in cinema. First, hordes of Congolese soldiers came pouring pell-mell down the road, tearing off their military insignia and throwing their weapons into the lake as they raced across the bridge to the safety of Rwanda. Half an hour later the sun shone on something that was pure cinematic cliché, a scene that US movie maestro John Huston would have been proud to have directed. Round the bluff and etched across the skyline came the ragtag mercenary column, a single line of Jeeps, each with a heavy-caliber Browning machine gun mounted on the back. Flying from an aerial in the lead vehicle was the familiar old flag of Tshombe's Katanga.

"Once again I hurried across the bridge, this time to hitch a lift with the convoy as it wheeled and headed back to Bukavu. In a plush suite in a deserted hotel I drank looted wine with the mercenaries while waiting to interview Jean Schramme. The interview with the chain-smoking war dog was everything a journalist could ask for. Punctuation was provided by a couple of loud crumps as the Bukavu bank vaults were broached with explosives. The Frightful Ones were collecting an advance on their pay.

"As I'd predicted, I was the only newsman at the fall of Bukavu. I wondered how the 'experts' in London were explaining this coup."

My old friend Peter Hawthorne from Cape Town, a veteran of more African disputes than he cares to remember, has been writing for the international magazine *Time* just about forever. Hawthorne had it right when he declared in August 2001 that the new round of bloody turmoil taking place in parts of Africa was really no more than "the same ground, new faces."

"Memo to United Nations Headquarters, New York," wrote Hawthorne. "Does anyone out there remember Patrice Lumumba, Moise Tshombe, 'King' Albert Kalonji and 'Mad' Mike Hoare? And ONUC—the UN operation in the Congo—arriving with a flourish and a flash of blue berets to keep the peace when the country erupted after its rushed independence from Belgium in 1960? And the UN's withdrawal three years later—battered, disillusioned and brought almost to bankruptcy in the heart of the Congo's darkness?"

In Katanga, in the south of this vast country, Hawthorne went on, "The UN was up against a small but formidable force of foreign mercenaries recruited in South Africa by an Irish-born adventurer who ran the blue-clad troops ragged."

The antics of "The Terrible Ones," as Mike Hoare's mercenaries were called, became legendary. Hawthorne recalls how they stole tons of equipment from the world body, including an entire helicopter, which they then sold back to ONUC as spare parts.

He tells too, of a time when he made regular trips into this chastened land and suggests, forty years on, that not a lot has changed. Albert Kalonji and many of the original players were long gone, and a new bunch of tyrants had taken up residence—just as shifty, ruthless and bloody-minded as the crowd before.

Kalonji, a bibulous drunk albeit an important political figure during this upheaval, once declared himself king of the diamond-rich province of Kasai in the Congo's south. He had no map, Hawthorne explains, "So for visiting journalists he drew a shape in the sand with the end of his ceremonial fly whisk and would say, pointing: 'That's all mine.'"

Other stories emerged during that period: tales about the ordinary people in the Congo's cities as well as isolated villages in the interior where just maintaining a grip on life in the crushing hell of poverty was an achievement. If the rebels didn't get you, government troops did. The newspapers were full of this sort of thing at the time.

While United Nations debates about some of today's excesses in Africa get full treatment by the media, nearly all of these discussions are vapid. They are also pointless because the damage can't be undone. Apart from the occasional snippet, you rarely see anything about what's really happening at ground level.

An exception was a report by Declan Walsh that ran in the *Boston Globe* in August 2001. Headed "Horror in the Congo," it told of the mindless atrocities taking place, virtually under the noses of the latest batch of blue berets that had arrived on the pretext of another peace-keeping operation. Walsh reckoned that roughly two-and-a-half million people had died in that sad land in the past two or three decades, and most had succumbed from war-related famine and disease.

"The true nature of the Congo war has remained obscured, largely because it involves six countries and at least four armed groups, and because much of the country was out of reach of Western aid agencies for security reasons," wrote Walsh. Six Red Cross workers were hacked to death in a remote region four months earlier, another macabre repeat from the old days, he recalled.

Very little of this makes an impact anymore, especially now that worse catastrophes have blunted our sensibilities. We've all seen bits and pieces about the carnage in Rwanda, and more recently about how men representing the United Nations were raping children in the Congo. As another commentator suggested, Africa has been relegated to the back burner of history. "The West is weary of Africa's problems," was his final dismissive word.

With time, reports of Africa's eternal shortages, monumental mismanagement, corruption, fierce dissolution, and tens of thousands of dying children become repetitive. Similar to what's currently happening in Israel, people close their minds to horror when it goes on and on without respite. There are more pressing issues like al-Qaeda, Iraq, terrorist strikes, hostage dramas, and perhaps the threat of anthrax. The West is indeed weary.

Then out of nowhere, in October 2001, the very public broadcaster Ted Koppel—in a prelude to a five-part series on the Congo's plight—apologized to the nation on behalf of an America that had ignored the Congo's problems for so long.

"How can two-and-a-half million people die over a three-year period and we don't even notice?" Koppel asked in an interview. He went on to tell the American nation, "It's not as though we're looking at the story and saying 'Its far away, let's not bother.' It didn't even rise to that level." Koppel contrasted events in the Democratic Republic of the Congo with what had taken place in Kosovo, where an estimated twenty thousand people had perished.

There is a remedy to all this turbulence, but it's going to take a brave man to say it out loud. Mercenaries had brought a measure of order to the Congo several times in the past (as well as to several other African states). Today, with the major powers preoccupied with far weightier issues, perhaps the time has come for the international community to look once more at the alternative option of private military companies (PMCs), or possibly the more politically correct private security companies (PSCs).

Writing in Britain's *Guardian* about a similar tragedy, this time in Sierra Leone, William Shawcross did what some of his critics regarded as unconscionable. He suggested that properly supervised and controlled mercenaries (or private security forces, as he phrased it) might be the best answer to that crisis, and similar crises in the future. He wasn't at all certain about the Congo, if only because that country remains in a class of its own because of its size, unwieldy politics, and a brutal and avaricious array of tyrants the country has produced over the past forty years.

Author Frederick Forsyth went one better. In an op-ed piece in New York's *Wall Street Journal*, Forsyth explicitly stated that bringing order to some of the "hellholes of the world" meant combat, adding that you cannot keep the peace until you've restored the peace. He added that "the Bosnian fiasco was a timely reminder, and though United Nations troops may defend themselves, they are not mandated to aggressive fighting."

So what to do now? The always outspoken Forsyth had the temerity to provide a very effective solution: "Then into the frame, to politically correct cries of 'yuck,' steps the professional mercenary." Citing the Sierra Leone experience, the author of *Day of the Jackal* justified his argument by recalling that two professional mercenary outfits had been hired to end the previous round of bleeding horror in Sierra Leone. "First there was a South African concern that rejoiced in its delightfully euphemistic name of Executive Outcomes, followed by another, British this time, which called itself Sandline—though it preferred to use the title of 'private military company,'"

There was nothing strange or new about this kind of paid warrior, Forsyth suggested: "From Sparta to Athens, through ancient Rome and the Middle Ages, via the condottiere of Renaissance Italy to the 19th century, the soldier-for-hire graced a perfectly honorable profession. True patriotism only surfaced about two hundred and fifty years ago, and both Britain and America have been helping friendly governments with officers on secondment to this day. Let's also not forget our ex-soldiers who earn nice retirement nest eggs by serving abroad as "training specialists" on a nudge-nudge-wink-wink basis."

Forsyth can be candid when he needs to be.

It's worth noting that there are already many people helping belligerents, and while few are friendly, just about all are camera-shy. In an exchange of letters with Jim Rupert, former *Washington Post* West Africa correspondent, I was told that he had obtained the registration numbers of five of the aircraft that had been carrying weapons to Sierra Leone's Revolutionary United Front (RUF) rebels. These were the same people that Neall Ellis had been up against.

"When numbers were checked against an international registry of commercial aircraft compiled by Airclaims Ltd, a private firm, the registration of one of them matched that of a Boeing 727 owned by the government of Burkina Faso," Rupert wrote me. Earlier reports spoke about arms flights having been organized between airports in Libya and Ouagadougou, the Burkina Faso capital. Nigerian intelligence sources, continued Rupert, had been monitoring RUF efforts at rearming after the fiasco that led to the intervention of South Africa's Executive Outcomes a few years earlier.[1]

Rupert disclosed that the Nigerians—as well as a Western intelligence agency—had tracked aircraft they had seen transferring crates of arms at West African airfields. Most were Libyan and some of the flights had gone directly into rebel-held zones in Sierra Leone, although the majority landed at Liberia's Robertsfield. What is of concern here, suggested Rupert, was that apart from Sierra Leone, there had been Libyan involvement in several other African theaters of recent military activity, including the Sudan, Kabila's Congo, Zimbabwe, the Ivory Coast, the Central African Republic, Angola, Somalia and elsewhere.

After returning home from Freetown, Rupert reported that there were a variety of people involved in arms and possible helicopter sales, either to the Sierra Leone government or to Liberia. These included retired Israeli army officers. Also involved was a former South African army colonel who had business interests in Liberia (and whom Rupert briefly met at his hotel in Monrovia), as well as an executive with the Belgium-based Rex Diamond Mining Corporation. According to the Israeli paper *Yedioth Aharonoth*, this man acquired diamond-mining rights in Liberia in exchange for the purchase of a Mi-24 helicopter gunship from Belarus in the former Soviet Union.

In his dispatch, Rupert mentioned teams of South African soldiers operating with the rebels in Liberia and on cross-border raids in Sierra Leone. He would probably have come up with more information had his activities in the Liberian capital not attracted the unwelcome attention of some of Charles Taylor's spooks, true inheritors of a ghastly tradition initiated by Haiti's secret police, the inappropriately-named tonton macoutes.

Earlier, the *Washington Post*'s correspondent told me of an incident that had some bearing on how civilian communities in Africa affected by this kind of barbarism sometimes react, especially when pinned between the jungle and the sea. Before a last bout of fighting in Sierra Leone, the country's lone Mi-24 combat helicopter blew an engine. Obviously, the rebels creeping closer to Freetown meant potential disaster for the authorities and they couldn't simply let the matter lie, especially since the aging gunship had been the government's most effective weapon. Officials scrambled to repair the machine. Rather than rely on conventional arms dealers, however, they took bids from mining companies, gem brokers and mercenaries, almost all of whom had or wanted access to Sierra Leone's diamond fields.

The government finally decided to buy almost four million dollars worth of engine parts and ammunition through a firm set up by an expatriate. In the end, because of another fiddle, the parts proved unsuitable and the helicopter stayed on the ground. The rebels seized Freetown, killing thousands of residents and maiming even more, Rupert said. Once the government got back into power, it hired a group of Ethiopian technicians to work on the Air Wing's "antiquated" Hind. After that, the old Mi-24 was about all that Nellis flew.

During the past twelve or fifteen years there has been a spate of mercenary involvement in civil wars, revolts, coups and uprisings on just about every continent. In early 1999, news agencies mentioned that there were former Soviet pilots in the pay of Jonas Savimbi, the Angolan rebel leader who was killed in 2002. While this may have been an effective bit of misinformation on the part of the wily guerrilla leader, there were certainly Russian and Ukrainian aviators flying Mikoyan fighters on both sides of the Ethiopian-Eritrean war.

US News and World Report carried a report of Colonel Vyacheslav Myzin emerging from the cockpit of one of Ethiopia's newly acquired Su-27s after a demonstration flight. Myzin was labeled one of Africa's "new mercenaries." Similarly, in the Congo (both before and after the recently departed Elder Kabila ousted Mobutu), Serbs, South Africans, Israelis, Croats, Zimbabweans, Germans, French and other nationalities were deeply involved, some fighting for, and others against, the government.

More war dogs were seen in action with rebel contingents in West Africa's Guiné-Bissau, as well as in Senegal's lovely Cassamance Province. Reports out of Dakar speak of foreign veterans (possibly French) helping dissident Senegalese rebels. It was the same in Namibia's Caprivi Zipvel where, until Dr. Jonas Savimbi was killed, Unita rebel forces crossed the ill-defined frontier from Angola at will to drive government troops into the bush. These dissidents were recruited and trained by mercenaries working for Savimbi, who, until his demise—lured to his death, ironically, by another group of South African mercenaries—headed the Angolan rebel group.

It's no longer a secret that during the Cold War, this Lausanneeducated revolutionary who had a predilection for espousing Maoisms, took his orders from the CIA. In fact, when I visited his bush camp at Jamba in the extreme southeast corner of Angola, we were all aware that CIA operatives were hanging about somewhere in the bush and beyond. So too, for a while, was French mercenary Bob Denard.

It was the same story in the Sudan, where first Iraqi pilots and then Russian mercenaries flew war planes. This was a time when Khartoum salted its ground forces with members of the Afghan mujahadeen, Yemenis and al-Qaeda operatives, who, in the early 1990s, benefited from the presence of Osama bin Laden in the country. The Saudi Wahhabist's protection came from a deposed former Sudanese prime minister, Hassan Al-Turabi.

Other foreign nationals, including some former Executive Outcomes mercenaries who had originally been active in Sierra Leone and Angola, also eventually found themselves in the Sudan. The enemy was (and still is) a largely Western-backed Christian/animist alliance involving black tribes living along the Upper Nile, its members bitterly opposed to Islamic rule.

There were Russian, French and other mercenaries active during the war in Kosovo (and earlier, in Georgia, Chechnya and, more recently, Dagestan). Hired fighters were also identified in conflicts in Afghanistan, Armenia, Tajikistan and Azerbaijan.

Columbia's drug cartels employed IRA dissidents in some numbers, as well as South African and British mercenaries, including a handful of my old South African buddies from Angola's civil war. Some of these people were involved in combat and others in training anti-government militias.

There is a powerful groundswell of opinion against using hired guns to fight wars and kill people, particularly in the West. In this regard, critics point specifically at the use of mercenaries in Africa, the one continent that can least afford them.

The truth is that there will always be work for mercenary pilots in some African states. The reason for this is simple: local air forces seldom achieve the required expertise in flying sophisticated jet fighters and combat helicopters. While there are some fine black pilots around, they're hardly in the majority. So another source must be found. Using mercenaries also goes against the ethos of more traditional professional armies, which could be why Australia reacted so vigorously once Sandline had been awarded a contract to fight insurgents in Papua New Guinea. South African mercenaries—many of them familiar figures from EO's African contracts—were sent out there but had to be withdrawn following protests from Canberra and a revolt within the ranks of the Papua New Guinea military. They were all hastily sent home and the group's leader, Lt-Col. Tim Spicer, was held for a month before British pressure forced his release.

As David Shearer wrote in an article published in *Foreign Policy* (Fall 1998), for three centuries the accepted international norm had been that only nation-states were permitted to fight wars. The rise of private companies entering the business as a legitimate, profit-orientated activity has provoked outrage and prompted calls for them to be outlawed. The popular press, he stated, "has used labels like 'dogs of war' conjuring up images of freebooting and rampaging Rambos overthrowing weak—usually African—governments."

There are good reasons why the developed world is reluctant to get involved in fierce, distant, often ethnic-related brush-fire conflicts like those in Somalia, the Congo and Rwanda. With a few notable exceptions, such as Mozambique and Sierra Leone, most do not end decisively. Neither side is able to claim outright victory, despite body counts that are truly horrific. The majority of these wars are marked by horrific excesses, with large numbers of innocent civilians killed or displaced from their homes, and in some instances their homelands.

When the United Nations, under the auspices of Operation Just Hope, went into Somalia in the early 1990s, the gesture was motivated first by the suffering of a million or more civilians who were starving; and second, to try and stop the fighting. The scope of the operation was well intentioned, even though improperly armed US forces took the brunt of it. The initial idea was to bring a measure of order within a socio-military system that had gone crackers.

It didn't take the dumbest second lieutenant in the force very long to discover that nobody had factored in the ability of a handful of bloody-minded Somali warlords to offer such determined resistance. Nor that al-Qaeda, within record time, would be able to deliver to these barbarians boatloads of RPG-7 rockets and their launchers, which they promptly used with good effect against American helicopters.

An important long-term consequence of that disaster was that it will take a generation or more before the stark television images of bodies of US soldiers being dragged naked through Mogadishu's streets are erased from the minds of the American public. As the holo-caust in Rwanda proved, recommitting American troops into an African conflict won't be happening anytime soon.

The end of the Cold War has also shifted priorities, some of them fundamental. Backing one tin-pot dictator against another is no longer as viable as it was when Moscow and Washington were playing power games. Even more important, there is a very real reluctance in every Western country to intervene in other peoples' squabbles because nobody is prepared to put their own boys at risk. The "body bag syn-drome," as some pundits call it, makes not for popular domestic pol-itics. Politicians can no longer commit troops into "hot" wars without offering the public back home a damn good reason. This is why the Clinton administration refused to allow ground forces to be commit-ted in Kosovo.

Given all this, it only makes sense to take a hard look at alterna-tives. This could be one of the reasons why the idea of employing pro-fessional mercenaries to go where other armies won't is making a determined comeback. Britain agreed to formally license private mili-tary companies in 2002, and that's a start.

Sam Roggeveen, an authority on strategy at the School of Australian and International Studies, argued presciently in a thesis titled "The Case for the Mercenary Army," that "war is today less a matter of applying massive force across a wide front as it is of apply-ing intelligent force at carefully selected points." All things being equal, he declared, an efficient, adequately equipped, and well-moti-vated force should always achieve a good advantage in any Third World Struggle.

Even the debacle that became Somalia—weighted by its own set of internal contradictions—might have been averted by the use of merce-naries. At the core of that mess was a top-heavy, hideously bureau-cratic United Nations force in which no one made any attempt at lev-eling the playing fields. Force was never adequately matched with opposing force, and Somali irregulars got away, literally, with daily mass murder.

How different were developments subsequently in East Timor, where the UN intervention force—this time with Australians in the van—fired back without having to ask permission from New York (or, for that matter, from anyone else)? To do such a thing in Somalia (as in southern Lebanon during that sorry two-decades-long debacle) required a ridiculous set of prerequisites before UN contingents could

react to any kind of provocation. The locals knew it and they mercilessly exploited the situation. A mercenary force, in contrast, carries
no such baggage. At the same time, of course, the alternative of using
"hired guns" as a military solution to some of the developing world's
problems presents another set of parameters to watch over. Some are
of perception, others based on recent history.

That mercenaries are active in other peoples' wars is a reality of both
contemporary history and politics.[2] Two events underscore this development. The first involves an American organization called Military
Professional Resources Inc., better known in the trade as MPRI. Not
only is this one of the largest private American military training and
planning groups active internationally, it has strong, though indeterminate, links to the Pentagon. In November 1999 this Richmond,
Virginia company (whose directorate is composed almost entirely of
retired generals) dispatched a support group to Luanda to train the
Angolan Army of President Eduardo dos Santos. According to the
Johannesburg *Mail & Guardian* (and with some obvious prodding
from Washington) MPRI reached an accord with Luanda to take the
Angolan FAA (*Forcas Armadas Angolanas*) in hand, very much as
Executive Outcomes had so successfully done a few years before.

Even more ambitious at the end of the Balkan wars was an "equip
and train" contract worth almost a hundred million dollars to create
a Western-oriented Bosnian-Croat federation army. That was done,
literally, from the ground up. It was run by MPRI under the aegis of
the US State Department as part of the program for Military
Stabilization in the Balkans that followed the Dayton peace accords.
Tammy Arbuckle, another erstwhile military stalwart from the old
days, and a colleague of mine, put the MPRI Bosnian operation on the
line in a major article in Jane's *International Defense Review*, published in Britain in August 1997.

Though it was the subject of much speculation at the time, the
contract went off without a hitch. What was conspicuous was that
while the almost two hundred MPRI instructors were all ex-military,
they slotted into exactly the same groove as EO recruits might have
done when that bunch of freebooters was training soldiers in Angola
and Sierra Leone. MPRI, with all its lofty disclaimers, might argue
with this comparison, but then that is their prerogative.

Another interesting development shortly thereafter involved a private South African force that became part of the UN contingent sent

to Dili in East Timor at the time of the troubles there. Consisting mainly of people of mixed blood ("colored" in South African parlance), the intent was that the group blend in with the East Timor locals. The force was assembled and trained by two Durban-based security companies (Empower Loss Control Services and KZN Security) and their job—under the aegis of the UN—was to work mainly undercover. Jose "Xanana" Gusmao, leader of the National Council of the East Timorese Resistance, told South Africa's President Thabo Mbeki that he preferred the security guards because he didn't trust those that the Indonesians provided.

Angola has been the focus of a remarkable amount of South African mercenary activity in recent years. Former members of the SADF were involved on both sides of a civil war that went on intermittently in that battle-worn country for more than a quarter century. (Not counting the prior fourteen-year anti-colonial guerrilla war against Portugal.) Some of these war dogs stayed afterward to "mop up," as one of their former field commanders suggested.

What was different about this effort, compared to other African civil wars, was that some South African soldiers trained and fought alongside Angolan government forces in the mid-1990s, even though they had been blood enemies in the past. With the winding down of Executive Outcomes on January 1, 1999 (following South African government pressure to disband and an act of Parliament making any kind of mercenary activity illegal) a number of the organization's veterans surreptitiously switched sides. That done, they once again took to directing Savimbi's efforts against Luanda.

When one examines the bigger picture and has the benefit of hindsight, what becomes immediately clear is that at the end of the day, it was air power that prevailed against the insurgents, both in Angola and in Sierra Leone. And that was because the rebels didn't have air forces of their own.

In a series of concerted pushes, Luanda—with strong mercenary ground and air support—finally destroyed much of Savimbi's military infrastructure and forced him back into the bush. While he might have lost that phase of this quarter-century-long war (in an internecine struggle that had already notched up more than a million dead, some say more), the rumblings continue. While Angola's top brass live on a grander scale than do some Eastern potentates, and the vast majority of this nation of ten or fifteen million—nobody really knows the real figure—continue to survive on starvation-level rations, there must come a point where the masses rebel. For now though, with Angola supplying a fair percentage of U.S. oil imports, any disruptive force in that tragic country, where a billion dollars of oil money recently "disappeared," is going to get no support from Washington.

Another country that saw South African pilots flying helicopter gunships against a group of dedicated warriors was Sri Lanka, against the rebel Tamil Tigers. There were never many of them hired, and none lasted very long. If you discount a fairly substantial Israeli presence, it's of interest that in spite of an intense war (or perhaps because of it) very few mercenaries were hired by Colombo to fight their battles. Most of those who were involved seem to have come from South Africa, and even they weren't able to stay the pace. There wasn't a man among them who could cope with Sri Lanka's crippling bureaucracy. As one of them said afterward, it was Asian efficiency at its most bizarre. He added that it was also one of the reasons why the Tigers made the gains they did: in reality, they were only marginally more efficient than government forces.

Some mercenary pilots spoke of an underlying mistrust among Sri Lankan military commanders, particularly toward non-nationals and mercenaries. There was also a lot of obfuscation when it came to planning. More often than not, those involved were faced with an almost paralyzing inability among Sri Lankan officers to make quick decisions.

Some of the mercenary pilots felt that there were times when they were unnecessarily put at risk. Also, they were critical of the fact that the Sri Lankan infrastructure lacked back-up, which is essential in combat in this day and age. Instead, they were told that if any of them were shot down, they were on their own. It was a brief but hard lesson in how not to win the trust of mercenaries who fight your war.

The Israelis we encountered in Sri Lanka seemed to have managed better, but then they usually do because they do things their way. Also, in Sri Lanka their presence was quasi-official. Jerusalem has been supplying much of the island state's air and naval power including Kfir jet fighters and fast naval patrol boats.

Before that, during the Lebanese civil war, mercenaries—allied to one cause or another—were used both for training and as combatants by a variety of the hundred-plus factions involved in that country's sixteen-year debacle. Some of those hired by the South Lebanese Army (SLA) commander, Major Sa'ad Haddad, were, like my old friend Dave McGrady, American nationals.

It mattered little that it was Jerusalem that funded Haddad or that the SLA was the brainchild of an Israeli journalist and military reservist, Colonel Yoram Hamizrachi. The purpose of this force was to bolster numbers. Pay was nominal, not even a hundred dollars a month, and the conditions under which they survived austere in the extreme.

Not long afterward, the staunchly Christian Lebanese Force Command (LFC) started using U.S. volunteers for tactical and sniper training in and around Beirut. Some of these people were sent to Lebanon at the behest of Lt-Colonel Robert K. Brown, publisher of *Soldier of Fortune* magazine. Others, mainly French and German radicals, attached themselves to a variety of Muslim forces opposed to the LFC. It was about then that the Falanghists hired a former Rhodesian Air Force Canberra pilot. He was paid ten grand a month in U.S. currency but never flew a single sortie, which was just as well since Syrian SAM-6 batteries dominated all the approaches to Beirut's airspace.

Right now, well into the post-Afghan and Iraqi war era, circumstances for conflict have changed once again. Recent developments along the American East Coast, the Middle East, parts of Africa, Columbia, Peru and Central Asia have seen a paradigm shift in the very nature of war. Even before September 11, Martin van Creveld, one of the best military theoreticians of our time, postulated as much in his book *The Transformation of War.*

It was his view that the kind of conventional struggles waged by nation-states in the past were fading from the map. In the future, he suggested, "war-making entities" were likely to resemble those of the pre-modern era. These might include smaller, regional conflicts in which one tribal element might be pitted against another. It could also involve religious groupings, mercenaries, or perhaps commercial bodies like those that opened Europe's trading routes to the Far East four or five hundred years ago.

As he wrote, both the Dutch and British East India companies had their own armies and all of them were staffed with mercenaries, some excellent, others deplorably bad.

Van Creveld has a vision of his own, which he believes might very well become the norm for irregular conflicts in the future. He wasn't specific about a timeline when he wrote:

"As used to be the case, until at least 1648, military and economic functions will be reunited . . . much of the day-to-day burden of defending society against the threat of low-intensity conflict will be transferred to the booming security business." Indeed, he added, "The time may come when the organizations which comprise that business will take over the state."

9

MERCENARIES IN BOSNIA, LEBANON AND ELSEWHERE

"If there is a lesson to be learnt from merc work it's this—you are on your own. If you put your trust in others or possibly rely on outside forces for salvation, you're buying yourself a one-way ticket to the oblivion of a merc's limbo: a jail if you're lucky, and if you're not, a bullet in the back of your neck in some godforsaken backwater . . ."

Soldier of Fortune magazine, June 1987

Before Neall Ellis went into Sierra Leone, he spent some time getting shot at in the Balkans. His brief stint as an aspiring mercenary in Bosnia had a significant bearing on his life because fighting other people's wars has been his chosen career ever since.

Out of work and with the West African posting still more than a year away, things weren't happening for him back home. The entire Southern African sub-continent was in a state of flux: Nelson Mandela had taken over the government, which sent the post-apartheid economy into a downturn spiral. Nellis was looking for opportunities in the Cape when he got a phone call from Johannesburg.

"How does flying for a crazy bunch of Islamic militants appeal to you?" asked a fellow named Mario. Nellis had worked with "Mario" in the past while flying combat in Angola. He was one of the most experienced pros in the game.

"Depends on which bunch of Moslems," the former South African Air Force colonel replied. He wasn't exactly hesitant, but nor was he enthusiastic; the Balkans had long ago acquired the kind of reputation that caused most freelancers to shy away, not only because of the lack of money but also equipment that was sub-standard and poorly maintained. Even worse was the fact that both sides had little regard for the ethics of combat: you were lucky to survive if you were taken captive. Nellis was also testy because of the experiences of some of his friends who had volunteered for duty in the Balkans. Some hadn't been paid, others had been killed.

"There's a limit to what I will do for money," he told Mario.

"This is different though," the other man assured Nellis. "You'll be working for Muslim separatists in Bosnia. They're a tough bunch and they're reliable." Mario went on to describe the mission.

"Done!" said Nellis, unequivocally because he trusted Mario, though they still hadn't settled on payment.

"Where do you want me?"

"Jan Smuts. Four this afternoon."

This was no small task since the main international airport in Johannesburg was a two-hour flight away, with another hour on the road to Cape Town's airport. And he still had to make his booking.

When Mario called, Nellis was working as a farm manager in the Cape. While it offered marginal security, the job wasn't what he was looking for. As Mario described his new assignment, Nellis would be involved with friends. Two of them—Jakes Jacobs and Jaco Klopper—were still serving members of the South African Air Force. They would have to apply for leave in order to take the Balkan job, although they wouldn't be able to say where they were going or what they'd be doing. As in any regular force, flying combat for a foreign government was what the Americans liked to call an effective career terminator. Others on the team were Phil Scott, Pete Minnaar, and Mike Hill, all former SAAF chopper crewmen with years of combat experience.

The way Mario explained it, the men would be handling a pair of Bosnian Mi-8s in ground support roles in outlying areas such as the Gorazde, Bihac and other enclaves. Since the Serbian Army had cut these Islamic settlements off from the world outside, the opposition was using helicopters to bring in supplies. Although he'd agreed to go, the assigned worried Nellis—just as it did the others when they later discussed it.

It was a hazardous job with some tricky twists to it. For starters, it would be winter by the time they arrived, something a dozen Wehrmacht divisions discovered to their cost when they invaded the Yugoslavia of old half a century before. Such terrain would be difficult country to traverse, especially when clouds obscured towns and the tall ground looming over them, sometimes for weeks at a stretch.

Of course, there were also the Serbs, across whose territory they would have to gad about in their flying machines and whose arsenal included some of the most sophisticated anti-aircraft missiles and AAA weapons available. Only after they reached Bosnia were they to discover that there were no navigational aids to speak of, and that almost all flying was at night. It was a tough call.

Still, the pay was good. Weather allowing, the men would be required to fly as many missions as they could, two a day if possible. They would each get an extra $500 for each sortie completed, and, as was agreed up front, operational flights would be in tandem, two Mi-8s to a mission, very much as they had always operated in Africa. If one of the birds was forced down, the other could pick up survivors. That was the way it had all been detailed by Mario before the men left South Africa.

In Johannesburg, Nellis and the others were briefed by another SAAF figure from the past, Slade Healy. He had just returned to South Africa, having flown for his Bosnian friends. It was Healy's job to negotiate terms for this new bunch of aviators. His contact in the Balkans was Zarif, a "heavy Muslim political figure" from Zenica.

It was Healy who warned Nellis and company at that first briefing that the job was precarious. He emphasized it by detailing his first flight from Zenica, a city northwest of Sarajevo. The mission was to reach Gorazde, which was completely surrounded by Serbian forces. "Our chopper took some heavy ground fire, much of it sustained," he told the group. He added that there was more battle damage than they would have liked before they were able to make it safely into an LZ in the mountains. Also, the crew had to fly in both directions using night vision goggles (NVGs).

"This is going to be hard work," he declared. But it seemed worth it, considering that South Africa was in a recession and everybody involved needed the money. Universally, this kind of freelance military activity was in short supply just then.

Healy cautioned the new arrivals about the helicopters they would be flying. Though none of them had flown Mi-8s before, they wouldn't have time to convert to the Russian helicopters before going operational. There was really no other way. He suggested that if they didn't accept the contract, others would.

Zarif, a short, slim man with a mustache—the archetypal son of the Prophet—was at Zagreb Airport to meet the team members when they arrived from Vienna. He took them to a small hotel, arranged for dinner, and left them to spend the night on their own.

The following morning the group was driven to a Croatian Army military airfield on the outskirts of town, where they boarded a Mi-8MTV—the same designation Hip they had been hired to fly and which is used today by the American company ICI of Oregon in its deployments. Their destination was Zenica. After that, said Zarif, they would be taken to the Bosnian front line.

Along the way they stopped briefly in Banja Luka to pick up a couple of mysterious characters dressed totally in black. With their faces hidden behind balaclavas, they were obviously the local version of Special Forces. Neither man uttered a word for the duration of the trip, not even a greeting when they clambered onboard.

Nellis' first impression of the Hip was good. The helicopter was a lot smoother in flight than he'd anticipated. The machine came across as rugged and functional even though its instruments were dated. True, Western pilots were critical of the Hip, but then few had actually flown it. He had heard criticism that the helicopter was crudely built and that it lacked the quality of safety features usually found on their own equipment. Also, some said, Hips would surprise its handlers with an occasional in-flight hiccup.

His final observation about the Mi-8 was instructive: "That chopper can take a lot of damage under fire and that's what counts. Ask me about it because I know." After Bosnia, Nellis flew Mi-17s in Sierra Leone for Executive Outcomes, followed by Sandline International, which was then offering "guns for hire" services.

Coincidentally, it was Neall Ellis' chopper—parked on the quay alongside HMS Cornwall and being worked on by Royal Navy technicians in Freetown harbor—that caused the British Parliamentary rumpus that resulted in Sandline being ousted from West Africa. That improbable event—vociferous and vigorously sponsored by a radical political lobby and supported by several left wing newspapers—ultimately caused the deaths of tens of thousands of innocents in the subsequent war that dragged on for years. As we have already seen, it also cleared the way for Foday Sankoh's rebels to attack Freetown again, resulting in a million or more refugees.

On landing at Zenica, the team was taken to an apartment block alongside the river. It was large and comfortable, though Nellis remembers that while taking a shower around midnight some clown let a burst rip with his AK-47 on full automatic outside his bathroom window.

"I got a helluva fright and fell into the tub. All I could imagine was a round or two coming through the walls and ricocheting around the tiles," explained Nellis. "The South Africans had already tested their thickness in case their building was hit by a shell. The man was drunk and after an argument with his neighbors, he was finally convinced that sleep might be the better option."

It didn't take the South Africans long to accept that while morale within the Bosnian Army was at an acceptable standard, discipline was poor. Quite often, Nellis recalls, their soldiers would start shooting into the air for no reason. Or someone would throw a grenade or two because it was what he felt like doing. He sensed that it might have been a reaction to the nightly bombardments to which the population was being subjected. For their part, the Serbs were using 155mm guns against them, and Zenica was at the receiving end of artillery and mortar bombardments just about every night.

"Usually the Serbs would fire five or six rounds and then there would be a lull which could last minutes or several hours, when it would start all over again. While there was a steady flow of casualties, the city's inhabitants seemed to have become accustomed to rounds falling about their buildings," Nellis explained.

The situation was perhaps best encapsulated by an incident that occurred while the group was sitting in a restaurant on their second day. "Everybody was eating. Suddenly an artillery round—a big one—fell not too far from where we were eating. Yet almost everybody in the place just carried on as though it was a completely normal thing." Unless a shell landed really close, most did not even bother reacting.

The team's first few days in their new base were spent in the apartment acquainting themselves with their new choppers. Pete Minnaar had flown combat with EO in Angola and was familiar with the helicopter, but it was a different matter trying to master the mechanical intricacies of a fairly complex combat machine without being hands-on. The rest of the time it was briefings with army intelligence officers and planning acceptable routes in and out of Gorazde. From the start it was clear that each mission would involve a good deal of map planning: flying at night made this imperative.

"One of our immediate concerns was a pretty sophisticated radar-guided SAM system we knew the Serbs had set up in large numbers throughout the region," explained Nellis. "We had seen what these missiles were capable of in Angola and were familiar with the threat. The weapon was deadly, especially in the right hands." SAM-8s had always been one of the better Soviet anti-aircraft weapons systems, especially against low-flying aircraft, and they tended to nurture a healthy measure of respect within the flying community. Since the Muslim forces had nothing with which to counter or evade them,

Nellis reckoned that they would just have to get used to the idea.

"What really worried us was that NATO commanders claimed to have destroyed all Serbian radar guided anti-aircraft defenses, which was crap. NATO said a lot of things that were not true. There was simply no guarantee that they'd been successful. So we decided that the only way to operate was to avoid all daylight missions and to go into Gorazde at night while hugging the ground and using our NVGs for navigation."

Each pilot had his own GPS for backup and it was just as well that they'd brought them because there were none to be had in Zenica. "Zarif also managed to lay hands on two American ANVIS sets which suited us," declared Nellis. Notably, the NVGs issued to the South Africans by the Bosnians were Russian-made and, according to Nellis, almost, but not quite as good as anything comparable in the West.

The first task the Bosnians set the South Africans was to prove they could fly as well as they claimed they could. "Though we had all the necessary qualifications, they demanded a series of practical demonstration flights from each one of us. Individually we were given two thirty-minute check rides—first in daylight hours, then at night, and finally, with NVGs." And that, added Nellis wryly, "was the sum total of our Mi-8 conversions."

Even in the beginning, relations between the South Africans and their Bosnian commanders were testy. They had immediate problems with Zarif, who had broken a cardinal promise on which the entire operation hinged. Before leaving Johannesburg, the team had been assured by Slade Healy that every flight would be a two-ship operation. On arriving in Zenica, however, the promise was immediately countermanded by Zarif. He said it was not possible to fly two ships at once, arguing that his forces didn't have the necessary resources to deploy two choppers at a time. Further, he told the group that the matter was a fait accompli. The subject warranted no further discussion, he declared.

"That was that," said Nellis. "The man had said his piece and we were expected to accept. But since we'd always been accustomed to flying in pairs in some of the remotest corners of the globe, his backtracking on an issue that we regarded as cardinal caused our first big rift."

That was not all that bothered the South Africans. "The other matter we'd raised—and we'd been told was OK—was a high-frequency radio set at the apartment. We needed this equipment for the guys who stayed behind so that they could monitor the others' flights in the event of problems," continued Nellis. "One team would go out and the other would keep track as things unfolded. Instead, they gave us VHF, which was limited to line-of-sight reception. Consequently, once the aircraft went into the hills we'd have no communication with our guys at all. That bothered the hell out of us and we said so."

The fact that the helicopter was painted a combination of blue and white Aeroflot colors also worried the men. "This was definitely a no-no in wartime," explained Nellis. "We demanded that it be camou-flaged black, specifically for night operations. Of course this raised eyebrows and they made excuses about cost and timing, but they even-tually saw the light. By the time the paint job was done, the Hip actu-ally looked quite sinister."

For cockpit illumination—which had to be compatible with using NVGs onboard—Jacobs had the sense to bring with him from home some green LED lights. These were wired and taped onto the instru-ment panel by Phil and Pete. "It was primitive, but the modification worked." There were some frustrating delays while the team waited for the helicopter to be painted. Then, after an unexpected engine problem, the South Africans got themselves ready for war.

"We'd already agreed to drop the request for a two-ship opera-tion, realizing that if we were shot down we'd be on our own," Nellis stated. But since Jacobs and Klopper were still in the air force, their concerns about being captured if they were brought down were pret-ty damn real. If that happened, they realized, they'd have no support from their government. Worse, as active SAAF members, they'd face courts martial afterward. All that, assuming that they would emerge from the wreck alive.

The first flight was taken up by Mike, Jaco and Pete from a sports field in the heart of Zenica in late September, 1995. The helicopter was loaded to the gunwales with ammunition and medical supplies and they were hardly airborne before they had to return to base because a powerful weather front had closed in. They were stymied for the rest of the day and after dark a mist enveloped the hills. With winter almost on them, bad flying conditions were inevitable, but this was a lot worse than they'd anticipated.

The next evening things improved a bit and they tried a second time. This time they made it to Gorazde. Though the flight was only about thirty-five minutes each way—with another fifteen minutes or so on the ground for offloading—it was about as hairy as it gets, one of the crew remembered. Conditions weren't helped by the fact that the LZ they were supposed to go into was perched on the side of a hill. The reason offered by their hosts was something about protection against enemy snipers.

Mike Hill recalled afterward that it was a difficult approach: "We had ground fire coming up at us just about all the way." The helicopter was hit several times but there was no serious damage. In the end, they brought out a batch of sick and wounded troops and some civilians.

On touchdown back at Zenica, the South Africans became overnight celebrities. Everybody wanted to pump their hands and, Islamic or not, buy them hefty shots of slivovitz. "It was during the debriefing that we realized the mission wasn't as straightforward as we'd hoped. In fact, it was a lot dodgier than we'd anticipated because we had to cross several rows of enemy lines that stretched from the Yugoslavian border all the way to Sarajevo and beyond. Worse, there was nothing in a straight line. We were required to fly a jagged, winding course that more or less followed the road from the border," Nellis explained.

"A second, more persistent issue was the deployment of enemy forces around Gorazde itself. Once the helicopter had crossed the first hurdle, enemy troops dug into positions around Gorazde would have been told by radio that there was a helicopter heading their way," Nellis explained. "So the Serbs would be waiting for us, having been allowed about fifteen minutes to prepare for our arrival. Consequently there would be quite a volume of incoming fire heading for us as we approached." As Nellis said, getting to the target LZ was only half the battle. "Whether that first leg of the sortie was successful or not, we still had to bring the chopper back to Zenica, our home base. So the chances of us getting hit whenever we took the machine out were just about a hundred percent."

Because Serb defenses around Gorazde were not as concentrated to the immediate west of the enclave, the crew thought that the best route on the return leg would be over the mountains toward the coast. Just then, however, the weather turned nasty again. "So we had no alternative but to follow more or less the same flight path home that we'd used before. The other option was to go high and seek cloud cover, but that would have meant flying blind in the mountains and that wasn't an option. Also, Serb radar would have picked us up in a jiffy and they would have been able to use their SAMs."

It didn't take any of the South Africans long to accept that since there were no airfields or letdown facilities anywhere between Gorazde and Zenica their options were constrained. It was a hell of a way to be earning bucks, the guys joked afterward.

Writing about his experiences in the Balkans a few years later, Nellis said that the stark reality of almost certainly being shot down at some stage or other caused the beginnings of a serious rift within the group. "Going into a strange country about which none of us knew shit and dealing with people who didn't speak English, made us decide very early on that if one of us was unhappy with the situation, then we'd all be unhappy. It wasn't the ideal solution, but it did create something of a common bond," he continued. "It was also agreed that if we couldn't sort things out, we'd all leave. Obviously, it didn't help that we couldn't trust our hosts. They'd lied from the start, and we knew that in their eyes we were expendable."

Consequently, the mercenary group felt that if they stuck together, their chances of success would be better, especially if they had to make a dash for it.

Nellis continues: "A few nights after Mike's mission, it was our turn, with the crew consisting of Jakes and Phil and myself. Again, Gorazde was our objective. This time the weather was perfect and we left for the helipad just before sundown. "We'd already seen how these people operated so we decided to supervise the loading of the helicopter and do a proper pre-flight check ourselves before it became too dark.

The South African pilot continued his narrative of the operation:

"The helicopter had meanwhile been moved to a hilltop outside the town where it was out of sight of anyone who didn't need to know about our flights. Intelligence was coming through that the Serbs were being informed by their own sources or, possibly, observation posts in the surrounding hills each time we lifted off. Consequently, nobody had to tell us that the bastards would open fire the moment we approached their positions.

"Leaving Zenica that night was an event. We were just about to cross the first line of Serb defenses when we came under some really heavy fire. What was coming up at us wasn't just cursory; it was big stuff. We could hear the bird take hits, you couldn't miss it, like somebody using a giant hammer on the fuselage.

"I felt a heavy thump underneath my seat accompanied by a loud bang. A moment later 'Natasha' started screeching.[1] We knew enough about cockpit warning systems to be aware that something was seriously wrong with the helicopter. And while we couldn't detect any immediate damage because all the instruments seemed in order, Jakes decided that it might be better to take her back.

"It was a sudden, impulsive move. Though we were flying a bit high, he turned and dived toward the ground. Luckily there was a full moon and we couldn't miss the ground coming up at us. Once we'd leveled out, we stayed low to reduce the threat of incoming fire."

As it happened, Jakes' decision wasn't the best option facing the South Africans. What he'd done was turn the helicopter directly toward enemy gun emplacements. More rounds followed and after taking more punishment, the Hip finally moved out of range.

Nellis: "Back at base, nobody was chuffed with this performance. We'd come back without completing a mission. An immediate result was that we got nothing for our efforts, even though the flight was about as perilous as any that I'd experienced in my career. The passengers in back were even more shaken by the time they emerged: they'd been sitting on three tons of explosive mortar and artillery rounds." The team waited several days for the chopper to be repaired and then tried again.

"We had just got to the LZ when the weather started to close in once more. This time Jakes told the Bosnians that neither he nor anybody else was prepared to take her up in those conditions and we were promptly taken back to the house," remembered Nellis.

Zarif was furious. In the four weeks that the crew had been in Bosnia, the South Africans had notched up one successful flight. Apart from losing money, Zarif had also lost face with his own people.

"At a confab later that night, Jakes decided that he wasn't prepared to go on. He told us that he wanted to return home and that was that," said Nellis. The aircrews had sensed it coming over the past week or so because their relations with Zarif had deteriorated to the point where he had become both obnoxious and aggressive. He had insulted the men, including once or twice in public. At one stage he threatened the team with arrest if they didn't take the chopper up.

"We stood by our earlier decision that if somebody decided to pull out, the rest would follow," explained Nellis. "I wasn't too happy with the idea because I needed the money. Actually, I was desperate, but since none of the others were prepared to hang in there—and I didn't have the experience on type to try it alone—I ended up on the plane back to Zagreb with the rest of the gang."

For aspiring mercenaries, Neall Ellis offers a few off-the-cuff observations:

- When going to a strange country to fight somebody else's war, make sure that you have someone on your team who can speak the language;
- Be careful how you choose your companions. Serving members of armed services are stuck either in a career or a pension trap. You can be almost certain that they won't be prepared to take the same chances that you do because they're going to be worried about wives and children;
- Last, make sure you have an escape route. Most important, no matter where you're going, negotiate your return air ticket up front. We left Zenica almost penniless. If we hadn't had our return legs paid for, we'd have been in big trouble.

Over the years, the international community has been regaled by some interesting tales involving mercenaries. Indeed, no continent has been spared the chicanery so often associated with "guns for hire."

As we have seen, Europe's Balkans—in spite of the sort of difficulties encountered by Nellis' South African crowd—eventually became something of a mercenary haven while that war raged, though more often with ground forces than those operating in the air. This was perhaps to be expected since conspiracy and intrigue were as much a part of the Serbian or Croatian psyche as the disparate nations that Field Marshal Tito molded into yesterday's Yugoslavia. Throughout, freebooters were a part of it, though their roles were sporadic and opportunities came in spurts.

One event unlikely to hit the headlines when it happened took place in Africa during the late 1970s. It involved Libyan leader Muammar Gadhaffi and an American pilot, Dana Drenkowski, a youthful Vietnam veteran from San Francisco who flew more than two hundred combat missions in F-4 fighters and B-52 bombers during his deployments in Southeast Asia. One of his biographers described Drenkowski as "a small man, dark-haired and strung tight."

His unusual claim to fame was that, with strong encouragement from Washington, he had accepted a job as a mercenary working for the often-irrational Libyan despot. As Drenkowski recalls today, it was a remarkable experience, if only because the CIA was eager to get some of their people on the ground in this most secretive of nations.

In the end it didn't quite work out as everyone hoped. In fact, Drenkowski is lucky to be alive.

Drenkowski and two of his American friends—pilot "Johnnie," who had spent time flying CIA contacts in and out of Castro's Cuba after the Bay of Pigs debacle, and "Blue Eyes," one of the most intrepid U.S. Special Forces operatives of the time—were hired by maverick CIA agent Ed Wilson. Wilson had been stationed in Libya for several years and had a reputation at Langley as being something of a master of the unorthodox. Drenkowski remembers that the man's approach to just about everything was nonconformist. What became clear only years later was that some of what Wilson did never reached Washington's ears. Over the years, this agent managed to ingratiate himself with the Libyan leader, do his bidding and report back to Langley, for which he was rewarded by Washington with decades in an American top security prison. Only recently has Wilson been exonerated by the judicial system, in large measure because the CIA originally lied about his role in the rogue Mediterranean state.[2]

In the Drenkowski assignment, Wilson's role was to coordinate the operation from start to finish. He hired Drenkowski and two others, who preferred to be known as "Johnnie" and "Blue Eyes," as mercenaries, negotiated their contracts up front (between $75,000 and $100,000 each), and sent them to Libya. Time was critical so the entire deal—briefings, travel, transfers of money and the rest—was accomplished within less than a week.

Hurried through customs at Tripoli Airport and immediately sent south to the Republic of Chad in an unmarked Libyan Air Force F-27 twin-engined Fokker Friendship, the men were told that their job would be to lead a group of rebels on a raid on N'djamena, the Chadian capital.

Going by Gadhaffi's track record, this wasn't exactly something new. The Libyan leader, always the impulsive amateur revolutionary, had been trying for years to destabilize Chad, together with just about every other country in the region. In fact, he'd been at it almost as long as he'd been in power.

With Drenkowski and his friends in the country, Wilson told them that the Libyan leader already had a sizable force in the northern part of the neighboring desert country, which is more than twice the size of France. Some were deployed along the Tibesti's Massif at Zouar and were complemented by more ground and air elements at Faya Largeau, farther south, one of the Saharan towns that Drenkowski and the boys would have flown over to get to N'djamena. Wilson assured the three men in a final briefing that he would make sure they coordinated competently as things developed with "friendly forces" out of Zouar.

What Drenkowski and his friends weren't told was that two French fliers hired to do the same job two weeks earlier had been summarily executed for failing to carry out their mission. The French aviators had tried to fly a group of Gadhaffi's insurgents to N'djamena, but their plane was forced back because of a rare Sahara fog—the kind of natural desert phenomena that only envelops the region a few times a year. The mist completely blacked out the target area so it was impossible to land, the pilots reported. The Frenchmen were accused of lying and of having failed to achieve the objective for which they had been contracted. They were put up against a wall and shot.

N'djamena—Fort Lamy in colonial times—was the same town from which French General Jacques-Philippe Leclerc (who later achieved fame as the "Liberator of Paris') set out with his Free French army to counter Field Marshal Rommel's push eastward along the Mediterranean coast more than a generation before. It was a spectacular thousand-mile march across the largest desert in the world to link up with the British Eighth Army at Tripoli. Along the way, Leclerc captured several Italian garrisons.

Drenkowski faced an immediate problem in northern Chad within a day of setting out, a dilemma that ultimately derailed the entire operation. They had come halfway across the world to do what they were assured by Wilson would be "a quick job." The night before they got to their destination, however, desert tribal politics intervened.

There was a sudden and inexplicable change of allegiance on the part of the group that was supposed to be Drenkowski's main support force. Apart from finding themselves in a situation that under any other circumstances would have been regarded as comical, the affair was also an embarrassment for the government; the three foreigners were on a personal assignment for Gadhaffi. Worse, the moment the Americans stepped off the Fokker they were grabbed as hostages and told that would be executed in three days if Tripoli didn't comply with their demands.

Ed Wilson now had a problem on his hands. Although the Libyans had managed to disguise the deaths of the two French pilots—Tripoli had told Paris that after returning safely from the Sahara, their plane had ditched into the Mediterranean—the last thing Libya needed was for three more foreigners to be killed in what was already a botched cause. The fact that they were U.S. nationals compounded the issue.

Taking his typically tough line, Wilson warned Gadhaffi that if the worst happened, Washington's reaction might be severe. While this nonconforming Arab leader had glibly explained away the deaths of the two French pilots a short while earlier, the Americans, Wilson warned, would demand an investigation, possibly *in situ* and with witnesses.

Drenkowski and his buddies, meanwhile, were being held under armed guard in a Bedouin tent in the shadow of the same granite wall against which their predecessors had met their fate. Aware by now of what had happened to them, he had no intention of waiting for what the three men now regarded as inevitable. Working closely with their Libyan liaison officer, the group decided that whatever else, they'd go down fighting.

Together with their Libyan host—who was stuck in Zouar and who was also under constant threat from the turncoat rebels—Drenkowski and the other two mercenaries agreed that their best option was to try and steal the lone Dakota C-47 parked on the airstrip nearby and try to make a getaway. This was the same Gooney Bird that they were to have used in the raid. It was a long shot, but under the circumstances, there was no other option.

Their opportunity came on the fourth day of their incarceration. The main Libyan force was camped some distance from where the prisoners were being held. Perhaps to make a show of strength to impress the opposition, its leaders mustered every available gun and staged a powerful display of firepower against one of the rebel flanks. The diversion had the effect of concentrating attention away from the hostages. The firing had barely begun when Gadhaffi's aide rushed into their tent.

"Move!" he shouted, pointing to where the Dakota was parked a few hundred yards away across open ground. The three Americans raced toward the airstrip. Three or four minutes later, as the firing slackened, the Bedouins realized they had been duped and turned their attention toward the plane.

Drenkowski vividly remembers the ground fire coming at them on take-off as about as intense as anything he'd experienced. They managed to get the engines going in no time at all, but as the wheels lifted off the gritty lava, the aircraft barely cleared a large concentration of men who had taken up positions at the far end of the strip. "The bastards had a clear advantage and by the time we got going they were ready for us. In fact we were pretty damn lucky even to get into the air." As it was, the aircraft absorbed a huge amount of punishment and, as he recalled later, anything else but a C-47 and they might well have been brought down.

Once clear of the runway, Drenkowski checked around to see who was hurt and determine the extent of the damage. Even before they had lifted clear of the ground, all portside cockpit windows had been shattered by rocket fire. Glass splinters temporarily blinded Johnson and he needed help at the controls until blood flowing down his head and face could be stemmed. Moments before, while hauling up the undercarriage, the landing gear lever was shot out of Drenkowski's hand. Once they had some altitude, they had to physically crank up the wheels.

With most of their instruments knocked out, Drenkowski navigated the plane over the next six hundred miles of featureless Sahara Desert with only its standby "whiskey" compass to guide him. For ground drift he relied on experience and dead reckoning.

The final chapter in the escape saga played out when the three Americans made radio contact with Sabha, one of the largest towns in Libya's desert interior. Though fuel was at a critical level, they were told that if they tried to land they'd be shot down. After explaining everything over an open radio transmission—including the fact that they were they were on a secret mission in Chad for their leader—the Libyans finally let them land. Their liaison man at Zouar had obviously not bothered to tell Sabha that they were on their way, or he probably didn't think they'd make it.

The reason for the authorities' reluctance to let them land only became clear after they had been taken into town. Sabha, the Americans discovered, was one of Libya's most isolated military strong points. It lay in the middle of the Sahara, completely ringed by layers of security barriers that effectively cut it off from the world outside. At that stage of the Cold War, Sabha was one of the most clandestine places on earth.

What had made things even more difficult was that this large oasis settlement was at the heart of Gadhaffi's worldwide revolutionary program. International terrorists from a dozen nations were being trained there. Their numbers included members of the IRA, Iran's Communist Tudeh—possibly the most virulent of all anti-Ayatollah Khomeini revolutionary movements—a diversity of Lebanese and

Palestinian terrorist groups, as well as aspiring terrorists from Germany, Japan, Spain, Egypt, Belgium, Britain, Italy's Red Guard, and a sizable squad of South Africans, mostly ANC nationalists in exile.

Also in Sabha were squads of Russians and both East and West Germans, all of whom were eternally squabbling among themselves. The majority of the East Europeans were responsible for military instruction and what was innocuously termed the "political instruction" of their "students. According to Drenkowski, just about everybody in Sabha was operating under some form of cover. The Germans and the Russians, for instance, referred to themselves as "school teachers."

The newcomers settled in. Like the rest of the foreigners, the Americans were given new names: Jones, Smith and Baker, though they kept forgetting who was who. They were told that if anybody asked, they were to identify themselves as a traveling team of geologists.

While Drenkowski has never been shy to talk (and write) about his adventures as a mercenary in Rhodesia, or flying UH-1 Huey helicopter gunships in El Salvador (where he went operational for several months against FMLM guerrillas), he has never before disclosed details about his "Libyan episode." After a six-week "cooling off process" the Libyans released the men, who then made it back to America. Upon his own return, former CIA operative Ed Wilson was jailed for having recruited the three of them for the Libyan Secret Service work.

Because the mission was deemed unsuccessful, Drenkowski eventually had to pay back most of the money that had been deposited into a Swiss bank account by his Federal employers. In the end he got out about $12,000 for roughly eight weeks work, good money at the time. Totally unassuming decades later, and as of the writing of this book still serving in the US military as a reserve lieutenant colonel (though these days in Baghdad) Drenkowski used what he earned in North Africa to qualify at one of the best law schools in San Francisco.

When not in uniform, he works as a lawyer in that city.

Muddle-headed schemes to overthrow legitimate governments—in Third World states in particular—are not uncommon. Some have gone down in the unlikeliest places. What is astonishing is that so many of them have succeeded. Sometimes they have involved masterstrokes of planning, guile and military expertise. Other attempts, such as the addle-brained attempt by a group of South African mercenaries to unseat the president of Equatorial Guinea in early 2004, don't bear comment, except that some lives were lost along the way, all of them in prison.

But then you have more distinctive events that go down in the history books. In September 1995, for instance, infamous French mercenary Colonel Bob Denard, whose dogs of war had been leaving murky footprints in African conflicts for three decades—not always successfully as the aborted attempt in Togo showed—led a group of French mercenaries in battle against government troops in the Comores Archipelago. It was the third time that Denard had taken over the tiny island nation. Already in his sixties, he had retired two years earlier and publicly pledged that his warring days were over and that he was going to write his memoirs.

With a couple of dozen hired fighters supported by a squad or two of local dissidents, a band of French irregulars landed from boats in the capital Moroni, grabbed President Said Mohamed Djohar in his palace, and held him hostage. Thereafter, this modest force fought for the possession of the radio station, occupied the airport, released political prisoners from jail and continued battling with the Comorian Army.

One day and several hundred dead later, the "colonel" was bidding to become King of the Islands for a second time. Let it be said that his was a popular "homecoming" because this unconventional French freebooter had ruled the Comores benevolently through figurehead presidents from 1978 to 1989. While he was in charge, his supporters remembered, the islanders prospered.

Just as it had in the past, France put the kibosh on Denard's aspirations to stay in the Comores. Barely a week after the 1995 miniinvasion, French troops, backed by helicopters and an APC or two, landed on the outskirts of Moroni and took control. They laid siege to Denard's revolutionary band of brothers while terms of surrender were negotiated. Denard capitulated without a shot being fired. According to the Associated Press, the last public words uttered by this gray-haired limping veteran on his beloved islands were: "Today it's raining and today the Comorian people are crying." There were apparently a lot of locals sad to see him go.

Mohamed Djohar, the despot Denard was trying to overthrow, was a ruthless thug who reacted cruelly toward anyone opposed him.

With Denard gone the islanders were stuck with Djohar again, but not for long. Since his abrupt departure, there have been half-a-dozen more uprisings.

Many projects involving the use of mercenaries end in failure. One, in particular, that covered three continents—North and South America as well as Africa—and eventually garnered a good deal of publicity while it lasted, was no exception.

It involved eight hired guns trying to overthrow the government of Flight Lieutenant Jerry Rawlings of Ghana. Using a Ghana Tourist Board map of Accra as a guide, the arch-planner Godfrey Osei—a Ghanaian expatriate living in New York City—told Phil Foley, an enterprising American with seventeen years of service with the French Foreign Legion (linked all the while to an American intelligence organization), that he wanted to dislodge Jerry Rawlings, whom he described as an ogre. He was deadly earnest that the Ghanaian leader was to be killed, together with his entire family. That included all his wives and children. After that, Osei declared, they would take Ghana's Kotoka International Airport, the nearby Tema harbor, Accra itself and, ultimately, the country. In other words, for Africa it was business as usual.

What became a grotesque tale of high-level intrigue involving American hired guns (as well as an exiled Ghanaian entrepreneur, coupled to Hong Kong business and gambling interests) would have been quite remarkable had its participants not been a bunch of half-wits. Foley fortunately opted out of this crazy scheme not long after he had been contacted. It was a hair-brained, lunatic adventure, he told me.

Among others playing roles in the misadventure were members of New York's Chinese Mafia, Israel's Mossad, a mysterious bunch of Argentinian arms dealers, the FBI and finally, the ubiquitous Central Intelligence Agency. Clearly, the entire venture was so badly mismanaged that it really should never have happened. But it did, and it gave mercenaries a bad name—especially since the tale is riddled with money, greed, double-crosses, and a plethora of questions that will never be answered, at least not in public.

None of this kind of farce was evident among the war dogs fighting in Lebanon's frightful nine-year civil war.

Mercenary recruits were mustered on all sides. Muslim militias fought Christians, and Christian Falanghist forces used mercenaries as snipers and advisors against the Muslims. Among many other factions active in this tiny country at the time were foreign recruits in southern Lebanon doing their bit for the Israeli-sponsored and mainly Christian Army of Free Lebanon. That force, under the command of Major Sa'ad Haddad, the unofficial "governor" of the Israeli security zone, operated along a ten-mile strip running the length of Lebanon's border with Israel's northern Galilee.

Most of those who came to fight in and around Beirut were masters of one or other military discipline. Islamic forces liked to recruit Europeans—mainly German anarchists, with a sprinkling of Frenchmen familiar with mines and explosives, supported occasionally by a sniper or two. The Christians, in turn, came to depend on snipers from America. It was deadly work, as much motivated by ideology as the nonsensical urge to get involved in somebody else's bloodshed. Lebanon had become a killing field.

Except for the former South African Air Force Canberra pilot who received $10,000 a month for doing nothing, financial returns were almost always minimal. Dave McGrady, who had seen quite a lot of action as a bounty hunter in Rhodesia—where he was paid a hefty fee for each insurgent kill—earned $97 a month for the duration while with Haddad's two-thousand-man force.[3]

McGrady told me years afterward that while some of the Lebanese soldiers suspected him of being an American spy, most of those serving in the unit commanded by Major Sa'ad Haddad had a pretty high regard for his military professionalism. Unlike some of the soldiers around him, McGrady soon garnered a reputation as being someone who could be counted on when the shooting started.

"It was different with the majority of Lebanese civilians in the south of the country: they despised me. And, of course, there were other problems, like our rations, which were Israeli leftovers and my Israeli-made rifle, which looked like refuse from an Army ordnance film on weapons abuse, needed a lot of TLC. Add to that the fact that we were constantly short on ammo, just about everybody looked alike, I didn't understand three consecutive words of either Arabic or Hebrew, and there were flies everywhere. Yet when it came time for me to go home, Haddad came to me and said that I should send him a bunch of other Americans like me. We actually got on pretty well."

There weren't many foreigners in that region because the South Lebanese Army (SLA) was run on an almost primeval basis. McGrady's two best buddies were "Maurice," a Frenchman with seven years in the Legion, and "Tim," who had served in the Canadian Army and believed somehow that military experience in Lebanon might ultimately help him further his career. That kind of logic mystified McGrady, but he said nothing about it. Tim's real value was his completion of a basic first aid course in Canada, and weeks spent thereafter assisting medical personnel at the Israeli hospital in Metula, the country's northernmost town. Officially, he was the unit medic.

"Maurice," in contrast, Haddad hated, and he did so with a venom that was both unmitigated and in his face, probably because he was French. Paris had originally opposed the formation of the irregular Lebanese unit and "Maurice" became the major's whipping boy. Eventually he had the Frenchman arrested and sent him overland to Beirut, where, he knew, he'd have to cross both Syrian and Palestinian checkpoints. Because of his links with the SLA, his chances of surviving the trip were remote. McGrady never did find out what had happened to the man and, as he told me, it was one of the quirks that came with the job: you never knew when somebody would turn on you.

"Technically speaking, we were on twenty-four hour alert and had to stay near our quarters, which was an unheated room in what had once been a school," McGrady told me. "If the call came, and it was usually an emergency, we were out of there." His squad would move about in outdated Israeli armored personnel carriers, usually M-113A1s with forward-mounted .50 Brownings and two 30-caliber machine guns on both sides of the APC and another perched on its rear. If the shelling got really bad, they would move one of Haddad's aging Sherman tanks into position and, if time allowed, a captured T54 or two, though they did have the advantage of being able to call on Israeli Air Force jets for top cover.

I met Major Sa'ad Haddad in 1979, not long after he had been appointed commander of the force. My wife Madelon and I were guests of Yoram Hamizrachi, the man who had originally created the force as a counter to Palestinian incursions into the region. We spent time at his Metula home, which doubled as an improvised military headquarters and, indeed, he even took us across the border into South Lebanon—sans passports—to meet Haddad, with whom we had our picture taken.

In 1979 hostilities were sporadic. Muslim guerrillas did what they could to infiltrate the Israeli frontier. A few times they successfully ambushed school buses and attacked the occasional settlement, mostly moshavs or kibbutzims. Occasionally their attacks spilled a lot of blood, and invariably it was women and children they murdered.

Hamizrachi's idea was that his newfound force—composed almost entirely of Lebanese nationals (with a sprinkling of mercenaries)—would deter the Muslims by being active along the same border that the guerrillas were trying to penetrate. He was quite successful, even though Haddad's irregulars were really little more than makeshift fighters made up largely of deserters—quite a few of them Muslims—from the regular Lebanese Army. There were even a handful of Syrian soldiers who had absconded from their own military and wanted in because of rewards being offered by the IDF. Such can be the nature of some of these conflicts.

What this tiny irregular army did buy for Tel Aviv was more time to upgrade its security in the north. Very much as things are today in the Holy Land, if there were any evidence of a concerted thrust or artillery bombardment by the enemy in South Lebanon, the Israeli Defense Force would reciprocate ten-fold, including missions by its Air Force to pound positions on the opposite front.

The main Palestinian/Lebanese defense in the area was Fort Beaufort. This historic, once-beautiful Crusader castle overlooked much of the lower Litani River that, in places, formed the northern boundary of the security zone. Beaufort—named after a French noble-man who, the history books tell us, pursued noble causes by trying to drive the Muslims out of Jerusalem—changed hands half-a-dozen times from about the 1970s on. What's left of the structure has been pounded so often that today it is little more than a heap of rubble. But then, that's the story of so much of the Middle East over the ages. Even in 2005, to the chagrin of the Turks, the Saudis are bulldozing mag-nificent old Ottoman forts to make way for urban development.

Those hired guns that fought around Beirut, in contrast, encoun-tered a totally different kind of war. Theirs was an intense, bloody struggle that left the finest city in the Levant in ruins. Twenty-five years, tens of thousands of deaths, and billions of dollars later, they're still working at reconstructing a city the size of Prague.

This was the job Lebanese Shi'ite billionaire and former Prime Minister Rafiq Hariri set himself for more than a decade, and at which he was astonishingly successful. It remained that way until the Syrians assassinated him in March of 2005.

The debate goes on whether foreigners who fought in Afghanistan and elsewhere for al-Qaeda and the Taliban were mercenaries or motivated by a more noble spiritual cause. There is no debate about the answer to that question when it comes to the Libyan soldiers that got involved in Uganda's civil war. It was the late 1970s, and Tanzania had decided it had had enough of the rantings of the monster Idi Amin.

Julius Nyerere, Tanzania's controversially erratic socialist president, took a deep breath and dispatched his army in a concerted armored push toward Kampala, the largest city in Uganda. The twenty-five thousand-man force was about one-fifth irregular—guerrillas, really, who had been fighting the Ugandan Army in the jungle for years and who were part of the Free Uganda Movement.

Twice Kampala was stripped to a shell, first by retreating Ugandan soldiers who left blown-up safes and looted shops in just about every street, and then again after the war was over. The latter destruction was the work of Tanzanian troops who loaded everything that hadn't been bolted or cemented down onto the backs of trucks and hauled it all back to Dar es Salaam. Stolen items included refrigerators, air conditioning equipment, industrial kitchens, and even an entire aircraft maintenance unit from Entebbe Airport. But they accomplished this only after a large Libyan force had been massacred, the lot of them "volunteers for a glorious anti-imperialist cause," as Libya's national radio proudly crowed.

Much of what took place in Uganda during that period was termed rough justice by Western media. It was perhaps to be expected that being an African insurrection, any kind of convention—Geneva or otherwise—that covered the handling or safety of prisoners got short shrift. The result was one long series of mass murders. Corpses littered the fields and streets of the country and it went on for years. While walking Kampala's streets, I witnessed four people being executed for crimes real or imagined. At such times you step politely aside and say absolutely nothing. Arguing or intervening to any degree could easily decide your own fate.

At one stage, about a hundred and fifty Libyans tried to make a run for it. In convoy, they headed for Entebbe Airport where they hoped they could be airlifted home. It was a forlorn option: Gadhaffi had long ago abandoned them for fear of attracting more criticism for his role in a war that tended to label all foreigners involved as mercenaries—Libyans included.

I was attached to a mechanized unit commanded by a Major Onwu, who was later to be appointed Tanzanian commander of the

Southern Region. It was his job to ferret out Arabs who had initially been part of a three-thousand-man Libyan force. "We knew that they would try to break out, because my men had brought in one of them earlier and he told us so," explained the major. "Consequently, we waited in ambush on top of a gully on the main road to the airport from the capital."

Onwu wasn't certain that the tactic would work. The day before his men had ambushed a Libyan column in exactly the same place. He thought they would be more wary the second time around. But the Libyans arrived anyway. They came in several buses, accompanied by two or three Soviet-type APCs with heavy machine guns, troop carriers and jeeps interspersed.

"They'd push a jeep and an APC about a mile ahead of the main group and we'd let them pass," Major Onwu explained. With his men lying in wait they would open fire, and the effect was chaos.

The entire convoy ground to a halt in a cut in the road directly below the barrels of Ugandan guns. Heavy machine guns, RPGs, and grenades cut swathes through the Libyan ranks as they tried to escape from their vehicles, some of them choosing windows instead of doors. A body count afterward revealed that more than half of the Arab force had been killed in the first phase of the slaughter.

"The rest of this disorganized mob ran into the bush," Major Onwu announced proudly. "For the next three or four days we had thousands of villagers with machetes out there searching for them."

One by one the Libyans were hunted down and killed, usually after having their vitals cut off and displayed as trophies, often in their mouths, for all to see. Villagers competed with one another for the highest score. It pleased everybody that Gadhaffi's people had taken such a beating. Altogether, about six hundred of his men died in the Ugandan campaign.

After suffering such a disaster, one would have expected Gadhaffi to have learned something; to become involved in another African war was not wise foreign policy. But he'd been taught nothing.

A couple of years later the Libyan Army was again thrust into a series of cross-border adventures, this time in Chad. That also ended badly for Gadhaffi when his Libyan contingent—which included four or five Mi-8 helicopter transporters and a couple of gunships—were routed by a combination of Chadian troops backed by the French Army and Foreign Legionnaires. An entire Libyan battalion was destroyed at the Saharan oasis town of Faya Largeau.

More recently, in early 2002, a group of South African mercenaries, all formerly of Executive Outcomes, was hired by Gadhaffi to train his army. The company involved called itself NFD, which signified the first initial of each of the directors.

An authoritative London report published by *Africa Confidential* stated at the time that the Libyan contract included training in infiltrating rebel bases and intelligence gathering. Also, instruction included the use of helicopters fitted with infrared cameras obtained from among others, Eloptro, a South African government arms manufacturer. Many of these firms were subsidiaries of the huge Denel defense conglomerate, which at the time was doing contract work for various European aerospace firms including SAAB, the Eurocopter, and several British firms.

With Kentron, another arms manufacturer, the majority of South African scientists and technicians involved had originally worked closely with the Israelis to develop some of this hardware during the apartheid era. The night vision and infrared equipment being marketed by the company, for instance, was then similar to that used today by Israel's security forces. So were at least two versions of unmanned aerial vehicles (UAVs) which South Africa has been exporting to unknown recipients, quite a few of them Muslim.

All this underscores the homily that there are no friends in the weapons business, only contacts.

Many of the yarns that have surfaced over the years have appeared in one form or another in one of America's most unusual publishing ventures, a magazine called *Soldier of Fortune*.

Love it or hate it, this "Journal of Professional Adventurers" has a remarkable following, both in the U.S. government and in the military, though no self-respecting career officer would ever admit to reading it. It is also true that there probably isn't an intelligence organization worth its oats that doesn't receive at least one copy of SOF each month.

The magazine has produced some remarkable leads over the years. The Pentagon paid the magazine several times for Soviet bloc weapons and systems it clandestinely recovered in some of the wars that its correspondents—almost all of them freelance—reported on. As one might imagine, a lot of this stuff came out of Afghanistan when the Soviets were still there.

SOF has also been instrumental in blowing the occasional career by exposing what it terms "the real truth behind the story." It laid bare some of the excesses committed by ATF and FBI agents in the attack on the David Koresh compound in Waco, Texas. Exposés have been the magazine's staple diet over the years, and its writers have included some interesting people. Hollywood military technical advisor Dale Dye, Jim Morris (author of *War Story, Fighting Men, The Devil's Secret Name*, and *Dumbo Drop*—which first appeared as a story in SOF before it was filmed), and columnist Fred Reed, a writer for the *Washington Times* and *Harpers* are just some of the better known.

The magazine's owner, Robert K. Brown, is as blunt and innovative as they come. Crusty as hell at times, the meat-and-potatoes media style of his magazine has made the man an icon among his readers, the majority of them ex-servicemen.

While *Soldier of Fortune* remains a strictly American phenomenon, Brown has been shoving a finger in Uncle Sam's (and nearly everyone else's) eye for more than a quarter century. He has done so by pursuing a succession of causes over the years. These have included training insurgent forces in more than a dozen countries in Africa, Asia, the Middle East and the Americas, all of them beset with some form of racial, religious or civil strife. Some of the people he employed in this regard might have been labeled "war dogs" by the magazine's detractors.

Lt-Col. Robert K. Brown USAR (rtd.) admits that in putting *Soldier of Fortune* on the map he has tended to follow his own brand of "participatory journalism." He is also candid enough to concede that had he still been doing the same sort of thing in the United States today, he'd probably be behind bars.

In the time that Brown has been fomenting solutions to radical causes—some of them outrageous, others as controversial as hell—he has either personally led groups of his magazine's staff into these frays or sent them independently into a variety of wars. These have included conflicts in Afghanistan, the Sudan, El Salvador, Uganda, Rhodesia, Angola, the Congo, Lebanon, Mozambique, Burma, Laos, Chad, Nicaragua, Sierra Leone, Israel, Croatia, Afghanistan and Iraq—and a good few others, he confided, that he'd rather I not write about.

I first met Colonel Brown in the mid-1970s when he flew into South Africa to discuss the founding of his fledgling magazine. The trouble was that he never made it past the first control gate at the airport in Johannesburg. Because he had briefly been involved with Fidel

Castro during the Cuban revolution, the South Africans refused to let him in. It mattered little that by then, Brown—having tasted the consequences of Cuban-style socialism from up close—did a smart political about-face to become one of the most dedicated supporters of anti-Communist causes in the world.

Loved by some, abhorred by others, Brown has made something of an industry out of attacking what he has always referred to as "the Evil Empire." While it would be overly simplistic to label him anti-Communist, he has pursued the cause long enough for the KGB to call him an "imperialist propagandist." That pleased the man: there was a time when his favorite lapel button read "I'd Rather be Killing Communists." Brown, more recently, has mellowed a bit, though his mindset and worldview remain intractable. Some of his friends say he's still as irascible as hell.

Brown recently paraphrased a maxim coined by Churchill after the Boer War. The former Prime Minister put it this way: "The most exhilarating experience in the world is to be fired at with no effect." Brown tacked the following onto the end of the phrase: "and to fire back." That came after he'd led an SOF team into Afghanistan in May 1982 and returned with Russian military equipment that had been captured by the Mujahadeen. By then the war was heating up in all quarters. Everything went pretty much according to plan for Brown until one of the rebel leaders asked him whether he would like to be part of a group that was going to attack a Russian fort.

Always the opportunist, Brown replied, "Why not?"

His rationale for jumping at the prospect of firing into a Soviet strongpoint in the valley below was that such opportunities came neither easily nor often. It mattered little that Ivan might retaliate and that gunships would be searching for the raiders immediately afterward.

It has always been that way with this former Special Forces officer. He bears the unique distinction of being the only man to have been kicked out of the Green Berets twice. But that's another story.

With a captured Russian 14.5mm heavy machine gun perched on a ridgeline overlooking the valley below—the fort lay plum in the middle—Brown spent a useful half-hour of his life in Afghanistan trying to kill Russians. The Soviets retaliated—hard. The same thing had happened often enough in the past for the Russians to have the ridge from where the insurgents were lobbing their shells zeroed in. "Some heavy stuff started coming in within minutes," remembered Brown.

The Americans in this group of fighters didn't linger.

The next time Brown visited his Afghan friends, it was with a request that he bring along someone who could show them how "to work the landmines" that Washington had given them. These were intended to destroy Russian tanks and armored personnel carriers in the various theaters where the Afghan rebels were active; but the word was that they "didn't work."

Along with Stingers, mortars, artillery, claymores, booby traps, AA guns and training, almost everything the rebels deployed in their war of liberation came courtesy of America. As we now know, the Russians also provided their share of rebel hardware, most of it captured in battle.

At Brown's request, John Donovan, an Army reserve officer and a demolition expert, flew to Afghanistan to teach the guerrillas about mines. As he quickly discovered, the rebels were laying them everywhere, but few detonated when they were supposed to. They look good, the Afghan spokesman told Donovan: "Plenty of explosives inside, but they no work. No boom!" he explained, exasperated.

It took Donovan only seconds to work out the problem. He pulled a detonator from the pack and explained to the assembled group that in order for things to go "boom," they first had to screw in the detonator! He showed them how it was done. Things worked pretty well for Afghan mine-laying teams after that. Brown estimates that his magazine can safely take some credit for the number of Soviets killed and tanks destroyed from that point to the end of the war. And, by all accounts, that number was staggeringly high.

Brown's antics have also gotten him into trouble. He has been investigated—occasionally at the instigation of Congress—by just about every security establishment in the U.S., including the Justice Department. The FBI has questioned him a dozen times. He guesses that more than once they tried to set him up, using provocateurs to get him into absurd scams that would almost certainly have landed him in prison.

He remembers one such occurrence. A gray-suited adventurer "with the requisite short back-and-sides and patent leather shoes" offered Brown a container full of Armalite automatic weapons. He claimed that he had used his own oil money to smuggle them into America and that there was a lot more where that lot came from. On another occasion, someone presented him with a silencer for a firearm at a gun show. Brown wasn't interested either time.

The ultimate irony, perhaps, was that with the onset of Glasnost, the American colonel eventually cut a deal with a group of businessmen in Moscow to publish a Russian edition of the magazine. It crashed, together with the Russian economy.

An iconoclast to the last, this erstwhile armored car guard, health studio instructor, freelance photojournalist, ditch digger, cowboy, private investigator, trail crew chief, logger, and hard-rock miner usually responds by telling his critics to "go fuck themselves." And while Brown has had more than his share of enemies, there are also some heavyweights who have gone to bat for him.

Joseph Goulden, a former director at the self-proclaimed watchdog organization Accuracy in Media, admitted that he regularly read the magazine. "They report (on events) at a depth you don't find anywhere else . . . and I can't see myself spending a comparable amount of time with *Time* just to see what (its chief political correspondent) happens to think. I just don't care that much," he stated in an interview in the magazine *Folio* in October, 1993. The *Detroit Free Press*, in a piece titled "Leading the Charge," lauded Brown's role in blasting extremist militias.

The *St. Louis Post Dispatch* was possibly closest to the truth when it declared that SOF derived pleasure "from tweaking the nose, not only of the establishment but also the liberals."

It has been that way from the start. *Soldier of Fortune* was the new boy on the block when it started more than three decades ago. The magazine quickly proved a hit well beyond Washington's beltway and also made Brown enough money to allow him to do pretty much whatever he wanted. One thing he did was build an A-camp in Laos with a hundred and fifty-man army of Hmong tribesmen. The idea was to rescue a group of twenty or so U.S. Air Force pilots and navigators purportedly being held as POWs in the northern part of the country.

The Defense Intelligence Agency took Brown seriously enough to give him a list of all the pilots who had gone missing. It was agreed that once contact had been made, Admiral Gerry Paulsen of the DIA would provide secret call signs that only individual captured pilots would know: that way they'd be able to check whether they were dealing with the real thing. In the end nothing came of it, though the trip was hardly smooth. With China just then sparring with Hanoi, and Laos a client state of the Vietnamese, "we had our share of scrapes."

The popularity of the magazine allowed Robert K. Brown to do all sorts of things that others only dream about. These included operational visits to Africa, air drops over the South American Andes to rescue refugees, helping hurricane victims in the Dominican Republic, a succession of insertions into Afghanistan, training sniper teams with the Christian forces in Lebanon, visits to the Sudan to find out whether the Khartoum government was using nerve gas against the southern insurgents, support for dissident Karen tribespeople against the Burmese, and so on. During the Rhodesian War, Brown and his men were regular visitors to the front.

In December 1992, he led five- and six-man training teams into Croatia. A couple of years later—using one of George Soros' "Food for the Hungry" trucks—Brown smuggled dozens of Scott Air Packs into Sarajevo for that city's fire department, taking them in right under the muzzles of opposing artillery. Once that was done, he retraced the same route out.

What became manifest after the first handful of SOF issues appeared was that Brown had made an important breakthrough in the coverage of events that you don't normally find on your neighborhood newsstand. Within four years his circulation was more than a hundred thousand. A few years later it had upped by another fifty percent. As anybody involved in the business will tell you, this was unusual in the convoluted world of magazine publishing. The colonel had read his market correctly and most of his support—then and now—tended to come from people who had served in uniform. In both Iraq and Afghanistan, the magazine gets big play among the younger team members, many of them—or their families—subscribers.

Brown has this to say about the magazine's early days:

"The majority of the vets returning from Southeast Asia had few friends. Having lost the war in Vietnam there was a large section of the American public that had become totally unforgiving. With no grassroots support back home, they were also being castigated and, to be sure, the media saw to that.

"What you couldn't ignore was that, right or wrong, Vietnam produced as many heroes as each of the two world wars as well as Korea. We all saw the consequences: the denigration of an entire generation of fighting men. There were people in the streets of American cities that spat on men in uniform when they returned from Southeast Asia."

As Brown observed, once back on American soil the guys couldn't get back into civvies quickly enough. The "peace generation" wanted them dead and they proclaimed it in public, usually to the accompaniment of guitar music. Even today, Brown's reaction is succinct: "A pestilence on all their houses!"

Overnight, SOF became a meeting place for like-minded souls. The magazine gave them a voice and continues to do so. Through it all Vietnam has featured prominently in its pages and still does, though the current phase of hostilities in the Middle East has naturally received more recent scrutiny. While SOF readership these days is perhaps older, wiser, and certainly more reticent than before, Brown concedes, there is a younger generation of fighting men out there taking over.

Other events that made news in the pages of SOF over the years included a hundred-grand reward for the first Nicaraguan pilot to defect from the Central American state with an intact Soviet-built Mi-24 helicopter gunship. After a surreptitious meeting with Lt-Col Oliver North, that amount was upped to a million dollars. North's office agreed to underwrite the balance. While no Nicaraguan pilot ever availed himself of the offer, one of the immediate consequences—once the issue hit the newsstands—was that the Nicaraguan Air Force suspended all operations against the Contras for almost a month until they could bring in Cuban pilots as replacements.

Before that, Brown had offered $10,000 in gold for the return "in one piece" of the Ugandan tyrant Idi Amin. There were no takers there either, though an SOF staffer was one of the first foreign journalists to go through Amin's bedroom after it had been ripped apart by Tanzanian troops. What the looters didn't find (but the staffer did) was a bag full of gold-plated medals that he took back to his hotel with him. Some of these also ended up in Boulder, Colorado.

Another offer made in SOF not long afterward was $100,000 to the first person who could bring back a sample of "yellow rain" from Southeast Asia.[4] Though there were quite a few opportunists, including someone who delivered to the offices of the Australian Broadcasting Corporation an RPG-7 rocket that had been painted yellow, it was SOF staffer Jim Coyne who eventually brought the first "yellow rain" sample back to America. He handed it to a government office for analysis. Coyne was eventually called to testify on the matter before a Congressional sub-committee on security issues.

Among some of the security coups notched up by SOF over the years was the return to the U.S. of the first Russian 30mm automatic grenade launcher round. Deadly and versatile in close-quarter combat, this was the weapon that was then being used to good effect by Soviet forces in Afghanistan. Washington had known about the AGS-17— dubbed Plamya (flame)—for some years but had never been able to examine one up close. An SOF team solved that problem. After one year of negotiations and the crossing of many palms, the magazine bought an AGS-17 in Pakistan's Northwest Frontier district of Darra. SOF's gun buff Peter Kolkalis test-fired it, stripped it down and made an evaluation of the weapon on video that was eventually offered for sale in SOF for $39.95 a copy. (It is still available.) That came only after a complete report had been quietly passed on to the Defense Attaché at the U.S. Embassy in Islamabad.

Also to emerge from that effort was the first report, together with photos (which appeared in the SOF February '83 issue) of Russia's RPG-18, a direct copy of the U.S. Army's light anti-tank weapon (LAW). According to Soviet specialist and Jane's correspondent David Isby, who was then on the SOF masthead, Russian scientists had processed the RPG-18 by a very clever reverse engineering effort. One of his conclusions was that "It had greater penetration than would otherwise have been expected from a weapon of 63.5mm caliber."

The ultimate coup was the way a succession of SOF crews smuggled thousands of rounds of never-before-seen AK-74 rounds from the Afghan front to U.S. intelligence officials in Pakistan. The AK-74 was the much-vaunted successor to the ubiquitous AK-47, though much of its buildup proved little more than empty hype. By then Brown had struck up a good relationship with at least one of Washington's intelligence agencies, though he won't tell you which.

It is interesting to note that after the U.S. invasion of Grenada in 1983, Brown and his gang returned to the U.S. with a suitcase full of captured classified documents. These had been rifled from, amongst others, the offices of the Grenada deputy minister of defense as well as the prime minister's office. More important, Brown and his group hadn't been the first there: the place had already been gone over by U.S. intelligence agents who landed with the invading force and who had obviously not done their job properly.

The material Brown chanced upon indicated that Cuba and the Soviets were turning Grenada into a strategic military base: a Cuban/Soviet military and intelligence fortress in the Caribbean. All this was happening while the Cold War was on a boil. After the *Soldier of Fortune* story broke, *Time* magazine flew in one of their reporters and a photographer to Boulder to get the rest of it.

Brown's brainchild must be the only magazine in the world to run an "In Memoriam" column on its masthead. At last count, it had almost a dozen names, almost all of them victims of misadventure.

One of these men was Vietnam veteran Bob MacKenzie, who had been invalided out of the U.S. Army after being badly wounded during the war. That didn't stop him, once he'd recovered, from joining the Rhodesian Army. He ended with the rank of captain in that country's Special Air Service, one of only two Americans ever to achieve the honor. After working as a contributing editor for SOF for several years—jobs that took MacKenzie to the Balkans, South and Central America, Mozambique and elsewhere—he eventually accepted a position in charge of a group of Gurkha mercenaries in Sierra Leone. MacKenzie was the first white man to command a combat force in that country since its independence. His end was a terrible one. (See Chapter 19.)

The first man to die while on assignment for SOF was former U.S. Special Forces Vietnam vet George Bacon. Formerly a CIA case officer in Laos and recipient of the CIA Intelligence star, Bacon was the only American killed in action in Angola. At Brown's behest, Bacon had visited me in Johannesburg before heading north. His claim was that he was a freelance journalist, but since he couldn't show me anything he'd written I didn't pass him along the line, a necessary precaution since there were dozens of American "wannabees" floating about at the time. Some had even joined the Rhodesian Army. I learned later that Bacon was top drawer. Had he come clean, I certainly would have helped. Working for Langley, however, he could hardly have done so. Even Brown wasn't aware until later that Bacon was with the Company. While specifics about his death remain sketchy, it is known that he was killed in an ambush led by Cuban forces.

One of the Americans captured in that same battle was Danny Gearheart. He was later executed by an Angolan firing squad. The Angolans claim they had reason: they presented before the military tribunal in Luanda an advertisement found in his pockets. It was for the recruitment of mercenaries and had been published in *Soldier of Fortune*.

Thirty months later it was the turn of SOF's martial arts editor Mike Echanis. Having been chief military advisor to Nicaraguan President Somoza, Echanis died when the Aero Commander in which he was traveling was sabotaged shortly after take-off from Managua. It blew up in the air and there were no survivors.

A Burmese mortar impacted alongside Lance Motley, who was covering the extended campaign being fought by a group of Karen rebels operating out of Cambodia. SOF was among the first publications to use his articles. After a lengthy stint in Afghanistan, Brown nurtured Motley as a freelancer. He was an outstanding writer, commented Brown afterward. "We lost a good man there. Brave, too."

Others killed while associated with the magazine include Almerigo Grilz in Mozambique and Peter Bertie in Nicaragua.

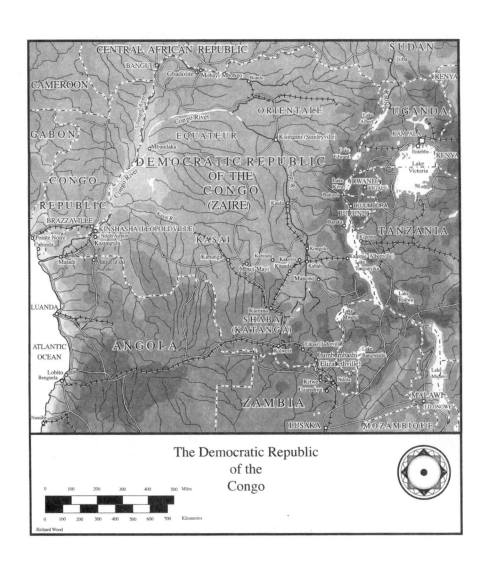

The Democratic Republic
of the
Congo

0 100 200 300 400 500 Miles

0 100 200 300 400 500 600 700 Kilometres

Richard Wood

10

EARLY MERCENARY ACTIVITY
IN THE CONGO

"Going up that river was like traveling back to the earliest
beginnings of the world when vegetation rioted on the earth
and the big trees were kings. An empty stream, a great silence,
an impenetrable forest. The air was warm, thick, heavy, slug-
gish . . . and this stillness of life did not in the least resemble a
peace. It was the stillness of an implacable force brooding over
an inscrutable intention. It looked at you with a vengeful
aspect."

Joseph Conrad: *Heart of Darkness* (1902)

The Congo has been cursed by its unmanageable and increasingly
ungovernable human infrastructure. What has been going on there in
recent years only serves to harden universal perceptions of so much of
post-colonial Africa: that it is little more than a continent comprised
of revolt, insurrection, corruption and instability.

In order to understand the Congo, it is important to realize that
it was there that the first real deployment of mercenaries in the modern era took place. The Congo was also the scene, in the early 1960s,
of the world's first armed aircraft hijacking, engineered by one of Bob
Denard's sidekicks named Jean-Louis Domange. After rescuing
wounded comrades from UN forces in Katanga, Domange commandeered a DC-3 at gunpoint and ordered the pilot to fly to Rhodesia. It
was a big story at the time. Aircraft had been grabbed in the past, but
not by a bunch of soldiers toting automatic weapons. Domange could
never have envisaged how this comparatively simple act would affect
our lives in the decades ahead. In a distant sense, it culminated in what
took place in New York City on September 11, 2001.

Almost one-quarter the size of the contiguous United States (or put
another way, five times as large as France), the Congo is one of the
least developed of the world's nations. The extent of the country's
"first class" road network could be joined together and dumped into

the middle of any medium-sized American city and barely be noticed.

Troubles in the Congo began long ago, many caused by the arrival of the white man in what Conrad called "The Heart of Darkness." Frontiers were shaped in the 1880s, a time when European leaders carved up Africa like an imperial game of Monopoly. Commercial interests vied for territory and the contenders played for people and zones of influence in an Africa that was almost entirely undeveloped. Examine maps of the period (you can do so in any public library) and apart from the more populated coastal regions, the interior of this vast continent—apart from the Arab states and a fair proportion of southern Africa—was largely uncharted. The largest share went to the best call at the table at the time. Perhaps Belgium was rewarded when the heads of state were passing the sherry around for the third time.

As it was then called, the Congo Free State was considered "beyond the pale of any civilized influence, untamable, its people primitive and restless," as a Flemish newspaper of the time summed it up. Nevertheless, tiny Belgium got stuck with it, though it has been suggested that Belgium's King Leopold II was bored and fancied running the place because he had little better to do. Nothing was seriously expected to come of a region that had already become a byword for chaos and savagery, though it was later discovered that trashing the place was just a clever ploy on the part of the Belgian regent. The Congo, in fact, offered its European conquerors the richest rewards of all.

As testified by official papers since released in Brussels, the shrewd old schemer Leopold had done his homework. While some decisions raised questions about his probity, he had quietly sent spies to a part of Central Africa that was almost totally without maps. It was their job to explore what was termed at the time "prospects." And what a windfall awaited them; their secret reports gushed with all kinds of possibilities.

The huge primeval region was untouched by modern civilization, but it was also wealthy beyond measure. Within its borders were huge reserves of hardwoods, rubber, gemstones, copper and other minerals, never mind the diamonds that would be discovered later. Indeed, its natural resources rivaled anything yet seen in Brazil or the East Indies. No wonder Leopold was eager to get his grubby paws on that part of the great continent, and he did so duplicitously under the guise of offering the locals what would later be referred to as "protection." It was a setup of course, and ultimately, a blueprint for disaster.

Unlike Britain and France, both of whom already had good experience in administering people in far-off domains (Paris and London tended toward a system of benign paternalism to keep their African subjects in tow), Belgium ruled its Congo with the gun and the whip. These Europeans had a callous disregard for the welfare of their African subjects. In today's world, Leopold, crown and all, would long ago have been hauled before the International Court of Justice on charges of human rights transgressions.

The Congolese, to the majority of the Belgian colonials, were nothing more than chattel and treated accordingly. As generations of their forefathers had done in the past, most residents had a patch of earth from which to eke out a living. It was a tentative, precarious existence, and now the land was no longer theirs. Everything in the Congo belonged to the distant king. Belgium's rule became more intrusive and a minor army of European officials began demanding taxes from a people who had virtually nothing to give. The country slid into corruption.

In August 1993, Bill Berkeley wrote a perspicacious piece about the country in *The Atlantic Monthly*. "Zaire: An African Horror Story" explains how Leopold used profits from the country's exports to build his own personal fortune: "Profits were extracted under conditions of forced labor that included killing workers and chopping off their hands if quotas were not met." Age-old tribal hatreds among the indigenés didn't help matters. The Lubas were (and still are) perpetually at the throats of the Bakongos. The same with the Bakubas, Pendes, Mangbetus and half a hundred other ethnics who involve themselves in often-frightful intrafactional struggles. Not unlike the Europe of old, many of the differences were a question of perception: there never was a village that didn't begrudge its neighbor something, even if it was only a trim ankle. The majority of these primitive people acted as they had always done and where might is right, the stronger invariably prevails.

The slave trade presented an altogether different dimension to this turmoil. With strong incentives, first from Arab and then European trading agents, African warlords were encouraged to sell their prisoners instead of killing them. And so untold thousands of these unfortunates were captured and marched off for sale to dealers who had built forts all the way up the West African coast as far north as Senegal. After having been paid a pittance for their pathetic human harvest—usually useless bags of cowrie shells that had been hauled across

Africa from the Indian Ocean on other peoples' backs—the slaves were locked together in chains and shipped off to the New World.

Joseph Conrad pictured the latter stages of these developments in his classic novel that, if some of its more subtle undertones are fully appreciated, is more of a documentary than a work of fiction. Conrad wrote from the point of view of a transient, for he was there only four months. His sojourn in the Congo, however, was long enough for him to be absolutely appalled by what he found and which deeply affected him for the rest of his life.

The character of the cruel, scheming Kurtz whom Conrad painted so vividly (and which Francis Ford Coppola adapted in his brilliant 1979 film "Apocalypse Now") was only one of scores of Belgian despots who could do as they pleased because they were answerable to no one. There were terrible abuses, all committed in the name of European enlightenment. In the end Conrad suffered psychological, spiritual, and even metaphysical shock. Even today, a century later, Conrad's epiphany has the power to deeply move readers.

In an interview on NPR, America's National Public Radio, Coppola admitted that instead of a prepared script, he used a copy of Conrad's classic to guide him. The old Pole would have been much amused.

Since avarice had so much to do with the Congo's modern period, it explains, in part, why—when independence was imprudently pushed through in 1960—the fledgling state could boast only five or six university graduates. One was a fractious firebrand named Patrice Lumumba, who believed that some of the answers to his nation's problems would be found in the peculiarly un-African credo then being proselytized by the Soviet Union. The CIA put a stop to that. Six months later, thirty-five-year-old Lumumba—the Congo's first popularly elected prime minister—was murdered at the behest of the Kennedy administration.

With Lumumba gone, a pattern of violence emerged from which the Congo has never recovered.[1]

Half a century after his death, that graduate of a Protestant mission school continues to enjoy a powerful, almost mystical following among black people everywhere. The Soviets even named a Moscow university after him. Although his name is barely recognized in the West, Lumumba continues to fuel Pan-African ideals. While the United States has its Malcolm X, Africa immortalized Lumumba.

Civil unrest which followed Lumumba's climb to authority was also a reason why the Congo attracted more professional—as well as quite a few unprofessional—soldiers of fortune than any other country on the continent. Because its government started to unravel within a day or two of independence, and the national army, the *Force Publique,* mutinied, someone in Brussels suggested to the fledgling state's new leaders that it might be a good idea to bring in the dogs of war. A short while later, Mobutu—by then head of the national army—grasped that nettle and what an abomination that can of worms bestowed on the country. But I am getting ahead of this sad saga.

June 30, 1960. The ink was not yet dry on the independence document that vectored the Congo toward its bloody fate before trouble started. Five days later the first recorded acts of violence took place within the *Force Publique.* The event took place in Leopoldville, the capital, or what is now known as Kinshasa. Us hacks simply called the place "Leo."

The soldiers were restless for several reasons. Belgium was tardy in handing over the instruments of power. Lumumba had promised his people dividends as soon as the Belgian flag was struck, but because of European intransigence he wasn't able to deliver. The majority of the colonial administrators still in place in the country's government offices resented having to make way for what some had taken to calling "a horde of savages." Some even used that kind of language in the presence of their Congolese staff, people who, in the past, had been their underlings.

The final affront came when Lieutenant General Janssens, head of the *Force Publique,* declared in a nationwide broadcast from Leopoldville that the military would continue as before, with him in charge. He was clear about the one issue that finally set the tinderbox alight: "There will be no black soldiers promoted to officers while I am in the country," he told the fledgling nation. Janssens' posturing, with the nation on the brink of civil war, was both mindless and insensitive.

Meanwhile, groups of mutineers roamed the streets of the capital causing panic. Let with no choice, Lumumba fired Janssens on the morning of July 6. A day later the entire Congolese officer corps was Africanized and the rank of private was abolished. The situation quickly turned farcical. Overnight the country was saddled with an army of officers and NCOs, every one of them issuing orders while nobody was listening.

Days later, the first throngs of refugees began streaming into "Leo" from the Congo's Equateur and Katanga provinces. The bloodletting had begun.

Les evénements was the first of contemporary Africa's disasters that had international ramifications. The situation was not helped by the fact that much of it was racially driven, with both sides guilty of excesses. Random killings, plunder and rape—with Europeans the principal target of all three crimes—made for some of the grimmest dispatches of the period. The Belgian Navy took the unfortunate step of bombarding Matadi harbor, which closed one of the few remaining avenues of escape to the settler community.

The unfolding drama produced several books chronicling the Congo's post-independence history. A classic in the field of developing world reporting was Ed Behr's *Anyone Here Been Raped and Speaks English?* Try pushing that one across an editor's desk today!

According to Behr, he boarded a ship on the Congo River shortly after the first batch of refugees began arriving. He wanted to interview someone who had been involved in the brutalities.

As he explained, members of the *Force Publique* had been on the rampage, and their deeds had been indescribably violent. Victims were brought to the river port of Matadi for evacuation to Europe, but since French wasn't exactly Behr's forté, he uttered his immortal phrase in English when he tried to talk to the first of the victims he encountered: "Anyone here been raped and speaks English?" he asked when he boarded the first steamer to arrive in port.

The rampaging *Force Publique* plunged the Congo into a crisis that seemed to confirm what many of Africa's friends believed: the continent did not yet have the ability to govern itself. Yet few pointed a finger at the people responsible for the spreading catastrophe in the first place, the majority of whom had fled back to Europe at the first whiff of violence. Still others went south to Rhodesia and South Africa.

Three events took place in the newly independent country about this time. Together, they were to set the scene in Central Africa for decades to come.

First there was Katanga—the country's huge, mineral-rich southern province that declared itself independent eleven days after the country had achieved *Uhuru*. That came with the backing and support of powerful Belgian business interests, notably Union Miniére, the colonial-era owner of the now-independent Congo's mineral assets. The mines, then and now, incorporate some of the richest copper and cobalt deposits in the world, and there's no question that had this not been so, the breakaway would never have taken place.

The second occurred nine days later when, with American support, a large United Nations force moved into the Congo to try to restore order. In some areas people were being slaughtered, sometimes in batches. Not long afterward, the first mercenaries arrived in Elizabethville, or Lubumbashi on today's maps.

This was done at the behest of the third factor in this deepening imbroglio, a man named Moise Tshombe, who was one of early independent Africa's most enigmatic political figures. In an Africa in turmoil, Tshombe had always been something of a maverick. For a start, as a member of the Lunda royal family, he was the self-appointed Katangese "president." Also, some of his cronies were critical of his role because this ebullient natural-born leader was as shrewd, erudite and charming as any cabinet minister in Europe. Those of us who met him sensed a winner. With all those attributes, it was no wonder that he made enemies in an emerging Africa.

Still, he not only managed to quell the revolt but he also got on well with white people. To the London School of Economics set of the 1960s and 1970s, the man was regarded as truly a product of imperialist blimp *pur sang*!

Whatever the sentiment, one has to give the man his due. When the country began to fall apart, who else was Tshombe to turn to in those most desperate moments? Considering the extent of the upheavals, he simply had to do something, if only because Katanga had no effective military force of its own. Almost overnight, the rebellion had become infectious and decisive action had become imperative. By the time that Tshombe made his move and hired the first of his war dogs, the entire country was teetering towards anarchy.

Although Brussels never allowed Tshombe to formally consolidate his position by according him recognition, the Belgians—unscrupulous and devious to the end—maintained that there was nothing to stop them providing him with assistance. Ultimately, these same Europeans played a crucial role in keeping Katanga viable, providing the secessionist state with military, economic and technical assistance.

Immediate steps were also taken to convert the newly created Katangese gendarmerie into a competent security force. Recruitment agencies were set up in Brussels for the enlistment of mercenaries.

Once the word was out, more of these opportunists arrived from South Africa.

These first groups of privateers were a bumptious, ill-disciplined bunch of ruffians, racist almost to a man and many with little military experience. Some of these thugs believed that having been picked, as one of them phrased it, "to protect Africans from themselves," they had license to do as they pleased. With that, another spate of killings followed since this ragged bunch of hired guns were armed as soon as they set foot in Katanga, but this time, it was white violence upon black.

An immediate consequence was to thrust Katanga's new-found military forces into a low-key, intermittent war with the United Nations, which in turn launched several operations to bring the rebel state into line.

"Operation Rumpunch," for example, which was launched on August 28, 1961, secured for the international body a variety of key positions in Katanga. These included the Katanga post office, its radio station and the residences of key European and Congolese officials. It culminated with the systematic rounding-up of mercenaries. All were expelled, having been offered free flights home. By then the mercs and the UN had exchanged fire several times and there were casualties on both sides.

Though there were some seasoned military men among Tshombe's European fighters, they were no match for crack Indian Army units that challenged his authority. It was a time when the UN was prepared to use firepower to achieve its objectives, even though the mercs shot down one of the UN helicopters. A few days after Christmas 1961, when Tshombe called for a general uprising against "the intruders," the UN responded by moving against other strategic Katangese positions and holding them.

After thirty months, Tshombe had no alternative but to concede defeat. By January 1963, his secession was crushed. The man who many regarded as one of the few accomplished Congolese leaders to have emerged during this difficult period—likable rogue that he was—fled to exile in Spain. But he wasn't finished yet.

Through a combination of unusual circumstances, Mobutu pardoned Moise Kapenda Tshombe and eighteen months later, in June 1964, the former Katangan leader was invited to return home to become the country's prime minister. Four months afterward, in what has since been referred to as "The Year of the White Giants," and this time with firm Mobutu support, Tshombe recruited mercenaries from South Africa, France, Belgium, Germany and elsewhere. More than a thousand answered the call and this time round, it was a program with a difference. All aspirant mercs were carefully vetted before they arrived in the country and only men with solid military experience were accepted.

There were even some Americans involved, as well as a squadron of CIA-sponsored Cuban exile pilots who flew an assortment of aircraft that included vintage B-26 bombers and T-28 ground-support aircraft. Though badly dated, all played a useful counterinsurgency role.

Some notables emerged among the mercenary commanders, and chief among them was Bob Denard. Also fighting for Mobutu was Jean "Black Jack" Schramme, the same veteran that Jim Penrith had written about earlier in Bukavu. Major "Mad Mike" Hoare, a professional soldier living in South Africa who had fought under General Orde Wingate with the famed Chindits in Burma against the Japanese, ended up taking command of his famed 5 Commando. Hoare's books *Congo Mercenary* and *The Road to Kalamta* adequately covers this historic period in mercenary lore and it is interesting that the first mentioned is into its umpteenth edition and continues to sell well. Notably, Hoare's command included the original "Wild Geese" contingent.

The question has often been asked what it was that possessed Mobutu to bring back from exile a man who was generally regarded as somebody who couldn't be trusted? Others called Tshombe a "political manipulator" who was far too close to whites. Further, he favored the unpopular deployment of war dogs to achieve his aims.

Tshombe, never shy to answer his critics, would give them a mouthful on all charges, the first being that he didn't need the job because he was already a very successful businessman. Also, he'd got there not through graft or undue muscle but rather as a consequence of hard work. Most important, Tshombe's links to the European business world were a huge asset to a Congo seriously strapped for cash, and it was this factor more than anything that eventually swung Mobutu around.

Politics, as he would say cockily of himself, only came later—and indeed, he'd concede, was opportunism.

Moise Tshombe was dealt two other powerful hands that had been denied previous Congolese leaders. The most important was that he was a Katangese nationalist and to cap it, he had access to a battalion or two of Katangese troops. Unlike the rest of the *Armée Nationale Congolaise*, these were orderly and battle-hardened soldiers who gave as good as they got, even against the UN.

Just then, their presence was essential: beyond the big cities the Congo had become rebellious following a major Simba revolution in the northeast. It was specifically to limit this threat—and the fact that the Soviets were surreptitiously providing the rebels with succor, military included—that he recruited freebooters.

The first thing Tshombe did on taking power was to integrate his Katangese fighting units into the national army. Then, by recruiting foreign soldiers (and this time he had more time and could be more select) he provided Mobutu with the much-needed leadership to conduct military operations against Pierre Mulele's disorganized but potentially-potent rebels in the east.

At that stage, the dissidents were concentrated largely around Stanleyville, though some of their cohorts were operating five hundred miles away in the south, and to a lesser extent in the sparsely populated northeast adjacent to the Sudan. It was to be expected that Khartoum would be involved: many rebel weapons and supplies came from there.

In an attempt to counter rebel successes, Hoare's 5 Commando—supported by air strikes—raced overland from the south and destroyed all rebel concentrations in their path. His force launched spearhead attacks against a number of Simba strongholds, and as his mercs took the offensive—using their technical superiority and discipline to good effect—the rebels couldn't match it.

Fighting grew progressively more brutal and, as we discovered afterward, the only time a man was captured and kept alive, it was because he had information to impart.

Meanwhile, the Simbas in Stanleyville had taken a thousand Europeans hostage, including scores of nuns and children, quite a few whom were subsequently murdered. Many were chained together and brought to the city's main square where they were violated. Some of the frightful images that emerged from this carnage eventually caused the West to take notice.

Gradually the word got about that some of the most ferocious of the Simba perpetrators were barely into their teens. Moreover, they were permitted by their more mature leadership to commit whatever savageries appealed to them. Raping nuns in public was only part of it. (An aside here was the problem subsequently faced by the Vatican: how to deal with the number of unwanted pregnancies among the Holy Sisters, some of whom went against their faith and had abortions.)

With its European allies and in conjunction with what Mobutu had to offer, Washington devised a rescue operation that is still regarded by military buffs as one of the most successful launched in the past half-century. It included both regular European forces as well as Tshombe's freebooters. Even today, the Congo's Stanleyville Raid is used as an example of what can be achieved with a well-disciplined, coordinated and motivated mercenary force working in conjunction with regular military.

In record time considering the logistics (many of the C-130s that were deployed had to fly all the way across Africa from Europe), a joint Belgian-American rescue operation codenamed *Dragon Rouge* was put on the drawing board at NATO headquarters. It was a massive effort that called for synchronized tactics involving U.S. planes and pilots and Belgian paratroopers. Also integral to the plan was a force of mercenaries moving up from the south in a flying column. Together, both forces knocked the wind out of what was left of Simba resistance, killing thousands in the process.

The media never properly reported some of the events that took place, largely because there were those among my colleagues who believed that much of what had happened was tainted because there were mercenaries involved. In fact, though a lot of lives were saved, the operation was disparaged by many of them. So much for the even-handedness of the Fourth Estate. In the end, Hoare's group rescued almost two-thousand white hostages. It didn't come easily though, and a number of his men were killed in action. There were others who were never accounted for: they just disappeared in the bush. A handful were killed and eaten.

During the course of these actions, 5 Commando took the town of Wamba with its two-hundred-and-fifty hostages, but not before the rebels murdered more than half of them. Some were shot, others were thrown, arms and legs bound, into the Wamba River where the crocs got them.

One of the most striking images to emerge from this period were groups of Simba rebels doing a demented war dance on the prone body of an American missionary, William McChesney They went on until ruptured organs and internal bleeding ended his agony. Then they gouged out his eyes.

Under the command of Hoare, Denard, Schramme, Siegfried Mueller (who was ex-SS and always wore his Iron Cross) and others, the mercs went on to mop up resistance across an area bigger than Florida. Anybody even suspected of having been involved with the rebels was "taken out." It was an obnoxious form of jungle law, as brutal as it was uncompromising, but it worked. By the following December, hostilities were about as "over" as anything was ever likely to be in an unsettled Congo.

The mercs who rallied to the Congo's (and their own) cause were not scheduled to get rich quickly. They did so for a paltry $360 a month, with an extra $16 a day "combat pay," which only applied if they were actually in a situation where they faced enemy fire. Hoare himself got $1,700, which wasn't bad for the time but hardly over-generous. The French and Belgians did better, with some of their senior officers getting $4,000.

Why did they do it? One battle-hardened South African professional replied: "I was somebody. All those people looked up to me. Even a Katangese major tried to salute me each time our paths crossed."

In general, the irregulars did a marvelous job, facing up to a fairly well-armed adversary at the almost overwhelming odds of twenty to one, sometimes more. With time, some of the legends created by this crazy bunch of mercenaries spread, even into the heart of Simba country. The rebels would often turn back in terror when they heard that the "White Giants" were coming. It eventually got to the stage where Hoare's people were able to capture towns just by phoning ahead to announce they were on their way. With all this mayhem, it was curious that the phones still worked.

An American mercenary Peter Simon, who was interviewed at his "retirement villa" in Mexico a few years later, told *Soldier of Fortune* magazine that he'd got into the business because of a flat wallet. He was in Johannesburg when the ad appeared in the newspapers.

"I went along to the address provided because I had nothing better to do. The outer office was filled with tough, hearty young men in open-necked sports shirts, a few grizzled middle-agers, and a selection of desperate-looking men whose whisky breath and bloodshot eyes indicated bad times.

"The room was small and stifling and almost nobody spoke until a good-looking brunette walked in and began to give us the gen. When she mentioned that there would be fighting, some of the guys left."

She told them they would be armed with the best weapons on the market and that beer would be plentiful. Because of limited time, she added, there would be only three weeks of training. Within a week Simon found himself in a tent town in the Congo surrounded by a thousand recruits from all over Africa and Europe, and the work began. Training soon weeded out the softies or those who had misrepresented their military experience, and they were sent back on the planes that had ferried in the next batch of recruits.

One of the problems facing Hoare was that some of his men didn't confine their activities to rescuing hostages. These freelance militants blew more than one bank once they became accustomed to "living off the land." Looting became so widespread that the first thing their commanders would do after taking a place was to post armed guards on the town's banks.

As American scribe Marc Segal explained in an article at the time, the mercs were a mixed bunch: "Off and running, ready to swear allegiance, temporary though it might be, to almost any government ready to lay cash on the line for a little sweat and a handy gun."

As we are to see in forthcoming chapters, things have changed a lot since then, with a multitude of smaller rebellions festering throughout the region. Unsettled conditions eventually formed the basis for individuals like Kabila to launch their own military campaigns against the Mobutu regime. But that only happened almost thirty years later and he succeeded where others hadn't.

Considering that the Congo is a land of countless lakes and rivers, a good deal more water operations were launched by mercenary commanders than is generally documented.

Early in the campaign, "Black Jack" Schramme, then leader of 10 Commando—popularly known as the Leopard Battalion—was tasked with control and pacification of the Lower Orientale Province. Gerry Thomas tells us in his book *Mercenary Troops in Modern Africa* that the region had fallen under the sway of roving bands of armed Marxist rebels.[3] Schramme created a small naval force along some of the rivers that flowed into the great Lualaba waterway, itself a tributary of the Congo.

For logistics, Schramme appropriated a small powered ferry capable of transporting armed jeeps—it eventually formed the backbone of his maritime strike force. For defense, he designed a speedy armed launch called a vedette, about thirty feet long. With a souped-up Chevy engine, machine guns fore and aft and a mortar tube amidships, it could roar along with a dozen troops onboard at about twenty-five knots. Generally, it worked well as a scout craft and made a reputation for itself by surprising a number of suspected enemy positions and knocking them out.

Other times Schramme would use it to provide supporting cover to ground forces moving on riverside objectives such as railheads, roadways, bridges and depots.

Hoare, too, got into the act. He commandeered a two-hundred ton tug which he renamed *Geri*, moved it up and down the Lualaba River, and was able to do some useful work containing rebel movement.

As Thomas writes, control of the major lakes in Central Africa was a priority for the mercs because so much enemy war materiel was brought across them—mainly from Kigoma in Tanzania—to ports on the west bank like Baraka. This harbor lay to the north of Kalemie (formerly Albertville) where more naval elements were stationed, all of them mercenary.

Other craft in Hoare's fleet included an eighty-foot radar-equipped gunboat named *Ermans*. There were also six high-powered, CIA-supplied thirty-foot Swift patrol boats—indeed, the same Swift boats of John Kerry infamy—which were capable of a silent thirty knots. Instead of being manned by soldiers of Mobutu's *Armée Nationale Congolaise*, all these operations were 5 Commando's business.

By the time mercenaries arrived in the Congo, the rebels had established a fairly sophisticated supply network. It employed three river transports as well as some fast motor launches which had mounted machine guns. An interesting departure from normal Simba operations was that they had Cuban volunteers as crew.[2] Cutting these supply links wasn't easy and they soon became one of the Hoare's priorities. By late 1965, his forces were able to interdict and sink four rebel craft in a night action that took place off Kabimba.

Before that phase of operations came to an end, several amphibious operations took place with mixed success. The first, in 1964, was dubbed "Operation Watch Chain," intended to be a lake-borne assault by a small commando unit in support of a two-pronged attack on Kalemie, then still in rebel hands. Dogged by mechanical failures, the much-depleted force eventually got ashore but were driven out with the loss of two men. The whole caboodle had been caught in an ambush. His shortcomings have been demonstrated by this setback, Hoare's second assault on the lake was on the port town Baraka. It was a critical target if he was to be effective in the north, especially after the previous debacle.

For this operation this former British Army officer tasked every boat he had on his books. He enlisted the help of the Belgian-run lake navigation company and they offered the use of four commercial ships. These were the lake steamer *Urundi*, a tug, *Ulindi*, a large barge that could carry a dozen trucks (as well as a Ferret scout car) and finally, *Crabba*, a flat-topped barge that ferried six jeeps.

In "Operation Banzi," 5 Commando deceived rebel spies by promulgating a land attack along a different axis. Within a week stories about a pending mercenary strike over the mountains began to circulate. When Baraka was finally hit, the six Swift boats were backed by Cuban merc fighter-bombers that helped pulverize the target. The entire force was ashore within forty-five minutes, even though they were pinned down on the landing area by heavy fire from higher ground. Taking the town became a formality later in the day.

Three years later "Black Jack" Schramme was to use these same improvised naval assets to try to force a mutiny in the Congo.

Involved in that crazy rebellion was an Italian former marine, Georgio Norbiato, who was later to make a name for himself in Biafra where he was killed in action. Schramme eventually holed up in Bukavu, until he and his rebel mercs—fighting off daily ground and air attacks—were forced to retreat into UN custody in neighboring Rwanda.

There were only a handful of fighters who had sided with this merc leader when he rebelled, but in the end and despite desperate odds, Schramme and his men held Mobutu's Congolese army at bay and continued to do so for months. It was a huge embarrassment to the Congo's leader and one of the reasons why African leaders today are so skeptical about using dogs of war to settle scores.

This Belgian mercenary later surfaced in Brazil where he was given refugee status.

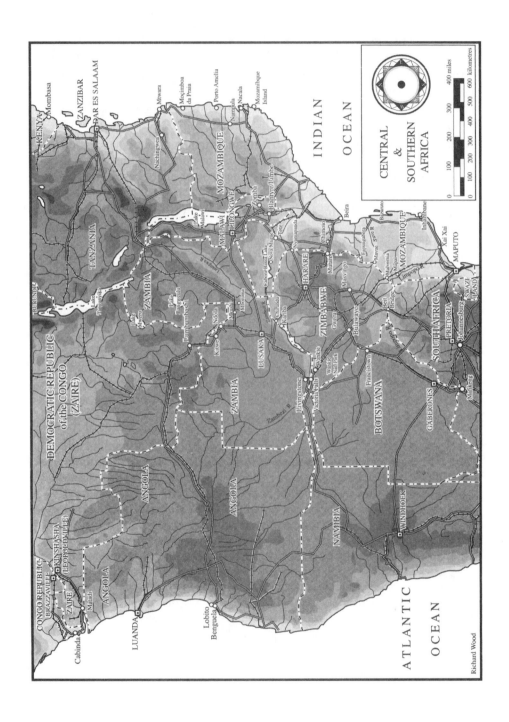

11

SOLDIERS OF FORTUNE DURING MOBUTU'S RULE

"Want peacekeepers with spine? Hire the world's fiercest mercenaries."

U.S. News & World Report, December 30, 1996

There was more intrigue in the final days of Mobutu's rule in the Congo than you'd find at a Papal conclave. It was a time of great uncertainty and heinous turpitude

In late 1996, when the country was still called Zaire, almost everybody was focused on the final phase of a long struggle that eventually brought another demagogue to power. His name was Laurent Kabila, since deceased at the hands of an assassin. One of a plentitude of problems was that the man who sought to replace the ailing dictator had the intellect of a pensioned army corporal. And of course, the Americans were involved; after all, Kabila was Washington's man. Following the Lumumba blunder of the 1960s, one would have thought the CIA would avoid making the same mistake twice.

Also implicated in the Kabila offensive were the Libyans, as was France's right wing *Groupement Universitaire de la Droite* as well as the DST, French internal security and SDEC, which runs that country's intelligence abroad and is regarded as the Gallic counterpart of the CIA.

There were hopes for this beefy revolutionary who, a long time before, had shown the ropes to Ché Guevara and his band of a hundred or so Cuban "military advisors" on their first visit to Africa. With Mobutu in decline, many Africa watchers believed Kabila might be the one to lift Zaire out of the debilitating political mire in which it had wallowed for almost a generation.[1] How wrong they were. According to the recently published Guevara diaries, even he regarded this uncouth Congolese as dim, with neither the acuity nor the guile of the man he succeeded.

"Bit of an idiot and not to be trusted," the Argentinian doctor wrote at the time, which underscored the argument that in Africa, the few who put themselves forward as avatars of a new democracy are seldom heroic. Most can't wait to get their fingers into the till.

Meanwhile, as long as Mobutu remained head of state, a hopeless interregnum prevailed. Instability—and an uneasy soporific lassitude that resulted from it—pervaded the entire community in a country already stultified by corruption. Zaire's problems attracted just about every charlatan known to Interpol, and many others who weren't.

Among those who arrived were gritty, fast-talking arms dealers from both sides of what was once the Iron Curtain. Others came from France, Israel, Yugoslavia and South Africa. Also poking about in the embers were all manner of "financiers," hopeful mercenary groups and a gathering of opportunists, each believing that he could cut a deal.

They had good reason for doing so. Despite the war, there was still a lot of money about. The mines around Mbuji-Mayi in Kasai Province never stopped churning out diamonds, with more being smuggled into Zaire by Unita's rebels from Angola. Add to this mélange corruption beyond cure or care.

When there was an occasional shortage of real money, gemstones replaced greenbacks. Prominent among those offering long-term financial and military aid on this basis were people from Russia, Ukraine, Israel, Bulgaria, France, Yugoslavia and others. None minded how they were paid as long as it was in a negotiable commodity they could easily carry on their person while boarding flights to Europe. There were no trickle-down economics here.

By this time the national currency, the Zaire, had been whittled away by inflation. Kinshasa had resorted to printing five million Zaire notes, which were nearly as useless as the pre-Nazi Deutschmark. Throughout, the black market dealers did their thing outside the Banque de Paris et des Pays-Bas on Avenue Colonel Ebeya or around the corner from the government-owned Union Zairoise des Banques. Others set up shop opposite the U.S. Embassy on the Avenue des Aviateurs. Some boldly operated within yards of local goons-cum-security guards posted specifically to prevent such things.

Two or three tiers down the economic ladder were a myriad of smaller operators, including Neall Ellis and his group of privateers. Only a short time earlier Nellis had returned home to South Africa, following his disastrous spell of trying to do his thing for Islamic militants in Bosnia.

Though Nellis was involved in the project only after it had been clinched, he was familiar with both the nature of the task at hand and its politico-military implications from the start. As he puts it, he and his friends had some aspirations for their new-found central African project. But Zaire, which would soon revert to its original name, the Democratic Republic of the Congo—not to be confused with the socialist-minded People's Republic of the Congo whose capital, Brazzaville, lies across the river from Kinshasa—was hemorrhaging.

A company called Stability Control (later abbreviated to Stabilco) was registered on the Isle of Man by a pair of South Africans: Mauritz Le Roux, a tough professional soldier with a background in the Angolan war, and his partner Harold Muller, who had dabbled unsuccessfully in military intelligence. Muller's wife was the linchpin in the venture, an acclaimed beauty who was both well connected in South Africa and a decorated intelligence operative from the apartheid era.

The company founders promoted the concept that their operation could effectively turn the tide of a quasi-guerrilla conflict that for a while now had been creeping inexorably toward Mobutu's capital. How they went about cornering a share of this volatile "guns-for-hire" market is interesting, because opportunists in a dozen or more developing states faced with instability use the same process today.

As Kabila edged toward Kinshasa, the security situation in Zaire became both fraught and newsworthy. This was particularly true in South Africa, where exports from that country were essentially keeping the Congo alive. It was an immense and profitable market. As was to be expected, the mercenary issue was also a topic. Despite denials, both sides were using freelancers and everyone knew it. In fact, it was reports about these war dogs that initially attracted Stabilco's interest.

"The guys obviously talked about ways of getting involved, but most of what they considered had been tried and discarded," explained Nellis. "Zaire was a formidable proposition, but once through the door, it became a treasure house." Diamonds, he suggested, were a significant part of it. So was gold, exotic tropical hardwood, emeralds, cobalt and a good deal more.

As Le Roux and Muller saw it, the key to unlocking Zaire's door and accessing its loot was to sell Mobutu on the need for close air support. At this time Kabila's rebels had no air assets of their own, even though he had been offered some by Uganda—flown by mercenaries, of course.

"We reasoned that probably the best tactic would be to approach

Mobutu's government direct with the offer of a couple of squadrons of gunships—naturally with our chaps in charge," recalled Nellis. "With such a force in place, it would be possible to argue that Kabila's advance could be stopped." Nellis, Le Roux and Muller had history on their side because what they were plotting had been done before in Angola and Sierra Leone. On both occasions it was Executive Outcomes that had been involved.

First, however, Stabilco's founders had to persuade the dictator's henchmen that their proposals were realistic, attainable, and could be implemented with a modicum of effort and a modest outlay of funds. But that was the difficult part, as was the last essential to their plan: speed. If Stabilco wanted to get into their game, it would have to do so quickly, for the burly revolutionary and his irregulars were making headway toward Kinshasa.

Both Le Roux and Muller initially had a hard time finding a Zairean who had clout enough to deal. They had to start at or near the top since any decision of consequence in Mobutu's Zaire was made at the highest level. A low-key functionary or diplomat simply wouldn't do.

The only entrée that offered a modicum of hope was the Zairean diplomatic mission in Pretoria. But even getting through that door without a connection was difficult. No one at Stabilco spoke French, and almost no one at the legation understood much English. Undeterred, Mauritz Le Roux "set up camp" on the doorstep of the Zairean Embassy each day until someone eventually agreed to see him: the ploy was characteristic of his style.

Having achieved his initial objective, a Congolese diplomat took careful note of what Le Roux had to say and then, to his astonishment, asked when he would like to go to Kinshasa to present it to his bosses. According to Le Roux, the phrase used was that he should "give it to them straight from the shoulder." Nellis was not surprised. "That's Mauritz Le Roux," he explained. "Skin's as thick as a rhino's and he's never afraid to push his ideas."

A couple of days later Le Roux and Muller arrived amid Kinshasa's torrid heat. The usual bunch of functionaries met them at Ndjili International Airport with shades and swagger sticks, one of which was a stuffed baby crocodile. The men were soon ushered into the offices of General Kpama Baramoto, Mobutu's security chief and one of the most feared men of the regime. Six months hence, Baramoto would fly to South Africa after Mobutu and his entourage fled Zaire, his suitcases filled with what some said was a hundred million dollars in American currency. There were also bags of raw diamonds, some of them checked through the airport as luggage. That was apart from his five or six wives, an indeterminate number of children, and who knows how many freeloaders who formed part of his huge extended family-in-exile.

Le Roux's presentation in Kinshasa was forceful and disarmingly simple. Apart from the heli-force, he explained to Baramoto, he and his associates could muster five hundred ground troops within a couple weeks. These would be former EO veterans with experience in conventional warfare as well as counterinsurgency operations. Many of the people he wanted to bring in had been blooded in Angola, Le Roux explained to the general. Consequently, they were well-experienced. He also had available any number of helicopter pilots ready for immediate deployment in Zaire Air Force gunships. With this force, continued Le Roux, Mobutu could drive back the rebel Kabila with ease. Once that threat had dissipated, he suggested, Le Roux and his team could train indigenous aviators so that the next time Zaire was faced with an emergency they wouldn't have to hire foreigners.

Once they had persuaded General Baramoto that Stabilco's contribution was the cure for what ailed Zaire, the South Africans were escorted to the office of another close military associate of the president: Special Forces commander General Ngbale Nzimbi. Le Roux made the same pitch, with similar results, and was then bustled off to meet with the Minister of Defense, Admiral Mudima Mavua. (Ironically, all three black officers later topped Kabila's "most wanted" military and civilian suspects list, but that was only after they'd ensconced themselves in lavish homes in Johannesburg.)

While in Kinshasa, Le Roux and Muller were introduced to General Marc Mahele Lieko Bukongo, an officer who struck them as one of the most astute senior commanders in the Zairean Army. Mahele was in a class of his own. He had already made a name for himself as someone who did what he said he would, a rare attribute in the Congo Republic, where it was generally all jaw-jaw with little to show for it. It was from him they learned that a small number of mercenaries had already been hired in Europe. It also emerged that Mahele was involved with a group of Serbians and French war dogs as a result of Bob Denard's secretive efforts. Unable to handle the contract himself (he was still under close surveillance by French Intelligence), Denard subcontracted the work to his old friend and business associate, Belgian-born Christian Tavernier. Their ties stretched way back.

Tavernier's father had served with Denard as a mercenary officer in the post-independence Congo army of the 1960s. He had actually led 14 Commando, part of Mobutu's former *Armée Nationale Congolaise*. This was the same group of fighters used to suppress the leftist revolt of the dreaded Antoine Gizenga. It was significant that both Taverniers (father and son) had honed their military skills in Belgium's colonial army in Africa.

Thirty years later, history almost repeated itself. Gizenga's "spiritual inheritor" was none other than the illustrious Laurent Kabila. Meanwhile, in line with the new Zairian contract and under Denard's guidance, Tavernier Jr. recruited the French element for the new foreign force in Zaire. At the same time, the offices of Paris' DST in Belgrade were instrumental in bringing Serbs to the table who, because their own economy was in tatters, came a lot cheaper than the market rate for French military veterans. This was the dual force that later became known as *Legion Blanc*. While Zaire had its mercenaries under Mobutu, they were small fry compared to what would arrive after Kabila finally seized power.

Kabila's rebel efforts meanwhile were being bolstered by several African states, each of them one eager to see the last of the aging ogre Mobutu. Uganda, for instance, threw a sizable force into the melee. So did Rwanda, whose soldiers displayed excellent combat skills. The Rwandans eventually became a major factor in the subsequent bid to oust Kabila once he had achieved power and dumped his former allies. The Sudanese also arrived, but in the end everybody agreed that it might have been better had they stayed away. Their efforts throughout the conflict were a sham. In fact, Khartoum—seemingly always at war with somebody—has never been able to achieve much in the military line. This has been more than adequately demonstrated over several decades by that country's inability to deal with a black Christian rebellion in the south of the country, a conflict that has been ongoing since the 1950s, which makes it the world's longest war.

There were also reports that Libyan Air Force planes were ferrying in supplies and men, first to Kabila's forces and later to Mobutu's forward positions. Like everything else, most of what was going on was veiled in a web of secrecy, intrigue and innuendo. No one discussed Arab involvement in the Congo. In addition to the Moroccans and the Libyans, Zaire received military aid from Egypt, Saudi Arabia and other Gulf States. London, Washington, Berlin, Beijing, Moscow and a host of other countries also had their fingers on the Congolese pulse. In fact, there wasn't a major intelligence agency in the world that did not have someone active there, with South African Military Intelligence more active than most.

A few of the more bizarre events of the war received media mention abroad, usually in a roundabout, "eyewitness report" sort of way. Much of it was broadcast by the BBC, with other reports carried by Kenya's broadcasting stations and South Africa's SABC. Some of the news even made it on-air in Zimbabwe, though that ended after Mugabe sent his air force and army across two thousand miles of Africa to fight for Kabila in exchange for diamond concessions (see Chapter 13). None of this was ever made public in Kinshasa, though obviously those involved were fixated by every broadcast (most coming from Europe) that mentioned their country and how the consequences might ultimately affect them personally. With each rebel success Zaire's currency plummeted further.

The one element that might have turned the war around but didn't, because Mobutu's generals (and the President himself) were reluctant to spend their money, was the Zaire Air Force (ZAF). Judging by routine Jane's reports and some of the studies offered by London's International Institute for Strategic Studies (IISS), the ZAF, on paper, appeared to be in fairly good shape, at least by African standards. Not everybody was aware that neglect, a lack of spares and an almost total absence of funding had resulted in the air force being pared down to a handful of operational aircraft.

Apart from the usual bevy of cargo planes—these were a priority and were kept operational no matter what—Air Zaire's civilian jets were increasingly brought into play, as were charter flights, the majority from abroad, South Africa in particular. Most were flown by Russians and Ukrainians and tasked to supply forward positions close to the front, which was inexorably shifting to the west. Toward the end of the Mobutu era, the inability of the ZAF to retaliate was caused by an inexplicable inertia that made no sense at all if you consider that hostilities escalated all the time.

After Le Roux had hired Nellis, the pilot's first job after arriving in Kinshasa was to assess the situation for himself. It didn't take the South African long to discover that there were almost no operational helicopters in the country. The spare parts and the like had been bought, but most of the crates hadn't even been unpacked. Critical elements like electronics or gear applicable to rotor operation were missing.

To those who were nominally responsible, none of this mattered. What did was the customary rake-off passed on to the responsible minister or general after money had changed hands.. Occasionally one of the Mi-24s that could still fly would go out on a sortie, but ammo and fuel were limited. In a tight spot, the Hinds could be used for ferrying troops, but that was only a stopgap measure. By the time Kabila's forces began to close in on Kinshasa proper, no trained pilots could be found to man the Hinds. There was also a persistent fear within Zaire's military command that its own pilots couldn't be trusted; some generals felt that one of them might take an Mi-24 into combat and land it behind enemy lines. According to Nellis, had they been able to, one or two might have done just that, especially once the situation had become critical.

In the last months of this conflict there was only a single operational Puma and a few combat-ready SA-341 Eurocopter Gazelles. The rebels found and burned the Puma at Kisangani Airport because it had an engine problem that couldn't be fixed in time to get it out.

There was reason for what some observers termed a "galloping malaise." This kind of lethargy has been seen elsewhere in Africa, especially during periods of upheaval. And while there are conflicting views, much of it stemmed from the inability of the country's defense force to communicate internally. Fundamentally, Mobutu's staff officers had become alienated from the main body of the armed forces. The result was that generals who should have been prosecuting the war sat comfortably on their backsides in the capital. As far as they were concerned, there was little that needed urgent attention: "It's out there in the bush somewhere . . . doesn't matter now . . . perhaps later," one of them was heard to say after a few drinks with the South Africans.

Most of these army commanders believed that Kabila's rebellion—though a niggling and sometimes heated subject of discussion—simply didn't warrant any kind of radical action. In their minds, as Nellis and other South African mercenaries later recalled, it seemed impossible that a crass and untutored clown like Kabila could lead anybody to victory. For years Mobutu's intelligence services had been downplaying the threat. Opportunities arose to assassinate Kabila, at least twice by poisoning, but were not acted upon. Any proposals to do so were scotched on the basis of "better the devil you know . . ."

There was no rational explanation for the torpor, especially the failure of the Zairean high command to do their jobs. Despite horrendous hardships being suffered by their troops who had been deployed to hold the line in the interior, these sybaritic sycophants went on living the good life as if there were no tomorrow. Their staff officers sometimes returned to Kinshasa to try to argue that disaster was only a step away, but it made no difference. In any event, for a major or a colonel to imply that his boss wasn't doing his job wouldn't have been worth his pension (or, in some cases, his life). The last person to be made aware of the situation was the big man himself. Nobody had the courage to suggest to an ailing Mobutu that matters really were falling apart. As one member of Kinshasa's peripatetic diplomatic corps commented, "You needed a really big pair of balls to bring any sort of bad news to the old man."

There were several more meetings between the two South African mercenary leaders, Le Roux and Muller, and the Zairean High Command in the days immediately after their arrival. Usually it was at the home of one of the generals and very late at night. But for a time nothing of substance developed, or even looked as if it might. The South Africans quickly discovered that among the Congolese hierarchy, time actually meant very little; expatriates they spoke with put it down to the heat. As Le Roux told Nellis, during those early days it was unusual to find someone willing to make a decision. And if the outcome in any way involved spending money, that was another reason for delay. This was peculiar, he admitted, because almost everyone with whom he dealt was wealthy beyond care. Finally, about one month after they arrived, the two men were asked how long it would take to prepare their forces, beginning with pilots for the gunships.

"Immediately," Le Roux replied.

"And the cost?"

No one has been able to draw out of either Le Roux or Muller what they asked for a fee, though the figure of about five million dollars—realistic for such work—has been mentioned. It has also been suggested that Stabilco demanded thirty million dollars for the first year's work, but this has never been confirmed, even though it's roughly ballpark in today's world of contract combat.

Once the process had been initiated, Le Roux remained behind in Kinshasa to keep up pressure on the generals, but it still took a lot of cajoling for the first payment to appear. And when it did, it was very reluctantly dished out and in dribbles. Having clinched what looked like a deal and receiving a down payment of $80,000 from General Baramoto, Muller left for South Africa to initiate stage two of the plan. Le Roux, meanwhile, remained in Kinshasa as "security."

Nellis had meantime contacted some of his former compadres and asked them a simple question: "Do you want to fly combat for the Mobutu regime?"

Ryan Hogan, who had spent time with EO in Sierra Leone, didn't need to think twice about it; nor did flight engineers Grant Williams and Phil Scott. Salaries offered were $10,000 a month for the pilots while the techs got $8,000.

Nellis reckons the Zairean adventure was one of the more surreal experiences of his many years of work in Africa. Nothing prepared him for the myriad of frustrations, obfuscations and lies they encountered at every turn. The contact lasted six months, ending without notice (or money) on the day that Mobutu fled. But at least he got out alive, as he put it, luck having played a major role. Nellis and two of his associates fled on foot and eventually paddled their way in a dugout canoe across the Congo River to safety in a neighboring country. When they got to the other side, the other two were clad only in their underpants. Since Nellis didn't believe in wearing jockeys, he was left with his pants on.

Stabilco's efforts in Mobutu's Zaire began slowly. According to Nellis, "We rushed like hell to get the whole thing going, and that was already late November, but nothing came of it. If you consider that the Mobutu regime crashed the following May, there should at least have been some urgency about the task ahead, at very least the need to get something of a counteroffensive going."

To most Kinshasa residents, its generals included, the war was little more that a remote phenomenon. Granted, there were a lot more troops around than usual in the city itself, but otherwise hostilities in the interior had no immediate bearing on life there. Food was plentiful, good French wines could still be had at the local supermarché, and things went on as they always had. In time, the military threat became more acute but the locals were uncomprehending, or, as Le Roux described it, "dazed"—often at the same time. "But not the rebels," emphasized Nellis. "They just came headlong at us and nothing seemed to stop them."

At this time the South Africans were spending most of their days in their hotel rooms or sitting at the bar of the Kinshasa Intercontinental kicking up their heels rather than flying combat missions. As a diversion, they managed to wangle two brief "inspection" sessions in Gazelle helicopters with Mobutu's *Forces Armées Zairoises* (FAZ) out east, around Kinda and Kisangani. But that was it. The prospect of combat didn't enter into the picture.

Getting into the interior on the inspection trip was an experience of its own. Nellis flew to Kisangani in an Air Zaire Boeing 707, piloted by a quirky Australian who had been living in the country for several years. He was something of a character—someone compared him to a personality from a 1950s Hollywood adventure series—and invited Nellis to sit in the cockpit once the plane was airborne. The South African spent the rest of the flight in the co-pilot's seat. "I ended up flying the plane just about all the way to short finals," Nellis reminisced. "It was the first time I'd handled a four-engine jet and since there was no autopilot it was a handful for someone accustomed to the lighter touch of a chopper's controls."

On first arriving back in Kinshasa—after Le Roux had received Stabilco's initial payment—the South Africans were appalled to find that they had been left by their high-ranking "friends" to fend for themselves. It irked, because that hadn't been part of the original arrangement clinched with General Baramoto. From the start, this black officer had been effusive about the help that would be forthcoming—not only from him personally but from his office. He promised to provide the team with a place of its own and everything that went with it, including servants. The men would be given all the Western food they required, almost all of it flown in daily from Europe. Despite the pledges, nothing materialized. The men would have to make do with what little they had.

By then Roelf van Heerden had joined the team and between them they managed. But only just. A quiet, taciturn man, Van Heerden was one of those professional soldiers who allowed little to faze him. Already something of a fixture as a field commander with Executive Outcomes in Sierra Leone, he was one of a small band of former SADF officers who saw action in the mercenary organization's first operation at Soyo in northwest Angola in which four of his group were killed. (See Chapter 15.)

Taking Baramoto's lapses on the chin, Nellis and van Heerden booked themselves into a grungy little downtown hotel on the fringe of what had once been the "tourist" area. It typified everything that was derelict, down to the hotel staff swapping sheets between residents rather than washing them. It also took the men all of twenty minutes to discover that Hotel Super doubled as a whorehouse. A few days later, with almost all their money gone, the men were forced to survive on what little credit they could scrounge. At one stage they had to make do on a loaf of bread and a can of pilchards a day. It was all they could afford.

At this point Nellis delivered a letter of demand to Baramoto's office. If Stabilco didn't receive confirmation of its contract, he wrote, he and van Heerden would leave Zaire. Muller was gone, finally allowed to follow Le Roux back to South Africa. "These people knew that they were screwing us since their spies would long ago have told them exactly what our position was," complained Nellis. "They were also aware that we were hurting, so we had to call their bluff. It was that or nothing."

Baramoto's reaction was immediate. That same day he had the South Africans transferred to the Intercontinental, which was then still very much part of the international chain. The Ministry of Defense began picking up all their tabs, including bar bills and anything spent in the downstairs disco. For Nellis and van Heerden, life suddenly became very much easier; this was one of the few hotels in the capital where you could use plastic.

As the guidebooks stated, at $350 a night (or three or four times as much as the average Congolese earns in a year) the Intercontinental was in a league of its own. Nellis still talks nostalgically about his room on the fifteenth floor, with its magnificent view over the capital and the great brooding river that had always been called the Congo. From that height, after dark he could make out the lights of Brazzaville, another of Africa's fine cities that just then was being ripped apart by civil strife.

"Each morning, for want of anything better to do, I'd sit on our verandah," remembered Nellis. "At ten minutes past eight, exactly, I'd watch the Prime Minister being escorted to work in a convoy bristling with guns. Monday to Friday it was always the same and the man's routine never varied. By nightfall I'd still be there and observe him being taken home again. We waited for calls that never came from Baramoto's office."

"I'd bite my lip and there were times that I'd seethe. To pass the time, I'd take to planning a small team attack on the ministerial entourage. It would have been easy—a couple of RPGs to neutralize his escorts and then have the guys move in to complete the job. We couldn't talk too loudly about it between ourselves because we weren't sure whether the rooms were bugged. Roelf and I shared a few smiles about the option."

For Nellis the process was largely therapeutic, the planning helping to sublimate his rage. The worst part was that while he and van Heerden waited for the minister to phone, they didn't dare move about the hotel for fear of missing a call. They discovered the very first day they were there that they couldn't rely on the front desk to take messages.

"We'd go two weeks without getting a word from anybody. That was exceptional, because everybody was aware that Kabila and his army were approaching the capital and, I suppose, it tells you something about how this part of Africa operates in times of crisis."

In his personal dealings with the mercenaries, Baramoto was both courteous and friendly. Socially, he was scrupulously correct. A tall man with grayish hair and spectacles—and unlike so many of his colleagues, not too heavy for his height—the general projected a confidence that reflected power. Whether in uniform, traditional African dress, or in a formal suit, Baramoto was always impeccably turned out. A non-smoker, he liked a good whisky, especially Scottish single malts, but he never overdid it, at least not in their presence.

Although Baramoto understood English, he confided to one of the South Africans that he felt he could better express himself in French. Consequently, there was usually an interpreter in attendance. Nellis realized from the outset that the other man was more than just a linguist: large bulges under both arms gave that away immediately. Judging from what the other generals used for protection, Nellis thought he was carrying something in the Heckler and Koch range.

Baramoto's house was a single-storied villa surrounded by high walls and ranging clusters of bougainvillea. The house itself wasn't as flamboyant as some might have expected, especially since when Mauritz Le Roux arrived in Zaire he had been shown a room piled almost to the ceiling with bundles of cash, mostly large-denomination US dollar bills. The general lived well, however, and he and his family wanted for nothing.

Furnishings were sumptuous and included several leather-covered lounge suites in the sitting room set against magnificent silk drapes. Nellis never met any of Baramoto's wives, but he was introduced to two of his daughters: "Quite lovely girls . . . very well dressed in chic

European outfits that seemed to be mostly designer," he remembered. In cars, Baramoto's tastes were orthodox oligarch: the inevitable black Mercedes limo with tinted windows, of which there were several, together with a couple top-of-the-range Landcruisers. Another distinctive feature, Nellis told me, was a SAM-14 ground-to-air launcher, complete with a missile in the tube, propped up precariously against a wall in the entrance hall. It seemed to be a permanent fixture because nobody ever moved it. If it had accidentally detonated, it would have demolished the building.

There was always a crowd of soldiers and civilians hanging about the place, including a contingent of guards who must have been as well kitted-out and efficient as any in the country. Splendid in their camouflage uniforms, most sported shiny AK-47s, though there was invariably a clutch of RPGs somewhere out back Nellis could see that these troops knew what was expected of them, like keeping a wary eye on everything going on in the vicinity, including monitoring traffic. Somebody else suggested that that might have been a result of the Israeli touch.

It was obvious that some of these troops had received South African training, and two men recognized a former reconnaissance officer who arrived with Le Roux one morning. The "reunion" ended up being quite emotional, with big smiles all round, Baramoto included. (The minister's ties with South Africa's apartheid leaders were once referred by an American diplomat as "all but intimate.")

Notably, most meetings between the South Africans the Zairean top brass took place late at night, almost as if these people were afraid of being seen in public with white people. At the same time, warned Nellis, "While I was with Baramoto, I couldn't help sensing that under the brittle crust of his amicability lay a boiling magma of paranoia."

For years, French freelance fighters had taken the lead in offering their services to fight for one government or another—in Africa especially. Thirty years after independence there were still Frenchmen playing behind-the-scenes roles in countries such as Gabon, the Cameroon Republic, Senegal, and Niger. It stayed that way until large numbers of South African military personnel were made redundant after President Nelson Mandela and the African National Congress took over in Pretoria. The border wars having ended, most of these mainly Special Forces personnel were given severance options.

Some of the French veterans recruited to help Mobutu only found out once they got to Kinshasa that it was the ailing dictator and not the rebels with whom they had thrown in their lot. Not to worry, they went ahead anyway and did what was expected of them.

This thirty-odd strong largely French and Belgian squad was part of the White Legion, as they called themselves. It included a Portuguese, a Chilean, and an Italian, and did well for itself even though they were only active toward the end of the war.

The group arrived the day after Christmas 1996, and was sent forward immediately. The French met stiff resistance that included exchanging shots with an opposing bunch of mercenaries from Israel and Ukraine, and still more from South Africa, many of whom Nellis knew quite well. One of the first surprises to greet this modest squad of French fighters was the aggressive nature of the enemy they faced in the eastern sector of Zaire to which they had been dispatched. Opposing them were Rwandan regular forces fighting for Kabila, a well-trained and aggressive lot who could mix it with the best. Nobody had told them before they left Paris that these same Rwandese troops were regarded by their adversaries as the most tenacious of all the rebel components.

The reality of the revolt against the government troops was that Kabila's war was being run by his mercenaries. The corpulent revolutionary leader expected his foreigners to do more than just fight. Unlike Mobutu's lot, Kabila's were responsible for almost all day-to-day decisions and, in many instances, the course of the war itself. Their influence became more apparent as rebel concentrations—sometimes twenty-thousand strong—swept through the country toward Kinshasa and the west. Even without air support, these mercenaries could be seen in planning, communications, battlefield coordination and execution (such as it was in this primitive fighting environment). Most important was their logistics role, for which Kabila had hired excellent support. Without that component in this huge remote land, the rebellion would quickly have spluttered and died.

Despite government claims that Kabila himself was a sham, he and his bush fighters were achieving remarkable results. They had the better of the Congolese Army in just about every department. Unquestionably, his people fought a hell of a war and Mobutu's people— with or without French or any other mercenaries—couldn't match them.

As one of the Frenchman commented afterward, "These guys aren't simply run-of-the-mill fighters. They would come at us again and again and we'd beat them off. Also they'd take losses, but that didn't stop them. Not long afterward they would be there again, fighting hard and sometimes keeping at it all day." The crux of the matter was plain to see: "The real rebel advantage was that while their supply bases were just over the next hill, or possibly alongside a ferry crossing nearby, ours were half a continent away," explained the French mercenary. "Everything we needed to keep fighting had to come all the way from Kinshasa."

Even then, the material often didn't get through because just about every possible aspect of FAZ operational planning was deplorable, including logistics. When a government unit or some of the French mercenaries in isolated bases needed support, the presiding general would either prevaricate or simply do nothing. When later asked about the hiatus, the man would say something about the aircraft having been taken out of service because of technical problems. No one bothered to pass the news on to those waiting at the other end. It was simply no way to fight a war. One of the French mercenaries went on record at the time claiming that Kabila didn't need secret agents to help him with his cause. He already had them in Mobutu's bunch of ham-fisted generals.

When the rebels were able to shoot down a government or charter flight, all aircraft would be grounded, sometimes for a week or longer. Things eased marginally when Kisangani was upgraded as a forward staging post in the final phase of the war, but by then it was too late.

Some remarkable stories emerged during this period. In one action at the Nzoro Bridge in early February 1997, Kabila's forces suffered heavy casualties after having been hit hard by Denard's 60mm mortars and Drugunov sniping rifles. But that didn't stop the enemy using their customary steam-rolling tactics to continue the advance.

Using binoculars and their sniping scopes, the French irregulars would watch in disbelief as more rebel troops, this time without weapons, would come up from behind and take the guns from the hands of their dead comrades. Then they would throw themselves into the fray. Accepting the futility of a deteriorating situation (as well as the possibility of being cut off), the French mercs withdrew.

At one stage, after finally pulling out of Watsa—a vital army communication station in the north—Tavernier's men marched almost a hundred miles through swamps and open savannah grassland to link up with another mercenary group at Faradje, a remote outpost near the Sudanese border. All the while, roving guerrilla bands followed up, snapping at their heels.

The first squad of mercenaries to arrive in Zaire consisted mostly of regulars who had been involved with Bob Denard in the Comores. Their number included "Titi" (who came to the archipelago from Burma by way of Cambodia), as well as a few who had fought in Angola and Rhodesia. Direct from Paris, this lot was designated Team Alpha. The second batch, Team Bravo, was commanded by a Belgian. It came in through Brussels a few hours later, more in an effort to keep French intelligence guessing than for any practical reason. In fact, French military intelligence knew everything from the start, including who had been responsible for recruiting as well as who was picking up the tab.

The head of the first group was a man I ran into while visiting Denard in the Comores. He was known simply as "Charles." A strong, trenchant fellow, his dislike for media types often fringed on paranoia. We didn't get on well at all when I first met him in the colonel's office in Moroni. I'm certain that, introductory letter or not, he would have sent me back to Johannesburg on the next flight had "Uncle Bob" not been in Moroni when I arrived.

Every one of Charles' men had been recruited independently in Europe, some from the "old boys" network, others by answering ads in newspapers. They traveled to Africa independently and were not gathered into a group until after they arrived. Zairean Army officers discreetly separated them from the rest of the passengers after their aircraft landed at Ndjili.

The money was good—perhaps a bit more than the going rate at the time: 30,000 French francs per person, per month, for a ninety-day stretch (or more than $5,000 at prevailing exchange rates). Team leaders got more, but what made this job different was that everybody was paid in advance. Contractually, the men were committed to renew for a further three months should circumstances warrant it.

The second, larger contingent, which numbered about a hundred, were all Serbian. Almost everyone in this party had been, or was still, a regular soldier in the Serbian army. This group included a handful of fixed-wing fighter and helicopter gunship pilots.

Commanded by Dominic Yugo, a Serb colonel from the Kosovo region, they had originally been assembled in Belgrade by Lieutenant Milorad "Misa" Palemis, another controversial figure who, word had

it, commanded a notorious commando unit during the Yugoslav civil
war. There was an unconfirmed report that he had been involved in
the massacre of civilians in Srebrenica.

Despite vigorous denials, including several delivered at the UN,
there was no doubt that the Yugoslav government was directly
involved in putting this force together to fight in an African war. That
much was obvious to everybody, including the Americans. The recruiting operation, for instance, had the undisguised blessing of Jovica
Stanisic, Serbia's internal security chief. Official passports had been
issued to the men at Belgrade's Turist Hotel a few days before departure. The documents were then sent on to Paris for Zairean visas.

Once on African soil, according to Thierry Charlier, a regular con-
tributor to *Raids* magazine, the Serbs' sole mission was to protect the
two airports at Kisangani, one of them civilian (ten miles northeast of
the city beside the local FAZ military headquarters) and the other military. These lines of demarcation became progressively blurred as
Kabila's forces drew closer to this once-fine city commanding the
northern bank of the Congo River. When it still appeared as
Stanleyville on the world's maps, it was regarded as one of colonial
Congo's most beautiful postings.

Operating in the heat and humidity of Kisangani, with its resinous
air that was usually thick with insects and wood smoke, wasn't easy.
The jungle loomed on the outskirts and it was child's play to infiltrate
agents (and often entire groups of fighters) from the outside. Rebel
front-liners—many of them originally from that part of the country—
would wrap their uniforms and weapons in rags and strap the bundles
onto their bicycles. They would then ride innocently into town. Once
a sizable group had penetrated, this clandestine force would gather at
a prearranged spot in advance of an attack, and before the defenders
knew it, they'd have the enemy among them.

The ploy was used so often that one wonders why some of the
Zairean commanders didn't consider implementing countermeasures.
Obviously the jungle helped. In the tropics it mostly starts at the edge
of town and is all but impossible to cordon off. As other tropical
wars—including Vietnam, the Philippines and Angola—have demonstrated, an entire army can sometimes find it difficult to control the
strategic approaches to any large city.

Joseph Conrad had traveled upriver as far as Stanleyville—and
possibly beyond into what was then still uncharted territory. He
described it well in *Heart of Darkness*:

The reaches opened up before us and closed behind us, as if the forests had stepped leisurely across the water to bar the way for our return. We penetrated deeper and deeper into the heart of darkness. It was quiet in there. . . . The dawns were heralded by the descent of a chill stillness. . . . We were wanderers on prehistoric earth, and on an earth that wore the aspect of an unknown plant. . . . We were cut off from comprehension of our surroundings, wondering and secretly appalled . . .

Anyone moving across this great green African mantle today, either north or south of the giant river and farther afield into Congo (Brazzaville) and Equatorial Guinea, will discover that very little has changed from what this great scribe recorded more than a century ago.

The towns are larger, more dilapidated and, in places, hopelessly forlorn. Yesterday's ordered communities have become sprawling camps where throngs can intimidate if that mood prevails, which is often in much of present-day Africa. There are also a lot more soldiers about than there were twenty or thirty years ago, but that's to be expected as the appendages of modern-day society grope inexorably toward the remoter regions of our globe.

Out in the bush, things remain as they always have because the jungle rules. Generally people don't go there unless it is to their homes or for a specific purpose, such as to hunt, trade or prospect. Invariably, strangers are treated with suspicion. The bush is also a world of shadowy isolation. Bad roads aren't just dreadful, they're beyond repair. Few have seen a grader for forty years. In many places the "highway" has deteriorated so much that the forest has reclaimed what was once part of the Trans-Africa network. Long stretches have reverted to jungle.

When Mike Hoare and his men sped north to join up with the U.S./Belgian rescue force at Stanleyville—not all that long after independence—most of the roads they used were passable. No more. Move cross-country through parts of the lower Congo in what was then still Shaba, as I did in the early 1970s, and there were places where we had to build our own primitive bridges. Things since have only grown worse.

And then there is the water—lots of water. Some of it stands stagnant in great pools that seem to go on forever, from which mosquitoes attack you in battalions. Elsewhere it's fast-moving and treacherous in an environment where, if you don't take care, the climate will sap your strength within days. A British river expedition tried to pass through this territory in the 1980s; some of its members were lost, not to rebels but to the turbulent waters. It was in this tropical hinterland in the Congo's northeast region that French and Serbian mercenaries found themselves at war against Kabila and his rebel army early in 1997.

In contrast to the French, Yugoslav mercenaries in Mobutu's army were badly paid, especially considering the risks. The average Serb merc received $1,000 a month (admittedly not unreasonable by Balkan standards), and then only upon completion of his tour of duty. Most of the rest was creamed in Belgrade. Otherwise, both teams were adequately equipped.

Almost everything, including weapons needed by both groups of mercenaries, came from Yugoslav arms factories and were flown to Kinshasa from Belgrade, usually by way of Luxor in Egypt. Stocks included Serbian copies of a variety of weapons, including the Yugoslav version of the AK-47 (M70B1 and M70AB2), MG-42s (the M53 GPMG), RPG-7 rocket launchers, the ubiquitous 64mm LAW anti-tank weapon (though Kabila had no armor to speak of) and, of course, the equally ubiquitous SAMs. According to a London *Sunday Times* investigating team, there was even a Yugoslav Army "directorate for supply and procurement" office set up for the purpose in Cairo.

A report in Jane's *Intelligence Review* mentions that the Serb fighters also had the more sophisticated SA-14 man-portable "Gremlin" surface-to-air missiles, but photographs taken at the time show SA-7s. Either way it didn't matter: the only air power Kabila had was an ancient Dakota C-47, which hauled him around the countryside to positions occupied by his forces.

Apart from what was sold by Belgrade, Mobutu bought a lot of weapons from the Ukraine and Russia as part of some totally inadequate improvised defensive measure. Toward the end, people were more concerned with the percentages they were earning than with the hardware, a good part of which was never delivered.

Among the first items to filter into Kisangani after the mercenaries arrived were four Mi-24 attack helicopters, supposedly "leased" from Ukraine. Other aircraft intended for the newly arrived Serbian pilots included several Yugoslav Galebs and Jastrebs, as well as a handful of Italian-built Aermacchi MB-326 Ks. These were light attack aircraft, normally used for training rather than combat. The Serbs promised Tavernier the full range of air support (including top cover), but little materialized. Flights between Kinshasa and Kisangani were in Air Force Antonovs with Russian pilots at the controls. A temperamental bunch, they'd laugh off a flight if they believed the war was getting too close to a designated airstrip.

For a short while the French had the use of a Pilatus Porter, but it crash-landed after arguing who had the right-of-way with a ten-foot-tall ant hill that destroyed the plane's undercarriage. After that, everything hinged on a "civilian" Andover that had been hired to ferry men and cargo between the various French mercenary bases, one of which had been used by Executive Outcomes for casualty evacuations a couple of years earlier. French correspondent Thierry Charlier identified the pilot as an American who called himself "Roland," but who seemed pretty tight-lipped about everything else. Another source suggested he might have been one of Langley's people.

Whatever his origins or real job, there were times when "Roland' would take some heavy fire. According to some of the French, he never flinched when he was required to pull them out of call signs that could only be regarded as marginal. Some of these attracted a lot of attention from the rebels when his plane appeared. Though he took more hits than might otherwise have been necessary, Kabila's fighters were never able to bring the Andover down.

When the fighting in Zaire ended, anyone who had anything to do with Serbian mercenaries agreed that their role in Mobutu's war was a disaster. Their contribution to the country's defense began in mid-January 1997. It ended with the fall of Kisangani two months later. During that eight-week period Kabila's rebels wiped the floor with these supposedly tough veterans.

Because of their loudly proclaimed experience back home in the Balkans, seasoned Congolese FAZ veterans at first dubbed them "specialists of warfare." Toward the end, they were disparaged by just about everyone as *ces cochons-la* ("the bastards"). Charlier declared in his writings about this phase of the Congo's war that all the Serbians had to offer was illusionary. A lot of fast talk with little substance. "As for providing air support for French mercenaries," he declared, "the Serbs were noted mainly for their absence." On the rare occasion that they did make made an effort, it was often from such an extreme altitude that they were almost useless to those facing the enemy on the ground.

Loud of mouth and abysmally short on courage (except when there was hard stuff about), the Serb component of the White Legion tarnished a lot more than any mercenary ideal in Africa.

12

NELLIS AND HIS WAR DOGS IN THE CONGO

**"Civil war is the worst event that can befall a nation, and
no one understands this more than a soldier, for it is
he who bears the brunt."**

Lt. Colonel Ron Reid-Daly, founder-commander of the Selous
Scouts, Rhodesian Army, in his book *Pamwe Chete*[1]

Once Neall Ellis and the boys became better acquainted with the
Congo's generals, they spent a lot of time chewing the fat at the home
of General Likunia, the Congolese Minister of Defense. Sometimes
they popped along to General Mayele's place. It was similar to Baramoto's but seriously needed a fresh coat of paint. As Chief of the
Armed Forces, Mayele preferred to do his entertaining in his garden,
usually under an Oriental pagoda that had been left behind by some
forgotten colonial functionary. It weathered well in the tropics.

The conversations between the South Africans and the Congo officers were similar: endless talk about the best way to tackle Laurent
Kabila and his *Alliance des Forces Democratiques pour la Liberation
du Zongo-Zaire*. Carefully choosing his moment, Nellis would invariably try to swing the conversation toward bringing to fruition the project that mattered most. After all, that was why he had come to
Kinshasa.

Getting anybody in Kinshasa to do something constructive was
not easy and, with time, it became more difficult. Issues were always
the same: the war, the lack of resistance on the part of government
forces, the inability of the air force to make headway and so on.

But there was a solution to it all, Nellis would urge for the sixti-
eth time. "There is an immediate way of turning the war around!"
That would get everybody's attention for about forty seconds. Brows
would furrow, the generals would stop what they were doing and, for
a few moments they'd listen, though the South African admits that the
degree of interest was usually proportionate to the amount of grog

that'd gone down. Then one of them would make some comment, usually trite, often stupid, and everybody would laugh. With that, the party would go on as before, while Kinshasa's deceptive fog of war enveloped them all. Again!

The reality was altogether something else. Nellis was astonished that the threat—real, tangible and inexorably heading their way—was not something that these people with more confetti on their jackets than an American two-star wished to grapple with. They must have known by then that the military situation had become precarious. By now Kinshasa—Mobutu's cherished capital for thirty years—was within Kabila's sights and everyone in the city knew it. Everyone, that is, except the generals and colonels who were supposed to be fighting the war.

One of the key issues facing Zaire was that the army hadn't been paid for more than six months. Nobody, least of all the generals, was prepared to remedy the situation. Each had money in abundance, but not one of them was prepared to part with any of it. The sums involved were not that significant. The average FAZ soldier's basic wage was about two dollars a month, in a country where a pack of local cigarettes cost two weeks' wages. With government forces estimated at about a hundred thousand men, the amount of money required to keep them happy—and loyal—was modest compared to the millions that were being squandered by these autocrats on the most absurd luxuries imaginable. For instance, flowers for Mobutu's dozen residences were still being flown in daily from Europe. So was fresh dairy produce and container-loads of milk-fed veal, some all the way from Japan!

One little aphorism attributed to the local stringer of Paris' le Monde said it all. "For most of these people," he said, "it's only recently that some of them have been able to tell paté from toothpaste . . . and even then there has been confusion." The jibe was unkind, but considering these excesses, in a country where the majority of the population didn't possess a cake of soap, it wasn't off center. Even the village idiot could have told these splendidly uniformed buffoons that if cash was not found to pay the troops and pretty damn soon, everyone would go down. What mattered most to these morons was money, most of it stashed abroad. At the time of his death, Mobutu was estimated to be worth somewhere between five and eight billion dollars. Not shabby at all for a man that had never held an honest job. Curiously, the ailing tyrant had always been generous to those close to him—especially his topmost military figures. Now they had every-thing, more than they could ever hope for, but it obviously wouldn't last.

"Looking back, none of it makes sense," Nellis says today. "The security, the longevity of all of these people was at risk, but nobody bothered to challenge the system, probably because they feared for their lives if they did."

There was one exception, and as might be expected, it bore a distinct Middle East imprint. Squads of Israelis (they, too, denied that they were mercenaries) had been hired to train and lead the DSP, the *Division Speciale Presidentielle*. The former brigade's principal role was to guard the president. An intelligence unit known as SARM supplemented it. In contrast to the rest of the Congo's armed forces, both organizations were well paid. It surprised no one that all the troops in the DSP security element were of the Ngbandi tribe from the Congo's Equateur Province, the same geographical region that had originally produced Mobutu.

One of Nellis' first observations after arriving in the Congo was that many regular army soldiers, having been paid so little for so long, would, given the opportunity, defect to Kabila. At least the corpulent rebel kept his men fed. Being Africa, this was not the first time that something like this had happened. In the Central African Republic the lunatic Bokassa—still regarded together with Idi Amin as one of Africa's most ruthless demagogues—had also neglected to pay his army. Like other African dictators, he wasn't short of cash, either. The result was that a group of rebellious junior officers ousted him. The same eventually happened to Amin, though with some help from a Tanzanian invasion army.

Mobutu could have bought ten squadrons of modern Russian fighter jets and ended the war in a month. The best helicopter gunships were available to him on the arms market, and no government would have minded a jot, not even if he acquired foreign pilots to fly them. Certainly Moscow would have relished the opportunity of earning hundreds of millions in arms sales. More to the point, much of it was ready and waiting: surplus stocks lay rotting in dozens of abandoned former Soviet bases. All Mobutu had to do was get one of his functionaries on the phone and order him to get hold of some of Kinshasa's resident Russian *biznesmeni*. They would have sold their grandmothers if the price was right.

Looking more closely at what was taking place in Kinshasa then, most nations trading with the Congo were desperate for Mobutu to reach some sort of accord with his enemies. The impetus was that apart from diamonds and precious metals, the Congo, for more than half a century, had been a major producer of about two dozen essential metals, including copper, uranium and cobalt. In coltan alone— short for columbite-tantalite (a heat-resistant compound used in electronics to make things like mobile telephones and Sony Play-stations)—Zaire had half the world's reserves, until new supplies were discovered in Siberia.

As the war dragged on, the instability that came from this impasse suited no one. It is fairly certain that no trading nation would have stood in Mobutu's way to counter Kabila no matter what he did, including the hiring of mercenaries. That Zaire topped the international list in human rights atrocities was no longer an issue: peace was, and at any price.

Mobutu's hometown of Gbadolite was stuck away in the northern part of the country within sight of the great lethargic Congo River and an ill-defined frontier with the Central African Republic. General Baramoto told Nellis that the place was out of reach of the war, one of the reasons why it became Mobutu's last-ditch center of operations. Not a big town, Gbadolite would fit comfortably within the confines of a place like Makeni, Sierra Leone, or Warri in the Niger Delta.

What made Gbadolite different from other cities in the country was its magnificent boulevards and well-kept roads boasting a feature found nowhere else in the country: streetlights. For the first-timer stepping off the plane, it was obvious that a good deal of planning had gone into its layout. Some of the homes were truly stunning. A visiting British journalist called it "Versailles in the Jungle."

In a strange, African sort of way, I suppose he was right. The fortune in national resources that Mobutu and those around him had squandered on what had been a riverside village stunned everyone who saw the place. For instance, the house in which the South African mercenaries stayed when they first arrived there belonged to Baramoto and it was like something out of a commemorative issue of *Architectural Digest*.

The flooring was white imported Italian marble. Persian rugs were almost casually scattered about the floors in each room. Even the toilets had air-conditioning. The faucets in all four bathrooms were gold plated, and while the beds were king-sized doubles, only satin was good enough for the duvets and sheets. Just about everything carried the signature of a French department store.

To the average Zairian, all this garish grandeur was beyond comprehension. Few had experienced anything but an existence barely above starvation. They had no point of reference with regard to such embarrassingly gaudy opulence. These same people also looked askew at some of our own traits. For starters, none could fathom the concept of pay toilets; the running joke among them was that we Westerners paid to pee. As far as Africa's poor folk are concerned, a Persian carpet is simply a spread of soft multicolored tarpaulin. The same was true with marble—merely another type of stone. Inviting the average Congolese into the villa for an evening respite would have been analogous to taking a bushman from his kraal in the Kalahari and asking him to comprehend the contents of London's Victoria and Albert Museum.

By now another helicopter pilot, Juba Joubert, had arrived from South Africa. He and Nellis, together with a French pilot named Jean-Jacques Fuentes, whom everyone called J.J., were designated by Baramoto to work something out to stem Kabila's advance.

The three men reached Gbadolite well after midnight, but that didn't stop their host from hauling his chef out of bed to prepare a meal that would have done justice to Berlin's best—and that on the periphery of Africa's darkest forests. It was comprised of an entrée of smoked salmon and fresh lettuce, a lobster thermidor main dish, followed by a choice of Italian and Dutch cheeses. Also on offer were a dozen flavors of Ben and Jerry's ice cream. Yet another array of servants arrived with an assortment of fresh fruit, none of it tropical. Almost everything had come in from Europe. So much for the vicissitudes of war.

Mobutu wasn't alone in these excesses. Creating living monuments seemed to be a trait of some African rulers at a time when there was still a lot of money available for such things. Ghana's Nkrumah had his effigy raised in just about every town in the country, which was a pity because they all came toppling down after he had been ousted while attending a meeting of Commonwealth heads of state in Singapore. Felix Houphouet-Boigny of the Ivory Coast squandered tens of millions that might otherwise have been devoted to the educational or medical needs of his people. This man built himself edifices that would almost have rivaled Disneyland, including a monstrosity of a palace, all of it to impress his fellow tribesmen at Yamoussoukro. As if that wasn't enough, he then had to erect a Roman Catholic cathedral that, in size, rivaled St. Peter's Basilica in Rome. And that in

Abidjan, the West African capital of a nation that is preponderantly either Muslim or Animist.

Jean-Bédel Bokassa went a step further and anointed himself emperor. He awarded himself hundreds of grandiose titles and decorations and wore them simultaneously on his formal military jacket. Because of the weight, the garment hung around his shoulders like sackcloth.

Like Mobutu, Idi Amin, and the socialist Kwame Osajyefo Nkrumah, with his muddle-headed "Consciencism," the actions of these people insulted African tradition, mind and culture, as well as the aspirations of millions of black people all over the world. Those of us in Europe and elsewhere in Africa who followed these crazy antics, would guffaw up our sleeves as new absurdities came to light. Few said anything publicly for fear of being branded a racist.

Despite his shortcomings, Mobutu's amazing life story, like that of so many of the political misfits of the last century, is fascinating. Born in poverty and educated at mission schools (which seems to be the norm for so many of the continent's tyrants), Joseph Desire Mobutu rose from the rank of a lowly enlisted clerk to sergeant-major, the highest rank open to Africans in Belgium's colonial forces. Mobutu first attracted Washington's attention shortly after the Congo became independent, when he was made commander-in-chief of his country's armed forces. He was appointed by an Idi Amin look-alike, Joseph Kasavubu, the man who replaced the murdered Lumumba.

Evidence indicates that Mobutu was in the pay of the CIA from very early on in his career. Those ties held until the end, especially during the Cold War when two of his closest neighbors, Angola and Congo (Brazzaville) became Soviet client states. Without Western help after he seized power in 1965, Mobutu would never have survived. In the 1970s he twice had to ask for foreign military intervention to repel cross-border attacks by Angolan-backed Katangese. (These same troops were still being linked to uprisings in the eastern part of the country against the Kabila dynasty while Unita remained active militarily in the former Portuguese colony.)

Invasions of Katanga, Congo's southern province, in 1977 and 1978, brought French, Belgian and Moroccan troops to Mobutu's rescue. Many were ferried by American military transport planes. The effort underwrote Katanga as a key strategic outpost in U.S. eyes. Apparently the CIA used the Shaba military base at Kamina to channel weapons to Unita rebels, then fighting an internecine war of their own against a socialist MPLA government in neighboring Angola.

On the one or two occasions that President Reagan was obliged to say something official about the Congo, he hailed Mobutu as "a voice of good sense and good will," which was the kind of dross being bandied about in Washington at the time. The absurdity had reached a peak in the late 1970s when Mobutu—by now as ruthless a manipulator as anyone on the world's stage—deified himself. He was depicted on the nightly television news in Kinshasa as a divine being descending from Heaven: the graphics were complete, halo and all. By then he had also changed both his and the country's name: Congo became Zaire, and Katanga was renamed Shaba.

Mobutu also adopted the grandiloquent title of "Mobutu Sese Seko Koko Ngbendu wa za Banga," which, I'm improbably told, means "The all-powerful warrior who, because of his endurance and inflexible will to win, will go from conquest to conquest, leaving fire in his wake." Of course, there was also his penchant for dealing harshly with messengers who brought him bad news. Most of these poor souls were hauled off to the headquarters of his hated secret police, the *Centre Nationale d'Documentation*, never to be seen again.

Those who had regular truck with the man said that Mobutu's mood was changeable, which was perhaps one of the reasons why he managed to stay on top for so long: you never knew what he would do next. Somebody once wrote that he had a presence as mysterious and terrifying as an Aztec priest.

Like Stalin, Mobutu trusted no one. Even members of his family were suspect. He made a fetish of keeping people close to him off balance. If he thought one of his ministers had exceeded his mandate, he was dumped. One moment the man would be a national figure, living the good life and appearing nightly on TV, and the next he and his family would find themselves relegated to a village in the jungle. Once that guillotine fell, there was no appeal.

Then again, Mobutu could be charming to people who might be of use to him, and when he regarded it appropriate, he would proffer the velvet glove. Underneath, wrote an American journalist who was accorded a rare interview with the oppressor, "It was jungle red." As one scribe commented, if the man read only one book in his life it had to have been by Machiavelli.

Ensconced in the Intercontinental, Nellis and friends found Kinshasa unlike any other African city. Even with the hard hand of war reaching toward the city's ramparts, the conurbation crawled with foreigners eager to do business. To the majority of these transients, it didn't matter that the current regime was becoming increasingly embattled. Though the pace at the hotel was leisurely, it was booked solid. You had to check in well ahead of time to get a squash or tennis court, Nellis remembered. The casino, too, was busy around the clock.

In addition, other needs were catered to, as they always are in a city where women come knocking at your door at all hours. Drink in hand on their balcony, the South Africans watched the street girls doing their thing below. Business was good, and things didn't slow down until nearly dawn.

For those staying at the Intercontinental, normality ended at the hotel gates on the street, which were usually well guarded and for good reason. "The world beyond our hotel walls was perilous, which was to be expected in a city where the man with ten dollars in his pocket was considered rich," explained Nellis. "It was an aspect of society that we would only glimpse fleetingly as we were shunted between one ministerial office and another, usually with heavy weapons front and back in our four- or five-vehicle convoy. For obvious reasons, you never went out on your own at night. You'd lie in your bed and hear shots over the hum of your air conditioner."

In Kinshasa, people were frequently murdered for small sums of money, for their clothes, or for the flimsiest real or imagined slight. Passersby were sometimes shot by accident. There were political slayings galore, though that was mostly restricted to the townships. If Baramoto's goons thought somebody was being subversive or even acting in a peculiar manner—or possibly had had too much contact with strangers or foreigners—he or she was simply killed. As one old warrior observed during my visit, "To be outspoken in Zaire was to dance on razor blades."

Within days of their arrival, Nellis and his comrades witnessed a riot involving the army. Several people were shot dead as they watched from their vantage point in the hotel. Nellis remembers, "It was all a bit hairy because the firing went on for a while and rounds went cracking past us." Another time, as they were being driven through town, squads of troops moved in and opened fire, scattering a demonstrating mob. "Our driver didn't even touch his brakes. Hours later, on our return along the same route, the bodies still lay where they had fallen." When he inquired about this at the hotel, one of the guests, an old-timer who had been coming to Zaire for decades, suggested he take no notice. "That happens at least twice a week, sometimes more," he told him. Most times their families would only retrieve the carcasses after dark.

As the South African pilot commented, you ignored a lot of what was going on in Kinshasa, unless, of course, it affected you personally. And you certainly never stopped to ask questions.

Referring to those Europeans who had stayed too long in the tropics, somebody told Nellis that living there eventually became a kind of malaria of the soul. "Like Lagos, Freetown, Accra and Douala in the Cameroon, Kinshasa can be draining, emaciating and debilitating."

The end for Mobutu, while hardly painless, came quickly once Kabila's troops broke through the government's last line of defense at Kikwit, about sixty miles from the capital. With the barbarians at the gates, Nellis could observe from up close that decisions being made by the Zairian high command were about as spontaneous as watching molasses melt. Any kind of precipitate or unexpected action resulted in a collective shudder. Even at this eleventh hour, Nellis told General Baramoto that the South Africans could still do something to stop the enemy's advance. This was when the three of them were sent north to Gbadolite. Their job, they were told, was to try to muster the remnants of the Zaire Air Force for a last-gasp effort.

Before leaving for the north on a military transport, there was a quick meeting with General Likunia, who by then had taken over as Mobutu's last Prime Minister. He told the South Africans that there were four Mi-24 combat helicopters, a pair of Yugoslav Jastreb ground attack jets, and five MiG-21 interceptor fighters, all of them sitting on the ground at their destination and fully serviceable. Nellis was assured they could go operational as soon as they were ferried to Kinshasa.

While hesitant to dampen Likunia's optimism, Nellis was skeptical. Point-to-point he estimated that Gbadolite was more than seven hundred miles from the capital and that the trip would almost certainly involve a refueling stop. And that could only happen if there were ferry tanks available.

Originally there had been two Jastrebs. But Nellis knew that one had already been written off when a drunken Serb mercenary pilot decided to roar back down the runway after take off. He came in a few feet off the deck, clipped a lamppost, and careened into a column of troops on parade. He took a lot of soldiers with him when he was killed. As Nellis noted jocularly afterward, "It was a helluva cure for a hangover!"

The MiGs that Nellis and Juba found at Gbadolite might have been useful for some kind of holding action—even if they could have got them south in time to be of any use. But they were hardly the kind of weapon needed to stop an invasion force. While they made a lot of noise and their rockets and machine guns would have been useful in a ground attack role, there was an additional problem: Zaire didn't have the pilots to fly them. Nor had any money been put on the table to recruit South Africans—the one group of combatants that might have been able to achieve something. By then, nobody was handing out any cash except for priorities, like airline tickets for government members and their families to get out of the country.

The last thing Nellis did before leaving for Gbadolite was to organize a final meeting with General Baruti, chief of the Zairean Air Force. The bad news, he was told, was that instead of four Hinds, there were only two that flew. One had crashed and another was being pirated for parts. Nor was Baruti sure about ammunition.

How to bring them through to Kinshasa was another matter. One would have thought that with Kabila on the outskirts, Mobutu's military leaders would have prioritized the problem, but even that didn't appear to have been given any kind of serious consideration.

As Nellis saw it there were two immediate options. The Hinds could be brought down to the capital in a couple of support planes. This was an essential component anyway, since Jet A1 would have to be airfreighted in, if only because he'd heard on the grapevine that Ndjili Airport was down to its final reserves of fuel.

Alternatively, if the necessary clearances could be obtained, the Mi-24s could be routed through Brazzaville and from there flown across the river to Kinshasa. That opportunity disappeared when an American military advisory group in Brazzaville commandeered all available aircraft fuel in the neighboring state. The Yanks also put out the word that permission for the Hinds to transit was, as they like to phrase it, no longer an option. Someone in Washington wanted to see Mobutu's back.

The situation in Gbadolite itself was discouraging. The MiGs were there all right, but they were in kit form. Russian technicians were still assembling them, and that could take weeks. Also, special oils and greases ordered from Moscow to complete the task never arrived. There were more problems. The MiGs needed special batteries, but none could be found. That meant it would have been impossible to start the jets even if everything else fell into place. And then came the news that the Jastrebs' batteries were missing and there was only one serviceable Mi-24 battery where two, working in tandem, are needed for an internal start. The entire air force was a shambles.

The crunch came when Rudi, a Russian technician in charge of the air force base at Gbadolite who spoke passable English, told Nellis that the ground power units that had been sold to Mobutu's people didn't have the correct fittings to plug into the aircraft, so they were useless too. Hands in the air, the normally unflappable Nellis asked what else could go wrong? Lots, he was to discover.

Neither the aircraft technicians nor the unit armorer had arrived at Gbadolite as instructed by the head of the air force. Undeterred, Juba Joubert—who had a pretty good technical knowledge of the Mi-24, having flown them in Sierra Leone for EO—clambered over the aircraft for a makeshift inspection. Everything looked fine, he told Nellis. But there was still a question about the helicopters' weapons' systems. While there was enough 12.7mm ammunition for one sortie, there were no links or feed belts for the Hind's magazines. Nellis explained this to the base commander, a half-colonel, adding that the gunship's weapons were inoperable until the armorer arrived because only he had the tools necessary to fix them. The officer brushed the pilot aside. He would fix it himself, he bellowed angrily before rushing off to the hanger.

With a couple of none-too-sober soldiers in tow waving their weapons about, the colonel descended on the helicopter in a fury. He used a mallet followed by a crowbar in a bid to pry open the Mi-24's securing catches, each blow inflicting more damage than the last. The only way Nellis could stop him was by warning the officer that once the repairs had been completed, it was air force policy for the man who had done the job to make a test flight. The colonel threw down the tools and left. They never saw him again.

Finally, the ground crew and weapons technician arrived from Kinshasa. But then it was found that because the choppers had been parked in the rain, there was water in one of the main rotor blade drag damper water indicators. This would cause the helicopter to vibrate during flight. But Juba took her up anyway. He flew a while and then turned back when he couldn't get sufficient operational speed.

The next day, Friday, May 16, 1997, Mobutu arrived at Gbadolite in his presidential jet. His entourage of more than a hundred people included ministers, wives and children. Later that afternoon, Rudi, the Russian technician, quietly cornered the South Africans in one of the hangers. "I got a call from friends," he told them. "Things are really bad. If the government hasn't already collapsed, it's about to." Kabila was on verge of taking Kinshasa and members of the government had either fled or were preparing to do so.

The news didn't exactly come as a shock to Nellis, but he hadn't expected things to move quite so fast. More intimidating was the reality of being stuck in one the darkest reaches of central Africa. An hour later they got word that rebel units were moving up on Gbadolite and, it was said, they might reach the city within twenty-four hours. Rudi told Nellis in hushed whispers that he'd heard Mobutu was preparing to leave the country that night on an Ilyushin Il-76. The plane was expected to land at Gbadolite any time so the remainder of the Zaire Air Force mobile missile systems still positioned around the airfield could be removed.[2] They should all be sure to be on that aircraft when it left, the Russian warned. If they didn't, he shrugged and made the symbolic cut across the throat.

Nellis and Joubert met Mobutu later that afternoon when the old and obviously very ill leader ambled around the airport with a couple of bodyguards. To their surprise, he stopped to talk and asked in a quiet, dignified voice what they needed. When they told him of their problems with the Hinds, Mobutu said that everything would be delivered the next day. He also confided that he was expecting several arms shipments from Libya. His manner reflected real confidence, something that astonished the pair. The relief flights were part of a done deal, he continued.

"There was no reason to doubt the man," Nellis explained, though at that late stage the ailing African was ready to believe anything. Mobutu warned the crew not to return to Kinshasa and promised that if he had to leave, he'd take them with him. With that he shook hands and moved on.

An hour later they heard that their old friend General Mahele, by then the Commander of the Army and Minister of Defense, had been shot by one of Mobutu's sons, an army colonel. The story put out was that Mahele, arguably the best of Mobutu's top command, had intended to defect to Kabila. At least that was what a Kinshasa radio bulletin suggested. It was an obvious option, Nellis ruminated afterward, though the South Africans doubted its veracity because Mahele had appeared to be a consummate professional. The turncoat general been "dealt with," the radio announcer crowed. The South Africans had gotten to know Mahele quite well during the course of their many evenings together, and thought his murder a great pity. Mahele was the only real soldier Nellis met during his six-month stint in the country.

The South Africans were also unaware that just then, Mauritz le Roux was in the air in a chartered Lear Jet heading toward Gbadolite. He told his wife that he intended to pull the two men out, even though he believed he might be too late. When he arrived at Brazzaville, he was not only denied fuel but was arrested and his plane impounded. The next morning le Roux was allowed to refuel, but he and his crew were warned that if they returned they would be jailed. They had no option but to head back to South Africa.

At about two in the morning, on the same night that insects were devouring Le Roux in one of Africa's filthiest jails, Nellis was awakened by the sound of a passenger aircraft gunning its engines. He didn't have to be told that Mobutu and his entourage were fleeing Zaire. A couple of hours later the thumps of heavy explosions and small arms fire reached the house. The noise came from the edge of town and intensified as dawn approached.

The two South Africans grabbed their clothes and went outside. The first hint of an African dawn had barely begun to filter through the jungle when strings of tracers arched across the sky. There were troops shooting in every direction. Worse, it was impossible to distinguish between a rebel attack and returning fire. Meantime, the guards at the compound gates had disappeared. That left Nellis, Juba and J.J. the last three white men stranded in a region that was coming apart and five hundred miles from civilization.

"There wasn't an officer in sight," Nellis recalled. "The only troops we saw were on the rampage, many of them drunk and firing their weapons at random, sometimes into the air, other times at shadows that they perceived around them. Some were as aggressive as hell, furious at having been abandoned by their leaders. All we knew was that we had to get out of there. But how?"

Obviously, Nellis reckoned, with everybody around them going berserk, there were almost no options left to them. A remote chance existed if they could get to the last remaining Mi-24 at the airfield. The gunship wasn't altogether airworthy, but Juba said that it had enough fuel to get them to the Central African Republic. The idea was discarded when firing picked up again. This time it was heavy automatic stuff—12.7mm or possibly even 14.5mm—coming in from the direction of the airport. If they were spotted heading that way, it would have been obvious to everyone what they were trying to do. They would have been shot on sight. What else to do then? Nellis and the two others put their heads together.

Having been in these parts before, Nellis knew that the closest border post was at Mobayi-Mbongo, about forty miles away. But that was along a road that by now would be packed with Zairean refugees, never mind troops fleeing Kabila's people. The army was in mutiny and already there were reports of soldiers shooting strangers. Some of the mutineers—including a few who had already discarded their uniforms—had come by the house earlier that day. Most were already high. While not hostile toward the war dogs, they certainly weren't their usual unctuous selves. If the shooting continued, the three of them concluded, matters would only get worse.

There was one other possibility, J.J. suggested. He was aware of a bush track leading straight north from Gbadolite to the frontier. He had spotted it on several occasions when circling the area prior to landing. Though there was no border post at the end of it, the route made straight for the river and, as he explained, the Central African Republic lay just beyond. Left with no other viable option, their decision was made. Meantime, Nellis used his satellite phone to call home and tell Zelda of their plans while J.J. spoke hurriedly to friends in Paris. His contacts there said they would advise the French Ministry of Defense about their predicament. He was also assured that French Army units in the CAR would be watching for them. In anticipation of a full-scale military rebellion in Zaire, France had already deployed squads of troops along the CAR's north bank of the Congo.

At this point, some soldiers who had stayed behind came into the house and forced open the general's cellar: the party began in earnest. More soldiers arrived with a truck and began loading furniture, drapes, TVs, kitchenware and mattresses. One even ripped a bidet from the bathroom floor and carried it outside on his head.

A woman in the general's compound approached the South Africans and told them in a hushed voice that she was worried about their safety. "You will be killed if you stay in the house," she warned, telling them that the word had gone out on the local radio for the army to be on the lookout for three white men. The story being put about, she told them, was that "You are enemy mercenaries and had infiltrated Gbadolite." She suggested they take refuge in her shack, explaining that it was away from the main house and at least they'd be safe there until the main body of soldiers left. She also promised to divert the attention of anyone who came looking for them.

Nellis' escape from Zaire into the CAR with Juba and J.J.—all of it on foot except for the final leg in a leaking dugout canoe—lasted two days. Along the way they were beaten, spat upon, robbed, shot at, and pistol-whipped. They hadn't even reached the far side of town before they were grabbed by some of the troops who had manhandled them earlier and told them that they should prepare themselves to be executed. Even today Nellis isn't certain why it didn't happen, because "the bastards seemed to be pretty set on it." Hardly a religious man, the South African pilot admits to having prayed more in those forty-eight hours than in all the previous years of his life.

Looking back, Nellis believes that it would be impossible to do it again and get away with it. Just too many things hinged on chance, he reckons today.

After talking themselves past the first few roadblocks on the edge of town, the three men headed cautiously toward the river. There was no food and if they needed to drink they had to resort to any one of hundreds of steams traversing the region. Occasionally they were forced to make wide detours around groups of soldiers gathered in the road. Other times, caught short, they left it to J.J. to argue with these thugs in French. It says much for his ability that he was able to talk enough temporary sense into a bunch of drunkards that they let them proceed, though not without being beaten because they had nothing to offer in the way of a bribe. Then, for no reason at all, they would suddenly be allowed to go again.

Eventually they reached the south bank of the Congo River, where they were made to strip. Even their shoes were taken from them. Only Nellis was allowed to keep his trousers because he wasn't wearing shorts. Eventually, following some of the most unlikely escapades imaginable, the three men managed to get out of Zaire with Juba and J.J. clad only in their underwear. How they ultimately got away with it, none of them is certain. They must have done something right, they acknowledged. Even before leaving Gbadolite all three had written off the possibility of ever seeing their families again. As a last resort they stole a dugout canoe from one of the villages along the Congo River and rowed it to the other side. By the time they were spotted it was too late, but that didn't stop soldiers lining the bank sending volleys of shots after them.

Nellis' biggest regret is that apart from having everything that he possessed taken from him by armed thugs, he also forfeited $8,000 that he'd secreted in his trunk back at the Intercontinental Hotel in Kinshasa. As had always been his custom while in Zaire, whenever he left town he arranged with the manager to have it secured in the basement for safekeeping. Nellis had expected to be back in a couple of days. Today he shrugs it off: like everything else they had on them, the money would have been taken from him anyway by the mutinous troops they encountered along the route to freedom.

They even took Juba Joubert's last $100 bill. In a final, desperate act, he'd secreted it between his toes. When some smart-assed corporal found it, Juba got a clip around the ear with a rifle butt for the effort.

13

ZIMBABWE'S MERCENARIES
IN CONGO'S WAR

"Zimbabwe's deployment of more than 10,000 troops to support the government of the Democratic Republic of the Congo (DRC) is the most significant costly drain on the country's resources. . . . Moreover, some reports have claimed that a few well-connected Zimbabwe business people as well as elements of the military are enriching themselves through the Congo war."

Zimbabwe: Current Issues—Congressional Research Service Brief, Washington DC, March 2001

The Congo entered a new and bizarre phase once Laurent Kabila marched his radical Alliance of Democratic Forces into Kinshasa. The rebel who toppled Mobutu was now himself on the hit list.

Again there were rebels from all over Africa crossing into the country: from Uganda, Rwanda, Burundi, Tanzania, Congo (Brazzaville), and the Sudan, every one of them of a single mind: to topple this burly thug-cum-president in a country almost half the size of Western Europe. Essentially it was the same scenario as before, only the participants were a more diverse and desperate bunch. There was also a new crowd of mercenaries, including some from Zimbabwe, a country that had never previously involved itself in this kind of business. Once again, diamonds were the lodestar.

The new "liberation" conflict started barely months after Kabila had been sworn in as president in May of 1997. It took him just two or three weeks to prove to everybody that he was every bit the tyrant his predecessor was, and then some. After changing the name of the country from Zaire to the Democratic Republic of the Congo, Kabila postponed elections indefinitely and then turned against anyone who spoke out against his actions. Those of his former allies he had not already betrayed or alienated turned on him. The sudden turn of events created a vacuum that could only be decided by another civil war.

Kabila took over a shaky economy that had deteriorated even further in the final days of Mobutu's rule. By late 1998, after he had instituted his *Franc Congolaise* (FC), the only thing that was of any conssequence in the Congo Republic was the American dollar. The name Zaire was dropped because that was Mobutu's old fief, not Kabila's. Planeloads of the successor's newly printed banknotes arrived in the capital and the official exchange rate pegged: one Congolese franc for a dollar. A week later, that same dollar bought you ten: after a month, the dollar fetched a hundred or more.

Dave Atkinson, a South African war dog who flew gunships in the Congo for Mugabe, took notes during his time in-country. Conditions were so bad, he wrote, that an egg—if you could find one in Kinshasa—fetched the princely sum of a dollar. In a letter home Atkinson added: "A small packet of corn right now is going for about ten times that amount . . . suddenly there are people starving." The food was there, but nobody could afford it. "Soldiers were supposed to earn $100 a month, but the only troops who got anything were those who were the first in line on payday," he continued. "Troops in the bush were subject to their officers' whims and most got nothing."

It was a repeat of what had taken place before, only it was much worse, and the consequences were not long in coming. Before President Kabila was ousted, the Congo and its economic decay escalated well beyond anything Neall Ellis and his buddies could have imagined when they hung about Kinshasa's Intercontinental Hotel waiting for a combat deployment that never came.

Kabila's opponents, having gained the support of Uganda, Rwanda, Burundi and several other countries in the region, kicked off in the east and militarily thrust their way toward Kinshasa. Vigorous, resolute, but badly equipped, they made the most of striking hard at an ill-prepared Congolese Army.

No longer the aspirant guerrilla, Kabila was now stuck with running a country that was not only dysfunctional but one of the most sinister in all of Africa. On top of which, he had to contend with an increasingly disaffected military establishment.

Within a year the rebellion had spread throughout the country. There were persistent reports of skirmishes near the Atlantic Ocean in the Congo's minuscule coastal areas to the west of the capital, followed by the most extensive military campaign of all, the battle for Kinshasa itself.

Meanwhile, for a variety of reasons—one of which was Kabila

instituting draconian security measures—troops that had been loyal to begin with switched sides. There came a stage when about half the rebel army consisted of Congolese Army troops who had defected. As with Mobutu's troops, money—or the lack of it—was the principal gripe, though serious shortages of food and equipment featured heavily among the malcontents. Obviously, if Kabila didn't turn the situation around he would lose his presidency. What his opponents hadn't factored in was that the old battler had fought too long and hard to allow that to happen easily.

The crux of the new president's problems centered on his lack of liquidity; Kabila could not immediately get his hands on Mobutu's massive resources, most of which were stashed abroad in Swiss banks, the Channel Islands, the Caribbean and elsewhere. Geneva had most of it. One credible story claims Kabila had a staff of diplomats living permanently in Switzerland concentrating on nothing else. Until the EU intervened, the moneyed Swiss mandarins gave these Congolese functionaries a right royal runaround

The situation facing the war-weary civilian population weakened Kabila's popular support still further. After almost a generation of conflict, the Congolese people were tired of war. Now more of it was in sight. Even more incapacitating was the familiar African malaise which, like a virus, riddled the administration to the point where it was difficult to get anything done, bribe or no bribe, not that Kabila had ever been among the more energetic of Africa's leaders.

Kabila's hard-suffering subjects were mostly simple tribal folk who had years before learnt to regard the despotic actions of their leaders with a suspicion based on long experience. Most of his appointees—a brigade of regional governors, mayors, magistrates, deputies, police, security chiefs—were his cronies. Almost all had come through the war with him and the majority ruled by decree and often brutally. It was never a question of doing the right thing or of more subtle interactions like fair play or conscience. These autocrats had no regard for the needs of the populace. If somebody resisted or complained, he was summarily dealt with.

As with previous administrations, some dissidents ended up in the Congo River with their hands and feet bound. Or they were dumped in the jungle. We'll never how many, because predators or crocodiles devoured almost all of them. Kabila's hoodlums went to extraordinary lengths to avoid any kind of contact with their underlings, even though they had been uplifted to high station from the very same circumstances. The situation was macabre enough to be almost medieval.

Still, caught short as the rebellion grew, Kabila needed military help to counter the insurrection, and he had to have it quickly.

While Angola had been taking out diamonds and tropical hardwoods ever since this tyrant came to power, he now offered Zimbabwe and Namibia similar incentives. He also offered his friends substantive trading monopolies: to get their share all they had to do was come to his aid and bring their fighting men and machines with them.

For all three countries, the rewards were richer than anything they had experienced before, which was one of the reasons why Mugabe pushed everything he had into a war that was not only remote but made absolutely no sense to the majority of his people. Within a month of coming onboard, the Zimbabwe leader began running discreet jet shuttles between the Congo and Belgium: their cargoes were packets of gemstones for the international diamond market. Mugabe's actions were motivated not so much by concern for a fellow African leader as by what he could make on the deal.

In many respects, the conflict that followed was almost identical to the one in which Kabila had originally been involved in his own bush campaign. But this time around there were more mercenaries involved.

On the government side, war dogs arrived from Angola and, to begin with, included former Executive Outcomes personnel as well as Russian pilots flying Angolan and Congolese Mi-24 helicopter gunships. Others, like "Double Dave" Atkinson, flew helicopters for the Zimbabwe Air Force (ZAF).

Unable to handle many of the transport missions that were vital to the war effort, the ZAF soon found it impossible to meet demands. Consequently almost all air shipments—including troop movements— were eventually contracted to a succession of energetic young Zimbabwean entrepreneurs. They were so successful that one of them was able to buy his first Boeing 747 freighter with the proceeds.

In retrospect, Zimbabwe's involvement in the Congo was massive, especially for a young African state that had only recently emerged from a civil war of its own. There were twelve thousand Zimbabwe troops deployed in the Congo at any one time. With air assets, it cost Harare about $1.2 million a day. By January 2003, Mugabe's foreign assets were depleted and his diplomats spent much time pressing Kabila for the almost $2 billion that Zimbabwe had so far "invested" on the war. Being Africa, they never got any of it.

When the war began in the late 1990s, Zimbabwe had roughly thirty five thousand troops mustered into five brigade headquarters of which one, the fifth, was Mugabe's crack presidential guard unit. The rest were geographically based, spread about the country. Broadly speaking, the Zimbabwe Army included an all-purpose artillery regiment, an armored regiment and twenty or so infantry battalions, none of which were ever up to scratch strengthwise.

The Zimbabwe Air Force, we are told by Adam Geibel,[1] had four thousand personnel as well as thirty-two Mi-24/35s, a couple of dozen Alouette IIIs and eight Augusta-Bell 412s. What Geibel did not tell us was that a number of the country's French choppers dated from the Rhodesian War and were barely operable. So too with many of the Hinds, which—apart from those shot down—ended up on the scrap heap after Harare couldn't find the foreign exchange needed for spares.

Fixed-wing assets included Shenyang F-6s (the Chinese version of the Soviet MiG-21) as well as Hawk fighter/trainers and short-haul CASA cargo planes, all of which were used in trooping configurations at some stage or another.[2]

The final episode of the Congo's civil war still has to be written. Somebody will eventually tackle it, if only because it's an important part of contemporary African history. It incorporated a new breed of mercenary that had strutted onto the stage, and many of them, like Atkinson (and his colleagues in the Namibian Air Force), were serving members in the military of the countries involved, quite a few of them white.

An immediate result was that Kabila's Congolese war became so secretive that while it went on for years, there was almost nothing about it in the media in any of the participating states. Someone once described it as Africa's first real "non-event," even though many of the two-and-a-half million war victims that Ted Koppel spoke about in his very public *mea culpa* died of famine or disease or were slaughtered during this period.

Take one example. Zimbabwe's Central Intelligence Organization (CIO) did an extremely efficient job of keeping everything that took place in the Congo under wraps. The only news about the war to appear in the national press came from official handouts. Some of these were single-paragraph statements that often made no sense at all, considering that hostilities by then were devouring a substantial proportion of Zimbabwe's budget, together with all the foreign exchange in the country. Nor were questions about the conflict asked—or allowed to be asked—in the country's still-functioning Parliament. In any event, by then Mugabe was running the country as his own one-party state.

There were other issues. Photos of the war, for instance, were banned, which is why there are so few of them about. In fact, Atkinson told me, there were instances of soldiers found with cameras in their bags being taken out the back door of their barracks and shot. Nor were journalists allowed anywhere near the conflict. But that, to the chagrin of the CIO, didn't stop people from speculating.

Almost overnight, rumors became the stuff of substance and more than once there were bans slapped on newspapers that featured stories that, true or not, couldn't be substantiated.

There was never any confirmation about war losses, even though —three years into the war—there had been more than a thousand Zimbabwean soldiers and airmen killed. Battle casualties—at between three and four hundred—were relatively light, considering that at its peak the force that Zimbabwe deployed in the Congo numbered somewhere between fifteen and eighteen thousand men. Others succumbed to malaria and a variety other tropical ailments. Quite a number died after contracting full-blown AIDS, a disease that remains endemic throughout the region and is getting worse.

One question that immediately comes to mind, obviously, is how does a government hide the deaths of its soldiers who die in a foreign war? It cannot, for no other reason that people speak about such things. When a man is killed in action the word gets about. And while military funerals in Zimbabwe obviously happened, most were low-key affairs. Only officers of staff rank had their deaths acknowledged by the state. Normal burials for other ranks were rare because most times nobody bothered to bring the bodies home. In the soporific Congo heat that was often impossible anyway: usually the dead were interred where they had fallen in the jungle.

As the Zimbabwe Army was soon to discover, the Congo was also a land where such essentials as morgues or cool rooms for corpses did not exist outside the three biggest cities. Nor did daily power cuts help, sometimes six or eight in a row. Families would often only hear about the deaths of their loved ones a year or two after the fact—usually from colleagues who had served in the same unit and might have been allowed home on furlough or were being discharged.

The reason for these rather unusual multidimensional imbroglios was that the four leaders most intimately involved in the Congo's troubles—Kabila himself, Mugabe, Angola's Eduardo dos Santos and Namibia's Sam Nujoma—agreed from the beginning that what they didn't need was media publicity. News about the war, they concurred, made for domestic and, in the long term, international disruption. In any event, they'd learnt a good lesson from the rumpus that followed Executive Outcomes' activities in Angola and Sierra Leone.

Consequently, though all four governments employed war dogs for their purposes, the roles of these irregulars remained secret.

There was another reason. None of them were under any illusion that the use of mercenaries was negatively construed throughout the world. Also, they were bad for the economy. For any country to survive in Africa, foreign capital is essential for growth, and having cash killers on your payroll is no way of getting it.

So while the people of Zimbabwe at first accepted that its army might be involved in an obscure conflict more than a thousand miles from home—and that there were other foreign flags involved—Mugabe's factotums did what they could to minimize the extent of this complicity. One phrase routinely bandied about was "It's all in the interest of helping out a friend," a plausible enough argument while casualties remained low.

As figures mounted and the air force started to lose planes by the month, sentiment in places like Harare, Bulawayo and Mutare reversed. Things were tough enough with the declining Zimbabwe dollar, and now, the critics said, the country was being bled white by a foreign war.

By the time the Zimbabwe Air Force pulled out of the Congo in mid-2000, it had lost four Hawk jets (some say six), three Lynx (Cessna 337s) ground support planes, several Spanish-built CASA short-haul freighters, two Alouettes and two 412 helicopters—all that in addition to a squadron or more of Congo Air Force Hinds that were knocked out of the sky by the rebels.

Atkinson points out that almost all the aircraft involved in the war—especially those providing close support—were hit by AA fire. Other losses were from man-portable ground-to-air missiles. These were former Soviet SAM-7s and SAM-14s, though one source claimed there were also Stinger missiles smuggled in from South Asia, but this has never been verified and in any event, the extended time-line makes it doubtful.

In this regard Atkinson has issued a caveat of his own. Since a raggedy bunch of rebels like those opposed to Kabila had no problem buying supersonic ground-to-air missiles on the international arms market, what was there to stop other groups, elsewhere, doing the same? Al-Qaeda and its cohorts spring to mind.

The fighting in the Congo became really intense just as the millennium turned. By then Zimbabwean forces had seen action—in some places, a lot of it—in places like Ikela, the Mbuji-Maji diamond fields, Pweto, and at several points along the Congo River, as well as around the capital, Kinshasa. Because the ZAF was involved—and government assets included Antonov cargo planes on charter, flown by former Soviet Union pilots—the rebels regarded anything that flew, civilian or military, as fair game. Consequently, losses mounted steadily. The insurgents even shot down an Air Congo Boeing 727 trying to land at Kisangani Airport. Everybody onboard was killed.

It was then, too, that a succession of ZAF relief flights came to grief. The first of these involved the Zimbabwean general in charge of the sector who ordered two CASA liaison aircraft to fly his troops to Kamina, each with about fifteen men onboard. At the last moment the officer changed his mind and told the pilots there was a new destination. It was to be Kabalo, out toward the east, he told them.

According to Atkinson, Kabalo had been hot from the very start of the war. Strategically, the town overlooked a major bridge across the Congo River on the eastern fringe of where hostilities were taking place and it consequently attracted a lot of attention. Essentially, it straddled the main road to the Kasai diamond fields. Rebel bands had to pass through the place or make a detour of hundreds of miles.

With an all-weather airport of its own, Kabalo was also a target that constantly changed hands. Because it was difficult to get to, just about everything needed by the ground forces holding it had to be brought in by air. Consequently, said Atkinson, "There were many claims and counterclaims and about all we could be certain of was that nobody really knew who was in control at Kabalo at any given time."

Shortly before take-off on that operation, one of the CASA pilots did what any sensible aviator would do under the circumstances: he questioned his orders. He told the general that more recent information was that things weren't too good on the ground at Kabalo. With a bunch of junior ranks present in the command center, this observation didn't go down well at all. Furious at what was perceived to be insubordination, the general turned his back on the flier.

Moments later he spun around and faced the pilot: "You obey your orders or take the consequences," he snarled, adding that Kabalo was safe. It had to be because it was under the control of his forces, he declared. "And I know exactly what is going on. Is that clear?"

As a postscript, he told the pilot: "If this wasn't so, I wouldn't be ordering you to fly there, now would I?" The aviator had no option but to take the senior officer at his word.

With nothing untoward indicated, the two CASA aircraft went into finals on arriving over Kabalo. The first plane hardly had its wheels on the ground before the place erupted: it had come down in the vortex of a rebel ambush. While the second aircraft was able to overfly the target and escape—with holes in its fuselage—the contact that quickly developed on the ground around the stricken plane caused the deaths of three soldiers onboard while several others were wounded.

In the end—more by luck than design—a dozen people onboard the fated CASA were able to fight their way out. Considering the circumstances—and the fact that they took out all their wounded—it says much for the tenacity of this tiny group of fighters. After almost a month of wandering around the jungle, sometimes aimlessly, they made contact with their own people and were brought back to safety.

Another story to emerge from the war about the same time involved Mike Enslin, a 21-year-old pilot from Harare who was flying a ZAF British-built Hawk ground-attack jet. He took a hit from a missile while bombing a target southwest of Kabalo. Forced to bail out over a heavily foliated area near the river, his became the third ZAF Hawk to be shot down in an area where, according to the Zimbabwe generals, the "rebels have nothing in the way of anti-aircraft weaponry."

Enslin got down in one piece, but his leg was burnt in the crash. Afterward, he told his buddies that the hit came while pulling out of a dive at about a thousand feet. He was certain that he'd spotted the man on the ground firing at him: a white and obviously a merc, he stated at the time. A year later his attacker was fingered as a Serb.

With nothing but his flight kit, a 9mm pistol and a GPS, Enslin spent the next three weeks hobbling through the jungle somehow surviving on roots and leaves. Though never short of water—he would sip moisture off folds in leaves or from the hollows of tree trunks—he had nothing with which to purify it. The result, within days of coming down hundreds of miles from safety, was a debilitating diarrhea that sometimes left him almost totally incapacitated.

His gut constrictions, he told Atkinson, were like giving birth. He'd rest a while, catch his breath and move on. On his second week alone in the bush, he went down with malaria. But Enslin was a toughie and he struggled through, even though he was sometimes delirious with fever. Talking about the ordeal back at base, Enslin thought that he'd been lucky. Certainly, the gooks did what they could to find him. There were times when they came within feet of where he was lying in the undergrowth.

"They'd obviously found the plane so they knew I'd got out," he recalls. And since nothing in the African bush goes unreported—he bumped into villagers from time to time—those looking for him were aware that he'd been hurt because he limped. In spite of the odds, the young pilot stayed on the run until he eventually reached safety.

Using his compass, the always-smiling Enslin—who has since emigrated to Australia—finally made contact with a Zimbabwean unit at Kakuyu. But even then he wasn't in the clear because they, in turn, were surrounded by a rebel force. Daily, the besieged group, with Enslin in tow, was obliged to fight a rearguard action. Worse, with so many Hawks lost—and now one of the CASAs—any prospect of resupply from the air was out. In addition, they were still a long way from home and desperately short of supplies. Even before he got to that unit, the men who greeted him were short of ammunition.

Finally, within a week of his emerging from the jungle, a decision was made to try to dash to safety. With their wounded in tow, the group slipped out one evening after dark.

By now Enslin, too, was walking wounded, his leg having become infected. But somehow he held on, managing to walk without support. The little column trudged the fifty or so miles overland to a larger Zimbabwe force at Kitanda, which was also under regular attack.

Even though the base commander at Kakuyu was able to radio headquarters that Enslin had come in, no such message was ever passed on to the pilot's family. They had been told he had crashed but the Zimbabwe government provided little detail, or even that he had been in the Congo when it happened. By the end of the first week there was almost no hope that they would ever see him alive again. When he did eventually walk through the door, his mother said it was like a miracle.

From the start, Laurent Kabila's Congolese Army faced two large insurgent fighting groups advancing toward Kinshasa from the south and the west. A twenty-thousand-strong Rwandan strike force had been airlifted from Kigali in Central Africa to the large port of Matadi, in Kabila's rear. These flights were handled by Russian mercenary crews in the pay of the rebel command and on a flight-by-flight, pay-in-advance basis.

Obviously, moving thousands of troops halfway across Africa would have been a hefty exercise and it was astonishing that nobody in Kinshasa was able to latch on to what was happening until it was too late. That was especially so since these flights would have taken them well within range of Ndjili Airport and its sophisticated navigational and radar systems.

The shortcoming also underscores the lack of basic military intelligence on the part of Kabila's people, something which seemed to bedevil the government war effort from the start. Kabila didn't even have anybody on the ground in Kigali to report on troop movements out of Rwanda. With so many soldiers on the hop, obviously heading somewhere, someone's curiosity might have been aroused

Shoving all these rebel soldiers into Matadi immediately wrong-footed Kabila. It was possibly one of the reasons why the Angolans rushed to his aid as quickly as they did. While there had always been deep mistrust between the two countries as long as Mobutu was alive, Luanda's newfound friendship with Kabila—tentative and not a little uneasy to begin with—was more a case of the Angolans supporting the enemy of one of their old enemies.

Luanda reasoned that with the rebels taking effective control of Matadi—the same place where Ed Behr had asked his outrageous question of fleeing Belgian women forty years before (and which is only half-a-day's drive from the Angolan border)—a vital link in an overextended defense chain might have been breached. The Angolans also feared that the former Unita rebel leader Jonas Savimbi—always the steely opportunist looking for a gap—might open a new front in northern Angola. A veteran tactician, he'd done so before when Mobutu was running the show.

Meanwhile Ugandan Special Forces—also working with the rebels —took possession of the Congo's largest hydroelectric facility at Inga, on the Congo River about thirty miles from the capital. That, too, was a blow because almost all of Kinshasa's power came from there.

Consequently, one of Luanda's first steps to counter the rebel

insertion was to send a mercenary group across the border to bolster
the new dictator's defenses. These were almost all former Executive
Outcomes personnel and they quickly dispersed the Ugandans. It was
a quick, decisive strike that gave credence to the rumor—by then circulating in the West—that a revived EO was back in action.

Meanwhile, there were also South African merc pilots flying
Angolan Air Force Hinds as well as Sukhoi jets. In the interim, Luanda
moved several mechanized tank battalions toward the Congolese border, most of them former Soviet T54/55 MBTs.

Zimbabwe Air Force Alouette helicopter gunships—one of them
with Atkinson at the controls—arrived in the Congo not very long
afterward. These were the same French-built machines that had been
used to good effect in Rhodesia and in South Africa's border wars. All
were flown out to Kinshasa in chartered Ilyushin jet freighters.
Another six British-built ZAF Hawks, four Lynx and two CASA transport aircraft were flown in through Zambian air space.

The original intention had been to deploy Augusta 412s, but without modifications these wouldn't fit into the bellies of the Russian
cargo planes then available. Also, time was tight. The operation
turned into a costly enterprise, with the cargo planes having to be
flown out from Russia. In the end, Angola paid for it all.

According to Dave Atkinson—he was accorded the rank of squadron
leader in the ZAF and fought on and off in the Congo for almost three
years—the first six or eight months of his new war were bitterly contested.

Had the rebels not split their forces in half as they crept forward
toward Kinshasa, he reckons that they might easily have prevailed.
Even so, their momentum appeared to have been unstoppable—government troops would disappear into the bush as they approached—
and it began to look the same as before when Mobutu's regime was
the target.

But then, quite unexpectedly, the rebel command blundered. They
divided their combined army into two separate spearheads at
Kasangulu just south of Kinshasa (not to be confused with the better-
known Kazangulu ferry crossing between Botswana and Zambia). The
way Atkinson tells it, half the force was designated to take Kinshasa,
while the balance pushed on through a great natural valley south of
the river to occupy Ndjili Airport.

"To our delight, we then discovered that the other side's spies hadn't done their homework." Not many people were aware at the time that Ndjili Airport, built by the Belgians before independence, had the longest runway in Africa, he explained. "So while the rebels were able to take the eastern half of the runway, there was still enough of it to allow our guys and their Hawks to operate."

Within a day the rebels had dug themselves in along miles of trench lines across the perimeter of the airfield from which they proved almost impossible to dislodge. Atkinson and the rest of the chopper gunships—together with the Hawk fighters—would bomb, rocket, strafe and napalm enemy lines, but without success.

It was a novel move in any African military theater, and for the defenders, totally unexpected. It's worth remembering that similar tactics were put into effect at about the same time in an equally bloody war between Ethiopia and Eritrea. Obviously, while the terrain in Africa's Horn is very different from the rain forests of the Congo, the effect is the same: it becomes inordinately difficult to dislodge your enemy from such a solid defense.

Atkinson: "In the past, we'd always had a pretty good idea of what was happening out there in the bush. The rebels would move in on a target, try to take it if they could, or, if unsuccessful, move on to the next one. But what was happening at Ndjili was all classic trench warfare. Eritrea or the Congo, it had the same effect: the impasse brought movement to a halt.

"In a way, I suppose that it was almost like World War I with the enemy digging in and operating from fixed positions. It took us two tough months of committed fighting to get them out of there. God knows who taught them, but it was effective. Their presence paralyzed activity throughout the region for long stretches at a time," said Atkinson, who among his buddies is often referred to as "Double Dave."

Operating from designated, fortified lines in what was sometimes an almost impenetrable jungle environment, was the pattern of conflict adopted by the rebels for the duration of the war. There were intense battles in and around Kinshasa itself: "Four hellish days, when thousands died on both sides of a very indistinct frontier that separated the two armies, much like the Green Line in Beirut at its worst," was the way that Atkinson remembered it. A lot of the fighting included close-quarter work in the streets, he stressed, "and that often became pretty grim with troops on both sides sometimes dying in their hundreds.

"We had gooks taking over churches and using their steeples as observation points. Then we'd send in the Hawks with cluster bombs, keeping fuel to a minimum so that they could carry four thousand-pound loads. Other times we'd fly over areas where we knew they were and wait for them to start shooting. Then we'd talk the jets down onto them."

Overnight it became evident to Atkinson and his fellow pilots that the enemy was having a hard time, and resupply was at the crux of it.

Fighting a series of extended campaigns so many hours flying time from their supply bases in Rwanda and Uganda, it was the Rebels' turn for attrition. First they ran out of food, and later, ammunition. Everything they needed had to be brought in overland. Since most of the country's roads were beyond saving, they ferried in supplies from Kisangani by boat after their own people were able to overrun that city. It was the reverse of the situation that the French mercs had faced a few years before out east. For his part, Kabila was fighting a holding action on his doorstep.

On the morning of the fourth day, Atkinson detected a sudden change. It was a clear, sunny morning and as soon as he woke, he could hear little of the crash and crackle of gunfire that had characterized the days before. Hostilities had become sporadic, with some rebel units pushing back toward the rear. Others consolidated their assets away from where the fighting had been most intense.

"Then, thank God, we got word that they had abandoned the prospect of trying to take the city. Instead, we were told they were going to concentrate the balance of their forces around the airport. And that's what happened.

"Because the rebels lacked just about everything they needed to intensify their push, the rest of their forces had pulled back into northern Angola where they waited to be evacuated. Here, too, in spite of critical shortcomings, the Rwandans excelled," recalled Atkinson.

Over a period of weeks, this large but emaciated rebel army of many thousands—with almost no remaining food or ammunition reserves—fought a series of rearguard actions all the way to Maquela do Zombo in Northern Angola. There were battles all the way through, one of which was a brush with an Angolan Army armored division that had been sent north from Kintanu. Then, from about September 15 onwards, Russian charter planes worked around the clock to airlift them all back to Rwanda, sometimes crowding four or five hundred men into the fuselage a single plane.

One of the Russian pilots told me later that it was one of the most unusual experiences of his life, which was interesting because he'd also been involved in both Afghanistan and Chechnya.

"There they were, thousands of them lined up under the palms, single file, silent and uncomplaining as they waited. They stood there patiently even though they were obviously all hungry and men were wounded or sick.

"There wasn't a whisper among them when I arrived that first night . . . they were like ghosts standing in the moonlight, long, straggling lines that seemed to disappear into the dark. Our planes were their only link to life, I suppose, and that was sobering, rescuing an army that only a short time before had been part of a proud, tough fighting force. By then they were completely broken."

He and his friends speculated afterward about how many of them had been sent back into the Congo once they'd recuperated and been rearmed. He'd seen some of them since, around Bukavu in the east, he added. Most were as cocky as prizefighters.

Rebel soldiers who were prepared to speak about the evacuation afterward said it was harrowing, even though they left all their weapons and equipment behind. The transport aircraft provided were little more than great hollow aluminum tubes with no seats. Also, with no air conditioning, there were some who could barely breathe: Every square inch onboard seemed to be crammed with bodies. The worst of the stretcher cases were secured. The result was that the majority of the troops had to remain standing for the entire trip home: no small ordeal since it took hours.

Some were suffering from tropical diseases, including malaria and amoebic infections. Others who collapsed in the stultifying heat were kept vertical by the bodies of their mates pressed hard against them. Like the wounded they weren't treated with any particular care and the men simply defecated or retched where they stood. By the time the doors of the plane were slung open at the other end, the stench was indescribable.

What mattered most though, was that almost all who had made it to that northern Angolan airstrip in the jungle were brought home. It was also tough on the aircrews. My pilot friend said that they kept their cockpit doors sealed, but that didn't stop things malodorous from seeping through.

In a sense, recounts Atkinson, "There was no other way. These people were half a continent from home. Had they not been evacuated, every one of them would have been massacred."

He refers to it today as "Africa's mini-Dunkirk."

The ZAF didn't come out of the Congo unscathed. The Alouettes and Hawk jets had a difficult time coping with some of the heavier weapons fielded by the rebels. These included hundreds of 12.7mm Dshka heavy machine guns, many of them twin-barreled, and a sprinkling of quad ZU-23/24 cannon as well as 37mm single-bore AAA. Almost all of it was East European.

The ZAF had lost one of its Lynxes early on in the campaign, which in the minds of the pilots involved, set the scene for what was to come. Then three of the original Alouettes that arrived with Atkinson were so badly knocked about they had to be sent back home for repairs.

According to Atkinson, Mugabe's air force also had to learn to adjust to an entirely new set of circumstances. While almost all of Zimbabwe is semi-tropical—and there is thick bush in places like Kariba and the lower Zambezi Valley—a good deal of the country is savanna or farmland (or was). In contrast, the Congo is very different. Although his squadron tended to operate at low level - usually in three or four-ship formations - this wasn't always possible along the Congo River.

'What we didn't discard was our classic G-Car and K-Car mode for shoot-ups: the same configuration that we'd used during Rhodesia's eight-year bush war,' he explained. Though that war had ended almost twenty years before, these same attack profiles were found to be the most effective way to work in this heavily foliated region. Ideally they would have liked to have the enemy visual at all times, but that was impossible in the forest.

Consequently, a single K-Car in the helicopter strike force performed the usual command and control duties during all of these operations. Classically, it was armed with a single MG151 20mm cannon on a fixed floor fitting, with the engineer/gunner firing out of the rear port doorway. With only two crew onboard, it wasn't the most practical arrangement, but it did allow them to load heavily with fuel and ammunition. Using a shorter 20mm cartridge than normal (with less than the normal amount of propellant) it effectively lowered recoil and muzzle velocity. The crews found that the reduced rate of fire was adequate for suppression purposes.

By contrast, G-Cars (gun-cars, as the name implies) were armed with twin .303 machine guns that had a faster cyclic rate of fire.

The usual pattern of attack would be three or four Alouettes in a line-ahead formation, with a fire fight commander in a K-Car hovering above. Most times the combination would be enough to neutralize almost any ground force, especially where the enemy's AAA capabilities were limited by forest overhang.

While the Alouettes were badly dated by the time that Mugabe decided to send them north, they were still good enough for a scrap in the bush. Fragile by contemporary standards and with almost no protection from ground fire, they could deliver effectively in skilled hands. Also, as the South Africans, Portuguese and Rhodesians proved in their respective bush wars, they could weather punishment. A notable shortcoming was that the Alouette didn't have the rocket capability of Russian helicopters, or the more recent French Gazelles.

Originally built by France as an interim measure, there's hardly a European, African or Asian air force that hasn't deployed Alouettes in a military or police role in the past. Relatively easy to maintain, this is a machine that normally burns jet fuel (paraffin), though in emergencies it will fly on petroleum, though only for short duration. In brief, the 'Alo' - as aficionados like to call it - is a rugged and well-built little craft that can absorb fire. On occasion this gunship would survive hits from anti-tank rockets. In the Rhodesian War, for instance, Ted Lunt's K-Car took a blast in the tail section from an RPG-7 rocket and he was still able to fly the old girl home.

Not long afterwards, in 1978, Dick Paxton's K-Car was riddled with automatic fire when he flew over a hidden insurgent camp. With all his instruments shattered and a rotor blade punctured, he ignored the damage, climbed to an operational height of about eight hundred feet and put down a curtain of suppressive fire before heading back. This was the same Dick Paxton who, after the war, was hired by Christian forces to fly Canberra jet bombers in Lebanon's civil war. He also served for a while as a merc pilot in Sri Lanka.

There was also the incident involving the celebrated Mike Borlace - still on choppers and not yet transferred to Ron Reid-Daly's Selous Scouts. After an action against guerrillas in the bush, Borlace brought his Alouette safely back to Fort Victoria with its tail rotor drive shaft severed. That said, if an Alouette took a hit in the engine or main rotor gearbox, it was over.

An amusing story to emerge from the Congo debacle concerned an event that took place shortly after a disgruntled bodyguard assassinated President Kabila while he was sitting at his desk. The explanation of his death remains inconclusive but it was the official line and who can argue? Kinshasa's grapevine has since suggested that members of Kabila's family were involved, in particular, a favorite son.[3]

Atkinson, having resigned from the Zimbabwe Air Force was back in Harare from flying combat in the Congo and one of his last jobs in uniform was to arrange for a ceremonial fly-past by ZAF fighter jets at Kabila's funeral. It was the usual transparent Mugabe effort to ingratiate himself with Kinshasa's new order. What followed was a jape, especially since almost the entire ZAF had been grounded for lack of spares. By then, Mugabe, a racist of some fervor, had begun to feel the effects of Western-imposed sanctions for underwriting a series of crazy land grabs that all but crippled his nation.

Not surprisingly, some mammoth logistical problems began to emerge during the planning stage. It was not only the first time anything like this had been tried, but the first time the ZAF had tackled a one-off mission so far from home. The scheme as initially mapped out went ahead anyway, the idea being to get five of the F-6 Shenyangs (Chinese versions of the MiG-21) to Kinshasa to perform the prestigious duty. Most of those involved regarded the idea as insane; however, nobody was prepared to cross Mugabe and tell him so.

The first problem encountered was that while the majority of senior ZAF fixed-winged pilots were "technically" licensed to fly the Shenyangs, few had completed much more than a routine mission or two in a long while. Some hadn't flown for years.

"Even "rusty" would have been inappropriate in these circumstances," Atkinson recalled. "These guys were way past it, but too proud to admit to it. Most had been flying desks and living the good life for so long that they'd forgotten most of the basics, and you know what they say—'If you don't use it, you lose it.' Also, nobody listened when I insisted that while the F-6 was great on short-hop ground support or fighter roles, it wasn't intended for the kind of long-distance flying then being contemplated. The bird just wasn't designed for it."

He explained to his superiors that the journey from the ZAF base at Gweru to Kinshasa—a distance of about fifteen hundred miles—involved four refueling stops for aircraft that had limited range. In the end Mugabe's people had to spend scarce foreign exchange to charter an Antonov tanker from Moscow to provide the jets with juice.

It wasn't long before other variables began to creep into the equation, the first being that the Antonov is a slow, lumbering cargo plane. The F-6 fighters, by contrast, flew at several times its speed and had to wait for it to catch up at each refueling stop. Also, the Shenyang has a notoriously slow turnaround time in the fueling process.

"Consequently," he explained, "the journey northwards across Africa took forever, with the last leg flown in the dark."

One of the Zimbabwean wing commanders had no night flying experience and became disorientated somewhere south of Kinshasa. Though he managed to eject, everybody thought he'd been killed because there was no parachute sighted and no radio comms with him afterward. He was later found, debilitated and more than a little disorientated, having walked around in the jungle in circles for five days. But at least he was alive.

The remaining four Shenyangs then did what they had come for—flying across Kinshasa's skies in close formation in a show of homage—and after a civilized break, all set off on the return leg. One of them crashlanded at Lubumbashi after the group captain heading the operation misjudged his approach. Because his wreck was blocking the runway, the fourth fighter was ordered to divert to an alternative airstrip thirty minutes away.

"Can't do," he told the control tower at Lubumbashi. He only had twenty minutes' fuel left. He had no alternative but to try to put the fighter down as originally planned and, as Atkinson recalls, the landing that took place was quite something.

"The last three hundred yards of runway was not only wet, it was also hugely strewn with wreckage. Give the man his due, he got down OK, but then spoiled it by skidding off the runway and going nose-first into a tree."

That made three F-6s destroyed, an achievement of sorts, since none of the jets had been involved in combat.

Though details remain sketchy and reports are often contradictory, President Mugabe continued to maintain a substantial military force in the Congo long after Kabila had been assassinated. The thirteenth or eighteenth peace treaty might have been signed with the rebels, but diamonds were still a president's best friend and that attraction continued to motivate the fighting.

Actual numbers of Zimbabwean troops deployed in the Congo at the beginning of 2000 were variously estimated at somewhere between

twelve thousand and eighteen thousand, with the UN opting for the
lower figure. By international standards, it was a sizable contribution:
the UN force in Sierra Leone, for instance, steadied at about the fourteen thousand mark during the last year of hostilities.

Keeping an army that size supplied and in condition to fight very
soon exposed Harare's modest logistical support capacity. Accentuating the problem was the fact that most Zimbabwe Army strongpoints were centered about the diamond-rich enclaves of Mbuji-Mayi
in Kasai Province. There were other outlying positions far to the north
along the Congo River near Kisangani, as well as a few positions out
east, all originally established to try to stop more rebels from rein-
forcing the insurgents already there.

The bulk of Mugabe's army, consequently, worked out of two
Congolese garrison towns at Kananga (on the western fringe of the
diamond diggings) and at Kabinda, a modest place in the jungle to its
east (not the oil-rich enclave north of the Congo River with a similar
name). The Zimbabwe Army headquarters, in turn, was about three
hundred miles to the south at Kamina, an old military barracks that
dated back to colonial times.

While the air war around Kinshasa's Ndjili Airport began well
enough, conditions deteriorated because of a lack of trained personnel. There was also a persistent shortage of spare parts, exacerbated
by Zimbabwe's shortage of real money.

In another development, Mugabe ordered his Chief of Staff to
upgrade training in a bid to cope with new demands. A large ZAF contingent of pilots and techs was sent to Rostov in Russia in 1999 for
training and upgrading, though ultimately, this and other measures
seem to have had little effect on the outcome of the war.

It took the ZAF three years of hard fighting before it pulled out
the remainder of its planes from the front and sent them home. By
then most had become inoperable anyway.

Tactically, according to Atkinson, one complaint consistently
raised by Zimbabwe pilots who flew in the Congo was the almost
total lack of ground support for the air effort. There were times when
aircrews felt they were regarded as intruders and that some of the
Congolese even resented having them around. This, despite the fact
that the ZAF's contribution toward maintaining an effective fighting
front—such as it was—was vital. It took Harare ages to develop some
kind of day-to-day working rapport with the Congo's military bosses.
Mercs who have flown in these remote conflicts, be they the Congo,

Angola, Ethiopia or Sierra Leone, reckon that that's the way it goes in most African military struggles.

Resupply was always the biggest headache. For several years, the ZAF used its own CASA aircraft—moderate-sized cargo planes—for this purpose, but their role became limited once Mugabe began to alienate the international community: there was no cash for spares. Meanwhile, the role of the ZAF was steadily being downgraded. Finally Harare had to charter Russian Ilyushin and Antonov cargo planes flown by East Europeans.

There were other problems. Having been stung by unfulfilled promises about payments in the past, the foreign pilots who were doing this cargo work eventually insisted that their fees be paid up front. As Atkinson recalls, it ended up being something of a farce.

"Crews would be ready to take off at the end of the runway at Harare and a car with ministry license plates would arrive. A black-clad figure clutching a bundle of American bank notes would hop out and disappear into the plane for a minute or so and then reappear empty-handed." Transfer done, car and plane would depart.

For Zimbabwe aircrews, a Congo posting meant trouble, sometimes serious. There were all sorts of language, cultural, security and political issues. Having gone in several times, Dave Atkinson is able to give us a fascinating picture of what took place in the Congo in the late 1990s. As a contract fighter, he was in the thick of it from the start.

Early in August 1998, for instance, on his first deployment with the Zimbabwe Air Force, he was told that he'd be operational for about three weeks. Four months later he was still at it—either in Alouettes or the larger 412s operated by the ZAF. The second deployment was an eight-month call-up, this time working out of Kamina.

"That's the way it went—we were never sure where we would be tomorrow. Our leaders—such as they were—constantly changed their minds.

"It wouldn't have mattered had we been comfortable. Instead, living conditions were abominable. All we had for quarters was half of a burnt-out house. The lights were either on all the time or off and it stayed that way for the duration because there were no switches," he reminisced afterward with a twinkle. The base's previous occupants had ripped out everything that was electric. They also took the ceiling boards.

"That in itself wouldn't have been too bad had we been properly paid. But we weren't." In Kinshasa to start with, the pilots got $12 a day, paid in American dollars at the end of each month. After six months, half of that was in American money and the rest in Congolese francs, a currency that was becoming more useless by the day. And remember, almost all of us had family back home, some with kids still at school or at college.

"To crown it, we got local money at the official rate which, by then, was far below par if you had to exchange dollars on the street outside. By the time I left, the fliers were getting about a third of what was owed to them, their senior commanders obviously pocketing a hefty chunk off the top."

At about this time, other problems started to surface—like evacuating war wounded from the front. According to Atkinson, taking casualties out of exposed, forward positions just wasn't on unless it was a senior officer, and he apparently had to be in perilous shape to justify the risk.

"At one stage I was ordered to go into a base way out in the jungle and evacuate a colonel who was down with malaria. When I got there, to my dismay I found that there were sixteen more cases, some of them really bad: two or three of the men were already in a coma." Though already overloaded and against orders, Atkinson brought them back to Kamina in his 412 as well.

Another time, four ZAF Hind gunships were ordered to provide top cover to a Zimbabwe CASA that was scheduled to go into a forward base near Manono—Kabila's home town. The cargo plane had to pull out some seriously wounded troops. Three of the choppers took so much flak from ground fire that they had to be shipped back home for repairs. The CASA barely got away, and then only with one engine.

A week later, the same officer ordered Atkinson to go into Manono with his 412 and pull somebody else out. Atkinson hedged. The place was rotten with gooks. It would be a suicide flight, he remonstrated. His superior countered by rolling out his operational map and pointing out that there wasn't a single red marking in or around Manono. As in most ops rooms, a red pin on a war map indicates enemy presence.

"The bastard had removed them earlier because he knew I'd query," said Atkinson, who had long ago learnt to carefully examine all options. He refused to fly the mission.

Then Atkinson got tasked to take his machine way north near the border with the Central African Republic. He was required to give top cover support to a small Zimbabwe force at the river port of Mbandaka, not far from Kisangani. Harare had deployed the company there almost a year before and the ZAF job that day was to go into action against a rebel group that numbered ten to fifteen thousand: the Zimbabwe force was completely surrounded. Again there were arguments, but in the end the pilots did as they were told.

That little venture resulted in more loss of life and the shooting down of a helicopter. In retrospect, Atkinson maintains today that nothing ever happened quite as it should have done in a hinterland where so many aircraft had gone down over the years and never been found.

"Often we were surprised by a turn of events in this African war that was as unforgiving as it was brutal. Prisoners were rarely taken. POWs were dealt with as individual field commanders saw fit. To these officers—some of whom would boast that they'd been on staff training courses in Britain or America and knew very well what was expected of them—the POW Charter could just as easily have been a gambling concession of sorts.

"Obviously, we gave a lot of thought to the possibility of becoming casualties ourselves. If we were shot down in some remote spot five hundred miles from base we would have had to walk home. But, being white, that would have been almost impossible." It was also a land devoid of the kind of navigational equipment that pilots take for granted elsewhere.

As one of them commented: "Getting about relied a lot on what the seat of your pants told you and the kind of experience that comes with many hours in the air." Fortunately, all the South Africans involved in Mugabe's air force had flown for the SAAF during the Angolan war where, of necessity because of the terrain, each one of them had become accomplished navigators.

So it wasn't altogether surprising that the pilots had GPS navigation sets brought in within a couple of days of arriving. Later these were supplemented by the GARMIN III (moving map) and HFI (horizontal situation indicator) systems. That they needed these devices was an understatement since some of the maps issued by the Kinshasa government dated from 1951. Many still showed old Belgium place names.

Radio communications, too, were if not tentative, often non-existent. The VHF system in the control tower at Kamina, for instance, had a twenty-mile radius, but everything transmitted in or out of Ndjili was supposed to be in French while the majority of Zimbabwean pilots only spoke English. Swahili would probably have helped, but this *lingua franca* had never penetrated that far south from East Africa's coastal regions, and certainly not as far as Zimbabwe.

Weapons were another issue. While the majority of ZAF aircraft were modern and adequately serviced, the stuff they were supposed to throw at the enemy wasn't. So it didn't take long for the air force to exhaust just about all the ordnance they'd originally arrived with. This shortfall included five-hundred and thousand-pound cluster bombs.

While the first batch worked well enough, the second lot was flawed and not all of it detonated on contact. With Swiss markings, they had cost the Zimbabwe government a mint.

More worrying was the fact that when the bombs arrived in the Congo almost all their casings were waterlogged. Nobody back home had bothered to cover their rail trucks for the long haul through Zambia in the rainy season. Then someone discovered that the ordnance they were using against the rebels was ten years past its expiration date. No worry: Harare's Aeronautical Inspection Service insisted that the bombs were good and had to be used up anyway. In the end they were, but again not all did the necessary.

By late 1999 advance enemy units were showing up in strengths of anything from six to ten thousand men at a time. And since all these rebels were very well armed and boosted by a succession of victories behind them as they swept toward the west, they were powerfully motivated.

The most disturbing development to the likes of Atkinson and his pilot friends was the sudden appearance of large numbers of mercenaries among the rebel ranks. And that despite former President Mandela having brokered his fifth or sixth Congolese peace treaty.

These irregular forces are still around and hostilities continue on and off to this day. And they will continue to do so as long as there are diamonds in quantity in Kasai's fields. Indeed, as we are told by Geibel, it was these same diamonds that caused the Zimbabwe military effort to eventually come unstuck. At the end of that phase of hostilities in the Congo, senior Zimbabwe army and air force officers were interested in nothing else.

The Zimbabwe *Standard* reported in an article headlined "Army Chiefs Loot Congo Diamonds" that jets ferried them from Harare to Mbuji-Mayi at night, from where they were escorted by their own soldiers to the Makumbikumbi Hotel.[4] There they would spend the night before going to shop for diamonds the next day—again under armed guard—in the center of town. Others would collect these precious stones from the nearby Senga Senga Mine. The newspaper was shut down shortly afterward for making these disclosures.

Things eventually got so bad, wrote Adam Geibel, that UN investigators accused Zimbabwe (with Uganda and Rwanda) of deliberately prolonging the war "to loot the Congo of gold, diamonds, timber and coltan." The United Nations report had no effect on this activity whatever, he adds, "and was barely noticed in the West."[5]

So much for international cooperation or transparency . . .

14

BIAFRA'S WAR AND MORE FOREIGN INTERVENTION

"The first mercenary pilots hired by the Nigerian government
arrived just after the fighting had started . . . most had
left the Congo only weeks before."

Michael Draper in *Shadows: Airlift and Airwar in Biafra
and Nigeria, 1967–1970*[1]

I was in my cabin on board the Swedish merchantman *Titania* when
the first salvo struck: two powerful blasts in quick succession. It was
like a car backfiring, only up close. The impact of exploding rockets
reverberated throughout the ship and my immediate impulse was to
get up top.

Two, three steps at a time, I shot up the companionway and
emerged on a deck washed in bright tropical sunlight. I just had time
to see two small single-engined aircraft turning low on the water
about a quarter mile away. We were only to find out afterward that
the planes—single-engined Swedish-built MFI-9B Minicons—had that
morning scored their first major strike against maritime targets in the
Nigerian civil war. Just then, though, they were heading straight back
at us again.

Two more spurts of smoke from their underwing pods told me
everything else I had to know. I'd seen enough war movies to be aware
that more rockets were heading my way. There was no thinking about
it: my only option was to hurl myself right down the same companionway from which I had just emerged. Moments later, more blasts
erupted behind the bulkhead, one of them eight or ten feet above my
head. For a second or two, I had the air knocked out of me and it took
a little while to get back on my feet.

Meanwhile, another projectile hit amidships and moments later,
one more above the waterline. Whoever was using these things knew
what they were doing.

Though neutral, the Scandinavian merchant ship on which I was a

321

passenger had become a casualty. So had the American steamer moored ahead of us in the roadstead off the Nigerian oil port of Warri. Both freighters had made their way the hundred or so miles up the estuary of the Niger, West Africa's biggest river, and gotten themselves caught in a conflict that was already into its third year.

Comparatively speaking, the *Titania*—the ship I'd boarded the week before in Ghana and which was taking me to Douala in the Cameroons—had come off lightly. Not so the *African Crescent*, then in the final stages of a West African run out of Houston. Though there were larger-than-usual Stars and Stripes hanging fore and aft—and she sported a Farrell Lines crest on her smoke stack—the American cargo liner had two of its crew members killed and seven wounded.

Only afterward was I able to put together some of it. Having watched the Minicons do their turn over the river and fire a second salvo of what we later discovered were 68mm rockets, I'd thrown myself down the same narrow set of stairs from which I'd emerged a short while before and landed on top of two female members of the ship's crew making their way up. The three of us collapsed in a heap at the foot of the companionway.

The rocket that had detonated nearest us had exploded in the ship's linen cupboard, right under the stairs behind us. A year's supply of sheets, blankets and towels absorbed most of the blast and we weren't hurt, though my ears zinged for a week afterward.

As "fighters" go, the Biafran Minicons involved in that attack were modest little aircraft. They'd originally been designed for training and were never intended to see action in any war.

"Von Rosen's Vengeance," as the minuscule prop-driven ground-support aircraft were called, had been named after Count Gustaf von Rosen—a swashbuckling Swedish philanthropist with obscure delusions of "changing Africa." Circumventing stringent arms sanctions in his own country, he'd clandestinely bought six of them and, with a group of volunteers in his employ, flown them all to France. There the two-seaters—originally built by SAAB—were fitted with underwing hard points that allowed them to carry rocket pods, one under each wing. That done, they were secretly shipped to Gabon.

It was an eventful morning for everybody. Having gone into action against us at Warri, the Minicons pulled away and banked toward one of four of five tiny airstrips where fortified concrete bunkers had been built deep inside Biafra. But not before they struck again at several oil storage tanks on the outskirts of the port, sending plumes of black smoke thousands of feet into the air. By then two merchant ships were dousing their fires and I was taking pictures.

Though damage was real and there had been casualties, as far as the Nigerian government was concerned, these were events that never happened. Nor were a million Biafran children starving. And since I was stringing for the London *Daily Express* and this was an event that needed to get out, I was faced with the dilemma of trying to communicate the news from a country at war.

No, said the captain, his ship was neutral and he wouldn't do it. He wasn't going to allow the radio officer to send "war" reports from his radio room. I countered with another request: what about me transmitting my own copy? I'd done a spell of telegraphy in the navy and suggested that I could push it out to one of my ham friends in Nairobi for forwarding to Fleet Street. That was also unacceptable, answered the Swede, reverting to his customary taciturn mode. He was a mean bastard; the only time I ever saw him smile was when there was skirt about.

Undeterred, I went ashore to try my luck at the local post office, irrespective of the fact that government spooks were to be found at every street corner in town. While the local postmaster was prepared to take my story, as well as the Cable and Wireless card that went with it for payment (sweetened by a $20 bill), my report was never sent. I shouldn't have been surprised. The country's military censors used blue pencils to impose a blanket ban on any news of Biafran air activity. Officially, they maintained, the Minicons did not exist.

Not long after the disaster that created the Congo that we know today, the rebel Nigerian "state" of Biafra became a rallying point for mercenaries from just about everywhere.

Their numbers included soldiers of fortune from many European countries, South Africa and Rhodesia, Australia, Canada and Britain, as well as Chinese Nung fighters. There was even a CIA operative or two eager to get in a bit of action at company expense. Experiencing the goings-on in a beleaguered Biafra must have been better than propping up the bar at the Federal Hotel on Lagos' Victoria Island.

There was also twenty-nine-year-old Nick Bishop from Philadelphia, who added Biafra to the notches on his belt after he had served a while under Colonel Mike Hoare in the Congo. With him in this desperate West African enclave was British "Major" C.C. Watson, a claymore mines specialist who went on to develop the appropriately dubbed "Ojukwu Buckets" that carried enough explosives to fry an armored car.

Another character to arrive shortly afterward was a hefty forty-two-year-old American, Barry "Hawg" McWhorter. A big man in all departments, he flew an obsolete B-26R bomber for the breakaway Biafrans for a time and then went on to look for something that paid better money. Tipping the scale at three hundred pounds, McWhorter was hardly your typical swashbuckling war dog, though he had lots of swash and more than enough buckle. By the time he got to the west coast, he'd already made a name for himself as an opportunist of repute in several theaters of military activity on the African continent.

Barry joined the American-based organization Joint Church Aid to help fly in relief supplies to the rebel enclave from the former Portuguese island colony of São Tomé at what he claimed was $5,000 a month. Most mercs flying cargo planes ended up there, while others flew from Libreville in the former French colony of Gabon. Only a handful of this rum bunch worked from Fernando Pó in Spanish Guinea—Equatorial Guinea today.

Not long afterward, word had it that McWhorter had moved on to Chad to provide support to French units fighting rebels in the Sahara. Totally mercenary, all of these aviators, though quite a few were also motivated by their Faith.

To understand the complexities of the civil war in Nigeria, in which numbers of foreigners eventually became involved—including erstwhile RAF as well as Egyptian Air Force pilots, Soviet anti-aircraft specialists, a South African Special Forces group, former French Foreign Legionnaires, and an assortment of other nationalities—one needs to understand both the people who took part in these hostilities as well as the reason why war happened.

Former Nigerian Army officer Colonel Ojukwu—the man who ultimately led the rebellion in the oil-rich eastern region that he ended up calling Biafra—was the son of Sir Louis Ojukwu, a transport mogul and one of Nigeria's first native multi-millionaires. It was not coincidental that he was a member of the Ibo tribe, and proud of it.

With a powerful tribal orientation, which, in the tradition of Africa of old has always been more of a *Gemeinschaft* than a *Gesellschaft*, he started life as a working class man. He was a good, solid, middle class sort and, at an early age, invested all his assets in a single truck from where he built up a pan-national chain of transport vehicles that ended up making him a very large fortune during World War II. For his services and aid to the Empire during wartime, Sir Louis was knighted.

The eternal entrepreneur, it was taken for granted that the majority of people he would gather about him were from the better-educated and not-afraid-of-work Ibo, Ibibio and Ijaw tribal grouping from which he hailed. The trouble was, that while this was fine for easterners, other Nigerian tribes tended to consider the Ibos as individuals who, if not pushy, over-ambitious and self-important, liked to regard the rest of their compatriots as inferior. Not for nothing were Ibo's sometimes called "The Jews of Africa," and uppity ones at that. In a word, the Ibos were considered snobs. But unlike the Muslim people in Nigeria's north, they were competent snobs.

Sir Louis' son, bright and outgoing like his dad, was born into this community in the early 1930s, educated in Britain at Edison, and moved up to Lincoln College, Oxford. Termed by his contemporaries in the UK as both likeable and energetic, young Odumegwu Ojukwu played rugby for his house and was regarded by his seniors as one of those rather Anglicized young black fellows who would eventually come to prominence politically in his home country, especially since it since it was presumed that he would take over his father's trucking empire. He surprised everybody when, instead, he joined the Nigerian Army.

With the backing of the pre-independence British military establishment on the West African coast, the always-smiling Ojukwu rose rapidly in seniority. He had done a good deal better than the majority of his contemporaries by the time independence came around in 1960.

Then, in January 1966, the country's first military coup d'etat took place. With it, there was some bloodshed, but not an inordinate amount of violence. The first putsch was more a matter of getting rid of what the youthful Nigerian officer corps referred to as the old guard.

What was of concern, as far as Nigeria's Muslims were concerned though, was that the mutiny was orchestrated by Christian "southern" officers. More ominous, to these devout followers of the Qur'an, quite a few were of Ibo tribal extraction.

Frederick Forsyth was there at the time and he points out in his excellent history of the Nigerian Civil War how and why mercenaries became involved in this struggle. It was also, he maintains, a development that set the pattern for quite a few other African wars thereafter.

He makes the point that far from being an "Ibo revolt," there were officers from other Nigerian groupings involved in the putsch, including a good few Muslims. Much of it he details in *The Making of a Legend*,[2] regarded by the majority of African scholars as the first, and best, of several books on the Biafran War.

The orientation of these plotters, says Forsyth, was actually much more radical, more left wing than tribal. The bulk of those involved had returned to Africa after having been educated in Europe and most had inculcated a distinct Socialist, egalitarian bias that reflected popular institutions like the London School of Economics.

Though not exactly Communist, some of the plotters viewed the Marxist-Leninist view of life preferable to the kind of corruption and nepotism then just starting to take a grip on Nigerian society. They wanted change, they declared in statements issued after they had taken over. Rather pointedly, their spokesmen maintained that they were compelled to topple what they viewed as a doddering, out-of-touch bunch of potentates that Britain had chosen to run this West African state after independence.

The politicians in the mainly Islamic north of the country weren't buying any of it. For a start, what the young officers wanted was contrary to the most fundamental precepts of The Prophet (May He rest in Peace). And if ever more proof was needed, in the eyes of Moslem leaders and their retinues in Kano, Maiduguri, Sokoto and the rest, that the January army mutiny was a set-up, then what about the fact that General Aguiyi Ironsi, the army chief who took over from the civilian government, was Ibo?

Ironsi ran the country for about six months, when the second coup took place in July 1966. The northerners had carefully planned their revenge, and they did so in spades, in the process murdering Ironsi. Unlike the January revolt, the carnage that resulted from the second coup was both bloody and widespread. It was also worse than anything Africa had yet seen and more than a million people were to die in its aftermath.

The bunch of northern officers responsible for countering the initial army revolt struck their first blows in Lagos, at Ikeja Barracks, headquarters of the Nigerian Army. Every Ibo officer in the place was dragged out of his quarters and butchered on the parade square. Concurrently, a massive pogrom erupted in the north where some thirty thousand easterners—men, women and children—were taken out of their homes and massacred, African style. Still more were hacked to death on the roads, in villages and towns, and in many a *Sabon Gari* (marketplace) of big population centers

As Forsyth emphasizes, there was not much gunfire involved: "We are talking about machetes and clubs. The outcome, clearly, was traumatic. It was also deeply shaming for the British government, because it was totally unforeseen. In fact, there wasn't an American or European intelligence service that had any idea it was going to happen." Therefore London's attitude was to suggest that things "weren't as serious as some observers said they were," he reckons.

"Play down the violence, play it down," British ministers told their press, stating that it was all just unrest. It was a phase and nothing would come of it, London told the world. We know now, of course, declares Forsyth, that it was nothing of the kind.

The pogrom was so bad that almost two million Ibos fled. These were people who had been living throughout Nigeria: in the midwest, the western regions and in the north of the country. One and all, they headed back to their eastern tribal homeland which was then under the military governorship of a man who had been appointed after the first revolt the previous January, Colonel Odumegwu Ojukwu, Sir Louis' son.

Curiously, it emerged afterwards, Ojukwu Junior had absolutely nothing to do with the January coup. The officers of the first revolt specifically left him out of it because, as one of their number told Forsyth, they regarded him as an establishment figure. He was more of a pan-Nigeria man, they reckoned. In the eyes of his peers, Colonel Odumegwu Ojukwu was above tribal conspiracies and in a sense they were right.

The youthful military governor of Eastern Nigeria now found himself trying to cope with a refugee problem the likes of which neither he nor anybody else had seen in any African country before, at least not in the modern period. Desperate people were resorting to desperate measures and were entering the eastern region in hoards. For a while, he was finding it difficult not only to maintain law and order, but to provide succor to a society that had lost just about everything.

Totally unprepared for this scale of emergency, because nobody believed that a catastrophe of this magnitude could ever happen, his fledgling Biafra, overnight, needed a huge injection of funds. There were not enough schools, a chronic paucity of clinics and hospitals, no basic transport infrastructure, which, in turn meant that there was not enough food or the means to distribute what there was. Coupled to this, Ojukwu lacked the administrative infrastructure to counter these inadequacies. In fact, says Forsyth, there was not enough of anything.

The basic population of the region under Ojukwu's command, he explains, was close to twenty million, of which by now a large proportion was fugitive. The problem was made more acute by the fact that the majority who got back to Biafra arrived penniless.

Forsyth: "They literally left behind everything. That included their houses, their workshops, their stores, and their little cars. They traveled on mammy wagons and trains, while others walked or cadged lifts home, some of them badly wounded because they had lost arms and legs. One woman arrived with her husband's severed head in her lap. Clearly, this was a severely traumatized community. They needed medical facilities far beyond what was available in Ojukwu's fief. He, in turn, needed all sorts of things, but there was nothing forthcoming out of Lagos and certainly no funds.

"This went on until finally the clamor for the secession of the eastern half of the country from the Nigerian Federation became more pronounced. It started with the tribal chiefs and the call was soon echoed by the refugees. Then it was sounded by those who were not refugees but who roundly sympathized with the two million people who had been displaced.

"'If we are to be treated in this way,' they shouted, 'and if we are not to be given any recourse from Lagos for our misery, then what are we doing in this country. Why don't we just pull out of the Nigerian federation and go our own way?'

"Eventually Ojukwu did just that. He declared his so-called unilateral declaration of independence (or what the Rhodesians subsequently referred in the politico-speak of the day as UDI) in April 1967, having delayed ten months. Because of fading memories and more often a total ignorance of the violence and the atrocities that had originally caused all this, the international media came down hard on Ojukwu's decision to go it alone.

"Ojukwu and his Ibos, some journalists wrote, were just a bunch of maniacs, idiots. . . . Ojukwu was an opportunistic power seeker, they wrote, which couldn't have been correct because he already had the power.

"Lagos' response came three months later, on July 7, when the Nigerian Army invaded.

"The immediate reaction of the north, when the eastern region went off on its own, was that the loss of that part of the country was good riddance. Most Hausa and Fulani in northern Nigeria were happy to see the Ibos go. They didn't like them, nor did they want them. They'd expelled them, almost to the last man and woman and that was that.

"Which was all very well, until somebody realized that the new state of Biafra, very strategically, was perched on almost all of Nigeria's oil reserves. And this, suddenly, became the key: Nigeria's oil was (and still is) its wealth. It was now under Ibo land. Most of the producing areas were along the Imo River, around Port Harcourt, in the creeks and along many of the tributaries of the Niger River, all of it essentially under Ibo control. And when this horrifying revelation finally entered the skulls of the Hausa colonel who commanded the Nigerian Army, when they realized that without Ibo oil, Nigeria was nothing more than a huge impoverished country, a complete about-face took place. It all happened in hours," records Forsyth.

So too in Britain and the United States. There, the collapse of the Nigerian federal political structure was viewed with alarm. The Cold War was hot and, in West Africa any kind of upheaval that upset the political and economic status quo tended to dominate headlines. More salient, Nigeria was one of Britain's principal sources of crude oil. Who knew what would happen if that flow was disrupted by war, it was asked, and that, basically, was the gist of some of the editorials that started to appear in the British press.

Also, argued Whitehall, if Nigeria were to fragment, hostilities there could ultimately affect other states in the region. Remember, this was a time when the Domino Theory was very much in the vogue, even though, in those early days, it pertained more to what was going on in Southeast Asia than Africa.

Barely mentioned, even in the financial press, was the fact that London and Washington were alarmed that Ojukwu, a young military upstart who nobody had heard of before, was threatening their investments.

Almost overnight, from all the clatter about good riddance and bad rubbish, emerged the shout: "We must again reunite Nigeria." "Ojukwu mustn't be allowed to secede," they bellowed. Which was a farce, as Frederick Forsyth suggests, because the whole concept of Nigerian unity was one great big invented fiction.

"There never was any unity in Nigeria," he declares. "It was a most divided country. Under Britain's colonial rule, the country was deliberately divvied up into what was essentially the north and the south (with the Yoruba nation being the other half of the south). In a makeshift effort, the country was cobbled together, literally five years before independence, and we were all told that it was one country. But in the hearts and minds of the people, it never was the 'One Nigeria' that its politicians said it was, because tribal groupings predominated. And it still isn't to this day.

"So the war began, and we were all told—I was a journalist at the time, working for the BBC—this whole thing was going to be over in ten days. We were also rather candidly informed by London that the Ibos were a bunch of incompetent bottle washers, and that we had this magnificent British-trained Hausa army of the north that would sweep down and make a meal of Biafra in a week.

"What was overlooked was two things. First, the so-called 'magnificently trained army of the north' was rubbish. It couldn't fight its way out of a Human Rights convention in Blackpool. Second, as we know today, the Ibos had become a desperate group and with all the things that were happening around them, they were suddenly given a large dollop of courage, which was something they'd never really before thought they had.

"The kind of fear and anxiety that the Biafran people were then experiencing really can offer an individual or a nation a remarkable level of audacity. And let's not forget, it can also result in an astonishing amount of obstinacy.

"For its part, Biafran propaganda immediately began to say, 'If we surrender, then we'll all be killed: they'll end up finishing the job.' This was not helped by many voices in the north replying, 'Yes we will! We will wipe you out!' So basically, it was a war of genocide.

"Apart from that, the British made two more mistakes, both crucial. If London had realized this was going to be a thirty-month war that resulted in a million children dying of starvation, I don't think the British would have taken the position that they did. In fact, I'm certain of that. The other was for the Prime Minister and his advisors not to realize that the rebel Biafrans were just as pro-British, and as much a part of the Commonwealth, as the Nigerians."

Frederick Forsyth was in Biafra when the Biafran Army decided to invade Nigeria westward, toward Lagos. It was a bold step, recalled this former BBC correspondent. (He broke with the news agency soon afterward because of its biased reports about the war.)

"Yes, I went in with them. We swept across the Onitcha Bridge and very soon we could see that it was a crazy amateurish kind of war, a conflict, in a sense, of boy scouts.

"Here was this huge bridge spanning the great Niger River that effectively connected the Biafran eastern region with western Nigeria. There was a sort of gentleman's agreement in place between the leaders of both sides not to use it. They had another agreement not to destroy it. Certainly, it was accepted by all the participants that it would not be used for any kind of invasion.

"Ojukwu was regarded by the Nigerian military leader Colonel (later General) Yakubu Gowon as an absolute bastard for breaking that concord by crossing the bridge with an invasion force. In a way it was a bit like the mouse that roared. How, Gowon asked, thoroughly perplexed, could the tiny little Eastern Region invade Nigeria? But it did. And it was a remarkably successful venture because the newly appointed Nigerian leader's strategy was a disaster.

"Gowon, by now at the head of the rest of Nigeria, took the entire professional Nigerian Army of only six thousand men and hurled them across the Benue River (a tributary of the Niger) to the north of the rebel enclave. He then ordered them to turn their guns toward the south, towards Biafra, where they promptly bogged down. The result was that there were barely any troops between the bridge and Lagos, Nigeria's capital.[3] The Biafran strike force was faced with an absolutely empty, open road to victory.

"Someone got to Ojukwu and said to him, look we can be in Lagos in forty-eight hours of hard motoring. That would end the war at a stroke. I don't know how much persuading he took, but certainly that was what he finally decided to do.

"Since Ojukwu had no armored columns of his own, the Biafrans got together a bunch of trucks and oil tankers because they would need fuel supplies. They also grabbed just about every Land Rover in the country and commandeered oil company vehicles and virtually the entire region's agricultural four-wheel drives. And what a motley collection that lot soon became, though all these shortcomings didn't prevent the force from calling itself 'Ojukwu's Undefeated.'

"They hadn't enough soldiers in their territory, because broadly speaking, Ojukwu apart, the Ibos had never really been among the country's soldier class. Nigeria's army in fact, was overwhelmingly from the north, much as it is today. So what this fighting colonel got in lieu of a combat force was a bunch of ragtag, bobtail volunteers, many of them schoolboys.

"So too with his officer corps, which was mainly composed of technical officers. The head of the Biafran Army, for instance, was a former Nigerian Signals Corps man. He was very good with radios, but sadly, he didn't know a damn thing about guns, though they had some artillery officers because that was a technical discipline. But there was no armor at all. They were literally riding to war in trucks, lorries, tankers and Land Rovers.

"So this column, before dawn one morning—as I was to see for myself because I was with them—drove across the bridge at Onitcha and took the war to the rest of the nation. Without formality, they swept aside the two-dozen or so Nigerian soldiers on the western side and plunged on towards Lagos.

"They reached Benin City, the capital of the Midwest within twelve hours where, amazingly, they lost their nerve. They just couldn't believe that they had managed to penetrate so deep into Nigeria without encountering any kind of opposition.

"Yet even then they didn't stop. This improvised, totally makeshift force—still with me in tow—went beyond Benin, actually to the border between the Midwest state and Western Nigeria, which is a little village called Ore. It was there that some of us realized that the reality of reaching the capital, Lagos, was almost in sight.

"Then too, the word 'cut off' began to circulate. 'Cut off from what?' I asked several of them. 'What are you going to be cut off from, in your own country?'

"'We're cut off,' they answered, adding that there might be Nigerian troops suddenly appearing behind us.

"So I would question where these supposed Nigerian troops were supposed to be coming from? There really aren't any there, I told the commander and his staff. 'Oh,' they answered, 'still, we might be cut off.' Very soon, the expression 'cut off' became obsessional.

"At the start of the invasion, Colonel Ojukwu did something rather unusual by appointing one of the very few Yorubas in his army, Brigadier Banjo, as the commanding officer of the entire expedition. He thought that because Banjo was a Yoruba, he would be made welcome once he entered his own Yorubaland. What the Biafran leader didn't recognize was that Banjo had his own agenda. The original intention of this Yoruba officer—with all this power play then going on—was that he earnestly intended becoming the future ruler of Nigeria.

"So Banjo turned traitor. Once the column stopped in Benin City, he used the radio of the British Deputy High Commissioner in Benin City to call up the British High Commission in Lagos and ask for Gowon to be brought to the microphone. His intention was to negotiate with that Nigerian military leader a handover of the country to himself. Banjo wanted to call himself President of Nigeria.

"That bit of duplicity stopped the invasion in its tracks, though frankly, I could never understand why. I could never comprehend why this extremely successful invasion force with an empty road ahead of it had been halted.

"Of course, there were two reasons here. The one was a total loss of nerve. There was also the treachery by Brigadier Banjo, its commanding officer," explained Forsyth.

Throughout it all, the experience—as that experienced British author will tell you—taught Nigeria a very hard lesson. It set in motion the effort, as he states, to recruit, recruit and recruit. "Within almost no time at all, General Gowon ran his army up from the original six thousand to something like a hundred and fifty thousand."

Forsyth: "The newcomers came from all over. They scraped dregs out of the prisons, like Lagos' awful Kiri Kiri Prison, which was nearly emptied of every thug, gangster and killer. Murderers were summarily released and put into uniform. Then they virtually emptied Lagos University. They put the students in uniform, gave them a rifle, and, as was the case in Angola thirty years later, all these men were pushed to the front. There was never any question of training this new group of improvised soldiers.

"Suddenly, further afield, there were other effects. There were people in London and Washington who panicked when they realized that perhaps this Nigerian civil war thing was not going to be as easy as they'd originally suggested."

By now, Ojukwu had secretly launched a fairly extensive arms build-up of his own involving people like the American Hank Wharton and Rhodesia's enterprising Jack Malloch. Both men—together with arms merchants from France, Holland, Germany and China—worked hand-in-glove with several European governments including France, Portugal and Spain to give Ojukwu just about all that he needed.

By linking itself to Paris' subterfuge, South Africa also got involved. The plan orchestrated by Jacques Foccart, the Elysées' shadowy eminence grise in charge of African affairs for President de

Gaulle, was to try to help Pretoria out of the isolation that had resulted from its years of race-motivated policies.

Soon after hostilities in the Congo ended, France persuaded
Pretoria to provide the secessionists with arms and ammunition, largely because French ammunition didn't fit "British standard" Biafran
weapons. The South African Army eventually gave Ojukwu hundreds
of tons of ordnance as well as a squad or two of Special Force troops,
all of it flown illegally across Nigeria's borders.

Contact had originally been made with the future President Botha,
who was South Africa's defense minister at the time. He delegated
responsibility for the liaison to General Fritz Loots, the original
founder of the elite Special Forces unit, the Reconnaissance Regiment,
or in local parlance, the Recess. Coordinating developments in
Libreville meantime was Neels van Tonder, a brilliant young staff officer who was eventually to leave his mark on the outcome of the
Angolan War.

Other South Africans who got involved included such luminaries
as Colonel Jan "Bruin Man" Breytenbach, one of the finest unconventional counterinsurgency specialists fielded by the SADF (and,
surprisingly, the brother of arch anti-Apartheid activist Breyten
Breytenbach).

There was also Chris Moorcroft, Alan Heard and another old
hand at this sort of thing, Paul Els, all of whom became involved in
the Biafran War. Still more South Africans were linked to training and
tactical issues. It suited the Pretoria regime to cause dissension in
Africa, largely in an effort to take the focus off domestic problems
back home. It was all part of South Africa's continent-wide program
of destabilisation.

At one stage there was an operation planned to get one of the
South African Daphne class submarines off Lagos harbor and send in
an underwater demolition team to blow up Russian freighters then
bringing in arms for the Federal offensive. Inexplicably, it was called
off at the last moment, which was perhaps just as well.

In the end, there were mercenaries from many nations in Biafra.
For several reasons, which included the isolation of the rebel state,
lack of communications, shortages of food and munitions, coupled to
a harsh tropical climate in a region that for decades had been dubbed
"the armpit of Africa," these people ultimately had little impact on the
outcome of the war. Mercenary cadres would also be faced with an
entrenched level of bias from Biafra's officer corps; most believed that

they could do a damn sight better than a nondescript bunch of hired guns, and they weren't afraid to say so.

That the people arriving to take up arms against the Nigerian Army were white didn't help either.

Among the foreigners involved, not everybody turned a coin. Count Gustav von Rosen, who created an instant air force for the near plane-less Biafrans during one of his summer vacations, didn't charge a penny. When he flew his squadron of second-hand MFI-9B Swedish trainers into Biafra from Libreville, they were so heavily loaded with extra fuel tanks, rockets in wing-pods and radio equipment, that some of the aviators on the ground when they left said they wouldn't fly. They did, and within a day or two these modest little ground attack aircraft had notched up their first strikes.

In their first three raids after arriving in rebel territory, on airports at Benin City and Port Harcourt, the Minicons bagged several Nigerian Air Force planes – including a MiG-17 or two as well as an Egyptian Air Force Ilyushin-28. All were blasted while still on the ground. By then the Nigerians had started using Egyptian mercenaries to fly some of their larger jets, including Ilyushin bombers. After that, the Biafran pilots became a lot more circumspect: there were any number of Nigerian Air Force planes—including MiGs—out looking for them and their bases.

Another illustrious figure who arrived in the war was Rolf Steiner —the same man who was later captured by the Sudanese government while fighting for the Christian rebels in the south. In Biafra, Steiner was appointed brigade commander, and mercenaries from many nations fought under him.

An austere, engaging figure, he'd enlisted in the French Foreign Legion after Germany's surrender in 1945. He claimed to have spent seven years in Indochina, where, he said, he'd lost a lung at Dien Bien Phu. Forsyth, after doing a bit of detective work, said that wasn't true, though he did actually have only one lung. This handicap didn't prevent Steiner from scrapping for five years in Algeria, after which he broke away and joined the anti-Gaullist OAS. While living in Paris, he got wind of merc opportunities in West Africa. It took him only a few months to make Colonel in Ojukwu's army, a nice touch since he'd never been more than a sergeant before.

For all his faults, of which insubordination toward his Biafran colleagues was among the worst, Steiner was hard on his troops. Black or

white, they found him a ruthless, demanding taskmaster. But somehow they also seemed to respect him, and though he was unconventional in his approach to most things, he got results.

Invariably the proponent of the unexpected, his favorite ploy was
to haul out his Browning Hi-Power pistol and fire into the air whenever he demanded attention. In Africa, he would tell the occasional
journalist who asked why he did that, such quirks work. For his personal credo he adopted the Legion's motto: "Long live death, long live
war."

Throughout the Biafran War, the fighting, though sporadic at
times, was as intense as it gets. It was also very often confused. A town
might change hands three or four times in a couple of months, and
eventually the sheer preponderance of Federal might prevailed. It did-
n't take long for Ojukwu's people to lose their foothold along the
coastal areas and be pushed back into the remote interior. Finally this
tiny recalcitrant nation became trapped in a combination of loosely
linked enclaves, almost all of them heavily forested.

What was also notable about this struggle was that from the
beginning there were very few prisoners taken on either side.
Government atrocities perpetrated by what had become a northern-
dominated, mainly-Islamic force soon convinced the rebel nation that
secession from the Federation was no longer the issue. It had become
a desperate struggle for survival.

Early in the war, the German mercenary Rolf Steiner became involved
in an aborted attempt to form a Biafran Navy.

With Biafra ringed by conflict on three sides out of four—and the
great Niger River and its tributaries running through most of it—it
was to be expected that Ojukwu would do what he could to ease the
Nigerian naval blockade. Federal forces by then included a Dutch
frigate, five Ford-class seaward defense boats (SDBs) and three Soviet
P6-class patrol boats. At one stage, a Biafran contingent tried to seize
one of the SDBs in Port Harcourt harbor but they were thwarted by
quick action by a Nigerian support group who sank it at its moorings.

In a bid to outdo them, Steiner and Georgio Norbiato, a former
Italian marine commando who had previously fought in the Congo,
commandeered three fast Chris Craft from the Port Harcourt Sailing
Club. They mounted machine guns on their prows and set to work.
Each could carry four commandos plus a pilot, the idea being that
they would ambush small freighters moving upriver.

Their first sortie provided excellent dividends: the booty included five Land Rovers, thousands of uniforms and millions of 7.62mm cartridges. A subsequent haul brought in ten tons of Soviet 81/82mm mortar shells and a good supply of grenades, as well as several 20mm Oerlikon cannon that had been mounted specifically to thwart such actions. Then everything ground to a halt after Norbiato was killed in a contact. Until the end of the war, merc elements continued to use the Niger Delta to perform early warning patrols.

Hostilities gathered pace during the latter part of 1967. Having left Nigeria the year before, I was determined to get back to West Africa and cover the war. Apart from the *Daily Express* there was also the Argus Africa News Service in Johannesburg and several French photo agencies.

But, as I was to discover, getting yourself into Biafra presented problems, some of them intractable. By the time I made my move, the place was landlocked. It could be reached only from one of two neighboring territories—the Portuguese island of Sáo Tomé (from which most relief flights into rebel territory operated) and Gabon, formerly a French colony and once home to the venerable Dr. Albert Schweitzer.

There were also relief flights from the Spanish island colony of Fernando Pó just off the Nigerian coast, but Madrid rarely allowed them to take passengers. Europe was cagey about what kind of support it gave "the rebel Ojukwu" and there wasn't a nation among them that did not become distinctly gunshy when there were journalists around.

Biafra at that stage was recognized by only four countries, and then only circumspectly. These were Gabon, Haiti, Mauritania and another revolutionary hotspot on the Indian Ocean pursuing its version of a half-baked Soviet ideology, Tanzania. It was hardly an impressive international line-up. Having gone to Nairobi, I'd made my way by road to Dar es Salaam and, using my *Express* press card, applied at the office of the Biafran legation for permission to enter Biafra. It took a while, but eventually a visa came through.

In theory, I might have covered the war from the Nigerian side, but things there had become difficult for us freelancers. The media, as usual, was suspect and individual Nigerian commanders weren't hesitant to react if somebody reported negatively.

One senior Nigerian Army officer, Colonel Benjamin "Black Scorpion" Adekunle, commander of Nigeria's 3rd Marine Commando Division, was among the most vituperative. A basket case, he would sometimes shoot his own men if he thought he needed to make an example, and he did so at least once in the presence of foreign journalists. Then he dared them to file their stories.

Adekunle would blast off about the kind of journalism then emerging from the front lines, blaming his nation's woes on the CIA, Westminster, the Pope and a host of others besides. It was worse if the perceived transgressor happened to be white. He was strident in the view that Europeans were responsible for all of Africa's ills, and when he'd had a few toots, he could become really menacing.

British foreign correspondent Mike Williamson, in his book *A Measure of Danger,* mentions a dinner at which Adekunle drew a pistol. In turn, he pointed it at each of the scribblers present. Eventually he pressed it against Williamson's temple and pulled the trigger. The gun went click. "Black joke from the Black Scorpion," somebody said afterward.

When such things happen, especially among hacks, the word travels. Consequently I wasn't all that eager to work with the Nigerian Army, especially since I'd been stuck with them for several months while working at Ikeja. Also, a short while before, Priha Rhamraka, a Nairobi pal—then working as a cameraman for a British network— was killed in an ambush. Also, my South African connections seemed to foster an unhealthy interest among some Federal intelligence agencies, particularly after a Biafran officer who had turned traitor made public Pretoria's role in the war. Finally I decided on Biafra, and in any event, Ojukwu's efforts against Africa's most populace state were just then starting to look laudable, at least from a distance.

But how to get into a country under siege? Since São Tomé was too roundabout an approach and, in any event, took too long (it meant going back to Europe and catching a plane to Africa out of Lisbon) I finally settled on coming in from Gabon. The trouble was that most flights out of Libreville were military, which often meant using an aircraft loaded with weapons and explosives.

That had already became a dangerous option after one of the mercenary pilots working for the Nigerians at the controls of a Soviet-built MiG-17 purposely shot down an International Red Cross DC-7B loaded with baby food. The incident was regarded by many of us as one of the more tragic events of the war. The freighter, piloted by American Captain David Brown, had taken off from Santa Isabel, capital of the island of Fernando Pó.

The Nigerian government afterward claimed that its fighters had challenged the cargo plane after it had entered Nigerian air space and ordered it to land either at Port Harcourt or Calabar, near the Cameroon frontier. When it refused, Lagos said, the MiG pilot "positioned his fighter to the rear of Brown's plane and fired several short cannon bursts." This caused the DC-7's nose to rise sharply before entering a stall. Shortly afterward it crashed.

Frederick Forsyth provides a more likely version:

> At 1738 hours on that Thursday evening Captain Brown took off from Fernando Pó with his cargo. . . . If he made any mistake, it was in leaving too early for Biafra. The sky was a brilliant blue, without a cloud and the sun was still well above the horizon. It was habitual for planes leaving Sào Tomé to depart at this hour, for with the longer journey they only came over the Biafran coast after 1900 hours, that is, after dark. Dusk is very short in Africa. The light starts to fade around 1830 and by 1900 it is dark. But with the much shorter journey (only sixty miles) from Fernando Pó to the coast, he came over the coast about 1800 in broad daylight. At 1803 his voice was heard on the Fernando Pó control tower and by other Red Cross pilots on the same run. He gave no call sign, and the voice was high-pitched with alarm. He said: "I'm being attacked . . . I'm being attacked." His switch went dead, there was a moment's silence, then a babble on the ether, with Fernando Pó asking for the identification of the caller. Thirty seconds later the voice came back on the air. "My engine's on fire . . . I'm going down . . ." Then there was silence.

Uli Airport—codenamed Annabelle—was the destination of all relief flights headed into Biafra. Within months, the airstrip became a legend among the airline pilots of the world. It also fired the imagination of a thousand adventurers.

Everything that went on at Uli was improvised. The runway—lined on both sides by forest—had once been a stretch of main road between the towns of Aba and Onitcha in eastern Nigeria. When the fuses blew, which happened often, they lined the runway with cans of palm oil with lighted wicks floating on top to show incoming aircraft where they had to touch down. It was a fragile arrangement, especially when the wind blew. Somehow, though, it worked.

Forsyth also captured the scene best in his introduction to another book to come out of the war, Mike Draper's *Shadows: Airlift and Airwar in Biafra and Nigeria*:[4]

> It was crazy, it was hairy, it was impossibly dangerous; it should never have worked. But somehow it did, night after night. When the planes landed and taxied into the welcome darkness by the side of the motorway-turned-landing-strip, willing hands hauled sacks of milk powder and bundles of stockfish out of the fuselages and away into the feeding centers. That done, the pilots taxied back to the take-off point, the lights flickered on for a few seconds and they were gone...

He recalls that this was the story of the strangest air-bridge the world had seen. The airplanes used by aid people were "a ramshackle collection of time-expired or phased out workhorses of the skies, culled from boneyards all over the globe." Had it not happened, he reckoned there would have been another million Biafran children starved into oblivion because by then the rebel state was blockaded.

The Nigerians were just as active. Apart from their shooting down the Red Cross cargo plane, mercenary pilots flew hundreds of MiG-17 missions for the Nigerian Air Force. Most were against Biafran ground targets, though occasionally they would turn their attention to the airlift.

What was interesting about the jet fighters (which came from Moscow) was the proviso that no Western pilots were to get near them. The indeterminate nature of this grim war soon changed that, which was how Ares Klootwyk, a South African pilot originally trained by the RAF, became the first Westerner to take a Russian MiG-17 into combat. Obviously it didn't happen by accident. Both London and Washington were more than interested in what Russian jets could (and could not) do.

The upshot was that there were British and American spooks all over the place. They operated along the various fronts for the duration and especially where there was a Nigerian Air Force base. Some almost became fixtures in the bars out Ikeja way and along Lagos' Ikorodu Road. Others worked Port Harcourt.

By the time it was over, Klootwyk—who I got to know well after the war—had spent more than two hundred hours flying sorties in MiG-17s in almost as many combat missions. More merc pilots, such as Britons Paul Martin and Mike Thompsett (who drove his MiG-17 into the ground shortly after the downing of the Red Cross freighter) were just as active. Other adventurers came from Australia and several European countries, all recruited through a single company in Switzerland.

Egyptian mercenaries, by contrast, flying NAF Ilyushin IL-28s were notable for a somewhat marked incapacity to achieve anything at all. For fear of ground fire, they would rarely drop below ten thousand feet.

For much of the conflict, Uli remained the tenuous lifeline between Biafra and the world outside. The "miracle of Uli"—as some people had dubbed it—hosted about twenty flights a night, the first arriving just after dark. If conditions allowed, these could be upped to as many as forty. Almost every one of these missions operated beyond safety limits: the aircraft were overloaded with tons of food, weapons and ammunition, all essential if Biafra was to survive.

Some of the planes were hit while on the ground taxiing. Others were bombed by the NAF using World War II-era cargo planes that had been crudely fitted with bomb racks. There were also some that were accidentally shot down by Biafran ground fire, though the rebels denied it. They said it couldn't happen, but it did. We were nearly hit by machine-gun fire as we came in, long lines of tracers reaching up at us, almost touching-distance away, it seemed. And it wasn't Nigerian guns either. At that stage their lines were miles away.

Look at the figures. In church relief flights alone (never mind the arms runs out of Gabon, which was itself a sizable tally each night) there were more than seven thousand freight flights into Biafra in the two-and-a-half years that war ravaged eastern Nigeria. In this time almost a million tons of supplies, including arms, were taken into the beleaguered territory. For the duration, there were fifteen aircraft lost and twenty-five aircrew killed, all of them buried at a small cemetery adjacent to Uli Airport. There were large jagged pieces of shiny aluminum lining both sides of the runway at Uli: until the war ended nobody ever bothered to move them, or rather, they had neither the energy nor the resources to do so.

The Nigerian Army bulldozed the graves of these aviators when its troops overran the place. The reason, as one bucolic Nigerian field commander declared to a gathering of foreign correspondents, was that "they will be eternally forgotten . . . we don't want their families poking about here for their remains afterward."

Getting to Uli that first time was an event. Suddenly, on day six or seven, the Biafran representative in Libreville told me: "You're going in tonight. Make sure you're at the airport by three this afternoon and bring along something warm. It gets cold up there."

My pilot was a German. "Herman the German," we called him, a laconic barfly whose breath cleaved the air like sewer gas. He was much given to brandy—good or bad, and word had it that Herman drank day and night. When he reported for duty that afternoon, he'd obviously already had plenty. I couldn't object: Herman was my passport to an unusual war. It was rumored among the crews that in another war he'd flown supplies into Stalingrad, but it was something that he wouldn't talk about.

Once onboard the unmarked L-749A Super Constellation with its unmistakable triple tail fins, there were no formalities. My place was at the back: a solitary seat immediately ahead of the tail and fractionally ahead of a toilet that probably hadn't been cleaned in months. Our cargo wasn't anything lethal: a mountain of baby food in plastic bags that separated me from the cockpit. Only I couldn't speak to those up front because there was no intercom.

Herman had warned earlier that "zey" would be waiting for us and, indeed, they were. As soon as we crossed the coast somewhere near Port Harcourt, I spotted flashes of artillery fire on the ground. While I watched through the porthole nearest me, these immediately became brilliant orange balls of flak as they exploded a few thousand feet below. I'd never experienced being directly shot at like that before and for a brief while it was like being at a show.

Only after the war did it emerge that the nightly shuttle of aircraft from Libreville and São Tomé had very early on become a charade. It was a game of chess that the Superpowers played when it suited them and, as with events transpiring in the Middle East today, the prize was oil.

Nigerian anti-aircraft guns and the people who manned them were either Russian or Russian-trained. The crews that made the nightly flights into Biafra were aware that the fuses on their AAA shells were always set for fourteen thousand feet: so they flew four thousand feet higher, a standard operating procedure. In reality, had the coastal gunners wanted, they could easily have shot us down. But they didn't, and so it went throughout the war.

It surprised us all that the Nigerian High Command never protested at the lack of results, even though Moscow's anti-aircraft efforts must have cost this African state plenty.

Once we'd crossed onto the mainland, there wasn't a light to be seen anywhere. Nor were any of the aircraft approaching Uli using their navigation lights even though there were eight or ten and sometimes more aircraft stacked in the immediate vicinity of the runway below. There was a half-serious joke among relief crews: if all the pilots were to simultaneously switch on their navigation lights, half would have died of heart attack from shock because they were flying so dangerously close to each other.

Getting down onto that primitive airstrip took some skill. Herman told me before lift-off that our approach into Uli would be made in the dark, not that it made much difference because by the time we got there, with a moon that was almost full, it seemed like all of Africa was clothed in a brilliant glow.

Our descent was ultra-steep, with pilots eager to get in and out as quickly as possible. They would maneuver their aircraft into position before sets of improvised runway lights were switched on for about four or five seconds, six if you were lucky. It was all the time they were given to get their bearing and go into finals.

Meanwhile, it was the job of a Nigerian Air Force bomber labeled "Genocide"—also flown by mercs—to give these relief planes a battering.

The bomber would break into the cargo planes' radio chatter and taunt them: "This is genocide, baby . . . come on down and get killed."

The man's South African accent was unmistakable: obviously another war dog. As Forsyth recalls, "Anyone listening in on the same wavelength could hear merc pilots flying the Nigerian bombers jeering at them, daring them to land when the lights flashed those few elusive seconds."

To begin with, "Genocide" was an antiquated Dakota C-47 "Gooney Bird" that had been adapted to carry canisters of explosives. Later the Nigerians would acquire surplus American B-25s. But that old plane would hover at about eighteen thousand feet and wait for things to happen, the idea being to drop its canisters just as an approaching aircraft came into the approach. Ideally, the explosives would go off just as the plane put its wheels down.

At the end of it, Nigerian aircraft rarely succeeded in causing much damage. When a plane did take a hit and blocked the runway, the Nigerian propaganda machine would spin into action and the newspapers would crow that Uli Airport had been crippled. It sometimes took a week to put things right again. Meantime, an alternate airstrip would be prepared or, if that wasn't possible because of fighting, other open stretches of road. Then the process would begin all over again.

Whatever else was taking place at Uli, the pilots always had something to talk about the next morning. In the final approaches to Uli Airport, some of them would come in so low that their fuselage would clip the tops of palms. Later, back at base, aircrews would compare notes about "green props."

There was also the occasional "red prop." Since most loading teams were made up of bush people who knew little about the dangers of modern aircraft, there were those who would walk into the propellers. Once on the ground at Uli, none of the planes ever switched off their engines. Instead, they would disgorge their cargoes, load up with whatever was there and shoot off again. With "Genocide" overhead there was an urgency about it all and cargoes would often be cleared within minutes.

Once landed, Biafran ground crews—many of them malnourished because there was so little food in the country—got busy and it was tough work. It sometimes took four of these sadly emaciated creatures to shift a single hundred-pound ammo box. If it were food, Roman Catholic White Fathers in their long cassocks would direct operations. Munitions belonged to the Biafran Army and those canisters and crates would be hurried away in trucks.

While this was going on, other Biafran officials would indicate what or who was to go out that night. Most of the outgoing consisted of starving children, mostly orphaned, being sent off to camps in other parts of Africa. The main clearing house for these waifs was "Kilometre Onze" in Gabon, though there were also Roman Catholic institutions run by Caritas in São Tomé.

The São Tomé side of the airlift—a tiny place about twice the size of the Isle of Man and which lies about three-hundred miles off the Nigerian coast—was started by Hank Wharton, a genial cigar-chewing Yank with a penchant for unusual flights and dubious cargoes. Officially he presented himself as a director of The North American Trading Company, a title that could hardly be more vague.

In 1968 he took a contract with the Catholic relief organization Caritas to fly six chartered flights into Biafra at $3,800 each. As part of the deal he would make one flight free. At that time about two thousand Ibos were dying of hunger each day, most of them children.

Gradually a number of European governments and the International Red Cross became interested in their plight, though it took a while.

Prior to bringing in his Minicons, Count von Rosen had been flying cargoes of food across Nigerian territory in daylight, about three hundred feet up. His navigator, Father William Butler, was a missionary who had worked in Rivers Province and knew the waterways like he'd been born there. It didn't take long for the Count and Ojukwu to become fast friends.

As more religious entities took part in the humanitarian work, they came to ignore sectarian differences. Catholic and Protestant churches pooled efforts and resources in São Tomé, working under the aegis of what became known worldwide as Joint Church Aid. For their part, the Americans became involved through Catholic Relief Services and Church World Service, and they ultimately provided four Boeing C-97 Stratocruisers.

All were sold as surplus for the peppercorn sum of $4,000 each.

None of us who went into Biafra at night will ever forget the heat and the noise that cloaked us like a sauna immediately we stepped off the plane. That first night I crouched for hours in a split-pole bunker beside the runway waiting for somebody to fetch me. I'd been warned earlier that it might take a while and that I should be patient. I was.

Time, one soon discovers under such circumstances, means nothing. You are simply too awed, too overwhelmed by what's going on around you, and the musty, unwashed immediacy to it all. Our senses were constantly sharpened by the stutter of automatic fire along the runway. Alongside our position were several tall palms, their foliage almost blown away. This was all that was left of a palm oil plantation from the colonial era.

Alongside, perhaps thirty paces away, was the barely recognizable tail section of a Globemaster C97 that had crashed the month before.

These sights, together with priests in their white cassocks, the intermittent rattle of war, the roar of aircraft constantly landing or taking off, and the babble of voices shouting in strange tongues, made for a surreal assault on the senses. Herman didn't even bother to wave goodbye when he left. He was airborne in minutes, intent on making a second run that night.

Then, for a little while, an uneasy calm descended on the jungle around me, broken now and again by more machine gun fire and a bunch of infants hollering in a trench across the way.

Hostilities ended abruptly in early 1970, after the Biafran people, literally, had been starved into submission. What was notable was that the slaughter of the Ibo nation—something we all expected after Federal forces had overrun the rebel territory—never happened. All credit here must go to General Yakubu—"Jack" to his friends—Gowon, the Nigerian leader at the time. More's the pity too, that he was ousted in a military putsch after the war ended. It was interesting that he ended up attending a British university as a student, and till now has been the only former African head of state to have pushed back his personal clock.

In the interim, not a great deal has changed in Africa's most populous nation. Thirty years on, there are disturbing trends that could very well be the precursor for another civil war. Once more the imbroglio is Christian against Muslim, and again there have been internecine clashes that have been mindless, bitter and ruthless. In early 2005, the Nigerian government admitted that in the previous three years there had been fifty thousand deaths in religious and sectarian violence and, sadly, there's barely a region of the country hasn't been affected.

Things aren't much better in the old Biafra either. After spending decades in exile in the Ivory Coast, Odumegwu Ojukwu, no longer a military man, is back in his home country. On occasion, he can be remarkably outspoken about the plight of his people in the modern era. Several times he has pointed out that despite the country's oil industry, easterners today are more distressed than ever before. All those hundreds of billions of dollars earned in fuel exports in the past half century, and almost nothing to show for it. As he also said, much of it ended up in the foreign bank accounts of his country's leaders. The deposed Nigerian President Sonny Abacha siphoned off a billion or three, only a small proportion of it ever having been returned by the Swiss banks where it was lodged before he died.

It was actually Ojukwu that publicly warned three or four years ago that if things did not improve, the region could very easily find itself embroiled in "another Biafran war." Harsh words, or as somebody else was heard to say, "war talk, and not to be ignored."

What he said though, made good sense. Especially to those of us who have kept our fingers on the pulse of a nation that seems to be eternally in transition.

PART IIII

"Military companies are not a passing phenomenon. Military force can stabilize a crisis, challenging the view that negotiation in the absence of coercion is sufficient to reach a settlement. . . . States and international organizations need to rethink current perceptions of the private military sector as an unpleasant aberration."

David Shearer, in his introduction to
Private Armies and Military Intervention[1]

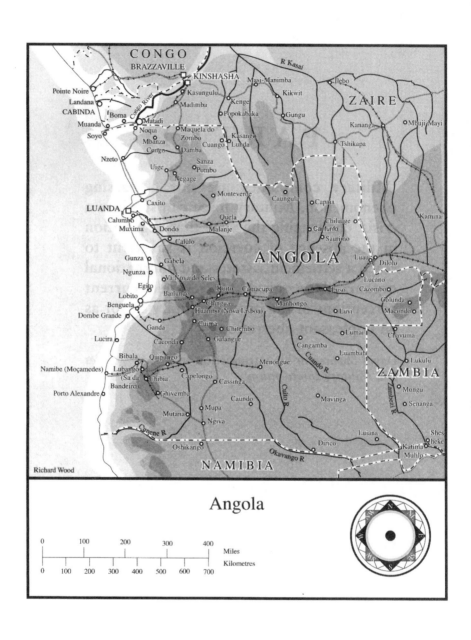

Angola

Richard Wood

```
0        100       200      300      400
|---------|---------|--------|--------|   Miles
                                          Kilometres
0    100  200  300  400  500  600  700
```

15

EXECUTIVE OUTCOMES
IN ANGOLA

"Executive Outcomes gave us this stability. In a perfect world of course, we wouldn't need an organization like EO, but I'd be loath to say that they'd have to go just because they're mercenaries."

Canadian General Ian Douglas,
negotiator for the United Nations

The bedrock on which the reputation of Executive Outcomes was built came from the bitter two-month battle for the Soyo oil installation at the mouth of the Congo River in Angola's far north.

The operation lasted from early March to the end of April 1993. It was fought against the rebel movement National Union for the Total Independence of Angola (UNITA), led by Jonas Savimbi. In the process, three South Africans lost their lives, though everybody who stayed the distance was hit at least once, some a dozen times over. Quite a few of the men suffered life-threatening wounds, a few injured seriously enough to be evacuated to hospitals abroad. In contrast, the rebel group lost several hundred men, including two of their top field commanders

A consequence of that tough, resilient action was that the Luanda government liked what it saw. It was impressed by a group of men who, until a very short time earlier, had been their hated enemy. An equivalent sort of turnaround might have been an American Ranger Battalion fighting for Hanoi at the end of the Vietnam War. Further, these South Africans were dead serious: among their number were men prepared to put their lives at risk to achieve their stated goals. As a consequence, the Angolan government hired five hundred more of these former veterans for an estimated $40 million a year. Executive Outcomes was on the map.

The job, according to the deal signed by company representatives in Luanda, was to train five thousand Angolan troops in both counterinsurgency and conventional military warfare, and the contract was to last from September 1993 to January 1996. At the same time Angola bought numbers of T-54/55 main battle tanks as well a hundred brand new BMP-2 infantry fighting vehicles from Moscow. The air component that would support these operations included MiG-23 and Sukoi jet fighter-bombers, Pilatus PC-7 and PC-9 ground support aircraft (with underwing rocket pods), as well as Hind helicopter gunships and Hip multi-role transport choppers. All flew under the banner of Angolan Air Force.

The arrival in Angola of EO, a small Pretoria security company with no previous record of military activity, happened to coincide with the lifting of the international arms embargo on the Luanda government. Ultimately, in a series of military adventures that spanned almost the entire country, the company was instrumental in forcing the Swiss-educated, Mao-espousing Dr. Savimbi to the negotiating table.

But it was the Battle of Soyo that set the scene for these events. There, at one of Angola's principal oil facilities—perched precariously on the south shore of the estuary of the Congo River—the scene was set for a force of forty men (often less than half that number) to fight a series of battles against a hugely preponderant Unita guerrilla army numbering more than a thousand. What made the event significantly different from previous Angolan government efforts in its war against Unita, was that almost all of EO's fighters had formerly been members of elite South African Defence Force (SADF) Special Forces units.

Having been airlifted into Soyo by Mi-8 helicopters in what should have been a surprise attack, this tiny but "highly effective work force"—as the company later phrased it—battled for the duration to hold on to the oil facility, the military base guarding it, and eventually to take the nearby ancillary port of Kwanza. The ordeal developed into an immense test of endurance, guts, improvisation and tactics as the South Africans countered everything that the rebels could throw at them.

There were days—and nights, especially—when Unita would send its irregulars in relays often hundreds strong, four sometimes six times in a row.

To the sound of whistles blown by their commanders the rebels would go in screaming "*Avante! Avante!*" and the fighting would last for an hour or two. The rebels would withdraw and the next batch would follow a short while later. Though the guerrillas attacked, probed, shelled, rocketed, mortared and regularly threw themselves at the defenders in numbers, sometimes getting to within yards of EO's defense perimeter, the tiny Executive Outcomes squad held on. As former Reconnaissance Regiment Major Lafras Luitingh was to comment years later, "We were able to contain it all OK, but believe me, only just . . . it could as easily have gone the other way."

It didn't help that many of the Unita regulars battling the South African perimeter were originally attached to Savimbi's own Special Forces, the brazenly bold *Groupos de Bate*. Nor that this accomplished and experienced unit had been fighting the Angolan Army for years and had originally been trained by South African insurgency specialists in times when Pretoria was still at war with Luanda.

Though the Angolan Army, or FAA,[2] offered some help (one of its tanks was brought ashore to bolster EO defenses) many government troops had no training whatsoever. Indeed, only after it was over was it established that most of these youths had been shanghaied off the streets of Luanda, put in uniform and had an AK thrust into their hands. Without further ado, they were then promptly shipped off to the front. At the first sign of a Unita attack, many of them would slink off into the jungle, sometimes doffing their uniforms and weapons as they did so. They would only return to the base when the odors wafting through the undergrowth told them that food was being prepared.

Though their officers shot them out of hand if they were caught—there were about fifty FAA soldiers executed that way, the majority by Angolan Colonel Pepe de Castro himself (who otherwise stayed well away from any actual hostilities)—the South African defenders accepted very early on that an unwilling troop was invariably more of a hindrance than a help.

Then, once the fighting had ended and the South Africans pulled out—with the oil facility again in government hands—Executive Outcomes signed a formal agreement with the Angolans. And over the next two years a lot more battles followed. These included the eventual recapture of Angola's diamond fields at Cafunfo (one of the largest diamondiferous pipes in the world) and the ousting of Savimbi and his command structure from many of the major centers in the border regions adjacent to Zaire.

Through it all, the reputation of this tough, resolute band of South African mercenaries hardly ever faltered, even though there were times when there was dissension within their ranks as to their actual purpose in the war.

In fact, the link was further cemented when, halfway through the Angolan campaign, EO's management was approached by an embattled Sierra Leone government anxious to quell its own escalating insurrection. After EO's directors accepted a contract price of "about $25 million," almost two hundred men were sent to Freetown, again at very short notice. With that, company personnel—this time using their own weapons and helicopters—set about hammering Foday Sankoh's rebels into submission wherever they could be found.

Not everybody was happy with the way all this came about. There were many critics of Executive Outcomes, its methods, and the kind of business it quite blatantly propagated. According to David Shearer in his substantive prognosis on the use of mercenaries, *Private Armies and Military Intervention*, the South African "guns-for-hire" organization represented the unacceptable face of mercenary activity.

Yet, added Shearer, while EO was condemned in liberal circles, the firm proved in its few years of operations that it could "create a climate for peace and stability for foreign investment, focusing chiefly on military training and including a particular emphasis on Special Forces and clandestine warfare." Shearer reckoned that it also saw "a role for itself in peacekeeping (persuasion) services and was prepared to buy equipment appropriate to a client's needs".

Not for nothing did EO describe itself in its promotional literature as a company with a "solid history of success."

Executive Outcomes began its business innocuously enough by handling private security back at its home base in Pretoria. Its founder, Eeben Barlow, originally qualified as a sapper in the SADF Engineers Corps, where he trained in mines and advanced explosives warfare. From there he was posted to 32 Battalion, one of the more aggressive South African units in the Angolan War, that made something of a specialty of unconventional methods of warfare. White officered, most of its members were disaffected Angolans who, having fought against the Marxist MPLA in a protracted civil war, ended up in exile in present-day Namibia (formerly the League of Nations mandate, South West Africa).

After South Africa's twenty-one years of border conflicts came to an end in the late 1980s, Barlow did unspecified work in a covert South African Defense Force unit called the Civil Cooperation Bureau, or CCB. Only after he'd resigned from that clandestine force did he and his partners establish Executive Outcomes, which operated as a normal security concern involved in private and corporate protection in a country where crime had become endemic following Nelson Mandela's election as President. Under Barlow's tenure, EO managed to recruit several weighty clients, among them the mining conglomerate Anglo American Corporation.

What happened next is regarded by some of those involved with EO in its early days as more of a fortuitous turn of events than anything that might have been planned.

While with the CCB, Barlow became fairly well known to British Intelligence and he, in turn, familiar with some of their operators. His role within the apartheid-era secret group was the opening of both local and foreign front companies to be used in the kind of furtive work in which CCB was then embroiled. He was also charged with handling bank accounts for these firms, some of which had links to South African sanctions-busting operations.

With EO innocuously on the map in South Africa, Angola just then was having serious military problems of its own, with Savimbi's guerrilla force managing to extend its influence throughout the country. At that stage already, Unita dominated all but the major urban centers. It had yet to penetrate secure security swathes around the main cities of Luanda and Lobito, but it was the guerrilla strike on Soyo that eventually emerged as the most urgent threat.

Though not the biggest of Angola's oil exporting facilities, Soyo represented an asset that was of vital importance to a number of oil companies operating in Angola at the time. These included Italy's Fina, Elf of France, and Texaco, one of the American oil giants, all of which—including Sonangol, Angola's nationalized oil company—used Soyo as a logistics base for their offshore operations. There was also Ranger Oil West Africa (ROWAL)—a joint venture between Ranger and Heritage. With the rebels holding the place, all oil shipments came to a halt. Financially, as a consequence, Luanda was hurting.

One item which fell into the hands of the guerrillas was a prototype of a rotating buoy which was being tried out by ROWAL. An extremely complex and expensive item worth "several million dollars," its owners wanted it back. Thus, through a series of intermediaries, ROWAL's directors made a formal approach to Unita's representatives in Paris and asked whether permission could be requested from Dr. Savimbi to have the buoy returned.

The reply that almost immediately came back from Africa was a very determined no. The burly guerrilla leader was of no mind to help his enemy balance its books, and he said as much. He had the buoy and was keeping it, was the gist of the message

Enter Tony Buckingham, a former SAS operator-turned-oil entrepreneur who had links to London's Heritage Oil and Gas.[3] According to Lafras Luitingh, Barlow's partner in EO, Buckingham—astute as they come in this kind of business—was (and still is) extremely well connected in Britain, Westminster included. The gist of it was that he had come up with a solution to defeat Savimbi's Unita.[4]

By then, Buckingham had already been in contact with the Angolans in Luanda, where he approached Joaquim David, head of Sonangol to do something about getting the buoy back. David replied that he couldn't authorize anything to do with the military and suggested that he talk personally with Angolan President Eduardo dos Santos, which Buckingham did. That this British operator was able to gain access to the notoriously reclusive dos Santos—and at such short notice—says a good deal both for his influence and tenacity, even though he had done a number of successful deals in the country in the past.

Together with a group of military advisors, the President listened to what Buckingham had to say. The argument that he presented centered on the possibility of hurling back Unita's forces at Soyo and recapturing the oil terminal. That done, he suggested, their joint aims would have been achieved: he would get back his buoy and Luanda would again dominate the high ground at Soyo. Buckingham was promptly given $1 million to prepare a feasibility study.

Once back in London, Buckingham contacted some of his former SAS pals and suggested there was good money to be made if they were to help him launch an operation to effect retrieval. It would be a short, snappy operation, he said, perhaps accomplished over a weekend. He also disclosed that the Angolan President had confided that the facility was lightly guarded.

It didn't take long for his old Hereford friends to give him a thumbs-down. The proposal was absurd, they told him. Having studied the implications of what the venture would entail and spoken to individuals who were familiar with the region, they told him that the mission was not only unfeasible, it was suicidal. Elaborating, they explained that with the Atlantic Ocean fringing the area on one side and, right next to it, the Congo River, the second largest river in the world, even getting in there would be difficult. Coupled to that, there was triple canopy jungle just about everywhere else. Even moving about the area off-road was difficult: the grass was eight feet tall and there were swamps everywhere.

So, his friends argued, should things go wrong, escape, while not impossible, would be, as Anglos like to say, dicey. EO was to discover later, to its chagrin, that whoever made that initial study was spot-on.

It was said, but not confirmed, that some British operators had been trying to get two of their own companies, Saladin and KMS (Keeny Meeny Services, the name stemming from an incident in Malaya) into Angola for the job and had been unsuccessful. Operating much on the same paramilitary basis as EO, their personnel weren't familiar either with the terrain or the local people. The South Africans, in contrast, on both counts were.

Significantly, Saladin/KMS already had good experience in such matters. It was their people who trained the army of the Sultan of Oman and others. Indeed, they had been "involved" in Aden, Malaysia and other traditionally British areas in much the same way that EO became embroiled in Angola and Sierra Leone. They also guarded British embassies in South America during the Falklands War and, it is said, EO was modeled on them. Because these people use primarily (and, in some cases, only) former SAS and SBS operators, the companies are sometimes referred to in the industry as the "SAS Reserve."

Having established the parameters in Angola, Buckingham flew to South Africa to talk to another old contact from the past, Larny Keller, an SADF Colonel from the apartheid era who was just then involved in developing night vision equipment with Eloptro. It was Keller who brought Eeben Barlow's EO into the picture.

By now Tony Buckingham had linked up with another of his friends from his Special Forces days, former SAS Captain Simon Mann. This was the same Simon Mann who, in mid-2004 was to find himself incarcerated in Zimbabwe's Chikurubi Prison with sixty-something like-minded mercenaries after organizing a botched coup attempt in Equatorial Guinea.

Ostensibly, while being briefed on the nature of the job and what might be expected of them, both Barlow and Keller were told that the project was extremely sensitive, which was why no other corporate player had been contacted to do the work. One option that might have been considered would have been to use the American private military company MPRI. But while that Washington-based concern is composed largely of former US Special Forces personnel, MPRI focuses its efforts on training, not fighting.

Within days in mid-February 1993, Larny Keller's house in Centurion, a large conurbation south of Pretoria, became Executive Outcomes' new "center of operations."

As Harry Carlse, one of the former Recce operators who was eventually to become a section leader at Soyo tells it, "Eeben called me on the Wednesday and asked me to bring along some of my friends. I took four guys and a fifth joined us later."

Five "platoon commanders" were contracted to handle recruitment, training and planning. All of them accepted the job. The men were Buks Buys, a former Reconnaissance Regiment major; Harry Ferreira, one of Barlow's old oppos from 32 Battalion; Phil Smith, a former Rhodesian who had also served with Barlow in 32; Lafras Luitingh, another Recce major; and finally, one more individual from Barlow's sapper past, Mauritz le Roux. The first four were each tasked with recruiting thirty of their more experienced military buddies from the past, while le Roux had to bring in a dozen SADF engineers.

At this point, the team was warned that what lay ahead would not be easy. There would be a good bit of fighting, they were told. In fact, Barlow suggested, there would be "a lot of action and that it would be heavy going." What they weren't told was where all this would be taking place, except that the country involved "spoke Portuguese." Since there were ongoing civil wars in all three of Lisbon's former African territories—Angola, Mozambique and Guiné-Bissau (formerly Portuguese Guinea)—it might have been any one of them.

Le Roux was further tasked to find a good supply of explosives, preferably C4, since all that was being offered by Luanda was some out-of-date TNT. He was cautioned that there would be "some blowing of bridges," and possibly mines to be laid. Training, too, would fall within le Roux's brief.

Barlow stressed that since he was already getting strong pressure to move things along from Buckingham and friends, "Whoever you guys hire will have to be ready to go within two weeks." Once on location, there would be the same period of training and familiarization with Soviet-bloc weapons, which were standard issue throughout the Angolan forces.

The initial contract was for thirty days, he explained, and should EO be able to hold the target for that period, there would be a thirty-percent bonus at the end of it. For that first month's work—the contract could be extended—everybody would get from a third to a half of their cash up-front, together with a full kit allowance that would be used to buy what was needed locally. With that, the five-man leadership group set to work recruiting the roughly hundred men required for the job.

First results were not only encouraging but enthusiastic. "Yes," said just about everybody who was approached. They were all for it. "When do we leave?" many of them asked. But then interest waned. That came after the men had been told that there would be "quite a bit of fighting." It went with the kind of money being offered, the five recruiters explained.

Altogether, about eighty men were interviewed for the job. While preference was given to former Special Forces personnel, only about three-quarters of the applicants passed first muster, among them, surprisingly, a few who had never been to war. One was an air force clerk who, like others in the group, had never seen any action. Also, "while some of the men were in good shape, others weren't anywhere near combat ready," Carlse told me. Looking back a year or two later, Luitingh reckoned that because the job was so rushed—all of it at Luanda's strong insistence—there wasn't as much attention given to detail as there might otherwise have been. "Which could be why some of the chancers got through," he thought.

"It worried some of the men that nobody was saying much to start with about where it was or what we had to do. We'd only be given the specifics once we arrived at our destination. What they did make clear from the start was that it would be no walkover," recalled Harry Carlse.

While some recruits failed to make the grade, others backed out. For the rest, there was no waiting around once papers were signed and formalities had been completed. Each man was given the equivalent of a couple of thousand dollars and taken to the local outdoor store to buy tropical gear.

Ground troops for the operation were offered five hundred rands a day (at the time, about $150) for the lowest-ranking participant, which was excellent money in South Africa just then. EO's leadership element was paid between fifty to a hundred percent more and though it might have been expected, nobody who signed took the money and ran. Many of these former soldiers had been like "family" while still in the SADF. Everybody knew everybody else and being a fairly closed society, that kind of illegality would have been difficult anyway.

By South African standards, the emoluments offered were outstanding, and that at a time when you could do roughly the same with a single rand in South Africa as a dollar would buy you in America. That meant roughly two or three times as much. Also, the economy was in a downturn and it was expected that EO would be inundated with applicants.

There were initially no ranks within EO, the men being broadly graded according to positions held while still in the SADF. Barlow appointed team leaders, and to start with the men were allowed to choose their own section leaders. All were warned that there would be no death benefits for members' families. Nor, he stated, was there to be any medical insurance.[5]

Unbeknown to Eeben Barlow and the others running the show, Tony Buckingham just then was fending off heavy pressure from Luanda to get the show on the road. In the simplest language he was told that he had taken their million dollars and they expected results, like, they said, "within the following week!" In turn, Buckingham pressured Barlow to turn on the heat, to the extent that the departure date to Angola for those who had signed was put forward to the next day, February 21st. That was barely a week after the recruitment program had started.

More serious, the biggest problem for everybody just then was that instead of the more than a hundred men envisaged for the operation, all the five recruiters had been able to come up with was thirty-five combat-ready volunteers.

True to his promise to Buckingham, Barlow dispatched Mauritz le Roux and four others to Windhoek. They flew to the Namibian capital on a commercial flight, from where, in a Cessna 404, they were taken to the old Cuban Air Force base at Cabo Ledo—about an hour's drive south of Luanda. Later dubbed "Ghost Rider"—with the registration number V5WAA painted on its tail—this aircraft would serve EO regularly for the next few months. But since travel to Angola required clearance from air traffic control, the pilot lodged a phony flight plan to the former military town of Rundu, in the northwest corner of the recently independent Namibia. Interestingly, the ruse worked for duration.

Back in South Africa, Barlow was encountering more problems. Some of the original group had opted out and the team had to scratch hard for replacements. At the end of it, the total number still hovered around forty, all of whom were being sent to Angola in groups, some in small charter planes from Grand Central Airport in Johannesburg, others on regular South African Airways flights to Luanda.

As one of the men commented, "There were sections coming up to Cabo Ledo whereas we'd been expecting platoons." Still, by the end of the week, just about the entire crew had gathered at EO's new Angolan base.

As Harry Carlse explained, nothing took place quite so simply either. "At Jan Smuts Airport—on the way to Windhoek—some of our guys who were traveling South African Airways were pulled over by airport security. We were a tough, rough-looking bunch and that immediately raised suspicions. They even queried if we were a military group.

"It didn't help that we claimed to be hikers. Nor that almost every one of us was wearing similar kit and that our tickets showed us heading for the same place. But we'd been briefed and the boys stuck to their story. In the end we got through."

EO established a temporary headquarters adjacent to the Cabo Ledo terminal's living quarters where, on the first morning, the men were briefed. Unita had attacked Soyo late the previous January, the spokesman explained, and shortly afterward the Angolan Army had been bundled out of the enclave with fairly heavy losses. All expatriate staff and local workers at the facility had been evacuated.

"We were also told," said Carlse, "that within the first day or so, the insurgents had been able to destroy many of the offices. So too, with communication equipment in the complex. A week later they trashed Soyo itself, a town of about four thousand people." It puzzled EO management that much of the Soyo oil facility and the adjacent port as well as its ancillary offshore supply base that had been used to service offshore oil rigs were all left intact.

Since the new headquarters at Cabo Ledo was adjacent to an existing Angolan Army military headquarters, with a detachment of FAA Commandos, the men took a good deal of interest in how their future compadres conducted themselves. What they found wasn't reassuring. The Angolan troops were a rum bunch. Most were ill-disciplined and lacked the most basic military skills. Many didn't even know how to hold their weapons properly, never mind march. As for their shooting skills . . .

Which prompted Buks Buys to suggest that since they were all going to war together, perhaps they should spend some of their time putting these black soldiers through their paces. Simon Mann, having arrived only a short while before, scotched that idea. His argument was that since British and French soldiers were alike, their Angolan

counterparts were likewise, since all armed services operated to roughly the same professional criteria, which of course was absurd. He also
told an EO gathering he had received good assurances from Luanda
that the FAA troops accompanying them into Soyo were "totally up to
scratch," a statement which got him some odd looks from the South
Africans present. Also, he confided, he'd been told that the opposition
they were likely to encounter at Soyo consisted solely of nine Unita
policemen armed with .38 Special revolvers.

Talking to a few of the men afterward, one got the impression that
it didn't take Simon Mann—an Old Etonian – very long to be labeled
by all as an arrogant and obnoxious prick. In spite of his previous so-
called Special Air Service experience, he seemed hardly to have a grasp
of what the operation entailed. Nor did things change once the fighting started, with a tiny group up against huge numbers of the enemy.

What annoyed most was Mann's habit of constantly having to
remind people of his role in an elite British unit. In dealing with this
altogether South African force, he could be disdainful, even insulting
to anyone or anything from that country. It perhaps tells you more
that he took absolutely no part in the hostilities that followed, even
though the manpower issue remained perilous from the start.

(Which also makes you wonder how he ended up fitting in with
the guys in a Harare prison a decade later, especially since some of the
inmates in Chikurubi were also part of the Soyo mob?)

With the entire group gathered at Cabo Ledo, a command structure
was quickly sorted out among the men. Roelf van Heerden (he of
Koidu, Sierra Leone notoriety) helped with the planning, while Lafras
Luitingh came into the picture because Barlow moved Buks Buys into
the position of commanding colonel, though he too, by the time it was
all over, never once set foot in Soyo.

Altogether four Executive Outcomes majors were appointed for
the three sections planned. These were the Rhodesian War veteran Phil
Smith, 32 Battalion's Harry Ferreira, Lafras Luitingh, and finally,
Mauritz le Roux, the unit's engineering specialist. Many of the
younger Special Forces men found themselves with Luitingh, while
Ferreira seemed to attract the more mature but still-active vets.

For his sins, Smith was stuck with what some of the more experienced operators termed "the plebs": those with the least military
know-how or combat experience. He only had three SF men in his
unit—an ex-Koevoet veteran, a Recce vet and a former Foreign

Legionnaire—while many of the others were physically out of shape and seemed more interested in the money.

Tactical planning for the operation was in the hands of Luitingh, Phil Smith and one of the section leaders.

While it wasn't Lafras Luitingh's job to liaise with Colonel Pepe de Castro, the Angolan commander who would be in overall control— the same man, incidentally, who was to lead EO's attack on the diamond fields at Cafunfo a while later—he appeared to slip into that capacity as things progressed. All agreed that it was a convenient arrangement, especially since Luitingh had many years of Special Forces combat experience.

For his part, partly because he could speak English, de Castro was to become a familiar figure among Angola's mercenaries. He was also designated by Luanda to be involved in all subsequent EO campaigns. Meanwhile, he tasked Lafras Luitingh with the job of ground commander of the operation.

The next day the group was issued Angolan Army uniforms and identity cards. All showed them to be "Advisors," though as one of the men asked at a briefing session, since few of them spoke any Portuguese, who should they say they were advising if they were captured?

Weapons provided by the government included AKs, RPKs, PKMs and RPDs, as well as Dragunov sniping rifles. Training included sessions with former Soviet 60mm and 82mm mortars, as well as an update on section attacks, contact and grenade drills. There were also house-clearing exercises and some of the more arcane stratagems with which Special Forces like to amuse themselves. According to Carlse, the experienced men quite enjoyed it all, but it was hard on those who weren't prepared for anything really physical.

On March 3, with all preliminary work completed at the old Cuban base, the entire group, together with all their equipment, was flown north to the Angolan enclave on Cabinda, which lies on the north shore of the Congo River. En route, they passed over Soyo and the men crowded around the Antonov-24's port-holes to catch a glimpse of their ultimate destination. They were not disappointed. The plan was to spend the night at the Cabinda base and attack the following day.

Two large self-propelled barges operated by the Angolan Navy were to leave Cabo Ledo for the north at the same time, each with five hundred Angolan soldiers onboard, together with the bulk of the heavy stuff, their ammunition and other hardware. There were also four T54/55 tanks, two to a vessel. But on pulling out of Cabo Ledo, one of the barges had mechanical problems, which meant that everybody onboard the crippled vessel had to climb over on to the second barge and bring everything with them. The tanks, of course, stayed.

But the mishap meant that the expected time of arrival of the remaining barge was delayed. With its increased load, it could only manage a few knots and would arrive off Soyo a day late.

Taking Soyo with such a small force was an inordinately tough call. Certainly, had EO been aware of what was waiting for them on the ground, the job would never even have rated consideration. As we now know, they faced a long, hard battle to win back the town as well as Kwando port. They were eventually required to also clear much of the surrounding areas that had been infiltrated by guerrillas. But first, they had to take the main military base, and that lay south of two large oil storage tanks at Quefiquena.

The harbor was included in this configuration because, until then, it had served the needs of this vital enterprise as well as the even larger military base at Campo Oito that was supposed to guard it.

As indicated by its name, Campo Oito—in Portuguese, Camp Eight—lay eight kilometers south of Soyo. What made it doubly difficult was that the entire complex was surrounded by some of the most magnificent primeval forest in Africa, which though "triple canopy spectacular," sometimes made combat extremely hazardous.

Under normal circumstances, trying to displace several hundred well-entrenched enemy forces from positions that had been reinforced for more than a month should have required something like a force of brigade strength. Armor and close air support would also have backed the effort. Indeed, Luanda promised it all, but in the end, very little materialized. An Angolan Air Force Hind did make the occasional cursory pass, mostly at heights in excess of five thousand feet, but that was useless.

In his initial discussions with the Angolans, Barlow made several stipulations that he felt were critical to the venture's success. The first was that the Luanda government pay for the operation in advance. Another was that, while it lasted, EO would not be interfered with, either by the Angolan Army or the country's politicians. The same held for government commissars and political functionaries, a feature of the country's Marxist establishment. There was no argument from Luanda on any of the points raised by the South African.

Consequently, instead of attacking Soyo on March 4, Buks Buys sent in a three-man reconnaissance team to infiltrate the area the night before. Until then, the EO squad had to rely solely on intelligence provided by the Angolan Army, which, they soon realized, was sketchy. Most of it was obscure and invariably based on second- and third-hand sources. Usually they got it all wrong.

"FAA couldn't even give us the coordinates of the town," one of the men recalled. The men were thankful for the delay because apart from being able to recce the target area from up close, the supply barge with its support force and ammunition had still not pitched. The supplies onboard were to become a critical asset during the early stages of fighting. In fact, without them, the South Africans would almost certainly have been overrun.

Finally, a briefing for the entire group—together with final preparations—took place the next day at Cabinda's airfield with both Simon Mann and Tony Buckingham present. Also there was Colonel Pepe de Castro, who was to follow the attack group to Soyo after the initial landings.

By now there had been several joint planning meetings involving the FAA and EO command. It was agreed that the two tanks would provide immediate back up, together with the thousand Angolan troops, their ammunition and food. Since the South Africans would go in first—with the FAA element being landed from the sea—all forty men, in three Mi-17 helicopters—would come in by air from the north.

One issue raised at that final meeting by some of the men was concern about the non-arrival of the on-site medical support team that the recruiters said would be in place before they set out. The company had promised to set up a field hospital alongside the runway with Dr. Francis Smit, the first MD to be badged as a Special Force operator in the SADF in attendance. But, as they were soon to discover, he was only to arrive weeks later and then after much prompting by the men as casualties started coming in. Those fighting across the water were kept in ignorance of this fact, which was to have serious consequences later.

Undeterred, the force finally set out early on the morning of March 5, flying the entire leg across the Congo River barely three feet above the water. Buks Buys would have liked to have the men on the ground before dawn, but none of the Angolans could fly at night. So first light it was.

Composed of three sections, which included two twelve-man stopper groups deployed to east and west, the fourteen-strong Assault Group—including Harry Ferreira, Luitingh, Phil Smith and le Roux— went straight in with the Angolan chopper pilot, who put his load down on the beach about a mile short of the oil storage tanks. The original plan was for him to land directly behind the tanks, but having reached the opposite shore and aware of a potential for trouble, a rather wild-eyed, trembling pilot would go no further.

This immediately presented the attackers with a raft of problems, not least being that their packs were extremely heavy with extra ammunition, food and water. They'd never expected to have to hike anything like that distance through dense undergrowth, compounded by a swamp and puddles of mud sometimes feet deep.

The answer was for them to drop some of their heavier stuff, which was not the best idea, but, as Lafras Luitingh admitted afterward, there was no alternative. The first items ditched were their 60mm Patmore mortars and shells. The attackers were not to know it yet but it was a bad mistake: waiting for them at Quefiquena was a Unita force at least three hundred strong.

EO's initial target, explained Harry Carlse, was Unita's living quarters at the Quefiquena base. "But being dropped so far away, it was a while before we could make contact with the original Recce team: it was their job to lead us in," he explained. "We'd also agreed beforehand that the stopper group, Team One, would provide early warning to the west of the LZ. Team Three took up a position to the east. Our group was responsible for the first assault."

Instead of attracting fire immediately, the first of the EO teams moving forward took the Unita guerrillas by surprise. They found a bunch of rebels congregating at the main gate of the target compound, obviously intrigued by the unusual helicopter activity in their area, "but when we sneaked up alongside one of the big storage tanks, they never even saw us. We opened fire and within twenty minutes we'd overrun their positions and forced them to vacate the compound and make a dash for it into the jungle.

"They left in such a hurry that their radios were still playing. There was money, clothes and weapons strewn about. Surprise was absolute, and obviously that pleased us."

What also surprised the South Africans was that the defenders had secured their AKs to the steel fence surrounding the complex with wire. "So when we hit them, they left it all behind. It was obviously a measure to prevent troops from grabbing their guns and bolting." Still, fire from the base remained intense and after a short consultation with the others, Mauritz le Roux decided to head back to the LZ and fetch the mortars.

Two men were designated to accompany him, but he hadn't been on the track for minutes before they disappeared. Only later did he discover that they had returned to the rest of group; neither had regarded the trip back to the LZ as a good survival option.

"That was probably the loneliest walk of my entire life, as much as was possible in that difficult terrain, I moved at the double. Swamp waters prevented me from getting up any speed and naturally I was aware that I could have run into the enemy at any time. But I didn't and so I retrieved the tubes and a bunch of bombs and headed back, most times with the jungle within touching distance on both sides. It was pretty hairy."

Having got back to the others, the additional weapons came in handy for finally routing the remainder of Quefiquena's defenders.

At about this point, one of the stopper groups a few hundred yards down the road toward the west ambushed a green Renault, killing its driver. Inside they found the vehicle stuffed with piles of kwanza banknotes, three feet high. Worth millions in the Angolan national currency, Executive Outcomes had hijacked the enemy battalion's pay for the month. Similarly, a white Mitsubishi trying to flee the base was destroyed shortly afterward and all its occupants killed.

After that, things didn't go so well. With surprise lost, Unita opened fire on one of the other teams from about three hundred yards, but fierce retaliatory fire drove that group back. The respite didn't last, though. Unita quickly regrouped and launched a counterattack that halted any kind of forward momentum.

Carlse: "Worse, the barge with all our reinforcements and armor hadn't arrived as it should have. It was six hours late and we had to fight hard to retain what we'd taken. When it eventually got there, the naval units came under concerted fire when Unita forces—sitting on a patch of high ground that overlooked the region—laid down a hail of fire that included recoilless rifles, RPGs, mortars, and light and heavy machine guns." By now the South Africans were running short of ammunition.

Finally, about noon, the three-hundred-strong contingent of government troops arrived, and none too soon. The 82mm mortars they ferried ashore provided immediate relief. With the South Africans taking charge, the Angolan soldiers were spread around the outer defenses, though it was immediately clear, with some of them wandering aimlessly and dangerously about, almost like schoolboys on a stroll, they had absolutely no concept of what danger they faced.

More problems followed. Because of sustained fire, the barge captain, in bringing his vessel onto the beach, forgot to drop his retaining anchor. That meant that while the troops were able to clamber ashore, the vessel ended up broadside to the beach. Worse, it couldn't land its tanks.

One of these T-54s, a noisy, smoke-belching beast, was eventually brought ashore on the fourth day, but because it attracted so much attention—coupled to a hopelessly incompetent crew—the single piece of armor made marginal difference to the outcome of the Battle for Soyo, though it did eventually help EO to take the adjacent town. The other tank ended up buried in soft sea sand up to its turret and couldn't be dislodged. It is still there.

The additional FAA support, for all its shortcomings, did result in Unita halting its retaliation for a couple of hours. A second attack followed when several hundred Unita troops came forward in platoon-strength groups. According to Carlse, it was an extremely determined effort, backed by mortars and rockets from further back. The defenders could immediately detect a new and single-minded discipline among the attackers coming at them. Clearly, these fighters were Savimbi's Special Force Groupos and they knew what was required of them.

Mauritz le Roux: "They headed right at us, with the issue being made more difficult by a ring of ten- or-twelve-feet-deep oil retaining canals that had originally been built as a precautionary measure to prevent spills from the oil storage tanks. They completely surrounded the complex.

"When the rebels popped into these culverts, we couldn't see them, nor they us because they were at a much lower level than our positions. But they were actually only fifteen, twenty yards below our lines and we could hear them talking among themselves." That didn't stop the infiltrators from hurling scores of grenades from down there and, as le Roux recalls, it was then that some of the men started to get hurt.

"We retaliated, of course, but our numbers were small compared to theirs," said Carlse, adding that the battle lasted about ninety minutes before Unita pulled back again.

Then the unit's only medic, "Bossie" Bosman, was hurt when, in a bid to escape sustained mortar fire, he hurled himself headlong into one of the culverts. It wasn't an intentional option: rather, he thought he would land on grass, so dense was the undergrowth. Bosman was fortunate to clamber out before the enemy grabbed him.

At about this point, said le Roux, some of the men realized that they had been short-changed by Buckingham. "We were obviously in very serious trouble. There were very few of us and huge numbers of the enemy. Our Angolan allies were all but useless. All we had between us were small hand-held radios. Where were the nine policemen with revolvers that Simon Mann had talked about at Cabo Ledo, the guys asked. The most serious shortcoming of all was that there was no way that we could tell those people waiting in Cabinda what conditions on the ground around us were like. The radios the groups had been issued were short-range and contact with headquarters across the water was impossible.

"Consequently, there could be no back-up at short notice and obviously, no casualty evacuation should the worst happen. Also, we'd been told that there would be 'an open-heart surgery' clinic made available on one of the oil rigs, but we never saw anything like it. There wasn't even a doctor waiting on the other side for those wounded who were ferried out the next day."

Le Roux is outspoken about the way he and the other South Africans were "exploited" by their British bosses with almost no regard for safety. As he commented bitterly, "They would never have done that if the boys had been British . . . they wouldn't have been allowed to."

Some really serious business started not long afterward, with the guerrillas probing attackers' defenses towards the south and east of Quefiquena. That affected some of the EO groups who had followed the initial group in, with them taking hits and having to make do with a precarious defense.

The section leaders felt that the biggest problem facing them at that point was the foliage that surrounded much of the complex. As le Roux recalls, the entire area was fringed by heavy jungle, so any kind of clear field of fire was out of the question. In places the jungle actually overhung their positions, so that some of the men could barely see fifteen yards into the undergrowth. Unita ruthlessly exploited this advantage.

The Soyo campaign was a close-quarters operation throughout. Said one of the men, "The rebels would infiltrate right up to our positions at night to attack. Or they would toss some grenades at us. Then they would call and taunt us, telling our blokes that they were going to die."

Another recalled that there were times when rebel fighters showed no fear: "Their perseverance amazed us all. Also, their combat tactics were excellent," he declared.

Then Jeff Landsberg was wounded in the foot and his mates had to haul him to cover. With a small squad under Harry Carlse, this team had been trying to get at one of the enemy's artillery pieces—a D30—but eventually that effort was abandoned. They were not only visual to the enemy but also badly isolated from the main force. As Carlse reckons today, it would have been crazy to go on.

He takes up the story: "With darkness that first night approaching fast, all three sections regrouped in an attempt to establish some sort of procedure. We knew that there would be a night attack because it was the way that Unita operated. But at about this point, some of the EO guys said they were worried about being sucked into something that none of them could handle. Obviously they were worried about casualties and they had a point. We'd been at it from the time we'd arrived.

"Others declared that it hadn't been made clear to them when they took the job that there would be so much fighting. A few argued that, rather, they'd envisioned training the Angolans. These were a bunch of rattled men.

"As section leaders, we believed that our best option lay in setting up a defensive line alongside the compound that we'd captured earlier. By nine that night—almost within touching distance of the jungle—everybody had dug themselves a foxhole, most of which were spaced perhaps five or ten yards apart. Elsewhere there were large open areas that needed to be dominated and for which we knew a large body of government troops had been deployed and were waiting for orders to attack."

At midnight, Unita arrived and the guerrilla movement launched its biggest attack, lasting more than two hours. With all forces on call, the EO leaders were confident that they could hold their positions. However, when their FAA allies didn't react when ordered to open fire, it took the South Africans about a minute to realize that they were on their own. The Angolan troops had disappeared into the night.

As some of the men reflected afterward, they should have expected it since so few government soldiers had been issued with more than a single magazine for their AKs. As for their illustrious officers, almost all of them hotfooted it toward the rear after the first shot.

During this attack the South Africans took their third casualty with Harry Ferreira wounded in the arm. A short while later Theuns Kruger took shrapnel in his head from a grenade, though neither wound was serious. But it was certainly indicative of how close the two forces were to each other because the grenade that wounded Kruger had been hurled from only yards away. By now, all three section leaders were aware that if they didn't react more forcefully, Unita had enough manpower and seemingly unlimited supplies of hardware to eventually breach their lines.

One of the more revealing comments about this attack was that incoming fire was so fierce that those of the men who didn't have their kit bags in their foxholes with them had them shot to ribbons where they'd placed them, just above their heads.

With daylight, work was immediately started to reorganize MPLA defenses. Barely an eighth of the original FAA force was still around at sunrise, though they were joined by another group who slunk in guiltily when additional ammunition and water was handed out. It had originally been arranged before leaving Cabinda that a helicopter supply drop would be sent on the second day, and this was the most welcome sight of the operation so far. They also used the opportunity to ship out the wounded.

All the while, the EO fighters were able to observe a white van moving backward and forward between Unita's rear echelons and Campo Oito. It soon became clear that the vehicle was resupplying the guerrilla forward lines with ammunition and taking back the wounded. Le Roux reckons that they would have been able to do something about it, but the vehicle always remained just out of range.

By now Unita had also started lobbing heavy mortars at the defenders—none too efficiently because most landed wide. For the rest of the time, they fired artillery salvos of four or five shells at a time. After dark, the previous night's drama was repeated, only this time defending FAA troops were a little more responsive. There wasn't a man among them who wasn't aware that if the South African position were overrun, they'd be the next to be slaughtered.

Mutterings among some of the EO men was now becoming audible. More than half the force wanted out. This wasn't what they had come to Angola for, they insisted. Also, they argued, they weren't all infantry trained and things could only get worse. As one of the more experienced fighters concluded, "They resented having to work hard for that nice big paycheck which, with all the percentage incentives now being offered, had become very fat indeed."

At the same time, things were going badly for the government's troops. While the South Africans helped where they could, their Angolan counterparts were simply not able to withstand protracted fire. Some FAA soldiers became disoriented. Others broke ranks and fled. Language, too, was a problem, even though four EO members could speak good enough Portuguese to make themselves understood.

That night brought more of the same. Though the EO officers had extended their lines forward about three hundred yards, largely to avoid Unita getting into the retaining canal around the base, and had placed a large FAA squad in position, when an attack came at about midnight the South Africans were again on their own. Once more all the Angolans fled.

On Sunday, the 7th of March, EO had planned in conjunction with the FAA commander to launch an early-morning retaliatory raid against the rebels, but none of the Angolan troops appeared. Instead, those who were left—about a hundred of the original thousand—wandered into camp shortly before noon. As Mauritz le Roux says, it was a monumental disaster.

Having spread the recalcitrants out in an extended line along the front and urged them to dig themselves in, everybody could do little more than wait for the next attack. It didn't take long in coming.

To Harry Carlse, it was obvious that their lines could not hold indefinitely. The Angolan soldiers lacked both the tenacity and incentive to face seasoned guerrillas. So grabbing seven of his mates and calling the tank forward, they moved in among the FAA ranks, with a man stationing himself every ten yards or so to fight alongside them. They quickly got these irregulars into something of a routine, encouraging them to coordinate magazine changes and to try to make an effective stand.

As he recalls today, the presence of this small group of South Africans right there among the FAA worked wonders. "Suddenly, with us shouting orders, showing them how and retaliating accurately, it started to have an effect. We gave them the courage to do the same. And in the end, that's exactly what happened. When they looked again Unita was on the run and our lines were able to move out even further." The tank, meanwhile, was blasting merrily away at anything that moved and became a powerful rallying point in the battle that followed.

With that, more of the EO men started to move up while others began to prepare food. Earlier, Le Roux had cut some forty-four gallon drums in half, cleaned them out and used them to boil water for cooking rice.

"We distributed great globs of rice while handing out ammunition. We also passed around extra magazines that were desperately needed by some of the African soldiers. Many of them still had only one with which they had been issued and, considering the circumstances, that was ridiculous," le Roux commented.

What was also a little absurd, he added, "was that once the rice was on the boil, more and more of these FAA troops would emerge from the jungle." At one stage there were so many stragglers arriving that le Roux thought a bus might have stopped close by and disgorged them all.

"We told them they could eat only if they stayed and fought, and with that, we probably doubled our numbers."

That evening, the third, Carlse remembers, presaged the first quiet night of the campaign.

With the helicopter bringing in the casualties from across the water, shock immediately set in among those waiting in Cabinda. Buckingham was appalled, especially since some of the wounds were stultifying. And there was still no doctor!

It stayed that way until some of the men were flown to Windhoek four days later, by which time Landsberg's suppurating foot had started to rot in a climate that is a constant hundred percent humidity almost year round. The story given the Namibian hospital to which he and some of the others were admitted was that he was part of a group of South Africans lifting mines in Angola. Looking back, Landsberg was lucky to have avoided gangrene.

What soon became apparent to those watching this debacle that was growing more intense each day, was that the so-called control group in Cabinda had almost no conception of what was going on across the water. In fact, with no comms in place, apart from messages passed back and forth by the helicopter pilots, they had no way of knowing. This was another of Simon Mann's blunders, since it was he who had originally vetoed buying more elaborate communication equipment that could have kept everybody in the picture.

For their part, Keller and Buys were distraught at what the wounded were telling them. For a start, the numbers against which the tiny force was up against stunned them. Luanda had told them it would be a walkover (underscoring, too, how little the average South African knew about Savimbi's Special Forces). Even Buckingham was perplexed enough to use his satellite phone to call his SAS contacts to again ask for volunteers for a parachute drop. He offered good rewards for any takers. There were none.

Despite the brief measure of relief that the Mi-17 brought each time it went across, conditions within EO's ranks continued to deteriorate. By now about the half the team wanted out, especially since they had been almost continually under attack ever since they got there.

On the morning of the third day, consequently, rather than have a mutiny on their hands, the section leaders—who had been forced to accept a more aggressive, independent role—made the decision: those who wanted out should go and there should be no delay. They agreed that the dissenters had become more of an encumbrance than a help. Also, they sensed that a negative approach within the ranks was affecting the ability of the others to perform. In any event, while contributing little, they were also using up valuable food, ammunition and water.

Luitingh asked his Angolan counterpart to request an airlift out for those who wanted to leave and the quitters were back in Cabo Ledo by nightfall. This immediately prompted Buckingham to offer an extra $3,000 per man bonus if the EO force could hold Soyo for thirty days. At the same time, EO was now reduced to less than twenty men on the ground and still facing a most determined enemy.

But the mercenary group still had a few advantages, one of which was in the air. EO had one asset that offered superlative support throughout the operation. That was "Ghost Rider," the same twin-engined Cessna that originally ferried the men from Windhoek to Cabo Ledo and which was now based in Cabinda. Its job was to scout opposing forces' positions and, where possible, provide ranging and other observations for the mortar teams.

It is worth mentioning that the plane was originally bought at a DEA auction in Miami after being seized for drug running in the Caribbean. Its role in the skies over Soyo just then was every bit as dangerous; in fact, even more so, since Unita would use all the Triple-

A it had, and in particular, its Chinese-made 14.5s to try to bring the plane down.

At this juncture we should take a closer look at the enemy faced by Executive Outcomes throughout the operation to recover Soyo for the Angolan government.

Opposing the company on the ground was, in part, a powerful adversary—Savimbi's Special Forces—that had originally been trained by the South African Defence Force. This was an elite group of experienced combat veterans with years of jungle fighting behind them and they made up perhaps nearly a quarter of the Unita force at Soyo/Quefiquena.

During the South African/Angolan war of the 1980s, these same specialist guerrillas had been put through their paces and gone into battle with some of the most experienced South Africans. The latter were skilled tacticians including senior officers like Fred Oelschig, Les Rudman, Bert Sachse and Jan Breytenbach, as well as Eric Rabie, a 32 Battalion Reconnaissance Wing officer. All these people had mixed it with the best that the Angolan Army had to offer for more than a decade.

In the view of a confidential CIA report compiled at the time, Savimbi's Special Forces and Penetration Battalions were rated to be among the best of all guerrilla combatants. They had to have been because at one stage in the 1980s, Unita had occupied almost all of the country. And while they might have lost some of their verve with their old South African allies out of the picture, they were still a pretty formidable combat group.

Having taken Soyo with the intention of crippling Luanda financially, Savimbi had no intention of having his troops pushed out of the area by a group of people that for years he had trusted and regarded as his friends, some of them quite intimately.

Previously, during the South African/Angolan war, SADF personnel who instructed and worked with Unita were part of the elite Directorate of Special Tasks within the "Directorate of Intelligence Operations." It was they who brought Savimbi's Penetration Battalion into line with modern insurgency procedures, the thrust being to conduct small team guerrilla operations against numerically superior enemy forces well into the interior of Angola. Such elite Unita squads were known as *Commandos Especial*.

Consequently, those South Africans who worked with Unita

(against FAPLA,[6] as the Angolan Army was then called) had about as good a measure of rebel capabilities as anybody. Former Special Tasks operators had been into battle with them and quite a number were wounded in action against Luanda's troops.

Within Unita's own ambit, these cadres would refer to each other as *Groupos de Bate* (Striking Groups). Composed of a fifty-man fighting unit—divided in turn into four ten-man fighting teams together with a ten-man command team (consisting of the group commander and second-in-command, plus eight men carrying platoon support weapons)—they were effective under almost any conditions. This last element sometimes acted as a reserve and was occasionally placed in a security capacity for the group commander.

Said one of the operators who handled Unita training: "They were structured so as to have the capability to conduct long-range reconnaissance missions, either in ten-man teams or their more compact four-man 'sticks,' which was something their instructors had learnt in Rhodesia's guerrilla war."

Alternatively, they could launch aggressive, hard-hitting attacks or extended offensive operations when operating as a full fifty-man group, often going out for a year at a stretch. While this might be regarded as excessive elsewhere, there was often no other way of getting about in a country where, most times, Unita had only their legs to get from A to B, even if it was sometimes on the far side of the country. In earlier years South Africa would use its air force to move Unita contingents and supplies about, but with Mandela taking over the Pretoria government, that support soon ended.

"The personnel for these Special Commandos were initially selected from seasoned guerrilla units. They were then given seven months of intensive special operations and guerrilla warfare training," the South African operator explained.

It was a harsh regimen, he recalled, and it took guts to qualify. Armed with the best weapons available on the international market and trained to the highest standards in guerrilla warfare, as well as conventional offensive operations, Unita Special Forces squads were responsible for many notable successes that Savimbi notched up over the years. Ultimately they showed themselves to be especially good against fortified FAPLA, Cuban and Soviet positions wherever they encountered them.

Now, since Savimbi desperately wanted Soyo re-captured, some of the Unita attacks grew in intensity. According to FAA radio intercepts that came through afterward, his instructions to the *Groupos de Bate* was "Do everything you can to retake Soyo,"

However, there was no "fighting to death." Unita's South African instructors had long ago instilled in their cadres the maxim that lives should not be wasted. In true guerrilla fashion, it was argued that it was better to live to fight another day. Savimbi was also aware that while his guerrillas had taken a lot of casualties, they also killed a lot more Angolan government troops.

The biggest battle of the campaign kicked off at first light on the morning of the fourth day.

Throughout the night, Mauritz le Roux and other EO men on watch thought they heard an unusual amount of rustling in the grass around their position, but being exhausted from days of fighting, they put it down to wind. Only once the battle had been joined did they realize that Unita had spent hours positioning its force for the coming onslaught.

It was extremely well organized, le Roux told me years afterward. "They moved quietly and competently into place. Not one of them allowed his position to be betrayed by the noise of metal upon metal. Nor did we hear a whisper among any of them . . . these guys had been solidly trained . . . they knew their stuff."

Also during the night they could detect engine noises, possibly the white van moving about behind Unita lines, but thought nothing more of it. It had been doing that from the start. A Unita officer captured months later by an EO Recce team admitted under questioning that more than a thousand new men had been brought forward that night, many of them *Groupos de Bate*, he declared proudly.

The EO officers were confident that, whatever happened, they would be able to hold the four hundred yards or so of frontline along which their forces were dispersed. They'd also distributed a huge amount of ammunition the previous evening for just such an eventuality. There'd be no shortages when the attack came, they reckoned. Nor was there.

One of the mercenaries, J.J. de Beer, had just been wakened for his watch when he stood up on the edge of his foxhole. In a passive, sleepy gesture he stretched his arms out above his head. With that, just about every enemy PKM, RPD, RPG rocket, RPK and mortar within a half-mile opened up. Without even thinking about it, he buckled his legs and plopped full-length into his hole. He remembers it being the first time at Soyo that they had come up against rifle grenades.

Though the battle raged on the verge of a series of cassava fields for about three hours, it seemed to slacken a little every thirty minutes or so, which allowed both sides to take stock. Unita used the break to haul back their wounded and dead, something at which they were adept. It was a Maoism that Savimbi had adopted from the very beginning of his guerrilla campaign: he'd argue that the enemy became demoralized if they had nothing to show for their efforts, particularly after long periods of fighting.

EO too, had incurred losses. One of the men, Oosthuizen, had the sights of his RPG blow back into his face. The heavy steel rim on the weapon cut him severely. In fact, when you meet the man today, you can still see the extent of the wound. Blinded and in pain, Roelf van Heerden briefly got out of his foxhole to help him reorient himself and when he returned to his tiny piece of turf, he found that a rifle grenade had exploded where he had been lying minutes before.

There were many close encounters in the battle that served to remove just about every leaf in the trees and bushes above and around the defenders' trench lines. Louis Engelbrecht, a Koevoet veteran from the old South West Africa, was using his PKM when he suddenly found that it would no longer fire on full auto. He'd cock his weapon and fire a single shot. Then he'd have to cock it again. That went on a while, until he discovered that an AK bullet had neatly lodged in the PKM's gas chamber. It had entered just below the supplementary barrel that operates the PKM's blowback system. An inch up, down or sideways, and he would have taken the bullet in his head. Lucky man.

At this point Carlse remembers some of the men starting to act peculiar. There were distinct signs of shell shock among a few of them.

Their eyes would quiver from side to side and a few would act and talk irrationally, but not enough to get themselves killed. The ongoing attrition was affecting the guys, as it had some of the FAA troops. A few tried to bolt into the jungle before being cut down by automatic fire. Altogether fourteen Angolan troops were killed in the attack, with more than a hundred wounded, several dozen seriously.

For several more hours the battle went on. Then, gradually, to the surprise of all, it slackened. According to Mauritz le Roux, something totally unexpected then took place. The defenders were astonished to see the Unita commanders pull their men back and it didn't take long for the entire area to be clear. The guerrilla force, too, it seems, had had enough, though word later came through that their senior commander had been killed by a mortar bomb which exploded right next to him.

It took a while longer for the dust to settle. Though elated to have survived that turmoil, the merc officers checked defenses and pulled back those that needed attention. Others were relieved of duty when their distress became obvious. But it all took time. Meantime, more ammunition was handed out and preparations were started to cook the morning meal.

Throughout the Soyo campaign, which went on intermittently for another two months (and afterward as well, when EO marched toward the diamond fields) there were consistent reports coming through that indicated Unita, too, was using mercenaries, possibly South Africans.

There was no question that Savimbi had used mercs in the past. Bob Denard had spent a brief time working with the rebels earlier in the war. More recently, Pretoria was abuzz with stories about agents recruiting seasoned soldiers for the other side, right there in the South African capital city. At Soyo, Angolan Army intelligence spoke about four white mercenaries having come across from the Congo during the first few days of the action.

As a result, it was no surprise after the final battle that some of the EO officers were shown part of a scalp recovered from a soldier who had had half his head blown away. The blood-matted hair was blond while the bandana that the dead man wore was red.

EO sources subsequently claimed that more than a thousand Unita died in the battle for the Soyo oil complex. However, this didn't make sense since Savimbi—at the height of his strength—never had more than thirty thousand men in the field. In their most vicious battles against FAPLA, Cuban and Russian brigades—with artillery, tank and aircraft action combined—they never suffered more than three or four hundred of their soldiers killed in any single conflagration, though there could often be a dozen of those on a dozen successive days.

Unita never did come back to Quefiquena in any kind of numbers, though attacks would take place there sporadically. Somehow their cast-iron doggedness had cracked in a contest of resolve, where luck probably played as big a role as expertise. After all, up to this point, no South African combatant had been killed.

About half the remaining South African force also decided not to push their options unduly and asked to be sent back. To the majority, it was a sensible choice and Lafras Luitingh and the others didn't argue. Those that wanted out were put on the first Mi-17 to touch down later that day, though they were told to leave their food, water and ammunition for those who stayed.

With the departure for home of that batch, Executive Outcomes strength at Soyo was down to twenty-four men, though the absconders were soon replaced by a fresh bunch of recruits. The newcomers were markedly better at playing at war than many of those previously recruited because EO's command structure could now be fastidious. They chose carefully who would do their fighting for them and it showed in subsequent campaigns in Angola and Sierra Leone. For a start, all future recruits had to have Special Forces experience and have taken part in at least one major military campaign.

While the oil tanks at Quefiquena had lost their luster for Unita, the guerrilla force didn't totally withdraw. Rather, with many of the main force having been sent back to bolster defenses around the diamond fields, there were still groups of rebels sporadically attacking FAA convoys and strongpoints. EO was constantly being called out to help.

One of the first of the areas that needed to be cleared of an enemy presence, Luitingh and the others decided, was the town of Soyo itself. Unita had spent good time and effort in a bid to ingratiate itself with the civilian population. Using the old TM 54/55 as well as a bulldozer that had been left behind by the oil contractors, about half the squad moved into town where they promptly annexed every civilian car.

One of the best of the lot was a white Toyota Corolla which immediately had all its doors ripped off, including the one over the trunk. With that, the company had made itself an improvised "troop carrier" that could ferry eighteen FAA troops to battle at a time.

On the sixth day, the entire EO force moved closer to town and occupied Cuanza Base, a small hotel-type facility that had previously been used by employees of the oil companies waiting for dispatch to their postings, vacation or home. It was an improvement on what they had made do with before, with a fully-equipped kitchen and, to the delight of some, their own gym and pool.

The Unita threat continued to manifest itself, though. Each day there were more attacks. Though minor compared to what the teams had gone through at Quefiquena, they were a reminder of why they were there. The main problem, the section leaders decided, was that the guerrillas were still infiltrating the area from the east and were still being supplied from the south.

With that in mind, a decision was taken to try to blow a large bridge to the south of Campo Oito which was still being used as a headquarters by Savimbi's people. They would use two of the zodiacs to take the men in. Permission was sought from the local FAA commander who passed it on to Luanda.

Meanwhile, Phil Smith asked to do a recce of the area in one of the Pilatus PC-9s that were now able to use the "liberated" Soyo airport and which, from time to time provided top cover in outlying areas where members of the company remained active. With its relatively low speed and underwing rocket pods, these Swiss trainers proved ideal for close air support throughout the campaigns that followed.

Having flown over Campo Oito, Phil Smith asked the pilot to do a turn over the first small town to the east of Soyo from where Unita had consistently been lobbing 100mm shells at both Quefiquena and other positions held by either EO or FAA. They had barely circled the place the first time—from the air it looked minuscule, consisting of little more than some old colonial structures, surrounded by clusters of mud huts—when Smith spotted a white man running out of one of the buildings. He was surprised to see him carrying a Manpad in his arms. A moment later, he aimed it at the circling aircraft.

With attack imminent, the pilot didn't need to be told what to do. He immediately thrust the stick forward and took the plane down low, but not before a couple of hundred rebels who had been hiding in the surrounding bush opened fire on the turboprop. As Smith told the others afterward, they had RPGs self-destructing all around them and the sky was peppered with green tracers.[7] Indeed, he admitted, they were lucky not to have been brought down. But then they took a hit somewhere midships.

From what he could make out, the aircraft's fuel line had been punctured and the next moment, the engine cut. It was all that the pilot could do to look for somewhere to put down.

Fortunately the river was close by and a stretch of open beach seemed the only alternative to crash-landing in a casava patch. Radio comms with base meanwhile had one of the Hips heading toward them from Cabinda in an attempt to snatch the two men to safety. It was none too soon: following lift-off, the chopper pilot did a circle over the damaged aircraft and already there were figures emerging from the jungle toward it.

The fact that the enemy was using white mercenaries from South Africa disturbed a lot of the men. They could never come to terms with the fact that they now faced some of their own people—former colleagues and, in some cases, friends, recruited by Unita. As they were to discover much later, some of these dissidents had served in the same units. But it didn't prevent one of the EO officers, J.T. Erasmus, a former Commandant in 1 Reconnaissance Regiment, passing the word around that if any of the whites fighting them were captured, they were to be assimilated into their own ranks and discreetly returned to South Africa.

As Mauritz le Roux explained, "We were there for the money, not vengeance. So that decision made good sense. After all, we were all South Africans doing a job as best as each of us saw fit."

What did worry the Executive Outcomes guys, though, was that word had filtered through of offers being made by Savimbi. He would apparently offer anyone—Unita or FAA—thousands of dollars for every EO combatant killed or captured. It was to be a repeat of the situation later in Sierra Leone with Foday Sankoh offering his gooks rewards for bringing in mercs, dead or alive. Apparently the Angolan guerrilla leader believed that if enough examples were made of those war dogs that fell into his hands, EO would have difficulty with its recruiting program.

More EO follow-ups took place in subsequent days, with the South Africans gradually gathering around them more seasoned FAA soldiers than they had encountered in the past.

Those Angolan soldiers that showed promise were coached in a variety of disciplines, including operational procedures, weapons handling and tactics. Basically they were shown what was expected of them under fire. Much attention was given to marksmanship: troops were weaned off the customary Angolan bravado of firing from the hip. It pleased Lafras and his buddies to discover that there were some enthusiastic learners and quite a few of the brighter Angolans chose to stick close to the South Africans as long as their contracts lasted.

The first target to follow the battles at Quefiquena and Soyo was Campo Oito, which a column headed by EO's men took on March 13th. It was a tough slog, with Unita reluctant to vacate its strongest positions.

It was also there that the company took its first mortality. Buks Erasmus, a former 32 man and a mortar specialist, was killed while some of his troops from Section One—with a FAA detachment in tow—were headed toward the Unita headquarters. Struck full on by a HEAT Strim, he was a brave men and, under the circumstances, irreplaceable. For the next ten days, EO's people were almost completely surrounded by enemy regulars.

Meanwhile, the news that Unita had had been driven out of Soyo was beginning to make headlines abroad. So too were reports that there had been mercenaries involved.

What soon became clear was that while the events at Soyo were a departure for the Angolan Army who, for a while now had suffered a succession of defeats, the media wasn't being fooled by Luanda's claims that its own troops had been responsible. Too many of the original EO squad had returned home to regale friends with stories. The word was out: War Dogs had done it again.

The normally-unforthcoming Eeben Barlow even did the unexpected by inviting a media team to northern Angola to "meet the boys" and explain what had taken place. That resulted in further coverage with several of the world's biggest weeklies giving EO credit for driving out an insurgent army and helping to turn on the oil faucets once more. The Americans seemed especially pleased.

By now, a new group of recruits had arrived in Soyo, and with some of the old timers who decided to stay and collect a second check, one of the first tasks they were given was to smack a small town which Unita was reported to control.

The group set out early in the day in two trucks containing a bunch of EO volunteers together with a squad of FAA troops. Reaching an area where attack was possible, some of the troops dismounted, with EO sending some of its own men ahead to cover all eventualities. They hadn't gone far when Unita troops, concealed in dense bush at the side of the road, opened fire. The men were caught completely off guard: Harry Carlse was shocked enough to drop his AK.

The first man hit was a relatively new arrival by the name of Cornell Taljaard, a former 4 Reconnaissance Regiment veteran. He took a hit in the leg and went down. Phil Smith immediately ran forward to give support, but was shot in the neck from up close and killed. With that, the rest of the column pulled back, leaving two of their own behind. Though reports about what happened to Taljaard are sketchy, it is known that he was tortured before being beaten to death by the women of a village in which the Unita force was billeted.

For EO it was a heavy loss. Two of the best company men had been KIA and suddenly things again started to look grim. Up to that point, the tally was three dead.

The perpetual uncertainty of what lay ahead worried most of the men, coupled to a manifest lack of support from the Angolan command that sometimes fringed on either indifference or negligence. Though Soyo was theirs, all these things together had a severe effect on morale. In a sense it was dereliction on the part of the FAA commanders. Still worse, there was nobody present who could—or would—do anything about it. Also, it wasn't lost on any of the mercenaries that they'd initially been tasked for forty-eight hours. At first that had been extended to three days, then ten and finally to two months. There simply didn't seem to be an end to it.

At that point, about half the remaining EO force, including many of the newcomers decided that they'd had enough crap and asked to be repatriated.

After days of continuous fighting, including reinforcements having been brought in to supplement the main force, EO's presence finally did prevail. It took another month, though.

At the crux of it all, looking back, is that whatever Unita handed out, they got back with interest, or to paraphrase Eric Linklater in an earlier conflict: the South Africans fought with dashing assurance.

Unquestionably, much of it was due to the efforts of the original group that had stayed on longer than they needed to. Again, money motivated most of them. Together with the newcomers, they had used experience gained earlier to push the main Unita force out of the oil areas.

Once EO pulled back and its members had gone home, the company left the Angolan Army in place to take care of things. At least that was the general idea. Within weeks, the rebels were back and had retaken Soyo.

What was immediately apparent to everybody in Luanda was that the experiment of employing mercenaries had worked. Not only that, it had been an unmitigated success. A difficult task had been accomplished. Moreover, it was the first real demonstration not only of EO dedication in achieving results against extremely heavy odds, but also of the unit's demonstrable combat abilities. More important, the effort showed some skeptics in Luanda—and there were many to start with—that the South Africans were not only serious but that they had outstanding military skills.

As the insurgency continued, Luanda had to make a decision. Were they to hire a larger, more effective mercenary force, or, as they had been doing all along, with questionable results, go it alone? The issue was decided for them by more guerrilla successes. Not only was Savimbi by then in control of about ninety percent of Angola—all that eluded his grasp being the larger cities—but his army soon occupied Soyo again.

Finally, in August 1993, Eeben Barlow signed a multi-million dollar contract to train five thousand troops from FAA's 16th Regiment. The company would also bring in thirty experienced pilots with solid Border War combat experience.

More significant was the proviso that, with immediate effect, EO would start to advise Angolan Army commanders on front-line operations against Savimbi's forces. One result was that some EO officers eventually ended up directing the course of several major battles against the rebel force. In the end, the tide would swing completely the government's way.

Part of EO's deal with the government was to help it acquire some of the more sophisticated items of weaponry, which included thermobarics or, more commonly, fuel air explosives.[8] These are the same enhanced-blast weapons used to good effect by the Russians in the past to dislocate the terrorist threat in Chechnya, especially in Grozny, the capital.

It is interesting that several sources have since indicated to this author that the Luanda government employed enhanced blast/fuel-air bombs in some of their battles against Savimbi, in particular in dislodging the guerrilla leader and his entourage from his main fortress in the hills around Bailundo in the Central Highlands. In all probability, this was achieved with the remnants of an EO presence.

Certainly, Executive Outcomes subsequently intended using thermobaric weapons against rebel strongpoints in the mountains near the Liberian border in Sierra Leone. I was present in Freetown when the implications of using fuel-air bombs was discussed. But before that plan could be implemented, EO's contract in Sierra Leone was canceled.

Since then, Colonel Bert Sachse, who for a long time ran the show for EO in Sierra Leone, told me that all that really prevented his people using this weapon was the reluctance of some senior commanders to wipe out Foday Sankoh's entire staff. In truth, apart from the fact that many of them had relatives among the rebels, quite a few were themselves on the RUF payroll.

In Angola, it is significant that video footage of thermobaric explosives being used against Unita exists, though the source of these controversial bombs has never been traced, at least not conclusively. Obviously they came from South Africa but nobody is saying how, why or when.

At the end of it all, the role of the two former British Army veterans who created Africa's first Private Military Company must give us something of an insight to the way that things are likely to be handled in the future.

Both Tony Buckingham and Simon Mann were well-acquainted with both Angola and its government. They had worked with these people in the past. Had that not been the case, EO wouldn't have got a foot in the door. Since Luanda welcomed people with whom they had done business and showed goodwill, the original link engendered confidence.

But it didn't happen overnight. The South Africans had to travel to Luanda—and elsewhere—to do the necessary. Indeed, they went in many times to thrash out the small print and much of this side of things involved General Luis Faceira of the Angolan Army.

It didn't take long to become clear to everybody involved in the venture that EO's future role in Angola would hinge on a successful Soyo operation, if only because Luanda wanted to be certain that the "Boers," as the South Africans were sometimes disparagingly referred to—could do the job.

General Faceira's approach, which changed with time and became much more favorable, indicated to Barlow and his friends that the company's actions at Soyo had impressed the Angolan High Command. "Immensely," he told Lafras Luitingh. Not only had these foreign fighters acquitted themselves well under the most arduous and dangerous of conditions, they were prepared to risk their lives to make it happen. The implications of a relatively small squad of twenty-eight former South African Special Forces personnel being able to evict a much larger Unita mobile force from the vital oil facility wasn't lost on any of them.

Those twenty-eight were all that were left after a large part of the group had opted out once things became hot. Of this number, only about fifteen had formerly been front-line fighters, though there were many times when the rear-echelon had to do some shooting, if only to avoid being overrun.

As Barlow's associate, Michael Grunberg, told me, "One must bear in mind that at that stage, the Angolans really knew very little of the internal machinations of EO—or, for that matter how they went about their business. Instead, it was a case of them keeping their fingers crossed."

More important still, he pointed out, nothing like this had ever happened in Angola before and Luanda wanted more of the same. Especially since Savimbi's people were then still in control of some of the country's most lucrative diamond fields.

16
HOW EXECUTIVE OUTCOMES
RAN ITS WARS

"Although the numbers involved were small—Executive Outcomes never had more than 500 men in Angola and were usually fewer, compared with Angolan armed forces of more than 100,000 men—it is generally regarded as having played a critical part in securing victory for the government forces . . ."

British Government Green Paper *Private Military Companies: Options for Regulation*, Feb 12, 2002

Executive Outcomes' Soyo adventure was eventually to become synonymous with what a well-disciplined bunch of war dogs can achieve in a regional Third World conflict. To other PMCs that might be active in remote, distant lands, it also offered what Kipling said of the Boer War: "No end of a lesson."

While the Battle for Soyo ranks right up there with Executive Outcomes having pushed Sierra Leone's RUF rebels from the precincts of Freetown, not much has appeared in print about either of these events, even though a lot of lives – the majority of them enemy—were lost in the process. What has been published so far about this extended African campaign has either been fragmentary or inaccurate, or in one notable instance, plagiarized.

Mauritz le Roux's very personal impressions in the previous chapter, in contrast, are remarkable. Not only was he there, right in the thick of it, he was also one of the original movers behind the founding of Executive Outcomes.

An organizer with guts and an indomitable spirit, he has since gone on to nurture one of the most successful Private Military Companies active in today's Iraq. In keeping with his no-nonsense, low-key approach—and unlike most American companies of a similar ilk—he neither seeks publicity nor does he get it. He was very specific about me not using the name of his Baghdad company in this book, a confidence that I intend to honor.

As he said when he, Nellis and I spent time together at the mouth of the Columbia River in the Pacific Northwest in the spring of 2005, "Anybody can talk. I just like to get on with the job."

With that kind of approach, and a face that remains incognito, Le Roux has had protection teams working the "Baghdad Beat" for more than two years. He has yet to lose one of his men to hostilities. At the same time, he and his team have battled their way out of several scraps with Sunni fundamentalists. That included an attack in Falluja in the spring of 2005, when his group, traveling in convoy with no military escort, was hit by a sixty-strong rebel group.

In the contact that followed, his attackers were routed. Le Roux's only casualty was his American client who, despite pleadings for him to travel in one of the protected vehicles, preferred to ride up front and exposed alongside one of the machine-gunners.

"A great guy. It was a catastrophe to lose him. But sadly, he wouldn't accept my advice. He was determined to be a part of it and we saw what happened. You need to be discreet rather than macho in the Sunni Triangle, and my friend, great pal that he was, paid a terrible price."

Le Roux flew back to Houston with his client's body and attended the funeral. It says something that the Texas concern remains a client.

As might be expected, there are quite a few notables who were involved with him in the Soyo operation that now work for him in Baghdad, including Harry Carlse. Neall Ellis has also joined him.

All of this underscores one of Mauritz le Roux's many strengths: he prefers people working for him who have fired a few shots in anger during the course of their professional careers. It is much the better if they have seen real combat. When push becomes shove, he likes staff members who are able to extricate both themselves and those who they are paid to protect from situations that can sometimes be fraught.

Compare that approach with the exploits of Blackwater USA, one of the most illustrious PMCs of the modern lot. At last count, in late 2005, Blackwater had lost twenty-six of its people in contacts, ambushes and the like. The majority of the fatalities occurred in Iraq.

What Executive Outcomes proved during the course of its activities in Angola was that with a solid command structure coupled to the correct choice of combatant, discipline that fringes on the exemplary, and a level of dedication you don't often find among the ranks, it is possible for a commercial concern to achieve good results under austere conditions.

In an article that I did for Britain's Jane's Information Group, I illustrated another reality: unconventional conflicts sometimes demand unconventional solutions. With decades of bush war combat behind them, this South African group managed to open doors that had been shut ever since Africa was vacated by the Colonial Powers in the 1960s and 1970s.[1] Some considered Soyo as arguably the toughest single campaign fought by any group of mercenaries The tragic economic situation was made even more horrific by an outbreak of Marburg, a deadly hemorrhagic fever related to Ebola. (See Colonel Mike Hoare's final days in the Congo in the 1960s, Chapter 10.)

Subsequent EO participation in Sierra Leone might have come close, but the level of competence among the rebels facing this mercenary group in the jungles beyond Freetown and in the approaches to the Kono diamond fields were no match to what Savimbi threw into the fray.

Considering the fact that there were a dozen or more battles fought in the sixty days that Soyo lasted, and the exceptionally low casualty rate among company personnel, what took place at this isolated oil installation in the jungle was both a tribute to their tenacity and a remarkable display of professionalism under fire. EO certainly vindicated any doubts that the company's adversaries might have had as to their efficacy outside the ambit of a conventional military force. And make no mistake; EO had critics aplenty, in Angola itself as well as in Britain, the United States and South Africa.

As Lafras Luitingh told me on the plane that took us to Sierra Leone not very long afterward, what happened at Soyo was often emulated but never surpassed. In terms of sheer numbers and the paucity of equipment available, he said, a tiny group of South Africans managed to keep a far superior Unita force at bay. The company played a significant role in preventing a major guerrilla force from neutralizing one of Angola's most valuable assets. That Savimbi's people took Soyo again after the South Africans had pulled out was of no consequence. EO, Luitingh declared, had done what it had set itself and that was what mattered.

Ousting Unita from Soyo a second time became a formality because this time around the attackers had support from both armor and helicopter gunships.

Once launched, the initial Soyo operation was the start of a most demanding regimen for the mercenary force in Angola. Within months of their return to this West African state, EO was very much in the thick of it. Their activities took them to the north and to regions that adjoined the Central Highlands in the interior. Only then did they tackle the east, though from the start, the company had an advanced operational base at Saurimo, the country's principal diamond city. (See Chapter 17.)

Looking at the broader scenario, some of Executive Outcomes' successes are said by insiders to stem from what Duncan Rykaart—a senior member of the company's original command group—termed EO's "four interlocking principles."

This codification—informal but strictly adhered to throughout the expanded campaigns that followed in both Angola and Sierra Leone—was much discussed during my two visits to EO positions in Angola in 1995. They were also to become the basis of many of the core values established by management. As such, declared Rykaart, himself a former Special Forces operator,[2] they were sacrosanct. Any EO member ignored them at his peril.

Briefly, these fundamentals included air support for all ground operations, reliance on the individual in the field for good level of personal initiative and basic common sense, and finally, logistics. Since most of EO's men had served long and hard in their own country's guerrilla struggles—many of them having seen action in Special Forces regiments—they weren't unduly taxed by these demands.

It was interesting that much of what ultimately took place under EO was dictated as much by the need to run an efficient business as to prevent loss of life in combat. The issue is perhaps best encapsulated by the credo, crude but emphatic, that was printed on some of the T-shirts issued to the men at Angola's Rio Lomba Special Forces training camp (about an hour's drive south of Cabo Ledo). Emblazoned across the back, in bold Day-Glo letters four inches high, were the words "Fit In or Fuck Off."

The first of the four EO basics, that there was to be no ground operation without close air support, was routinely observed in Angola where there was never a shortage of government Hips and Hinds. These Russian rotor wings were used extensively in every punch-up into which the company was thrust. Angolan Air Force pilots flew some of them. Others were piloted by South Africans working for EO, though as the war progressed, the company itself increasingly played a more dominant role in air ops.

In Sierra Leone, by contrast, things were different. Because that tiny West African state had no combat pilots of its own, EO at first made use of the government's solitary Mi-24 gunship (the Hips only arrived afterward). A big obstacle that needed tackling after their arrival in Freetown was that the South African company was obligated to employ those Russian pilots who were already there since they were contracted directly to the state.

In order to establish a more effective, versatile system, Executive Outcomes commanders had to find a way of bringing the air asset under their control. This was not easily achieved. The Russians balked—as was expected they would—because it put a rather abrupt end to their monthly paychecks. They argued that they were doing a competent job, when in fact they weren't. Their idea of top cover was, as at Soyo a short while before, hovering somewhere above five thousand feet. South African gunship pilots, in contrast, thought fifty feet might sometimes be too high.

The issue was resolved, according to Barlow's financial mentor Michael Grunberg, by EO using the clout it had accumulated from organizing the supply of pilots, parts and ordnance to protect Freetown. Thus, the company took the helm and the Russians were ditched, but not before they sabotaged the Hind's electronics. In this spooky world of point and counterpoint, one of the Russian pilots was later found murdered, though another source maintains that the death had more to do with diamonds and the Russian *mafiya* than mercenary activity.

Notably, it helped EO's cause that there had also been a fairly serious language barrier between the components. With former Soviets flying these machines, EO's ground forces couldn't communicate properly with the men who were supposed to be providing air support. As they explained to Valentine Strasser, the Sierra Leone leader, "when people are shooting at you, you don't need to waste time with translators." Strasser was usually too spaced out on cocaine to comprehend very much of what was going on around him, but that message came through loud and clear.

EO eventually brought its own Mi-17s into play. Two Hips bought from the UN in Angola (and still in that organization's white livery) were flown halfway across Africa, though that didn't prevent them from being "arrested" in Nigeria while in transit because their pilots were South African.

The second EO canon centered on initiative and good common sense—values for which the majority of Third World forces are not especially renowned. EO's command and control approach encouraged resolute, often independent action to achieve these aims. As Hennie Blaauw, another of EO's combat commanders in Angola pointed out: "That sort of thing doesn't feature in the handbooks."

The third element comes back to discipline, enforced with a very strong arm. Anyone who stepped out of line—which excluded getting drunk as many times a week as you liked as long as you weren't smashed on duty—was put on the first plane home. Every unit, no matter how remote, had its rules, which were rigidly applied, even if it meant ousting someone from a pivotal position. Liquor-inspired fisticuffs was the main culprit here.

Two of EO's best and most valued combatants were peremptorily kicked out of the organization after they had attacked the British manager of Ibis Air—the airline founded by Buckingham and friends and used to bring in supplies—in a bar in Freetown. In a vicious attack that was described by one of those present as reflecting "a pit bull mentality," they broke the poor man's jaw and some ribs. He was rushed home on an emergency flight.

Later, in both the Angolan and Sierra Leonian diamond fields, several of the men were fired for illicit dealings in precious stones. There might have been more, but diamonds are easily hidden and anyway, it was a difficult charge to prove.

The last was logistics. The key to EO's philosophy regarding conflict in Africa was, quite simply, that nothing happened unless it was made to happen. The South Africans had been dealing with African governments for a while by now and, without exception, government support throughout had been found wanting.

Said Lafras Luitingh, in charge of EO's operations: "All governments with whom we've been associated make promises. They make lots of them. They always do, especially when the bottle is being passed around. But we've found, sometimes to our disadvantage, that these promises were rarely kept. By morning they were forgotten. Consequently, if we were to deploy a force on the ground in some remote region, we'd have to keep it supplied."

If anything were needed by the men in the field—from a toothbrush or a *sjambok* (quirt) to a toilet roll—it had to come on the weekly (and eventually fortnightly) Boeing (Ibis Air) flight that was allowed unimpeded access to Lungi. It was also part of the deal that EO was not subjected to any immigration or customs controls. As hostilities developed in Angola, the same system was adopted and relief flights became twice-weekly events after they commenced in 1994.

Michael Grunberg actually remembers being on the tarmac at a military field outside Luanda when the first of these passenger jets was delivered: it was still in its American Airlines livery. He also recalls that after regular flights between South Africa and Angola—and further north—had been introduced, EO pilots instituted a sophisticated logistics structure into the Sierra Leone operations envelope. It was passed on, together with the requisite international component, to the West African air controllers at Robertsfield.[3]

Basically, in all theaters of military activity in which EO was active, the organization worked on the principle of the host nation providing the main component of military "muscle" in order to get the job done. With the odd exception, this included arms, ammunition and land support vehicles, together with the basic military infrastructure that any army should be able to come up with. Men in arms from the host nation were part of the equation. At the end of it, the company took with them everything else that might be needed to keep its force in the field.

Its main menu included direction, the men needed for the task at hand, their personal equipment and food, plus helicopters for close air support.

The movement of EO troops, replacements and casualties were also the responsibility of the company. Apart from the two Boeing 727s, two other aircraft came from Britain: former RAF Hawker Siddeley Andover CC Mk2 twin turbo-prop transports that had previously been operated by No 32 Squadron for the Queen's Flight. Depending on criticality, these were used to evacuate casualties either to London or South Africa, with one stationed at Luanda and the other at Lungi. Both had full aircrews on the company payroll and were maintained on the basis of a twenty-four hour standby. It was a notable advance from the Cabinda debacle where the first doctor only arrived weeks into the campaign.

The Andovers ended up playing a crucial role in the war, even though they weren't tasked that often. For a start, the troops had the reassurance that if things did come unstuck, they would be airlifted to the best hospitals abroad, almost always with a company doctor in attendance. They could be airborne and on their way within an hour of a contact in the jungle, the Hips handling the first transit.

Consequently, lives were saved by flying some chronic malaria cases to the tropical fever hospital run by Canadians in the Ivoirean capital. More than once a Boeing was diverted to Abidjan if a doctor believed a case was life threatening.

As Grunberg observed, you had to give the company its due: when it came to health issues. "Cost was never an issue."

There were several more EO planes, including two King Airs, but these mostly worked Angola and the rest of Africa. One of them crashed in Uganda in bad weather, killing a senior EO director. Also on company books was a Westwind jet located at Lungi and used by EO personnel for airborne surveillance work.

Things developed quickly following the two thirty-day deployments in the Soyo area early in 1993. While producing nothing spectacular, the EO presence had achieved its aims.

Once the new contract had been signed with Luanda, the Angolan Army (FAA) immediately thrust numerous responsibilities at the organization. Almost overnight, a lot more men had to be recruited, every one of them South African. The EO directorate was aware that they needed to be much more discriminating with regard to the caliber of their recruits than before. Also, it became a *sine qua non* for the newcomers to have had good combat experience, preferably with a Special Forces or an elite infantry unit and over a period of several years.

A significant aspect here is that Luitingh, Barlow and their cronies were interested not only in individual operators, but also support personnel with whom these people had been linked during their period of military service. They reckoned it was axiomatic that shared hardship bred trust.

Race was never a criterion. Despite apartheid, elite SADF units that had fought the Border War and in Angola were totally non-racial. In fact, they had just as many black troops as whites in their ranks and, in some cases, in command positions over white soldiers as well.

The majority knew and understood the strengths and foibles of their officers and NCOs; after all, they had taken a lot of flak over the years in each others' company in operations that spanned more than a decade. What mattered a great deal to EO's bosses was that during that period, these people had not only fought together but had sometimes saved each other's lives.

Luitingh viewed his company's black troops with immense respect. He regarded their welfare as his personal responsibility and would tolerate no officiousness towards "my manne" (Afrikaans for "my guys"). He'd actually served with quite a few in his Recce days and was on first name terms with many.

The company would be that much poorer without these black troops, he would say. They were strong, likable and every one in the team had seen a good bit of action in his day, which made them invaluable when things got rough.

He also liked to emphasize that there were few soldiers anywhere who were able to display such remarkable versatility with squad weapons as the African troops under his command. In this regard, one of the men quipped, it was ironic that EO was now handling the same guns while working for the Angolan government that FAPLA and FAA had used against the South Africans when they were opposed to Luanda's Marxist regime.

A fundamental mistake made by the majority of critics of private military companies—and one which never escaped the attention of EO—was the pigeonholing of those who were prepared to do this filthy work as criminals. The press used various epithets, almost all of them unflattering. Others called them retards, contract killers or worse.

The perception in the civilized world, generally, is that mercenaries are semi-literate psychos with no scruples. And while EO always conceded the experience bit, it was only because that was what the majority of these veterans had been doing all along.

The truth is that some dogs of war could probably slot comfortably into all of the categories mentioned. Granted, there is also the occasional psychopath and over the years I've met a few: in Rhodesia, the Congo, Angola, Uganda, Sierra Leone and elsewhere. But then most military establishments have the occasional loose cannon.

Looking at the broader canvas, it's axiomatic that the concept of killing people is repugnant to civilized people anywhere. While EO might have done an excellent job in destroying the rebel infrastructure in Sierra Leone, and before that, in forcing Savimbi to the negotiating table in Angola, the subject nonetheless remains unsettling.

There are those who feel that mercenaries indulge in violence for the sake of it. Yet anybody who has seen these people at work from up close knows that that is not true. At the same time, one has to accept that the ideal is blurred by perceptions spawned by the events of recent history, like Callan's mindlessly brutal role in Angola and what went on in the Congo before Colonel Mike Hoare pulled the operation up by its bootstraps. Obviously, there is an image factor here that needs to be dealt with. It is hardly flattering.

What went on in the Congo in the early days is perhaps at the core of it, compounded more recently by the doings of some American free-lance operators who have since been charged with killing dissidents in Afghanistan. Mercenaries everywhere were done another disservice by the large group of South Africans who, at the behest of Mark Thatcher, the son of the former British Prime Minister, and his side-kick Simon Mann, tried to bring down the government of Equatorial Guinea in 2004. Almost all of those involved in that fiasco ended up in jail, with some of them subsequently dying in prison.

In the earlier phase of the Congo's war, reports were reinforced by the show-and-tell photos of smiling mercenaries who held aloft the decapitated heads of black men. This gory display of trophies was disgusting and it didn't help that some of these pictures appeared in the news magazines of the time, particularly in Europe.

Fast forward to the twenty-first century and just about everything has changed. Today's professional soldier for hire, in the main, is a pretty ordinary guy. The majority probably wouldn't be out of place in your local police force. About the only thing that sets the contemporary soldier of fortune apart from the rest is that he is a veteran with a good run of experience to show for it. He's seen combat and he's survived.

These are also folk who are not only familiar with the multi-disciplined precepts of most regular armed forces, but are able to handle themselves with deftness under fire. Indeed, many have half a lifetime of military service and, to be blunt, they're dinkum proud of it.

Neall Ellis, who, on his own, twice turned the war around in Sierra Leone, is a case in point, though admittedly he is not your typical hired gun, if only because most combat pilots are a good ten or fifteen years younger by the time they return their flying helmets to the ready room for the last time. Still, there are few combat pilots who have had as much experience as Nellis.

In Executive Outcomes' first new phase in Angola, the first deployments took place to the east of Luanda and around the diamond fields of Lunda Sul. Soyo too, once again required pacifying.

The company chose as its headquarters in the east the airport at Saurimo, not far from what was then still the Zairean frontier (today the Democratic Republic of the Congo).

While this contract was renewed a year later, and then extended again for a further three months, it was officially ended early in 1996. By then EO had about five hundred men in the field, the majority of whom were either in combat or busy training the FAA. South African mercenary pilots were also active throughout, and whether they were providing support for their own people or assisting the regular army, Angola couldn't have managed without them.

Several developments contributed toward Dr. Jonas Savimbi finally signing an accord with the Luanda government in November 1994. The first, in February 1994, was the recapture by FAA—with a strong EO presence in support—of N'dalatando in Cuanza Norte. Until then, this little junction town, which lies about halfway between Luanda and Malanje, had been pivotal to the guerrilla penetration of the oil-rich northwest.

Four months later EO was engaged—in conjunction with FAA's 16th Brigade—in a three-month operation to retake the Cafunfo diamond fields (see Chapter 18). It was a blow from which Unita never recovered.

The alluvial diggings encompass miles of Angola's northern forest regions along the Cuanza River, and at that stage this valuable resource was supplying the rebels with about two-thirds of their diamonds. If Savimbi was of half a mind to continue with his war, he couldn't do without it.

Finally, when Huambo—Angola's second largest city—fell to the government after battles that left thousands dead in September of that year, the Unita leader sued for peace.

There was another issue constantly being raised by the media whenever contact was made with the mercenary force. That centered on whether any mercenary in the pay of a foreign government could actually be loyal.

In Freetown, where journalists and mercs shared the same nightspots, the specter of divided allegiances would be raised more often than was necessary and, once or twice led to blows. As some of the hacks were to discover, a tavern is not exactly the place to ask a tanked-up war dog about whether he's likely to defect to those whom he's fighting against. Lafras Luitingh phrased it rather neatly when he said that while both Freetown and Luanda might have been pleased with what EO had achieved on the battlefield, "That didn't mean that we were always above suspicion."

He explained: "The black leaders who hired us would invariably judge us by their own standards. Of course, in their minds, that often made us complicit. We are, after all, marketable commodities and obviously, that would make us suspect."

Luitingh accepted that governments for whom his people (and other groups of mercenaries) fought had been "bought," as it is usually phrased, by a higher bidder. It happened within the ambit of the major powers as well, he pointed out, only there, turncoats are called spies.

Because of this, he suggested, there was sometimes a real fear among African leaders that if a better offer came along, these hired guns might switch sides. "Our problem," he stressed, "is that we do what we do not for any cause, or ideal, but for money."

But, he declared, there were limits. The financial motivation was obviously something that any African leader could understand. But it was also true that he and his EO colleagues sometimes encountered suspicion about what some of them termed "real agendas." He accepted, too, that some of these misgivings stemmed from recent events. As he pointed out, "History has left the world with a legacy of betrayals."

This former Recce operator illustrated his argument by citing the Angolan experience. EO had won several key battles in a country that had seen decades of war. Soyo was a part of it. But it hadn't gone unnoticed that in achieving its objective, Executive Outcomes had lost several of its best men. Yet, he said, there were still senior Angolan officers who questioned, if not the company's allegiance, then that of several former SADF officers who were directing EO's efforts at winning the war.

"For instance, they would pose questions about our motives for coming across. After all, they argued, the two sides had been blood enemies for a generation. The switch didn't make sense, they liked to aver, and as a result the suspicion bogey continued to worry us."

At the time we discussed it, Luitingh hadn't been prepared to discuss this option in such depth before, though he'd alluded to it once or twice. It was a serious matter once we got into it and his voice assumed a conspiratorial urgency.

"As contract people—PMCs, mercenaries, war dogs, whatever—our motives are always going to be suspect, if only because we fight for profit. So, the argument goes, what the one side offers, the other, feasibly, can top."

But that was not the way the company worked, Luitingh insisted.

EO, throughout its brief career, maintained stringent codes of conduct that were inviolable.

He used himself—well dressed, clean shaven, reasonably well read and informed about matters military—as an example of today's corporate soldier of fortune. As one of the top men in the organization, everybody who had anything to do with Luitingh had to concede that he was hardly what one would have expected of a mercenary leader.

Lafras Luitingh joined the army after leaving school, and for more than a decade, following his selection for South Africa's elite Reconnaissance Regiment, he did nothing but fight. His operations would sometimes take him on deep penetration insertions into Angola or Mozambique, either on foot or in vehicles. Other times his unit would be put ashore in kayaks, launched from navy submarines or make clandestine high altitude HALO/HILO entries from SAAF C-130 freighters.

A tall, powerfully built man with a perennial smile, Luitingh had long ago learnt to become uncompromisingly aggressive when he had need to. EO was formed after he had left the SADF with the rank of Lieutenant Colonel. To his—and to everybody else's surprise—he found it relatively easy to combine the art of survival of a fighting man with the battles sometimes encountered in the rarefied atmosphere of Yuppiedom. Clearly, this tough and fit erstwhile combatant was a quick learner.

Very early on, Executive Outcomes established its own brand of definitive criteria when fighting a war. Being in the business of war, everything that the company represented stood or fell by the core values it advocated.

Executive Outcomes offered Sierra Leone a feasible military solution for the kind of insurgency the nation faced, in much the way that it approached the same issue before that in Angola. Basics were coupled to good old-fashioned experience and a solid gumption to implement such programs to good effect.

Financial considerations, said Luitingh, were obviously the basis on which everything turned, or as he declared, "Just about all we do starts and ends with money. Consequently, it's good to accept that we're not into welfare. In fact, we charge what we think the market will bear. And to get to that figure, we do our homework."

There was a time, he suggested, when the people of Freetown really did think that the company might switch sides, which was possibly to be expected because almost nothing in Sierra Leone was based on a handshake.

Also, he added, "the Russians had been running the Air Wing before we arrived and they had screwed the government so often that there were some who queried whether the South Africans wouldn't do exactly the same. And when you're faced with that kind of dilemma, a very real danger materializes when someone believes that you might betray him. They start to see shadows where there are none." It was the story of Africa, he believed.

As in Angola, Luitingh and his colleagues quickly countered that perception by getting into some of the most aggressive battles against Unita that its military leaders had yet observed, with their own people taking still more fatalities. After that, things changed markedly, especially once the group had clocked up a succession of strikes that began to hurt the rebel movement. That included killing some of Savimbi's most experienced field commanders, including some of the generals who were closest to him.

Luitingh: "As soon as we could show that the other side was taking some serious losses, things began to ease up. Also, you don't easily disregard casualties among people who are fighting for you." It took a while, he added, but by doing what was expected, these "Demon Boers"—as they had been described in Angolan newspapers and radio broadcasts in the past—were able to show the Angolans that they had themselves a bunch of fighters that were both professional and reliable.

Similar problems were sometimes encountered in Sierra Leone. Luitingh took matters in hand at his first meeting with Chairman Strasser at State House by arguing—with some aplomb, one of his sidekicks commented—that to betray the Freetown government would irrevocably destroy the credibility that the company had worked so hard to foster. This applied not only to Sierra Leone, he told the youthful head of state—who was then still only twenty-five years old—but to governments on three continents to whom EO was then talking.[4] It was a point well made and even the usually verbose Strasser couldn't argue.

"I told him that we couldn't operate in this business without trust. We might be a band of brigands, I said, but we were an honorable band of brigands." The Sierra Leone leader seemed to enjoy the quip.

Still more important, Luitingh explained, the company offered its services only to recognized governments. It wasn't interested in factions, or political parties trying to unseat rulers, no matter what kind of money was being put on the table. A year before, he disclosed, a dissident Nigerian group had approached EO with an offer of a hundred million dollars to train a guerrilla army to overthrow the tyrant Abacha.

"You can do a helluva lot with a hundred million US. But we refused. We had no option. Once you get into that sort of thing, you're going to have the international community on your neck."

Such actions might also be classed international terrorism, he believed. "Then you're into something that involves big government, Washington, London, the United Nations, war crimes commissions at The Hague, Interpol. And then what? In the end we convinced Chairman Strasser that it was just not on and I know he believed us because he never again questioned our motives."

While Executive Outcomes lasted, it was active in almost a dozen African states. Apart from Angola and Sierra Leone, it accepted contracts in the two Congos, Uganda, the Sudan, Mozambique and elsewhere. For a while, toward the end, it guarded South African farmers from cattle rustlers, though that option eventually became too expensive for its client base.

Prior to going into any country—and while still negotiating the contract—EO would state very clearly and in writing what they were able to offer and exactly what it was that the company intended to achieve. Having agreed on something of a template, and with a contract price settled, other needs would be explored. These would include the extent of the threat, exactly who would fund what, together with a timeline, sundry expenses and so on.

Discussions always involved the company's British associates, and Michael Grunberg's experience was a reliable adjunct from the start. At a very early stage, these would detail finance, the apportionment of assets and what needed to be procured, as well as liaison with local forces. The small print would contain specifics concerning equipment and weapons systems. Ancillary issues included support aircraft, logistics and exactly what EO would be expected to bring into the country.

Other aspects detailed security, internal movement, bases and airports to which the mercenary unit would have access. To get a permit each time a man entered a security area would have been impractical. Consequently, the company demanded blanket clearances, and though it took a while in Angola, they got them in the end.[5]

There was also the matter of accommodation, which, in places like Freetown and Luanda, included serviced apartments with attendant domestic staff. All this would be tabulated, and after a bit of a haggle, both parties would sign.

Perhaps the strongest attribute shared by senior EO personnel was that, as a group, the men all had intimate knowledge and understanding of the continent on which they worked. Just about everybody in EO had grown up in Africa.

On arrival at Freetown, the men were to discover a remarkably empathetic environment. Freetown's kids weren't all that different from those in the "Far South," as some Sierra Leone newspapers would refer to South Africa. Consequently, none of the men who went into Angola or Sierra Leone labored under any of the misconceptions that might have encumbered Europeans and Americans who suddenly found themselves among disadvantaged folk.

It was that way in Somalia after the U.S. Army arrived, something graphically depicted in Mark Bowden's *Black Hawk Down*. The book is a classic example of what takes place when you don't understand the people and the ambiance into which you're thrust. In such circumstances, mistakes lead to fatalities.

Also, the people around Freetown were indigent, as are the majority of black people in kwaZulu-Natal or the former Transkei. Almost from the time that Sierra Leone got its independence from Britain in 1961, the nation had been abused by a string of despots, as had South African blacks under apartheid. Similarly, these west coast people were little different from throngs of Angolans or ethnic Namibians among whom these former South African soldiers had worked and fought in the past.

And as Luitingh also pointed out, Africa is the ultimate leveler. EO personnel didn't have to be told what the region could—or could not—offer. It was taken for granted that conditions would be tough, to be treated simply as part of the job's demands.

To take one illustrative example: consider the British Army major who, with ten of his men, blundered into Magbeni, the Sierra Leone village controlled by lunatics with guns in late September 2000. Had this been an Executive Outcomes operation, nobody would have gone near the place until they'd taken the trouble to find out who or what was there. Reconnaissance was necessary not only in the face of the enemy but at all times. This simple precaution is essential in any conflict environment in the Third World. American troops recently returned from Iraq and Afghanistan are likely to echo the sentiment.

The consequences of the Magbeni catastrophe were serious. Apart from millions spent in getting a rescue effort off the ground, the operation that followed caused the death of an SAS bombardier and the wounding of almost a dozen more British troops, two of them seriously. The British Army is not likely to make that kind of mistake again.

So, too, with relations with the people. From the President down, any kind of social interaction between EO and local folk had to be exemplary. If a man couldn't relate comfortably with Africans—an EO recruit was routinely warned on signing up—he had no place in the organization. And while there were examples of interracial strife elsewhere on the continent, and South Africans—as we are constantly reminded—are hardly paragons of racial virtue, EO would always stress that its people were required to be empathetic toward those with whom they had contact.

This was not a problem for the men who had been in elite units of the SADF. For them a man's race had never been an issue—even in the days when the severest racial strictures bedeviled life in South Africa. In any event, that country's Special Forces were always more than half-black. In fact, the elite, partly-Angolan 32 Battalion was eighty percent African, and the Ovambo 101 Battalion had only white officers and some white NCOs.

At the same time, while EO executives would quickly ingratiate themselves with a country's leadership, there wasn't all that much socializing between EO officers and the host country's military. That was in marked contrast to the cavorting that went on in Sierra Leone's bars once the newcomers discovered some of Freetown's wilder nightspots.

In the upper echelons of Angola's armed forces, in contrast, "gifts" would feature prominently. There was always something on the plane out of South Africa for key generals. A new Range Rover and a $32,000 electric generator went to the three-star headquarters general that ran their show when I was there. Most times, such things were kept to practicalities.

Further down the ranks, life was informal, with the result that the people of both Luanda and Freetown soon embraced these newcomers. During the time I spent with Luitingh, the locals looked after us exceedingly well. Whenever the two of us drove around the city after dark—without an escort—we were never checked at roadblocks, even though security controls in those days (as opposed to during Nellis' term) were letter-of-the-law as far as the rest of the population was concerned.

17

THE MERCENARY AIR WAR
IN ANGOLA

"An air force of mercenaries has turned the tide of battle
against insurgent rebels in Angola and West Africa."

"Gunships For Hire," *Flight International*,
London, August 21, 1996

The Angolan capital that became Executive Outcomes' new base of
operations is one of Africa's most unforgiving conurbations. The
poverty there is of apocalyptic proportions. Perhaps for this reason,
Luanda was once described by Jon Jeter of the *Washington Post*'s
Foreign Service as a city "awash in oil and mired in poverty." The
tragic economic situation has been made even more horrific in recent
years by outbreaks of Marburg, the deadly hemorrhagic fever related
to Ebola. One of our colleagues, having visited the place, once said
that it was like Mumbai's Jhopadpathis, only worse, if that were possible!

Approach Luanda from the air during the rainy season and you're
greeted by an awful mishmash of muddy pools, wrecked cars and ten-
foot high piles of garbage. And pullulating crowds that for all this, will
greet you with a smile. At its heart, this is a place of nebulous neglect.

Getting up close doesn't help much either. The city is a hive of tens
of thousands of nondescript, mud-colored shacks and shanties, many
of them roofless. This conglomeration stretches from one unbroken
horizon to the other, a monochrome copy of Lagos without its
Victoria Lagoon. In an enlightened moment, British scribe Sam Kiley
talked about some African cities having become "grand Guignol horrors." That's Luanda!

We arrived on one of the company's Ibis Air Boeings a little after
dawn. Parts of the city were cloaked in a cold, clammy mist that sometimes creeps across the bay from the sea, especially in the cooler
months. Frenzied movement on the ground below looked like something out of an old newsreel film: everybody scurrying about, build-

ings, tin shacks, favelas, slum tenements and roads pushed out sporadically like amoebic pseudopodia that ended in a congeries of bush
or jungle or at a stream on the outskirts. To those who lived there,
pain must have been a solvent.

In the middle of this apparition appeared Luanda's *Aeroporto de
4 Febereiro*, the country's only international air terminal. A bright
neon sign on the roof announced in bold letters, "Bem Vindo:
Welcome."

Even while taxiing, it became apparent why the UN regarded
Luanda as its most important staging post in Africa. By six in the
morning, the roar of scores of aircraft—mostly ex-Soviet Tupolevs and
some high-slung Ilyushin-76s—could be heard through the sealed
bulkheads of our 727. There were also a few of the more familiar
Antonov-12s, looking deceptively like American C-130 Hercules
transports. Not for nothing did the crews refer to them as "Hercskis."

This same routine was repeated unwaveringly seven days a week,
Christmas and Good Fridays included. Angola's starving millions were
waiting for their bowls of gruel.

Because of the war in the interior—as it then was—many of the
country's population centers were either cut off from the outside
world or under siege. The way Jon Jeter described it, "Just about
everyone was half a step away from starvation." He painted a succession of vignettes that were uncompromising and grim.

Writing from Kuito in the Central Highlands—it was a busy place
thirty or thirty-five years ago when the Portuguese were still in control
and trains ran between Benguela at the coast and the Congo's
Copperbelt—Jeter set the scene:

"The cargo planes that keep this city alive land every few hours,
trembling to a halt amid cracked concrete and yawning potholes. With
the roads already close to impassable, relief workers worry that the
approaching rainy season will shut the airport as well, hobbling their
efforts to deliver food to thousands of peasants who pour into Kuito
each month, chased from the countryside by an unyielding civil war."
And that in a country the size of Texas.

Coming in to refuel, you couldn't miss the detritus of war. Like a
giant knackers yard, it lay about everywhere. On the verge of the airport were great heaps of rusting radar towers, scanners and reflector
dishes. There were scrapped generators and pylons, all of it once
Soviet, reminding everybody that, in its day, Luanda was as strategically important to Moscow in the South Atlantic as was Castro's Cuba

in the Caribbean. The airport was a junkyard and as such shared a kinship with Mogadishu's airport across the continent at the Horn.

Some of the revetments that had previously sheltered Sukhois, MiG-21 and MiG-23 fighters had collapsed. Others had been washed away by tropical downpours that in fifteen minutes can turn large swaths of Luanda into a swamp. Similarly with the military barracks at the southern end of the runway: it too was in ruins. So were airport repair sheds, their technicians having long ago returned to Mother Russia and the new order that there awaited them. In between, more wrecked Soviet jets and helicopters littered the periphery. It was a panoply of senseless waste, more so than at any other airport I'd seen.

Yet, in the middle of it all, there was a clear-cut division between civilian and military, and the best part of the terminal was reserved for the air force. It was immediately apparent that South African mercenaries were allowed to come and go at will.

Driving into town was something else. There were soldiers everywhere. We had been warned before leaving South Africa to be polite. If we weren't, they told us, Executive Outcomes couldn't help. Or rather, they wouldn't.

A month before, an Angolan Army colonel had had an AK magazine emptied into his chest; he'd refused to show his ID card at an airport checkpoint. The entire scene was neatly encapsulated by a comment from John Edlin, another old Africa hand, then working for Associated Press: "While Angola is a land of extremes, Luanda is populated by psychos."

We had barely left the airport when we saw a glistening pair of aircraft wings straddling the roadside. The fuselage of what was obviously a passenger jet lay half-a-mile on, occupied by squatters. The pilot—drunk, of course—had put the plane down short of the runway. Several passengers were killed but he survived long enough for a military squad to smell his breath, frog-march him to a clearing and shoot him.

Though the accident had taken place several years before, nobody had bothered to move the wreck. There was no need to, an official explained. If they did, he argued, they might be depriving *povos*[1] of their homes. It was rumored that two of the three engines were found to be repairable and both were sold for a hundred crates of beer to a Lebanese businessman who, in turn, passed them on to an airline in the Middle East for real money.

Angola's civil wars—five or six of them by now, nobody's counting—have been hard. For five centuries the country was ruled from Europe with an exploitative efficiency that rarely masked its brutality, and like it or not, much of the suffering that followed independence in 1975 was Lisbon's fault.

While Britain and France prepared its African subjects for the inevitability of *Uhuru*, Lisbon would have none of it. Portugal's three African colonies—Angola, Mozambique, and today's Guiné-Bissau—were as much a part of "Greater Portugal" as any city back home, they would argue. With solemnity, these Lusitonian apologists would declare that after five centuries on the "Dark Continent," it was Divine Will that they were still there, which, on reflection was arrant dribble. It is notable, though, that Lisbon stayed on in Africa twice as long as the British held on to its American colonies.

And make no mistake; the majority of these Europeans really believed that God was on their side, which is why they fought so hard for fourteen years from 1961 onward to keep a grip on their colonies. In the end, proportionate to their respective populations, Portugal lost more men in its African wars than America in Vietnam.

One of the more bizarre consequences was that just as the Belgians had done in the Congo, Lisbon handed over to a people, totally unprepared for self-governance, one of the largest and richest countries in Africa. There was only a handful of university graduates among the indigenés.

Almost three decades after independence, the Portuguese imprint on these African states is ineffaceable. For one, the official language is Portuguese. So is much of the culture in the cities. There were a couple of excellent little *Fado* bars in Luanda when I was there with EO. So is the food: most meals (for those who can afford restaurant fare) offer *caldo verde* for starters, usually with an excellent Dáo on the table.

Forgotten is the trauma that resulted when the Portuguese were eventually bundled back to Europe in 1975, the majority leaving only with what they could carry.

That happened shortly before independence when Angola declared itself Marxist. In the civil wars that followed there have been a lot of people killed. Though Savimbi is now dead and Unita, as a consequence, has been emasculated, the killing hasn't stopped. Each day there are people dying in some of the biggest minefields on earth.

From Luanda we were taken by small plane to Cabo Ledo,

Executive Outcomes' first major headquarters in the country once it had achieved a foothold.

As the aircraft banked over the coast, we spotted irregular groves of topsy-turvey baobabs. Beyond, almost like a sentinel on a promontory that jutted into the Atlantic, stood a lighthouse that Lisbon's engineers built more than two centuries ago. There weren't too many houses along this stretch of coast but the Iberian imprint among those that stood was unequivocal. When Portugal colonized Angola in the fifteenth century, they brought with them their distinctive red clay roof tiles, still today as much a feature of the homes in Lobito and Luanda as in Coimbra and the Azores.

Cabo Ledo was originally taken over by former SADF Parachute Regiment Colonel Chris Grové. Not long afterward the first FAA battalion of eight-hundred men were being put through their paces by South African vets in preparation for the series of battles that eventually ended in the recapture of Cuito, Huambo, Uige and Soyo.

Little had changed at the old air force base. The runway was lengthened to accommodate larger Soviet jets and to receive some of the overflow when the main runway in Luanda was obscured by fog, but its terminal building was still an unpainted wooden shack about the size of your average garage.

As we stepped off the plane, we were met by Brigadier Nick van den Bergh, a powerfully built man with a full beard who had been a staff officer with 44 Parachute Brigade during the Border War. A pivotal figure in the company, he had been appointed by Eeben Barlow to handle EO's interests in this West African state. Though he did the two-hour road trip to Cabo Ledo often enough, Van den Bergh and his wife had made a home for themselves in Luanda: a simple triplex on a terraced block with few redeeming features. Situated in a noisy street with broken down cars outside, the place cost the firm three-quarters of a million dollars. It was a rip-off considering that the place was jerry-built and cluttered, and he blamed the oil companies for contaminating the economy.

We stayed at the van den Bergh home whenever we visited the capital and would lie awake each night listening to automatic fire reaching up from the Luanda docks. The army had instructions to kill anybody who entered the area. Pickings must have been good because there were casualties in abundance.

For all that, the South Africans shared the Cuban penchant for creating a reasonably comfortable environment for themselves at the base. About all that was missing was air conditioning.

To one side, spread over about a square mile was a FAA airborne training base with enough BMP-2s scattered about to give it the appearance of an armored headquarters. From our verandah, we would watch them cluttering off on the day's exercises and clearly nobody seemed to bother with maintenance; the machines belched fumes like old steam engines each time they were started.

By the time I got to Cabo Ledo, EO had about twenty men stationed at the base, half of them white, mostly communications, logistics and transport techs. There were also a few pilots like Namibian-born Werner Ludick of Lone Hill, whose job it was to ferry unit commanders about in the company King Air. His photos of the Pilatus Porters used by EO in combat are still the best of the bunch.

The big event of the day was invariably the barbecue—or as the South Africans preferred, *braai*. Bottles of Red Heart Rum would be hauled out and the fellows would talk about home, the latest rugby scores and, of course, women. In circumstances where you didn't dare touch the local sluts because a third of the population was infected with HIV, every night was party night.

On the third day, we went to what was eventually to become EO's main training facility in Angola, a Special Forces base at the mouth of the Longa River, or as it is featured on the map, Rio Longa. The trip was an hour-and-a-half by road and we stayed the night: you don't travel around this country after dark, especially with roadblocks armed by troops who are almost always plastered.

We followed the coast for part of the way through the Quicama National Park, which had been almost totally eviscerated of wildlife. Important visitors would come to Angola a quarter of century ago and be awed by the range of animals: elephant herds that were sometimes hundreds strong, lions at every watering hole, buffalo, leopard and even the occasional rhino. By the 1990s, however, there were more people in Quicama than animals.

The elephants went first, for their ivory. Then most of the antelope, because Luanda was tardy with victuals for their troops. Finally the big cats were hunted for their skins, for which there was a big demand in Cuba. It seemed that every one of Fidel's pilots couldn't return to Havana without at least one photo of something he had shot. Nobody said anything about them having used automatic weapons to do so.

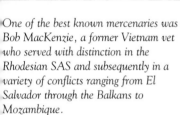

One of the best known mercenaries was Bob MacKenzie, a former Vietnam vet who served with distinction in the Rhodesian SAS and subsequently in a variety of conflicts ranging from El Salvador through the Balkans to Mozambique.

Above right: Sibyl and Bob MacKenzie with Renamo guerillas in Mozambique.

Right: Bob MacKenzie with equipment in the jungle.

Below: The long, lonely road to Camp Charlie (with the detritus of previous convoys) where this American privateer was eventually killed and eaten by the rebels.

Photos: Courtesy Sibyl MacKenzie

The Biafran War was one of the biggest conflicts experienced in post-independence Africa.

Above: The first western pilots to fly the MiG-17 did so in Biafra; one is seen here at Nigeria's Port Harcourt Airport.

Right above: Four-engined Super Constellations were among the cargo aircraft used to keep Biafra alive, and eventually both sides acquired a few surplus American bombers (right below).

Below: Swedish and Biafran crewmen with their tiny but extremely effective Swedish-built MFI-9B Minicons.

Photos: Courtesy of Michael Draper, author of Shadows: Airlift and Airwar in Biafra and Nigeria, 1967–1970

Above: Biafran troops in training. This force was eventually starved into submission.

Left: A British Ferret armored car in service with the Nigerian Army.

Below left: The author came under rocket fire onboard the Swedish merchantman Titania from Minicons while the ship was lying at anchor in Warri roadstead.

Below right: Rolf Steiner, who fought his own kind of war.

Author's collection

Above: Two of Executive Outcomes top field officers, Colonels Duncan Rykaart (left) and Hennie Blaauw on Luanda's once beautiful waterfront. Both men were former senior officers in South African Reconnaissance Regiments (Recces) and went on to plan and implement successful strategies against the rebel Angolan leader Dr. Jonas Savimbi of Unita.

Below: Executive Outcomes and senior Angolan Army officers at the Rio Lomba Special Forces training camp south of Luanda run by South African mercenaries. Author's collection

Above: In the presence of senior Angolan Army commanders, Executive Outcomes personnel display a selection of rebel weapons at the Rio Longa Special Forces camp.

Below left: Former South African No. 1 Reconnaissance Regiment Major Wynand de Toit putting his Angolan charges through their paces in a training session.

Below right: Granite memorial to Executive Outcomes personnel who were killed in action in Angola and Sierra Leone. It stands on the grounds of a house in Pretoria, South Africa. Author's collection

Above: Xangongo bridge across the Kunene river was knocked out in an air strike by South African Airforce jets during the war.

Right: Some of Savimbi's men celebrating after taking a town.

Below left: A Russian-built tank knocked out by Unita commandos in a raid on Saurimo while EO was active there. The company took casualties in that attack, including a fatality.

Below right: Dr. Jonas Savimbi, Unita's mercurial leader. He was killed in action in 2002.

Author's collection

Above: An EO "stick," mostly former South African Special Forces, onboard a Mi-17 helicopter ready for deployment. The mercenary force operated in sticks of four men, usually dropped behind enemy lines by chopper. Their pilot (below left) is "Juba" Joubert. Photo: courtesy Cobus Claassenss

Below right: An Angolan Air Force Sukhoi Su-25 (Frogfoot) flown by mercenaries out of Saurimo in the diamond fields. Photo: courtesy Hennie Blaauw

EXECUTIVE OUTCOMES
— CC —

Above: EO's Jonny Maas in a training session with Angolan Special Forces at Cabo Ledo. Author's collection

Above right: Angolan Air Force Pilatus PC-7s (with rocket pods) like the one flown by Lourens Bosch when he was shot down. Photo: Werner Ludick

Right: A mixed bunch of former SAAF pilots with EO. Back, from left: J.C. Linde, Sonny Janecke, Lourens Bosch, Arthur Walker. Front: Pete Minnaar and Carl Alberts.

Below: A BMP used to strengthen Saurimo's defenses. Photo: Hennie Blaauw

Above: The rugged Russian BMP-2 infantry fighting vehicle proved itself often enough in these ragtag African wars. These were tough, dependable amphibious machines that often turned the tide of battle in Angola and Sierra Leone.

Below: Al J. Venter (left) with Cobus Claassens in the jungle after the attack on Baiama.

Above: Special Forces training group in the presence of EO personnel and a senior Angolan general. Wynand de Toit is pointing out detail to Duncan Rykaart on the bench. To his right, standing, is Hennie Blaauw.

Below: A view of Saurimo—filthy, ramshackle and often under attack, but still Angola's diamond center in the northeast of the country. The photo was taken from one of the Hips flown by EO pilots.   Author's collection

Above: Colonel Hennie Blaauw conducting an informal order group with his command elements during the blitzkrieg operation to take the Cafunfo diamond fields.

Right: A member of the EO squad checks the road ahead of a squadron of Russian-built T554/55s for land mines.

Below left: Carl Alberts (left) and Hennie Blaauw return from a recce in an Angolan Air Force Mi-17.

Below right: Blaauw takes the salute beneath the Angolan hammer and sickle flag.

Author's collection

Top left: EO officers who took the diamond fields, including Simon Witherspoon (left) next to Raymond Archer, Rich Nichol, Cobus Claassens and the du Preez twins, Nico and Louis. Photo: courtesy Cobus Claassens

Top right: Formal photo of EO's Koidu commander, Roelf van Heerden (standing center) with Cobus Claassens kneeling (left) next to Jos Grobelaar. Author's collection

Above: One of the Nigerian Air Force Alpha Jets gunned up and ready to roll at Lungi Airport.

Below: A trio of mercenaries among those involved in taking the Sierra Leone diamond fields—Raymond Archer, Cobus Claassens and Simon Witherspoon. Photo: courtesy Cobus Claassens

Above: Carl Alberts (in flying suit, back to the camera) with the Hind that was eventually sabotaged by the Russian mercenary contingent.

Photo: courtesy Arthur Walker

Below left: An informal Land Rover patrol (with AGS multiple grenade launcher mounted) in Koidu after EO took the town from the rebels. The mosque it is passing remained undamaged throughout the war.

Bottom left: An Executive Outcomes BMP on the way to Koidu.

Photo: courtesy Cobus Claassens

Below right: A British Army patrol on the outskirts of Lungi Airport.

Author's collection

Top left: Side gunner onboard EO's Hip.

Top: Louis and Nico du Preez with Cobus Claassens (center) on ops near the Kono diamond fields in Sierra Leone.

Above: Russian technicians in Sierra Leone who often did more harm than good.

Bottom left: Heavy jungle foliage hampered the attack on Baiama in eastern Sierra Leone.

Below: Executive Outcomes was composed mostly of black South Africans Special Forces veterans under the command of white officers. One of EO's squad leaders in the Sierra Leone conflict.

Author's collection

Sierra Leone's Marine Control and Surveillance unit was originally established with the help of ICI and taken over by Southern Cross Security. Though moribund for lack of money and spares, it is a successful example of how mercenaries have been used to counter illegal fish poaching and pirate activity along the African coast. Run on a shoestring budget, this maritime unit has become an effective presence, even though some NGOs are vocal in their opposition to the use of mercenaries.

Above: The occupants of this Pam Pam have their hands in the air after being intercepted on the approaches to Freetown.

Below: Cobus Claassens would take his armed semi-rigid hulled inflatables in close to any fishing craft in Sierra Leone waters, sometimes firing a volley across their bows to stop them. Some of these crews—mostly Asian—were arrested for illegal fishing, for which the company was paid a bounty.

Two examples of present-day PMC deployments in the world's trouble spots. ICI was contracted by the U.S. State Department within hours of the Northern Pakistan earthquake disaster to go in and provide logistical and air support.

Above: ICI's Danny O'Brien with Pakistani villagers in the Fall of 2005.
Photo: Courtesy of Danny O'Brien

Below: Private security operatives on the main road to Baghdad Airport in Iraq.
Photo: Courtesy of Gregory Lovett

EO's base on the river was one of the best on the continent. It fringed a great, tropical waterway and might have been an appropriate setting for a remake of one of Rider Haggard's great yarns. At one point near the estuary, the river was a quarter mile wide. The camp itself was gathered like a *safari boma* around clusters of tall palms while lianas dangled everywhere. We could hear the monkeys cavorting as we arrived. The thirty-odd South Africans based there lived in tents, their metal beds raised several additional inches off the ground because of scorpions and snakes.

It was always a topic of discussion when newcomers arrived. The men took a devious delight in telling us about the numbers of mambas, puffadders, gaboon vipers and cobras that slithered in. Being so close to the river, pythons were also a problem, and apparently in that area they had become something of a threat to humans.

On my first evening, while visiting the unit's water purifying plant, I was escorted down "Python Alley." It was too dark for photos, so we had to return the next day. When the time came, we made a wide detour to get there. "Snakes," my escort explained, and I didn't argue.

The officer in charge at Rio Longa was Wynand du Toit, a legendary figure from South Africa's war days in Angola. Still in his thirties and like most of the others, with requisite beard, he'd devoted his life to conflict. Wynand's claim to fame was that as a member of an elite Reconnaissance Regiment, he had led a strike force into Cabinda in an attempt to sabotage Angolan oilfields.

Though things went well enough after being brought close inshore by one of South Africa's submarines, things went sour because there was a squad of Cuban Special Forces waiting for them. During the course of the operation some of the South Africans were killed while Major du Toit was wounded and taken prisoner. He was to spend years in solitary in the worst of Angola's military prisons, though he actually thanks Cuban doctors for patching him up.

Curiously, not long before the Cabinda episode, he'd led a similar raid up that very same Longa River where he was then based. Once again a submarine had been tasked to take them about two miles offshore, from where they paddled the rest of the way in kayaks.

"It was a dark night and we entered the estuary, right under the noses of the guards . . . could have blown the bridge if we'd had the right stuff, but I decided after the first recce that the structure was too big for what we had. Couldn't carry too much in those little craft." he explained. For two nights, the combatants secreted themselves among thick reed beds that stretched out hundreds of yards from the bank. Through it all, they never spotted a single serpent.

"If I'd have known how many there really were, I'd never have tackled the project," he smiled.

In the aftermath of the South Africans having settled in at Cabo Ledo, work began in September 1994 to prepare a battle plan to oust Savimbi and his forces from their strongholds in the north and northeast. Prime targets were the diamond fields, then under rebel control. While this was happening, EO instructors trained a battalion of FAA troops at several locations within a few hours' drive of the capital.

The envisioned combat force was divided into three elements: an offensive group (including air assault units with Mi-17 and Mi-24 helicopters); a mobile mechanized group that was equipped with FAA's new T-62 Russian tanks, and the Rio Longa training contingent.

In November, the Angolan Chief of Staff, General Joao de Matos, summoned EO's leadership to Luanda for a conference that centered on the biggest prize of all, the recapture of Cafunfo. It was a particular difficult assignment, since all roads leading to the diamond diggings were in Unita hands. There were in excess of ten thousand guerrillas and their supporters on the banks of the Cuango River.

The Angolan command was aware that Savimbi had ordered all bridges leading to the approaches to Cafunfo prepared for destruction, should government forces try to take the place. Thus, the attack would be two-pronged: one pincer headed out east from Luanda and the other came from Saurimo, headed northwest.

Because of landmines, once conjoined at the junction town of Cacolo, the column would avoid all roads, itself a difficult decision because of the nature of the country that needed to be traversed. This part of the Angolan interior was still primeval, the kind that early explorers had always romanced about, a tough, unforgiving terrain. That it fringed the Congo to the immediate north underscored its isolation.

Instead the strike force would "bundu-bash" its way toward Cafunfo, roughshodding over whatever obstacles remained. Bridges would be built or temporarily laid with Russian TMM bridging equipment brought along for the purpose. Those present at planning agreed that while the task was difficult, it could be done. This pleased de Matos, a bluff, chubby fellow who had already proved to the South Africans that he could be both ruthless and outspoken.

By the following January, another mechanized group was being prepared with BMP-2s at Cabo Ledo under EO Col. Roelf van Heerden, formerly of the SADF's 82 Mechanized Brigade, who was later to play a pivotal role in the Kono diamond fields in Sierra Leone.

Meanwhile, by mid-February, Grové, assisted by Colonels van den Bergh and Duncan Rykaart, got their heads together with members of the Angolan General Staff. Heading the group as theater commander of the operation was FAA General Marques, and it was he who issued orders to prepare for an armored thrust against Unita at Cafunfo.

This was all pretty tough stuff. The plan included moving men and armor—almost a full division—from their two points of origin to the northeast corner of the country, a distance, as the crow flies from Luanda, of almost six hundred miles. In fact, with Unita doing what it could to interdict any kind of movement that included surrounding the air strip at Saurimo—with men armed with SAMs and rocket launchers—it ended up a good deal further.

To begin with, they had to move twenty-two new T62 tanks—in stages and on seven low-loaders—a hundred miles to the crossroads town of Dondo, about halfway to Malanje. Beyond, they'd proceed through the badlands under their own power.

By now other EO men had assumed key positions. Col. Hennie Blaauw formerly commander of 5 Reconnaissance Regiment, was placed (together with his FAA counterpart, Brigadier Sauchimo) in charge of Combat Group Alpha. The order was reversed shortly afterward when Blaauw was detached to take command of the Saurimo sector as well as Combat Group Bravo. His immediate boss was de Castro, who by then had taken most of the credit for what had happened at Soyo and been promoted to Brigadier. De Castro, good Party man that he was, took it upon himself to monitor all EO activities, a security measure that came down from the top.

The force eventually included a motorized infantry battalion, which included thirty-two BMP-2s. Two at a time, these amphibious armored vehicles were flown out east in droop-winged Ilyushin 76s.

In the later stages, Saurimo became an indispensable cog in the envisaged program of attack. Though remote and with few facilities (or even a proper hotel) this dirty, dusty little outstation with no sewage system, few shops, banks that seemed to exist in name only, and a road grid that ended in minefields on the edge of town seemed to attract diamond dealers from all over.

Like most other settlements within a five hundred-mile radius, hygiene hardly rated, which might be one of the reasons why two of the worst Ebola outbreaks in the past quarter century occurred just across the border in the Congo. Both were within half-a-day's drive of the place.

If you stayed a week at the decrepit old Hotel Lisboa or frequented the market—a huge, open-air fanfare of filth and cacophony where the entire community would gather during the day—you were likely to meet as many Israelis and Russians as French and South Africans. Each one of them was eager to crack the "big one," though most of the larger stones moved surreptitiously. Angola has never been shy to tax its transients.

Diamonds ruled just about everything that happened in Saurimo then as they still do today. In an environment about as enervating as it was dangerous, all talk seemed to center on cut, color, clarity and carat. Mention Saurimo back in Luanda and again you could end up discussing diamonds. You drew attention if you mentioned going there: Angola is a police state and the authorities like to keep tabs on what foreigners are doing in their country, especially where it concerns precious stones.

For all that, Saurimo wasn't the easiest of places to get to. Since Unita dominated most of the countryside between the diggings and the coast, a charter was one of the few options left to reach the place, and that could cost an arm. Or you might cadge a lift from one of the Antonov pilots hauling in food for the U.S. The going rate at the time was about $100 for a single journey if you were lucky enough to find someone willing to take the chance. That also needed muscle because nobody with clearance was allowed to enter an Angolan Aeroporto. It had to be arranged up front with more "incentives" to the military running the show.

Even then there were risks. On our flights into Saurimo, EO's 727 would descend in a sharp, righthand spiral from about twenty-five thousand feet. We'd virtually swoop out of the sky and glide down onto the runway, often holding our breaths and seats to keep our breakfasts down. It could be unnerving, but as Werner Ludick explained, it was either that or missiles.

It was not only SAMs that concerned him. "Friendly fire" from FAA troops manning anti-aircraft guns around the perimeter of the airport happened too often to be ignored. Most times such incidents took place late in the day when cheap liquor or hash had taken effect.

For that reason Ludick repeated the process on his departure. For ten minutes or so, he'd spiral upward, making tight circles in the sky and would go on doing so until we were out of range of ground fire. Only then would he set course for home.

There were other problems that not everybody spoke about. Only months before I arrived, a Russian Antonov-12 was hit by one of Unita's SAMs while preparing to land. Though the plane came down within sight of Saurimo and the Russian crew was able to walk away from the wreck, two of them were killed because they ended up wandering into a minefield. Both the town and its airport were completely surrounded by them. Even today, with the war over, there are still mines all over the place.

Unlike EO's air crews, Russian pilots rarely bothered themselves with anti-missile precautions, was Ludick's view. "Some of their pilots begin descent a hundred miles out and, let's face it, to some gook in the bush, that must present a pretty inviting target at ten thousand feet when you're handy with a Manpad," he commented.

It was the dominance of Angolan air space that finally turned the war around.[2] That and a vigorous ground campaign spearheaded by several hundred Executive Outcomes mercenaries.

The South African aviators were all SAAF veterans. Many had cut their teeth on Dassault Mirages or Buccaneers originally bought from Britain just before the anti-apartheid brouhaha became earnest. Some of the pilots, like Arthur Walker, Charlie Tate and "Juba" Joubert—one of the few helicopter pilots to have taken a direct hit from a Strela missile and still bring his machine down—had seen years of action in chopper gunships in Angola's earlier wars. So had Neall Ellis, who at some stage or another flew with them all. These aviators all did their share of combat in Sierra Leone afterward.

Initially, the Angolan high command seemed reluctant to allow the South Africans unrestricted access to the Angolan Air Force (FAPA's) fleet of MiG-23s, Sukhois and helicopters. So too, with the PC-7s to start with. Equally abruptly, as plans neared fruition, some of these restrictions were lifted.

The Swiss-built PC-7 Pilatus turboprop trainers went on to provide valuable service in close-quarter ground-support work in some of the remoter areas in which EO operated. Obviously slower than the jets, they gave the pilots the ability to do the kind of reconnaissance work that would have been impractical from larger aircraft. Also, during ground operations, one of them would sometimes be tasked as an improvised Telstar relay station to relay messages between ground units and headquarters or air assets moving into the attack.

For combat, their underwing hard points had originally been adapted for weapons systems by technicians in Luanda shortly after the aircraft arrived from Switzerland. This allowed them to field either two or four sets of eighteen-round 68mm SNEB rocket pods.

The Mi-17s fielded by the Angolans were also armed. They could handle an even heavier load and a variety of systems were experimented with on its four racks, including UPK-23-250 pods containing GSh-23L twin-barrel 23mm cannon. Also tried were GUV pods with the AGS-17 Plamya 30mm grenade launcher, which went through a prototype stage.

Not everything worked. More successful on the Hips were two four-barrel 7.62mm 9-A-622 machine guns. Because of technical problems, some of the crews of both the 8s and the 17s eventually settled for pintle-mounted 7.62mm PKMs firing from port and starboard and, once the clamshell rear doors had been removed, another from the rear. As for the pilots manning them, conversions were improvised. Former SAAF Mirage or Impala jet jocks would go solo after a few hours of orientation.

The South Africans were impressed with all these machines, the choppers especially. Former SAAF Colonel Arthur Walker, who had survived two decades of combat in Rhodesia, Namibia and Angola and who did several tours with EO (never once being wounded) found the Mi-17 rugged and reliable. Charlie Tate told me at Denel Aviation that on one of his first orientation trips with the Hip, he and Carl Alberts uplifted a four-ton container at the Rio Longa base. That was about two thousand pounds more than the manufacturer's permissible load.

The same with trooping. Hip specs allowed for about twenty fully equipped troops to be loaded. Never fazed by what the book said, the Angolans would raise that tally by half as much again. In one emergency near Cafunfo, a Hip was forced to aid another helicopter that had been forced down by ground fire, and by the time it got into the hover again, there were forty men onboard. All were hauled those last few hundred miles or so to EO's staging post at Saurimo totally in the dark.

Without an air force of his own, Savimbi still managed to inflict serious damage. Airports were mortared whenever possible. His people proved their superiority in mortar barrages by using their NATO 81mm bombs (supplied through an intermediary dealer by France) to good effect. With a greater range than the East European 82mm issued to FAA, the rebels usually attacked from just beyond the range of what the Angolans had.

The rebels excelled in getting past enemy defenses. Employing techniques taught by South African Special Forces instructors during the earlier Border War, they would use defectors' know-how and come straight on through any minefields in the way. Once, while EO worked out of Saurimo, a Unita commando group—dressed in FAA uniforms—was able to penetrate airport security and destroy several aircraft on the ground. Two of the Hips then in EO employ were written off, one of them burnt to a frazzle after it took an RPG blast. The other, riddled by gunfire, was still standing, stripped of anything useable, in the base grounds when I was there.

In a remarkably well-orchestrated Unita house-clearing operation at the same time, EO lost "Blackie" Swart. Badly wounded, the company airlifted him to Johannesburg but he was dead on arrival.

Unita commandos who'd been responsible for this attack were members of Savimbi's crack Special Forces *Groupos de Bate*. Absurdly brazen, they would slide in just about anywhere and cause mayhem. According to Blaauw, his men had to be "extra-alert." Once, after 45 Brigade had moved to Lucala, guerrillas penetrated a well defended perimeter and slit the throats of eight men as they lay in their sleeping bags. They came and went like shadows, the bodies only being discovered in the morning.

Aircraft and armor were Unita's two main targets. Earlier, prior to the 1992 cease-fire, the Angolan government had taken delivery of eight new Mi-24s. Without spares the deal was worth about $40 million. The rebels destroyed most of them as soon as the talks were halted because they were shrewd enough to site their camps near important airfields.

Other aircraft knocked out on the ground included several C-130s, two or three AN-12s and at least one Ilyushin-76, blown away in a rocket attack. About a dozen more were accounted for by ground fire—12.7mm and 14.5mm heavy machine guns as well as SAM-7s and SAM-14s, quite a few in the Huambo area. It could have been more because Luanda never credited Unita with kills if there were no survivors.

Like the Nigerians in Biafra, Luanda would barely acknowledge

Unita's prowess. Grudgingly, they would admit that the rebels were bothersome, but to concede to any kind of successful strike or even that they might have lost aircraft as a result of their efforts was out. When a plane did go down, Luanda's spinmasters would remonstrate with the international press and they did it well.

For instance, a King Air was brought down with a missile at the Cafunfo diamond center in late 1994. In the attack, shrapnel fragments killed and wounded several passengers and crew. For a while afterward, Luanda claimed that mechanical failure had been the cause.

Executive Outcomes' aircrews were linked to some remarkable tales of courage as the war progressed. Consider events that took place after the company had relocated part of its force to Saurimo.

At one stage Hennie Blaauw tasked a pair of Mi-17s—one flown by Tate and Sonny Janecke and the other by J.C. Linde and Joubert—to "hot extract" an EO reconnaissance party that was about to be overrun by Unita Special Forces.[3]

Earlier, another recce team comprised of two whites, Renier and Steyn, a black tracker by the name of Handsome Ndlovu (a veteran of the Rhodesian War) and one of his pals had been dropped by helicopter near the small but strategically situated hamlet of Cuango.[4] Almost immediately their radios went silent. After a search that lasted days involving every available helicopter as well as a pair of PC-7s, it was accepted that they had either been killed or captured.

EO maintained strict radio schedules and there had to be good reason for the men not to call in. They never did and there was not a whisper about their fate. Only afterward did word come through that "two white mercenaries" had been captured by the rebels and executed. There was no mention of the two Africans.

Unofficially, the word went out that they had been compromised by one of EO's radio operators at Saurimo who had been "bent" by Unita. It was said, but never confirmed, that the radioman was killed in an "accident" shortly afterward.

According to Colonel Duncan Rykaart, much of the early work of the mercenary force in the east entailed a program of destruction and disruption of enemy command and control centers. Small, long-range penetration groups would be dropped by helicopter and picked up after the job was done at designated LZs. The object was to survey Unita camps, supply dumps and strongpoints, as well as headquarters and, ultimately, to prepare a route for an attack by land forces.

Only occasionally did these small teams go on the offensive.

An example of the remarkable ability to retaliate swiftly came when Saurimo received an urgent call from Simon Witherspoon, a former Recce and in his day, one of the best operators in any man's army. It was sent on the second night of an operation in distant parts.[5] Having been inserted near Cafunfo, Witherspoon, Rich Nichol and their two trackers were running hard from a Unita follow-up team through an unusually-dense stretch of jungle. The undergrowth was so thick that they could barely manage to cover five hundred yards an hour. Worse, they were making little headway in a black night and the enemy was gaining on them, which was unusual because these were the fittest men in the unit.

It didn't take Witherspoon long to realize that their Unita adversaries were closing in. And since the South Africans weren't familiar with the area, there was also the possibility of them being ambushed by other enemy soldiers deployed further out. As he was to report afterward, they all had radios.

At that point several members of the chase team were about three hundred yards behind, close enough for the South Africans to spot the reflections of their pursuers' torches off the wet foliage. He said later that they had considered an ambush, but from the noise being made, they were hopelessly outnumbered. Whenever he stopped he could hear the enemy's scouts chopping away at the undergrowth.

At that stage they were near the village of Sacassambia, about twenty miles north of where Renier and his group had disappeared. EO's policy in these matters is clear: if they asked to be extricated, it was assumed that the situation was critical. Such requests were serious and the unit reacted accordingly. In any event, all these men had been involved in combat for years and were highly experienced.

Consequently, at four in the morning, a pair of Mi-17s left Saurimo and arrived at the designated LZ at first light. Heavy mist obscured visibility, which—according to the pilots—was scary because the region was undulating and there was also a mountain or two. Since the crew hadn't brought night vision goggles, they were forced to rely on the fleeing party's strobe light. Finally, using their GPS sets, they were able to close in and establish comms.

With Linde at the controls and Tate's machine offering what support it could, the drama that followed was about as hairy as it gets. Though it soon became light, a heavy mist still clung to the slopes.

"It was really tough," Joubert remembers. "We would feel our way across the top of the forest and then suddenly a mountain would sort of appear out of the mist in front of us. At last Charlie spotted the strobe and he gave me bearings." As he tells it, the hillside sloped from left to right and the bush there was almost impenetrable. Meanwhile, the guys below had reached a small clearing but it wasn't big enough for his rotors to make a clear descent without causing some kind of damage.

The South Africans took the helicopter in anyway and Joubert used his rotors to carve a passage through the bush. It would have worked but for one tree that was sturdier than the rest which ended up damaging the blades.

"But we still weren't down on the ground. In trying to hover, I found that the machine had become seriously unstable. Meanwhile, Simon and the boys had emerged from the bush and shouted that we were still too high, so I beat the trees for a few more seconds and finally we were able to get them onboard.

"As I pulled power, the chopper began to vibrate and it was quite violent. The shaking continued as I gained altitude and I was forced to pull back on the throttle. It was then that I decided to put her down. If I didn't, I was sure that the old bird would break up," he said.

Joubert spotted a stretch of water ahead. To buy time from his Unita pursuers—they must have been within RPG range by the time they lifted off—he decided to put his wheels down on the far side of a river. The moment they touched, he knew that he'd brought the helicopter down in water. They'd landed in a swamp.

"The tail boom immediately began to sink." With Tate still circling nearby and having been given time to inspect the damage, the crew decided that they might just be able to make it back to base, more than a hundred miles away. Finally, the men set about extricating the machine from the mud and though it took time, they got it all clear in the end.

"We had to fly at reduced speed the rest of the way. Anything over ninety knots and the chopper began to vibrate almost uncontrollably and yaw all over the place. Obviously our light load helped."

The same mistake wasn't made when another EO group was inserted with SAM missiles near Luremo, another diamond town on the Cuango River to the north of Cafunfo. With its own airstrip, using chartered C-130s and DC-6 transports, Unita regularly hauled in supplies, armaments and equipment, most of it out of Kinshasa. The idea was for the EO squad to take up a position on the outskirts and try to bring down one of these aircraft. The problem was that though they were there for some time, the "stick" was always in the right place at the wrong time.

In the end the four men had to be pulled out because just about all of them contracted malaria.

Preparations for the attack on Cafunfo progressed steadily at Saurimo and each day also brought something new. EO's first casualty in the eastern sector of the war was one of them.

By early 1994, the town of Xinge—an important command post just north of the strategic crossroads of Cacolo—was increasingly being fingered in intelligence reports. What became clear was that the place was rank with Unita troop movements. Under the command of Brigadier Bule, a competent though unconventional Unita officer, this small town caused enough headaches for Hennie Blaauw to do something about it. Thus, in concert with his FAA bosses, two mortar sections were landed by a pair of Hips some miles to the west of Xinge. The intention was for them to spend the night in the area, set an ambush and hope for the best. At some stage they would mortar Bule's headquarters.

The plan was that they'd be extricated on request, probably the following day, Blaauw explained during one of the evening *braais*. The usual precautions were taken: LZs in several categories were marked on the maps, with a specified pick-up point together with one or two alternatives. Also listed were emergency locations where the choppers might go in if things got desperate.

This time round, the men had barely exited from the Hip in the dark before some kind of movement was observed by the men onboard. It was a short distance away in the surrounding bush. Not being certain if it was enemy, nothing was radioed to the choppers. In any event, with the men on the ground having been infiltrated, the choppers were already on their way back to Saurimo. Throughout the night, reports that came in of unusual activity around Xinge. Unita talked of the movement of helicopters. Radio reports claimed that they had fired on them, the usual inter-unit claptrap.

In debrief afterward, the aviators admitted that they had never been aware of coming under fire during the insertion. In fact, things might have taken a very different turn if they had. And while the situation on the ground was not yet serious, it didn't take long for things to turn nasty.

By morning, Braam's team had had their first contact with the enemy and Polly van Rooyen, formerly of 4 Recce, almost had his leg blown off. Holding off a bunch of Unita attackers, the South Africans went ahead anyway and mortared Xinge. Though it took a while to make comms with Telstar—the plane by then having taken up a monitoring position in the sky above them—they called for the Mi-17s to haul them out. They reported that van Rooyen, a big, robust man, was in excruciating pain and losing blood. Still, he never uttered a sound throughout the attack or during the subsequent extraction.

It was Carl Alberts who eventually brought his Mi-17 and pulled both mortar teams out. As he recalled afterward, it was done in extremis, almost within sight of Xinge, with "Tattie" Tate's chopper in support.

Airlifted back to South Africa within hours, Van Rooyen's leg was saved and he stayed with EO in a non-combative capacity until the company folded. We went on to have a few rums and cokes in Pretoria where he told me his story.

Not long afterward, Blaauw was ordered to organize a fairly large force composed of mortar teams with protection elements to harry Unita forces at Camaxilo. Not a big place to the immediate south of the Zairean (Congolese) diamond town of Kahembe, it was an essential part of Savimbi's supply chain. Much of what he used for his war effort was routed through there.

Former Recce trooper Carl Dietz was charged with getting the attack together while the first helicopter involved in the operation was again crewed by "Juba" Joubert and J.C. Linde. They were the first to drop their component. Charlie Tate and Sonny Janecke—with Dietz sitting between them in the jump seat—followed. Two PC-7s monitored the operation to provide top cover if required.

One of the PC-7s had already gone ahead to scout the LZ, and though he chose a position only about a half-mile from town, the pilot said that it'd have to do because there wasn't anything else suitable for some distance. It was a one-off, thought the pilots, so what the hell. They would go in, drop the men and pick them up again immediately afterward. The show was expected to last thirty, forty minutes max.

The job done, the helicopters went in again to bring out the men. There were no problems with Juba: he lifted out his team and headed southward to wait for Tate and Janecke to do their thing. Tattie had barely touched down when the jungle exploded. Not only were they picking up fire from the direction of town, but from behind as well. Though the side gunners were supported by more PKMs on the ground, the Mi-17 was taking some serious hits.

Within a minute, there were three men inside the chopper wounded, including one of the EO operators, Billie Erasmus. Dietz remembers seeing a solid stream of fuel running down the inside of the helicopter's windscreen and into the cockpit. They'd obviously been blasted in one of the feed tanks, probably by an RPG.

In the babble of messages that followed, coupled to more shouts from the back about incoming, all of it muffled by the screams of the wounded, one of the engine oil pressure lights on the console flashed an emergency signal. With "Natasha" screaming her customary warning that things were amiss, Charlie Tate had to make a decision: it was a matter of fight or flee.

The first, he recalls, was never an option because it was obvious to everybody onboard that they were outnumbered. He had serious doubts about the second.

Unaware of little but the immediate problems in his face, this former SAAF Alouette veteran took it for granted that none of the men would hang about outside. It was *shaila*[5] time so he pulled collective and got airborne. But only just, because the helicopter barely responded to its controls.

By the time that Juba's Hip had joined forces, Tate's chopper was limping across the top of the jungle. Also, it was spewing volumes of fuel. Meanwhile, retaliation from the ship's gunners had ceased because the men feared that a spark might ignite fuel vapors which had enveloped everybody onboard. As it was, Juba recalls, the crippled machine billowed a huge white cloud of vaporizing fuel.

Barely two miles from where the ambush had taken place, Tate put his machine down. It was an LZ that had tree stumps everywhere.

"What we had to do in double quick time was get everybody off, talk Juba down and hope to Christ that he'd be able to get off the ground again with the additional load, which was huge. It would have been about forty men, together with the remainder of their equipment. To his credit, Juba didn't even have to think about it: he landed his machine, loaded up and took off again, the entire operation being completed in two, perhaps three minutes.

With Telstar in a low-level formation, they flew together until it got dark. Both aircraft arrived at Saurimo about an hour later.

The biggest tragedy of the event was that in the flurry and confusion of what was taking place when Tate was trying to get off the ground, four of the original group had been abandoned on the ground. Worse, though it was unintentional, the quartet of PKM gunners—on their own volition—had taken up defensive positions on the ground outside. They were actually protecting the helicopter from further attack, and by all accounts were doing a pretty good job of keeping Unita heads down.

As one of the men commented afterward, paraphrasing the familiar maxim, "They died so that the rest of our group could live." It was a pithy comment because for such a small unit, the loss was massive.

There was never anything forthcoming from Unita about the fate of the four men who had been abandoned.

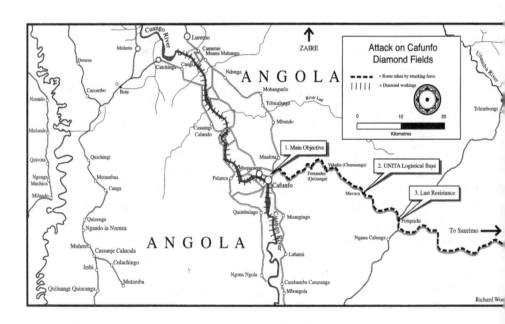

18

TAKING ANGOLA'S DIAMOND FIELDS FROM THE REBELS

"Private armies are a far cry from the Sixties dogs of war."
John Keegan, Defense Correspondent,
The Daily Telegraph, London.

With Angola's armor, ground and air assets preparing for battle, Cafunfo became the magic word. Nobody had any doubt that the rebels would eventually be dislodged: there was a new bearded bunch of toughies on the block and Luanda was confident that, as with Soyo, they would do the trick.

Several years earlier, Unita had taken possession of the huge alluvial diggings on which Cafunfo stands, and it was those gems – "blood diamonds" as the politically correct like to call them—that continued to fuel Savimbi's war.

The task ahead was daunting. There were innumerable delays, false starts and cancellations, and much of the obfuscation could be sourced to Luanda's mind-blowing bureaucracy. At one stage a group of MPLA political commissars[1] arrived at Saurimo. Like a gaggle of Auschwitz *uberleutnants*, they jackbooted about the base and demanded to know about things that were not only of no concern to them, but had nothing to do with the campaign ahead. A quick radio call to Luanda from Hennie Blaauw got them back on their plane.

In Saurimo, during the preparatory stages of this coming series of battles, there were endless messages, contradictions, debates, and not a few heated arguments, as well as a question or two that sometimes made sense. Forms had to be completed (sometimes in quintuplicate), much of it coupled to order groups and staff meetings. Additionally, strings of military brass would flip in and out of the capital. Kafka would have loved the place, especially since most of the senior Angolan commanders had been put through their paces in the Soviet Union. They liked to do things by the book and the South Africans didn't.

That, in essence, was how the operation got started. Issues were further compounded by delays in the supply of men, equipment and machines, none of which was helped by the fact that Luanda lay on the far side of the country.

To cap it all, EO had to contend with staff officers who sometimes nurtured their own agendas, petty jealousies that became squabbles, equipment that didn't perform, and spare parts that would disappear within an hour of arrival, or didn't fit because they weren't the ones that had been ordered. Not to mention an army that seemed permanently smashed or, more often, was smoking something noxious.

Even Angolan pilots who, with their South African counterparts, were to be part of the show, weren't immune to inanities. There were a number of aircraft involved in accidents, with those at the controls later found to be drunk. One of them took an Mi-17 out and after cutting enough of a crooked line across the skies above Saurimo to have everybody on the ground gaping, he brought the helicopter down with a thud. Several rotors snapped and the chopper's undercarriage buckled on impact. Unlike civilian air crews, this crowd wasn't regarded as expendable and such transgressions were ignored, most times, anyway.

Weather in that part of tropical Africa seemed to have a priority all its own. Though it was technically winter in the southern Hemisphere, the occasional storm—black, billowing cu-nim—would roll in and make things miserable. There would be downpours that would make quagmires of areas half the size of the Netherlands.

Finally, there was the rebel leader Savimbi. A tough adversary whose entire career revolved around taking absurd chances, he had never been a pushover. Together, all these factors in concert seemed to contrive to deny success before the operation even began.

Whenever things looked hopeless, however, somebody would recall that EO had done it before. Never mind that the circumstances at Soyo were different, it had already been demonstrated that the Unita nut could be cracked. Throughout, even when there were sharp differences between Blaauw and the FAA high command—which was often, because the approach to most things military by so many of these black brigadiers was cumbersome and intransigent—it was taken for granted that this tough bunch of mercenaries would repeat the process.

In reality, Cafunfo would be a critical test of the firm's ability to counter Unita's insurgency across a huge swath of the interior. Every one of those involved knew that without his diamonds Savimbi would falter. Thus, should the boys fail in their efforts, the implications weren't lost on any of Eeben's people. Future PMC contracts stood or fell by the outcome of this encounter.

Hennie Blaauw explained some of it shortly after I arrived in the diamond capital. He pulled out a set of Angolan government maps of the northwest. Marked in bold capital letters across the top was the word, in Portuguese, SECRETO.

The Cuango, the river on which Cafunfo lay, he explained, emptied into the Congo. It also drained much of the huge Malange basin. Penciled in across the chart were tiny shields of crossed picks and shovels—geological markings that identified diggings: gold, diamonds, iron ore, aluminum and the rest. Many of these highlighted diamondiferous pipes, which, though largely alluvial, stretched all the way to the Congo's frontier and beyond. A source at De Beers confirmed afterward that the entire riverine region was regarded by some geologists as among the richest diamond deposits in the world.

With a stubby, nicotine-stained finger, Blaauw poked at a few places until he finally found what he was looking for and chortled in Afrikaans: "*Ja. Hier's dit!*" ("Yes, here it is!").

That place was Firiquichi, he declared, pulling himself up to full stretch. A hefty scotch in one hand and the map in the other, he added that I probably wouldn't find it on any conventional chart. He and the others who went in with him weren't to know until later, but just about everything that eventually took place in a succession of battles that lasted a month hinged on that tiny anonymous cluster of grass huts in the African jungle.

When the armored column eventually did transmogrify itself into a potent fighting force—part of it having moved overland across Angola from Luanda with the rest coming out of Saurimo in the east—it consisted of about a hundred vehicles. Apart from the twenty-eight BMP-2s, all of them brand new, there were an additional sixty logistic and fire-support vehicles, among them several Russian bridge-building TMMs.

In terms of manpower, there were about five hundred FAA troops altogether, many of them trained at Wynand du Toit's Rio Longa base. They, in turn, were supported by a couple of hundred EO mercs, the majority black.

Also in this array was a group of a hundred Katangese regulars, hard aggressive combatants who years before had fled Zaire and taken refuge in Angola. Though older than the rest, everybody knew that they could dish it out when they had to. Blaauw regarded them as a rather odd, irascible, French-speaking bunch, but as everybody knew, they kept themselves in a constant state of readiness for the day they could return in triumph to the old country.

On the road to Cafunfo they were to prove their worth many times over, even though Colonel André, their leader, was sometimes unnecessarily castigated by his Angolan counterparts. For Blaauw that ached, because it was sometimes done in the presence of junior officers and as far as this veteran was concerned, that just wasn't on. But then, as even he would admit, the Angolan military code of ethics was very different from his own. This former Recce commander was old school and he played by the rules.

There was no doubt, he recalled afterward, that the Katangese had seen a lot of fighting. With Angolan support, they had launched three bloody invasions of Zaire against the hated Mobutu regime in the previous twenty years: the last time they'd tried to take the copper mining town of Kolwezi in what was once called Katanga. Twice they were beaten off, but only after the tyrant had appealed to Europe for help. Both times a combined force of French parachutists and Legionnaires was sent to Africa to sort things out.[2]

The armored thrust on Cafunfo would eventually cover hundreds of miles across some of the most difficult bush country on any continent.

As Blaauw commented: "We knew from the start that it would be as tough as anything we'd experienced." And since there was no way of predicting events, they could only guess what Unita would pull out of the hat.

In the end, the operation—in its various disjointed phases—lasted three months, though the final stage out of Cacolo took only twenty-five days, during which the Angolans had to literally carve their own route through the bush. Throughout, the column was harassed by a succession of attacks, ambushes and mortar standoffs, an average of about four or five assaults a day. At one stage Unita was hurling 60mm mortars at the column as if they were firecrackers. There were also landmines laid by Savimbi's people but because the attackers covered virgin ground almost from the start, there was no way that Unita commanders could predict which route the mobile force would follow.

A glance at the *dagboek* (diary) kept by Hennie Blaauw for the duration provides something of an insight. This extract is from the final stages of the march on July 25, 1994, the day before Cafunfo was overrun.

His measurements are metric while notes in brackets are for the readers' benefit:

0829 Mortar fire from 100 meters ahead. Line of Unita infantry behind. BMP throws a track. Scramble MiGs (MiG-23s)

0940 MiGs in air taking heavy 23mm fire from positions around us. More Unita troops in trenches near thick bush. BMPs overrun them. 250 kg aerial bomb falls 100 meters behind us. Close! Mortars incoming!

1126 Move column forward. Prepare mortars and artillery for reaction. Unita on left flank and hitting us. Nick wounded in lung. [Presumably Nick Hayes who later died in a South African hospital.] About 60 enemy dead

1215 Move into town, More mortar and small arms. Heavy going!

1320 Another contact. FAA soldiers fired rifle grenades at enemy from behind us and almost hit our BMPs! Gadaffi wounded. [A black EO operator who was also seriously wounded in Sierra Leone fifteen months later.]

1410 Stopped for eats. Instructed drivers to go on both sides of the track rather than on it because of mines. Two sections in front, one in depth. Caught Unita patrol on open ground. All killed

1455 Mortar and small arms incoming.

1537 Reach Alberto Fernandez. Go round town. Heavy incoming. Hatches down. Just go! Mines!

1600 Into TB [temporary base]. Overnight.

Colonel Blaauw made two further observations. The first regarded night flying activity by the Pilatus Porter PC-7. Louwrens Bosch—using his 68mm rockets—hit two Unita trucks moving through thick bush, having targeted their lights. "Huge explosions" was scribbled in the margin. The other mentioned the enemy using their ZSU-23s in

ground support roles in conjunction with mortar fire. That took place
a few hours later. As usual, *die waens* (the wagons), as he phrased it,
had been pulled round into a traditional Boer laager position. Earlier,
Blaauw had ordered his men to dig slit trenches at least two feet deep
though most, because of the intensity of incoming fire, went down half
as much again.

It was a complicated process getting all the components together for
what was to become the biggest single FAA operation of the war. The
airlift of BMP-2s to the east began in February 1994 and even that
took longer than anticipated because there was always something else
that needed shifting.

Originally, EO Management had put forward the proposal that
for logistical, maintenance and other reasons, the entire force be marshaled at Saurimo. But this proved impractical and the onslaught
became two-pronged. Thus, once FAA's heavy-duty Russian-built Ural
logistics vehicles arrived, Combat Group Bravo with Brigadier Pepe de
Castro in command—together with Roelf van Heerden and the rest of
the mercenary force in tow—departed Saurimo on April 21. The PC-
7s had arrived the previous month.

An immediate problem facing Luanda was that most of the bridges
linking Saurimo with the west had been destroyed. Also, all approach
roads were mined, which was why the column struck out first toward
the east, then south and finally northwest toward the junction town of
Cacolo, where they would integrate with Combat Force Alpha.

Mines were more of a problem than at first anticipated, and within a week several BMP-2s had been knocked out. Every single road
that the enemy thought might be used by the attacking force was peppered with these bombs, many of them command activated from higher ground. UN specialist teams said afterward that it would take years
to clear the main roads, never mind secondaries.[3]

Also, fuel for the air support element became so much of an issue
that the MiG-23s (which only became operational in the sector in mid-
May) were grounded halfway through. Eventually the problem was
partly solved by aircrews tapping fuel directly into their fighters from
the tanks of the cargo planes that regularly flew into Saurimo.

Totally unexpected, Roelf van Heerden—major offensive or not—
decided that he had to go back to South Africa. His wife was having
a baby. The always-affable Blaauw was delighted. He'd been kicking
rocks back in Cabo Ledo and he wouldn't have missed what was to

turn out to be some of the best action of his life. Always keen for a scrap, Blaauw probably would have paid the Angolans to let him go.

Flown to Saurimo on June 1 and having been familiarized with what was going on in the field at EO's command center, he was taken in one of the Mi-17s to join the column at Tchicuza the next day. As it happened, Blaauw was to become de Castro's most valued counselor: in fact, it wasn't long before the South African led most of the day-to-day planning sessions in the field. Blaauw also countered some of de Castro's more debatable decisions. Irrational man that he was, the Angolan Brigadier often let emotion rule.

The first phase of the operation—after several punch-ups with Unita at Dala, Alto Chicapa and Cucumbi—was the capture of the crossroads town of Cacolo from where all routes, such as they were, led to Cafunfo. But first the Alto Quilo River had to be bridged by a TMM team. Only two of these mechanical systems were allocated to the force and they were carefully husbanded. Without them, the column would have been halted dozens of times, and in the end, probably wouldn't have got anywhere near the target.

Also included was what some of the South Africans regarded as their most valuable asset of all: a Caterpillar front-end loader. At one stage it was almost discarded in a sloppy recovery operation that had been directed by de Castro. On a whim, the Angolan officer decided that because the machine didn't work quite like he thought it should, it would have to go. He'd already given instructions for it to be blown up and it took a hefty argument from Blaauw to persuade de Castro to desist.

And it was just as well he didn't. Several times the column ground to a halt, paralyzed because of obstacles. This usually happened at rivers where vehicles might have tumbled into the water because bridges weren't level or they hadn't been built strong enough to take armor. Then this extremely versatile, reliable old machine would be hauled forward to remove whatever was causing the commotion.

Supplies were a problem from the word go. Everything had to be flown in to a mobile force that could never predict in advance where it would be at any specific time. For this reason, EO personnel spent long hours prior to the operation planning air drops with former Soviet pilots who were flying Ilyushin-76s on contract for the government.

"We couldn't afford mistakes while we were out there. So we would improvise as we went, usually working with our pilots when looking for safe drop zones. They'd do an aerial recce for us and come back with suggestions about likely places where a drop might be able to happen. At the same time, the guys bringing the stuff to us had to be scrupulously familiar with our routines, which were always flexible. Everything that might be needed was listed. We prepared pages of detailed instructions: where everything was stored or from whom it could be ordered. Then followed complicated delivery arrangements, which also had to be coordinated, a nightmare in a city like Luanda. With all these factors in mind, we established some good parameters for the drops." Blaauw detailed.

Supply drops were made from about twenty thousand feet with between sixteen and twenty drogue-stabilized pallets per flight. Each time about twenty tons of fuel, food, spare parts and medical needs would freefall to about a thousand feet where KAP-3 systems would automatically open the chutes. Obviously, altitude had to be strictly maintained because of the threat of SAMs.

"It was all very professionally done. The Russkies dropped their cargoes spot-on and never missed a drop zone. Actually, they were a real pleasure to work with," said the former Reconnaissance Regiment Colonel, speaking of his former enemies.

Unita threw everything they could into the war which, as some of the men commented afterward, might have become a rout had the rebels been anything of a lesser adversary. Though Unita hardware was every bit as good as that used by the FAA, Savimbi's combatants —many of them crack specialists with years of bush war experience— were in an altogether different class.

At the same time, there was evidence of extreme hardship endured by many rebel units. As they could see from casualties after a battle, nearly every Unita soldier was malnourished. Also, in many instances, their uniforms were threadbare. They would use rucksacks that were made of sacking and sometimes didn't even have slings for their AKs. So they made their own of a rough bark that had been treated and made malleable.

Unita would attack wherever and whenever the opportunity presented itself, a fact that underscored not only their ferocity but dedication. According to Blaauw, though, while the rebels caused damage, their efforts had very little effect on the BMPs in the end. "We would shut our hatches and plough right through their lines, sometimes right over the top of their bunkers and trenches . . . they suffered terrible losses," he declared.

"We'd be traveling along in the bush in line-ahead and as soon as we heard their distinctive mortars, 'plop...plop...plop,' we'd close down everything and go. Sometimes their aim was well off but even when they homed in on us, their sixties had little effect. The BMPs were built to take a 60mm hit and when that happened, the guys inside would be deaf for a week, their eardrums blown. Were 81mm mortars used instead, it would have been another story."

The route to Cafunfo chosen by Blaauw and de Castro was a series of remote bush tracks to the north of the main Cacolo-Cuango road. A second, smaller column made a perfunctory feint westward from Cacolo to keep the enemy guessing. In fact, said Blaauw, either of the forces could have ended up in the diamond fields, so it was a good, practical approach to anything Savimbi might have planned in the way of interdiction.

"They'd actually expected us to hog the road. So Savimbi planned accordingly. He ordered that huge supplies of mines and booby traps be lugged south from the Cafunfo area in preparation for the confrontation. More significant, they never believed that we'd go in a straight line right across Africa."

That had also never been tried before in the war, even though the South Africans had used the tactic often enough in decades past in their cross-border raids against the Angolans and Cubans.

One of the immediate effects of these developments, observed Duncan Rykaart, Blaauw's deputy, was that Unita's crew-served weapons—artillery and some of the heavier stuff—was invariably out of position. It would usually end up a day or two from where the real action was. "Also, they couldn't move it about that easily because just about anything mobile on the roads was blasted by our pilots."

"Of course, those guys helped enormously." The MiGs and Porters flown by Bosch and Pine Pienaar and the others would plaster a Unita town long before we got there. Then they'd zap them again as we approached." The ploy underscored one of the fundamental principles of modern warfare: the field commander who controls the skies dominates everything.

Not everything went to plan, though. On July 15, shortly after Unita had been ousted from Cafunfo, the usual two Mi-17s arrived at the town from Saurimo. They did a dummy delivery to confuse Savimbi's artillery spotters across the river and subsequently proceeded to the real LZ. Just about then a call came through on the radio from Louwrens Bosch, who had been circling an area to the north of them all in a PC-7.

"I've been hit," he snapped into the intercom, adding that the plane was on fire. He was going to have to put her down, he shouted, because there were flames all around him in the cockpit. Even more disconcerting to those listening was that Bosch had been operating alongside the river, well within the Unita orbit of activity. With Walker and Alberts in the one Hip and Joubert and Linde in the other, the situation was critical.

As Arthur Walker said afterward, it was probably a SAM-14 that had caused the damage. He had flown with Bosch often enough in the past and knew that the Pilatus pilot would always joke about having eyes behind his head. In any event, stressed Walker, the man wasn't one to take unnecessary chances.

By Walker's reckoning, Bosch was one of the best pilots with whom he'd worked: "Good man, brave, competent and resourceful, and I don't only say that because he's gone. He really was one of the best. Whether at the controls of a Pilatus or a MiG-23, Louwrens would always reconnoiter a position beforehand and decide on what action to take. For him, it was that kind of war," his old buddy reckoned.

What happened afterward developed into a tragic sequence of events. Not only did Bosch crashland his PC-7 in thick bush—which resulted in a wipe-out of his aircraft—but he and his observer, Skeurkogel, were able to get out of the wreck and make their way to a nearby road for a pick-up. All this time he was able to stay in touch with the choppers heading his way. To do this, he used his little hand-held VHF Bendix King.

Quietly, methodically, Louwrens Bosch guided the incoming Mi-17 toward the two survivors. The area, as he characteristically phrased it in Afrikaans, was "*vrot met die vyand*" (rotten with the enemy). He could hear them coming, he told Walker and Alberts breathlessly, indicating that he'd been hurt in the crash landing. A short while later Bosch told them that he had their Mi-17 visual. The enemy was also approaching fast, he warned. "They're coming in hard . . . the bastards are really after us," he told the others.

"The odds were impossible," was Walker's contention several years afterward. Undeterred, Louwrens Bosch set about trying to find somewhere for the approaching helicopter to put down in fairly heavy bush country, but by then Unita forces were closing in on all sides.

Looking back on what was to have been a rescue, it's Walker's view that their Mi-17 might have been better off had their regular sidegunner been with them. But this was an emergency and the moment the order came, they went up "cold" with only themselves and their Angolan tech Tito Nunes to help. Ideally, they might have carried a search and rescue team, but there was no time to get it together.

Walker: "The last two clicks were what I suppose you'd call a hell-run. We were flying fairly low and were taking fire along the entire distance. They threw everything at us—even a couple of 12.7s and 14.5s. Of course, everybody and his uncle had his AK and they were shooting at us too. Meanwhile, we kept talking to Louwrens and by the time the two of them came into view, he was able to direct us almost right on top of his position."

What happened next is not altogether clear. Because of the volume of fire, Alberts headed in at a steep rate of descent. As he flared, the ground was suddenly enveloped in billowing dust. The last thing they'd expected in a terrain covered in thick vegetation was a "brown-out." Also, comms with the Angolan tech Nunes didn't work well because he understood little English.

The three of them felt the chopper shudder as their wheels touched. The crew thought they might have taken a hit. Moments later the Hip began to shake violently and then veered uncontrollably to one side. Since they were on the ground anyway, Walker urged Nunes to hop out and lead the two men onboard.

"This was really one helluva situation, because by now we could see squads of Unita troops racing down the road towards us," said Alberts. The first group of enemy soldiers was coming at double pace over a small rise only two or three hundred yards from where we had put down and they were firing their guns intermittently as they rushed in.

Nunes was back onboard the Hip almost immediately afterward. The men weren't there, he screamed, indicating with arms raised that they should get away. More volleys came whistling by.

Alberts needed no encouragement. He lifted his chopper off the deck but the shuddering became so severe the moment he pulled power that for a moment or two neither he nor Walker were sure whether they'd actually be able to control the machine. Somehow Alberts managed. Walker thought they'd lost their tail rotor, or at least part of it.

In those few moments in the hover before pulling away, the two pilots spotted a prone figure lying face down on the ground alongside the LZ. Both agreed afterward that Bosch's blue flying jacket was unmistakable. From what little they could see from the cockpit, it seemed as if he'd taken a hit from the tail rotor.

In the investigation that followed back at base, it was concluded that because of the volume of dust whipped up in their descent, Bosch might have become disoriented and possibly walked into the rotor. Visibility on the ground was almost zero at the time and the chopper wasn't completely stationary, so it was feasible. Of the other man, "Skeeries" Skeurkogel, there was no trace.

It took about a minute before Walker and Alberts were able to get clear of the commotion, but again, there was stuff coming at them from all over. At one stage they even clipped the tops of a row of trees to get away.

Though the entire episode had lasted perhaps two minutes, Alberts had a tough time controlling the machine. In retrospect, it says a lot for his experience that he managed to get back to base. At one stage the vibrations got so severe that they thought the machine might rip itself apart. Eventually he put the Hip down on a road about three or four miles north of the town, but still behind enemy lines. By now "Juba" Joubert and J.C. Linde were circling in the other Mi-17.

Once down, the two South Africans did a quick damage assessment and decided that it was pointless to linger. The helicopter was in a bad way but not totally incapacitated. They would chance it, they told the other two, but suggested that they stay real close.

As Walker recalls, the tail rotor had obviously hit something. The blades were twisted and one had all but been ripped off. In fact, looking at it afterward, it was clear that the entire rotor was off kilter. In theory, they shouldn't even have been able to get airborne. But they did, which is also a tribute to Russian engineering ability. The machines they make are not pretty, but they work under the most arduous conditions, even when damaged.

On van Heerden's instructions, two BMP-2 IFVs were dispatched to the site the next day. They had to fight hard to get in and, having poked about a bit, get out again. In the end, nothing was found. The Pilatus wreck, by now incinerated, was still where it had come to rest among the trees. There were scraps of flesh and some blood marks on the ground at the LZ where a body seemed to have been dragged to a vehicle. But of the two men, not a trace.

Radio intercepts later spoke of a capture, but there never was any word of "Skeeries'" fate.

It was ironic that it had to happen to him because Skeurkogel was an EO non-combatant personnel officer based permanently at Saurimo. It was also his first operational flight. As the pilots later recalled, he'd sit in on some of the debriefs and watch the proceedings through his thick "coke bottle" glasses. Afterward he'd ask to be allowed to fly with the guys.

"Just once," he would plead. But there were always other priorities, and anyway, the brass didn't want anybody taking unnecessary risks. On that fateful day, with Duncan Rykaart in Cabo Ledo, Louwrens Bosch thought, what the hell. He'd give "Skeeries" the experience of his life.

In the end, sadly, he did exactly that. Skeurkogel had craved long and hard for his "spin with the boys," but his wish had disastrous consequences.

On the ground a short while before the Bosch affair, the column had made remarkable progress. Colonel Blaauw attributes a lot of it to what he regards as one of the most remarkable fighting machines of the modern period: the Soviet-era amphibious BMP-2.

A product of the Cold War, this fourteen-ton infantry fighting vehicle (IFV) first appeared in public in Moscow during a 1982 parade. Since then it has found its way into many Third World conflicts. Although originally designed for the battlefields of Europe, this classic tracked troop carrier with its distinctive pointed nose and almost horizontal ribbed glacis plate has always performed well in difficult African terrain. Usually carrying ten men, which includes a three-man crew, the Angolan versions came with 30mm cannon mounted together with a co-axial 7.62mm machine gun.

In all, said Rykaart, it's a pretty formidable weapon and only a direct hit with an armor-piercing RPG grenade or a heavy mortar can cause serious damage. It was his view that the BMP was the best vehicle for the job. Also, the terrain being primeval, its tracks were an advantage over wheels whose tires were vulnerable to bullets and mortar shell fragments. Its secret, said Blaauw, was that it needed almost no regular maintenance. "As long as it's kept greased and its water and oil kept topped up, the BMP-2 will accomplish everything that is expected of it, including lengthy safaris across the face of Africa."

Like many other Western force commanders who only got the feel of Soviet hardware in later years, Blaauw always talked well of this IFV, as did a subsequent group of South Africans who used it to good advantage in Sierra Leone.

Trouble was, only days out of base, the engines of at least three of the machines seized because their FAA operators didn't bother with routine upkeep when they pulled over the covers at night. They'd allowed their machines to run dry, with the result that they had to abandon them where they ground to a halt in the bush. After that, Blaauw put the word out: "If your BMP-2 fails because you didn't maintain it, you stay behind with your crippled vehicle." The prospect of being picked off or taken captive by the rebels had the required effect.

As might have been expected, the last twenty miles in Cafunfo ended in a series of land battles that were both intense and, by African standards, classic. What was obvious was that Savimbi, by now, was desperate. He threw at Combat Group Bravo all that remained of his reserves. As one of the EO officers recalled, these bush fighters would sometimes come in waves with a total disregard for their fate. Some Unita attacks were nothing short of suicidal because, "Let's face it, guerrilla or not, men on the ground or in soft-skinned vehicles were no match for armor."

It says much that this burly rebel leader, who was killed in the summer of 2002 after a betrayal by somebody he knew and who, in all probability, had formerly worked for him, could inspire such dedication.[4] It is also one of the reasons why Dr. Jonas Savimbi is regarded as one of the best guerrilla leaders of the last half century. Internationally he has been acclaimed, and though now gone, his standing rates high. In the eyes of many African revolutionaries, it's way up there with people like Mao and Giap. In Africa's insurgent wars there is nobody close to him in terms of ability, pertinacity and resolution.

Luanda couldn't kill the man so they put a large amount of money on the table and brought in a group of whites—South Africans, no less, who had worked with this guerrilla leader in the early days—to do the job for them. In trying to avoid making a martyr of the man, they ended up creating a hero, and on a continent that so desperately needs a few idols of its own, to boot. Savimbi's star, as a consequence, will continue to shine bright in the firmament.

Over a thirty-year period, where guerrilla operations were concerned, Savimbi repeatedly showed the international community—

first against all that Portugal could muster in its insurgent wars and then against the MPLA—that he was a master of the unforeseen.

By the time the Cafunfo operation took place, both Unita's senior commanders, General Bok (Chief of Staff, Logistics) and General Ben Ben (Head of Operations and Savimbi's deputy) were driving the war from a set of bunkers in Cafunfo. In the northern sector was General Luzamba, a fine tactician with much experience of battle. Personnel from the apartheid-era South African Directorate of Special Tasks had originally trained them all.

The last resistance offered by Unita was at the village of Firiquichi, where a huge rebel force had gathered together for a "Hail Mary" ambush. This was the same place that Blaauw, the former Recce officer, had pointed out on the map to me when he detailed the campaign. As Blaauw recalled, they took some fire and there were a handful of FAA wounded. But in the end, it was no different than before.

As soon as the Unita whistles sounded—another trick taught by the boys from Pretoria—the Angolan BMPs made straight for Unita lines and overran all resistance. With that, the attackers scattered. Almost a hundred bodies were counted afterward, including one of Savimbi's most resourceful field commanders, Colonel Antonio Neves. Acknowledged as an expert in unconventional warfare, even by FAA's senior commanders, it was a huge loss for the rebel command.

Just after the Firiquichi line had been breached, the column had a remarkable run of luck. They were approaching Muvuca when Louwrens Bosch—overhead in his favorite PC-7 and flying one of his last sorties before he was killed—suddenly took Triple-A fire from an area of thick bush about ten miles to the north. This was unusual, Bosch reported afterward. Unita never wasted ammo.

The South African pilot immediately felt that there had to be something there, and being curious, he went down to have a look. Though there was nothing immediately obvious, except a partially camouflaged blue truck, he did spot a lot of tracks. Specifics were passed on to Blaauw.

The next day the South African commander decided to investigate for himself. Having been given coordinates, he detached two BMPs and with Jos Grobelaar, a former Koevoet regular, led a sortie into the bush. For once there was no resistance. Shortly afterward they came upon those same vehicle tracks that Bosch had noticed. Having reported back to de Santos, Blaauw pushed deeper into a remote, largely unpopulated and undeveloped region.

Then things began to happen. Sending his own BMP into a crag-gy outgrowth, Blaauw's people stumbled on to what must have been the biggest supply dump of the war. It was immense. As Blaauw said, it easily covered an acre, with as much below the ground as above it. The material that had been accumulated must have taken Savimbi years to get together. Every single item had been hauled overland through the Congo, itself an often impossible task considering the state of that country's roads. In terms of raw diamonds mined at Cafunfo, the cache must have cost Unita tens of millions of dollars.

"There was everything there that an army might hope for," Blaauw recalled. Carefully hidden from curious eyes were hundreds of fuel drums—at least six months supply for the column.

Apart from more TM-57 mines that anyone had ever seen stacked together, there was hardware for 106mm recoilless rifles, crate upon crate of ammunition for B-10s and B-12s, and mortar bombs by the thousand, together with millions of AK rounds. "You could have started another war with all that stuff," reckoned the South African.

Topping off the lot was a hundred tons of food: canned meats, hams, fish, vegetables and the rest, all of it in cans and good quality, like you might have found in any European supermarket. It was gone in a stroke because one bored rebel soldier had fired a burst at a pass-ing aircraft.

The reality of this catastrophe really came home when it was reported later that with those supplies alone Savimbi might have kept the war going for several more years. It was lost, in part, because the guerrilla leader never envisioned that the attacking force would move overland through some of the most difficult terrain in Angola. Nor that their route would take them within a rifle shot of his most valu-able strategic reserve.

Though Savimbi remained steadfast, not so his commanders. Some of them lost the will to continue the struggle, said one of his senior officers after it was all over.

It was in the final approach to Cafunfo that Hennie Blaauw had what was possibly the narrowest escape of his career as a fighting man.

"I called the column to a halt fairly early one afternoon a couple of days out of Cafunfo. Because there had been harassment from Unita after dark, some of it pretty concerted, involving mortars and encirclements, we were in the habit of bringing our vehicles round into a defensive laager. We'd arrange the BMPs so that their guns would point outward: if we had to retaliate, we would be quick to do so.

"The forest around us was thick, typically jungle and almost impenetrable in places. The bush encroached right up to where we'd parked. It was also the season for mist, that would roll in across the valleys within an hour or so of sunset and only lift again the next day about mid-morning. Although Unita tended to mortar us whenever we stopped, we weren't overly bothered because we'd all dug slit trenches. Or for those who preferred, they could sleep inside their IFVs.

"It wasn't quite light when I got up the next morning and did the usual rounds. If a man was asleep at his post, it was better that I should find him than his bosses. Angolan officers and NCOs would shoot a sleeping man where he lay. We only docked their pay."

The Colonel asked his signaler-driver Paul Ditrich[5] for a roll of toilet paper. He then did what he'd spent a lifetime in Special Forces telling others not to do: he set off into the bush for a dump alone.

"I ambled off toward a clump of bushes. By then Ditrich was headed back to the perimeter of our defenses. Moments later, facing outward from the column and having just undid my belt, I was watching something on my flank and not paying too much attention to what was immediately in front of me when suddenly, a rebel pops out of the bush, right there, only yards away.

"He was as surprised to see me as I was him: we had eye contact for about a second." Armed only with a toilet roll, Blaauw threw himself sideways and sprinted for the nearest BMP.

"I had perhaps twenty yards to cover when the ground erupted all around me as the enemy targeted me on full auto. A second later the entire column came under attack as a huge rebel force that had crept up close during the dark hours opened up. I got back OK, but I reckon I must have been pretty lucky to have done so."

Blaauw was to establish later in the day that it was an attack in battalion strength: about two hundred and fifty of the enemy were involved. His own people were able to retaliate immediately, something they'd learnt to do many times over. Looking back, he reckons it was probably their quick reaction time that saved them.

"Meanwhile, Ditrich, who hadn't seen me cut and run, assumed that I'd been killed. When he heard the first volley, he turned toward where he'd left me and all he could see was a Unita soldier, AK in hand, letting rip. He promptly threw himself down on the ground shouting 'The colonel's been shot! The colonel's dead!'"

Indeed, Blaauw didn't come out of it unscathed: he took a flesh wound in his arm, probably from an AK. He's convinced too, that the attack had been pre-empted.

"I'm pretty sure that the entire group was not yet in its final position. In fact we heard that afterward from a capture. There were apparently some Unita troops that were held up for some reason or other in a shallow defile to the north of our position. Had they been there as well, things might have been a little different because they were pretty well on top of us when the shooting began . . . some of the enemy were lying three or four yards from us.

"Yep! I was lucky," was his comment, adding, "It's the first time that the outcome of a battle was decided by someone needing a shit."

Only after Unita had withdrawn was he able to evaluate his good fortune. The BMP behind which he had taken cover took the brunt of the onslaught. Thousands of rounds were fired at it. The firing was so intense that you couldn't put two fingers together over any patch of armor without touching a dent where the paint had been sheared, he said.

"Also, all the trees around our positions were cut down by the salvoes that followed. Most were completely stripped of their leaves. But then it ended as suddenly as it began because a few minutes later, when more IFVs got into the act, our attackers dropped everything and ran."

Blaauw was pulled out later by one of the helicopters. He had his arm dressed at Saurimo and was back with his unit before nightfall.

Another equally unlikely survival story to come out of the war involved "Juba" Joubert, who was later to fly combat in Sierra Leone with Nellis. As one of the stalwarts of the Cafunfo campaign, his Mi-17—with John Viera as his co-pilot—took a hit from a SAM-14 a few days after the column had occupied Cafunfo.

Though the air crews had been assured that the area around the diamond town was clear of threat, including missiles, these veterans of several wars tended to remain a little circumspect, and it was just as well that they did. When they were required to head for the sharp end, they flew high and came down fast—invariably in a spiral, as steep as the rotors would allow. It was the same on the way out again: straight up and then a swing away when the required altitude had been achieved.

Cafunfo presented the same problems as anywhere else in this ongoing war. The pilots noticed that as soon as they got anywhere near to the town, Unita guns and mortars from across the river would open up. Rebel gunners would shell the landing strip and they would keep hammering away as long as there were Hips on the ground. On that day, Walker consequently decided to put down at an old disused airstrip on the southwestern side of town.

Flying in support of Walker and Alberts, Joubert's Hip had just delivered its two-and-a-half ton load and taken onboard about a dozen casualties for Saurimo. With that, the two Hips took off again. As Walker always said, "There's no hanging about when you've got people hurling things at you."

The two machines were about six hundred feet in the air when several people on the ground saw the brilliant white flare of a missile being launched from the opposite bank. It was a SAM, somebody shouted, and its contrail showed that it was heading straight for the circling choppers.

Walker saw it first but it happened so fast that there was no time for evasive action. At Mach-2, the missile shot right past his nose and headed for Joubert, hitting his chopper's exhaust just above the starboard engine. The South African recalls an enormous explosion above his head.

Talking about the incident later, both pilots extolled the ruggedness of this Soviet-type helicopter for not being immediately knocked out of the sky. Walker has always been of the opinion that no Western helicopter would have been able to weather that kind of punishment and come out of it airworthy.

Having got onto the deck again, shaken but safe, the crews were able to examine the damage. Altogether five pockets on one of the rotor blades had been blown away. The blast missed the main spar by a fraction of an inch. If any one of the Mi-17's five blades had been sheared, it would have torn out the gearbox and they would have crashed. Exactly that had already happened to fifteen other Angolan Air Force Mi-17s in the war by the time Joubert's incident took place. Worse, there wasn't a survivor among any of them.

Nor did three more Hip crews get out alive when Unita SAMs destroyed their Angolan Air Force choppers over the following six months. To the guerrillas, of course, bringing down a helicopter with a high-visibility hit was one of their biggest thrills.

It's interesting that during the period that the South Africans manned Mi-17s in northern Angola, each of the three helicopter teams was picked up at least once by other crews after having been brought down by ground fire. This was why they always insisted on two-ship sorties. The same policy held afterward for Sierra Leone.

But not for Neall Ellis, who, for almost two years, fought Sierra Leone's war from the air almost totally on his own. Most times he didn't even have a co-pilot.

19

AN AMERICAN WARRIOR DIES IN AFRICA

"EO's workforce was largely made up of battle-hardened soldiers, most of whom had been at war for over fifteen years, fighting for a way of life that they believed in deeply, however objectionable it may seem to the rest of the world."

Elizabeth Rubin, *Harpers Magazine*,
New York, February, 1997

While Executive Outcomes was busy countering a major rebel insurgency in Angola, more of its soldiers were fighting in Sierra Leone, a country that was almost toppled by revolutionary forces backed by both the Liberian warlord Charles Taylor and Libya's Gadhaffi. Indeed, this modest little West African country was the third nation to hire a strictly mercenary force to rescue its government from iniquity.

Aware that its soldiers had sunk three or four tiers below normal where training, capability, know-how and motivation were concerned, Freetown decided in late 1994, even before Executive Outcomes arrived on the scene, to recruit a private military company to help them counter the rebel threat. The job description was kept purposely vague, though it did mention the need to cope with a national security situation that had gone critical.

Sierra Leone's leaders had watched similar developments in Angola with interest. Through its own contacts, diplomatic and otherwise, it kept abreast of what had been taking place, first at Soyo, then Cafunfo and on to the northeast and elsewhere in that vast, potentially wealthy land. Obviously, they matched the situation in Angola, especially in regard to diamonds, with their own insurrection.

The trouble was that, unlike the FAA, Sierra Leone's army, or as it was then called, the Republic of Sierra Leone Military Forces (RSLMF) was regarded by Western sources as among the most incompetent and corrupt military establishments of its kind. It was a force that couldn't even muster a decent parade on Independence Day.

445

Also, Sierra Leone wasn't the only entity on the continent to appreciate the implications of EO bringing conflict in Angola to a timely end. Nigeria, the Congo and even the United Nations—following the horrific loss of life in Rwanda—had given serious thought to the option. Secretary General Kofi Annan admitted years later that when the killings in Rwanda had gone into overdrive, he'd considered hiring mercenaries to stop the slaughter. But he didn't take that final step, he said, because he didn't believe that the international community would have been able to accept the consequences. A million deaths later . . .

Sierra Leone was different. Here was a government about to be toppled. After some debate in Freetown, there were those who argued that if Executive Outcomes could do what was needed for Luanda, then surely the same might be achieved with one of the groups that had already approached Freetown with an offer of a "rescue mission." It was worth a try, said the country's military, for once admitting that they weren't able to do a damn thing about what was then taking place in the interior.

Immediately afterward, a diplomat attached to the Sierra Leone High Commission in London met with the directors of a Channel Islands-based company calling itself Gurkha Security Group (GSG). The question posed was whether this commercial concern could provide a squad of its Nepalese troops to turn the tide in what appeared to be a "galloping insurgency," as one Freetown newspaper called it.

Within days, all the details had been discussed, an operations plan agreed upon and the price settled. Almost overnight, a group of professional-looking businessmen in well-cut Saville Row suits of a texture and quality totally unsuited to the tropics began to arrive in Freetown. Weeks later, the first bunch of Gurkhas stepped off a charter jet at Lungi. GSG meantime contacted American Bob MacKenzie, one of the most illustrious figures in the business of freelance soldiering, and offered him the job of commanding this new combat unit.

Brilliant and innovative throughout his career, MacKenzie was regarded by those who had spent time with him as the ideal candidate. Though still in his forties, he had fought on three continents, sometimes with his wife Sibyl in tow. Apart from Rhodesia and a spell afterward with Colonel Ron Reid-Daly in the Transkei Army, MacKenzie had spent time with Renamo rebels in Mozambique, rescued missionaries in East Africa, done reconnaissance work for a U.S. intelligence agency in Guyana, fought in El Salvador and trained Bosnian militias in the Balkans. He also handled a few other projects that we'll probably never know about.

As a correspondent for one of the Jane's publications, I'd been on ops with MacKenzie in El Salvador in the mid-1980s and was able to observe what he did from up close. He was a good operator with a solid grasp of all things military and he put his knowledge to good use for this Central American state. I also quickly learnt that in this business, Bob MacKenzie wasn't somebody to be trifled with.

Although he started his career as a grunt in Vietnam, he had been invalided out of the U.S. Army because he'd almost lost an arm in combat. And since his own government wasn't interested in what MacKenzie himself called "damaged goods," he decided to try his luck in Rhodesia.

There Bob not only served with distinction in the Rhodesian Special Air Service (and was involved in numerous strikes against that country's enemies—usually behind enemy lines), he also became one of a handful of Yanks to achieve commissioned rank in the Rhodesian Army. That he managed to successfully complete the tough, hazardous SAS selection course, crock arm and all (it was partly withered because of his war wounds) tells you the rest of it. MacKenzie was not only an extremely determined individual, he was also strong, obstinate and resolute.

As with most things in the sometimes erratic and somber world of contract killing, MacKenzie's choice of Sierra Leone was not altogether fortuitous. GSG was partly owned by Mike Borlace, one of his old Rhodesian buddies, who, apart from being a qualified Alouette gunship pilot, had served with Ron Reid-Daly's Selous Scouts. Like the SAS, the Scouts was an ultra-clandestine unit that did most of its work on cross-border operations and much else besides, including an array of dirty tricks that might even have awed Iraq's "Chemical Ali."

Inevitably, the catalyst that brought them together was precious stones, and the fact that Sierra Leone was—and still is—a major producer of quality diamonds. Historically, several of the world's largest gems have come from the Kono diggings in the southeast of the country, including several that are today part of Great Britain's national heritage, the Crown Jewels.

Though nobody has been able to pinpoint a time frame or a specific link between a group of mercenaries and London's Central Selling Organization—the biggest diamond marketing cartel in the world—

anybody who knows African politics accepts that such a connection was implicit in the arrangement. Somebody at the CSO's office in Charterhouse Street, a short walk from Hatton Garden—where many De Beers clients cut and polish the company's products—suggested that since Libya's maverick leader was bankrolling Sierra Leone's revolution (as he had Liberia's), it was not impossible that all those precious stones could eventually end up in Tripoli.

Horror of horrors, must have been the conclusion. That simply could not be allowed to happen. Things then began to happen quickly in West Africa.

A contact at De Beers spoke to somebody in the Foreign Office who, in turn, tickled the fancy of a minister in the Freetown government, which was probably how Borlace eventually got into it. Being a taciturn, uncommunicative sort of character, as I know him—we attended MacKenzie's memorial service together at the U.S. Navy's amphibious base at Coronado, San Diego—he'd admit to nothing.

MacKenzie and his wife Sibyl arrived in Sierra Leone shortly afterward. As Bob's "other half," Sibyl admits that while they didn't initially regard the posting as particularly tough, almost nothing originally promised by London was forthcoming. The Freetown job, they'd been assured, was a cinch. All activity would center on a local version of "Special Forces." But the only thing special about the unit, they discovered, was that it was completely dysfunctional.

The government—at the behest of Sierra Leone's baby-faced leader, twenty-five-year-old Chairman Valentine Strasser, and his right hand man, Major Abu Tarawali—had formed an elite group called the Sierra Leone Commando Unit (SLCU). It was MacKenzie's job at the head of a group of sixty Gurkhas to teach these West African soldiers how to fight. Initially the idea had come from U.S.-trained Major Abu Tarawali, who had done a stint at Fort Benning. As one of the few competent professionals in uniform in the country, his men affectionately referred to him as ABT.

It took MacKenzie about eight minutes on his first morning at Aberdeen Barracks to discover that the hundred and sixty "hand picked" men allocated to his command were about as rum a bunch as any he'd encountered. Most were louts, enticed off the streets with offers of regular meals, uniforms, weapons and drugs. The idea of transforming them into an effective force within weeks was ridiculous. MacKenzie told his bosses: he needed six months. None of the senior commanders with whom he tried to reason would listen.

By anybody's standards, this was a right bunch of mothers. Most would fire their weapons on full automatic and from the hip without regard for either accuracy or who might be standing in the way. He lost two men in accidental discharge incidents in the first three or four days. Others removed the wooden stocks from their AKs because they thought it looked "cool." None of them could read a map. As for "zeroing" a rifle, there weren't three men in a company who could.

Sibyl MacKenzie recalls that the compasses the men were issued were worn as decorations around their necks. To top it, just about everybody was smashed, and it was that way from the first muster on because a supply of marijuana came with daily rations. For lunch, they'd also get huge dollops of the local rotgut gin neatly packaged in plastic sachets.

Other imponderables soon surfaced, the first being that nobody in Freetown knew anything about the rebels, including how many there were, what automatic weapons they had (if any), their command structure, logistics and the rest. They weren't even aware that most had infiltrated the country from neighboring Liberia. Part of the problem lay with the fact that the few that had been taken captive in the past had been executed. Consequently, the possibility of using these men to find out more about the people they were up against didn't get a look in.

To the majority of senior Sierra Leone Army commanders, military intelligence was equated on a par with rumors. In fact, there was no department handling intelligence in the country until after EO arrived, some months later. The little that Strasser's General Staff did know about the rebels was what they'd been able to glean from foreign news reports.

Calling themselves the Revolutionary United Front, or RUF, this almost mystical group of killers had acquired a larger-than-life status, and they'd achieved it in an astonishingly short time. Some claimed that the rebel fighters had mastered supernatural abilities. They were reincarnates of great warlike creatures from the past, it was suggested, and even had auras around their heads to prove it. This skewed perception was reinforced while the guerrilla force increased its numbers by grabbing every young boy of seven or eight years old to do its bidding. Obviously, the movement was getting stronger all the time. Meanwhile, the nation's army that should have done something about all this remained base-bound.

Certainly, voodoo was a feature of many of the RUF's rituals, almost all of which were cruel. Some were unspeakably barbaric. Rites could include anything from pouring a libation of gin on a weapon to "give it accuracy" to human sacrifice, usually the younger the better and preferably female.

But then, to a lesser extent, the same applied to some of Sierra Leone's military, where nothing was done until "the gods have been appeased." No journey was started without dousing the radiator of the vehicle you were riding with juice. Having slaughtered the enemy, RUF cadres would sometimes cut out the hearts of their victims and eat them raw, as they did with MacKenzie's after he was killed. Sierra Leone troops, according to Colonel Bert Sachse—who went on to command EO in Sierra Leone—were known to follow suit more often than the authorities believed.

British expatriates living in Freetown at the time, though skeptical about the ability of the rebels, couldn't counter any of this nonsense because they weren't allowed to be involved. They would argue that, for all its problems, Africa seemed to breed revolutionaries like most other countries produced prodigies. But there was no way they could convince the locals. Even in the civilized world, it is difficult to knock success.

What soon became clear was that as a guerrilla force, the RUF could match anything fielded by the Sierra Leone Army and still have room to maneuver. Indeed, by the time MacKenzie arrived, a village in the interior only had to hear that an RUF force was approaching and everybody would flee. Freetown was starting to feel strain because of all the refugees who came flowing there.

Bob MacKenzie had hardly gotten off the plane at Lungi Airport when the first of many issues awaiting his arrival had to be addressed. Most notable of these was that Strasser (like Mobutu) didn't pay his troops. Consequently, it was not entirely unexpected that many government soldiers had either revolted or defected to the rebels.

Another was that the rebel leader, Foday Sankoh—a former army communications corporal who had been dishonorably discharged a decade before—was a good deal more efficient than the government in pursing his military objectives. Sensing a gap, this C-4 radio-operator-turned-mass-murderer exploited every schism imaginable, within both the armed forces and the political establishment. Moreover, he did so with vigor that astonished everybody. It was curious that some of his friends had written him off years before as a dope-head.

Most serious was the fact that apart from Gadhaffi, the succor that Sankoh was getting from Liberia—Sierra Leone's traditional English-speaking partner in that corner of West Africa—had tripled in the previous six months. Charles Taylor had smelt blood and he believed his friends were poised for victory. Consequently, he upped the anté, which meant even more weapons being sent across to the rebels. Most of the stuff had originally been flown into Liberia from Libya and was then hauled across the border, usually on the backs of rebel troops or civilians shanghaied for that purpose.

It was no accident that Charles Taylor—then orchestrating his own grotesque civil war in Liberia—had also been a recipient of Libyan aid, lots of it. Only afterward did it emerge that both revolutionaries had been trained in a secret military camp to the south of Tripoli, the Libyan capital. (In all probability, the same one visited by Dana Drenkowski and his friends at the Sahara town of Sabha—see Chapter 9.)

The situation was perhaps best characterized by what somebody wrote in a Freetown newspaper at the time: Sankoh's relationship with Taylor, it was said, "was a brew concocted in Hell." On the one hand there was Taylor, a jailbird-turned-president who had escaped from a Massachusetts prison, skipped the country and used a civil war that he had orchestrated to bring him to power on the continent of his forebears. On the other hand was Sankoh—a certifiable psycho—who wished to do the same in Sierra Leone.

What is remarkable is that Sierra Leone remained as stable as it did for so long. It gained independence from Britain in 1960 and because its leaders began dipping into the till almost immediately, the country had been bankrupt for decades. Also, its politics were a mess. The first army coup d'etat had taken place years before, which resulted in decades of an interregnum that all but paralyzed the country. Schools, hospitals, the civil service, police, social institutions, pension funds and the rest were systematically stripped of their assets and downgraded.

Most appalling was the graft. Every strata of Sierra Leone society—in government and out—had been corrupted. Because avarice extended to the highest echelons, nothing could be achieved without what was euphemistically termed "a little encouragement," usually indicated by an outstretched hand. Sometimes, when there were diamonds involved, such encouragement could be sizeable.

It had often been said by those who knew Africa, that of all the capitals on the continent, the measure of avarice in Freetown simply did not rate comparison. So it's not all that surprising that the people of Sierra Leone eventually turned against their rulers. It is also one of the reasons why so many people regarded the RUF as a "liberating" army, rather a brutally destructive military force run by violent thugs who cut the hands and feet off children.

At that time, too, the rebel movement was referred to by its critics as Africa's Khmer Rouge—though thankfully, without the ideology.

Eager to get things moving, the MacKenzies weren't inclined to spend much time in Freetown. They did the usual rounds, diplomatic and otherwise, were introduced to people who mattered, and within days, were shunted off into the interior with the unit. By now the men had been issued new French-cut uniforms of Portuguese camouflage, splendid green berets and crates of Kalashnikovs still packed in their original grease.

As Tarawali phrased it, the force was "to prepare for the confrontation." The Gurkha contingent, together with Andy Myers—a British freelance fighter and a veteran of the Balkans—had already gone ahead to prepare a camp.

It is worth mentioning that while still in London, MacKenzie was told he would have five or six months in which to train the men and make them ready for war. Five days after arriving at his new base, the American—who by now had been given the rank of Colonel—got a call from one of the defense chiefs at Cockerill. Peremptorily, he was told that he should muster his men and attack a rebel base in the Malal Hills. It was to be done "within days rather than weeks," was the instruction. While he was able to deflect that one, more instructions kept coming.

The MacKenzies' new home at Mile 91 on the road to Bo was called Camp Charlie, an abandoned agricultural facility. Sibyl MacKenzie described the place in one of several articles she wrote at the time.

As a military base, she thought, Camp Charlie was probably the best available option, with good and bad points. Some twenty solid houses stood along three sides of a road network a quarter-mile square. A headquarters complex, motor pool and security gate lined the other side, while palm and mango trees dotted the base. There was also a central grassy field where the men would play football most afternoons.

"There were some sorry remnants of a fence, no cleared fields of fire and no defensive positions. All of these were to have been addressed before we and the Gurkhas arrived, but nothing had been done. The enormously deep well, which should have supplied us with fresh water, remained completely dry, though there were promises of water bowzers and a bulldozer."

After Sibyl MacKenzie returned to America, she spoke about camp security. There was none, she said. Soldiers, civilians, men, women—and who knows, an RUF spy or two—came and went through the camp gates as they pleased. Nobody asked them for any kind of identification. It didn't take MacKenzie and those helping him in this isolated jungle posting long to realize that the job he was being ask to do was impossible in the extremely short time available. After three days he discovered that there weren't half a dozen men in the entire group who understood the rudiments of combat. They weren't even able to fire their weapons properly.

"They couldn't walk quietly through the bush, set up or maintain an observation post, lie in ambush or even conduct small group discipline," wrote Sibyl afterward, adding that most of them wore civilian clothes under their uniforms.

"At the first incoming, they would shuck their uniforms, hurl their weapons into the bush and sneak back into the camp as civilians."

Mile 91 wasn't an altogether unmitigated disaster. In getting there from Freetown, their convoy was ambushed about halfway to the destination. Their column was a big one. Because of the war, everybody grabbed the opportunity to travel with an escort, with the result that civilian cars and trucks tagging along stretched out a mile or more behind the military elements traveling in front. As it turned out, the ambush, not entirely unexpected, brought some unexpected dividends.

As Sibyl tells it, Bob didn't hang about after the first shots sounded. Instead, he accelerated through the kill zone and when he saw that civilian trucks coming along behind had stopped and were trying to turn around, he immediately marshaled his troops and started to flank the attackers. Under heavy return fire, the rebels turned and ran. Blood trails afterward showed that some had been hit, but in acting promptly, the convoy had been spared serious casualties.

To the people, this was one big victory. The enemy had been dispersed. Even better, it been achieved on home ground. Once the news got back to Freetown the city rejoiced. The American mercenary had shown that the RUF could be beaten!

More circumspect than the rest, MacKenzie warned that one success didn't win the war. It was early yet, he said, and a lot remained to be done before the troops would get the hang of it. After all, Sankoh's people had been doing this sort of thing longer than anybody, he told his bosses.

MacKenzie was a tactician born. Not a big man, some would have called him slight. What he had in abundance was tremendous reserves, both physical and mental. Not tall as Americans go, he was lithe and fit. Curiously, this amiable, balding, round-faced professional wasn't into jogging or press-ups but he could walk the pants off any man half his age, as he did when I went on patrol with him in El Salvador's Morozan province near the Nicaraguan frontier. I never once heard him complain, even though he was carrying twice as much as any of us, including the unit's field radio.

As a leader, he seemed to have the unerring ability to inspire men under his command. He instilled confidence where there had been none before. A scenario would look dismal and he would immediately come up with something that looked hopeful. Instinctively, he knew how peoples' minds worked and those under him responded accordingly.

Most of all, Bob MacKenzie wasn't afraid to take risks. On the back of the helmet he wore in Bosnia, he had stenciled the words "Follow Me." He was always after slaying the elusive dragons, for these were the things that drove him.

About MacKenzie's final battle—which provided something of an impetus to Sankoh's aspirations at the time—very little is known, except that he was the first white soldier to be killed in that war. One report states that the group stumbled into an ambush, possibly close to an RUF camp. With that, government troops under his command broke ranks and ran "as if they we were being chased by the devil," one of the survivors admitted afterward.

What has since been pieced together is that the American colonel was wounded very early in the first contact with Sankoh's gooks. One of the Gurkha soldiers saw MacKenzie take two bullets in his legs and, he thought, perhaps one in the back. Then he went down. It was Andy Myers who knelt down to attend to him and he became a casualty immediately afterward. Also hit was Major Tarawali, though it would appear that only MacKenzie survived long enough to be taken prisoner. Presumably the other two died before anybody could get to them.

While there is no clear picture of what subsequently took place, we do know that once they had him, MacKenzie—badly wounded as he was—was tortured by a group of children. This is not unusual in some parts of contemporary Africa where you haven't earned your spurs until you've taken a life. In the hands of those juvenile savages, he didn't last long. One report to emerge said that they strung him up and shoved wooden stakes into his side, as well as into several of his orifices, after which they spun him around like a top. This must have taken a while, but it is notable that all this was witnessed by a group of Roman Catholic nuns who had earlier been taken hostage.

With MacKenzie dead, the rebels set about dismembering him. First they plucked out his heart and devoured it raw, with a number of them squabbling for bits of it. In one sense, in more primitive times (even in our own societies) this might have been regarded as a tribute to a very brave man. The group then cooked and ate parts of him, including the flesh lining the palms of his hands. Those who indulge in such perversions are said to regard that part of the body (as well as the haunch) as a culinary delight.

Reports made by the Holy Sisters after their release tallied in one specific detail: the nature and extent of MacKenzie's earlier wounds. You had to know the man pretty well to be aware that while in Vietnam, his upper arm had been badly scarred. Some of the nuns subsequently mentioned this disability; the only way they could have known about it was to have seen it for themselves.

According to one of the Sisters who was there when MacKenzie's body was brought in, *ju ju* priests officiated during the ceremony while drums sent messages across the hills into the nearby towns of Yonibano, Bo and beyond. It was a macabre, frightening ritual.

The death of my old friend MacKenzie was one of the reasons why I'd returned to Sierra Leone with Executive Outcomes in 1995. Originally I believed that I might be able to bring back to America something that might identity him and confirm his death: part of his jawbone, perhaps. He and Sibyl had a house at Port Angeles in Washington, not far from where I lived in Chinook. Right then, she needed to verify that he was dead: the insurance people demanded proof and it didn't help that the FBI suggested that MacKenzie's "purported death" was a scam to collect insurance money. They harassed her for months.

Once I got to West Africa, I'd have had to have my head read even to contemplate going anywhere near the Malal Hills. The area within a few miles of Mile 91 was heavily contested and even when I returned to fly combat in the summer of 2000, RUF units still dominated parts of the region.

It is of interest that on my return to the U.S. after the earlier visit, I was called by a State Department official who asked what I knew about MacKenzie's death. I thought it odd that he should have called me, and I said as much. The U.S. Embassy in Freetown had all the details and more, I told him, especially since he'd been in government service at the time. I also took it for granted that whoever was making these inquiries had seen what the Vatican released. Or perhaps somebody in DC was fishing.

By the time it was over, nobody was able to prove anything, if only because the jungle tends to guard its secrets.

There are still a lot of unanswered questions about the American's role in this and several other wars in which he was active. While MacKenzie would have gotten good money for the Freetown contract, there were always issues raised, like how he managed to support himself when he went into remote regions, sometimes for lengthy periods. There were stretches, sometimes for as long as a half a year at a time, when he apparently earned nothing at all.

Since his death, there has been a lot of speculation about the work done by Bob MacKenzie, alias Robert McKenna, Bob McKenna and the rest, with some avering that he was on somebody's payroll back home. One of the U.S. intelligence agencies has been mentioned in this regard. That was reinforced in London a few years later when I spoke to Peter Cole, an old SAS associate.

Cole, by then working in security in the UK, disclosed that several years after leaving Rhodesia, MacKenzie had recruited him and a couple of the others for what he termed "a little adventure" in Surinam. As Cole understood it, the CIA had initiated the project because Surinam had embraced Cuban support to establish a military presence in the former Dutch colony.

Once it was over—inconclusively, as it turned out because the mission was overshadowed by the Iranian "Arms for Hostages" scandal —Cole flew back to the U.S. and discovered that MacKenzie either owned or had the use of his own apartment in Washington DC. They stayed there for the subsequent debrief.[2]

The pieces start to come together when you discover that MacKenzie was married to the lovely Sibyl, daughter of Ray Cline, a much-heralded former Deputy Director of Intelligence (DDI) at Langley. Cline's postings for the company took him away for extended periods to many countries, including Taiwan and West Germany. In fact, Sibyl was fifteen when she left Taipei and she admits to having been able to speak fairly good German by the time she eventually got back to the States.

It was one of Cline's jobs on his return to the United States to set up a CIA affiliate "think tank," appropriately called the Global Strategy Council. MacKenzie's little jaunts into Africa, Asia and elsewhere must have slotted in rather well.

When the events in Sierra Leone were all over, three good men had been killed in an action that was not only futile, but should never have been allowed to happen. If all the facts be known, it's not impossible that some of those who initially feted MacKenzie might ultimately have had a role killing him.

Many of the players in Sierra Leone's civil wars eventually switched sides, perhaps not directly to the rebels, but as sympathetic fellow travelers to their cause because of the hopeless tangle in which the country's affairs then floundered.

Yet MacKenzie was an accomplished warrior. He understood the vagaries of modern conflict. He was also sensitive to the unforgiving nuances of turmoil, if only because intrigue had become integral to most of it. More important, he had enough combat under his belt to understand war, as well as the duplicity of the men who often fought them.

After the events at Malal Hills, MacKenzie's Sierra Leone Army unit—as well as the Gurkha group that had been hired to provide support—went to pieces. It was almost as if they had been hexed, said one of the officers afterward. At the first shot—almost as if it had been rehearsed—the African troops panicked, discarding their weapons. The Gurkhas followed in their tracks, but at least they held on to their arms.

The Times of London possibly encapsulated the drama with what Sam Kiley wrote from the training camp Benguema Barracks on the outskirts of Freetown shortly after eleven British soldiers were kidnapped by The West Side Boys. Sierra Leone's soldiers, he commented, are "best known for their combat tactic of blindly loosing off a few rounds against their rebel enemies before rushing to the rear." By the time British military training teams under Brigadier David Richards arrived in Sierra Leone early in the new millennium, not very much had changed.

Since reports of MacKenzie's death involved children abusing him as he died, it is worth looking at this phenomenon. It seems to be fairly widespread on the continent wherever there is trouble.

One of the sad realities to emerge from the Liberian and Sierra Leone conflicts is that those involved in the mindless violence that seemed to grip so much the country were pre-teen. Significantly, a British news report in March 2005 disclosed that with more blood-shed in the offing in the neighboring Ivory Coast, Liberian youths were being recruited by both sides in this largely Muslim/Christian war because they were regarded as "fearless." "Without conscience" would perhaps have been a more appropriate term.

Indeed, both Foday Sankoh and Charles Taylor actually went out of their way to recruit children. As one of the RUF leader's aides declared, "Some are mindless and will do exactly what you ask." Nellis would agree. As he was to observe firsthand, it was kids that committed some of the most barbaric acts. Several observers have stat-ed that many of the worst acts of terrorism in Liberia's civil war were committed by the very youngest combatants, noting too that the more widespread the conflict, the greater the use was made of these pubes-cents.

In recorded instances of child violence in Sierra Leone, Liberia, the Congo especially, and Rwanda, as well as in parts of South Africa over the past forty years, it is now acknowledged that there have been many acts of terrorism committed against innocents in which imma-ture killers were instrumental. In Freetown, for instance, the authori-ties concede today that a lot went on in the interior that "we will never know about." A Swiss social worker pointed to the much-feared Small Boys Units (SBU) of Sankoh's Revolutionary United Front, a notorious bunch of malcontents that committed untold numbers of grisly acts.

And yet, this trend has support from an unexpected quarter. Martin Coker, a neo-Marxist, British-educated spokesman for the RUF, told Steve Coll of The Washington Post in Buedu that he not only supported the use of children in war, but actually abhorred the West's criticism of "child soldiers." These were "elitist human rights activists," he declared, adding that those who protested such things were out of touch.

"They fail to understand that in a people's army, families had to move together on the front lines—husband, wife and children, all fighting the people's war," he said. It had nothing to do with terrorism, he is reported to have subsequently broadcast on "Radio Freedom: The Voice of the People's Army of Sierra Leone." This was an FM station in Buedu in the eastern corner of the country that he helped establish for the RUF Command.

Some of the acts perpetrated by armed youths have been indescribable. Many involved mutilation and dismemberment. Elsewhere, youths cut unborn children out of the stomachs of pregnant women, the smiling perpetrators often laying bets on whether a male or female fetus would emerge.

These are all acts that have been listed and categorized by UN investigating teams in Sierra Leone and since been branded as terrorism by a variety of authorities in Europe and America.

This senseless carnage includes rape and the lopping off of hands and feet of people who had nothing to do with the war. In one case, an infant of two months who was brought to me in Murraytown, the Freetown suburb that ended up hosting such victims, had her arm severed by a youth. It was ugly.

In Sierra Leone, there have been instances of youngsters between nine or ten and twelve or thirteen years old involved, and there is a move afoot to identify the perpetrators and possibly bring them to trial, as has been the case with war criminals in the Balkans. But it is unlikely to happen: age limits are an effective shield against retribution in the civilized world.

John Sweeney, reporting from Freetown for the Johannesburg *Mail & Guardian*, interviewed three twelve-year-olds who had been taken by the RUF at ages of eight or nine to fight. They were specifically recruited for one of the organization's Small Boy Units. While all sides involved in this carnage had SBUs, "People tell you that the RUF were the worst," wrote Sweeney.

One of the problems now facing the world is whether these underage terrorists were actually aware of what they have been accused of doing. Most perpetrators claim they were drunk or on drugs. Meantime, the debate goes on.

Significantly, this is a recurring problem in Africa. In the early 1960s, the Congo's "Simba" rebels that took European hostages in Stanleyville (today's Kisangani) allowed children to torture their victims. As we have seen, nuns were raped by them and it often took place in public. Following the accession to power of President Mobutu

Sese Seko, all prosecutions for these crimes were put on hold because it was maintained that adults had unduly influenced the young people. Some Belgian social workers objected and said that that was not the case. They maintained that psychotic children initiated many of the brutalities—including several hostage deaths, and that they reveled in the unbridled power they wielded.

The same holds for Uganda. In early September 2000, a group of Lord's Resistance Army (LRA) rebels based in the Southern Sudan killed nineteen people in attacks around the town of Kitgum. LRA cadres near Gulu massacred others. Local villagers said at the time that "quite a few" of those involved were juveniles. Like adult LRA members, they were armed. Like their seniors, they took part in ritual killings of civilians who were suspect of being pro-government. According to the Geneva Convention, such acts are of a terrorist nature and are thus categorized as war crimes.

The same situation held in South Africa during the apartheid epoch. While children did not spearhead anti-government protests, they instigated much of the violence that followed. Very few of these juveniles have ever been tried in the country's courts, even though it was gangs of children that murdered many of the victims.

Following a cease-fire in Sierra Leone and the surrender of many child soldiers, the government was assisted in the task of reintegrating them into normal society by organizations that included several United Nations bodies. Those who came forward—in age from about nine or ten to sixteen (accurate birth records are not often kept in remote areas, others were destroyed by war)—maintained that they had been coerced into acting as they did.

They also seemed to have survived their ordeals on regimens of little food and large quantities of alcohol and drugs. Among the latter were marijuana (*Ganga*) and a cocaine mix, colloquially termed "brown-brown."

As the British would say, sounds like a cop out to me . . .

20

EXECUTIVE OUTCOMES
MOVES NORTH

"[Executive Outcomes personnel] went where no one else
would go, to do a job that no one else would do, to end
(for a time) two senseless African wars."

James R Davies in *Private Armies and the
New World Order,* Canada, 2001

Apart from those on the flight deck of the Ibis Air Boeing 727, only
two other people onboard were aware of our ultimate destination.
Lafras Luitingh had given me the details over dinner the previous
evening. The rest of the men got it after we'd left Angolan airspace.

"Destination Sierra Leone," was the call over the intercom. He
hadn't been able to disclose anything earlier because of security, he
told them. "We didn't even tell the Angolans what was up, even
though we had a contingent fighting for Luanda at the time."

He explained the problem, saying that if they weren't careful, the
whole of Africa would know what EO was planning before its forces
got anywhere near the place and there'd be an uproar. "You can just
imagine it, whites fighting blacks! The connotations to emerge from
that little scenario would be horrendous. They'd be rattling fences all
the way to the Security Council. But once we're in place and doing our
thing—as in Angola—well, that's different. We're saving lives, right?
We're there in numbers and doing our thing . . . nobody can say a
word . . . nor did they when they eventually found out."

That was in the early summer of 1995, and initially the word was
that the group was headed for Burkina Faso. Others thought they
might end up in the Ivory Coast. Once the real destination was
known, it could as easily have been Timbuktu. Almost to a man, these
fighters—white and black—though born in Africa, knew precious little about the continent on which they were born. To some, Sierra
Leone might have been a record label. But then if you were to ask the
average American what Sierra Leone is, I'm being generous if I say

461

that perhaps ten percent of the population would get it right.

Once the banter onboard started—and there was a lot of it—nobody was sure what they would find waiting for them, or what the country would be like. Everything about the place was vague: the terrain, the people or even whether or not they spoke English. Because of the name, the consensus was that they didn't. Some thought it might once have been a Portuguese colony.

In this respect, they were half-right. Centuries before, Portuguese, Dutch and British mariners had circumnavigated the Cape of Good Hope, and the hills behind the tropical inlet on which Freetown is perched was dubbed Lion Mountain. Or so cartographers out of Lisbon recorded it. This choice stemmed not so much from the presence of any big cats, of which we are told in history books there were plenty—along with elephants and leopards—but rather from a hollow rumbling that would echo across the valleys during heavy rains. The same sounds can be heard today, in season.

The first of Prince Henry's navigators who went in search of a sea route to India stopped in Freetown's great bay for water. According to his diaries, there weren't many crew members on board his pair of three-masted Lusitanian barques who were enamored of the place. Others who followed were similarly inclined: they stayed only long enough to replenish stocks.

For its part, Executive Outcomes had its own ideas about what it had to do once its men got to Freetown. Under the auspices of their British contacts, some had already visited the place and met the youthful Chairman Valentine Strasser and his deputy, Maada Bio, the Chief of Defense Staff (CDS). All of this happened after Bob MacKenzie had been killed.

Tony Buckingham—always the entrepreneur—had been looking for alternate options and he took it upon himself to introduce Strasser to EO's directors. Meanwhile this former SAS operator and his friends provided assessments of their own, based on reports gleaned from contacts in British Intelligence and elsewhere. The situation, EO was told, was critical. The organization would have to move quickly to have any hope of countering rebel advances.

Back in South Africa, Eeben Barlow and the boys put together a team and in no time at all produced a working blueprint for the operation, which was rushed to London and Freetown. Already the first elements of an RUF advance guard were on the outskirts of the capital, and the government was very much aware that it was up against a movement that relied on bludgeon, long knives and intimidation to achieve its aims.

Until then, nobody from EO had been able to assess the situation because none of them had been further than the city limits. Everything they'd been told about the rebel army, the war and the circumstances surrounding MacKenzie's death came from State House. And an already desperate Strasser was hardly likely to level with the newcomers about what was really going on in the interior of his country. He wouldn't want to frighten them off.

At that point, former SAS operative Fred Marafano—who had been living in Freetown until a short while before—offered his services. EO grabbed him in London after Michael Grunberg had checked his contract. Marafano was of immediate help because he was not only familiar with what was going on in Sierra Leone; he'd been living there, on the periphery of some of the earlier fighting. What he had to say about the rebels was sobering. The situation, he stated, had all the ingredients of a long-term guerrilla struggle. Being ex-SAS, and having been faced with this kind of insurrection for a good part of his professional life, it was agreed that he should know.

Luitingh immediately formed two combat groups—a Mobile Group and a Fireforce Group. Instructions were passed down the line to his field commanders to prepare for action.

Heading EO's mission in Freetown was Bert Sachse, a former Rhodesian SAS and Selous Scouts veteran who, until approached by EO to run the Sierra Leone mission, was a serving officer in South Africa's Reconnaissance Regiment. As he says today, "I didn't even think about it. I'd made Colonel and when the offer came, I wasted no time in resigning my commission. Then I took six weeks leave." A couple of days later Sachse was headed for the west coast of Africa. He was to return to South Africa after that brief session to finally check out of the SADF, and went back to Freetown in overall command of the mercenary operation immediately afterward.

Sachse was the obvious choice, not only because he was an experienced warrior but he'd seen an awful lot of fighting in his day. As a senior field commander in Angola, he'd crossed swords with Soviet and Cuban-backed battle groups on numerous occasions. Invariably he came out on top, though in his last encounter with Cuban forces in the Cuando, a shell fired by a T-54/55 tank exploded in a tree above his IFV and he took a hefty chunk of shrapnel in his back. He's lucky to be alive, he concedes.

For all that, Bert Sachse —who was the recipient of the Sword of Honor at Sandhurst—has always been the thinking man's soldier. His vision, as one his colleagues who had fought alongside him said, was never clouded by immediate demands. His views would come across clear and dispassionate, with the ability to view conditions from the perspective of both sides, blemishes and all.

By the time that I arrived in Freetown with Lafras Luitingh, South African Special Forces Colonel Duncan Rykaart—the same man we'd met earlier in Saurimo, Angola—was temporarily in charge. Rykaart had been promoted to Brigadier, because in Third World conditions, the amount of clout you had in a country where the military ran the show was dictated solely by how much brass featured on your epaulets.

Once Sachse had returned to Freetown, the war went into overdrive. With Rykaart and others, it didn't take him long to turn the conflict around.

Among the first of the deputies to be appointed was P.P. Hugo, another former Reconnaissance Regiment major who had thrown in his lot with EO. It was a handy arrangement, with Rykaart responsible for planning and Hugo handling operations (a position the peripatetic Roelf van Heerden was later to fill).

EO's air contingent hadn't yet been activated because the Russians were still running their show from Lungi.

Conditions on arrival in Sierra Leone were described by one of the men as "antediluvian." All that the men were handed at their improvised headquarters base at Cockerill was a stretcher and a mosquito net. The base sergeant-major—the geriatric local senior NCO—was appointed to look after the interests of these men, occupying a room next to where they all slept dormitory-style. It had previously been a warehouse and both looked and smelt it.

"That old bugger was our first contact. Apart from ordering about squads of half-drunk troops who, though tasked with off-loading our equipment, did nothing, he remained a passenger throughout our deployment, which shouldn't have been surprising because he wasn't really with it either most of the time," Rykaart recalled.

Having been flown to Aberdeen from Lungi in several shuttles on a commercial Mi-8 helicopter operated by Soros Air, the men were given an hour to settle in. Immediately afterward a handful were delegated to get some hardware together, take a squad of local troops and see what lay beyond the cement walls of the military headquarters.

"We'd brought no weapons of our own," recalled Sachse when I spoke to him in Cape Town, where he'd gone to live after the war. "The original agreement signed by Luitingh, Michael Grunberg and Chairman Strasser—and at which both myself and mining engineer Alan Patterson[1] from London were also present—stipulated that Freetown would provide the necessary firepower. But there was nothing waiting like there should have been. We had to go and scratch the stuff out of some of the bunkers and back rooms where it had been stashed. Even then it wasn't much."

Looking back, Sachse reckons that had the rebels known all this, they could have launched a night attack and probably taken the base in no time at all. That, in turn, would have given them Freetown. "There wasn't any sort of platoon support weapon, or even heavy or medium machine guns. There were no pyrotechnics or basic 60mm mortars. Only AKs and, here and there, a PKM."

The mercs were able to filch some RPGs from one of the strongpoints when nobody was looking, but as one of the men said later, nobody was sure what was really expected of this unusual group of newcomers. "There was obviously a limit to what we could achieve with only small arms," was Sachse's view.

A patent lack of enthusiasm on the part of Strasser's government—never mind almost zero support for what was intended to be a critical rescue operation—was of immediate concern to EO management. Some of the men concluded later that it was probably just as well that things started the way they did, because the impasse set the tone for much of what followed. In truth, said the man in charge, after the first day at Cockerill, nothing surprised them anymore.

He went on: "What they did have was a pair of not-so-new BMP-2 infantry fighting vehicles that were a part of army inventory. There were two more guarding Valentine's residence and we couldn't touch them. Like everything else, the machines had done a lot of time without maintenance . . . the tracks on one were pretty worn, while the other 'was sort of OK,' though the turrets wouldn't turn. Also, the guns looked like they'd never been cleaned and their electrics were stuffed."

That meant that if EO intended using these IFVs operationally, just about everything onboard would have to be manually controlled, including physically cranking the turret around. Jos Grobelaar got to work and did a good job sorting out some of the problems. A Cafunfo veteran, he'd already demonstrated his ability to repair things. In the end, it was no big deal, the men agreed. Quite a few of them had worked with BMPs in Angola and had mastered the weapon's idiosyncrasies. Also, they'd quickly learnt to keep them mobile, sometimes while fighting raged all around them.

"So we reckoned we'd do the same here," said Andy Brown, who deputized for Rykaart for some of the time while I was in-country. One of his first jobs was to try to stem government brutality, especially among those suspected of helping the enemy. They didn't need proof to call you a collaborator; somebody just had to whisper it and you were grabbed.

Brown had hardly arrived in Sierra Leone when he discovered a jail where fifty-seven people were being held in a cell designed for four. The prisoners, including children, slept on top of one another, and over previous weeks some of the inmates had suffocated.

"'They're all rebels,' said the base commander when I asked about them. 'Every single one of them,' he exclaimed, adding that they were all condemned to death. Then I looked a little more closely and saw that there were some older people in the cell, including one old patriarch of about eighty. He was so doddery he could hardly walk, never mind fight. There were also some pregnant women.

"Obviously these weren't terrorists and I told him so. I called the office of the president and we managed to get just about all of them released except for eight hardliners." Brown later talked to the old man. He showed him an AK, but the fellow didn't know how to hold it properly.

The army was no less severe with its own malcontents. Anybody convicted of a breach of military discipline was arrested and had his arms tied behind his back forcefully enough for his elbows to touch. "Try that one for size; the pain is excruciating. Some men pass out with the agony," said Brown, explaining that at the same time, legs were secured at the ankles and the man was placed on the ground, belly down. Then, a final brutal touch: they'd secure ankles and elbows, sometimes with wire. It was a bestial torture, he reckoned

The Nigerians were the most callous and their people used that practice often, never mind that Nigerian Army rules specifically forbade it. Brown recalls finding three Sierra Leonian soldiers who had been trussed up like that for days. Two of them took about eight months to regain partial use of their limbs, and then only after massive physiotherapy. The other took a year but never came right again.

When Brown accosted the Nigerian officer about these inhumanities, he scoffed.

Brown: "It's often easier in Africa to look the other way when you encounter some of these things," he stated, adding that it's often worse in some Arab states, Saudi Arabia in particular.

At first, Sierra Leone troops at the base were wary of the South Africans. While the civilian population was ecstatic about the new arrivals, the soldiers of the Republic of Sierra Leone Military Forces (RSLMF) weren't so sure. Hadn't Bob MacKenzie been heralded as a savior? So too was EO. The entire city turned out to greet them when they drove through town that first time. It only took these tough South African veterans about a day to quash any doubts about their ability.

Commented Sachse: "The guys who came from Angola were more than useful. They not only looked fit and strong, they were all that and more. Nobody who had anything to do with them could dispute that this was one capable bunch of fighters: you could see it by the way they handled their weapons." Things took a turn for the better when their hosts discovered that they'd been fighting Savimbi for a year. Moreover, from what little they'd learnt about the rebels in the bush outside, it was also clear that Foday Sankoh's men were not in the same league as Unita's seasoned guerrillas who could sometimes, when pressed, stay on the trot for a day or more at a stretch.

"We should know. It was our guys that'd originally trained those Unita guys," he declared.

Contrary to the earlier agreement, there were no vehicles at EO's disposal at Cockerill. Undeterred, Sachse commandeered a bunch of Land Rovers. Among this batch were four that had been shipped out of the UK for use by a mining subsidiary linked to EO. He also "acquired" a couple of heavier trucks from the Sierra Leone armed forces and the men did what they could to make them ready for ops. Others were sent to scout town for spare parts. More vehicles were expected, he explained, but since they were coming in by sea, it would be a month or more.

One of Rykaart's first jobs was to create an intelligence unit together with an operations room, complete with operatives in the field. An old hand at the game, he told senior Sierra Leonean staff officers—with whom he was in daily contact—that he needed to train and integrate interpreters and analysts. It was an essential part of the war, he explained to them, though he shouldn't have had any need to. It took him no time at all to appreciate that hardly any of the indigenous senior staff officers had the vaguest idea of what he was getting at because, for most, it was something that had never been done before. Nonetheless, he kept at it and an "Int" network gradually started to take shape.

For all that, conditions at Cockerill Barracks remained bizarre. Accommodations that had been promised the men never materialized. On the contrary, living conditions, if anything, deteriorated to the point where, because of the food, the place was inundated by rats. There was also no air conditioning, which, because of mosquitoes, made sleep difficult. And since the men had no place to secure their personal belongings, pilfering became an immediate problem.

There was a lot more that wasn't up to scratch. A single tap serviced the entire garrison, together with two modest-sized bathrooms, all for eighty men. Rations weren't much better. The bulk consisted of homemade packs that had been flown out from South Africa, a lot of it commercial packets of sugar, coffee and other perishables that had been bought in supermarkets back home and bundled into manageable "kits" by their wives. The problem encountered here was Freetown's humidity—which can be both clinging and fetid—and which meant that everything quickly deteriorated because it was contained in paper. Within a week, for instance, a half-pound of coffee became a lump of brown rock. The same with sugar.

There were other surprises. Initially, said Andy Brown, Executive Outcomes' senior management had been told that the terrain in the interior was very much like it was in Angola. In a sense, it probably was—particularly in some of the northern regions adjacent to the Congo—but this was Equatorial Africa and consequently much more luxuriant, more tropical. Worse, the country's rain forests were almost impenetrable. What also made for a couple of surprises was that someone in South Africa had told the men that it would be possible to fight a mobile war in Sierra Leone. In theory, it was suggested, they should be able to line up a bunch of mine-protected vehicles like Casspirs or Ratels[2] and chase the enemy through the jungle.

This was absurd, Brown declared. In fact, nothing could have been more disjointed. Sierra Leone, he explained, could just as easily have been Indonesia or Guyana. It was totally different from anything the men had experienced before. For a start, he said, "Any movement in the interior meant keeping to the roads, and it stayed that way for about half the year, or at least for the duration of the rainy season.

Those who ignored such precepts got bogged down. And then, should someone go bushwhacking—and some of the men eventually had to do exactly that—vehicles could easily disappear, sometimes permanently." The jungle oozed with mud that could quickly incapacitate a vehicle if you weren't careful, he recalled.

"The first inkling of what we faced came a few days after we'd arrived. The helicopters hadn't yet arrived, so, to give the lads a bit of a break, some senior officers took us all to a local holiday resort at Lakka. It had been a lovely spot before the war, a few miles down the coast towards Cape Shilling." As he explained, Freetown's Peninsula Mountains backed the entire coastal area and though they weren't yet aware of it, Sankoh's irregulars had already infiltrated the region.

"But what made an immediate impression that first time was that, barely an hour out of town, we were able to see from up close the difficult conditions in which we were expected to fight. People had been living along this coast for centuries, but it made no difference to the terrain because there was little cultivation: just about all of it was primeval. Around us—on both sides of the road—was the same dense, heavily foliated jungle that we would later encounter in the interior."

As one of the men commented, "Great stretches of bush seemed to be impassable." But then, some of the South Africans reckoned, if the rebels could cope, then so could they.

What was of concern to Luitingh and Rykaart was that none of the men had any real experience of this kind of equatorial forest. While there had been jungle in Angola, a lot of the war there had been fought across a savannah-like terrain where movement with heavy trucks or tracked vehicles was manageable. One of the first warnings issued was that it was extremely easy to get lost in this kind of jungle where the unsuspecting could quickly become disoriented. Indeed, cautioned Rykaart, if anybody was to move away from the main force and the forest closed behind him, he could have a problem getting back. It was worse in a firefight where one sometimes loses track of time, space and distance.

Meanwhile, in Freetown itself the rebels were getting closer. At night the men would hear the rumble of some of the heavier stuff and the occasional mortar in the hills around Aberdeen. With some Army regulars who appeared to be trustworthier than the rest, several tentative probes were sent out to assess the threat. But even that became a chuckle.

It was difficult at the beginning to persuade government troops to use stealth or to even to stop talking when out on patrol. These black troops would arrive near a village beyond Hastings, or perhaps near Mama Beach, and with rifles raised would stare intently toward the greenery and jabber excitedly among themselves. Since they spoke Temne, Mende or one of the other local languages, the South Africans had no idea whether this was just normal conversation or whether they'd actually seen something. It was soon apparent that this was the way they did things. As Carl Dietz was to tell me later at Koidu, there could be no question of his men doing any kind of effective reconnaissance work with them.

"They didn't understand the basics of counterinsurgency. And when you work like that, chances are that the rebels would have been aware of our presence long before we had any notion of theirs. It was a serious shortcoming, never mind that most of them were on a constant high," he declared.

By then the rebels were already at Waterloo, close to the Benguema Training Camp, a huge encampment which lay on the far side of the hills that surrounded Freetown. This was the same military base used by squads of British instructors to train the Sierra Leone Army in later years.

Things began to change—marginally to begin with—when some of those involved in gathering information about the enemy started to offer incentives such as money or beer. Good intelligence, Brown stressed throughout, was essential: the defenders would not manage, could not manage without it, he told his Sierra Leonean counterparts. Gradually a few leads started to come in. It was the company's job to piece it all together so that it made enough sense on which to act.

What was soon discovered was that the rebels appeared to have a fairly extensive training base somewhere in the forest, not far from that same Benguema that had been pinpointed on the ops room map as an insurgent gathering point. Nobody could provide specifics such as numbers or size, but evidence began to accumulate that the base was there. The question then, was how to find the place?

For the moment, EO was stymied because the helicopters still hadn't arrived and the Russians who were at the controls of the only serviceable Hind were useless. There was even talk that the rebels might have "got to them" in a bid to thwart reconnaissance work. Certainly they were unwilling to go anywhere beyond Freetown, never mind low-level reconnaissance over no-man's land. What a different bunch they were compared to those former Soviets who worked with ICI of Oregon (or, for that matter, who continue to work for Danny O'Brien's crowd, as they are doing today in Darfur).

In retrospect, it was amazing that the RUF could maintain and operate a large military base so close to the capital. It also says a lot for the efficiency of RUF security that their command structure was able to keep wraps on the place throughout. It was discovered later that Sankoh had warned that anybody who talked would be executed. The RUF "political police" even murdered some innocents as an example of what would happen if anyone did.

As the men were to discover later, the rebel camp was huge; about half a mile long and five hundred yards wide, well laid out and professionally secreted in the bush. But as Sachse explained, "The rebels didn't factor our ability to do aerial reconnaissance and our own pilots easily spotted these positions once they'd been activated." It was strange, he mused at the time, that the Russian aviators hadn't come up with a single lead, which underscored the argument that they were on the RUF payroll as well.

Nobody was certain about numbers, but EO estimated at one stage that the camp could easily have housed two thousand people. What ultimately emerged was that it was a staging area from which the rebels operated in their efforts to infiltrate Freetown and its environs. At any one time, Andy Brown estimated, there were several hundred insurgents holding the place.

The daily routine at the rebel base, though primitive, was well orchestrated. It was patrolled and there were musters at dawn and dusk. Though surrounded by forest, it consisted of a perfectly functional barracks, a clinic with medical staff, tailors complete with their sewing machines to make uniforms, administrative offices, a small parade ground under an overgrown area adjacent to a stretch of heavy undergrowth, and a lot else besides. Along the perimeter there were even stalls with women selling basics such as cigarettes, aspirin and palm oil, much as one would find in any West African village.

Rykaart: "When we first got there we thought it was a town, which I suppose it was. We couldn't help thinking how strange it was that nobody within government had any idea it was there. But of course, there must have been quite a few that did but who said nothing." Not unusual, that sort of thing, he added, since most people in the capital hedged their bets in case the rebels really did capture the city in the end.

The first big move before EO's choppers arrived involved a group of the South Africans being sent to Camp Charlie—the same abandoned agricultural college near Mile 91 that Bob and Sybil MacKenzie had used as a headquarters. A column with BMPs together with a scattering of trucks and Land Rovers set out from Freetown, some with heavy machine guns mounted on the back. Traveling in convoy, it took them several hours to get there.

Andy Brown said that it was disconcerting to begin with because the men were expecting an ambush. In fact, some of the officers at Cockerill had warned him: "You are going to be attacked on that road! You are going to die." "We had a driver who we ended up calling One Mile," said Brown. "Every time we asked him how much further, he would smile quietly to himself and say 'one mile'." So in the end, Mile 91 became a bit of a conditioning experience, he recalled.

According to Brown, "Once there, the group started doing patrols and making contact with the locals, who had no problem recalling the drama surrounding MacKenzie; after all, it had happened only a few months before. It was all they talked about at first, adamant that it would happen again to this EO contingent.

"It was there, too, that the lads started to eat and enjoy African dishes like cassava, plantain and other native food. Some of it was primitive and distinctly African, but it had an appeal, was reasonably nutritious and everybody made the best of the change," he said. Actually, they had no option because there was nothing else in the larder.

Links with Freetown were tenuous and, until EO's choppers got to Sierra Leone, everything needed at Mile 91 had to be hauled through by road convoy. For the moment, nobody was chancing it.

What they did have was a lot of beer. "We'd brought enough to completely fill one of the local houses. But there was no refrigeration. So the men had to get used to drinking warm ale, but then there were those among us who'd polish off drain fluid if there was nothing else available," he joked.

Meanwhile, Rykaart and P.P. (later Colonel) Hugo transformed one of the buildings at Camp Charlie into an operations center. But even there, little was allowed for comfort. Some of the walls had collapsed and come nightfall—midge-speckled with clouds of mosquitoes and other insects that would arrive with the bats—you remained outside at your peril. It wouldn't take long for the men to disappear behind netting.

Eventually some of the men used beer crates to make cots for themselves on which to sleep. Also, the first malaria attacks had rolled around and that was to become a serious issue. All EO personnel were required to take anti-malarial tablets at first, but it was difficult to enforce the regimen. Discussing it afterward, Michael Grunberg recalled that there was always frustration about the matter, even though it was enforced with threats of dismissal for non-compliance. He said that some of the operators felt that the risk of not taking anti-malarial pills was less of a concern than the side effects of long-term usage.

Rykaart: "While we were at Mile 91, there was a squad of RSLMF junior officers being put through their paces by one of their majors. He was doing a fairly good job, but it was all by the book. His knowledge of drills was thorough, British Army stuff, straight out of WWII."

"Very professional, with his uniform always spotless, he had good things planned but it just wasn't working, not in that climate, at any rate. His men were getting up at five, doing some PT and so on. And because it was a genuine effort and our guys appreciated his enthusiasm, we decided to help.

"Eventually we sat down with him and offered a few pointers. Within days there was improvement all round."

A second squad of Sierra Leone's semi-trained troops had meanwhile arrived and these were designated EO's responsibility. Though training routines began immediately—the idea was to take them into action when they were ready—there were a few problems that almost proved intractable.

"There was absolutely no discipline within their ranks . . . a bunch of raging zombies because everybody in the squad got his daily issue of marijuana. Others were hooked on booze." Part of the problem, Sachse explained, was that a hefty liquor ration was included in the daily handout. The most potent of all was something called *Peka Paks*, which consisted of a sachet or two of local gin, or something that passed for it, and which obviously contained quite a bit of wood alcohol. "This was some seriously rough stuff, at least fifty percent alcohol," he added.

"For reasons of their own, some of these soldiers got more than others, which meant that for most of the day they were useless." Others couldn't follow basic orders. Consequently, because a man with an AK and live ammunition can be lethal, some of EO's operators took precautions of their own, which had nothing to do with any rebel threat.[3]

"What was really dangerous was the idiot who started to believe that we were fucking him about, which, of course, we were. It was part of the process. That and the *ganga* that they smoked until their eyes glazed.

"Eventually we ended up putting some of the men through the ropes and moving the worst cases aside. We'd show the good ones the drills and initiate a guard system, but even that needed a constant round of inspection because we'd find them asleep at their posts. But at least we had a handful that we regarded as sort of alright. Also, we'd begun to get something resembling an early warning system working. The biggest job was familiarizing them with the regular stand-to and stand-down at dusk and dawn and that was really tough going."

Without air support, communications with Freetown remained a problem. Finally, Rykaart used Soros Air's commercial Hip in its distinctive white livery to fly to Camp Charlie, where he told the squad they would return to Freetown the following day. After that, the group was split into sections as a prelude to start proper counterinsurgency operations.

By then too, Roelf van Heerden—another EO veteran from Angola—had arrived in Freetown. His job was a combination of chief of staff and SO1 Operations, with Brown processing and offering whatever intelligence came in. Much of it was trial and error, which was strange since soldiers from Sierra Leone had fought in two world wars alongside British Tommies. As the records show, they had always acquitted themselves well. But what a bundle of trouble this new bunch was.

The Executive Outcomes squad got back to Freetown about the same time as their two Mi-17 choppers arrived. Unexpectedly, they had been arrested and held for a while at Lagos' Murtala Mohammed Airport and the crews were glad to get in. Nigeria had clearly been a grind and it showed. Nonetheless, the pilots began to prepare for their first sorties.

Freetown by now was almost deserted. Just about everybody had left because there were RUF cadres all over the place. And because the rebels didn't wear uniforms, nobody knew exactly who was who.

"At the same time,' said Sachse, "you had to be pretty wary of moving about on your own. We'd go around town and people who were obviously rebels would sidle up and you couldn't miss them kind of assessing our worth in the Sierra Leone currency. Much of it was based on what we were wearing at the time and we'd hear them tallying: 'Nike's 20,000 Leones; watch 30,000 Leones' and the rest. They'd be quite blatant about what they would do to us if they caught us on our own. Ruthless bastards, the lot!"

Sachse: "Once the day's work was done at Cockerill, some of the men would go to Paddy's and the guys would be the only whites there, which in itself was peculiar when you see the place today. Paddy's usually zinged the moment the sun began to dip. And of course, with no other business in the offing, the guys were constantly being approached by local women who were desperate for business because in a city preparing for war, we were the only 'scores'."

Though there might have been an occasional exception, very few of the men availed themselves. There were black women galore back home and it wasn't something that the majority of these sometimes staunchly Christian South Africans were, as they would inappropriately put it, "into." Having emerged from a racially conscious, strictly-delineated South Africa, they were being thrust headlong into a society where just about everything black and African was in their face, women included. But for the majority, such things—as well as narcotics, of which there was a lot about in Freetown—remained forbidden territory.

Not that some of the men weren't tempted. West African women, especially when young, are lovely. Fulani and Mandingo girls were not only beautiful, but lithe, pencil thin and statuesque as well. When "working," they'd accost the men and come right out with it, often making a point with their hands in appropriate places. According to Sachse, though, it never became a problem. In any event, the majority of his EO force was black. "Obviously, since we got on very well with our own African fighters from Southern Africa, I suppose it was something of an extension of what we'd experienced in the past."

As an alternative, there was always Laguna Casino, one of the few large centers not affected by the war. It stood at the end of the Aberdeen Peninsula and soon the fellows would alternate their routine and go there on a Saturday night where they would lose their money and end up fighting with Chinese fishermen off the commercial boats.

The first EO strike against Sankoh's rebels followed six weeks after the vanguard arrived in Sierra Leone. The bulk of the force drove from Cockerill Barracks to the BTC base at Benguema while the choppers took others in. At last, the two long-awaited Mi-17s were ready for action.

It was also at Benguema, south of the Bunce River, that Rykaart set up an operations center. With that, Roelf van Heerden was appointed Fireforce commander with two English-speaking South Africans, Simon Witherspoon and Rich Nichol, as platoon commanders, both former Recces who'd been involved in EO strikes on Unita positions out of Saurimo.

The racial composition of the unit was interesting. Of just over forty troops, six were white. These men comprised the leader element: section commander, his two platoon commanders, a medic, a signaler and another South African.

The Mobile Force, in contrast—similarly divided—would be under the command of Jos Grobelaar, a former Koevoet combatant from the Border War days. Aggressive and uncompromising as a fighter, in Sachse's view, he was ideal for the job. "You told him what you wanted and he would go for it," he recalled.

What was important about the way Jos operated, he said, was that he had a close, almost intimate rapport with his black soldiers. They'd all experienced a lot of combat together over the years and, to a man, were used to the kind of mobile operations then being planned. It was notable that apart from the officers, quite a few of Sachse's force had formerly been Swapo "terrorists," many of whom had been captured in the Border War. In the tradition of the earlier Malayan and Mau Mau emergencies of the Fifties, these enemy combatants were "turned" to fight for those who had been trying to kill them.

In the old days, once taken prisoner, they would be brought back to the "Fort" at Oshakati in Ovamboland where Koevoet had its main operational base. Customarily, the captives would be given two options: either you join Koevoet or . . . Almost all of them took the gap and defected to fight their erstwhile comrades. In the long term, Koevoet was molded into one of the most successful anti-guerrilla squads in Africa: the unit had a higher kill-rate than any of the army units, including 32 Battalion and various Special Forces elements, though some Recces might argue otherwise.

When Grobelaar decided to opt for an EO contract, he was encouraged to contact some of the black troops that had worked with him before. Not many declined. In any event, they would be earning a lot more than the going rate in Namibia, even if they could get a job. Former South West Africa had also recently gotten its independence and was facing unemployment.

The plan, as Rykaart detailed to his order group, was that Jos and his men would deploy from the training base at Benguema with the two BMP-2 infantry fighting vehicles and some Land Rovers. By now these had been fitted with Dshkas as well as AGS-17 grenade launchers. Tactics would be basic. The entire Mobile Group would drive down the road toward the suspected enemy base not far from Waterloo. Once there, they'd put out feelers and wait for a reaction. At least that was the idea, he explained. The column set out the next morning, with Fireforce on stand-by at Lungi.

The squads had hardly deployed when they encountered an observation post manned by rebels. It happened perhaps minutes after they had stopped at a small village.

As Rykaart explained, the enemy would customarily push a small group of fighters forward from their main base. These men, two, perhaps three of them, would act as an "early warning alert team." It was more of a listening post in the jungle than a fighting group, he reckoned, but it had a critical role: most times you didn't see the outpost until it was too late. Their primary task was actually to stop civilians getting too close to the main camp. Anybody else and they might fire a few shots and that would be enough of a deterrent. Or if the opposing force was preponderant, they'd slip into the jungle as they did this time. Meanwhile, they'd use their HF radios to report back to base.

"While that was going on, I was on standby at my own little company HQ. I'd divided my Fireforce into two twenty-man platoons, each with their respective commanders. We'd agreed that as soon as Jos made contact, we'd react in strength with the choppers hauling us in. It was all classic bush war stuff that we'd used scores of times before when we'd been operational during Border War days, and also subsequently, in Angola."

As he explained, the basics involved first getting to grips with the enemy, even if it was an ambush, which was invariably the case. Fireforce—flown in immediately afterward—would cut off any line of retreat and follow-ups would result until, hopefully, the rebels were dispersed.

According to Arthur Walker, one of the Mi-17 pilots involved throughout the campaign, it was more of a game-plan than a set piece action, largely because the unit's appreciation of enemy activities was poor. The men had to act on their own volition: initiative, instinct and reaction in the Wehrmacht tradition, was how he declared it.[4]

In effect, the force under Rykaart's command was an extremely versatile fighting group and then only because they remained flexible in their approach to the kind of problems that might arise. Each situation was handled on its own terms. Nothing was predetermined or fixed.

"If needs be, we could make a hundred-and-eighty degree change of plan in full flight and the platoon leaders would know what to do. They'd been in the thick of it like that often enough in the past, so it was nothing new," Walker commented

By now, the rebels were obviously aware that the South Africans were coming and they were making a few plans of their own. In all likelihood, details about numbers, armor, helicopter support and so on had been passed back to the rebel command in Benguema. Without ado, Grobelaar asked for Fireforce to be deployed. Shortly afterward the two Hips dropped Hugo and his men, the two groups keeping in radio comms with each other in anticipation of a contact.

Rykaart continues: "We were now about eighty men on the ground, including some trained RSLMF soldiers. Opposing us—we had been briefed earlier—were probably several hundred of the enemy, though others had heard that the majority weren't in camp. We really didn't know because, no fault of Andy Brown's, our intelligence was abysmal.

"Following plans formulated earlier, Jos, our platoon commander and I went to work observing the broader precepts. In essence, it meant spreading most of my troops out among the fighting vehicles and using the bunch that was left ahead and to the rear as stopper or interference groups." It wasn't long before the column began to move forward again.

Until then, remembers Rykaart, it had been a fairly slow process. Movement had been severely impeded by terrain that was so furiously overgrown that it sometimes reached right over and onto the road. It also encroached on ground level from both sides. A man could be standing yards from you and you'd miss him completely. "That worried us all, because it limited options," said Sachse.

To the majority of the South Africans this wasn't quite what they'd experienced in Angola, even though adaptation to these new conditions was easy enough. Some of the men did find the brooding forest intimidating, particularly the South African blacks. Everybody was also aware that the rebels must have had a pretty good idea of the size of the force they were up against. For this reason the column stopped for the night at the next village. The men got together and pulled their vehicles into a tight laager, like they'd done on the long road to Cafunfo. There was little sleep.

The following day started early, without the usual security patrol sent out for a preliminary recce. With the column barely a mile from where it had slept, it surprised nobody when the first shots rang out. Some of the men said afterward that they thought there would at least be some mines, but there were none. How unlike Angola, where there were always a couple of APs to be found in roads and tracks the next morning.[5]

Sachse explained that the rebels had used the darkness to prepare a fairly elaborate ambush at a cutting alongside the road. It was almost within rifle shot of where the group had bedded down. The moment the contact happened, the South African phalanx went onto the offensive and turned directly toward where the enemy had positioned themselves in the undergrowth. But as the bulky BMPs turned, both threw their tracks in the loose sand. Within seconds, the situation had been reversed and it was the South Africans who were now on the defensive.

Suddenly the EO contingent was facing a support problem that was serious. Both heavy vehicles were out of action and though they could be fixed, it would take a while. Worse, it hadn't been a big ambush and Jos wasn't pleased with the way that some of his men had reacted under fire. When his troops deployed from the BMPs he could see that some of the gunners, the Sierra Leone troops especially, were nervous. At one stage he had to stop some of them just short of firing into their own lines.

"So we pushed out the Fireforce, made a line and went forward on our own." For the moment, this seemed to have an effect, since the rebels were quickly dispersed and disappeared down a narrow lane into the jungle," Sachse told me.

Earlier, the group's field-force heads had agreed that whatever happened, a follow-up would be mandatory. Since it had been established during training that this was something that the locals had never contemplated, it was hoped that the tactic would surprise the enemy and keep him off balance.

"So I took my guys and we went right in behind them, splitting ourselves into two groups to possibly gain a better advantage of the enemy in full flight," said one of the section leaders. Jos, meanwhile, stayed behind. His job was to set up a defensive line to protect the vehicles, now totally immobile and stranded.

"It was just as well he did: we'd hardly pushed into the undergrowth when a fairly large group of rebels—having gone out perhaps five or six hundred yards—did an abrupt about turn and headed right back." Their attacks came in silently, except for the sudden bursts of AK fire that revealed their presence in the jungle.

By now Jos was surrounded and his men were fighting hard. His own men were tearing gaps through the surrounding foliage with a constant stream of fire. He was also aware that he was up against an enemy force of about two or three hundred fighters and, judging by their firepower, pretty well armed. Once Hugo heard the firing behind him on the road, he quickly figured out what had happened.

In theory, Jos should have been able to communicate by radio with the others, keeping them in the picture. But he couldn't.

"Call it nerves, inexperience, whatever, but one of the vehicle commanders—he was sitting an arm's length away from his driver—decided to communicate with him by fucking radio. He could have reached over and talked to him in sign language if he'd wanted to, but he used his radio instead. And because both men were wearing headsets, they dominated the airwaves for the next five or six minutes—all of it critical time while the firing went on. Meanwhile, nobody else could talk.

"We couldn't even tell the choppers what was happening or where we were." It ended with Jos, realizing that things were going haywire, shutting them down.

Before that could take place, Hugo, unchallenged, managed to get his force back onto the road. He ended up doing so in an extended line through some pretty formidable undergrowth. "It was dangerous work," he recalled afterward, and admitted that a box formation might have been the better option. Masses of clawing thorns had made that difficult.

"So there we were on the far side, with the rebels between us and Jos, who was letting rip at them with everything he had. One immediate result was that a lot of his outgoing fire was coming straight at us. Quite a few times the guys had to go down hard because Jos' shells would overshoot the rebels and land among us. We were lucky nobody was hit. Because comms were down, Grobelaar didn't know we were out there. Nor could we tell him.

"Eventually we were able to move into a position where we could dimly make out some of the rebels ahead of us. They were only yards away but the bush was rank and they didn't know we were looming over them. Using my hands to signal, I quickly formed up a line and hit them from behind. The moment Jos' people heard us they held back and let us finish the job." In Rykaart's view, it was a turkey shoot.

In the subsequent debrief, it was established that the EO squad was on top of the enemy unit before the rebels realized their predicament. Those who could ran off down the main road past the squad's right flank. The Hind meanwhile, having been kept on standby at Lungi with Carl Alberts and Arthur Walker at the controls, was called in to provide top cover as soon as the action began. But being on the other side of the bay, it took a while, which was possibly just as well.

The Mi-24 arrived about the same time that the rebels were pulling out and though heavy bush precluded them from following everything going on down below, clumps of rebels running through the jungle presented the pilots with targets of opportunity. Also it was the first air strike against RUF cadres with South Africans at the helm. To help the aviators differentiate friend from enemy, the government force had been issued with strips of orange "Day-Glo" that they stuck onto the tops of their bush hats, another old trick from the Border War.

With the main attacking force dealt with, both EO groups set up defensive lines around their crippled vehicles. They also called down the choppers to take out casualties and have their techs flown out to retrack the IFVs.

Rykaart: "Our casualties weren't serious. There were quite a few shrapnel wounds from RPG rockets, though one of the men, Henry Engelbrecht, lost an eye and he was lifted out to Freetown by helicopter. His wounds were first dressed by EO doctors and the same night, in the company of Alan Patterson, he was flown to London on a commercial flight."

With the first day's fighting over, the teams closed ranks. That night everybody slept close to their vehicles, which, by now, had been repaired. Early the next day, the Hips airlifted the entire Fireforce to a new position some miles up the road, the idea being to use them as a stopper group while the Mobile Force continued down the road. But first the men had to slash back half an acre of jungle to create a landing zone for the helicopters.

There was also a debrief session before dark. With the help of additional input from the chopper jocks, everybody had a better grasp of the area where much of the fighting had taken place. The pilots spoke of irregular lines of tracks that all seemed to be heading in the general direction of where the Fireforce was headed. At the end of it, it was surmised, was the rebel base.

"It was only after we linked up and, later on the second day moved down almost parallel to the road that we'd originally used, that we found the camp. The entire area had been abandoned by the rebels," said Rich Nichol.

The enemy camp, once the Executive Outcomes force was able to get there, was a revelation. There wasn't anybody who wasn't awed by the size of the place.

It was vast. It also gave the mercs an inkling of what they were up against. What became immediately apparent was that these people were much better organized and disciplined than any government force with whom they'd had to deal, which was not saying much. Still, the men had had their first real brush with the rebels. Also, as Sachse suggested "EO was feeling its way in an unfamiliar environment."

According to Walker, the base must at one time have accommodated a brigade of rebels. Curiously, in spite of a battle that anybody within a range of eight or ten miles would almost certainly have heard, groups of RUF stragglers would keep arriving at the camp. The mercs were waiting for them and for once, Andy Brown got his prisoners for interrogation.

It puzzled everybody why the rebels had fled, because in terms of size, they outnumbered the attackers perhaps a dozen times over. Only afterward did it become clear that the RUF command not only knew that Executive Outcomes was on its way, but it was the first time that a military force had resolutely come after them. Doing so immediately after an ambush was also something new. Moreover, interrogations revealed that the rebels had been confused by some fundamental battle tactics employed by EO. Until then, the war had been fought piecemeal: a minor scrap here, a skirmish there, always with lengthy breaks between.

Duncan Rykaart had told me back in Angola that psychologically it helped that EO was never afraid to trade blows. In fact, it was their style. Thus, his men would take the war to the enemy, which was a first-timer for the rebels. Also, the other side had never been confronted either as doggedly or on such a scale before. Nor had it experienced such a defeat. Naturally, the gunships made a difference. As Arthur Walker would always say, the Hind was still the ultimate killing machine.

Once back home in Johannesburg, Walker was able to take a long hard look at what had taken place. He stressed that the tactics that Executive Outcomes employed were actually pretty basic. It was all classic, counterinsurgency stuff, he reckoned, coupled to superior discipline.

"Until then," he told me, "the rebels would creep up to a government position, open fire and—more often than not—the Sierra Leone forces would either make a half-hearted attempt to fight back or they would take the gap." That was what had happened so many times in the past. As Nellis was to observe at Lunsar, it was still essentially the pattern of hostilities years later.

"But even when our boys were in danger of being hit by Jos's troops in the first ambush, and since we couldn't communicate with him by radio, they went down and stayed put until the pressure was off," Colonel Sache explained. Others in a similar predicament might have tried to get out of the line of fire.

Soldiers toward the rear of his extended line were especially vulnerable because nobody knew who or what would emerge out of the jungle behind them. "So we covered that contingency as well by having our guys face outwards. And it wasn't long before some of the enemy started running straight into our people. Tail-end Charlie was a PKM gunner that I'd moved there for that purpose."

While this was going on, none of the men had any idea what a crucial little path it was. They only discovered afterward that it led all the way into the enemy camp.

On casualties, numbers remain vague. Initially the group counted about a dozen dead, but after the other troops arrived, the men kept finding more dead, many of them having died of their wounds after holing up somewhere. You don't do that in the tropics, warned Sachse: septicemia sets in within hours.

Going over the rebel town afterward was an education. The rebels had built hundreds of little shacks. For cover they'd take roofing sheets made of zinc that had been looted from nearby villages.

The first thing that Executive Outcomes figured out as a consequence was that whenever they found a town where many of the roofs had been removed, there was bound to be an RUF camp nearby. That rule became inviolable later in the war.

For structural supports, the rebels were equally cunning. They'd take young saplings, and instead of cutting them down, they'd bend them into shape, with the result that their huts would be secreted under natural cover that was difficult to spot from the air. As somebody else commented, it was possibly another trick borrowed from Southeast Asia.

"At camp headquarters, there were still vehicle batteries and solar panels lying about. So we knew how they powered their radios," Brown recalled. Because solar power is common throughout West Africa, they could buy it anywhere. It was also easy to spot from the air in the future. Five years later, Nellis regarded solar panels in out-of-the-way places as the biggest rebel giveaway.

At the camp's sick bay, dirty bandages were found lying about everywhere. "We were later able to figure that a lot of their medicines had been looted from non-governmental organizations like *Medecins sans Frontieres* or the Red Cross. They would grab whatever they needed when these NGO convoys moved into the interior.

"Because we saw ICRC and MSF logos all over the place, we thought at first that these organizations had donated goods to the rebels: there was such an incredible amount. Inquiries in Freetown afterward indicated that the rebels just stole everything they needed.

The mercenaries also got an idea of what the rebels were eating, how they slept and the basic structure of the camp. It had been extremely well laid out, with the camp headquarters on one side, sleeping quarters and drill areas elsewhere and ablution blocks and latrines well away from the rest. Overall, it seemed to have been very well managed.

After the camp had been taken, EO got its pilots to fly over the place so that they could have an idea what to look for in the future. This turned into a useful exercise.

Both EO contingents slept in the enemy base that first night, having put up defensive positions all around. Throughout the dark hours, small rebel groups, and once or twice squads of twenty or more—totally oblivious of the fact that the place had been abandoned—wandered in.

"We'd thought this would happen, so one of our more enterprising operators, Raymond, made dozens of booby traps out of grenades with their pins removed. These were then gingerly placed inside tin cans. There were also some very clever other devices. He set them up—complete with trip wires—along many of the approach paths. We had that stuff going off all night," another of the operators remembered.

The only serious accident took place then. It was one of those tropical nights with a dark, new moon. As Carl Dietz remembers, in that West African jungle you had to have an altogether different appreciation for the word "black": "You'd lie on your back and you couldn't see your hand before your face."

What happened was that one of the EO men got shot while trying to wake his buddy. He had walked the ten or so paces to where his relief was lying on the ground. The moment he touched him, the other man turned and shot him through the chest with his rifle. It was altogether a reflex action and also resulted in EO's first death in Sierra Leone.[6]

The final phase came the next morning when Walker and Alberts, out on patrol in the surrounding jungle in their gunship, caught sight of the tail end of the fleeing rebel army trying to cross one of the rivers in dugout canoes. They lined up the *pirogues* in their sights and sank the lot with automatic fire.

The effect of driving the rebels into the interior after EO's first battle in Sierra Leone had a significant effect, not only on Freetown, but much of the rest of the country as well. As the word spread, the people felt that they could breathe again. Also, it stymied Sankoh's hopes of occupying the capital, though it was not the last time he was to try his luck.

After Freetown had been secured, about half of EO's men went home on leave. Those who stayed continued with the mopping-up process. Rykaart finally handed command over to Sachse to continue with another project, this one secret.

The war was far from over. The RUF still had a sizeable force in the mountains around the capital and one group after another was dealt with piecemeal in the weeks that followed. Also, for the first time good intelligence was coming in, sometimes arriving in bundles, which eased things for the gunships. About then the aircrews began using night-vision goggles for operations after dark.

The Kono District to the east—with its huge diamond diggings—was suddenly within the sights of the mercenary group. Essentially, the existence of those rich fields had been the cause of this war in the first place.

21

GUNSHIP COMBAT IN
WEST AFRICA

**"Like it or not, when you're up there coming to
grips with an enemy that's throwing things at you,
the adrenaline pumps."**

Neall Ellis, Cockerill Barracks, Freetown, August 2002

One of the immediate concerns that needed to be dealt with on the
arrival of Executive Outcomes in Sierra Leone was who would crew
the gunships. At that stage of the war, the Sierra Leone Air Wing had
an Mi-24 Hind, complete with Belarusian air and ground crews, plus
a vintage Mi-17 support helicopter that could get aloft, but only just.
The two EO Hips that the company had bought from the United
Nations in Angola only arrived afterward.

Before the South Africans landed in Freetown, aviation in this
West African state had been something of a Russian monopoly, and
since it was lucrative, nobody doubted that Moscow's boys would do
all they could to hang on to it. In spite of their efforts, the South
Africans eventually took over flying duties for the duration of that
phase of the war.

To start with, EO's primary concern was enlisting people who
could make good use of their machines, especially in combat. It was
felt—perhaps with justification—that the Russians did not have sufficient motivation to do what was needed. Michael Grunberg's wry
comment was that "The Russians wanted to save 'their' machines
from having their paint chipped."

After much conniving and intrigue, the East Europeans were eventually sidelined. Certainly, they were not much pleased, and ultimately they would choose their own time and place to retaliate.

It was swift in coming. Soon after EO took over air operations, the
Hind's electronics were sabotaged and although an engineer was
brought out from Moscow to fix it, the bird flew only intermittently
thereafter. However, the gunship did last long enough to play a semi-

nal role in the Battle for Freetown. There was more drama after a
Russian pilot was found dead alongside one of the helicopters. The
circumstances were suspicious. Though the former Soviet had been
murdered, the authorities eventually determined that it could have
been the consequence of a diamond deal that had turned turtle.

The most serious attempt to undermine South African influence in
the Air Wing was initiated with a particularly nasty piece of work by
a man called Nosov. This former Soviet pilot worked to a two-phased
program, the first involving the partially disabled Hind. Then Nosov's
technicians began to tamper with the armaments, and finally the
rotors, causing malfunctions in them all.

When Walker, Alberts and the others first started flying the gunship across rebel-held areas, the enemy would scatter as soon as they
appeared. After Nosov's bit of mischief, things changed almost immediately.

"It was odd how it went," said Walker. "One day the gooks would
run for their lives as soon as we arrived over a position. A day later,
they would stand there and laugh, pointing at us. They obviously
knew that we couldn't fire our guns and, of course, there was a good
reason for it all because it happened directly after one group of technicians had arrived from Russia and replaced another."

At about this time reports started to filter through of Sankoh
offering diamond concessions to anybody who was prepared to help
his people. Though nothing was ever proved, things fitted together too
tidily not to implicate the Russian group. Subsequent inquiries in
Freetown following Sankoh's death proved this to be the case.

Animosity directed at the South Africans by the men from
Moscow became even more pronounced when Nosov was appointed
to a government board of inquiry after Charlie Tate's Mi-17 mishap
with a bird that July. The fact that Tate was able to land his machine
without injury to crew or passengers was due solely to his flying skills
because the helicopter was wrecked.

Carl Alberts, then serving as a lieutenant colonel of the Air Wing,
was appointed president of this board. Also included in the line-up
were two Nigerian squadron leaders, a Sierra Leone major from Army
HQ and two Russians, of whom Nosov was one. Alberts' report on
the sequence of events is interesting:

On Sunday 23 July, 1995 at 1045Zulu, a formation of three
helicopters departed from Lungi for Sefadu on a logistical sup-

ply mission. The aircraft routed at low level in a loose battle formation. The lead aircraft roused a large flock of birds that massed in the path of the number-three helicopter. Despite evasive maneuvers, a bird strike was heard and observed above the cockpit. This was followed by engine fluctuations with associated aircraft yaw and a drop in rotor rpm.

Tate brought his disabled helicopter down in a heavily foliated patch of jungle. In the process his main rotors struck a palm, which swung the Mi-17 a hundred-and-eighty degrees. That caused it to hit several other trees and lose its tail boom.

Nosov did what he could to have Tate declared incompetent. But the Muscovite hadn't reckoned with the South African's years of combat or with the fact that EO was being briefed by a confidential source in Moscow, with whom the pilots were in daily contact. The Russian's performance was not improved by his fondness for the bottle, often arriving at the morning sessions with a couple of beers or a glass of vodka in hand. His African colleagues, more accustomed to British traditions, took a dim view of his habit. Even so, none of them had the gumption to tell him to hold off until after the meetings and Alberts, as chairman, couldn't do anything that might have been interpreted as partisan.

Nosov's erratic behavior became more pronounced as the inquiry went on. Sometimes he wouldn't turn up at the morning session, surfacing only after lunch. It was Alberts who eventually suggested that because this was an extremely serious issue somebody else should replace him, preferably another Russian.

In the end Tate was exonerated and Nosov was reprimanded for trying to influence the board.

Initially, there was also the matter of South African combat crews having to learn to fly a machine that dated from the Soviet era. Though not unlike other combat whirlybirds, Hinds had idiosyncrasies of their own.

Working in Africa, the men had obviously seen a lot of Mi-24s. The Angolan Air Force had squadrons of them, and during the Border War era they had used them, often successfully, if not against the South Africans then against Savimbi's Unita forces. In subsequent EO operations on behalf of the Luanda regime, former South African Air Force types—at the insistence of the Eastern Europeans—had been excluded from operating them for most of that war.

Nor was Ivan going to lift a finger to help in Sierra Leone. Why should they, they would ask. They might very well end up being replaced by the South Africans, which, in point of fact, they eventually were.

Compared to the ubiquitous Mi-17 Hip, the Soviet Mi-24 Hind—obviously intended for a totally different combat role—is a superior machine. It is more versatile, more aerodynamic and, with a maximum speed of roughly two hundred miles an hour (and more powerful engines) a good deal faster than the Hip. Those who know the machine are aware that, like the American Apache, its aviators sit in tandem under a pair of front bubbles, the pilot positioned behind and slightly above his gunner, as I was to discover when I flew combat with Neall Ellis five years later.

EO's salvation arrived in the shape of former Soviet pilot Nikolai Kagouk, a much-decorated veteran of the Soviet war in Afghanistan. He'd spent years at the controls of Mi-24s hammering Islamic fundamentalists in the mountains adjacent to Pakistan. However, the hard-drinking Kagouk could speak no English and the best that the South Africans could muster in Russian were *nyet* and *Stolnichnaya*, though never consecutively or immediately before a flight.

A solution was found when a diplomat arrived at Cockerill Barracks accompanied by the Russian-speaking wife of a Lebanese trader. She immediately offered her services as an interlocutor. As far as EO was concerned, the woman was a godsend.

Originally hailing from the Ukraine, this unusual woman was immediately dubbed "Madam Chernobyl" because her home was in that area. The crews would joke that when she walked past a television set the screen would go fuzzy because of the amount of radioactivity in her body.

With steely determination, Madam Chernobyl surprised everyone by getting the library of Moscow's Embassy in Freetown involved in the exercise. In no time she was able to master the intricacies of Russian aeronautical dynamics and interpret results in a way that the South Africans could understand. In a sense, she'd assumed the roles of both flight instructor and engineer. She also translated into English all the factory manuals that had arrived from Moscow in Cyrillic script. It says something that they were still on Nellis's desk years later. Long after EO had departed, he'd call her whenever he was stumped and she'd come down to Cockerill and sort it out.

The first South Africans to be put through the Hind's complex conversion basics by Kagouk in 1995 were those two illustrious veterans of South Africa's Border Wars, Arthur Walker and Carl Alberts. Space constraints at Cockerill forced them to move almost all orientation work to Lungi, and within a week or two both men were flying solo.

Kagouk then familiarized them with the Hind's weapons systems and the South Africans mastered those as well. Another few days at the controls and Walker and Alberts were ready for their first combat assignment. Afterward, it would amuse those on the flight line that there would always be a bit of banter before take-off about who would do the flying and who would handle the days' "hunting."

Meanwhile, the two Mi-17s that belonged to EO arrived from Angola. Both had seen extensive service against Savimbi and came equipped with the usual hard points for weapons under their winglets. But they hadn't been wired up or mounted, so the choppers had to be fitted with side door-mounted automatic weapons built into harnesses and hurriedly fabricated at workshops in Freetown.

To fly the two choppers across Africa was a bind, especially since most African states—even today—are nervous about people ferrying war planes through their air space. As EO quickly discovered, this applied especially to white mercenaries. Still, there was no other option short of dismantling both birds and having them shipped first to Europe and then dog-legged back to Africa. Grunberg pointed out in one of his missives that this was a hideously expensive alternative.

So fly halfway across Africa they did. Internal ferry tanks were fitted and the crews set off for from Luanda to Nigeria. Then things went nuts. On touchdown in Lagos, the authorities seized both aircraft and the pilots were accused of being "racist warmongers." Why else had they come to Nigeria, it was asked. The Nigerian press had its day with headline banners such as: "South African mercenaries held captive at Murtala Mohammed Airport." It was of no consequence to Nigeria's military rulers that Nelson Mandela had recently been elected president of South Africa. Or that the Hips were being taken to Sierra Leone to provide support to Nigerian soldiers fighting a war against a common enemy.

For almost a week the machines remained impounded. Their crews were forced to camp out under their rotors next to the runway of the busiest airport in West Africa. Meanwhile, "a cocky a bunch of pie-eyed goons" guarded them. Automatic weapons were shoved in their faces if they wandered more than a few yards. The palaver that followed became acrimonious and went on for days; in the meantime, appeals went out for help.

One of the pilots, "Juba" Joubert, has never counted Nigerians among his favorite folk, and it has nothing to do with race because he also looks down his nose at Americans. It was he who recounted afterward that they actually had to beg for water, while food wasn't even a consideration:

"We were treated like animals. And let's face it, they were really after our money. But we were damned if we were going to give those bastards anything." Eventually, following appeals by the Sierra Leone High Commissioner as well as a direct approach from Chairman Valentine Strasser to the Nigerian president, the helicopters were released. Cash and coercion carried the day.

The first operational sorties in which EO pilots were involved in Sierra Leone followed a pattern not unlike those instituted by company crews in Angola. There was one major difference though and that was the jungle. Like Nellis, they had to adapt to new circumstances.

The equatorial forests of the West Coast were unlike anything the South Africans had experienced before, and the pilots had to adjust to a totally new game plan if they were to survive. If Angola was primitive, then Sierra Leone was a suburb of hell.

For a start, mixed crews serviced the aircraft. Consequently ground checks prior to take-off had to be meticulous: the lives of the pilots depended on it. Also, there were no flight or survey maps of the country. For some time the pilots were obliged to rely almost solely on Sierra Leone road maps published by Shell Oil and bought from the local Lebanese store. Michael Grunberg afterward told me that this had been a problem from the start. EO's original country appraisal— its tactical appreciation of the situation prior to the company accepting the contract—had to be done with the aid of a rudimentary Michelin map of West Africa, the kind that is offered for sale in Foyles or Barnes and Noble.

It didn't take anybody long to appreciate that, when it came to air operations, bush war tactics used down south simply wouldn't work along this stretch of tropical coast. Sierra Leone's rainy climate and its sometimes-impenetrable triple-canopy forest screened just about everything going on below. "The gooks could see us, but for much of the time, particularly when there was fighting going on, we couldn't see them. Effectively, we were blind," Alberts recalled.

"For instance, if somebody on the ground remained motionless when our choppers passed, chances are that we'd miss them. Six or eight rebels could easily hide behind a single mahogany trunk and nobody would be the wiser."

"Tatties" Tate—also a veteran from the Angolan War – said that there were huge stretches of rain forest which were so dense that the RUF could have secreted a brigade in the bushes around Freetown. Consequently, the pilots had to concede that Sierra Leone was a more dangerous theater of war than anything they had experienced in the past.

As Nellis explained, you had to factor in a variety of obstacles, some natural, others tactical. You had the terrain, he said. Then you had to consider friendly forces, fuel supplies, rebel concentrations (the ones you actually knew about) and half a dozen other imponderables. Coupled to all this was the eternal tropical luxuriance of it all, allowing for few distinguishable features when flying across jungle at fifty feet. The result was that some pilots would become disjointed. As he was to comment, "Events on the ground had a disconcerting way of presenting newcomers with the unexpected." It was a prescient observation.

Walker: "We were sometimes called out to give top cover to our guys who were completely surrounded by rebels. Like us, our ground forces were new to this kind of terrain and, as we discovered, they faced a pretty resourceful enemy." The situation wasn't ameliorated by the fact that they hadn't been allowed a shakedown period: some of the men were put to work within hours of disembarking from the Boeing.

"As for combat, we struck at the terrs[1] wherever we found them," said Tate, "and that was just about everywhere." Some, he explained, had taken up offensive positions in heavy bush country overlooking the city even before EO arrived.

It didn't take long for this conflict to gather its own logic and momentum. Confused at first by conditions which made both flying and navigation difficult, the pilots quickly worked out fresh sets of operational priorities.

Tate recalls that discussions would take place on a day-to-day basis. Afterward, usually over a couple of ales at Alex's, ground and air commanders would get their heads together and mull over problems encountered that day. Communications between air assets and the men on the ground—or more likely, the inability to properly coordinate them—was the first issue. Others followed.

"Basically," said Tate, "you learnt pretty soon how to react when somebody is shooting at you." It was his view that if EO didn't take the initiative at every opportunity the rebels would almost always exploit the situation. The kind of excessive caution displayed by the Russian pilots that they replaced, he reckoned, was used to good advantage by Sankoh's people, especially if the enemy believed the helicopters had been neutered.

Also, because of security lapses, it wasn't something they could discuss with their Sierra Leonean bosses. Within days, to their cost, they learnt that very little that crossed the desk of Maada Bio, the Chief of Defense Staff (CDS) didn't end up in the hands of the RUF, which was one of the reasons why all EO radio transmissions were in Afrikaans (as are some communications involving South Africans working for private security concerns in Baghdad today). Neither the enemy nor the government could understand it. In any event, argued Colonel Bert Sachse, it was a comfortable way of keeping security intact since even our own black troops understood the lingo.

That was to change eventually, especially when word arrived that the rebels had hired some Afrikaans-speaking "coloreds" (people of mixed blood) from the Cape.

From the start, Arthur Walker and the boys were astonished at the intensity of some of the contacts. There were missions where they were literally right on top of the men on the ground—perhaps fifty or eighty feet off the deck—and when that happened, he recalled, "You couldn't help but see green tracers coming up at you in volume." The only good thing about it, he admitted, was that when the enemy used tracers, they'd quickly be able to zero in on the source.

Walker: "It was nothing big—lots of RPG-7s, PKMs and AKs. We were hit more often than we liked, but there was actually very little that we could do apart from strike back. And we did with interest," he declared with a smile that would inevitably emerge whenever we discussed exploits past.

"There was also a huge difference between the way we fought our war and what the Russians had attempted previously in giving close air support. We would hear from Sierra Leone officers afterward that more often than not, instead of homing into where the fire was coming from, the Russkies would just veer away. They'd go high and wait for the commotion to subside."

Not that the Russians were cowards, he averred. "It was just that they didn't believe they were being paid enough to take risks in sticking about, especially when the ground forces they were supposed to be covering were getting clobbered. Which they were—a lot—before we arrived."

Walker: "We took a different approach. In fact, our South African chopper guys were in a class on their own. Not only that, but they were accomplished aviators and they were damn good at dishing it out," he reckoned.

"The same with our guys on the ground—our brothers. They needed us right there, able to react at a moment's notice, and we were, because basically that was how we'd always fought our wars. Anyway, that's what the job was about and in the end our efforts prevailed."

Most important of all, he elaborated, it was also the first time that the rebels had come up against any kind of retaliation from the air, "and it didn't take long for them to realize that if they exchanged blows with us, they were going to die." Fanatical followers of Sankoh or not, he reckoned, "The alternative of ducking and diving while we were hovering over their heads became a much more realistic option— at least then they would survive."

Some of the fiercest battles took place during what is now referred to as the "Battle for Freetown."

Walker reckoned that the sheer volume of fire exchanged by the two adversaries was often more intense than anything the Alouettes had experienced in Angola under similar conditions. "It's then, with little or no leeway for error, that accidents happen, though it was much more comfortable working in a Hind." The titanium bath which is a feature of the Hind cockpit and which protects both the pilot and his front gunner, was "mighty comforting." Certainly, it offered better protection against ground fire. he declared.

It's worth mentioning that though the government lost a few Mi-17s as a result of enemy action, the RUF never managed to bring down one of the Mi-24s.

For all that, though, this was also a time when EO began to take casualties. In fact, as Colonel Sachse pointed out, this was inevitable when contacts would sometimes drag on, quite often at extremely close quarters. Perhaps half a dozen company men died in action during the course of EO's involvement in this West African war, though none were aircrew. Malaria also took its toll.

At the same time, the forces working under Executive Outcomes' banner in Sierra Leone saw very little of the kind of extended ground operations that the men had experienced earlier against Unita in Angola.

During the Border War days of the 1970s and 1980s, Koevoet—the SA police anti-terrorist unit—would clock up hundreds of enemy killed and wounded during the course of a year's fighting. Much of this happened in a region that included most of northern Namibia and a large portion of southern Angola, for the loss of handful of their own men.

In that campaign, any kind of tactical thrust with ground forces would involve mobile, mine-protected Casspir infantry fighting vehicles. In turn, these would be backed by helicopter-led close air support sorties using Alouettes.

Swapo insurgents, in contrast, were invariably on foot. They legged it into the operational areas—carrying all their weapons, ammunition, medical supplies, water and food on their backs—and they would hotfoot it out again when they thought they'd scored enough points. Most times they'd have security forces hot on their tails and it says a good deal for the caliber of rebel resistance that South Africa's border conflicts were to extend over more than twenty years.

In fact, as Walker and the others will admit, Swapo guerrillas, as one of them phrased it, "were one tough bunch of fighters." More's the pity then that so little has been published about this long military campaign that in phases, covered an area almost the size New Mexico.[2]

In those days, ground and air cooperation was such that individual pilots were able to follow developments on the ground from a distance, often from the ops center back at base. They eventually became so good at it that they learned to anticipate moves while the chase developed. Then, once there was the prospect of a kill after a successful follow-up, they'd be overhead.

It was a scenario that had played itself out untold times, first in Portugal's colonial wars in Mozambique and Angola, and then in Rhodesia's bush war, where many South African Air Force pilots were blooded in counterinsurgency operations. The border wars came afterward and it was this kind of experience that they brought with them to EO.

What also emerged among those correspondents who were able to cover South Africa's two-decade-long bush war was the remarkable level of camaraderie between the "brown jobs" (ground troops) and the "blues" (pilots), as they liked to refer to each other. There are few places where the two arms interacted as intimately as they did in southern Africa and this, too, became a feature of Executive Outcomes' activities.

Consider the alternative: in Algeria, the French Air Force, a haughty, opinionated elite who believed they were better than everyone else, fought their own isolated air campaigns. And though this trend, of necessity, eventually changed, the country paid a bitter price for the accumulated hubris of the country's aviators.

Similarly, while Lisbon was fighting its three separate wars in its African colonies (Angola, Mozambique and Portuguese Guinea—today Guiné-Bissau) in the 1960s and 1970s, Portuguese Air Force pilots would rarely share any kind of confidence with the men on the ground unless they absolutely had to. Never mind split a bottle of wine with them after a successful contact. It happened, of course, but not more than was needed.

Former Selous Scouts founder Ron Reid-Daly told me that he was sometimes perplexed at the way the Portuguese fought their bush campaigns. "You'd have very little interaction between respective assets, be it on the ground or in the air." Pilots wouldn't talk to the army, and neither would talk to the police or security services who, in turn, wouldn't pass on good intelligence. They all eventually turned on the Portuguese secret police, PIDE,[3] he said, adding that it was small wonder that the terrs were successful in driving Lisbon out of Africa.

Though not a fraction as serious, the beginnings of similar shortcomings seem to prevail in some sections of today's American armed services. While different elements might mix during furlough, it is rarely an easy-going association. Inter-service rivalry in the U.S. forces is often intense. Marines tend to associate with Marines when off base and Army pilots with Army pilots, though clearly, there is some overlap, especially when abroad.

Where they do have a common denominator is that you won't find many American soldiers on active duty today who believe that the CIA is fulfilling its potential in gathering humint.[4]

On the technical side, Langley is the best there is, but real intelligence on today's obscure battlefields—as Iraq, Afghanistan and many other places in Asia, Africa and the Near East have unequivocally demonstrated—depends on realizing every little village and town, every gathering of religious leaders, and just about each maddrassah you might encounter along the way is a potential recruiting point for Islamic terrorists.

The pilots who landed at Freetown were an experienced bunch of professionals. They drew no distinctions about who did what, because everybody had a common objective. Each one of them was bent on the destruction of a violent, unprincipled and often irrational enemy. At the same time, they knew and understood the needs of their compadres on the ground. Like Nellis, Walker, "Tatties" Tate, Joubert, Alberts and the rest, these were the original war dogs in this mercenary war.

Walker had a few other attributes that set him apart. He is the only man ever to have twice won the South African *Honoris Crux* (HC) in gold,[5] having earned these credits in Angola while flying Alouette helicopter gunships. The first time, when he landed his frail-looking machine alongside a huge enemy force to rescue a fellow pilot who had been downed by AA fire, he doesn't know how they survived. Talk to Arthur today and he won't admit to either courage or luck, though he'll concede that it was possibly a bit of both.

In all, the South Africans lost about seven hundred soldiers during the course of its insurgency conflicts, including many of Walker's associates.

Those who were able to walk away from it at the end expressed surprise that Walker had survived. Those of us covering these wars—as with his own pals—were aware that he had an almost cynical disregard for danger, a trait that served him well when things got tight. It also underscores another of his traits: Arthur Walker rarely entertained the possibility of defeat. To him, death was never an option. He estimates that during the course of his career (which, briefly, included a spell of flying combat in Rhodesia) he'd been in more than a hundred actions, the majority exchanging some kind of fire with the enemy. There were also scores of minor scraps and follow-ups, all of which eventually became part of an almost daily routine as the Border War dragged on. Even more astonishing is the fact that Arthur Walker was never wounded.

Lean, tough and, like his good buddy Neall Ellis, having survived the first critical "half century," Walker in his prime had a great love for things that moved fast—sleek cars and trim aircraft included. And as he will candidly admit, lots of good American whiskey, preferably Jack Daniels.

Following the accession to power of South Africa's African National Congress (ANC) in the early 1990s, Walker stayed in the SAAF only long enough to see Ronnie Kasrils, a card-carrying communist and Kremlin protégé, take over as Deputy Minister of Defense. Like Nellis, he left the force in disgust.

As he says today, "Who cared a fuck anyway whether I stayed or went?" Then, when EO began to recruit pilots with combat experience, it was to be expected that one of the first of the veterans they approached was Walker.

Others included Louwrens Bosch, Sonny Janecke, Pine Pienaar and J.C. Linde, together with a handful that didn't make it. Neall Ellis only arrived later. When EO first went into Angola, he was into fishing and very much embroiled in the process of losing his pension money. Like both Walker and Ellis, most of the crews recruited by EO signed up because the money was good. With the political transition from white rule to black, coupled to a sudden, not altogether unexpected economic downturn in South Africa, things back home were tight.

Overnight there was work "up north," as these veterans started to refer to West African combat opportunities.

The problems that the South Africans encountered with the Russians who had flown Strasser's gunships centered as much on basic counterinsurgency procedures as on a patent unwillingness to get to grips with the enemy.

For example, the East European idea of close-quarter top cover for government forces was hovering somewhere between two thousand and five thousand feet. From there, they would fire their weapons at random, if at all. Since neither Strasser nor his CDS (or any other member of headquarters staff at Cockerill Barracks) knew any better, they couldn't argue. So they had to accept the glib assurances of these former Soviets that it had been handled like that in Afghanistan. There was simply no other way.

What these Russian hustlers didn't add was that such tactics were one of the reasons Moscow lost the Afghan war

"Most of their targets were in their heads," commented another of the South African pilots. Brigadier Maada Bio, the CDS at Cockerill, had earlier picked up on what the Belarusians were doing, but until

Executive Outcomes came along, he was powerless.

EO pilots discovered in their first week of combat that they were up against fairly large groups of rebels, usually in company-sized groups: "They had adequate numbers, but were fragmented. Their forces never gathered together in any one place, except at night when they looked to each other for support against the demons of the dark," explained Walker.

In any event, nobody fought at night in Sierra Leone; in African tribal lore, it was a time when the spirits of their forefathers walked.

Walker believed that it was a mistake to underestimate the power of the supernatural in scoring points with these people. Their fears, he felt, could easily be turned against them. For instance, if their witch doctors concocted a potion which they believed would make them invisible, "They'd go into battle actually believing that we couldn't see them."

"It didn't matter that the rest of their buddies, similarly 'sanctified,' were dying in clusters each time they connected with us. They go on fighting believing irrationally that they had the 'protection' of their forefathers.

"That was our job, to try to correct this stupid folly. If we did that, we were aware that we would have achieved two objectives: first, the rebels themselves would take care of their bogus, in-house 'medicine makers.' And in so doing, psychological deprivation would result among many of them . . . ultimate they'd lose the will, the rationale, to fight."

While this might sound like hocus-pocus to the average Westerner, there are primitive perceptions that reach deep into the psyche of some of these tribesmen. They end up becoming totally fearless, at least in the initial stages. Many, after the daily dose of drum-thumping, hollering and indoctrination, are often ready to take on just about anything. "Then they fight with an almost indomitable will, because they really do believe they're immortal," which was Bert Sachse's explication.

"Of course, as the day wears on, many become even more 'substance inspired,' usually on booze and ganga. Then their actions become even more crazy," reflected Walker. "They'd lose all sense of cohesion . . . like zombies, and they'd cut off a child's arm just for the hell of it, or split open the bellies of pregnant mothers."

In this, the RUF seemed to share just about everything evil in Africa with Uganda's equally mindless Lord's Resistance Army that is still out there killing people, and which today still relies heavily on child soldiers, the majority of whom are what one psychologist described as "mind blown." If the war were to end tomorrow, the authorities would face a major uphill task in trying to assimilate these pubescent psychopaths back into society.

Variations of these and related issues were faced by everybody in this West African war, including us hacks who were covering it. By then, Phillip van Niekerk had joined us. He was to go on to edit Johannesburg's *Mail & Guardian*, and after that, accept a position in Washington's Center for Public Integrity. Even in those early days we would be circumspect about who we mixed with after hours in Freetown, plus where we went.

Years later, following the deaths of two of our colleagues in an ambush at Rogberi, most of the media would avoid going out after lunch. In that heat, rebel groups fortified by the usual combination— as well as the latest talisman from the witch doctor—would become almost inhuman in their actions. We'd been nobbled often enough by nondescript groups of fighters, many of whom were so far gone that they didn't know the time of day. With guns shoved into our ears, as would happen sometimes, situations like that could get tricky. As a result, we would stay put and spend the afternoon dozing, reading or writing. In any event, it was stupid to take more chances and at least the beer was cold.

The pilots discovered soon after they arrived that it was rare for the rebels to split into smaller sections, which made them easier to spot from the air. They'd stay in their groups, often fifty or eighty strong and sometimes the gunship would be "talked down" onto these targets by EO operators on the ground operating in four- or eight-man sticks.

"Of course the gooks knew exactly when we were in radio contact and headed out towards them," Walker recalls. "As we got close to where it was all happening in the jungle we'd come under fire from fifty or eighty barrels at a time. Or the guys would fire a flare to try to pinpoint enemy positions and we'd follow the smoke trail in with the Gatling."

When things went well it wasn't long before it was like old times. That was when the experience of past encounters helped.

The pilots had no illusions about what would happen if they were to be brought down by enemy fire. Bob MacKenzie's story had done the rounds and it had a marked effect on them all. What made it more immediate was that a lot of the boys—Walker and Tate included—had worked with the American during periods they'd done some fighting in Rhodesia. They'd even had ales together when they met up afterward in Harare.

In the final stages of that bush war quite a few South African pilots gave close air support to Rhodesian SAS cross-border sorties in Mozambique or Zambia, and now and again in Botswana. Reid-Daly's Scouts were also recipients of this bounty, as were RLI fighting groups when they hit some of the larger insurgent camps like Chimoiyo or Mepai.

Sierra Leone presented some astonishing contrasts compared to earlier African conflicts. Once, when a dozen or so of Simon Witherspoon's men—completely surrounded—had taken refuge in a wooded defile on a hillside and couldn't move, Walker and Alberts were scrambled to provide top cover.

Witherspoon, a former member of South Africa's elite Reconnaissance Regiment had already indicated earlier by radio that whichever side his people probed, they came under concentrated fire. Some of it was from a 12.7mm AA gun used in a ground attack mode and which was causing worry. As he told us later, heavy rounds were coming in clusters and some salvos would clear a passage though the bush. Worse, his group was outnumbered by something like a dozen or more to one.

"After a couple of hours trying to extricate them, by which time they were almost out of ammunition," Walker recalls, "we considered a 'hot extract'—pulling them straight out with our winches. But with an Mi-17 in the hover over such heavy country, that wasn't really an option. It wouldn't have taken long for the enemy to have spotted what we doing and they would have brought us down. You can do that with a big caliber gun like a fourteen-five."

Like his EO boss, Lafras Luitingh, Witherspoon was an experienced combatant and aware of the ultimate consequences if things deteriorated further. As the second wave of choppers approached, he spoke to Walker. "He had me visual but I couldn't see him," the pilot explained. "So he talked me down. It was a slow, deliberate process, until we were almost on top of him. When he asked me if I could identify a small crossroads at about ten, eleven o'clock. I answered, 'Below me and to the left'."

"Affirmative!" Witherspoon replied, adding that his group was holed up in a clump of bushes on the other side of the road. The rebels were in deep foliage about a hundred yards or so to the north. "Simon couldn't have been more specific."

Walker put his nose down, switched the Gatling to full-auto and sprayed. Radio intercepts that night referred to about thirty kills.

Firing at the enemy with your own forces directly below wasn't a simple matter. As Tate had always warned, the problem facing crews was that in firing its quad, the Mi-24 ejected a shower of brass shell casings on to the men below.

"And matters weren't helped by the fact that the boys on the ground weren't wearing helmets; the climate was just too hot and humid, not that there were any to be had in Sierra Leone anyway.'

Said Alberts: "If any of those chunks in full flight hits a man, there could be injuries: a quarter pound of metal dropping from a hundred feet up might crack a man's skull. Consequently, our attack direction and profile had to be perfect."

The gunship crews rarely worked to any set routine. Like resistance to more recent RUF incursions involving Nellis, Walker and his friends flew as and when they were tasked. Looking back, Walker reckons that each op, while unique, was always hellish exciting. After a week he started looking forward to seeing what each day would offer.

"Looking down those sights was great, especially since the rebels had killed so many innocents. This was payback time!"

Some of the most memorable missions flown by the South Africans during their earlier deployment involved the Nigerian Air Force.

About noon one day, Andy Brown popped into the pilots' ready room and asked whether they could take the Hind up. Headquarters had made an intercept about sacks of rice and other supplies being delivered to a gook camp about ten minutes' flight from the base. "One group was apparently resupplying another."

The Nigerian Alpha-Jets deployed in Sierra Leone and then operating out of Lungi were to be brought into the act, but before getting airborne, both groups of pilots met to coordinate the strike. It was agreed that the Mi-24 would "talk" the fighters on to the target where, it was hoped, they would do what was needed with their five-hundred-pound fragmentation bombs. Afterward the gunship would skulk around and pick off survivors.

The sortie went off without incident and radio intercepts later confirmed six or seven dead together with more wounded.

Walker: "The Alphas came in fairly high. Normally their attack profile involved dropping their loads from about five thousand feet AGL, and given the problems we'd already encountered—cloud cover, lack of visibility on the ground and the jungle—it was very professionally done. Their bombs landed only yards from the cache that we'd spotted through the trees."

The South Africans were impressed with their young, enthusiastic Nigerian "jet jockey" friends and, unlike the army, both groups of aviators got on famously. All had been British-trained, "and you could see by the way they approached the day's problems that they knew their business. In bearing, speech, attention to detail, together with the kind of questions asked in the morning's briefing, some of these sessions might have been held at RAF Brize Norton.

"If you closed your eyes, you felt that a few of them might have been wearing RAF uniforms."

It wasn't the first time that Alberts and Walker had worked with the Nigerian Air Force. In an earlier attack, Army HQ had pinpointed a fairly large rebel camp in the hills beyond Waterloo. A combined Mi-24 and Alpha strike was planned for early the next day, with the chopper boys providing coordinates with their GPS system and the jets coming in from five thousand feet.

Then followed one of the remarkable events of the war. It involved Nigerian pilots who had been trained by the British, flying German fighter aircraft armed with French munitions in an operation involving South Africans at the controls of Russian helicopters. To further compound the mix, their targets were Sierra Leone nationals whose leaders had been trained in Libya and had originally set out from Liberia.

Cloud ceiling on the morning of the strike was down to about four hundred feet. According to Walker, it was the usual thick, impenetrable tropical soup that often grounded flights at Lungi. The Nigerians wanted to cancel, but Walker and Alberts flew across the bay to talk to them at their "tent city" base on the far side of the runway. Walker proposed that they launch anyway, with him and Alberts going ahead in the Hind and pinpointing the target. The jets could follow, he told them, hoping they'd bite.

Throughout, Walker suggested, the jets would remain visual, just below cloud cover: instead of five thousand feet it would be something like three hundred and fifty. If they didn't come in low, he warned, it wouldn't work.

The objective, he explained to the Nigerian squadron leader, was, as before, to "talk" the Alphas all the way down to the target at tree-top level. At the right moment he would signal them to let go their bombs.

The Nigerians were incredulous. The scheme was hare-brained, they said. They'd never done anything like it before. And tree-top flying? "Not on, old chap!"

There was another problem. The Nigerian officer said that cluster bombs were expensive. They only had half a dozen or so of them left and they weren't too keen to waste them, which, he implied, was what he thought of low-level bombing. The attack wasn't going to happen, he declared. That should have ended the discussion but, undeterred, Walker carried on, as usual oozing charm like glycerin.

"Trust me," he told the squadron leader. "We'll get you down the throat of those bastards. Just aim straight for and below us and we'll coordinate the whole thing." Walker could be persuasive when he set his mind to it, especially since he assured his Nigerian friends that what he proposed was something his own people had done often enough in Angola in the past. That really got the Nigerians' interest. What probably swung it was that these pilots were impressed with Walker's unreservedly gung-ho approach to something that he regarded as "merely a matter of routine."

The Mi-24 took off and headed for the hinterland. Using their GPS sets, the South Africans made straight for the enemy camp. Once there, they took up a position beyond, but within sight of the target so that nobody on the ground would know what was up. Alberts called the Alphas to prepare for their approach runs.

The Nigerian pilots were given a two-minute IP point for reference and the jets roared in just above the palms at about four-hundred and fifty knots while the helicopter moved into position over the target. "It was something marvelous to watch from right up close. It was also good that they went through with it because they didn't really have to," Walker recalls.

"They had their own peculiar flight language; terribly British, he recalled. I could hear them over the radio after I'd told them to stand-by to let go: 'Pickle...pickle...pickle...NOW!' With that they dropped their loads."

In the debrief afterward it was found that the Alpha-Jets could hardly have been more accurate had their bombs been smart. The French munitions were state-of-the-art and performed magnificently, opening up the jungle like an overripe avocado. A succession of blasts exposed an area the size of a football field, which only hours before had been an enemy camp housing hundreds.

Walker: "But somehow, the bastards got wind of the strike and the gooks had fled. It was obvious to all of us that someone at headquarters had tipped them off. Just about the entire group had left the area not long before we got there, which was the sort of problem that we had to live with for the duration." All that had been left behind was a tiny rearguard squad armed with RPGs. "They gave us a couple of sticks before they were killed," Walker concluded.

Mission accomplished, the South Africans radioed back. They invited the Nigerians to circle back over the target area for an up-close look at their handiwork. The Alphas made a wide arc and the pilots admitted over beers that evening that the tactic had value. Also, it was quite a novel experience and would probably be worth incorporating into future battle plans, their CO said afterward.

He was as good as his word.

In the earlier Sierra Leone deployment involving Executive Outcomes, Walker and his colleagues flew both types of Russian helicopters. While the Mi-24 Hind was used solely in combat, the Mi-17 Hip served as a gun platform when it wasn't hauling men, supplies and odds and sods like me into Koidu and other call signs in the interior.

Some of the operational equipment was based at Hastings, a small airport on the far side of the peninsula about forty-five minutes' drive from town, but that was supposed to be classified. During the UN deployment of 1999, it became the principle air base in the territory occupied by the international force. Historically Hastings had always played a role in defense. It was the first military airfield built in Sierra Leone during World War II, but had been little used until Sankoh crossed the Liberian border with his hordes. By the time EO arrived the airport had been declared out of bounds.

Not everybody was aware that in 1995 the American Embassy parked its six-seater Piper Apache there. Or that the local detachment of CIA operatives was using it. This detail emerged from a bit of reciprocal intelligence banter between the Americans and the South Africans.

Washington obviously needed to know how the war was going and Langley was prepared to give a little to get a little. The resident Chief of Station, Colonel Larry Reiman, was candid about his needs. As he said, that's the way things are done between "allies" in remote parts. He filled in some of these details at a function at the British High Commission in Freetown to which we'd all been invited, and our paths continued to cross for several years afterward.

The Friday night "diplomatic" affair was an unusual mix with a kind of "Year of Living Dangerously" piquancy about it. The British High Commissioner made no apologies for inviting senior EO members. While the international community might look down their noses at what they would regard as mercenaries, he would publicly declare that it was their boys who had secured Freetown and prevented the rebels from occupying the city. And if that hadn't happened, said the High Commissioner flatly, he, for one, wouldn't be there that night. It was not only crass to ignore their presence, he told one critic, it was also not being very clever. It was a classic understatement and it took a senior British diplomat to make it.

For their part, most EO officers seemed to get on pretty well with their hosts. They partied well and were usually the last to leave.

EO's mercenary activity in Sierra Leone was always in the spotlight. Military helicopters in camouflage with white men at the controls tend to draw attention in any African state, especially since a Hip or two—and occasionally the Hind—could often be seen refueling at Lungi. Nobody bothered to cover up the guns or ammunition belts when passenger jets parked adjacent to the main terminal.

Invariably those spectators who did haul out cameras, and were spotted by Nigerian military police who patrolled the airport with an often deadly enthusiasm, were promptly bundled off the plane, sans baggage. It could take days and a lot of diplomatic effort to extricate these poor souls from that bumbling quagmire of graft and obfuscation. Unless, of course, you were British or American and greased enough palms.

Through it all, the helicopters and their crews led a punishing life. Operations started early and often ended well after dark. Like Ellis, the EO pilots flew seven days a week with damage to fuselage and engine cowlings constantly being patched. Then there was that government Mi-17 lost in a bird strike. Another had to land after being hit by ground fire and its partner had to dash in under fire and haul everybody out. One of the guys had been wearing flip-flops and in the hundred-yard dash to the other helicopter, his feet were badly slashed by thorns and razor wire that proliferates in that jungle.

During my assignment the Hips were often loaded roof-high, with troops having to compete for space with stores before take-off. It occasionally surprised me that we actually got into the hover. Most often we carried cargoes in excess of the manufacturer's predicated limitations, and even Walker and Tate were heard to comment on the stresses to which the Mi-17 airframes were being subjected.

As Tate explained it when I saw him afterward at Denel Aviation in Johannesburg: "We did what the manual said, and then quite a lot more. But since it all seemed to work quite well, it didn't bother us much."

Just about every page of Walker's logbook for mid-1995 tells a story. Apart from conversion flights to the Hind with Kagouk, much of May that year was spent with the pilots familiarizing themselves with the machine, usually with the Russian or Alberts in the other seat. Shortly afterward, Tate and Joubert did conversions, with Walker and Alberts handling instruction. Those who converted would admit later that when they returned to flying Hips, they missed the protection afforded by the attack chopper's armor plate.

By June 1995 the air war in Sierra Leone had entered a more serious phase than anything experienced before. Recognizing that they were now on the defensive, the rebels made desperate moves to counter air superiority. Hundreds of RPG-7s were brought in from Liberia, and there was also talk of Libya having supplied SAMs. Walker's logbook for the period is instructive.

On the first Thursday of that month, he records, there was a gunship strike north of the Freetown area, near Ma Gbaffi. It was to be a major EO attack against the insurgent groups assembled there. A reconnaissance flight to Mile 91 followed. The next day there were more strikes against rebel positions, this time toward Port Loko. The number of flights intensified as the weeks progressed.

It began with a two-casualty evacuation from the Waterloo area with the Hind giving top-cover to one of the Mi-17s. Walker's notation mentions "an extreme situation" but gave no specifics. Another casualty followed on the eighth. The next day, he and Alberts flew several sorties offering protection to ground forces cleaning up in the same area. Apart from several other missions—like Neall Ellis's deployment in the same theater five years later—it could be as many as two or three sorties a day. For the rest, it was all fairly predictable.

A couple of weeks after arriving in West Africa the pilots settled into something resembling a routine. It stayed that way until a reconnaissance-in-force was ordered at Kamalo on June 16. Two more medevac flights were ordered to bring out the wounded the next day.

Woes then seemed to come, as Shakespeare phrased it, "in battalions." In one strike a BMP got stuck in the mud, resulting in serious casualties. As the tracked vehicle faltered, a well-entrenched bunch of rebels peppered it with RPGs—many of them HEAT.[6] Within minutes an EO combatant went down with a head wound. Another was splattered by shrapnel and both needed evacuation. Shortly afterward, some government troops were killed. Andy Brown ordered Joubert to take his Mi-17 and bring out the wounded, with Walker and Alberts giving top cover.

It was hazardous work. Although the jungle along that stretch of coast was pristine, the area in which the EO units were then coming under fire had once been farmland. Parts of it had been used to plant rice and for once there was almost no ground cover. The area was seriously hazardous for chopper ops.

Joubert initially reported back to base that he thought he might be able to land on an improvised wooden bridge about a hundred and fifty yards from where the contact was taking place, but the ops commander vetoed the move. "Too exposed," he radioed. He suggested instead a small road, slightly elevated, where the Hip could touch down. It was just behind a patch of raised earth. Meanwhile, Walker and Alberts were instructed to use the gunship to saturate the surrounding area.

"It was really tight," recalled Walker. "Juba had to sort of feel his way in. Once on deck, there was no way out unless he did a hundred and eighty and slipped out the same way he'd arrived.

"We could see it was vital that he avoid several rebel concentrations that we'd established were clustered along the tree line just ahead of him. We weren't of much help because we were out of rockets and timing was critical."

In the debrief afterward, it was established that the insurgents were well dug in and no more than a hundred yards away from where it was all happening, which was one of the reasons why they remained relatively unaffected by the Hind. Nevertheless, taking the initiative, Joubert did what he had to: he dropped through a hail of rebel fire, boarded the wounded and was out again in perhaps a hundred seconds. The maneuver went off without a hitch, underscoring the remarkable degree of interplay between several experienced elements both in the air and on the ground.

When they checked his chopper afterward, they found that about all that wasn't punctured by enemy fire were his fuel tanks. Had he not been able to get out as he did, there was a good chance that the soldier with the head wound would have died. Twenty-four hours later he was in ICU in a modern hospital in South Africa almost four thousand miles away.

The value of the experience gained by all these pilots really came to the fore during night operations. After dark, the choppers would go out with night vision goggles (NVGs) and they'd look for enemy bivouacs in the bush. Walker recalls that, operating from a relatively moderate height, either he or Alberts would send in a combination of machine-gun fire and rocket bursts from their pods, which made for a serious concentration of fire.

Unfortunately, said Alberts, "We were never able to view the results of our work from up close. But not long afterward, the radio intercepts would start to come in and from what we could follow, it always sounded good." There would be six dead and who knows how many wounded on one strike. Another time it was eleven, and so on. In a night attack at about the same time, more than twenty insurgents were killed in our first pass. It must have been pretty grim on the ground, suddenly being hit in strength from out of nowhere. They hadn't a clue what it was all about.

"The assholes would try to retaliate with their RPGs and every automatic weapon to hand—usually aiming where they thought we'd be. But it was always wide. And then we'd target their flashes and go in again.

"Also, while they were shooting at us, good ammo was being wasted. This was valuable stuff, all of which needed resupply. It had originally been hauled into the country on peoples' backs, so they actually lost both ways."

Walker: "One of the battle plans that we perfected during this time was being able to pinpoint their bases with the use of our GPS sets. The gooks could never understand how we were able to 'see' them in the dark. We'd look for them in daylight too . . . search for path patterns in the bush, check the river line and so on, which would show whether an area was being regularly used or not. This was something else we'd learnt from our earlier bush campaigns.

"Later, aware that they were being tracked, they would only gather in numbers after dark, and then at specific points. We knew that these would have to be close to water where they'd cook their food and prepare positions for the night. So we'd fly over an area that we'd been told by intelligence or defectors that was 'hot' and we'd use the infra-red scanner to look for clusters of small fires.

"IR would pick them up in a jiffy. We never missed, no matter how thick the bush."

The series of operations against the rebels within a twenty- or thirty-mile radius of Freetown—which had kicked off EO's first successful strike against the rebel base near Benguema—lasted six days. Once it became clear that concerted resistance had become futile, most of the insurgents pulled out.

The mercenary force was to experience several more days of sporadic skirmishing, this time with smaller, isolated groups of the RUF on the fringes of where it had all taken place, but by now the enemy had taken to bivouacking in even smaller groups to avoid being spotted. As Walker pointed out: "Spill a bit of blood and it quickly teaches you the basics of survival." After that, the entire group withdrew en masse.

In retrospect, most of the pilots involved in the classic Battle for Freetown were certain that Sankoh's rebels knew nothing about IR imaging or NVG equipment. It was another example of white man's *ju ju* that EO had brought into the country, the fellows joked, and some of it even befuddled Sierra Leone Army officers back at Cockerill.

Judging from further intercepts of the rebels' messages, Tate told me later, it was obvious that the rebels were convinced that some sort of black magic was being employed. In one instance, after being hit hard two nights in a row, they chopped off their medicine man's head while he slept, thinking that it was he who had visited these catastrophes on them. This was confirmed when about forty rebels took advantage of the cease-fire and defected. Most came into government strongpoints with their weapons to surrender. The army—and EO—subsequently got their stories.

Neither Brown nor Walker were able to establish accurate enemy casualty figures, except that first guestimates—plus body counts—put the tally of enemy dead after the first fighting phase around the capital at about two or three hundred. Obviously there were also many wounded, few of whom would have lived for more than a day if their wounds were serious or had penetrated their torsos. In other words, Walker reckoned, in less than two weeks EO had accounted for about a third to half of the enemy force operating around Freetown.

These were big losses for the RUF and though nobody realized it yet, it was also the beginning of the end of that phase of the war.

22

SIERRA LEONE'S DIAMOND WAR

"Privatize the war against the rebels and help the Sierra Leone government pay a well-trained bunch of fighters to wipe out the RUF. It worked in 1995 when (less than two hundred) mercenaries and one helicopter came close to crushing the rebels."

Sam Kiley in *The Times*, London, September 13, 2000

The reason why Executive Outcomes was so successful in Sierra Leone, according to Colonel Bert Sachse,[1] was because he infused his men with the need to get at the enemy by every means possible. "Go and get them!" he would urge his troops at every briefing. "Maintain the initiative and don't even give them time to think," he declared.

In a subsequent briefing on how this dedicated former professional soldier had turned around that war in West Africa, he declared, "It was the basis of our policy to harass the rebels wherever we found them. We would attack their camps and force them to remain constantly on the move. Do that often enough and after a while you begin to observe an overwhelming weariness, a lethargy that almost defeats logic and that begins to creep up among those who are being pursued. They are under threat and on the edge. You actually saw the same kind of thing with the Taliban toward the end of that conflict in Afghanistan. This is not a conscious decision, but people that are caught like that on the back foot can't get rest. Also, they don't eat properly and their wounded cannot get the kind of medical attention they desperately need.

"Of course we used our air superiority to pretty good effect. If a pilot made a sighting while on a sortie, any kind sighting that indicated that there might rebels around, he would, if he had need to, go back to base for more ammunition and return immediately for a strike."

According to Sachse, there were other disconcerting touches implemented against the RUF by his people, like Lt-Col. Carl Dietz, a former 5 Reconnaissance Regiment intelligence officer who played back rebel messages that had been intercepted and appropriately "doctored."

"We'd use the voices of their commanders, people that they all knew—sometimes intimately—and had perhaps worked with in the past. Having edited new messages from material in hand, we'd go ahead and pass on utterly conflicting or confusing messages. Like we'd tell a unit that their comrades in an adjacent operational area had taken terrible losses. The unit in question would deny it when asked to confirm, of course, but then an element of doubt had been allowed to creep into the equation.

"Other times we'd hammer a specific field commander for real or imagined operational blunders. In the end, it had the effect we sought. Cumulatively it lowered the morale of everybody on the other side and they wouldn't really know who or what to believe. It was a means of effectively sowing dissension, but then, as they say about war, all's fair . . ."

As Sachse recalls, it really was a great big game, "and this was one that we won." Certainly EO saved hundreds, possibly thousands of lives in doing so, and subsequent studies of this West African conflict have confirmed this.

Following the action around Waterloo, Benguema and elsewhere, EO then took to devoting effort to preparing for the strike on rebel positions around Koidu and the Kono diamond fields. It was to be the biggest operation launched by the company during their twenty-one-month deployment in Sierra Leone.[2]

The first objective was to get the BMP-2s—by now reconditioned and "sort of running well"—to within striking distance of Kono. Very early on in the initial planning phase, was it agreed that only the final section of the route would be accomplished under their own power.

The convoy that eventually set out from Cockerill Barracks in August 1995—almost three months to the day since Executive Outcomes had arrived in country—consisted of about a dozen vehicles including Land Rovers with weapons mounted, including AGS Plamyas. One was designated a mortar carrier and played a critical role in the hostilities that followed. From Makeni onwards, it was dangerous turf and nothing was to be left to chance.

The column headed by Executive Outcomes led the way, with a larger RSLMF contingent following in Bedford, Mercedes and other trucks, all of them crowded to the rooftops with troops who brandished their AKs like brigands. In the old days such occasions would have required shots to be fired in the air, but with EO about, no more. A man who didn't follow instructions would get a clip around the ear, or worse.

Still, there were accidental discharges galore,[3] which was one of the reasons why the unit commander ordered local forces to hang back a distance from the merc vanguard. By the second day, most of these troops had tossed their weapons onto the floor, the prospect of ambush of no real concern.

The plan was that the South African squad would take out any likely ambush points on the road ahead with mortars. In the event of a real or suspected insurgent presence, a small strike force would be detached on foot with instructions to neutralize it. Not that they were called into action too often; a crack bunch of fighters suddenly emerging in that jungle was usually sufficient to send the rebels scurrying for cover, unless of course, they weren't killed first. So it went for several days, the choppers patrolling ahead to spot movement on the ground or providing close air support.

The night before the final onslaught—with Koidu still some miles away—the column turned off the road, bivouacked and took up defensive positions in the bush on a high point overlooking all approaches. It was the same routine that the boys had followed in Angola in anticipation of a night attack. It never came.

RSLMF government forces accompanying the column were different. Their commander decided that he would stick to the road. Come evening, the majority of his troops would dismount, settle down comfortably in one of the nearby villages, get drunk and fraternize with the women. Each day, EO's commanders would point out this folly to their RSLMF counterparts, but they thought they knew better. They'd also been warned that the rebels had radios: they would pass on this kind of information to units waiting down the line.

And that is exactly what happened. After scouting the area beforehand and establishing where the regular army was sleeping, the rebels simply waited until dawn and hit them. They scattered as soon as an EO rescue squad arrived.

They did it once too often outside Koidu. This time the guerrillas were unaware of the off-road presence of the EO element. In fact, they had to move right past their lines to get to their target, the support group.

As Sachse reflected afterward, "One of the men on watch spotted movement early on and woke us. So when their main group passed our position, we whacked them in a flank attack that left many dead. It was a big force of several hundred, so many, in fact, that there weren't enough weapons for them all."

The military operation that allowed EO to take Sierra Leone's diamond fields was a classic action. It also became something of a watershed in the war. Most important, the timing was right: it was almost three months to the day that EO had entered the war and in the interim the rebels had taken some weighty losses.

Indeed, before it happened, both Sachse and Luitingh told Chairman Valentine Strasser that they believed they had a pretty good measure of the enemy and that the force was ready to move into the interior.

Intercepts at Cockerill, meanwhile, had indicated that Sankoh's people were hurting and by all accounts—including those coming in from defectors—their leaders weren't nearly as confident as before. There were also indications that the RUF command had no battle plan of its own and was confused about how to react to the EO offensive.

Logistically, EO's diamond field operation presented the mercenary command with a series of tasks that were not only complex but difficult, considering that they were about to launch an operation in an area about which they knew little or nothing. While distances were modest, the job of subjugating and then occupying a strategic area that just then represented Sierra Leone's only viable source of income presented the attackers with some vicious obstacles.

The first of these concerned numbers. Because the defense of Freetown had been successfully accomplished, some of the men were sent home on furlough. The question, then, was who would replace them? As the most experienced military man in the country, it was left to Sachse to work it out. As he told me, he had the option of bolstering numbers by using local forces, but then not all of them had been trained. He got some help from the fact that just about everybody, in and out of government, accepted that the only reliable combatants were South African. The majority of RSLMF troops, in contrast, trained or not, could barely be trusted.

Second, there were doubts about whether the hearts of these government troops would be in the right place if the Kono area was powerfully contested. In fact, the consensus was that it would be, because, as Sachse constantly had to remind senior officers at Cockerill, it was also the enemy's main source of revenue.

Third, the interior of Sierra Leone, even today, is almost totally undeveloped. Because most of the country is blanketed in forest, it can be unforgiving in its tropical luxuriance that you can really only appreciate by flying over it, which EO did every day. Any thoughts of going cross-country (as had been done at Cafunfo in Angola) simply didn't rate consideration. In any event, there were only a couple of "major" roads in the entire region and these were dominated by large RUF contingents that had proved both reasonably adept and well equipped in the past. As was discovered once it was all over, the rebels, in anticipating this next step, had stockpiled huge supplies along the length of the route, whereas everything the column needed and which wasn't onboard their vehicles when they set out would have to be flown in.

Last, this final push into the interior was no secret. Everybody in Freetown was expecting it to happen "any day now." Through his own informer network—which stretched all the way to the capital—Sankoh would have known exactly what was being prepared for him and he would certainly have reacted accordingly. Intelligence leaks that had been a porous feature of the war still hadn't been plugged, nor would they be until after the British entered the picture in 2000.

Nevertheless, the South Africans had a few options of their own, such as close air support and, inevitably, the always invaluable infantry fighting vehicles. The problem here though, was that while the BMP-2s had been prepared for the job, they were barely up to the task ahead. The machines would cough and belch like a trio of witches each time their engines were turned over, but once going, they rarely faltered. Still, Kono was far away over difficult country and there was doubt that they would stand up to such a long haul.

Barlow and Luitingh would have preferred buying newer versions of the IFVs but Freetown maintained that there was no money; supposedly there never was.

So while their paint was worn, their armor buckled and with the front ends of all three providing good evidence of having disputed the right of way with some really big trees, they would have to do. Luitingh commented afterward that while he was stuck with them, they would probably have been relegated to the scrap heap in any Western force.

In the end, EO's command decided on a tactic that hadn't been tried before along this stretch of the West Coast. The government would commandeer three commercial low-loaders and use them to ferry the IFVs several hours down the road to the town of Matotaka. From there, they would go mobile and move on their own tracks.

Altogether about eighty EO troops headed the attacking force, with government forces coming along behind. At the head of this column, all except eight or nine white officers were black. Because there was very little rebel opposition during the early stages, the strike force did well during its first forty-eight hours on the road.

But then, with the first serious attacks by the enemy, problems emerged among some of the government soldiers, the most obvious being that they were anything but combat-ready. Also, though there had been searches for drugs and liquor, many of them seemed to be in a stupor and some had a difficult time keeping up with the convoy. The rebels would pick off the stragglers, which wasn't a bad thing, some of the EO guys reckoned.

Fortunately, not all the RSLMF soldiers were losers. Some had taken training at the hands of EO instructors seriously and it showed: they were alert, adept with their weapons, kept to themselves, and were grouped in what would probably resemble Sierra Leone's first modest "Special Forces" unit. Among them was Lieutenant Schenks, a tough, resilient fighter who was later to become Neall Ellis' side-gunner on the Hind. As their actions were later to prove, this home-grown unit was well motivated with a good leadership element. In Sachse's view, they would do what was expected of them, but as he was to admit, there was too few of them.

Having reached the Kangari Hills, the column encountered its first big ambush. Though it started with a bang, it quickly fizzled, though it did leave some of the Sierra Leonean detachment wounded. What emerged afterward was that during this skirmish several government soldiers shot each other. With that the South Africans increased the gap between their own people and the rear: there wasn't a man among them who didn't want this mob as far away from the sharp end as possible. What they didn't need was to have their own people killed by their "allies."

Lt-Col. Carl Dietz, second-in-command to Colonel Roelf van Heerden, had meanwhile arrived from Angola to take charge. He said later that he would have preferred going it alone, without any kind of RSLMF participation, but Cockerill countermanded him. The army needed to be represented in the push, the CDS stated, even if only for publicity purposes.

Having fought off the first enemy probe on the column, EO elements sought opportunities of their own by following up quickly on foot and causing more damage in several subsequent ambushes in the vicinity of several small towns like Makali and Makoni. They were able to keep the rebels at bay until they got to Masingbi, a junction town on the road to Falla where the vehicles were drawn around in the usual laager formation. The anticipated night attack never came.

Dietz recalled the time spent at Masingbi. "We could hear their drums in the forest after the sun had set . . . it was fucking eerie. The throbbing would reach us deep into the night and some of the Kamajor Hunter Detachment[4] guys told us that they were probably dancing around their fires and making their voodoo sacrifices for battles still to come." As he remembers them telling him, the rebels' *ju ju* priests were priming them for the battle ahead, the idea being to make them "invisible" to bullets. Dietz recalls it as a ritual involving a gory run of blood and guts.

"It sounded pretty grim and as primitive as hell. Our own black troops would exchange glances and say nothing. But then, apart from the color of their skin, they had very little in common with these West African folk."

The column encountered the first of three big ambushes near Masokary the next day. This was an area where the road ran through hilly terrain and, according to Dietz, had the rebels used a modicum of initiative, they might have done better. Instead, the typical RUF ambush-in-waiting would spend its time lazing about at the entrance to town in anticipation of the scrap ahead.

"We hit them—caught them with their pants down—with some of our guys moving quietly ahead, just off the road. You could see from their faces that few had experienced that level of aggression before. Until then, I suppose, they'd had it easy because the Sierra Leone Army had never operated like this. It was like we were battling a bunch of amateurs. We were actually chuffed as hell that things were going a lot better than we'd expected."

It is also worth mentioning that the South Africans had planned for an operation that would take upwards of three weeks. But by the morning of the second day, their objective was almost in sight.

Dietz went on: "Most of the rebels would fire their weapons like cowboys—usually from the hip, though that was also something government troops were prone to. Or they'd shoot at us from cover, hold-ing their AKs above their heads. Consequently, they were usually way off target. And when they did hit anything it was luck, not design. We ended up blowing them away.

"Then our troops killed a few more groups in several quick fol-low-ups. We went after them on foot and caught some of them camped a couple of miles into the jungle. Another time we came on some gooks with their weapons lying on one side tending to their bud-dies who had been wounded, obviously in a previous scrape. There were no survivors from that bunch either."

By now the column had moved into a succession of foothills that led toward a range of mountains in Guinea. "There was little in the way of a civilian population; just about everybody not involved with the war had fled. I suppose our biggest single advantage was that the rebels hadn't seen anything like this before either. To almost every one of them, it was a new and different form of combat, not made easier by the fact that, where possible, we employed aggressive, mobile 'Blitzkrieg' tactics. The shock effect must have stunned them all."

To Dietz, it was a case of do or die, "both for them and for us." He added that what really made the difference was that EO kept their heads while the rebels didn't.

EO's field commanders would adapt their tactics both to the cir-cumstances and to the terrain. When it looked as if the road would pass through a narrow cutting—or there was a row of hills where an ambush seemed likely—the convoy would halt and a six- or eight-man patrol would be pushed forward on foot.

Dietz: "The men would move fast, making as little noise as possi-ble, very much as they had been accustomed to doing when they fought down south. I'd keep the engines of the vehicles running and we'd potter about, make tea, bang a few cans together to make things seem normal, like we'd stopped the column for a meal or a rest. Meanwhile, the squad would move quickly through the jungle. By now the gooks would have known we were a mile or two away and would have begun to prepare for an ambush, usually on a high point or overlooking a river crossing. It was all predictable.

"And that's exactly how the guys would find them, prostrate and waiting, usually smoking dope or chatting among themselves, as if it were pay day." It was their way of hyping themselves up for the com-ing attack, he explained.

Surprise was often so complete that the EO squaddies would eliminate the lot before they knew what had happened. He reckoned that the scenario must have repeated itself at least a dozen times by the time the force reached Kono.

"Other times we'd hurl a few mortars at where we thought they might be. Our guys had a lot of experience with this stuff and they were accurate. They'd sometimes get them spot on. Then the rebels would disappear into the jungle and there would be no resistance." When we discussed the war later, he thought it was remarkable that RUF cadres never really learnt from their mistakes, especially because by then they had fought a score or more of actions against the South Africans. Just as well, he reckoned, because otherwise the operation might have taken months.

Column commanders would usually coordinate timing so that the gunship—with Walker and Alberts at the controls—would arrive at about the same time as a counterstrike. "Once that happened, it was over. The men would go out and pick off anybody still in the area," reckoned Dietz. On the rare occasion when his men would actually be involved in a firefight, according to Colonel Sachse, his people would prove to be very well disciplined.

"Our guys would stand their ground and hit back, always giving better than they got. That done, they'd follow up or launch a few probes in depth, and more casualties would follow. It was the standard routine and in Sierra Leone nobody had ever seen anything like it."

The column reached the crossroads at Bumpe just before three on the afternoon of the second day. Before them lay Kenema, and about five miles beyond, diamond-rich Koidu. According to some of the Sierra Leone regulars who understood what the drums said, the word had spread: the monsters were coming!

"We found Bumpe deserted: not a soul. There were no dogs in the streets. Nothing! It was a place, it seemed, where only ghosts walked," recalled Roelf Van Heerden. It was also eerily quiet, he said, with bodies everywhere. The town itself was in a shocking state. Buildings had been burnt and there was garbage strewn about everywhere, some of it many months old."

In effect, said van Heerden, it seemed that the clock had stopped. The only effort anybody seemed to have made over previous months had been in killing.

"There were skulls on stakes—hundreds of them—and more lying in heaps at several of the crossroads on the way into town, sometimes fifty or eighty of them in a pile. Also, lots of skeletons scattered about in the dirt. It was about as gruesome as it can get and just about everybody was sickened by the carnage and the stench."

More dead, many of them skeletal, could be found hanging from trees. Others had been staked out on the ground and left to die, just about every victim picked clean by the crows and vultures that perched on the roofs of buildings or the few bullet-scarred billboards that still stood.

It was the same when they got to their final destination, Koidu and its diamond fields, later the same day. There, more piles of skulls were heaped up at some of the traffic circles in the center of town.

"It made the hair at the back of your neck stand up," the Colonel said afterward. In a military career that spanned two decades and that had taken him across the breadth of Africa, he'd never experienced anything like it. Nor did he wish to ever again.

An interesting sidelight, recalled another of the mercs, was that many of the bodies appeared to have been white people. But this was not so, explained Van Heerden. "The crows would start by stripping the skin off a cadaver and it would come away in strips. Only then would they attack the flesh. This gave human remains something of an off-white appearance. It was a peculiar phenomenon and none of the troops ever got used to it. To some of us, Africa had gone dark again," he added.

Why the rebels had murdered, tortured or mutilated so many of their own people was a question that persisted. It still does. Among the people of Sierra Leone, it was an issue that sometimes became divisive, if only because there was no rationale reason for so much bloodshed. Also, cruelty, sadism and the like had never been something in which this nation reveled: Sierra Leonean folk, as history had shown the British and others, were a quiet, dignified and ordered people. They always had been, which was one of the reasons why the first West Africans educated in Britain almost four centuries ago came from there.

While their leaders might have been corrupt, it was argued, that was merely the African way. Murdering people and cutting off the hands and feet of children was something altogether different. That kind of abomination had never been experienced before, no matter how far back you searched in the country's history.

As one Freetowner told me, the rebels' concept of violence for the sake of it actually defied logic. In a sense, it was a total contradiction of "being like one with the enemy," as Mao had espoused, a maxim that Foday Sankoh was fond of using. Instead of being a part of the people, Sankoh's cohorts actually alienated them.

As rebel captives began to come in, some would explain that their actions were a defensive mechanism to drive terror into the souls of the populace. One of them, a little better educated than the rest had a bland expression on his face when he commented: "Our role was to make them not only fear us, but fear us totally." It was terror, he conceded: "We controlled their lives. We decided who would live or die. We could make them do anything we wanted and that made us powerful. We were gods," he told his inquisitor, beaming.

The uncontrolled, senseless level of violence became one of Foday Sankoh's most damning revolutionary precepts. After he was taken prisoner and interrogated five years later, it was determined that he must have been motivated by Liberia's Charles Taylor, who employed identical mind-numbing tactics. Taylor's brand of inhumanity was just as brutal and unthinking. Like Sankoh, it was implemented solely to terrorize the people and to achieve the absolute power he sought. In the end, it made him mad.

Meanwhile, Charles Taylor is still very much alive, living the good life with his retinue in splendid isolation. Officially, all are guests of the Nigerian government and they live in an extremely well-guarded luxurious villa in Calabar, a lovely riverside town in the southeastern corner of the country. Part of the exile deal was that Taylor would take no more part in his country's politics, but being the scheming bastard that he is, the Nigerian government had to warn him in 2005 that if he didn't stop stirring the political pot back home, he would have to leave.

That horrible little man has a price of some millions of dollars on his head, and one would have thought that there might be a group of freelancers somewhere tempted to snatch him to face a multitude of war crimes.

From the time the flying column left Cockerill Barracks it took EO just three days to rout a very substantial rebel force and cover the distance to Kono. Once there, reports of the rebel reaction started coming in.

One immediate aftershock that apparently rattled RUF cadres was the perception that they were up against forces that were either supernatural or were reinforced by some kind of serious *ju ju*. There were also whispers that the attacking force would never have been able to do what they did without "divine help." Mischievously, Van Heerden encouraged the notion. At the end of it, many rebels who survived headed back to their homes, a fair proportion crossing into Liberia.

Up to that point, Sankoh's murderers had walked tall almost throughout the country. Now, with Kono back in government hands, the insurgents had been subjected to a crippling defeat.

Meanwhile, messages directed at the RUF headquarters in Liberia and intercepted back in Freetown, started to come through. What had been dribbles before, became an unending flow of demands, insults, questions and altercations. It became worse as supplies became scarce: there was no longer a functioning supply line out of Liberia.

Some field commanders didn't even bother transcribing their messages into code. Trying to counter these failures, Sankoh executed a number of his officers, blaming them for the catastrophe. He had lost Koidu and the diamond fields, which was a tremendous blow, not only to his prestige but also to his fortunes. Still worse, he no longer had the ability to pay the Liberian leader for his support.

More seriously, the disaster tended to portray him in a very different light from before. Sankoh was now perceived to be vulnerable, which was bad for the image of someone who wouldn't do anything without making a sacrifice to his voodoo gods. An immediate consequence was that atrocities against innocent civilians became even more barbaric, and some of these rituals now involved a substantial proportion of children and infants. There was also an increase in cannibalism in the areas where the rebels were still active.

Roelf van Heerden was there to greet me when I stepped off the Mi-17 after it landed on a huge granite slab that towered above Koidu town. Lean, bearded and looking more like a recalcitrant schoolmaster than the tough bush fighter he was, van Heerden's gentle manner belied his single-minded determination to destroy the RUF.

Like much else in the region, the helipad used by the company was improvised. Being on high ground, it was a perfect site since it would be difficult to target the chopper from below, even if someone with an RPG was able to sneak up that close.

The Executive Outcomes base at Koidu was a makeshift affair. The main building had obviously taken a beating during the attack on the town when the rebels were driven out. One of the back walls was blown away and nobody had bothered to fix it. Not that it prevented anybody from sleeping inside, though it would have been easy for someone to get in once we'd all bedded down for the night.

The war made it a dismal posting. The walls were dirty, there were no proper windows, and all the frames and the wiring had been ripped out. Being the rainy season, there was mud everywhere.

The base's water supplies were fed by rain off the roof, leading into two tanks, one for washing and another for drinking. The only problem was that every second vulture in Sierra Leone seemed to perch on that very same roof. That was disconcerting, especially since those same birds—with cadavers everywhere—must have been among the best fed in Africa. Not that the killings had stopped, even though the rebels were supposed to have fled. We realized that when we spotted the scavengers feasting on fresh corpses on the outskirts of town.

The base must have once been a delightful country home. From its porch on a good day you could see for miles. You could also survey much of the town, spread-eagled untidily below, its dusty streets meandering off in all directions. It had originally belonged to a Lebanese diamond dealer but he had fled long before the rebels arrived.

While I bunked at "Casa van Heerden," the rest of the EO contingent was billeted in a couple of houses further down the hill. There was only one approach road, guarded in theory by RSLMF troops, but since they were smashed most of the time, security arrangements could only have been spotty. As it was, our backyard stretched hundreds of yards down the valley to a stream below, and anybody wanting to attack could just as easily have come at us from there. We were surrounded by jungle on three sides and the last security fence seemed to have been torn out of the ground when the British were still around.

Colonel van Heerden's role in Koidu's magisterial district—a huge area which, apart from the diggings, was almost all jungle but still had a substantial population—was as more of an *amicus curaiae* than a military commander. Day-to-day affairs were discussed each morning in the same communal bedroom for senior staff that doubled as an office during the day. It was officially termed the Joint Operations Center or JOC.

After breakfast, van Heerden would conduct a series of meetings that would include the army and the Sierra Leone police as well as a regional civilian representative. Also present was Koidu's secret service contingent, consisting of two Smersh types who never removed their hats or their non-reflective Ray Bans. Almost all the discussions centered on illegal diamond diggings, most of which took place after dark.

Within weeks of getting there, this South African colonel was accepted by all—civilians and military alike—as the unofficial "mayor" of Koidu. He was also the only de facto legal entity in the area, and once the government side of business was done, strings of civilians, local chiefs, diamond merchants, women's groups and others would trudge up the hill to seek either a judgment or his opinion. Each would be given time, and after pondering the matter, he would deliver a verdict. What was obvious to anyone who called at the base was that the most powerful man in town was held in very high regard for the way in which he dealt with the locals. His role was that of arbiter, military commander, lawyer, administrator, mediator, facilitator and judge.

It was not always easy, he admitted. Like Andy Brown, the Colonel was a good listener. As he commented, "You have to be if you are going to achieve anything at all in Africa."

I was to discover afterward that it was rare for his decisions not to deliver swift closure, especially since some of the issues had been dragging on for months. That he and his men were able to drive the rebels out of Koidu placed him in a rather special category among the residents and, as the American journalist Elizabeth Rubin said in her article about Koidu in New York's *Harper's Magazine,* they even prayed for him and his men in the town's mosques.[5]

The arrival of our pair of supply helicopters at this eastern base was an event for the couple of dozen EO personnel stationed there. For almost everyone there were letters from home. The jackpot was the usual bottle or two of Red Heart rum; it was a requisite and invariably arrived compliments of the missus. There was no problem getting it through in the post because Executive Outcomes was the post, first by Boeing 727 from South Africa and then by helicopter from Freetown. Along with luggage, spares, radio equipment and administrative material was a stock of beer: cans of Lion and Windhoek lager.

For some, the party started immediately. Others had to remain alert—a round-the-clock radio link was maintained with Freetown. Signals came and went, the majority of them encoded. It was soon clear to this observer that a minor bureaucracy had encroached even this far into the jungle.

For communications, EO used DET 175 sets. These could send a five- or six-line message in code, but it would only work with another DET receiver in place. One of the signals that arrived while I was there came from a mother wanting to arrange a fishing trip for her son to Swakopmund in Namibia when he came home on R&R.

When the rebels first took Koidu, about a million people from the Kono diamond region fled into the mountains. That happened after they had slashed a hundred throats. The survivors didn't hang around to discover who might be next. With EO in place, van Heerden airlifted a number of these victims to Freetown where they were handed over to the Red Cross.

The International Committee of the Red Cross wasn't at all happy to take charge of them. Geneva had already made up its mind about EO and had declared publicly that the NGO would have nothing to do with mercenaries. Consequently, even humanitarian issues were to suffer.

Then, with a huge area caught between warring groups and starvation in the northeast of the country, Andy Brown offered the ICRC the use of company helicopters to bring in food supplies. It was an obvious gesture at a time when the Hips weren't doing much, but Primo Corvaro, the local Red Cross representative, not only ignored the offer, he didn't even bother to return the call.

In a bid to seek clarity, I visited the ICRC's offices in the capital on my return and was told by Corvaro that it was really none of my business. Fair enough, nor was it, except that I would have liked a reason, "for the record, because I was writing about the country and this was an unusual development," I told him. There were hungry people out there, some of them dying. Moreover, the service was free with no strings attached. I stressed all this because the ICRC was always carping about being broke.

Corvaro—who on the face of it seemed to nurse a psyche as intricately self-absorbed as an anemone—was only willing to say that the Red Cross did not do business with mercenaries. I pointed out that what was being offered to the ICRC wasn't business but aid and had absolutely nothing to do with the war.

With that, Corvaro ordered me out of his office. So much then for the neutrality of the Swiss.

By the time I'd arrived in Koidu, the place was coming along nicely. It had been thoroughly rubbished by the rebels, which was surprising because the town was to become the most important source of funds for their revolt. Its diamond mining industry is as significant to Sierra Leone as gold is in South Africa.

Sankoh's people had gone to work with a will, systematically destroying the infrastructure, government or otherwise. Safes were broken out of walls, with the rebels using fire and water to crack the mortar. Or they'd take axes to get in from the back. The strongrooms of the local branches of the Barclays and Standard Charter banks were blown open with dynamite to get at supplies of uncut gemstones waiting for uplifting to the capital. These were eventually used to barter for weapons, with Liberia's Charles Taylor as the intermediary.

Most damaging, if incomprehensible, was the destruction of anything of value at the workshops of the National Diamond Mining Corporation at Yengema, a smaller town a few miles down the road from Koidu. Trucks were burnt where they stood while lathes and other machines were tossed off their bedplates. Each time one of the big machines crashed down, the rebels would cheer, we were told by a technician who was there at the time and who was fortunate to have survived.

Everything mechanical was demolished. This activity extended to innocuous items such as film projectors in the town's only movie house, generators, telephone exchanges and water pumps. Even hospitals and clinics didn't escape the attention of these thugs. To those of us viewing this wreckage for the first time, it hardly seemed to be the work of rational beings. But then, as one of the mercs pointed out, it wasn't. Sankoh's people had let loose an orgy of barbarism.

To van Heerden it was a nihilistic kind of destruction simply for its own sake. As he was to suggest, it was of no consequence to the lunatics that successive generations of the country's rulers—possibly even Sankoh himself—might ultimately need these same assets to bolster the country, never mind the workforce. In their addled minds, there was no tomorrow. The South African was particularly angry about medicines and the torched trucks because they would be expensive to replace in a country with zero foreign reserves.

Similarly, by the time the advancing rebels had reached the diamond area, buildings in towns they had occupied along the way were destroyed. They'd sent word ahead that the same would happen to Koidu, and that resulted in half the populace scampering, many into neighboring Guinea.

"Brick by brick the place will be taken apart," were Sankoh's words. The South Africans had interrupted their efforts, but by then the damage was already awesome. Asked months later in Abidjan about this depredation, Sankoh justified his actions on the premise that everything had to be smashed "before it could rise again." It was an off-the-cuff remark, but echoed similar actions by the deranged Pol Pot years earlier in Southeast Asia.

Unlettered and basically untutored, Sankoh liked to propagate the myth that the only solution for Africa lay in violence. In this he's not alone. Idi Amin was of a similar persuasion, and in a not altogether different way, so is Robert Mugabe. It calls to mind the Russian proverb that a fish rots from the head down.

An interesting sidelight here was an Italian technician I met the day after I'd arrived at Koidu. He had originally been working at Yengema and had decided to wait out the arrival of the rebels. Prior to the rest of the expatriates fleeing, he was entrusted with a large parcel of gemstones by another company man that he secreted under the floorboards of the main factory. That had been a year before EO arrived. As one of the first of the foreigners to return to the town after the Kono region had been liberated, he went straight to the hiding place and recovered the diamonds, which, van Heerden said, must have been worth several million dollars.

I never did ascertain whether the Italian was rewarded for his loyalty.

This wasn't the first time that Koidu had been retaken after being occupied by the rebels. They had held it for nine months in 1992, before a combined force of the RSLMF, Guinean Army and a Nigerian army detachment drove out the Sankoh dissidents. It was a notable event, if only for the fact that none of the Conakry people could understand English and the others knew no French.

Despite the need for pantomime, the operation was successful, even though it was said at the time that the soldiers were only fractionally better organized than the rebels. Also, the government had Alpha Jets flown by Nigerians to back their claim, though they habitually bombed the wrong places. Their aim had clearly improved markedly in the interim, though these lapses were usually blamed on faulty ground control, which didn't matter anyway because the rebels fled headlong into the bush each time the aircraft appeared.

While many of Sankoh's followers destroyed Christian churches, shrines and mission stations, they never touched a mosque. The one in the diamond fields—a striking, multi-minareted structure—was particularly imposing, and like others in Bo, Yengema and Makeni, it survived intact. This gave substance to early reports, since substantiated, that it was money provided by Libya that was bankrolling the revolt.

And Sankoh, for all his dabbling on the dark side of the occult, was said to be a Muslim.

On my return to Koidu after the Baiama attack (see Chapter 23), I was able to talk to Colonel van Heerden about diamonds.

There were obviously plenty about, he told me. It was the very reason why Koidu existed. In fact, he explained, there were so many gemstones in the diggings to the immediate west of where we slept that people would sneak across at night to steal a bucket of soil. "And they wouldn't be doing that if they weren't scoring, at least part of the time," he suggested.

"Go into town and you can buy as many as you like. They're selling them: big ones, small ones. Take your pick." It was like a diamond Wal-Mart, he reckoned. But he warned that what I would get for my money could be doubtful, adding that "you really do need jeweler's eyes to eliminate the dross, of which there is ample because everybody knows about glass substitutes." Similarly, he recalled, in Zambia the locals knocked the green reflector glass out of traffic lights, broke them up into pieces and sold "emeralds" to unsuspecting tourists.

"On the other hand, you can make a lot of money if you know what you're doing. But you can also lose a packet. However, that's not my game. Can't afford it, and it is certainly not on while I'm doing this kind of work."

EO, he declared, pulling himself erect at his makeshift desk, had an image to protect. The company was there to protect people. If he or his officers were to sully that commitment, "then you start to think like a rebel, especially when people around us believe in what we are trying to do here." There was little doubt that the man was engaged more by the minutiae of human interaction than the wheeler-dealer goings-on in his immediate environment.

Like Lafras Luitingh, Van Heerden had been fighting African wars for almost all of his adult life. Before Sierra Leone, it had been Unita in Angola; he was there as part of the EO contingent when Cafunfo was taken. He'd also been part of Nellis' team in Stabilco in Zaire. Before that it was Swapo in Namibia, where he was a specialist in armor. A forthright, uncomplicated individual, he was a man of simple piety. He never ate without saying grace—even if he was the only one at the table—and on his desk lay a well-thumbed Bible, its leather cover mildewed by the humidity.

We were sitting on the porch overlooking Koidu on my last night in the east. Below, a few lights blinked up at us from the village. The town was still waiting for a new generator but nobody knew when—or even if—it would arrive. From somewhere he had scrounged a bottle of Pernod; he enjoyed an occasional pastis.

Van Heerden told me the story of one of his sergeants who had bought a twenty-eight-carat diamond for next to nothing from one of the local people, and having sold it, retired in South Africa on the proceeds. The diamond was apparently a nearly flawless blue-white stone and he had taken it to Brussels himself after returning home on leave.

"But that's unusual and I want it to stay that like that," he said thoughtfully. "We can't have the men getting interested in that kind of business. There would be trouble for sure in the end and we would lose the trust of these folk. They respect us and I want to keep it that way."

For somebody with a reputation for being a bit of softie, Van Heerden could be as tough as old boots when it mattered. Within the armed forces that fell under his control—which included all government troops based in town—he was a disciplinarian of repute and the order that he brought to the community within a comparatively short time didn't happen by accident.

I was told that when he and his men arrived at Koidu, his fellow Sierra Leonean officers had difficulty controlling their men, quite a few of whom were notoriously insubordinate. At about that time one of the African colonels put his unit on short rations because they refused to go into action against a group of rebels that intelligence had told him were encamped not far from town. That meant no gin or ganga for as long as it suited him. One of his men shot him behind the ear while he was asleep and nobody was prepared to say who was responsible. A day later, the customary perks were again being passed around.

The South Africans went about things differently. It had taken a short while for the civilians in Koidu to realize that if they had a problem with the army they could bring their gripes to "Colonel Ruff," as they referred to him, usually with great deference. More often than not, he would sort things out. Some of these transgressions might involve RSLMF soldiers who had brutalized townsfolk or possibly raped somebody's wife or stolen a hi-fi. That happened while I was there.

Once the complaint had been laid, up on the hill, Van Heerden would send some of his own men, together with the aggrieved party,

to look for the culprit. Tough shit if he was found—as he usually was
—because Koidu and Yengema were fairly small communities. The
man would be brought back to camp and thrashed: usually a rump
and a dozen with a hippo-hide *sjambok*.

While being fitted out for the bush at Cockerill, I'd seen a pile of
these whips at the EO quartermaster's store. Though it was obvious
what they were for, I didn't dare ask because I was aware they can
draw blood if properly used.

There was nothing secret about these beatings. The men were
"brought to trial" at the base and questioned before witnesses, usually in the presence of three or four local chiefs who were always hanging about the HQ building waiting to see "the boss." It was they who
ultimately decided what punishment should be handed down, usually
a dozen lashes for more serious offenses.

Men from his own unit would hold down the guilty party over a
log of wood and the screams could sometimes be heard in town. Most
of the culprits fouled themselves long before it was over.

Primitive? Atavistic? Call it what you will. An almost immediate
result was that army discipline throughout the Koidu region improved
markedly. This was a language that the troops understood very well
and I wasn't the only one to observe that they quickly moderated their
activities accordingly. Naturally the RSLMF officer corps was pleased,
and small wonder then that they held this rough-hewn farmer's son
from the Free State in such high regard.

Years later, when I joined Nellis, there were several Sierra Leonean aircrew members at the base, including two lieutenants who had originally been trained by Executive Outcomes. Lt. Philip Schenks, with
whom I flew numerous times, was among them. Another was the
reserve sidegunner who would do duty when Hassan was called elsewhere.

Both men had the usual stock of yarns about the South Africans
who had put them so rigorously through their paces. It was Schenks
who observed that when he joined the unit he noticed that almost all
the recruits had their shaven heads adorned by little strips of band-
aids that covered cuts. When asked, a soldier explained that if they
didn't obey orders properly "We get de stick . . . on de head."

"We had our crowns banged together often enough," said
Schenks. "We still carry the scars," he added, pointing. Looking back,
the two men had fond memories of a difficult period that had result-

ed in them and their buddies being unceremoniously molded into an efficient fighting force. They were also candid about the consequences. As one of them told me, "We'd probably not have survived hadn't it been so. They were hard taskmasters. Tough but fair."

The only Afrikaans expression that Schenks recalled—and he did so vividly, because he would use it when he was frustrated by one of the men under him, was "*Ek gaan jou moer!*" which, roughly translated, means: I'm going to fuck you up!

I was to see the two men in action many times during missions against the RUF and it was clear that they enjoyed a scrap. Both still had a couple of scores to settle and neither were wearied by the confusion and utter futility of a conflict that had been part of their lives for longer than either had been adults. Unlike some of their compatriots, they were also physically strong and not afraid to use muscle when we went into forward operational bases and some of the troops would try to force their way onboard for a ride home.

They were fearless, too, and not just for my benefit. Schenks would see a target and go at it with a relish that surprised everybody who flew with him for the first time. Out of uniform, in contrast, he was a dapper, quiet-spoken man who would have liked nothing more than to see a bit of the world. Hostilities apart, people tend to forget that Sierra Leone was once the best-educated country in West Africa.

In late 1995, the Angolan contract was suddenly halted and a hundred more EO vets were sent to Sierra Leone to form a new unit under the command of Nic du Toit, a former SADF special forces major who was new to EO.[6] Seconded to him as his deputy was a former Parachute Battalion major, Cobus Claassens, who had also come to EO straight from the SADF. Brigadier-General Bert Sachse remained in overall command.

This force consisted of some infantry, several men with armor experience and some former policemen from special detachments. It wasn't a happy marriage because the very first firefight resulted in several of the newcomers resigning and being sent back to South Africa. Some had thought that a Sierra Leone posting would be a jolly and they were wrong. Things changed overnight when an EO column drove into a large ambush and suffered two killed and seven wounded.

Claassens: "By then we were back at the BTC training base and were given instructions by the EO regional head to move on Makeni."

The place where it happened was along "Ambush Alley" between Lunsar and Makeni. It was almost within sight of the stretch where Neall Ellis had thumped the RUF convoy on its way to a clandestine meeting with the Nigerian second-in-command of United Nations forces in Sierra Leone (see Chapter 6).

As Sachse explained, "This wasn't inordinately difficult country in which to operate and the place wasn't all that overgrown. The problem, basically, was road cuttings. There were dozens and the rebels would use them to good effect for their ambushes . . . it was all classic counterinsurgency stuff." The men would clear each cutting up ahead by laying down heavy machine-gun fire or possibly use mortars to dislodge anything planned by the rebels. Nic du Toit, meanwhile, in overall command, was overhead in a push-pull Cessna 337. And so it went, for several hours.

The ambush that caused the damage was very well planned. It consisted of three zigzag killing groups spaced-out at regular intervals over about half a mile. In the melee that followed, Claassens' Land Rover got seriously pummeled. His driver and side-gunner were killed and just about everybody else was wounded at least once.

As Claassens recalled when he told me about it, "What we did immediately afterward was drive into the bush in a follow-up operation and we killed quite a lot of them. But it didn't make up for our losses. It was also apparent that this group of rebels was more capable than the usual rebel raw recruit that we'd faced in the past. They were better trained, better equipped and, most significant of all, they were well motivated."

Their leader, they were to discover later, was one of the best field commanders in the RUF, Sam "Mosquito" Bockerie, who later moved to Liberia to take up a security position, first in the government of President Charles Taylor and afterward among RUF units inside the neighboring country.

He was eventually taken out in a hit organized by Taylor's people because his presence in Liberia had become meddlesome.

The Rutile operation followed not long afterward. About fifty EO troops drove to Moyamba Junction, a distance of about sixty miles, and from there to Rutile.

For some of the men Rutile was a disappointment because there was no pitched battle: the mercenaries simply moved in on the place and took it. While some reports talk about Rutile being "recaptured," this wasn't so. In fact, says Claassens, "When we got there, Sierra Leone Army detachments were busy looting the place."

In January 1996, barely a month later, the decision was made by the Sierra Leone High Command to push on to the RUF stronghold in the Kangari Hills, a strategic area in the center of the country, roughly midway between Kenema and Makeni. For this, the mercenaries were joined by remnants of the Fireforce, which would have given them a tactical force of about a hundred men.

What was significant about that operation—it lasted four or five days—was that EO never actually captured the base, or for that matter even managed to occupy it. But they did block the rebels' main avenues of escape, which forced them to leave the area on foot through the jungle. In so doing, they had to abandon all their vehicles and heavier weapons.

One other operation was launched by EO prior to the final push on Sankoh's HQ in the Gola Hills, adjacent to the Liberian frontier.

Sankoh had taken up residence in a jungle valley that most military tacticians and planners at Cockerill agreed was probably impenetrable. The site was protected by narrow gorges at both entrances. Sankoh originally chose the place because from there he was able to cross the Moro River into Liberia whenever he wished. It also doubled as a bolt-hole.

Like the Kangari area, EO never actually got into his camp because both Sankoh and the remainder of his RUF rebels fled before the mercenaries got near the place. As Claassens says, that was probably the result of the many ambushes that were laid along all the tracks leading to his HQ. "We took out some of his best people in that episode," he told me.

Bert Sachse has another view of that phase of the campaign. For a while he had been pressing Sierra Leone's military leaders to let him use thermobaric, or fuel-air, bombs against Sankoh's jungle hideouts. These were the same weapons deployed by the Russians against Chechnyan rebels while they were still very active in Grozny.

Known in the argot as "the poor man's atom bomb," the device would have been useful within the rugged mountain ravines which characterized much of the Gola Hills. Originally developed in South Africa, the bombs were made available to Executive Outcomes.

Sachse sensed strong opposition to this plan from the start, and in particular from Brigadier Maada Bio, the CDS. Only afterward was he to uncover the fact that many RSLMF commanders had family members among the rebels holed up in that rebel retreat. Maada Bio's sister, for instance—later fingered as an arch spy for the rebels—would have been among those who might have been killed had Sachse been allowed to go ahead with the plan.

This disclosure led many in Freetown afterward to believe that Maada Bio might have been the source of the majority of the leaks that were inexplicably being fed to the RUF while the campaign lasted. His sister was a regular caller at Cockerill Barracks for almost the duration of the war

Before the Gola Hills fuel-air bomb strike was to have taken place, there was one more operation in the panhandle north of Pendembu in the far northwestern corner of the country, directly adjacent to the border with Guinea.

Shortly after Sachse took leave and Nic du Toit went to headquarters, Claassens and his group were sent to Kenema, with the latter in charge of a mobile unit of several dozen troops with the former Recce officer P.P. Hugo commanding Fireforce. Their instructions were to support the Sierra Leone Army, then in the process—with strong EO backing—of driving toward Kailahun.

Claassens: "When we got close to the area, we found government forces stalled; most of them were decamped along the road leading to the north. Obviously, they were going nowhere. So after a few days of inactivity we decided to launch a heliborne attack. We flew one of the platoons with our 82mm mortars onto a patch of high ground to the south of the town, while two more platoons were dropped from choppers about four clicks from the target in what looked like knee-high elephant grass.

"In fact, it was nothing of the sort. The grass was over our heads and what should have taken less than hour to cover eventually took the attacking force half a day.

"It was a really tough slog. We were carrying heavy—our kit, weapons, ammo and water, and not only did we have to slash our way through this jungle grass to make any kind of progress, we also had to traverse extremely rough terrain across hilltops and gullies that had fast streams flowing through them. In other areas there were swamps.

"Finally, under mortar cover, we entered Kailahun, where we had two contacts with the rebels, though nothing major. They then abandoned their positions and hot-footed it toward Liberia

"The first thing we did was occupy the tallest structure in town. This was a three-story mosque with exceptionally thick walls and it was here that we set up our OPs. True to form it wasn't very long before the gooks started infiltrating back into town, and from our vantage point we were able to monitor their progress. They had seen our helicopters leave shortly before it got dark and surmised that we'd all gone as well.

"The bastards would walk down the main street with their little torches. Meanwhile we waited until there were enough of them in our sights and then let go. They took a lot of casualties," said Claassens.

The next morning a Sierra Leone Army detachment was flown in by helicopter, some of them without weapons, which surprised Claassens because this was still a very active area. With that, Kailahun was formally handed over to the RSLMF commander.

"The last rebel stronghold, Kailahun, is yours," I told the officer, a half colonel. At the same time I symbolically handed over the keys to the town.

"We didn't leave immediately but got to work in typical guerrilla fashion, setting up ambushes and harassing positions the rebels were known to frequent. It was important that we did this because the region immediately adjacent to both Liberia and the Republic of Guinea was the last real stronghold where RUF elements were to be found in any kind of number, and where they seemed to have good support among the locals. They did quite a bit of their training there as well and, because of the fertile terrain, it was also the region's grain bowl.

"We went back to Kenema after about a week and then on to Freetown. Five, six days later, true to form, the entire Sierra Leone Army force fled Kailahun and was finally airlifted to safety by the Hips. What a bunch of wankers . . ."

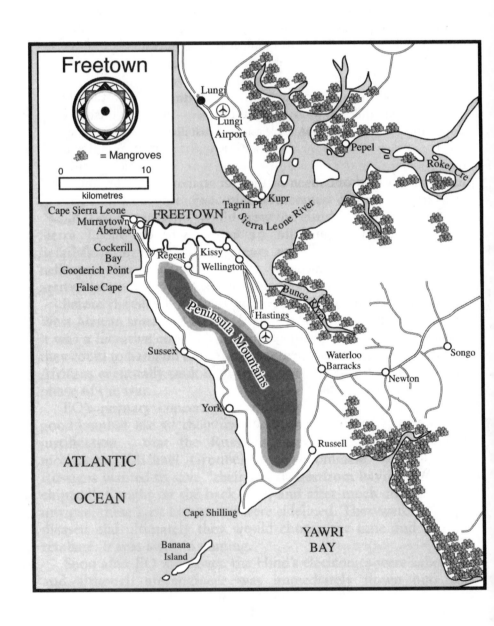

23

WAR DOGS HIT A
REBEL BASE

"When we had need of skilled soldiers to separate fighters
from refugees in the Rwandan camps in Goma, I even considered the possibility of engaging a private firm. I did not
do so because I believed that the world might not be ready
to privatize peace."

United Nations Secretary General Kofi Annan,
Annual Ditchley Foundation Lecture, 1998

Going to war with Executive Outcomes in 1995 was a defining experience. Twice I had spent time with the company in Angola, and in
Sierra Leone I was again to meet some of its major players. Almost all
had remarkable military credentials and many today are doing good
work in Iraq, Afghanistan and elsewhere.

Like everybody else who had contact with these people, I couldn't
help being impressed by the way they went about their business. That
was further reinforced at the end of my sojourn at Colonel Roelf van
Heerden's regional HQ at Koidu when an attack was planned on what
was regarded as a significant rebel base.

The operation had been given the go-ahead while I was still in
Freetown. With Bert Sachse out of the country, Andy Brown remained
in charge. Lafras Luitingh had meantime left the country to conclude
a deal aimed at settling the Chiapas issue in Mexico. As we were to
learn afterward, that little episode was canned once Washington got
word that the Hispanics were considering hiring mercenaries to suppress a domestic rebellion. What a stink it would have raised in
Washington had EO gone ahead with what was to have been a "pacification" program.

In Freetown meantime, according to Brown, Kamajor intelligence
had revealed details about what seemed to be an advanced RUF staging post at Baiama, a tiny settlement to the south of the diamond town
and not far off the main road leading to Gandorhun and Kenema. Van

Heerden had been waiting for me to get there so that he could send his boys in. Not that my presence was essential, Brown mentioned, since they were going to hit the place anyway. But it had been Luitingh's opinion that the company needed more media mileage, and just then EO's international image seemed to matter.

In a series of pre-attack briefings, Baiama was projected as a pretty innocuous sort of place; a pinprick on the map, as one of the officers called it. Its importance lay in the fact that all approach roads in an area that stretched to the frontier went through it. Before the war the village had been a typical little jungle settlement of a few dozen buildings. It had had a store, a church and at one stage its own post office. There had even been an elementary school that took in children from miles around.

The people who lived there were like millions of others in Equatorial Africa, only these folk grew coffee. The way the elders remembered it, everybody thrived. Then came the war and out of an original community of roughly a hundred, barely a dozen were still alive.

Getting to Baiama meant a journey through some difficult terrain, Colonel van Heerden warned. Thick bush and overhanging forest was just about everywhere; in fact, in most places the jungle began right alongside the road. Consequently, there were endless opportunities for ambush.

"You're going to have the BMPs with you," he told us. Without them, he reckoned we probably wouldn't get half the distance before being hit, and in any event he didn't need casualties. "So just don't wander away from the column, even for a piss," he stressed. A stickler for detail, van Heerden went through each possible scenario.

"Stay together while you're on the road. You'll have enough opportunity to split up once the business starts. And when you get there, don't go poking about because the place could be booby-trapped." The warning—ostensibly for everybody present at the briefing—was primarily for my benefit. What he didn't want was this non-combatant wandering around taking photographs because I could end up being separated from the main body.

I was issued with the usual olive green camouflage uniform, given several water bottles and, if I wanted, a machete—or *panga*, as he called it. Finally, my choice of weapon was either a brand new AKMS —Poland's version of the ubiquitous Kalashnikov (complete with collapsible stock) or a Russian AK-47 with standard wooden butt.

It was strictly for self-defense, he stressed, "but you'd be stupid to refuse it." At any moment, he suggested, somebody might step out of the bush, "and make no mistake, they're everywhere. They'll certainly be watching the column arrive and since you'd have cameras around your neck, that sort of thing makes you conspicuous. For the same reason the top guys don't display any rank.

"So, if one of them is tanked up and decides to do the obvious, you'd have to fight or flee. But where are you going to run to? Since it usually happens when you're within a few feet of each other you might have no option but to defend yourself."

The decision was mine, of course, and because the circumstances were so unusual, I had to agree. There was no disputing van Heerden's argument: we were a small force possibly going up against a much larger one. The weapon, should it come to that, would be a lot more useful than my laptop. So I accepted his first offering, a brand new AK still in its original oil paper and factory grease.

Van Heerden planned everything. He issued maps, GPS sets, a medical kit that included blood plasma, rations, signal rockets, fuel, gunship back-up radio frequencies and so on. I would travel on top of one of the IFVs rather than inside, he told me. While there was space in the troop carriers that followed behind, they were full of Sierra Leone troops, the majority of whom would already have been pretty tanked up before we set out.

That, in itself, he said, was not so bad, because the men got used to it. What did worry him were the inevitable accidental weapon discharges, or in the jargon, ADs, that came with every action. A month after taking Koidu, it remained one of the quirks of the war that government troops were still shooting each other by accident. It happened with alarming regularity, especially at night when they got nervous.

There were some who thought that these "shootings" weren't all accidental and that there must have been the occasional settlement of a personal score. Nobody could argue, especially when just about everybody involved was smashed. Moreover, the RSLMF, as we'd been told, wasn't immune to "fraggings."

Whatever the truth, van Heerden made the point that while traveling to Baiama, the drivers were to keep maximum distance between "them" and us.

We were up at dawn on that first morning. ETD was set for an hour after sunrise but it took a while longer for a clinging mist to lift. Just as well: the mechanics needed time to get one of the BMPs started.

Cobus Claassens would run the show once we got on the road. Though he had been in the country only months, this former SADF major had already been in several scrapes with the rebels in the hills and jungle around the diamond town. The attack on Baiama, he said, would be like most of the others. It was all routine.

Whenever possible, he told me, he'd use the Kamajor fighters to clear out the area in the immediate vicinity of any village or settlement that we'd pass through. The diminutive combatants arrived in a group of about a hundred about the same time that we emerged out from under our mosquito nets. Once ready and with the troops lined up, van Heerden inspected the squad.

The "hunters" were not big people. In fact, as a force, with their torn, almost threadbare clothes and antiquated shotguns, they were almost pathetic. Yet each one of them was eager to mix it with the rebels who had caused so much grief within their communities in the past few years. According to the EO vets, these people were good fighters; in fact, much better than the majority of RSLMF troops, though in any regular force they would have been regarded as frail and anything but soldierly. Almost to a man they appeared to be under-nourished. To compound the issue, van Heerden said, it would take the government at least another year to get them issued with automatic weapons.

Unconventional, almost uncaring about how they went about their lives, seriously ill-equipped and, on the face of it, not your run-of-the-mill bush fighter, these seemingly gentle folk—while polite and disciplined—were ruthless in combat. They gave no quarter and expected none in return.

Van Heerden confided that he had yet to see one of them return to camp with a prisoner.

We had to pass through the heart of the Koidu business area to get to the road leading south and it seemed that the entire town had gathered to cheer us on our way. Lining the road out of town, the people laughed and shouted and exchanged banter with some of our boys who, it seemed, they'd got to know very well in the brief time they'd been there. Some of the folk passed on baskets of mangos to the men as we drove.

Like the Kamajors, many of these people had been subjected to some pretty severe RUF excesses. Interestingly, while the army had abused many townsfolk after Koidu had been retaken—and almost everybody detested the arrogant and often brutal soldiers who were supposed to be there to protect them—RSLMF troops, in comparison to the rebels, were regarded as "gentlemen." They hated the RUF with a passion both bitter and unmitigated, due solely to the mindless inhumanity to which they had been subjected at the hands of Sankoh's people.

It took us about an hour to reach Woama where, as I'd been briefed earlier, we would turn off to Baiama. At that point we heard the first of the drums that sounded in the hills around us. It was like a film script, the enemy striking up on cue. The rebels were obviously not far away and they knew we were coming.

It was there on the approach road that we found the first of several sets of steel roofing sheets laid across the road: the RUF version of an early warning system. The overlapping corrugated iron sheets created a terrible din when the steel IFV treads crunched over them. It was a crude but effective measure. We were to see similar precautions in place in miniature along some of the footpaths leading out of Baiama. They could just as easily have been mines, except that this was one war where landmines barely featured as a threat.

Like everything else in Sierra Leone, the roads weren't what they'd been in peacetime. In places the jungle, with creepers, undergrowth and lianas going off in every possible direction, had partially overwhelmed the road. Another two or three years without maintenance or regular traffic would see it reclaimed by the bush.

Woama, our turnoff point for Baiama, had obviously been a compact, tidy little town in its day. When we got there it was derelict. There were none of the usual signs of life, no people and no smoking embers and, most eerie of all, not a single dog. In more settled times one of the first signs of habitation in these parts would be the presence of mangos: the kids would knock them off the trees with bamboo poles long before they were ripe. Here, the fruit was rotting on the ground. That was a good sign, said one of the men. It meant there weren't too many rebels around.

Like the roads, the town itself was in bad shape. Just about all the mud structures were damaged. Some had had their walls blown away and very few had roofs even partially intact. Part of the reason was that Woama had been the site of a rebel ambush the first time an Executive Outcomes column had passed through the area not many months before, and one of the BMPs had been knocked out by a

HEAT rocket. We'd passed its rusting hulk on the way in.

Claassens said that when they first arrived there, early in the day, they were greeted by scores of skulls stuck up on poles. It was a grotesque replay of what they'd encountered at Bumpe and Yengema when they'd taken those towns a month before.

"In a way, it was quite disturbing. Just as we got there, the area seemed to be washed by the same eerie mist that had caused our delay (earlier in Koidu). We'd never seen anything like this in Angola. Some of our black troops were convinced that the place was cursed."

Looking about Woama that first morning on the way to Koidu months before, Claassens and the others with him felt that there was something almost necrophilic about what had been done to some of the corpses they found lying about, almost as if a giant cadaver wagon had passed by and hurled them out at random. Quite a few of the bodies were still warm. They discovered this when the troops had to move them off the road so that the convoy could pass.

"Of course, some of our black guys went crazy. They just wanted to get out there and kill," he recalled. He had to restrain some of them, if only to prevent his force from being fragmented. At that time he had no idea who or what he was up against.

When the first of the mercenaries arrived, nine or ten emaciated survivors emerged from the bush. They had managed to stay alive by living off berries, leaves and grasses and the occasional small animals, usually rodents, which they ate raw because they were afraid to light a fire in case it alerted their persecutors.

For many of EO's new arrivals, it was the first time they had been exposed to this kind of atavistic barbarism. In their earlier experiences of conflict in Angola and Namibia and elsewhere, there had never been such excesses. "Not even when we fought Angola's government forces," said one of the men. Southern African wars were pretty self-respecting by comparison, he reckoned. Nobody defiled enemy dead. Nor did they eat them.

There had been a whiff of it at the beginning of Angola's anti-colonial revolt in the Sixties, among insurgents who invaded from the Congo in 1961, but those incidents, though sensational when they eventually hit the European press, were isolated. In several instances settler families had been fed into circular logging saws.

"They shoved them lengthwise through the rotating blades," recounted one of the rebels responsible for these atrocities, "*avec un grande sourire*" (with a big smile).[1]

Having checked Woama for booby traps, Claassens gave the order to mount up. We still had a distance to cover and it was almost ten o'clock. He'd hoped to get to Baiama by early afternoon because both the Kamajors and the Sierra Leone troops in the column would need time to mop up after we'd occupied the place. It would be tight, he declared. Also, we didn't know what the other side had planned for us.

Before leaving, Colonel van Heerden had warned that the rebels might attempt to hold us up by dragging tree trunks across the road; it would have taken twenty men to move one of those forest giants. Nor was it lost on the officers that this was the same trick that had been tried in most insurgencies from Malaya on.

"And if you've got logs on the road, you're also going to have an ambush," van Heerden confided.

Another rebel tactic was digging a big hole in the middle of the road. With light wooden supports, they would cover it with small stems and elephant grass. Over that would be spread a thin layer of soil. Essentially, the rebels hoped that one of the IFVs would fall into the trap, but it'd never worked, said Claassens. The rebels still had to learn something about concealment, especially on laterite. He did concede that if one of the BMPs was incapacitated this way, it would take days to dig out. They'd probably need to bring in some heavy lift equipment as well. "And all that would need guarding because then the fuckers would really try to cause us a spot of bother."

We were about three miles out of Baiama when Josh Groblaar, one of the mercenaries who had played a seminal role in the Battle for Freetown, called together his mortar team. Using open ground in the next village, he set up his tubes and struck at a pre-designated target. Half-a-dozen volleys of 82mm mortar bombs went out over our heads.

Meantime, the chopper jocks had been following our progress by radio. Josh's fusillade was the signal for them to swing into orbit over Baiama, with the Mi-17 side-gunners watching for movement on the ground below. Anybody there would be fair game because the town had been a rebel stronghold since the start of the war. It had also been identified as an advanced RUF training and recruitment area. Well placed, the main camp overlooked much of the terrain, which was why Van Heerden chose to clobber it.

Baiama had originally been uncovered more by accident than design. Apparently one of the pilots spotted a huge brown patch on top of one of the hills over which they'd been flying. He checked it out and came under fire. Only afterward was it found that the enemy had cleared an area about the size of a football ground to make way for the main camp. But nobody had bothered to remove the dead brush which contrasted sharply against the verdant green of the surrounding jungle after three or four days.

The first ambush came shortly afterward. A small rebel group had taken up position at a clearing around more abandoned huts, the last stretch of open ground before Baiama. But they didn't use the opportunity as they should have.

Because the attackers were close to the road and the BMPs were unable to depress their cannons, the men onboard were forced to deploy directly into the line of enemy fire. Through it all, nobody in our party was hit. Claassens observed afterward that most of the enemy fighters had their eyes closed when they pulled their triggers: he was that close to them. Then they all ducked back into the jungle.

After half a minute of shooting, a deep silence settled on the jungle, giving it an uncanny stillness. The men even stopped talking and for a moment or two everything around us was almost serene. Someone asked about a follow-up. "Negative" was the reply from Koidu.

We didn't linger, which meant that there was no time to check for kills. That would be left to those following behind. If lucky, they would strip the bodies while we were busy in the target town. At this point Claassens suggested that with the main attack imminent, I should move back a vehicle or two and choose a comfortable niche for myself. I found one on the Land Rover immediately behind the IFV and settled between a pair of unsmiling Ovambos.[2]

The jungle in the area we were then passing through appeared to be denser. It was clearly impenetrable in places, with tangles of thorn and foliage bound together by dense, stringy creepers, sometimes reaching upwards two or three hundred feet. There were places where it blocked out the light altogether and one couldn't help thinking that nobody could fight a clandestine war in such country for any length of time. The jungle restricted movement and the only way of getting about was to stick to existing roads or tracks. It really all boiled down to logistics: who could get what to wherever the action was taking place the fastest.

We'd gone five or six hundred yards further when they hit us again. Once more there was none of the vigor that we'd been expecting. Much of it seemed to consist of small groups of rebels erratically letting off bursts of automatic fire or an occasional RPG. Then, like the others before, they would disappear back into the foliage. The IFVs sent volleys of shells in after them and the heavy calibers caused damage far beyond what we could see from the road. By now both Mi-17s were over us, their PKMs chattering away. They flew in a broad circle and plastered every moving thing that wasn't part of our column.

Suddenly Baiama came into view, and with it our first heavy ambush. An RPG exploded in the bush above our heads. And then another and within a moment everybody was retaliating. Claassens called on the helicopters to check out where the firing was coming from.

Uncomfortable in my new position on the vehicle—and anyway, everybody around me was firing and I needed photographs—I jumped down and moved forward toward the BMP ahead. I was the only one in the group to do so and realized too late that it was not the wisest move. Camera in one hand and AK in the other, I traversed small bits of open ground between vehicles. The shooting slackened before I got up front.

I could hear Claassens speaking on the radio in Afrikaans. There were bodies around a brick building to our left, one of the gunners on the choppers told him, and he ordered somebody to get out there and check.

Another RPG exploded, then two more and our people retaliated. By then the show couldn't have lasted more than a couple of minutes, and as the cordite started to clear, the only sound we could hear was Claassens issuing more instructions. A burst of automatic fire followed from the rear.

I was to discover later that fighting in this kind of terrain was extraordinarily difficult for several reasons. First, it was almost impossible to establish exactly where your enemy was. Also, you had no idea of numbers. And then, when it was all supposed to be over, you couldn't be sure that the rebels had actually pulled out. Even more confusing, the jungle tends to deaden blast. So there could be somebody ten yards away shooting at you and you wouldn't be able to place him until you spotted a muzzle flash. Because of the undergrowth, that too was often difficult.

By now just about all the men had dismounted and were moving in line ahead on both sides of the column. The BMP ahead of us continued pushing out heavy stuff, but there was nothing more coming in. More reports of kills arrived on the radio. Intercepts later spoke about a dozen of the enemy having been killed by the Mi-17s, though it could have been more, Juba said when we got back to Freetown.

Baiama was disturbing. Once the BMPs had taken up their usual defensive positions and firing was limited to the occasional volley at the end of town, we were able to move about. But we tended to remain cautious.

I had to be especially so because each time I took pictures I had no option but to place my weapon on the ground. Usually it was next to me, but then I'd move on a short distance to perhaps take a lateral shot. Or perhaps enter one of the buildings and Claassens or one of the other officers would come running. There was nothing daredevil about it: this was my job and why I was there.

Even though it lay in the middle of nowhere, Baiama must have been an important little place in its day. The walls of the old Catholic Church were standing, but barely, and the roof had been all but stripped. On its walls the rebels had daubed slogans: "Give to God for Make" or "Jesus Jive he Save."

Much of the graffiti was incomprehensible. There were numerous crude sketches of copulating couples or individual figures with huge erections.

We found a *ju ju* shrine in a house that was still relatively intact. All its windows were shuttered and it was too dark inside for photos. An "altar" stood in the middle of the room, holding devotional items that had clearly come from the church across the street, such as it was, with the grass growing three feet high where there had once been a road. That alone indicated that the rebels had probably taken the place before the priest—or whoever else was responsible—was properly able to vacate it. These accouterments included a chalice as well as a bell and censer, all of them surmounted by a large wooden cross with a defaced Christ. Again, the walls were painted with primitive religious or animistic motifs, some of them provocative.

In a corner, a raised platform had been used for offerings. It dripped with gunge, blood and mucus from who-knows-what barbaric rituals. One couldn't help but get the impression that living creatures had been sacrificed because it stank of carrion. A bowl of palm wine stood on a small wooden stand. Few of the troops who entered the building stayed long.

Unquestionably, the place was imbued with a malfeasance that seemed to stick to you for a long time afterward. I still cringe when I talk about it, because one had visions of things lurking in dark corners. One of the South Africans said that he got a horrific sense of idolatry, almost as if the place was alive. I was glad to get into the fresh air again even though the humidity outside was somewhere around a hundred percent.

I had seen a lot of this sort of thing while living in Nigeria further down the coast, and had always been uneasy about black magic. In Badagry, near Lagos, I'd had a fleeting encounter with one of the voodoo priests and he'd intimidated me. Then, while filming in Liberia in the 1980s, we stayed a few days in a village that geographically couldn't have been more than a hundred miles from Baiama.

My camera crew—a bunch of professionals that included Charles Norman from back home—were made uneasy by some of the rituals. Most were forbidding and ghastly. All the village's dead were buried in graves that were traditionally dug between the huts in which everybody slept. It was a tradition that apparently went back forever. While the rest of the crew could hardly have been described as naïve—they'd been in the business a long time and seen and done it all—they, too, were convinced that "spirits pranced about," as our sound engineer commented with a healthy touch of irony.

At the end of it, the crew refused to sleep in the place and chose instead the unit's Volkswagen van parked in the jungle some distance down the road.

Immediately on arrival in Baiama we followed one of the Hunter scouts up a narrow hill path for about an hour in order to reach our original target, the rebel base. There were dozens of paths that led from the village into the jungle and we marveled at how these little people were able to choose the right one in that unending, overgrown tangle of green. That was also where we found more roofing sheets discreetly laid along the paths to give warning of our approach.

We ambled single file, first past three small clearings that resembled control points. Had we not taken the place by force there would probably have been someone waiting for us. As in other places, the previous incumbents had left in a hurry: all that remained were some rucksacks, neatly packed as if their owners had been preparing for a journey.

There were also some clothes, cooking utensils and other equipment lying around, but with the Kamajors about, all had new owners within moments of their first sighting. There was no stopping these people taking things, even though one of the officers had warned before setting out that some of the packs could be booby-trapped. So like anything else that wasn't nailed down, all was "liberated" by our escorts. Soon every man jack in the column was wearing two or three shirts, while others had donned several pairs of trousers.

The rebel camp came next. First impressions were that much effort had gone into its disposition and approaches. There was only one track in, and even that was crafty. The final hurdle was a single log across a fast stream: an imaginative measure and certainly not typical of the rebels we'd come to know. Only one person could get across the "bridge" at a time. Had there been an ambush, we could have been delayed indefinitely, or at least until a chopper arrived to do the necessary. At the top of the hill was the camp itself.

After Baiama, the base was a pleasure. It was neatly laid out with huts of sapling walls and grass roofs set in the middle of a small parade ground. The latrines were sanitarily laid out behind the living quarters. It was refreshingly clean after the putrefaction in the valley below. There was even a dungeon: a hole in the ground about ten feet deep covered by a grill of logs that could be guarded by one man. The place was certainly well organized.

Here nothing of value was left lying about. There were no pots, no stoves, nothing in the food lockers, not even an exercise book to show what was being taught in what looked like an improvised lecture room with logs raised off the ground for seats. There must have been a radio room somewhere, but we never found it. Everything had been removed before we got there, more evidence of betrayal.

It surprised everybody that the place had been vacated so swiftly, because the Hips had only started circling about an hour before. They'd obviously known we were on our way.

I had an impression at the time that whoever ran the camp was not local. All this organization was just too systematic, too methodical, while the rebel trademark was total disorder, often more in line with haphazard mumbo jumbo. There wasn't a scrap of paper lying about the camp, not even in the toilets. The paths had been swept, probably by the last person to leave the place. There had been reports about foreigners working with the rebels, but nothing concrete; not then, at any rate. EO would need to capture somebody to get it substantiated, but rarely was either side taking prisoners.

One of the South Africans said something about the place reminding him of some of those Viet Cong camps he had seen pictures of while studying at Staff College.

Originally we were to have spent the night at Baiama, but somebody back at Koidu changed his mind. We'd all brought sleeping bags and mosquito nets, so it would have been no hassle. In fact, I was quite looking forward to a night in the jungle under the stars.

But there was something that bothered Claassens and he wasn't talking. The enemy was still about, he told one of the others, and maybe there'd be a lot more than he'd first thought. Also, we'd get no air support after dark. Coupled to that, the horizon showed that there was a storm brewing.

By late afternoon the column pulled out, but not before some of the men had laid a few welcome mats of their own. Most were simple devices that would be triggered when the rebels returned to assess the damage. Several cans of food were linked to three or four grenades that would explode simultaneously across a fairly broad area. None had delay fuses; all would detonate when the first one popped. Almost all the bodies left behind had explosive charges placed under them. There was also a delay fuse on a cluster of mortar bombs hidden in the roof of the *ju ju* house and another in a structure that looked as though it was being used as a barracks. Both were timed to go off about three hours after dark the following night. The engineer who set these devices almost got bitten by a mamba.

Anti-personnel mines were spread along all the approaches to the camp: Chinese-type 72s with just enough explosives to blow off a man's foot. Hopefully the witch doctors with their vile potions would do the rest. Then some of the men placed POM-Z grenades alongside the approaches to the town. More were primed just off the junction leading to Baiama.

Only the rebels would be using these throughways, since all the indigenes and their families had fled, Claassens told me, and it would remain that way for about two weeks. "Then we'll be back and do it all again," he said. Significantly, no traps were laid at the base camp on the hill: Claassens had decided that it would be waste of ordnance. Whoever lived there knew their turf and they'd spot anything out of order in an instant.

We hadn't been on the road long when we heard the first big crump echo across the forest and the men on the vehicles cheered. I was told later that some of the Hunter Detachment who stayed behind to case the joint reported more blasts during the night.

Once back at Woama, "Juba" Joubert and Fred Marafano touched down their chopper just long enough to get me onboard before they headed back to Freetown. We got in after dark and made straight for Alex's Bar. I'd hardly ordered my first beer before Larry Reiman, my American friend, sidled up and asked me where I'd been. The last time I'd seen him had been at the previous Friday night's party at the British High Commission.

Give Larry his due: he was a good operator and Langley must have been pleased at his efforts.

24
A FUTURE FOR
PRIVATE MILITARY COMPANIES

"If soldiering was for the money, the Special Air Service (SAS) and the Special Boat Service (SBS) would have disintegrated in recent years. Such has been the explosion in private military companies (PMCs) that they employ an estimated thirty thousand in Iraq alone—and no government can match their fat salaries. A young SAS trooper earns about $3,500 a month: on the 'circuit,' as soldiers call the private world, he could get $16,000. Why would he not?"

The Economist, London: October 22, 2005

The term "private military companies" or, as some prefer, "private security companies," has only recently entered the lexicon. The issue became pertinent to a lot of Americans when the headline "Blackwater Mercenaries Deploy in New Orleans" appeared in a September 10, 2005 news report.

Overnight, we were told, squads of heavily-armed private security contractors were out on patrol in the streets of this stricken Louisiana city. That followed serious hurricane and flood damage in the wake of America's biggest catastrophe since the Civil War.

Details were sparse. What soon became clear was that some of these mercenaries—many who had just returned from stints of active duty in Iraq—had not only been "deputized" but wore gold Louisiana state law enforcement badges on their chests. That was in addition to their Blackwater USA photo ID cards. The pay, one of them intimated, was $350 a day, only a fraction of what the men were earning out east where a good operator can get anything between $80,000 and $180,000 a year depending on specialties and risk.

When asked what they were doing there, those who would talk to the media—there were many who wouldn't—said that they were part of a Homeland Security deployment. They had the authority to use lethal force to maintain order, they declared, though once the matter had become controversial, that was disputed by Eddie Compass, the New Orleans Police Commissioner.

Whatever the truth, Blackwater is no novice when it comes to operational matters. I know Gary Jackson, the CEO quite well, having visited him at his Moyock, North Carolina headquarters. We stayed in touch afterward and shared a few insights by e-mail including the fact that his men provided security to employees of the Coalition Provisional Authority in Iraq, including its former U.S. administrator, L. Paul Bremer.

British-born and a SEAL-team veteran, Gary's first choice of recruit for work in remote and dangerous parts is somebody with solid Special Forces credentials. He started out by recruiting many of his former SEAL buddies, though by now many nations are represented within the company's ranks. Essentially the market is something of a moveable feast, with supply dictated by demand, and in Baghdad these days, the need for such professionals remains desperate.

Also, it is no secret that Blackwater USA is one of the field leaders among PMCs/PSCs in Iraq and Afghanistan. The company has numerous government contracts. Its men provide security to American embassies, VIPs, government officials, workplaces and construction sites (including getting crews to and from them on often-dangerous roads) and so on. In fact, the list is extensive, especially when determined and competent groups of zealots are in the business of killing people.

Blackwater works extensively with private corporations in other parts of the globe. Indeed, Gary told me in late 2004, company contracts were rapidly edging up toward the billion dollar mark, which, he admitted, is nice work if you can get it.

More recently, the company was involved in a huge and complex retraining program of members of the U.S. Navy following the bombing of the USS *Cole* in Aden. Its members put several thousand sailors through their paces in an intense training program in the close-quarter use of firearms. For that purpose, the company built a mock ship superstructure on one of Backwater's extensive properties about ninety minutes by road south of Virginia Beach.

Significantly, the name Blackwater first rose to prominence when four of its staff members were caught in a road ambush in Fallujah, Iraq in March 2004. Who can forget the horrific images of charred and dismembered bodies strung up on one of the bridges leading into that city?

More recently, Blackwater was linked to the in-flight destruction of a Bulgarian owned and operated Mi-8 helicopter that was brought down during an action just north of Baghdad. The "commercial helicopter" was owned and operated by Heli-Air Services, a Bulgarian subcontractor to SkyLink Air and Logistic Support, a Canadian firm under contract to Blackwater in support of a Department of Defense contract. Though the pilot managed to bring the damaged chopper and everybody in it safely to ground, all eleven people onboard were murdered by al-Qaeda-linked insurgents immediately afterward.

Which begs the question: If the United States is in control of the situation in Iraq—and around Baghdad especially—why then didn't one of the many U.S. helicopters—gunships included—in the air around the Iraqi capital just then not hasten to assist when the pilot reported that his machine had been hit and he was going down?

Apart from the three Bulgarian crew members, there were two Fijian PMC contractors and six Blackwater employees onboard, which brought the number of Blackwater USA operators KIA in the Middle East in the previous two years to twenty-four, surely a record for any private military company.

Though the jury is still out on the future role of the hired gun in international politics, a landmark decision was made in London in early 2002, when Whitehall gave the nod to regulating Private Military Companies. The British Foreign and Commonwealth Office—in response to a request from a parliamentary committee—released a briefing paper on the subject which noted that in the post-Cold War world, "The demand for private military services is likely to increase."

More important, it advocated the advantage of relying on private companies rather than national militaries. Its thrust was that a "strong and reputable private military sector might have a role in enabling the (United Nations) to respond more rapidly and more effectively in crises." A rider almost perfunctorily added that the cost of employing such people for certain UN functions, "could be much lower than that of national armed forces."

It is fortuitous that British minister Jack Straw released the paper when he did. Five months earlier, the strategic international focus had been reversed by the events of September 11, 2001. Overnight, small wars like those that blighted Liberia, Sierra Leone, the Sudan, Liberia, the Congo, East Timor and elsewhere didn't get anything like the attention they warranted.

Shortly before that, Colonel Tim Spicer—today head of Aegis and a major PMC player in Iraq—made a comment that was both prescient and timely. Though he was talking about Africa, what he had to say was relevant to any country struggling with an insurgency, particularly in the Third World.

"Peacekeeping deployments in Africa are doomed to failure until the United Nations recognizes that issuing blue helmets to ill-equipped and inadequately trained troops from helpful nations is a futile exercise." Just because these were the countries that came forward and proffered help was not enough reason to use them, he declared to what must certainly have been silent applause in many of the West's corridors of power.

"Establishing, enforcing and maintaining peace in volatile regions of Africa requires a more robust and effective form of intervention," stated an employee of the British firm Sandline. The major powers should continue to accept the offers of other nations, he stressed, but they needed to supplement this with the kind of expertise available from private military companies that could provide cadres of experienced officers and NCOs. They, in turn, could plan, lead and enhance the skills of these forces in the field.

Looking at the game board today, it has become clear that, being composed almost entirely of former Special Forces, the majority of PMCs are ideally suited to accomplish peacemaking tasks, which is exactly what Sandline pointed out in its original policy statement. It wasn't lost on many observers that PMCs, mercenaries, hired guns—call them what you will—had on numerous occasions already proven their mettle, not just to monitor, but actually to end conflict. If they needed to fight to achieve their aim, so be it, since that is a capability that comes with the job.

This was aptly illustrated in April 2004 when eight members of Blackwater USA—together with a single U.S. Marine and four military policemen—fought off an attack by hundreds of Iraqi militiamen in the Shi'ite town of Najaf south of Baghdad. Most significantly, though the company men took three wounded and the marine was critically hurt, U.S. military forces only arrived when it was all over. By then Blackwater had sent in its own helicopters to resupply the embattled occupants and to take out the wounded. During the scrap, which lasted three-and-a-half hours, the defenders' house was completely surrounded and all the injuries apparently came from a single sniper on the roof of a nearby building.

Brigadier General Mark Kimmitt arrived at the battle zone shortly afterward and his observations at a press conference the next day
are instructive.[1] Of the Blackwater people he declared: "They knew
what they were here for. They'd had three of their own wounded. We
were sitting there among the bullet shells . . . the bullet casings . . . and
frankly, the blood of their comrades, and they were absolutely confident.'

In contrast, it was later established, the attackers took an awful lot
of casualties.

The modern-day mercenary falls into several categories and, for a variety of reasons, the world at large remains skeptical both of their role
in the international arena and their ultimate agenda. Bear in mind,
too, that this is an age when a large sector of American society still
cannot agree whether the use of atom bombs against Japanese cities
was justified. Or even if events surrounding 9/11 – should the master-
mind be identified – deserves any kind of retaliation. Thus, the question of using freelancers to fight wars remains contentious.

So, while Colonel Mike Hoare built his reputation on the rock of
what he set out to accomplish in Moise Tshombe's troubled Katanga
of the 1960s, he demolished it a decade or so later by trying to invade
the Seychelles in an operation botched as much by booze as bad planning. Since then, there have been mercenaries in a score of countries
including Columbia, both Congos, Angola, Eritrea, El Salvador, Togo,
Nigeria, Rhodesia, Sri Lanka Mozambique, Chad, the Sudan, Uganda
and elsewhere.

Some of the players we've already met. These are people like Neall
Ellis, Bob Denard, Bob MacKenzie and the Rob Marafonos of the
world. There are more, such as ex-French Foreign Legionnaire Phil
Foley, who at extremely short notice absconded from an illustrious
thirteen-year career in the service of the tricolor when his CIA cover
was blown in Tahiti.

Which brings us back to Robert Kaplan. In his timely 1994
Atlantic Monthly article, Kaplan predicted growth in the use of civil-
ian-based "Special Forces." Such a development would come about
partly due to cost, he believed. He went on to say that by buying "private" protection, the international community would get it as cheaply
as possible while warding off a new enemy: the skilled, high-tech terrorist.

Kaplan also saw elite former soldiers being able to meet the needs

of cities in North America, where the future will "be brutal to industrial-age armies with big tanks and jets, and kind to corporate-style
forces in urban settings." Then why not turn to corporate structures
themselves instead of changing the nature of the armies that our public pays for?

Then one must ask, will private security companies replace armies
at home as well as abroad? In some senses, they already have. These
organizations have proliferated worldwide. In fact, as we all know,
there is barely a large corporation, airport, building site, housing
estate, school, university, dockland or industry that has not got uniformed security people on its staff.

Private security companies can be very well "regulated" in the
public interest, a point already made by David Shearer in his seminal
work for London's International Institute for Strategic Studies.[2] The
history of regulation, however, bears frequent witness to how eventually the regulators have served the interests of the regulated. Only
transparency and understanding can prevent this, not only in the public interest, but also in the interest of the investors who form private
companies,[3] particularly those involved in resource development in
Africa, where mercenaries have been so much in the news.

Overnight, all this effort is tarnished by the actions of a group of
renegade "hired guns" such as the Southern Africans that intended to
dislodge the status quo in Equatorial Guinea.

As if to anticipate the possible resurgence of organized professional
fighters bringing order to areas devastated by civil war, there has been
a sudden market surge in mercenary recruitment in other domains as
well.

A television documentary produced in the Ukraine and shown on
Kiev's commercial station, ICTV, exposed a huge network of mercenary activities behind what was once known as the Iron Curtain. This
has taken place in countries such as Russia, the Ukraine, Belarus and
others. The film exposed a worldwide network created by officers of
the former Soviet Military Intelligence Directorate (GRU) and detailed
the hire of war dogs, arms smuggling and illegal sales to rogue nations
—and even more insidiously—human trafficking.[4]

It also dealt with supply and demand. The TV program showed
that whereas soldiers of fortune from the Ukraine had previously been
paid $5,000 a month to train and fight in Laurent Kabila's Congo,
there had been so much interest among Soviet veterans to get a piece

of that action that eighteen months later, the average East European recruit was lucky to be offered $900.

Brigadier-General Ian Douglas, a retired Canadian soldier, had his own views on the subject. He made the case for the UN to use "private security firms" to fulfill peacekeeping requirements. Citing the work of Executive Outcomes in Sierra Leone and Angola in 1995, this veteran soldier believed that there is a place in the international community for these organizations.

"Look at what EO did in Sierra Leone. Without them, there would have been no peace to pursue. They literally stopped the war," he declared. Both Ironically and tragically—considering the number of innocents who were to die or end up without limbs—that "peace" was soon overtaken by a coup, launched by the Sierra Leone Army in May 1997. The revolt was ended in February 1998 following armed intervention by ECOMOG, the West African peacekeeping force built around the Nigerian army.

At the same time, it is consistently (though hardly vociferously) argued that Turtle Bay needs to be more practical in its peacekeeping efforts. In 1995, Douglas helped to organize an $8 million UN operation that saw fifteen hundred Zairian troops hired to provide security for the refugee camps along their country's eastern border. That cost, he maintained, would have been $80 million if "traditional peacekeeping troops" were used. Indeed, he believed, it was a very practical solution to something that could very quickly have turned nasty.

As we are now aware, the UN did not follow up on their promises of additional support. They did absolutely nothing. As a consequence, hundreds of thousands of innocents were murdered in one of the worst examples of internecine strife the world has seen since the end of World War II. British writer Aidan Hartley was there and saw the carnage from up close. He spells out the scenario that led to this terrible catastrophe in his last book, *The Zanzibar Chest*.[5] Of all recent books on Africa's woes, this is essential reading, because if the world is stuck with the United Nations in its present form, we're likely to see such bloodshed again. The way events have been unfolding in Darfur in the Islamic Republic of the Sudan, it is likely to be sooner rather than later.

It is Hartley's view, that had a PMC like Executive Outcomes been allowed to go into Central Africa in what might euphemistically have been termed a pacifying role (this was actually debated behind closed doors at the UN at the time) its personnel could have halted the slaughter. It might have taken a bit of time and lives would have been lost, but nowhere on the scale that took place while the world community sat on its thumbs.

In a related article on post-Cold War mercenaries, *USA Today* reported that "private military companies are working hand in glove with various governments to fight their wars in a businesslike manner." That was followed by observations from Dianne Alden in an article titled "Soldiers R US: The Corporate Military." Among a raft of comments, she suggested that the modern mercenary force "is no longer an unkempt, unprofessional band of soldier wannabes."

Continuing, she said, "They are, for the most part, organized former military officers and enlisted men from all ranks and nations. Ostensibly advisers and strategists, they also conduct warfare in places where official government armies are not prepared to go."

Ed Soyster, a thirty-five year U.S. Army veteran and former director of the Defense Intelligence Agency, added his bit. He said that if you accept that there is a national treasure called retired and former military people, "and if you bring them together to form a company and give them the necessary resources and support, they can accomplish just about anything." Soyster's role as the erstwhile spokesman for Military Professional Resources, Inc. placed him in an excellent position to judge, if only because MPRI remains one of the biggest in the business of PMCs.

Regarding terminology, some prefer the acronym MSPs (military service providers) and still more, like Tom Valentine, a senior vice president of Control Risks Group's Washington offices, prefer the appellation Private Security Companies (PSCs). Like Gary Jackson of Blackwater, Valentine is also a former SEAL: in fact, the two men served together.

Strictly speaking, where MPRI is concerned, one needs to distinguish training from combat support, because the American company does not fight others' wars for them. Whatever they call themselves, all such entities do similar work and, were there no need for their services, they simply wouldn't exist. Underscoring that premise, the private military industry has burgeoned and there is a stock of them.

For its part, MPRI—run by a group of retired generals—handles anything from military training programs in countries facing war to setting up a coast guard service, as they accomplished in Equatorial Guinea. The company also supports the U.S. Department of Defense in the establishment and operation of the Africa Center for Strategic

Studies (ACSS). It used a $3.5 million budget funded by USAID, for instance, to "review the Nigerian military in order to formulate a plan for its professionalization and modernization."

Africa has not been the only theater where MPRI was instrumental in turning things around. During the 1990s the company showed its mettle when it took charge a bunch of ill-disciplined militias that passed for a Croat army and hauled them off to an island off the Dalmatian coast. There, in a remarkably short time they taught these hopefuls a lot of what there was to know about combat and they did it from the bootstraps up. Within a year, this same group—by now relatively responsible and much better disciplined than before—were formed into units under a single central command.

As Ian Bruce tells us in "Guns for Hiring and Firing," these same "one-time nondescript Croats launched Operation Lightning Storm, a counter-offensive which combined tanks, artillery and infantry in an unstoppable assault which drove the Bosnian Serb army out of the Krajina region." In fact, those efforts—coordinated by a dedicated bunch of American professionals—marked the beginning of the end of Serb domination of the Balkans.

The downside is what one veteran termed MPRI's "almost intimate relations" with the Pentagon. Among the majority of undeveloped nations in this unstable era of burgeoning "Washingtonphobia," that kind of conjunction in the long term is likely to become counterproductive. Politics aside, MPRI has acquired an enviable reputation as an organization that can deliver the goods.

Mercenary-related work can take many forms. For instance, more than two decades ago, contracts worth more than $170 million for training Saudi Arabia's National Guard and air force went to the Vinnell Corporation and a sister company, partly owned by Washington's Carlyle merchant banking group. And that in an age when you could do a lot more with a million dollars than today. It is perhaps not coincidental that the company's chairman was former U.S. Secretary of Defense, Frank Carlucci. Vinnell advisors subsequently provided "tactical support" and advice to the Saudi military when, in a spate of brief, bloody battles in 1979, it retook the Al-Haram Grand Mosque in Mecca after armed zealots had occupied it by force.

Although the operation was muddled and innocents died in the crossfire, things might have been very different in Saudi Arabia today had the fundamentalists not been checkmated. They directly threat-

ened the Saudi ruling dynasty, in much the same way that Osama bin
Laden managed to do in the mid-1990s. He was bought off with a
$200 million "incentive" from Riyadh. It is also worth nothing that
two Vinnell-trained Saudi armored brigades fought in the Gulf War
and by some accounts put up a reasonably good show.

More recently, according to P.W. Singer, a Fellow at the Brookings
Institution and author of *Corporate Warriors: The Rise of the
Privatized Military Industry*, during the period from 1994 to 2002, the
Pentagon entered into more than three thousand contracts with pri-
vate military firms. Companies like Halliburton, Vice President Dick
Cheney's former firm, he pointed out, now provide the logistics for
just about every major American military deployment.

"Corporations have even taken over much of military training and
recruiting, including the Reserve Officer Training Corps programs at
more than 200 American universities. (Yes, private employees now
train our military leaders of tomorrow.)," is Singer's view.

Not all the companies involved are American. One of the most
enterprising of the lot is Safenet Security Services, a PMC that started
with twenty men in Baghdad in 2004 and now employs more than fifteen hundred, a significant proportion of them South African. Operating unobtrusively and very low key, the company's unofficial watch-
words are "tactical prudence." Put another way, said Mauritz le
Roux, its chief executive, "Don't go looking for crap. Don't give anybody the opportunity to give you any either."

Safenet's policy appears to work. It has excellent relations with
Iraqis "on both sides of the fence" and gets the done job quietly and
methodically. It is perhaps significant that the company has yet to lose
one of its men in action. At the same time, company convoys and
patrols have come under fire numerous times, attacks that were both
concerted and well-planned and that sometimes took half-an-hour or
more to beat off. Since most of those providing support are veteran
Special Forces personnel who have seen a lot of action in conflicts all
over the globe, they invariably dispense better than they get.

In the long term, the Third World is going to see a lot more of this kind
of freelance military activity. Countries like Nigeria, for instance, offer
marvelous PMC prospects for the future, which is a good reason why
ArmorGroup, a global security consulting and services firm, has been
active there. The company has also worked in nine other countries in
sub-Saharan Africa, though its specialty remains countering threats to

oil operations in Nigeria. Much of the demand for commercial security protection over the past decade, said a spokesman, "was driven by
the need to provide a degree of insulation for expatriate employees
from the rough-and-tumble of daily life and petty crime in Lagos or
Port Harcourt, rather than to protect them against serious threats to
life, which were rare." The company has also dealt with problems
relating to hostage-taking (with dozens of workers being detained at a
time), especially around the drilling platforms in the oil-rich Niger
Delta region, where large ransoms tend to predominate.

Similar trends have been evinced in South and Central America.
According to the Mexican publication *La Jornada*, the U.S. company
Epi Security & Investigation hired a thousand Colombian military and
police veterans to work as mercenaries for U.S. forces Iraq. Salaries
offered were between $2,500 and $5,000 a month, or a good deal less
than what their U.S. counterparts were making. A U.S. source suggested that most of the people were retired military or law enforcement elements that had originally been trained by Americans. Before
that, the Bogota daily *El Tiempo* reported that the U.S. contractor
Halliburton had recruited twenty-five retired Colombian police and
army officers to provide security for oil infrastructure in Iraq. There
were also U.S. media reports that former soldiers from Chile and
Spain had been recruited to beef up Iraqi security forces

Then there is Levdan, one of a variety of low-profile Israeli firms
that peddles military assistance abroad. Not long ago the company
completed a three-year stint in the Congo (Brazzaville) where two
hundred Israelis trained the armed forces, together with the elite guard
that protected President Pascal Lissouba. This Congo Government—
not to be confused with the Democratic Republic of the Congo (DRC)
across the river—afterward agreed to buy more than $10 million
worth of Israeli weapons and military equipment. Not that it did
much good, because soon afterward Lissouba was ousted in a putsch
supported by the Angolan military.

The difference between Israeli PMCs and those from other countries is that the Jewish operators inevitably try to sell the products produced by their country's arms industries. Though more expensive than
similar items from Eastern European states, this material is of good
quality, though not always suited to primitive Third World conditions.

Another company, formerly British and now American
(acquired by the New York Stock Exchange-quoted L3 Communications) is Defense Systems Limited, or DSL, founded by former Guards

and SAS officer Alistair Morrison in 1982. In its day, DSL was a world leader among PMCs. It would provide a variety of services including mine clearing, training of military personnel and provision of security in Algerian oil fields, Columbia and many other countries, as well as administrative support for UN operations. DSL boat teams have been active in offshore counterinsurgency operations in Angola's Cabinda oilfields.

Looking at the broader, international perspective, it is Africa that could most urgently use help from the private security community. The problem, however, is that the majority of states that need assistance the most are broke.

In the case of Sierra Leone, for instance, Neall Ellis has been battling for over two years to get the million dollars-plus he is owed. In theory, the Sierra Leone government could, with American help, have used a company like the private security firm International Charter Incorporated of Oregon (ICI) to do its air work, but then they wouldn't have done the fighting. Instead, in the modern era, this organization is at the forefront of the kind of non-combat services that a PMC is able to offer. In a briefing, Danny O'Brien, ICI's chief executive officer, told me that his is a Civilian Aviation and Government Services company, at one stage the prime contractor in Sierra Leone after 2000.

"We worked directly for the United States Department of State, USAID, and OFDA," he declared. When ICI was involved in the evacuation of the American Embassy in Liberia and brought in reinforcements in 2002–03, that was a State Department contract, O'Brien said. While still operating in Sierra Leone, the ICI directorate had allocated about twenty hours a week to that country's army. Its Russian-built helicopters (see Chapter 3) also flew free hours for some NGOs such as Geneva's International Committee of the Red Cross.

PMCs and PSCs have also distinguished themselves in the aftermath of natural, as well as man-made disasters. When the damage following a series of devastating earthquakes in Pakistan and surrounding regions was still being assessed toward the end of 2005, ICI's Danny O'Brien sent me a brief e-mail which read: "Just checking in from Pakistan. We have been flying our trusty Mi-8's in support of The Earthquake Relief Mission."

The disaster had barely happened when O'Brien got a call from the U.S. State Department to move his men and machines into action, half a world away from where they had been operating in the Sudan.

Attached to his message were a bunch of photos, one of which is to be found in this book.

The projects embraced by this kind of PMC are remarkably cosmopolitan. Danny O'Brien traditionally uses Russian pilots to crew his Mi-8 helicopters, and for very good reason, he adds. "For a start, the Federal Aviation Authority (FAA) would never allow a civilian 'N' registered aircraft or helicopter to fly in the zones we work. In any event, American civilian pilots are sometimes impossible to work with, especially once the shooting starts. I have had this experience, and don't wish to repeat it.

"Also, you must accept that the Russian CAA does not allow mixed crews to fly in 'RA' registered aircraft.

"More important, as far as operational capability is concerned, we have the additional advantage that Russian aircraft design philosophy is such that it is possible for us to perform heavy maintenance in the field using in-house [Russian] engineers. We can repair radios down to the component level, replace engines and main gear boxes in the field. It would be extremely difficult to achieve that kind of versatility with Western machines. In fact, considering where some of our missions take us, that is a huge plus!

"Last, ICI's pilots are unmatched anywhere in the world. Our captains average twelve thousand hours as PIC. More salient, they are trained for conditions in the arctic, the desert, over water as well as for any kind of mountain operation. They have thousands of flying hours in uncontrolled airspace, most of it at low level.

"In addition, I can only say that they have big balls. They don't whine about money and many have run unauthorized cross-border missions with the company and have never said a word.

"But that is something about which I will not expand," were O'Brien's final words on the subject.

Asked about moral issues surrounding what an interviewer termed "Murder for Profit," British author and UN authority William Shawcross spoke candidly about the use of mercenaries.

"Obviously, money has always been the issue," he replied, adding that all soldiers are paid. "I don't see that it really matters whether they are working for the ministry of defense of, say, Bangladesh, or employed by a private security company that is regulated and is transparent.

"What we are arguing about here, is that these should not be mercenaries of the old traditional 'dogs of war' type. They would have to be private companies whose dealings were entirely open and accessible to the United Nations, or whoever it was that was employing them. . . . Now all these things are not easy, and I'm not saying that this is a panacea for all the world's problems. But I do think that if we in the West are confronted with horrible images on television and say that something must be done, then something must be done."

As a postscript he added that this was an alternative that global leaders should look at "very seriously and rather quickly." Also, if the international community wished to put the world to rights and were not prepared to sacrifice their own troops, "then governments like that of Sierra Leone should have the right to call upon forces from elsewhere." That seemed to him to be "not an immoral proposition in any way whatsoever."

Clearly the industry has flourished, though rarely to its credit because the civilized world is prone to be critical of people who are prepared to take lives for cash, even if they are fighting terror and losing some of their own in the process. Writing in the US Army War College Quarterly *Parameters*, Lt-Col Thomas K. Adams—an unusually prescient observer of these disciplines—declared that there were three basic types of mercenaries.

The first, he said, might be called the "traditional" type, consisting of groups or individuals that have military skills directly applicable to combat or immediate combat support. These are basic, industrial-age and hi-tech forces. An example would be Russian and Ukrainian ex-military aviators flying jet fighters for the Congo government. A generation ago, this group included individuals who responded to ads in macho, true-to-type magazines. Since then, things have changed.

Consider the deal by the Moscow-based Sukhoi Design Bureau to provide Su-27 jet fighters to Ethiopia for its war with Eritrea in the late 1990s. Although the Addis Ababa government was anxious to acquire modern fighters, it lacked the pilots to fly them. As part of the agreement, the firm included former Soviet military airmen and ground crews. They delivered a compact little air force to Africa's troubled Horn that in the end crippled Eritrea.

By the time it was over, there were former Soviet Union pilots flying MiG fighters on both sides. During a previous phase of hostilities, *US News and World Report* carried the story of Colonel Vyacheslav Myzin, depicting him emerging from the cockpit of one of Ethiopia's newly acquired Su-27s after a demonstration flight. He was labeled one of Africa's "new mercenaries."

The second type, says Adams, is a late 20th-century phenomenon: fairly large companies that provide the services of a "general staff" in one of the more developed countries. They provide high quality tactical, operational and strategic advice for the structure, training, equipping and employment of armed forces. This, he explained, was what MPRI had to offer. There are also specialized companies like AirScan, which offers "airborne surveillance and security operations" as well as specialized consulting services for a variety of companies, particularly those involved in government or the oil industry. Last heard, clients in its portfolio included the U.S. Department of the Interior and some multinational oil giants in Angola and elsewhere.

Other companies in this category—such as Freetown's Southern Cross Security—might have both military and civilian skills performing functions such as personnel protection, signal intercepts, computer "cracking," secure communications and technical surveillance. Until recently, Southern Cross also operated an anti-piracy and fish poaching division off the West African coast out of Freetown in conjunction with the European Union.

Obviously, says Adams, none of these skills emerged overnight. They took time to develop. Also, they tend to draw on the expertise and disciplines that could only come with close involvement in a sophisticated military environment.

South Africa's Executive Outcomes slotted very neatly into the first and second categories. In its day it effectively represented what Adams termed "the expanded model of the military contractor." It did spectacularly well in such a short time that it astonished everybody when it unexpectedly wound down its affairs at the end of the millennium. Those close to the organization say that South African government pressure had a lot to do with it.

One of EO's founders told me that there were quite a few ancillary factors that contributed to the closure: "We just felt it was time to pull down the shutters."

The move was apparently precipitated as much by a lack of new contracts as questions about how much had been earned, who was supposed to pay taxes, to whom and so on. Though almost all transactions were offshore, there were governments eager to claim their piece of the action. But this became rather involved, not least because the company had financial links to a variety of commercial organizations abroad. Even today those connections remain contorted.

Then there was the issue, possibly, that EO sometimes did not take as many prisoners as some would have liked. Because of this, there were those among its staff who believed that war crimes might eventually become an issue, though in the harsh reality of what has been going on in this distant West African jungle, that would be absurd. In reality, hardly anybody in Sierra Leone (or Angola, for that matter) took prisoners unless there was a very good reason to do so. More to the point, few of those involved in those bitter struggles—on both sides of the front—had ever heard of Geneva, never mind its namesake convention that dictates the actions of combatants in wartime.

While much of what took place in the back and beyond in Sierra Leone could probably never be condoned in terms of international or any other law, there was sometimes good reason for EO combatants to act as their own judges and executioners. One example will do:

In Sierra Leone's eastern hills, one of their units came on a village where everybody had been murdered. The women had had branches rammed up their vaginas in a particularly brutal manner that must surely have resulted in some of these pathetic souls dying of shock. It was truly dreadful.

A youngster emerged from the bush shortly after the EO squad got there and said that the rebels had terrorized them all. His entire family was dead, he cried, saying that he had only escaped because he was fetching water when the rebels arrived and he had heard the desperate cries. So rather than show himself, he hid.

The mercenaries—all of them black except for two white officers —were incensed. There was no question that these mindless atrocities cried out for vengeance. The child indicated a path that the perpetrators had taken and, at a trot, the group headed down it. Twenty minutes later, the rebels were found laughing and drinking at the next village. Seven of the eight-man insurgent group was killed. By this time the rescuers weren't looking to arrest anybody who might or might not eventually come to trial.

Sir John Keegan phrased this kind of circumstance rather eloquently in a recent piece for his paper, *The Daily Telegraph*. Quoting in the original Latin, he called it *inter arma silent leges*, which, roughly translated, says there is no law on the battlefield. That might be a useful precept for some of my more vociferous colleagues to remember when they report from Iraq. A ruthless enemy with homicidal/suicidal tendencies can not always be met by forebearance.

It's actually quite easy to offer your services to fight in some of the more obscure destinations of the world. Jim Penrith, then working for Johannesburg's Argus Africa News Service, was, as we saw in Chapter Eight, almost recruited in a Kampala bar to fight in the Congo.

These days, all you really need is a decent military background, preferably with good (and verifiable) combat experience and perhaps half a dozen friends with similar proclivities. Having spent time in uniform, you've probably read appropriate books, as well as magazines like *Soldier of Fortune* and Britain's *Combat & Survival*. No doubt you will have access to the right websites and there are a lot of them.

Having established your parameters—and perhaps even made a preliminary approach to a specific government—a single discreetly worded advertisement in the Johannesburg *Star* or one of the Moscow or Kiev dailies (in Russian) is likely to prompt scores of inquiries. Usually the return address is abroad because some countries, the United States in particular, have laws about its citizens fighting under foreign flags, though that does not seem to have affected PMCs in the Middle East.

Veterans from some former Eastern bloc countries are available for as little as $600 a month, though most aren't noted either for reliability or proficiency. For that, you pay what the British or American markets will bear and it doesn't come cheap. Remember that a British Army private earns about $2,000 a month and a major as much as $75,000 a year. But then you are getting top-drawer quality, backed by years of training and expertise.

South Africa has any number of experienced soldiers of fortune for hire. Because of a depressed economy and, for a long while, an unstable rand, many veterans of that country's insurgency wars were looking for jobs. These days South African war dogs come relatively cheap, though field commanders everywhere (except from Balkan states) are paid roughly the same as their counterparts in places like the Congo and Angola.

As for hardware, you can buy most of the basics off the shelf in countries such as Bulgaria, Romania and elsewhere in Eastern Europe. There's a lot of surplus about in the warehouses of some of the CIS states, where good military materiel can be had at much less than you'd pay for the same kind of thing in London or Paris.

A good Asian copy of the American M-16, for instance, comes at about $350. A crude crib of the AR-10 costs even less, though Thailand's version of Heckler & Koch's 33/93 needs solid input if you're going to force costs down. But, as one gun enthusiast suggested, why buy NATO calibers when there are AKs a-plenty out there, and they're going at about a quarter the price? Standard squad weapons like the RPK, the Degtyarev DPM light machine gun or the PKM might cost a bit more, depending where they come from and how many rounds have been through their barrels. Anybody with reliable Serbian contacts can get a container-load of the old Yugoslavian M76s wholesale.

Scratch a bit and you're likely to come up with a few Israeli, Ukrainian or South African dealers who handle more complex items such as claymores, grenades and mortars. Be circumspect about your dealings: they're usually under surveillance when they're in someone else's town and the activities of most of them have been highlighted not only on the web, but also by Interpol.

With armor, there's enough good surplus material floating about in Europe to satisfy most needs. You should be able to come up with sufficient BMP-2 infantry fighting vehicles to put a couple of divisions into the field and they're relatively cheap, too. Quality refurbished versions can be had for as little as $100,000, but that doesn't include shipping and their engines will probably need some attention.

Don't bother going heavier: tanks are usually more of a hindrance than a help in primitive terrain, a description that fits just about all of sub-Saharan Africa north of the Zambezi.

You can even buy what you need in South Africa, where there are six hundred companies vying for arms contracts.[6] A UN report accused the Pretoria government in April 2005 of ignoring international arms embargoes and supplying a host of countries that were involved in cross-border conflicts, insurgencies, internal suppression and other iniquities with weapons of war. Mentioned in this regard were Uganda, Rwanda, Zambia, the Sudan, Ethiopia and others. Because a finger was pointed at the biggest culprit of all, the state-owned Denel corporation, it is unlikely that the top echelons of government in South Africa—including the president—were unaware of the transactions. As the report implied, money was at the core of it, but then that is the story with most of Africa.

When I was last in Freetown, Neall Ellis had prepared a proposal for a small force of eighty-eight combatants (including sixteen Air Wing personnel). It was the size of a force that he believed he could put together at short notice. The proposal covered operations over a sixty-day period and involved communications equipment, protection, logistics, support, a small field hospital (with medical staff) as well as the positioning of personnel and equipment.

He listed a requirement of about fifty thousand gallons of Jet A-1 aviation fuel (at plus/minus US$1.60 a gallon) together with about three thousand gallons of diesel. To that, Nellis added capital equipment costs at $1.5m each for two Mi-17/7 medium transport helicopters plus their respective spares packages. Also essential, he reckoned, would be a light reconnaissance aircraft plus night vision equipment at $150,000. Overall, he believed that about half a million dollars would cover ammunition. Transport, probably from Eastern Europe, would be another $150,000.

Nellis' total package (with a ten-percent contingency for the two-month period) amounted to just short of $4 million, which is perhaps a little more than what Sierra Leone's UN operation cost the international community toward the end of that war for roughly forty-eight hours work. Extend this activity to a year—without having to spend on more capital items—and it would average out at even less.

A more elaborate breakdown for what he termed "A Proposal for Deployment of Air and Ground Forces—Two Months" such as what was offered to Mobutu's government toward the end of that rule was calculated as follows, though bear in mind that he had Africa in mind here. In the Middle East or Asia these costs could feasibly double.

And if these prices appear to be basement bargains, bear in mind that all this took place in the late 1990s. By early 2006, many of these amounts might have doubled, fuel and expatriate manpower costs especially.

TWO-MONTH DEPLOYMENT OF AIR AND GROUND FORCES
(In U.S. Currency)

1. Salaries – 72 ground force personnel	1,313,000
2. Salaries – 16 air wing personnel	240,000
3. Salaries SLA troops	187,500
4. Rations: two months—163 person @ US$20/day plus 20 percent[7]	202,120
5. Field Hospital, medical equip plus supplies	150,000
6. Charter fees/air fares for positioning and repositioning of personnel and equipment	225,000
7. Logistics, administrative and communication equipment	192,000
8. Jet A-1 Aviation fuel—53,000 US gals @ $1.62/gallon	188,730

9. Diesel – 3,000 gals @US$2.00/gallon	16,020
TOTAL:	2,714,370
"Contingency" payments at 10 percent[8]	271,437
TOTAL FOR THE GROUP FOR TWO MONTHS	$2,985,807

CAPITAL EQUIPMENT COSTS

1. Two Mi-17/8 medium transport helicopters plus spares package	3,000,000
2. One light reconnaissance aircraft plus night vision equipment	150,000
3. Mi-24 ammunition requirements	600,000
4. Transport costs	150,000
TOTAL:	$3,900,000

RENEWAL OF CONTRACT—88 TROOPS FOR ONE MONTH

1. Salaries 72 ex-pat personnel, Ground Force	536,500
2. Salaries 16 ex-pat personnel Air Wing	120,000
3. Rations for one month 163 personnel @ $20 per day/ per person	101,060
4. Medical equipment and supplies	40,000
5. Charter fees for positioning + repositioning personnel and equipment	40,000
6. Logistics, administrative and communication equip.	50,000
7. Jet A-1 Aviation fuel	94,770
8. Diesel and oil for vehicles	8,010
TOTAL:	990,340
"Contingency" fees	99,034
TOTAL REQUIRED FOR ONE MONTH	$1,089,374

Obviously, the majority of those involved would be locals who customarily would be paid less than expatriates. Second, the number of personnel for such an "Air Wing" would, of necessity, be flexible. It would vary according to the number and type of aircraft available.

The medical requirement that Nellis had in mind included medevac by air and hospitalization of wounded in South Africa, though (as with Executive Outcomes) it included finance for a personal death insurance fund payable to the dependents of Air Wing members killed in the line of duty. Also, there would be the repatriation of bodies as well as funeral costs. Any unused funds to be returned to government on completion of the operation.

Apart from medicines/equipment, food and communication systems, the client government would be required to provide all other logistical requirements, including vehicles, aircraft, fuel, weapons and ammunition. If these were not available, the contractor would be in a position to source all requirements for government account. All this stuff would remain in country on completion of the contract.

If the services of the "Air Wing" so formed, were required beyond the initial two-month contract period, the monthly contractual amount payable in advance would be US$4,700,000.

Why Neall Ellis remains a proponent of Russian helicopters has puzzled a lot of people who have done business with him. The answer is that he is not. He favors them in Sierra Leone, first, because they are there, and second because, like his old friend Danny O'Brien of ICI, they are low-cost, and spares can be found just about everywhere. In a worst-case scenario, if one of his Hinds was crippled because of the lack of a spare part, somebody from State House could fly to Guinea in a couple of hours and do a backhanded deal. With the right kind of incentive, he could be back with the item before nightfall.

Nellis has always said that if he could choose an alternate machine, his first option for a medium-sized transport chopper would be something akin to the French-built Super Puma, or even better, the South African Oryx, the latter an excellent upgrade on the standard Puma. These aircraft are easy to fly and visibility from the cockpit is better than from any Russian helicopter, particularly for night operations, which is vital for African conditions where helicopters often have to put down in bush clearings.

As for combat, he has good reason to stand by the Hind, which, for the price, is unbeatable. With a normal take-off weight of about twelve tons, it might be a little heavier than most, but that is offset by reliability.

"Look after it, keep it serviced, and it'll remain useful longer than most Western machines," he told one inquiring writer who was predisposed to what was coming out of the U.S.. Nellis asked him pointedly why he should buy an Apache for between $20m to $26m (depending on options)—which, granted, was top of the range—when he could get something similar from Moscow for a fraction of that figure? Anyway, he added, most times the Apache didn't slot into the kind of environment encountered in primitive regions. Albania—when Kosovo was in flames—was a case in point, he suggested, though since then Afghanistan has proved otherwise.

"Like most pedigrees, the Apache also needs a helluva lot of attention. It must be finely tuned and that becomes expensive when U.S. Air Force technicians are not around. Western ground crews in outlandish places cost a mint since most demand the same kind of facilities that they get back home."

The Mi-24 is different. "It flies anywhere at any time. It can do exactly the same work as the Apache with a quarter of the down time." It was great for Europe, he stated, "but Africa is something else: ask anybody who has fought out there." With the Hind, says Nellis, you can fly more than six hundred nautical miles by fitting four external fuel tanks, which is a comparatively simple task. "That's a lot of hours sitting cramped in the cockpit."

One of the principal characteristics that differentiate today's private military companies from the ad hoc groupings of freelance soldiers of the 1960s and 1970s is that they have a clear structure built along corporate lines. MPRI, for example, is a massive organization structured in the traditional American manner with a full executive, topped by a CEO. The same is true of Blackwater USA.

The new companies are defined, incorporated entities intended to continue in perpetuity. What they are not are bands of individuals who have been recruited to carry out a single contractual obligation. This is a fundamental rationale for reconsidering the definition and applicability of the term "mercenary."

At the same time, it is a difficult tag to shake. While with Executive Outcomes—an organization whose leaders vigorously discouraged the use of the word—most of the field commanders I encountered would relish the notoriety that it bestowed, though that revelation usually came after a beer or six.

"We're mercenaries. What else? It's fooling nobody to give us any other sort of name," said Hennie Blaauw, in his day among the best combat commanders in a Boer tradition that goes back two centuries. In the final stages of South Africa's border wars, Blaauw headed the most active of the five Reconnaissance Regiments.

As Sandline said in an insightful paper titled "Should the Activities of Private Military Companies be Transparent?," there will always be ad-hoc groups such as the unfocused and unruly bunch of Bosnian freebooters that were deployed to the former Zaire in 1996. "They are harder to control and regulate and also less likely to apply internationally accepted standards to operations of their own." Also, it was suggested that the growth of active PMCs had overtaken the embryonic regulatory framework, both at national and international levels.

As a consequence, PMCs for the most part, have developed their own set of operating principles and processes of self-regulation. Certainly the most important factor that distinguishes PMCs from the distant "dogs of war" is that they are prepared to work only for the "good guys," which means legitimate clients. Neall Ellis, for example, employed as a combat pilot on contract to the government of Sierra Leone, would not long ago have been damned as a mercenary.

Nellis, in the meantime, has traveled the long road. It says something that he has finally achieved acceptance by the international community, because he never took any kind of action in isolation from the war effort. In his role as the country's lone combat pilot, he operated directly under the command and control of the Chief of Defense Staff of the Sierra Leone Army. As he told me, if he didn't follow orders, he'd have been out of a job long ago.

Had Sandline been permitted to act—before Tony Blair's government stepped in and forced the company out of Sierra Leone—the international community would have been spared the carnage that followed in the wake of a rebel onslaught that lasted several years. Also spared would have been billions of dollars thrown away on a moribund UN operation that in the end yielded nothing but discord and irreverence. It was finally a British military presence, backed by powerful input from both the Royal Navy and Royal Marines that eventually put a close to the war, and it is no revelation that the United Nations spent almost all their time in Sierra Leone as spectators.

Push this concept up a notch or two and the real benefit would have been the saving of tens of thousands of innocent lives, never mind the untold number of amputations, mutilations, rapes, and the million or so souls that were displaced by ongoing hostilities. The true stories behind many of the atrocities and numbers killed by the rebels will never be known.

The only company, so far, to have come directly to grips with the kind of savagery espoused by the rebels of Foday Sankoh's Revolutionary United Front is Executive Outcomes, with whom Sandline's executives maintained close ties over several years.

As Michael Grunberg says, over a twenty-one-month period, an average of about a hundred and fifty EO soldiers, supported by a solitary gunship (and then only for part of the time) together with two transport helicopters, did their thing in Sierra Leone and turned the war around. Apart from retraining elements of the Sierra Leone Army, they drove the rebels back from the edge of Freetown and systematically destroyed their fighting capability in the bush. The cost was a modest $20 million a year, including provision of all the necessary equipment.

The result of EO's intervention was the signing, in November 1996, of a set of peace accords between the rebels and the government. Part of the deal, ultimately, was that EO's service should be terminated. And when that happened, the rebels abrogated the peace accord and sent their people back into the bush. Within a hundred days of EO's departure, the rebels were easily able to orchestrate another coup.

Enter Nigeria and the intervention of a ten thousand-strong regional military force named ECOMOG, again advised and assisted by Sandline. After the British company had gone, the UN stepped in and deployed a mammoth force totaling thirteen thousand, sometimes more. It also had a billion-dollar-a-year budget and more freeloaders that any comparably-sized force in the history of modern warfare.

The situation would have been a joke were the consequences not so serious.

From the earliest, ultra-critical days, the media attempted to monitor the activities of Executive Outcomes. South Africa had just emerged from the apartheid era and since the public face of EO was white and well versed in some of the more unsavory aspects of inter-territorial conflict, their motives, as some observers proclaimed, simply had to be devious. It had been so in the past, was the argument: so what made the new boys on the block any different?

It didn't help that the EO executive was almost paranoid about the press, as are almost all of these organizations that would rather get on with the job than try to justify what they do to scribes. And therein lies the rub.

Despite all the publicity surrounding the Gulf War, ten years of conflict in the Balkans as well as what is currently ongoing in the Middle East, quite a few so-called combat correspondents don't begin to know the difference between an Armalite and an AK. Still, EO did make tentative efforts to show the world how it had turned the war about in Angola and later, Sierra Leone.

Time magazine ran a major feature on EO in May 1997, where it described the company as one of the world's leading purveyors of private military muscle. Peculiarly for a magazine that usually takes a strictly politically correct line, it had kind words for chief executive Eeben Barlow, who was "fast becoming the soldier-of-fortune set's answer to GE's Jack Welch."

It described Barlow as a slim, fair-haired, forty-year-old "military marketeer extraordinary." The magazine went on: "He puts a cheery face on one of the world's oldest professions, mercenaries or 'military consultants' as most prefer to be known." *Time* highlighted Barlow's earlier work as a one-time intelligence agent for a South African military unit that, it said, carried out assassinations. "But now he prefers gray flannels to fatigues."

EO was high profile in those days. "At an arms show in Abu Dhabi in 1997, the Executive Outcomes booth quietly competed for business with mercenaries from Britain, France and the U.S.," the magazine reported.

Shortly before that, American journalist Elizabeth Rubin spent time with EO in Sierra Leone. Having returned from West Africa after she had gone into the diamond fields with the mercs, she told of her experiences in an unusually detailed article in New York's *Harpers* magazine.[9] EO reckoned itself to be "a kind of advance team" for the UN, she wrote.

"You cannot keep peace if there is no peace, as we saw in Bosnia," Eeben Barlow told her. Referring to the group's operations in Angola (and Sierra Leone, in particular) he went on: "But we can help the country achieve some sort of stability before the UN comes in."

Rubin recounts how EO was founded in 1989 and how, a year later, Barlow had already established the company as a counterintelligence consultancy, numbering among its client base his former employer, the SA Defence Force, as well as the De Beers diamond cartel. Barlow's links to a shadowy South African military-linked undercover group known as CCB, that had agents operating in all the countries in which the apartheid regime (and its enemies) had interests, appeared to help, she suggested.

She told how Barlow chose for his company logo the paladin, the same chessboard knight once featured in the old TV series "Have Gun, Will Travel," because "I like the way it moves on the world board." Like most people in the business, he deplored the use of the word "mercenary." Rather, he preferred to view the organization as "a team of troubleshooters, marketing a strategy of recovery to failing governments around the world."

She went on: "In exchange for millions of dollars, the company offers to do what the United Nations cannot and will not do: take sides, deploy overwhelming force, and fire 'preemptively' on its contractually designated enemy." With a force of between two and three hundred, the numbers could hardly be construed as "overwhelming," she stated. It was the same in Angola where EO turned around a civil war that had been on the go intermittently for the best part of a quarter century. There, EO deployed at most, perhaps five hundred men. At any given time it was usually less than half that.

For an American—a nation traditionally opposed to killing for cash—Ms. Rubin was remarkably forthcoming about EO's position in West Africa. Further, she was giving a firsthand report about a difficult subject, having made the effort get to EO's field headquarters deep in the interior. She ended up staying a while, living rough with a tough bunch of rugger buggers, sharing their food, beer and a lot else besides. In doing so, she was privy to much of what went on within EO that was otherwise denied the press.

Speaking of the people at the diamond town, "Many felt . . . indebted to the soldiers of Executive Outcomes, whom they rather fantastically imagined had come in a gesture of pan-African generosity. . . . The South African mercenaries, camped on a nearby hilltop overlooking Koidu, were unreservedly hailed by the chiefs, the businessmen and the street people as saviors."

Ms. Rubin quickly discovered that the local residents actually loved this peculiar band of brothers. Recounting, she was unequivocal that they had brought stability to the land. More important, they had done what they had been paid for and that was to drive the hated rebels back across the Liberian frontier. Pitifully, they were to return not long after EO had gone home.

An interesting aside is that one of her "sponsors"—a mercenary like the rest who had hosted her at Koidu—ended up in a British prison not long afterward. With Executive Outcomes disbanded and he out of work, he'd tried to smuggle a planeload of marijuana from Africa on to a deserted airfield in the south of England. The British police were waiting for him.

As they say, it takes all types.

EPILOGUE

At this writing it is the situation in Iraq, and to a lesser extent in Afghanistan and other Third World military deployments, that is of most immediate concern to the private military and security companies. Sources in Baghdad talk about thirty to fifty thousand of these people active throughout Saddam Hussein's former domain. Every one of them costs money and the United States is paying for much of it.

Gregory Lovett, a former police officer, has been in Iraq almost from the start of the current phase of hostilities, working security for Halliburton. We'd first made contact when he returned from Baghdad in the summer of 2004 and have kept in touch ever since. Lovett features prominently in a book I was working on at the time which deals with cops who had been shot and survived.[1]

In Lovett, I discovered a man whose mind could best be described as a series of locked cupboards guarded by the cherubs of self-discipline. Someone in Arkansas had suggested that he was the original no-nonsense cop. In Baghdad, he'd worked first with a K-9 Squad, and then in VIP protection against suicide bombers and like-minded religious zealots. Before that, he had been in Kosovo, operating with about a hundred and fifty others out of Ferzi, a small town just beyond Pristina. Lovett's views are instructive, in part because he sees things the way they are. Also, he likes the job and has no axe to grind. He is also astonishingly blunt about the industry's shortcomings. I quote:

"Overall the private security companies seem to fall into two areas now that things are starting to get 'civilized.' We have rules to follow and our activities are carefully monitored by a myriad of organizations, many of them eager to bring us into disrepute. Our hardest task masters are our own bosses. Step out of line and you're on your way home.

"You have your 'High Speed' companies such as Blackwater USA, Triple Canopy and the rest . . . all of which are reputable companies. They are doing everything from executive protection, K-9, to static

579

guard positions at embassys and palaces. These types of companies are usually hired by what is termed 'Other Government Agencies' as well as larger companies that are not necessarily hampered by budget restraints. Also, they have the political pull to get the large contracts awarded . . . they are here for the long haul.

"Obviously, they are very expensive but are usually very good at what they do. In this environment, you get what you pay for."

As Lovett explains, the vast majority of companies in Iraq are connected in some fashion with the United States program that has been termed "Reconstruction of Iraq." They provide protection for construction personnel, engineers, road convoys and ancillary activities. One example of money spent, as elucidated by Gregg Nivala, a spokesperson working out of the American Embassy in Baghdad, was that two million of nine million dollars budgeted to exhume a mass grave in the southern Muthanna Province of Iraq was paid to a security firm to guard the diggers.

But as Lovett points out, as with all private companies, the bottom line is profit. That, in turn, leads to another expression in the jargon of multifaceted security work called "acceptable losses": equipment and personnel which can be written off, all of which needs to be factored in against what a company can make out of a deal.

On the negative side, he points to some construction and security companies that are of the "fly by night" variety.

"On the face of it, some of these organizations come into Iraq and get a contract with the Defense Department. Or perhaps a security contract with the U.S. State Department. In achieving this, they underbid just about everyone, often by millions of dollars, knowing full well that they will only operate in the country a year or two at most. Then there are those who take the money and run, especially since in this business, companies get a large proportion of the contract cash up front, added to which they are also allowed a usually generous period of grace to get things moving.

"The truth is that some of the companies never even get off the ground, while there are others that operate—after a fashion—but are unable to provide services for which they were contracted. It is these companies that end up giving the rest of the people doing this kind of work an unsavory reputation."[2]

"What I have personally observed is a company that hires a security manager, usually a good experienced individual with solid Special Forces credentials, coupled perhaps to a string of good qualifications.

The bosses then rely on this man not only to hire security officers but also to train them, which is difficult when you're dealing with individuals with little or no prior military experience.

"And when you accept that the going rate for a 'qualified shooter' is earning anything from five hundred to a thousand dollars a day — which is average—you're talking about big bucks.

"But I also know companies here that hire what is known as 'Third Country Nationals' or TCNs for as little as fifty dollars a day as 'shooters' and pay even less for static guard positions at checkpoints. Then they wonder why the so-called 'bad guys'—the Qaedists or Sunni insurrectionists—are able to get into secured areas and blow stuff up."

According to Lovett, the majority of the TCN's are from India, the Philippines, and Nepal, though there are increasing numbers of potential recruits coming in from South and Central America. Most of these people, he concedes, are hard working people. They are doing a job in trying to provide for their families. But at the end of it, the majority of them shouldn't be at the business end of an automatic weapon.

Lovett: "As with a K-9 company I know . . . they were charging their clients two thousand dollars a day per dog. Multiply that by thirty and it comes to something like sixty thousand dollars a month per dog. And since they paid their handlers a paltry five thousand a month and provided only the most basic facilities and equipment, the profit margin is huge. That particular company had anything between thirty and forty dog handlers on their books and was/is making a killing."

The trouble is, he stressed, it is all being done with American taxpayers' money.

"What is happening," says Lovett, "is that many of the qualified and reputable security companies that arrived at the beginning of the Iraqi debacle established for themselves very good and reliable bases of operations. These were the ones that were instrumental in getting construction and trucking companies up and running and, in turn, got the funds for all these projects.

"But as everybody knows, each government contract lasts a year, As with every business involved in this scenario, they have to resubmit their bids on an annual basis. So now that these businesses are on relatively firm ground and running smoothly it is perhaps only natural that they should look at ways of expanding their profits. It is all part of the Western system.

"At the same time, these firms were good at what they did. Some of them were outstanding. Everybody would make mistakes, but generally things went well. Moreover, it was axiomatic that since qualified security companies provided good protection, hostile actions and losses were kept at a minimum and it wasn't long—in spite of a lot of things wrong on the periphery of the civil war—things appeared to be reasonably secure.

"Indirectly, you had clients now beginning to think that they no longer needed the same level of protection as before. So they would toy with the idea of saving money by cutting back on protection costs, which, of course, is absurd. It's kind of like canceling your car insurance because you haven't had an accident. Then things start to snowball.

"Enter into the equation a host of security companies that start by underbidding their competitors, the very same security companies that originally paved the way for this to be allowed to happen. These are security firms that pay their shooters and static guards fifty dollars a day (sometimes less) coupled to what can generously be termed 'less than stellar' living quarters. It really doesn't need a rocket scientist to see where all this is headed.

"Concurrently, with most people in the United States wanting to pull the troops out and questioning the billions of dollars that are being spent, Washington simply has to find a way to cut down on the spending and lower the troop numbers. The result is that the bids go to not to the most qualified companies or individuals, but rather to the most cost-efficient."

Greg Lovett's final comments, made in an e-mail from Baghdad on December 3, 2005 are instructive. The bottom line here, he said, "is that the overall security situation is far worse than it was when I got here in 2003. And it's not going to get better anytime soon.

"We have to face the fact that the civil war is here. It is just that nobody wants to put that kind of spin on it, with the media grabbing at anything that can make America and Americans look bad. Not yet, anyway.

"I used to drive from here at the airport area in Baghdad to the Green Zone on Route Irish by myself. I did so many times in the past. It was risky, of course, but that was the job—it came with the package. Now that very same Route Irish is proclaimed to be the most dangerous stretch of road in the world.

"Curiously, we have a bit of the old déjà vu here: the same kind of problem that our people experienced previously in Vietnam. Fact is, the enemy is constantly active. It changes its methods and tactics as well as its deployments daily. Being fanatical, it has a steady supply of human resources to draw on, which is why we've had so many suicide bombings: they take enormous risks and as a consequence they are able to cause enormous damage. On our side, some very experienced, extremely well-qualified people are brought in to cope with the war. They're the ones who are expected to turn things around. Then you hear them whisper about not being allowed to do their job. Others complain about the inability to complete their missions. But they're not too vocal about it, because such things aren't good for career advancement.

"Some people, I fear, would rather that we look good rather than be good. And heaven knows 'we' don't want to offend anyone while the nation is fighting a war.

"Right now I am involved with the mail convoy security, although I have been moved up the 'food chain' and have been riding a desk for sometime. I still manage to sneak outside the wire from time to time for some fresh air.

"Since 2003 our operation has lost nine personnel, all of them killed in enemy actions. And that doesn't include the wounded."

Some of Lovett's comments about moving about on Iraqi roads are instructive. As he says, "Drive like you stole it!" is the motto among those using Route Irish to get between the Green Zone and Baghdad Airport. He goes on: "The main supply routes (MSR) here in Baghdad are all patrolled by the U.S. military and the Iraqi military as well as the Iraqi police. All have checkpoints along each route.

"In theory, it should not be difficult to maintain some kind of control since the highways are much like the ones in the states—most of the main ones are four lanes (two each direction). But in the Baghdad area the routes are lined with houses, apartments, small villages and the rest, so it's not a problem for the Qaedists, Baathists, or just whoever wants to kill Americans to wait for the MSR patrols to go by, slip out and plant a bomb or set up an ambush. Sometimes these roadside bombs are planted in plain view of Iraqi troops or police. The Iraqi police and military have been infiltrated, though to what extent is anyone's guess.

"The distance from the BIAP (Baghdad International Airport) area to the Green Zone is about ten miles. The route has numerous on and off ramps and overpasses. Attacks are common along all parts of the route, but the on and off ramps where traffic has to slow down is the favorite. Like regular security forces, it is at these points where many of the contracting companies have taken losses. "And it's not getting any easier . . ."

Clearly, the concept of private military or private security companies is a modern-day phenomenon that has taken hold within the international security establishment. This becomes apparent from a paper titled "Expeditionary Forces for Post Modern Europe" delivered by Colonel James Wither to the Conflict Study Research Centre in March 2005, which makes a salient argument for the establishment of unconventional, privately run military forces.[3]

According to Colonel Wither, "Few governments are willing to pay the financial and political price of diverting resources from domestic health, education and social priorities in order to enhance military capabilities in an era of unprecedented peace in Europe. As a result, the bulk of the EU's soldiers may be ill-prepared both technically and psychologically for the kind of high intensity combat that might be necessary during an expeditionary operation."

Further, declares Wither, the response of some soldiers from EU states to the more demanding peacekeeping tasks on recent operations has already raised concerns about their combat readiness, although it is only fair to note that many peacekeeping contingents have had to operate within very restrictive rules of engagement imposed by governments anxious to avoid casualties that could undermine domestic support for their policies.

One of the immediate deductions made by Colonel Wither—and which is seminal to being able to make long security projections where these pertain to Europe or possibly some Third World conflagration, is that the armed forces of the new EU member states can currently contribute little to expeditionary operations.

"To a large extent they are still organized and equipped for general war, not limited intervention. Poland is making a serious effort to modernize, but as the preparations for deployment to Iraq revealed, its armed forces will need substantial investment to develop an effective expeditionary capability. In other countries, such as Hungary and the Slovak Republic, there is a lingering reluctance to shift from a military emphasis on territorial defense, mainly because of the political and economic costs of restructuring and force downsizing. Forces with a Cold War–era organization and mindset will be of little assistance to the EU as it seeks to develop an effective intervention capability.

"Currently only seven of the EU's member states have the all-volunteer, professional armed forces needed for rapid, combat ready deployment. For political considerations, conscripts from most countries can only be used for collective defense or in the most undemanding conflict environments."

While Europe's state militaries struggle with reform and re-structuring, the heirs of the *condottieri* are thriving, says Wither. Globally, the private sector offers the full range of military services from combat infantrymen to strategic consultancy. Between 1994 and 2002, as we have seen, the Pentagon entered into thousands of contracts with PMCs. In the U.S., contractors have been described as "no longer nice to have," but instead "an essential, vital part of our force projection capability—and increasing in its importance."

David Isenberg, a leading international authority on the subject. makes the additional point that the extent of privatization is illustrated by statistics from the two wars against Iraq. In the campaign of 2003 the ratio of civilian contractors to military personnel was 1:10, compared to an estimated 1:50 at the time of the Gulf War in 1991. A research project by the International Consortium of Investigative Journalists, completed in 2002, identified around ninety PMCs that had operated in more than a hundred countries throughout the world.

Colonel Wither makes other observations. The growth of PMCs, he maintains, has been driven by a number of factors, most of them peculiar to the post-Cold War era.

"Since the early 1990s there has been a significant reduction in the size of armed forces. The U.S. military, for example, is thirty-five percent smaller than it was at the time of the Gulf War. During the same period, North American and European soldiers have deployed on more military operations than in all of the forty years of the Cold War. These operations have covered the full spectrum of conflict from peace support to high intensity combat, demanding a range of military skills and experience beyond the capabilities of many states. Private contractors have expanded to meet the skills gap and also to fill the shortages caused by the reduction in the number of military personnel. This expansion has been assisted by the availability of individuals with appropriate expertise, made redundant through the downsizing of state militaries."

Further, "The sophistication of modern military hardware has also fuelled the growth of a small army of civilian specialists needed to maintain and service it. The UK deployed roughly fifteen hundred civilian contractors during the Iraq campaign in 2003, mainly to provide equipment and technical support, not least because British soldiers lacked the specialized skills required to support all of the technologically advanced equipment in theatre. As equipment maintenance is increasingly carried out by the original manufacturer, contractor support on operations has become vital for advanced Western militaries."

Colonel Wither then gets to the convoluted nub of the issue, one that is invariably controversial, contentious, sometimes polemical and consistently tackled by the media.

"For the United States in particular," he states, "the employment of PMCs has allowed military assistance to be supplied in situations where it might have been politically unpalatable to use the regular armed forces. American-based private firms have carried out clandestine operations proscribed by Congress or unpopular with the American public, most notably in Colombia."

In fact, posits Wither, "PMCs have already taken over many functions that were until recently the exclusive preserve of uniformed personnel. Formed units from military provider companies have also demonstrated the private sector's ability to intervene effectively in the kind of intrastate conflicts in Africa that the EU's battle groups are intended to tackle."

Since the mid 1990s, therefore, many officials and commentators have also advocated, or at least contemplated, "privatized peacekeeping" because of the persistent failings of the national military contingents deployed on UN missions. P.W. Singer has described the emergence of private firms as heralding "tectonic" changes in the way military capabilities are provided to both states and non-state actors.[4] American military analyst Steve Metz[5] has also predicted that "Corporate armies, navies, air forces, and intelligence services may be major actors in 21st-century armed conflict." Other commentators have even questioned whether the motivation and morality of soldiers in modern professional armed forces can really be distinguished from the so-called "mercenaries" employed by PMCs.[6]

As Colonel Wither maintains, the services of PMCs became increasingly critical to the success of peacekeeping missions during the 1990s. "It was therefore inevitable that employees of these companies found themselves placed in "harm's way" well before the current operations in Iraq. For example, contractors from Defence Systems Limited (DSL), a PMC based in the UK, supported the United Nations

Protection Force (UNPROFOR) in Bosnia-Herzegovina and undertook a wide range of combat support missions, defined by the company as transport, maintenance, communications and engineering. But DSL employees actually drove armored personnel carriers on peacekeeping operations and sometimes delivered supplies to bases under small arms and artillery fire.

"The Clinton administration broke new ground when it hired the Virginia-based DynCorp to supply ceasefire monitors for Kosovo in 1998. In an unprecedented venture for a PMC hired by a Western government, contractors were deployed in a potential combat area instead of regular soldiers, although there was no question of the DynCorp employees taking part in even defensive military operations, not least because, like those of DSL, they were unarmed.

"As non-linear battlefields and asymmetrical methods of warfare characterize contemporary armed conflicts, the distinction between combatant and non-combatant has become increasingly blurred. Although none of the PMCs in Iraq was hired to take part in combat operations, contractors providing military security services such as installation protection and convoy escort have been forced into direct combat with insurgents."

Given that most major security firms recruit former personnel of American and other Western special forces or elite combat units, it is hardly surprising that these personnel—including those from security firms such as Control Risk Group, Triple Canopy and Hart Group Ltd—acquitted themselves well under fire. In some cases, private contractors proved to be more professional and effective than coalition troops. Triple Canopy's operatives fought for three days to protect civilian members of the Coalition Provisional Authority in a facility in Kut after Ukrainian soldiers apparently retreated from their positions.

"While PMCs in Iraq have demonstrated their competence to fight limited defensive battles in low-intensity conflicts, elsewhere private sector forces have already taken a leading role in offensive military operations in theatres of war as far apart as Macedonia, Colombia and sub-Saharan Africa. It was the successful interventions by the South African PMC Executive Outcomes in the mid 1990s against rebels in Angola and Sierra Leone that brought the issue of the employment of PMCs in direct combat to the forefront of discussion. EO's operation in Sierra Leone in 1995, in particular, is widely viewed as a classic example of what a small force of highly skilled, professional soldiers from a military provider firm can achieve against the more numerous, but ill-trained, irregular fighters that make up the bulk of combatants in conflicts in much of the developing world. The company employed a battalion-sized force of infantry, supported by combat helicopters, light artillery and some armored vehicles, which completely defeated rebel forces of the Revolutionary United Front (RUF) in a few weeks.

"EO's success contrasted sharply with the United Nations Mission in Sierra Leone's (UNAMSIL) costly and ineffective operation and launched much debate about the possibilities of privatized peacekeeping and enforcement. An Adelphi Paper of 1998 argued for governments and international institutions to begin a "constructive engagement" with military companies that might allow them to supplement international and regional peacekeeping activities."

Other companies have the potential to fill the gap left by the demise of Executive Outcomes and Sandline. My old friend Gary Jackson, president of Blackwater USA, has been quoted as saying that he would like to have "the largest, most professional private army in the world" ready for peacekeeping duties in any country.[7]

Colonel Wither points to the fact that many other established PMCs such as DynCorp and International Charter Inc. could offer combat services, but are not currently in this market. Nevertheless, the Anglo-American firm Northbridge Services Group has claimed to be able to deploy a fully equipped brigade, including full logistical support, anywhere in the world within three weeks.[8] The same PMC, he says, offered to provide a battalion of peacekeepers for Liberia in 2003 to halt the fighting around Monrovia and arrest the indicted war criminal President Charles Taylor. The company's web site offers "Operational Support" services including Special Forces units, air assault capabilities and rapid reaction forces.[9]

Unfortunately, declares Wither, "as with Sandline, some of the company's business activities have courted controversy and undermined its claims to respectability. In April 2003, the British Foreign Secretary publicly accused the firm of jeopardizing the peace process in Côte D'Ivoire by reportedly recruiting personnel to intervene in the fighting. Currently, the absence of competition in the military provider field means that any government seeking these capabilities has few reliable options. It also remains to be seen whether many well established PMCs would want to enter the high-risk business of direct combat even if such a role was viewed as legitimate."

The important factor in the business of hiring guns is that military provider firms and top flight security companies hire from the same pool of elite soldiers.

Colonel Wither: "Such enterprises provide a source of employment for retired officers and soldiers, who often leave the armed services in the prime of life, with not only years of military experience but also a profound understanding of the norms of military behavior, civil military relations and the laws of war. PMCs can provide a means by which the expertise of these military personnel can continue to be leveraged on behalf of a state, albeit at a price."

But, he warns, recruitment by PMCs could have a negative impact on retention and morale in national armed forces, especially if private sector "soldiers" were to be deployed on a battlefield alongside regular troops performing the same tasks, but with lower pay and greater liabilities. The high salaries on offer in Iraq have already caused elite soldiers from armed forces on both sides of the Atlantic to retire prematurely in record numbers.

"The UK has even resorted to offering soldiers 'sabbaticals' from the Army to enable them to work for private security firms. While Iraq has produced perhaps a unique demand for private security operatives that is unlikely to recur on a similar scale, a growth in the number of military provider companies could cause a hemorrhage of critical military skills from leading Western militaries, as well as creating the unacceptable situation where a government funds the training of special forces and other elite soldiers only to end up having to buy back their services from the private sector."

A consistent media theme on the increase in violence in Iraq is that some private military contractors appear to be out of control, or at the very least, not subject to the same kind of discipline that regular forces maintain. There have been accusations of indiscriminate fire from people working for some of the major PMCs. While this might be true and verifiable in certain circumstances, the majority of these accusations simply do not stand up to scrutiny. In fact, each one of the firms I approached specifically stressed that every single infringement by staff was investigated. The consensus was that if somebody was found to have exceeded his or her mandate, they would not only be sent home immediately, but could conceivably be charged under civil law.

These issues are underscored by Washington's International Peace Operations Association (IPOA) a trade association of private contractors working in conflict/post-conflict environments and initially founded by a group of PMCs/PSCs "to ensure sound and ethical professional and military practices in the conduct of peacekeeping and post-conflict reconstruction activities." As Doug Brooks, IPOA's president told me when I visited his offices in the American capital, "Our mission is to promote high standards in the peacekeeping industry. We inform both the public and the policy makers about skilled private companies and their contributions to international peace and human security."

Since its founding, IPOA has been unusually active in the media world rebutting accusations that range from war mongering to the excessive use of force to implement control, as well as charges of unbridled mercenary activism. Following an article in *The Washington Post* on September 10, 2005, "Security Contractors in Iraq Under Scrutiny After Shooting," Derek Wright, an IPOA Research Associate, replied:[10]

[The report] was unclear about the mechanisms available to both the Iraqi and U.S. governments to control private contractors and the threats the contractors face in Iraq. Security contractors are regulated by both the Iraqi Interior Ministry and the coalition governments. In a report to Congress, the Pentagon made clear the chain of command in Iraq, oversight mechanisms, sanctions that can be imposed on contractors and disciplinary and criminal actions that can be brought against contractors.

With more than a hundred and fifty contractors killed and a thousand wounded (out of an estimated twenty thousand in Iraq) between May 2003 and October 2004, security companies faced casualty rates nearly identical to those of U.S. troops in Iraq during the same period. Despite the extreme risks, many companies and industry leaders believe that security contractors can and should be held to higher ethical standards than even our military. This is being done by working with governments and international organizations to improve laws, regulations, oversight and accountability.

Given that the private sector is playing a central role in the stabilization and reconstruction of Iraq, we should expect nothing less than excellence.

For his part, Matan Chorev, an IPOA Research Associate and a colleague of Derek Wright, was even more outspoken in what he had to say:[11] "If we are to get a handle on the myriad of difficult ethical and operational questions regarding the increasing role of private contractors in Iraq, we must commit to developing a nuanced understanding of the diversity of services offered by the peace and stability industry. Unfortunately, overly simplistic portrayals of the industry have thwarted progress in the public dialogue on privatization. Detractors of the so-called 'privatization of national security' label the industry as a 'coalition of the billing' who profit from the continuance of instability and suffering in Iraq. Advocates of privatization see the industry as filling the supply-demand gap for peacekeeping, providing logistical and support functions and other services in conflict/post-conflict zones.

"The fact is that the industry is multi-faceted. Delineation into its different service components is helpful from a conceptual standpoint for both the government and the industry for four reasons. First, it will assist the shared goal of refining regulatory mechanisms to address only those companies to which they should be made applicable. Second, the government will become a better client in that it will be more aware of what it is purchasing and more capable of relaying that information to taxpayers in a transparent manner. Third, understanding the fine distinctions of the private sector will allow for more thorough and meaningful assessments of its field implications. Finally, such review will improve war planning, as it will be easier to figure out when and under what conditions outsourcing to the private sector is appropriate and cost effective.

"The industry is essentially made up of three major types of service providers—Nonlethal Service Providers (NSPs), Private Security Companies (PSCs), and Private Military Companies (PMCs).

"Cleaning latrines and cooking meals is a vastly different task than guarding the head of the Provisional Coalition Authority in Iraq, but both act as crucial force multipliers that allow the military to focus on what it does best—to fight the insurgency. It does a great disservice to the industry and to consumers of news when reports do not clarify the service provisions of these companies. . . . IPOA has been working for greater transparency and accountability. Our elected officials must continue to demonstrate leadership and push additional legislation forward. Nevertheless, private contractors should be encouraged to clarify their service role.

"The diversity of services in the industry is not new. What is new, is the sheer volume of actors and the increased reliance on the private sector to assist in the different facets of military life. It is therefore all the more pressing to put forth an effort to make the industry more effective and accountable. A sober dialogue divorced from pundit-driven analysis is long overdue. A sophisticated understanding of the service provisions is an important first step to yielding a safer, more effective, accountable, and ultimately successful operation that will spare the lives of coalition forces, civilians, and the Iraqi people while ultimately minimizing the length of the U.S. presence in Iraq."

The deployment of private contractors to Iraq and Afghanistan has taken its toll. The website casualties.org has managed to keep a fair track of the number of PMC/PSC personnel killed in action which, by early 2006 in Iraq, was close to three hundred. It includes no Iraqi deaths, which, by this writer's account have been substantial. Nor does it include those killed who were working primarily for civilian contractors such as Halliburton, Bechtel, GE and some of the other big names.

Examining the list of fatalities in some detail, what comes across is that nationals from just about every country in the world are involved in the security business in Iraq. Apart from a large body of people killed and listed as "unknown," the tally includes almost a score of South Africans which, subsequent investigation has shown, is incorrect. There have been many more Southern African casualties than those listed.

At more than a hundred fatalities, United States casualties top the list, though Canadian and British nationals are very well represented, as are Turks. More recently the swing has been toward Third World countries as well as Eastern European nations. Though there are known to be a sizeable number of contractors from South and Central America, those deaths barely come into the reckoning, which accentuates reports that barely half of the deaths that occur are officially reported.

Interestingly, the number of wounded are not part of the equation. This can be deceptive because since the start of 2003 and the filing of the first hundred or so death claims, there were more than twelve hundred contractors wounded, quite a few seriously. For all of 2001 and 2002, in contrast, contractors reported ten deaths and less than nine hundred injuries, not all of them from enemy action.

All of which goes toward answering the question: who then is defined as a private military contractor, or, more appropriately, a fully fledged mercenary?

Part of the answer to that question emerged following the death in Iraq of Akihiko Saito, a Japanese national who had also served in the French Foreign Legion. Saito—working for a British concern—went missing in May 2005 during a fierce firefight and was captured by Ansar al-Sunna, one of the most feared Islamic militant groups.

In attempting to answer questions, IPOA's Derek Wright made the following observations about Saito's execution:

"The complex and often misunderstood world of private security contracting was brought to the attention of the Japanese public after private security contractor Akihiko Saito was abducted and killed in Iraq this May. Upon learning of Saito's involvement in Iraq, the government and media in Japan began looking for answers to questions about the nature of the peace and stability industry in Iraq and other conflict and post-conflict areas.

"How and why did a Japanese national come to be working for a British firm in Iraq? Confusion about the industry led some to condemn Saito's work as a mercenary, while others lauded him as a hero for fighting the Iraqi insurgency and sacrificing his life in the process. The truth is that both of these views of Saito are incorrect," wrote Wright.

According to IPOA, the man was neither a mercenary, nor was he "fighting" anybody. Rather, declares Wright, Saito was "a member of an industry that provides services crucial to reconstruction and stability in conflict and post-conflict areas. These services include providing logistical support, clearing mines, training military and police officers, and providing armed security to key infrastructures as well as civilian and government officials."

As he stated, contractors are in Iraq (and Afghanistan, the Sudan, Algeria, Angola, Colombia and a host of other states) to provide airlift capabilities, run mail and food services, build camps, procure equipment, supply armed security personnel, and provide many other essential tasks that have traditionally been carried out by the military.

In this way, says Wright, private contractors act as "force multipliers" for the military campaign by allowing the military to focus its talents on fighting the war instead of spreading its already limited resources to other, non-combat duties.

That's one definition of a modern merc. But as we have seen, there are other wars where the great military establishments of the West—supported by the limitless largesse of their governments—fail to engage. Though the Mideast has become a newly fertile playing field for PMCs, there have been, and always will be, many battles where freelance fighting companies will need to effect decisions by themselves. Whether this means operating a lone gunship against homicidal rebel hordes, stalking through the deepest jungles to root out ambush positions, or defending crucial resources in the savannah, the only alternative to success for these professionals will frequently be death, and in the event of their failure the deaths of countless civilians.

In those future conflicts in which the great powers of the West decline to become involved, others will from necessity look to the "war dogs"—that most inscrutable, and to many, admirable—breed of men.